HERTFORDSHIRE HOUSES

Selective Inventory

ROYAL
COMMISSION
ON THE HISTORICAL
MONUMENTS
OF ENGLAND

HERTFORDSHIRE HOUSES

Selective Inventory

J T Smith

Published by the Royal Commission on the Historical Monuments of England, Fortress House, 23 Savile Row, London W1X 2JQ

©RCHME Crown copyright 1993

First published 1993

ISBN 1 873592 10 8

British Library Cataloguing in Publication Data
A CIP catalogue record for this book is available from the British Library

Designed by Chuck Goodwin, 27 Artesian Road, London W2 5DA

Printed by The Alden Press, Osney Mead, Oxford OX2 0EF

Contents

Commissioners

Foreword

Hertfordshire Houses: Selective Inventory has been prepared by Mr J T Smith to accompany his synoptic discussion of Hertfordshire houses, published as *English Houses 1200–1800: The Hertfordshire Evidence* (HMSO, 1992). Although that book is designed to stand alone, many readers may wish to explore further the buildings selected for investigation. The *Selective Inventory* contains a brief historical analysis of each significant house and sufficient architectural detail to indicate the basis of Mr Smith's conclusions. The complete record for each building is available in the National Buildings Record (Fortress House, 23 Savile Row, London W1X 2JQ; tel 071–973 3091).

English Houses and the *Selective Inventory* are based on many years of detailed fieldwork and documentary research, the greater part of which was completed by 1982. The Commission would like to thank Mr Smith for his outstanding efforts in bringing this work to a conclusion and to thank all those who assisted him. These include the many owners of buildings, drawings and manuscripts, who were unfailingly co-operative throughout the survey; the librarians and staff of national and local libraries and record offices; the directors and staff of Hertfordshire's principal museums; the staff of the county and local authority planning departments; the staff of the brewery companies, which own many historically interesting buildings, and the members of various local history groups.

The Commission also wishes to thank particularly two of Mr Smith's former colleagues, Mrs Pauline Fenley and Dr Bridgett Jones, for the documentary research that informs the accounts in this Selective Inventory, and the three graphics officers who prepared the illustrations, Mr Nigel Fradgley, Mr George Wilson and Mr Allan Adams. For the preparation of the text, thanks are due to the editors, Ms Kate Owen, Ms Lizbeth Gale and, outside the Commission, Mrs Susan Whimster; and, for an heroic piece of typing, to Mrs Jan Cornell.

T G Hassall
Secretary, The Royal Commission on the Historical Monuments of England

Author's Preface

This book provides the evidence on which *English Houses 1200–1800: The Hertfordshire Evidence* rests. The circumstances prompting the work, and under which it was carried out, are described in the Author's Preface to that book.

The entries are intended primarily to justify the architectural and historical conclusions drawn for individual buildings. A second aim is to present briefly any evidence that exists about long-demolished buildings preceding the existing ones and so enable the reader to judge the relative importance of a house before and after the present one was built. Although such evidence is far too fragmentary to allow quantitative treatment, it may give some idea of the number and distribution of important houses prior to the Reformation, and of the instances in which new country houses replaced farmhouses.

Both these aims are part of an attempt to present architectural evidence derived mainly from the examination of buildings as a source for social and economic history. Doing such work within an organisation devoted to the recording of buildings imposes constraints not experienced by most historians; for example, documentary research and inquiry after graphic records have necessarily to be limited. However, by analysing standing structures, insights can be gained concerning types of building and their development usually denied to academic researchers, and these can extend to the interpretation of the graphic evidence. It is therefore hoped that the present work may stimulate discussion of the proper relation between documentary research and fieldwork, and of how both might be conducted.

Acknowledgements

It is both a duty and a pleasure to thank the many people other than those already mentioned who have been involved in the preparation of the *Selective Inventory*. First and foremost I have to thank Commissioners and four successive Secretaries, Mr A R Dufty CBE, Mr R W McDowall OBE, Professor P J Fowler and Mr T G Hassall, first for accepting that a survey of this kind was feasible, then for permitting it to go forward and bearing with the innumerable problems entailed in its writing. Two former members of staff, Mr R F Meades and Mrs L Titmus, prepared drawings at an early stage. Dr Bridgett Jones undertook valuable documentary research in Hertford and other record offices; Mrs Pauline Fenley acted as research assistant to the project for several years and searched out drawings and plans in museums and libraries; and Mr Stephen Croad interpreted engravings and drawings.

The research could not have been done without the most generous co-operation of many owners of drawings and manuscripts. The Marquess of Salisbury kindly permitted the use of plans and drawings of Hatfield House in the Hatfield MSS, and the publication of drawings based on them. The Marquess's librarian and archivist, Mr R Harcourt-Williams, gave generously of his time in producing documents and answering queries. Mr Godfrey Meynell kindly permitted the copying and reproduction of certain drawings in his collection, as did Mr David Lewis a book of plans and drawings of Newsells Park, Barkway, then in his possession. The staffs of the British Library and the Ashmolean, Victoria and Albert and Soane Museums were consistently helpful, but special mention must be made of the Society of Antiquaries and its former librarian, Mr John Hopkins.

Mrs Barbara Hutton's generous gift of a copy of the second edition of Chauncy's *Hertfordshire* was of great help. Mr Graham Bailey, Mr Stephen Castle, Mr Philip Coverdale, Mr Adrian Gibson and the late Mr Gordon Moody MBE were generous with information and drawings. Mr Guy Beresford provided information about Ashwell. Mr Peter Walne and his staff at the County Record Office were unfailingly helpful, as were the directors and staffs of the county's principal museums: Hertford (Mr A Gordon Davies); Hitchin (Mr Alan Fleck); St Albans (Mr D Gareth Davies) and Watford (Mrs Helen Poole); also the research librarians at St Albans (Miss Vivienne Prowse) and Watford (Miss Marshall).

Mr John Onslow, County Architect, and members of his staff, as well as the staff of several district councils, were of great assistance, notably Mr Alan Carter, Mr D Russell Craig, Mr William Dodd and Dr Mervyn Miller. Four brewery companies, Greene King, Ind Coope, McMullen and Whitbread, provided plans of the many historically interesting buildings they own. It is impossible to list all the people, especially those in various local history groups, who helped in many ways, notably by lending plans and old photographs. I hope they will accept my general thanks.

Finally, I thank the many householders who welcomed Mr Bassham and myself into their houses. I hope they will find satisfaction in having assisted in this enterprise.

J T Smith

Houses

❖ Indicates houses illustrated

Editorial Notes

The entries in the *Selective Inventory* supply essential facts relating to the dating and interpretation of the houses but without formal descriptions. For some houses the architectural and documentary evidence is discussed in the hope of clearing up confusion; Rothamsted Manor, Harpenden, and Rawdon House, Hoddesdon, are examples.

The *Selective Inventory* is arranged alphabetically by parish; within parishes, houses have been entered alphabetically according to house name or in numerical order under street name. The National Building Record number appears first followed by the name of the house or its number and street name, and its National Grid Reference number where appropriate. (The names and boundaries of the parishes are those effective after April 1974.) A brief history of ownership is given where known, followed by a physical description of the house and its main architectural features. If there are illustrations of the house in the accompanying *English Houses 1200–1800* volume, the relevant figure numbers are listed before the Notes. Unless otherwise stated, all houses are timber framed.

Extracts from contemporary inventories or documents relating to room usage too lengthy to be quoted in individual entries appear in the Appendix.

All references to the Victoria History of the Counties of England are to the Hertfordshire volumes unless otherwise stated.

Sir Henry Chauncy's *The Historical Antiquities of Hertfordshire* is a valuable source of information for houses in the county. References citing text are to the second edition of 1826 (reprinted in 1975 with an introduction by Carola Oman); references citing engravings by Drapentier and others are to the 1700 edition, superior for this purpose, in which the illustrations appear by parish.

`RCHME photograph' refers to postcard photographs taken at some time during the preparation of the 1910 Inventory, which were not published, but which are filed in the National Buildings Record.

`E Clive Rouse report' refers to reports in the house files on wall-paintings; they form the basis of Rouse 1989 listed in the Bibliography.

A large archive of photographs illustrating the majority of houses can be consulted in the National Monuments Record.

In the Bibliography the place of publication has been omitted for titles published in London.

Unless otherwise indicated, plans are of the ground floor of a building and are reproduced at a scale of 24 feet to the inch, the sections and elevations at a scale of 12 feet to the inch.

Where more than one plan is shown, the lower floors are to the left or below the upper floors. Plans show the state of a building as it was when recorded unless otherwise stated.

Initial letters have been used on certain plans to indicate former or conjectural room use. A key is given below:

B	Bedchamber/Bedroom	Dr	Dressing room	Pal	Pallet Chamber
Ba	Bakehouse	Drg	Drawing room	Py	Pantry
B Cl	Bed closet	Dy	Dairy	S	Saloon
Bil	Billiard room	EC	Earth closet	Sc	Scullery
Brew	Brewhouse	EH	Entrance-hall	SH	Servant's hall
Br R	Breakfast room	G	Gallery	Sit	Sitting room
But Py	Butler's pantry	H	Hall	St	Study/Office
By	Buttery	K	Kitchen	WC	Water closet
Ch	Chamber	La	Larder		
Cl	Closet	LC	Lodging chamber		
CP	Common parlour	Li	Library		
Cu	Cupboard	Lo	Lobby		(An arrow on a staircase indicates
Din	Dining room/Dining parlour/Eating room	Ny	Nursery		the direction of the upward flight)
		P	Parlour		

SELECTIVE INVENTORY

ABBOTS LANGLEY

(77178)
The Abbot's House (TL 094020)

was evidently of manorial or near-manorial status, although it cannot be identified with any of the several manors in the parish; the origin of the name is not known. Its architectural development is complicated and the earlier phases have to be inferred from scanty evidence.

The chimney-stack W of the entrance has on both sides creasings for a roof considerably lower than the present one (Fig 1); they may relate to a late-medieval open hall. In that case the present entrance-hall corresponds to the screens-passage and the E wing is either an addition or, more probably, a rebuilding of

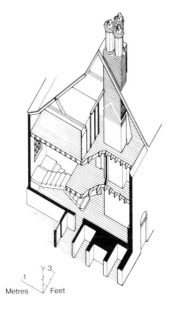

Fig 1 *The Abbot's House, Abbots Langley: axonometric drawing of previous roof*

an end bay (Fig 2). To this it can be objected that the roof timbers of the main range, most of them re-used, include none that are blackened by smoke; but the alternative, that the creasings relate to a late 16th-century timber-framed building, as the re-used timbers appear to do, would make the plan inexplicable.

The E wing is a well-finished range of two storeys and attics with ovolo-moulded beams; surprisingly, there are no signs of any original partitions, chimney-stack or staircase, while the lack of any original first-floor doorway into the rest of the house reinforces the suggestion that the adjoining structure was of a single storey when the wing was built c1600. In the third quarter of the 17th century the chimney-stack on which are the creasings mentioned above was built; it is dated by three octagonal shafts with moulded caps and bases and no break is visible in the brickwork below. Probably at the same time the chimney-stack E of the passage was built within the wing although it has no datable features; the ground-floor fireplace was 12 ft 6 ins wide (3·8 m) and the room it served must have combined the functions of hall and kitchen. An unheated room created at the S end of the wing was perhaps a pantry. The former screens-passage became an entrance-hall; the double-pile hall range presumably provided a dining room and drawing room; and a predecessor of the present staircase, of which a few balusters are re-used in the attic staircase, stood in much the same position. Towards the end of the 18th century the wing was shortened, the walls rebuilt in brick, and a new staircase built. In the late 19th and early 20th centuries there were various extensions at the rear.

(77179)
Cecil Lodge (TL 096023)

appears to have been built in the early 18th century; it is depicted c1800[1] as a small five-bay stuccoed house facing W, of two storeys and attics and with the two end bays projecting boldly forward as wings of one-room plan (cf Little Cassiobury,

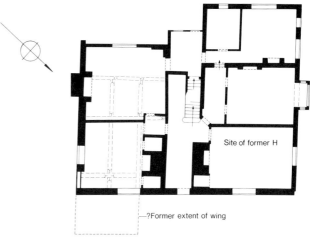

Fig 2 *The Abbot's House, Abbots Langley: plan*

Watford). Its original name is not known but in 1773 it was bought from Mrs Legrand by Lady Brown, born Margaret Cecil, granddaughter of the 3rd Earl of Salisbury and widow of Sir Robert Brown, diplomat;[2] she gave the house to Lord Cranborne, later the 7th Earl and 1st Marquess, on his marriage in 1773.[3] Lord Cranborne resided at Cecil Lodge until succeeding to the earldom in 1780 and from 1786 onwards it was leased to tenants. An early 19th-century drawing by J C Oldmeadow,[4] when it was the seat of P Mure Esq., shows it as a double-pile with large bow windows to N. By 1871 the space between the wings had been filled by a conservatory through which the entrance-hall was approached, and there was a large service wing to N.[5] A photograph shows that it had been enlarged beyond recognition in the present century.[6] It was demolished during the 1950s.

For an illustration, see *English Houses 1200–1800*, Fig 194 (plate).

Notes
1. Oldfield Vol IV, 452.
2. *DNB*.
3. *Granville Autobiography*, 5, 545.
4. BL Add MS 32348, fo 247.
5. BL maps 137a 2/14.
6. *CL* **74**, 2 September 1933, advertisement.

(77180)
Hyde Farm (TL 084040)

is associated with the manor of Hyde which, until 1546, was owned and leased out by a succession of important families and was then sold to William Ibgrave, who held the office of King's Embroiderer. Whether he resided there is not known; the form of the original house is consistent with the residence of a minor officer of the royal court. It descended in 1558 to his third son Ellis whose widow, after his death in 1563, brought the property by marriage to Robert Smethwick 'of Lees Langley',[1] ie Langleybury. She sold the manor in 1588; it reverted to lease and has so remained.[2]

The oldest features in the house, which is now faced entirely in brick, are in the N range. Patched brickwork shows that the chimney-stack serving the hall fireplace was once much larger than now, and the absence of smoke-blackening in the roof suggests that the stack is original; the binding-beam in the hall is housed awkwardly on a wall-post and its double chamfer would accord with a date in the late 17th century, showing that the first floor is an insertion; and there are two doorways, now blocked, with four-centred heads. All this is consistent with a construction date in the middle decades of the 16th century, perhaps *c*1546–63, and manorial status. The original plan is slightly uncertain. Probably the house was approached from S with a parlour E of the open hall and a chamber over it, and with service rooms and chamber above to W; the siting of the service doors implies that a staircase adjoined the S wall; of the parlour no trace remains. But the hall was not quite of the usual proportions, ie a square plus the width of a passage; either it was somewhat larger than usual or the lower end was arranged in some unusual way.

In the late 17th century the house changed its form and function. A first floor was inserted in the hall and a cellar was dug out beneath it, indicating that it had by then become a parlour or dining room. A S wing was added to produce an L-plan with a lobby-entrance; the principal room was a new hall with, behind it, what was, from its proportions and large fireplace, a kitchen. The cellar, hall and kitchen are coeval because the bearers have similar chamfer stops. A 19th-century staircase in the S wing may replace an earlier one. It would be reasonable to expect a principal staircase in the late 17th-century plan but the present one appears to be of the first quarter of the 18th century. Then, if not earlier, the entrance was moved to W, into the new hall and conveniently related to the staircase, and the house was refaced in brick and roofed with slate. Subsequent changes are not important.

For illustrations, see *English Houses 1200–1800*, Figs 170 (plate), 171.

Notes
1. *Visitations*, 21.
2. VCH II, 325.

(77181)
Hyde Lane Farm (TL 088041)

comprises a main range of two storeys and an E wing of one storey and attics (Fig 3). The late medieval wing has joists of large scantling and was probably always of two storeys; it has a clasped-purlin roof; the S wall-plate has been cut off above the staircase but formerly extended W; the tapering of the wall-plate immediately beyond the NE corner post shows that the building terminated there. Probably it was a service bay, the hall having

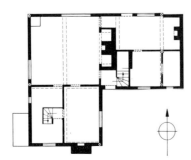

Fig 3 *Hyde Lane Farm, Abbots Langley: plan*

been rebuilt when the chimney-stack, possibly backing on to a cross-passage, was added in the 17th century. The new range may always have incorporated two ground-floor rooms in its S bay, one of them an unheated parlour. The present staircase may replace one beside the chimney-stack. Subsequent changes were of a minor nature until recently, when the house was damaged by fire and subsequent demolitions.

(77182)
King's Lodge (TL 083005),

formerly The Lawn,[1] incorporates part of a timber-framed house built in the late 15th century. Nearly all that remains of it is a two-storey service bay to W, of two ground-floor rooms with a staircase in approximately the position of its medieval predecessor. An open hall doubtless existed to E. In the mid 17th century the hall and whatever adjoined it to E was replaced by a three-cell lobby-entrance house; the chimney-stack has cruciform shafts; the binding-beam and bearers in the hall are concealed by ornamental plasterwork; over the fireplace a plaster panel bearing the Stuart arms and the date 1642 refers to the whole of this work. Later in the 17th century a chimney-stack with two square shafts was added; a moulding at the base of the shafts is much like that on the internal stack. A slight difference in the first-floor levels suggests that an E bay or cross-wing of the medieval house was incorporated in the 1642 work. Refronting in brick took place in the late 18th century and an E bay was added; other service rooms to W are 19th-century additions. In the present century plaster panels in 17th-century style, one bearing the date 1642, were added to the front.[2] In recent years, the building was stripped to its timber frame in the course of restoration.

Notes
1. RCHME 1910, 28.
2. Hussey 1943, 660–3, with plan.

(77183)
Langleybury (TL 077001),

the principal manor of the parish, belonged to St Albans Abbey from the time of Edward the Confessor until the Dissolution. In 1536 demesne corresponding to the Langleybury estate came into the hands of the Childe family[1] and remained with them until 1711 when Thomas Childe sold it to Sir Robert Raymond, the Solicitor General;[2] in 1554 the manor was granted to Sir Richard Lee. About the time Raymond became Lord Chief Justice in 1725 he began building the present triple-pile house; it has a rain-water head dated 1728. Originally it was joined by a covered passage to the detached kitchen block to SW which bears a rain-water head of 1727; parallel with the kitchen is a stable block of 1726 (rain-water head). Raymond willed the house to Beversham Filmer, with whose descendants it remained until 1838;[3] for a time it was leased to Baron Hotham, MP and Commissioner of the Great Seal.[4] A projection added to SW appears to have changed rapidly; Oldfield shows it as single-storeyed;[5] an undated drawing, perhaps of 1801[6] shows a three-storey, almost flat-roofed building; and by 1835 the large servants' hall was in being.[7] Some time before 1835 a ground-floor bow window had been added to E.[8] The most considerable alterations took place after 1885 when E Henry Lloyd inherited Langleybury, and before 1894 when he was Sheriff; Cussans remarks that 'the distinguishing features of the original have been strictly adhered to'.[9] Lloyd built a two-storey block to join the house to the kitchen block; enlarged the service quarters to W; replaced the original parapet by a balustrade; added new porches and a bay window and greatly altered the interior.

Virtually no original detail remains to identify room use. The entrance-hall to N[10] was still the largest room, and in discussing the function of other rooms it is important to decide where the secondary staircase was. The logical place is to SW where the passage from the kitchen came in (cf Bonningtons, Stanstead Abbots) because anywhere else would entail the servants going through a room and the staircase-hall to reach the secondary stair; and in that case the fireplace surround and overmantel, which are of 18th-century appearance, are late 19th-century reproduction work and some likeness between them and the obviously Victorian panelling confirms this. The middle window of the middle room to E extended to the ground,[11] to give access to the garden. The literary allusions conveyed by the medallion heads of Anacreon, Ovid, Sappho and Theocritus in the ceiling point to this being the library in the late 19th century; its precise size and function before then are uncertain.

In the 19th century the entrance was transferred to S; perhaps at the same time a new N entrance and staircase-hall were built by William Jones Lloyd who owned the house from 1856 to 1885.[12] His son E Henry Lloyd built the three-sided block connecting house to service range and forming on the ground floor a dining room separated by an L-shaped corridor from the new kitchen to W. Since 1947 Langleybury has been a school.

For illustrations, see *English Houses 1200–1800*, Figs 191 (plate), 192, 203 (plate).

Notes
1. VCH II, 323–4.
2. *DNB; Home Counties Mag* 1905, 7, 51–6.
3. VCH II, 324.
4. Oldfield Vol IV, 445; *DNB*.
5. Oldfield Vol IV, 444.
6. Meynell Collection.
7. HRO, SC, block plan.
8. Clutterbuck.
9. Cussans 1879–81, Vol III (ii), 91.
10. Oldfield Vol IV, 444.
11. Buckler, in Clutterbuck II, 170.
12. Inf. Mr Ian Bower.

(77184)
The Manor House (approximately TL 092016)

was separated from the site of the original manor of Langleybury in 1536, and under the will of Francis Combe Esq. (d.1641)[1] was acquired in 1644 jointly by Sidney Sussex College, Cambridge, and Trinity College, Oxford.[2] The house depicted by Oldfield[3] was probably built in the 1650s by a member of the Greenhill family, who had it on lease; Thomas Greenhill of Langley was a Parliamentarian and a member of the County Committee;[4] Mr William Greenhill paid for 13 hearths in 1666.[5] Originally the house probably had mullion-and-transom windows of three or four lights, but Oldfield appears to show sash windows. In the early 19th century a ground-floor bay window was added on the garden side to left of the front;[6] a lean-to and service ranges were added to right; and the brickwork was rendered.[7] It was demolished in 1953.

Notes
1. Chauncy II, 378.
2. VCH II, 324.
3. Oldfield Vol IV, 448.
4. Kingston 1894, 42n.
5. PRO E179/238/25.
6. Drawing, J C Oldmeadow, BL Add MS 32348, fo 27.
7. Old photographs from Mr Michael Hemming.

(77185)
Yew Cottage, Kitters Green (TL 094017),

is of the late 17th century. It is of two storeys and of two-room plan with lobby-entrance; a lean-to beside the W room is probably original. The larger E room was the hall and probably kitchen too, the W room the parlour, and the W lean-to a service room. The chimney-stack was of timber, the present stack being entirely of 18th-century brickwork. Bearers and joists are poorly finished and may have been intended for plaster ceilings from the first; a peculiarity of the joists is that they appear to rest on rails at back and front and are not tenoned into them. A S wing was added in the late 18th century, perhaps in order to provide a new kitchen.

For an illustration, see *English Houses 1200–1800*, Fig 300 (plate).

ALBURY

(77186)
Albury Hall (TL 426453),

a manor, passed in 1755 by descent to John Calvert, MP for Wendover (Bucks) and subsequently for Hertford,[1] who pulled down the old house, which had been the residence from 1661 to 1669 of Sir Edward Atkyns,[2] and built a new one nearby; this was done *c*1780.[3] It was a large double-pile house facing E, of three storeys and seven bays with two full-height bay windows to S; the drive was to N.[4] In 1799 both John Calvert and John Calvert junior, MP for Huntingdon, were described as 'of Albury Hall'.[5] A drawing of 1841[6] shows a quite extensive and complicated NW wing and also suggests that the drive had been much reduced in importance; perhaps the house was by then approached from W. In 1847 the estate was sold to Richard Dawson, who, in the following year, acted on a hint in the sale catalogue[7] that 'the House might be made more comfortable and still sufficiently spacious for a large Family, if a projecting North Office Wing were removed'; but he replaced it by a new and lower wing and added a carriage-porch and an Italianate tower.[8] It was sold in 1899 to H A Hare and again a few years later to M G Carr Glyn,[9] who was Sheriff in 1912. He rebuilt the wing and remodelled the W front in Queen Anne style at about that time.[10] The house was demolished *c*1950.

Notes
1. VCH IV, 6.
2. *DNB*.
3. Cussans 1870–3, Vol I (ii), 161.
4. Oldfield Vol I, 54.
5. *Court and City Register*.
6. Buckler Vol II, 7.
7. HRO.
8. Photograph, NMR; Gerish Collection in HRO.
9. *Kelly* 1912.
10. Photographs made available by Mr Jeremy Glyn.

(77187)
Albury Lodge (TL 440240)

is the house belonging to the half of the manor of Albury which was purchased in 1597 by John Brograve, by whom it may have been built shortly afterwards.[1] It descended to Simeon Brograve, at whose death in 1636, when his son John was living here, the outbuildings included 'hopkills with all other outhouses and buildings belonging and copper brewing vessels and mill in the brewhouse'.[2] The manor court was held here. After the two halves of the manor were reunited in 1688,[3] Albury Lodge ceased to be of much importance. A drawing of 1834[4] shows it still timber framed and plastered but in the 19th century it was encased in brick;[5] and in the 1930s and again more recently it was considerably altered. Buckler shows a house apparently of E-plan with gabled wings and a gabled two-storey porch in the middle, all of which could well be of the end of the 16th century; the two gables of the hall range and the attic windows look later, perhaps mid 17th century. The plan comprised a main range divided between hall and service rooms, with a passage behind the latter to the kitchen in the N wing. There are indications that the kitchen originally had an internal wooden chimney. The N cross-wing has a newel staircase in the re-entrant angle; the S wing had a chimney-stack on the rear (W) wall which, in Buckler's day, was flush with the hall. In the present century the W wing and its staircase in the re-entrant angle were rebuilt and any timber-framed walls remaining were replaced by brick.

Notes
1. VCH II, 4–5.
2. Inquisition *post mortem*, PRO C142/590/18.
3. VCH IV, 6.
4. Buckler Vol I, 84.
5. VCH IV, 4.

(77188)
House SE of churchyard (TL 435986)
is of two storeys, rendered, with thatched roof. Formerly the W gable had late 17th-century plasterwork with crowns and square fleurons grouped around an oval panel which may have been intended for a date and initials.[1] (Not examined.)

Note
1. Anderson, WCL.

(77189)
Hole Farm (TL 421260),
of two storeys, has a main range facing E with a modern cross-wing of two storeys to S and a lower E wing to N. The latter was formerly a cross-wing but the roof of the main range has been extended over it; it incorporates what was originally a single-storey structure in which, to W, a little above the first floor, is a tie-beam and to S a wall-plate (cf Cutting Hill Farm, Benington); and to S the first floor can be seen to be an insertion because it is carried on lodging-plates. This end of the former wing was probably an open hall with perhaps a service room or rooms to E. A range comprising two rooms and a timber chimney-stack was added c1600 to S and the older part was heightened and made into two storeys; an unusual mode of development, but cf Hyde Lane Farm, Abbots Langley. The present brick stack is probably of c1700; the first-floor fireplace and ceiling in the room to S are of that date. Probably the room to N of the stack was the hall/kitchen and the one to the S was the hall/parlour; a probable instance where the old functions were confused. The large S room may have been an unheated parlour. The site of the staircase is not known.

(77190)
The Hunting Box, Patmore Heath (TL 343293),
is a late 17th-century brick house of two storeys and attics; it has a cruciform plan of two rooms with lobby-entrance, two-storey porch and staircase turret to rear. A lean-to is a later addition, marked by straight joints, but probably replaces some earlier structure; the present staircase is modern and the whole house has been heavily restored.

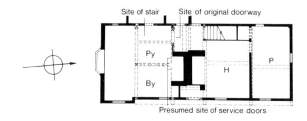

Fig 4 *Kennel Farm, Albury: plan*

(77191)
Kennel Farm (TL 428237)
is a three-cell continuous-jetty house built in the early–mid 16th century (Fig 4). The roof has clasped-purlins, part of it in the chimney-bay being apparently blackened as if by smoke; this could have been a smoke-bay, although no other example was recognised in the course of the survey; more likely there was a timber chimney backing on to a cross-passage to S. Mortises and peg-holes suggest an orthodox arrangement of two service rooms to S of the passage, with a staircase next to the W wall. In the late 17th century, when the stack was rebuilt in brick, the two service rooms were thrown together and a fireplace added to serve the new room, which was presumably a parlour; perhaps the room to N became the pantry. A fireplace discharging into a separate chimney-shaft was added in the chamber over the hall c1700, when attics were created in the roof. A fourth bay to S was added in the 18th or 19th century.

(77192)
Tudor Cottage, Upwick Green (TL 450244)
was built in the late 16th century and is a continuous-jetty house of three-cell plan. Originally a timber chimney-stack served fire-places in two rooms. The largest room to N was not divided structurally and the twin doors that might have been expected for a pair of service rooms definitely did not exist; it was prob-ably an unheated parlour. There being no obvious service room, it is possible that the lean-to at the S end or its predecessor always performed that function. Originally the staircase adjoined the lobby-entrance. Upstairs the N room was the prin-cipal chamber; its timbers were all brought to a flush surface internally; the remainder of the upper storey shows no sign of subdivision. The walls are close-studded throughout, with curved vertical-to-vertical bracing; the roof has clasped-purlins. Later alterations did not materially change the character of the house and it was extensively restored in 1974.

For illustrations, see *English Houses 1200–1800*, Figs 154 (plate), 155.

ALDBURY

(77193)
Nos 9–13 Stocks Road,
called The Old Manor House (SP 964124),
is likely to have been part of the manorial demesne, and the date of its earliest parts may fall within the tenure of Henry Winch, to whom the manor was leased for 27 years in 1485; alternatively it was built by the related family of Russell, who appear to have been tenants from 1495 onwards for about fifty years. It is unusual in having the upper part of the open hall flush with the jettied upper walls of the parlour and service bays. In the S wing a doorway with depressed four-centred head led into the cross-

passage; the W door has been reduced in width; the passage was at some time partitioned off from the service room but perhaps not originally, nor is there any sign that the latter was subdivided. The present stair by the W wall must replace an original one hereabouts. From the passage a wide chamfered opening led past the chimney-stack, which is an original feature, into an open hall. In the hall the fireplace, of stone, has a depressed four-centred head, in the E spandrel of which the date 1516 is inscribed in digits which are doubtfully consistent with that date.[1] The hall roof is not blackened by smoke. In the N parlour block the plate of the ground-floor wall appears to be housed into the hall framing, hence they are coeval. Of the original staircase here there is no trace. The narrow W wing was open to the roof originally; the two E bays have a smoke-blackened clasped-purlin roof; the W end was of two storeys. This was either a kitchen wing, although it appears too big for a house of this size, or served some unknown special function; its proportions deny the possibility that it was a separate house. The wing is undatable but the fact that covered access to it could be obtained only by blocking the cross-passage suggests that it is an addition. In the middle of the 17th century an upper room was inserted in the hall and given a small fireplace with a depressed four-centred head; generally similar fireplaces were added to the parlour and the chamber over the service room. The parlour fireplace is off-centre to the room, perhaps because the original staircase ran up beside the W wall; and the jettied and unheated N block may have been added at the same time as the chimney-stack to provide a service room. This work must have been completed by 1663, when Bennet Winch paid for five hearths; his initials are incised in the main chimney-stack. A staircase was added W of the parlour and a first floor and chimney-stack were added in the wing in the late 17th century. By 1722, when the property had been acquired by John Duncombe of Stocks, it was described as a `house and two cottages...part of Winch's estate'; James Partridge, whose name and the date 174(?) are inscribed on the lintel of the fireplace, was perhaps the first tenant of that part.[2]

For illustrations, see *English Houses 1200–1800*, Figs 61 (plate), 62.

Notes
1. Inf. Mr S E Rigold.
2. Inf. about owners and tenants from Mrs Jean Davis.

(77194)
Nos 39–43 Stocks Road (SP 965336)

incorporates a late-medieval cruck truss to N of a hall of one bay; immediately to N, in a shorter bay, are opposite doorways for the entrance; probably the house extended farther to N (perhaps for a byre). A parlour bay of two storeys was added to S, probably in the 17th century. The house was refronted in brick c1800, when much of the original framing was removed.

(77195)
No. 40 Stocks Road (SP 965126)

is of two-cell plan corresponding to two builds; all the longitudinal timbers show a structural break and neither part of the house is complete in itself. The N part appears to be the older despite the fact that some of its timbers are supported on those of the S part; it may be of the early 16th century. This was a parlour and chamber above; the original stair trap is in the NE corner; upstairs are remains of an early 17th-century wall-painting. The S part probably replaced an original open hall and is perhaps mid 17th century, the likely date of the large hall/kitchen fireplace. The position of the latter suggests that the

entrance has always been to S, and probably past a staircase to E of the stack; this in turn may imply entrance from a cross-passage in an inferior building which was replaced by the present one in the late 18th century.

For an illustration, see *English Houses 1200–1800*, Fig 71.

(77198)
Nos 16–20 Trooper Road

originally formed one house built c1500; the N part (No. 18) was a hall open from ground to roof, and the S part (No. 20) was an unheated jettied block, the whole being comparable to Nos 61/63 Park Street, St Albans. In the late 16th century a chimney-stack was built at the junction of the two blocks, probably in part of the site of the cross-passage, to provide fireplaces in hall and parlour and also a lobby-entrance. At this time a floor was inserted in the hall. The position of the original staircase in No. 20 is uncertain; a modern staircase at the N end, beside the chimney-stack, probably replaces one of the late 16th century. Over the ground-floor fireplace is a painted panel of that date. In the 17th century the ground-floor fireplace N of the stack was added or rebuilt; it has elaborate stops and bears on the lintel the initials I H with a device between them; above is a date which is either 1617 or 1677; on the evidence of the stops it should be 1677. In the early 18th century the S block was refronted in brick and a new entrance made into a lobby cut out of the original partition between the two rooms.

The relation of this house to the next building N (No. 16) is uncertain; the latter was originally open from ground to roof and of comparatively poor construction; it is perhaps of the 17th century and may have been built as a barn or other store. It was heightened to two storeys in the 18th century. Numbers 16–20 became three cottages in the 19th century and remained so until recent years.

(77196)
Royal Hotel, to W of Tring station (SP 950121),

was opened soon after the opening of the London and Birmingham railway from Euston to Tring in October 1837, to cater for travellers from a catchment area which for a short time extended as far as Oxford.[1] John Brown, a brewer of Tring, was under contract with the railway company to build the hotel known as The Harcourt Arms, and in 1845 purchased it for £232 10s. The present name was acquired between 1845 and 1851.[2] The building comprises a front block, of three storeys over cellars, facing the road to Tring, and a rear wing to SE of two storeys over storerooms and stables. The principal rooms are on the ground floor; how the front block, facing NW and now divided by two bars back-to-back, was arranged originally is not certain; the gable-end walls to SW and NE each have two fireplaces, perhaps for four small rooms. There is an entrance from the road and in the re-entrant angles of the wing are more important ones from the railway station to NE and the hotel yard to SW; both of the latter entrances lead to the entrance-hall, from which the principal staircase rises to a landing and a corridor facing the yard to SW. The two principal wing bedrooms nearest the staircase have small adjoining rooms, perhaps dressing rooms; two rooms to SE (now made into one) can have had no such provision; the end room of the range has two small rooms opening off it, perhaps dressing room and closet (probably in the sense of lavatory).

Notes
1. Inf. Mr G Goldsworthy, citing PRO Kew, Rail 384/21.
2. Inf. Mr C Goldsworthy, citing a conveyance in the possession of Benskins Brewery.

(77199)
Nos 42/44 Trooper Road,

of two storeys and of three bays, jettied to E, is probably of the 16th century; both floors appear to have formed two rooms, the larger one being of two bays; the roof has clasped-purlins; the original chimney-stack, presumably of timber, was replaced by brick stacks, one to S of *c*1700 and one to N of the 19th century.

(77197)
Town Farm (SP 965125),

of two storeys and attics, is now predominantly of brick. As built in the late 16th century it was timber framed and comprised two W-facing bays considerably lower than the present building. The longer S bay was probably an open hall; a mid–late 17th-century chamfer stop on the bearer suggests that the upper floor is a later insertion; on the first floor a shallow step up to the N bay confirms this. The hall bay is longer than usual, ie it is more than square. In the late 16th century the house appears to have belonged to the Barnes family.[1] The will of Owen Barnes, yeoman, dated 1587, mentions the hall and the `chamber where I used to lie', which implies a second chamber. In 1631 the inventory of another Owen Barnes, also yeoman, mentions hall, chamber, loft over the chamber, chamber over the hall, buttery and milk house, and kitchen, so that between 1587 and 1631 the house had been enlarged and an upper floor inserted in the hall. In the late 17th century it was heightened in timber-framing and a third bay added to S in brick, with wide vertical bands of blue headers; the S bay incorporates corner fireplaces on both ground and first floors; the present chimney-stack was built, and, if the bearer has been dated correctly by its stop, a new floor was provided for the chamber over the hall. The E wing was added or rebuilt at the same time to accommodate various service rooms. In the early 18th century the house was owned by William Ladyman, whose probate inventory dated 1 August 1736[2] can be related with some probability to the existing house. In the 18th century the ground floor of the N part of the house was refronted in brick and the timber framing infilled with brick. Subsequent alterations are of little importance.

For an illustration, see *English Houses 1200–1800*, Fig 162.

Notes
1. Details about the ownership of the house were supplied by Mrs Jean Davis.
2. HRO, 85 HW 38; transcript provided by Mrs Jean Davis.

ALDENHAM

(77200)
Aldenham House (TQ 168965)

can be identified with Wigbournes, a copyhold estate which, in 1621, passed by marriage to Henry Coghill who, in 1640, purchased the house variously known as Penne's Hall or Place or Aldenham Hall or Place. Penne's Place (TQ 166968) `is a small Mannor situated upon the Common where Henry Coghill Esq. built a fair House of Brick: He was constituted Sheriff for this County...1632'.[1] In 1662 Henry Coghill paid for 23 hearths.[2] A drawing of the present Aldenham House by Oldfield is captioned Penn's Place.[3] The subject of another drawing,[4] captioned in a deliberately archaic-looking hand `Front of Aldenham House/East part of the House', bears a stylistic resemblance to Rawdon House, Hoddesdon, but none to the present house, no part of which can now be inferred to be as early as *c*1630–50;[5] the drawing appears to refer to Aldenham

manor house,[6] the ruins of which are visible near the parish church, and was evidently copied from an earlier original since the house itself had disappeared by 1711.[7] Although there is no reason to link the present Aldenham House with Penn's Place, the drawing so captioned, or the `fair house of Brick' on the grounds that the Coghill arms are in the pediment[8] – the arms are equally appropriate to Henry Coghill the younger, who inherited Wigbournes in 1672 – it seems to have been built on the former common, as Chauncy stated. The younger Coghill was Sheriff in 1673 and that, on stylistic grounds, is an acceptable date for Aldenham House, which appears in a drawing of 1786 under the name Aldenham Great House.[9]

The late 17th-century house was of L-shaped plan with wings to W and S, the former being the entrance front. The width of the pediment corresponds to the hall and an important room above it, both of which which had fireplaces discharging into a now demolished chimney-stack set back behind the roof ridge.[10] This stack was flanked by two others now rebuilt with heavy corbelled caps; that to N serves a small parlour with corner fireplace and a similar first-floor chamber, whereas that to S may always have served two somewhat larger rooms. The staircase was perhaps to N of the hall chimney-stack. The E wing must always have been divided in its width more or less as now; and the middle room of this wing probably replaces a garden hall and one other room. The chapel to NE of the W wing, formerly a kitchen, may be of the late 17th century. In 1735 the house passed by marriage to Robert Hucks[11] and `In 1785...Robert Hucks, the younger, made additions to the house, and it is evident that alterations were made by his predecessors';[12] these include a two-storey bay window to S and a single-storey block to N, perhaps a library. In 1842 the house descended through collaterals to George Henry Gibbs, whose descendant Henry Hucks Gibbs made large additions and many improvements after 1869, `but in no way altering the character of the building'.[13] Much of the high-quality reproduction work is his. After 1869 large additions were made to N, while to W a single-storey porch was added along the whole front. The architect William Butterfield submitted designs for a dairy.[14]

Notes
1. Chauncy II, 369.
2. PRO E179/375/30.
3. Oldfield Vol I, 149.
4. Ibid, 139.
5. Cf VCH II, 152.
6. Brigg 1902, 190.
7. Salmon 1728, 97.
8. Hill and Cornforth 1966, 218.
9. Map, HRO, 63791/1.
10. Oldfield Vol I, 149; Clutterbuck.
11. Hussey 1924, 285.
12. Cussans 1879–81, Vol III (i), 249.
13. Ibid; Hussey 1924, 280.
14. V&A, Dept of Prints and Drawings, D55–7, 1908 (nd).

(39604)
Munden (TL 136001)

was a manor, formerly called Meriden, and was the property of the monastery of St Albans until the Dissolution. Thereafter it passed through many hands, no doubt always leased out, until in 1787 it came by descent to Roger S Parker.[1] A note dated 1795 records that `within 7 years he had built a house and offices upon his estate called Munden';[2] this was a plain squarish house in late Georgian style, facing E with a service wing to W.[3] On his death in 1828 the house descended by marriage to George

Hibbert,[4] who immediately proceeded to remodel it in Tudor style. In Cussans' words the house was `refenestrated, with stucco hood mouldsʼ;[5] full details of the new internal decorations remain.[6] None of the wallpapers appears to have had a Gothic or Tudor pattern.

An extraordinary feature of Hibbert's house was the way it was entered through a small lobby into the billiard room and so

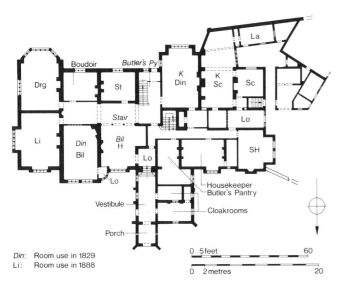

Fig 5 *Munden, Aldenham: plan (from plan of 1888)*

Din: Room use in 1829
Li: Room use in 1888

to the staircase-hall (Fig 5). This clumsy design perhaps resulted from a desire to give a quite small house an impressive appearance, so that the principal front had necessarily to embrace the service quarters as well as the principal rooms. It is perhaps equally extraordinary that Hibbert's removal to a house as small as Munden necessitated the sale of art treasures and a huge library.[7] His son Nathaniel succeeded him in 1837 and in 1851 proposals for altering the entrance were submitted by Richard Geldham, architect. They were for a single-storey addition, initially comprising only a porch and a long entrance-hall or vestibule; in a second proposal this was flanked by a large ground-floor room entered only from the house, and there were to be two first-floor rooms.[8] The outcome was a compromise: a porch, vestibule, two flanking cloakrooms and an enlarged butler's pantry, all in a more convincing version of the Tudor style.[9] In 1855 Nathaniel Hibbert was Sheriff.

In 1874 the house passed by will to the Hon Arthur Henry Holland, who rebuilt the stables in 1877 and, on coming of age in 1879, took the additional surname of Hibbert. In 1887 he undertook considerable alterations to Munden at a cost of £1,900 and in 1890 was Sheriff. The billiard room was enlarged and made into the hall; its rear wall was replaced by arches open to an axial corridor which led to a new main staircase; a large dining room replaced the old kitchen.[10] This created a nearly symmetrical garden front.

Notes
1. VCH II, 459–60.
2. *Munden Year By Year*, 199.
3. BL Add MS 9063, fo 235; before 1799.
4. *DNB*.

5. Cussans 1879–81, Vol III (ii), 181.
6. V&A, Dept of Prints and Drawings, Wallpaper Book, 780.
7. *DNB*.
8. Plans in the possession of Viscount Knutsford.
9. There appears to be no reference to the work in *Munden Year by Year*.
10. *Munden Year by Year*: plans by Charles J Ferguson, architect, of Carlisle and Westminster.

(77201)
Netherwild Farm (TL 152011)
is of two storeys, and was refronted in brick in the late 18th century; it was described as being of brick and tiled in 1798.[1] The earlier work, ostensibly of the mid or late 17th century, comprises a hall range with lobby-entrance flanked by two cross-wings and with a rear wing to W. The hall has an ovolo-moulded binding-beam; the fireplace is mid 17th century; and above the first-floor fireplace of the N (correctly NE) wing, which discharges into the same stack, is a heavily restored wall-painting bearing the date 1662. Although such timbers as can be seen are all compatible with that date, the rarity of the hall and cross-wing plan in the late 17th century, coupled with the unusual proportions and narrowness of the hall itself, suggest the piecemeal rebuilding of a small, late medieval house with an open hall, with which the short cross-wing to S may be coeval. A probate inventory of Anne Feeld of the Nether Wilde, widow, proved 1 January 1615/16,[2] mentions only the hall and an unspecified number of chambers. Certainly this wing, in which the upper floor is carried by binding-beams, is structurally different from the N wing, which has axial bearers throughout its length and is in all probability of the same date as the chimney-stack, ie mid 17th century. The postulated rebuilding seems to have begun with the addition of the hall stack and N, or parlour, wing; was followed by the heightening of the hall, because the hall eaves are higher than those of the wings; and concluded with the addition of the W or dairy wing, though this may not have followed the previous phase immediately. The S wing may also have been extended then. The owner responsible for this transformation recorded his and his wife's initials in the painting over the fireplace: N N A, probably for Nicolls; the flanking initials I N and S N are presumably for their children.

In the early 19th century the middle and NW wings were joined up to create a new kitchen. In 1847 the first-floor painting was restored by someone with the initials R S and probably at the same time the present staircase in the NE wing was built.

Notes
1. Guildhall MS 11937/24, 620.
2. HRO, 56 AW 10.

(77390)
The Nook (TQ 147994)
is now completely rendered outside, and inside all old features are concealed except in the roofs. It is of two distinct parts; to W is a late-medieval open hall of two bays with a smoke-blackened crown-post roof. It is separated by some 2 ft (0·6 m) from the slightly higher parlour block to E but since the timbers at the N end of the hall are unweathered the parlour block must replace something earlier. A staircase wing to N appears to be a 17th-century addition. The extensive late 19th-century alterations are said to have been undertaken when Lord Aldenham installed his gamekeeper here. (For a different interpretation of this house see Dulley 1978, 87–8.)

(79307)
Wall Hall (TQ 137995),

formerly Aldenham Abbey, was a manor and is referred to in the middle of the 13th century as the court of Walehale.[1] After 1633 the estate descended with the manor of Aldenham, with which it was sold in 1799 to George Woodford Thalluson;[2] at that time `it was only a large farm, and the present building was erected by him'.[3] In 1803 Repton advised on garden improvements.[4] In this first phase of alteration the house had a simple neo-classical front; the block to SE, which has lower ceilings with plastered bearers and simply moulded cornices, repeats what was incorporated of the earlier building. Either then or shortly afterwards a three-storey block was added to S, another to NE, and the N and W elevations received the `castellated front' mentioned in 1812,[5] when the house was sold following Thalluson's death. He is said to have renamed the house Aldenham Abbey[6] although it was sold as Wall Hall. From 1830 to 1874 the house was owned by William Stuart, who added the large library (notable for a ceiling 25 ft (7·6 m) high), the carriage porch and a conservatory;[7] all this before 1860 when the last two are depicted in an engraving.[8] Then or subsequently the service quarters were extended but the house itself has undergone little structural alteration. Early in the present century it was the residence of J Pierpont Morgan junior.[9]

Fig 6 *Ardeley Bury: plan*

Notes

1. VCH II, 426.
2. Ibid, 151.
3. Oldfield Vol I, 327; Cussans 1879–81, Vol III (ii) contradicts himself at 276n and 276–7.
4. Stroud 1962, 66, 173.
5. HRO, SC D/P3 29/9.
6. VCH II, 427.
7. Cussans 1879–81, Vol III (ii) 276–7.
8. Andrews Collection.
9. *Kelly* 1912.

ANSTEY

(77391)
Red Stack (TL 406331),

of one storey and semi-attics, is of the mid 17th century. The plan comprises, from W to E, an unheated room, two rooms with fireplaces and with lobby-entrance to S and stair to N, and what were originally two small service rooms. The room to E of the stack has the proportions of a kitchen (cf Causeway House, Braughing); the hall has to N exposed framing which includes long paired braces of shallow curvature, formally resembling

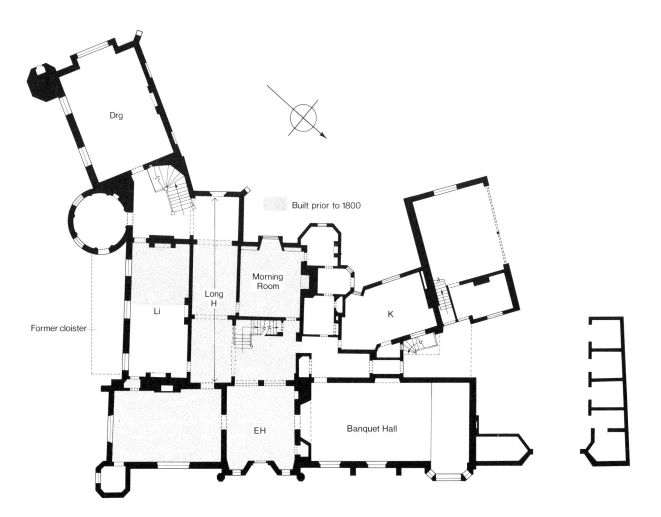

Kentish framing. The roof has clasped-purlins carried on collar-beams which are incorporated in partitions corresponding to those on the ground floor and two others to E and W of the chimney-stack; the latter has conjoined diagonal shafts.

ARDELEY

(39601)
Ardeley Bury (TL 301271)

is the house of a manor, apparently identical with Lite's Manor,[1] which belonged to the canons of St Paul's, London, from before the Conquest until 1808, except between 1649 and 1660 when it was sold off during the Commonwealth.[2] The manor house included in the 12th century a good hall, a chamber leading out of the hall and cloisters.[3] In 1610 Henry Chauncy of Ardeley, gentleman, leased to John Knight, yeoman, the `Owld House',[4] an expression which implies the existence of a second, new house. In 1700 the manor house was described as standing `in the Middle of an ancient Park, now disparked, well water'd with Fishponds, and heretofore moated round' and at that time manor house and demesne had been held by the ancestors of Sir Henry Chauncy by leases for lives for `above the space of two hundred years last past'.[5] No part of the present house can be said definitely to be of medieval origin, and although some parts existed in Chauncy's day, extensive alterations have made it difficult to say much about them. A number of rooms with lower ceilings than the rest form an L-shaped plan which corresponds to the late 17th-century house (Fig 6), but this, because it is not rectilinear, is probably itself of two builds. The ascription of this house to the late 16th century[6] appears to rest solely on the evidence of panelling. On the N (correctly NW) side of the L-shaped block are two chimney-stacks each with three octagonal shafts, and the roof of the E part of the N range has tenoned purlins; these are all 17th-century work and are the earliest datable features of the house. Chauncy the historian, a man very aware of building-works as a mark of family prestige, says nothing about his forefathers' activities of this kind, a point which, like the plan, argues that they altered and enlarged an old house without doing anything noteworthy. A Parliamentary Survey of 1649 describes the house as having `a Hall, a great Parlour, a little Parlour, a kitchen, two Butteries, a cellar...also one parcel of Houseing consisting of Five Lower Rooms and Five Upper Rooms'.[7] The kitchen of that date may well correspond to the present one, which is likely to have been a detached structure originally, and the `parcel of Houseing' sounds like a lodgings range which cannot now be identified. This work may have included the addition of a SW wing to the L-shaped building, because a chimney-stack to W retains the bases of three octagonal shafts; and with this must go the addition of a front hall between the wings. A drawing of c1800[8] and also a sketch of 1805 by the Revd J Skinner[9] show the half-H shaped house refaced in classical style towards the end of the 18th century, presumably by the lessee John Spurrier, auctioneer,[10] to whom in 1808 the dean and chapter sold it.[11] In 1811 Commissary-General John Murray purchased the estate and in 1820[12] remodelled the house in a castellated style resembling that of Panshanger, Hertford. A remarkable feature of this work is the Great Hall, complete with bay window, minstrels' gallery and a rather thin-looking hammer-beam roof. Within the pre-1800 house the principal alterations were the creation of a new entrance-hall and a long corridor or hall with a plaster vaulted ceiling. Some work was done in the late 19th century, notably a staircase in late 17th-century style which stands to N of the round tower; and in recent years some of the extensive outbuildings added by Murray have been demolished.

Notes
1. VCH III, 196; Chauncy I, 110–19.
2. VCH III, 195.
3. Hale 1858, 136.
4. VCH III, 195.
5. Chauncy I, 107, see also Gerish 1907, 67.
6. RCHME 1910, 36; VCH III, 195.
7. Guildhall MS 25631, fos 98–104.
8. Oldfield Vol VII, 470.
9. BL Add MS 33641, fo 215.
10. HRO, Land Tax, Ardeley L/T.
11. VCH III, 195.
12. Gerish 1907, 68.

(77392)
Chapel Farm, Wood End (TL 324254)

was built in the late 16th century; it is a continuous-jetty house of three-cell plan with chimney backing on to the cross-passage. Negative evidence suggests it may originally have had a timber chimney; the shaft above the roof is of the late 17th century and there is nothing below to suggest an earlier date. In the hall the binding-beams and bearer are moulded. The siting of the hall fireplace implies that the staircase, now modern, has always been in its present position. The W service room was not subdivided; the partition between it and the passage has been removed. The doorway from passage to hall has a segmental head moulded continuously with the jambs. Later alterations are not important.

(77393)
The Cottage, Cromer (TL 296282),

of two storeys, was built in the 16th century and was heightened to two storeys in the mid 17th century; the wall studs terminate in a rail, formerly a plate, over which the joist ends are halved; the bearer in the middle room is seated on a post rather than the rail in the partition; and upstairs the front (E) wall has the slight outward lean that appears to denote heightening. The framing is poor and was evidently intended to be plastered. The lack of principal posts in the wall between hall and service room suggests that the house was originally of three-room plan; moreover the N end was of only one storey in 1910[1] and its former wall-plates appear to continue those to S. By the late 17th century the hall, parlour and chamber over the parlour had fireplaces; at the N end was the service room. The staircase must have been in a turret or wing to the W, more or less where the present one is.

For illustrations, see *English Houses 1200–1800*, Figs 156 (plate), 157.

Note
1. RCHME photograph.

(77394)
Cromer Farm (TL 296282)

was built c1500 with an open hall and two jettied cross-wings. In the hall the rear (E) door of the former passage has a four-centred head; traces of the E window show that it was nearly 6 ft 6 ins (2 m) wide and 7 ft 6 ins (2·3 m) high, with a large middle mullion-and-transom; the wall-plate forms the lintel and is rebated for the full length of the window, as if for hinged shutters, though no trace of hinges was observed. The principal posts of the open truss have wide hollow chamfers and thin hollow-chamfered braces; the tie-beam has a plain chamfer; the clasped-purlin roof is smoke blackened; the rafters have assembly marks; there are no end trusses. The N wing has close-studding and braces with a slight reverse curvature. The ground-floor room, which was unheated, was presumably a parlour; a stair trap against the back (E) wall was approached from the N with the head of the stair lit by a window positioned off-centre. The S wing was no doubt always divided into two rooms. Both wings had one upper room and open clasped-purlin roofs. The windows had sliding shutters.

In the late 16th century or early 17th century a chimney-stack was built backing on to the cross-passage; the stack has a single hexagonal shaft and the front, facing the chamber over the hall, has a stepped outline. At the same time an upper floor was put into the hall, carried on a moulded bearer; the joists are chamfered and stopped. The stack allows of a stair on the E side. In the 17th century the S wing was enlarged to the E. In recent years a large NE wing was added.

For an illustration, see *English Houses 1200–1800*, Fig 307 (plate).

(77395)
Cromer Hall (TL 296282)
is a two-cell internal-chimney house with lobby-entrance (Fig 7). A fireback found behind a later fireplace in the parlour (now reset) was stapled to the original brickwork; since it had cracked and been bent by heat it was probably in its original position and thus the date 1635 upon it provides an upper dating limit for the house. The main range and staircase wing to W appear to be one build, and the wing presumably incorporated a service room since there is no other place for one. The chamber over the parlour has an original fireplace; the front ground-floor windows have shutter grooves extending the full length of the room. At the rear are extensions of various dates.

Fig 7 *Cromer Hall, Ardeley: plan*

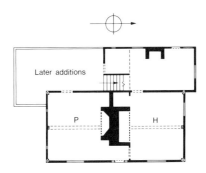

(79318)
High Tree Farm (TL 326254)
has a pebble-dashed late 19th-century appearance. Internally the original front wall-plates and the tie-beam can be seen at the level of the present first floor, showing that it was originally of one storey with an open hall; presumably it had an open hearth, because the existing three chimney-stacks are of the 18th century or later, but an earlier original and perhaps timber chimney-stack, of which there is no positive evidence, is a possibility. The heightening to two storeys probably took place in the late 17th century or even later, and has resulted in the top part of the front wall leaning in the same way as at Chells Manor, Aston.

(77396)
The Jolly Waggoner PH (TL 309272)
was built in the late 17th century and is first referred to in 1698 as `the messuage called Sheepcote Wick'; its owner was Sir Henry Chauncy and the occupier John Marshall. In 1765 it was occupied, together with various buildings including a blacksmith's shop, by George Paul. In 1823 James Camp bought the property and sometime before 1839, when he died, built a messuage adjoining as a grocer's shop. The first indication that Sheepcote Wick had become a public house is in December 1854 when, on admission of William Camp to the property, it was described as in the occupation of James Bray, publican.[1] By 1877, when it was sold to Joseph Simpson, brewer, it was said to have been `for many years past used as a beer shop called The Jolly Waggoners' and included a small amount of agricultural land, farm buildings, and a dwelling house adjoining, formerly used as a grocer's shop.

The house has a three-cell plan with a lobby-entrance; the middle and S end rooms have fireplaces and at the N end was a service room. There is an old and perhaps original fireplace in the S room on the first floor but not one in the middle room. The roof has clasped-purlins and appears to have been open originally. In the second quarter of the 19th century the house was refenestrated and generally refitted.

Note
1. Details from Guildhall MS 14247/3, Court Book of Yardley Manor.

(77397)
Moor Hall Cottage (TL 326268)
is a small house only 12 ft 6 ins (3·8 m) wide, of one storey and semi-attics with thatch roof; it was probably built in the late 16th or early 17th century but has so little old detail that its dating is problematic. Originally it had two ground-floor rooms, the E

Fig 8 *Moor Hall Cottage, Ardeley: plan*

with an upper storey above it and the W apparently open to the roof (Fig 8). In the latter, the larger room, are indications that the upper floor is an insertion: the cutting of the middle tie-beam (E of the stack) for a doorway; the slightly different relation between the chamfered binding-beam and the beams to E and W on which the joists are lodged; and a few re-used smoke-blackened rafters in the largely rebuilt roof. The W room was floored over in the late 17th or early 18th century, when the chimney-stack was built. The W bay is an addition, perhaps of the late 19th century.

For an illustration, see *English Houses 1200–1800*, Fig 13 (plate).

(77398)
Peartrees (TL 325253)
is a small house incorporating an open hall; the end bays are in series with it, that to W being roofed as a narrow two-storey

wing and that to E divided by an axial partition into two service rooms. Reverse-curved braces in the wing suggest an early–mid 16th-century date. A chimney-stack and first floor in the hall are possibly of the late 17th century and may be dated by a wood block in the house, which is now loose, inscribed W N < I > R S/1673.

(77399)
Spring Grange (TL 253324)

comprises a short cross-wing to W, probably late medieval, to which was added to E, *c*1600, an internal-chimney house with lobby-entrance, replacing an open hall. Perhaps at this time a narrow wing was added to N of the cross-wing to form an L-plan; the principal room adjoining the earlier house was a kitchen. The chimney-stack of the lobby-entrance house was rebuilt in brick in the mid 17th century. The house was restored *c*1932;[1] in 1947 that part to E of the main stack was destroyed by a fire.

Note
1. Extract seen in house from *Town and Country Houses*, April 1933.

(79317)
The Vicarage (TL 308271)

was built in 1685 as a completely new house. The first vicarage house is mentioned in 1297 when the vicar built, with the consent of the parishioners, a small house in the cemetery.[1] In 1625 the vicarage house comprised `one hall with a chamber

Fig 9 *The Vicarage, Ardeley: plan*

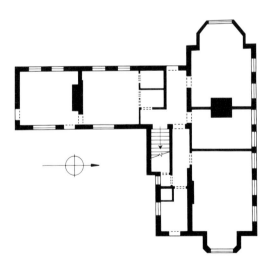

over it...a parlour with a loft over it...a study with a closet over it', all of which were tiled, and `a milk house and buttery with two lofts over them, thatched'.[2] This description varied slightly in 1638; `the Hall with a little chamber over it, one parlour and study with two little chambers and one closet over them, milk

house and one buttery with two chambers over them'; and the house was said to be of five bays. Possibly an older house survived, for `in the south-east corner of the parsonage close is a little tenement 30 ft [9·2 m] long and 14 ft [4·3 m] wide divided into three rooms with a loft over the parlour thatched all over'.[3] There was no change in 1664[4] but in 1685 Robert Strutt, the incumbent since 1682, `built a fair Pile of Brick for a Vicaridge-house [*sic*] at his Charge, which is a great Benefaction to this Church'.[5] The glebe terrier returned by Strutt in 1709[6] describes the house as having five lower rooms: parlour and hall, both boarded with deal boards, a little room S of the hall, kitchen and brewhouse; under the hall was a large cellar with four `apart-ments'; upstairs were four chambers, two closets and three garrets. A terrier of 1742[7] adds that the little room was `laid with red Pavins [tiles]', the kitchen floored with white bricks, and the brewhouse was simply `bricked', ie presumably floored with red bricks. Strutt's house comprised the present front range, a staircase-projection and the S wing as far as the chimney-stack (Fig 9). Later alterations have made it difficult to identify the named rooms. The 1709 terrier, after listing several outbuildings, notes: `All these built by the present incumbent 1685'.[8] Strutt is of interest as having procured a confession of witchcraft from Jane Wenham of Walkern as late as 1711.[9]

A drawing of 1800[10] shows a five-bay elevation (which faces N) with a rear lateral stack to left and an end stack to right; by then sash windows had replaced mullion-and-transom windows. Subsequently Edward Gerrard Marsh (vicar, 1824–35) built a music room which corresponds to the large room W of the former end stack. Father Mallet (vicar, 1843–85) built a nursery, kitchen and bedrooms.[11] Some of these additions have been removed recently. In the 19th century the staircase of 1685, which related to an entrance in the middle of the N elevation, was altered to face W to relate to an entrance on the W side; in doing so, the `little room S of the hall' disappeared.

Notes
1. St Paul's Cathedral Library, Liber I, fos 57–8.
2. Lincolnshire RO, Terr, Vol 6/47.
3. HRO, AHH/3/2.
4. Lincolnshire RO, Box 14.
5. Chauncy I, 128.
6. Lincolnshire RO, Terr/22.
7. Lincolnshire RO, Box 14.
8. Ibid, Terr/22.
9. Oman 1975, 15.
10. Oldfield Vol VII, 467.
11. Harbord 1952, 30.

ASHWELL

(77413)
The Rose and Crown (TL 267396)

is a late medieval house which comprised an open hall and two jettied cross-wings. The irregularity of the plan (Fig 10) suggests piecemeal rebuilding of an open-hall house and may have been necessitated in part by former plot boundaries or the need for access to the rear. An intermediate bracket under the jetty of the service (E) wing suggests either that the cross-passage was incorporated in the wing, or that the wing had independent access, as if for a shop. Only upstairs are a few of the principal timbers exposed; the hall roof has a rebated crown-post; the E wing, of three bays, has plain crown-posts with two-way braces. The final stages of rebuilding were the replacement of a putative bay in series with the hall by the W wing in the late 16th

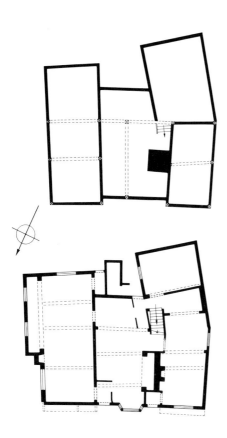

Fig 10 *The Rose and Crown, Ashwell: plans (based on a drawing by Mr Guy Beresford)*

century, and the building of a brick chimney-stack and upper floor in the hall in the late 17th century. There are now additions at the back.

(77405)
No. 55 High Street

was built in the third quarter of the 17th century to fill the gap between two earlier timber-framed houses. The framing was concealed from the first by bold pargeting of the kind found at Nos 3–13 Fore Street, Hertford, and is dated 1681.

For an illustration, see *English Houses 1200–1800*, Fig 272 (plate).

Fig 11 *Ducklake Farm, Ashwell: plan*

(77403)
Dixie's, High Street (TL 264395),

of two storeys, is probably late medieval and is a notable feature of the village street. It has a hall range flanked by two jettied cross-wings; the front is rendered, the chimneys, windows, hall roof and rear additions are of the nineteenth century, and internally all old features have been concealed.

(77401)
Chantry House,
formerly The British Queen PH (TL 263394),

of one storey and attics, is built partly of clunch but mostly of timber-framing, and has a thatch roof. The W half of the N wall is of clunch; it incorporates a blocked window of two cinque-foiled lights, which shows no sign of being reset and is probably part of a small 15th-century building. To the E the steep-pitched roof, which is plastered internally, has no visible purlins and may be of collar-rafter type; it was originally open to the roof. Two chimney-stacks were inserted in the 17th century.

(77404)
No. 29 High Street,

Anton Cottage, was built in the second quarter of the 19th century. It has a brick front but is otherwise of timber construction, rendered. The plan is approximately square with an entrance in the middle of the front, two rooms, both of which had a fireplace against the side wall, and a kitchen and pantry behind them.

(77402)
Ducklake Farm (TL 398267)

developed in an unusual way that can be explained only tentatively (Fig 11). The key element of any explanation must be the skewed transverse frame which originally formed a partition on both floors, and the truss above it; together they divided the house from top to bottom into two parts of identical size. This frame is an original feature of that part of the house to S because the face of the roof truss to N of it is slightly weathered. Although, as a result of removal of the partition, posts and a beam have been inserted to prop up the ground-floor part of the frame, the original wall-posts can be seen to be askew to the walls. This might indicate that two buildings were put up end-to-end at an angle of about 80° to one another, yet neither this nor subsequent realignment would be easy to explain. The alternative explanation offered here is that the two parts of the house were in separate occupation – effectively two houses – in the manner of Walnut Tree Farm, Pirton; this would account for the division in to two parts but not the manner of achieving it by a skewed partition. A possible analogy may exist at Eye Hall, Horningsea, Cambridgeshire, where the N wing appears to incorporate one of two houses similarly divided.[1] The earliest

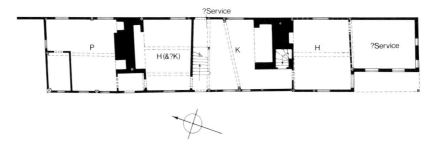

part of the building lies to N of the skewed partition; it has lower ground-floor ceilings than the rest and on the first floor to E a wall-plate now serves as a middle rail in a heightened wall; this was probably a late medieval house with an open hall. Formerly there was a studded partition where now is a wide fireplace to S; the absence of peg-holes to W shows that a doorway has always been there; the room extended as far as a partition to S of the main staircase, where a post and beam with mortises are exposed. The plan of this house is difficult to reconstruct. No clear signs of a coeval house exist to S and in this respect Ducklake Farm resembles both Walnut Tree Farm and New Hall, Ware Rural. Certainly by *c*1600 and possibly earlier the building had attained its existing length at that end. This is established by a partition some 37 ft (11·3 m) to S, in which the evidence is conflicting; the wall-posts have down-curved braces halved across the studs and apparently precluding a doorway, yet the ogee head of the doorway to W is tenoned and pegged and must be original; and since the wall-posts project to S beyond the flush face of the partition there was a further room. The partition appears to have formed the upper end of a hall; peg-holes for a bench exist. Thus the rooms from S to N were parlour, probably unheated, and perhaps with a small service room adjoining; hall and kitchen, forming a complete house. Everything suggests it is later than the part to N; it is probably datable to *c*1600 by a wall-painting in the parlour.

Although the development of the N house is uncertain it must have been joined to the S house by *c*1600 when the skewed frame was built. Its plan then appears to have comprised, from N to S, two service rooms, hall and parlour; the parlour may not have had a fireplace then. A large fireplace added subsequently in the house to S suggests the narrow and awkwardly shaped room it faced was a kitchen. Later alterations include a fireplace of uncertain date, perhaps late 17th or early 18th century, in the house to N, backing on to the original fireplace. The main staircase is part of extensive alterations in recent years when the room at the S end was completely rebuilt.

Note
1. RCHME 1972, 69, where explanation of the skewed beam as a dragon-beam seems untenable.

(77400)
Bluegates Farm (TL 256404),

of the late 16th century, was built on a T-shaped plan; the stem of the T, aligned E–W (correctly NW–SE) comprises two rooms, that to E being roofed as a cross-wing, with internal chimney-stack and lobby-entrance to N. To E of the stack the parlour and chamber above have moulded clunch jambs and timber lintel; the hall fireplace was similar. To W, forming the N part of the bar of the T, is a cross-wing of two-room plan with an internal chimney-stack and lobby-entrance to W; only the room to N had a fireplace originally; it was a kitchen, and was open from ground to roof. The reasons for supposing it was open are that the walls have large timbers unrelated to the present first floor; the bearer is re-used and appears to be an insertion; the floor joists are largely re-used and their ends rest on applied rails; and there was no access to E on the first floor. The kitchen wall-plate to W is cut away as if for a large window or shuttered opening. No evidence of the staircase remains but the proportions of the hall suggest it might have been to SW, serving both the main range and the S room of the kitchen wing. In the late 17th century the internal stack was rebuilt and a staircase wing added to S, the latter having ovolo-moulded windows and solid oak stairs; the kitchen wing was doubled in length to S for purposes not now evident.

(77406)
No. 56 High Street

was built on the former market-place in the 17th century; it is a narrow building, originally two rooms deep and jettied and gabled to N; it apparently had no fireplace (Fig 12). Little of the framing can now be seen. In the late 17th century it was extended to S and a chimney-stack built; the room to S was a kitchen. A shallow fireplace in the ground-floor room to N is probably later. In the mid 19th century the walls were heightened a little, the building was extended to S and a new roof of low pitch, slated, and parallel to the street, built.

Fig 12 *No. 56 High Street, Ashwell: first-floor plan*

(77407)
Nos 57–61 High Street

formed the hall of the Brotherhood or Guild of St John the Baptist in the church of the Blessed Mary of Ashwell; it was called le Guildhouse or St John's Brotherhood House.[1] Licence to form the Brotherhood was granted in 1476[2] and the hall was probably built *c*1500. It is jettied to N and comprises, on each floor, a large room to W and a smaller one, occupying one bay, to E; on the ground floor the latter is divided axially and has paired doorways as if for the buttery and pantry of a domestic hall. There are no original fireplaces. In the late 16th century a bay of virtually identical design was added to E, with a cellar beneath. In the 17th century chimney-stacks were built and the whole was converted into two houses.

For an illustration, see *English Houses 1200–1800*, Fig 242 (plate).

Notes
1. PRO SC 2/176/139 M9.
2. PRO C66/538 M10.

(77408)
Bear House, No. 77 High Street,

was built in the late 15th century (Fig 13); it had an open hall with the wall-plate to N running immediately below the sills of the three-light first-floor windows; the N (street) doorway has a two-centred head; in its jamb to E and in the corresponding jamb of the opposite doorway to S are mortises for the short screens of a spere-truss; in the N wall adjoining the spere-truss to E is the

Fig 13 *Bear House, No. 77 High Street, Ashwell: plan*

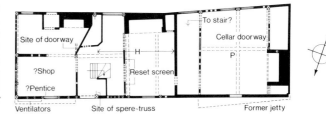

customary window, here of three lights; a wall-post to N is mortised for the arch-brace of the open truss. A panelled screen with moulded posts probably occupied the middle part of the spere-truss; it may have been movable originally but is now reset 7 ft (2·1 m) to W. The length of the hall is uncertain; a square hall (see *English Houses 1200–1800*, p 39), excluding the passage, would extend to the present featureless partition immediately to W of the middle chimney-stack. How this range joined that to W, and whether its W end was part of the hall, are not clear; no old internal features are visible in the short part to W of the stack but replastering of the front wall exposed briefly what appears to be a continuation of the low wall-plate to E. The bay to E of the cross-passage, which is partitioned into two rooms with a pair of adjacent ogee-headed doorways, has an unusually high ceiling and, in the wall to N, a row of quatrefoil wooden ventilators; these two features suggest that the N room at least was not the ordinary pantry or buttery. Studs between the ventilators have mortises for upward-curving braces or brackets but the height of the ceiling makes a jetty unlikely; possibly they supported a pent roof over a shop, the ventilators being needed at such times as the shop front was closed up by shutters. The location of buttery and pantry is uncertain; one may have been in the room to S and the other, possibly, in the puzzling narrow room to E of the hall.

In the early 16th century a cross-wing of two storeys was added to W; originally it was jettied to N; the binding-beam, bearers and joists are all moulded but revert to square at the present N wall,[1] ie the wall was always where it is now. The wing structure is unusual; the ground-floor studs are undifferentiated; the joists are pegged to a boldly projecting middle rail; the binding-beam and bearers meet the latter very awkwardly with the moulding projecting well below the rail and neither mitred to it nor stopped against it; the posts of the truss, which is arch-braced with a steeply cambered tie-beam, project proud of the studs and give the appearance of standing on the rail. In the bay to N on each floor is a clunch chimney-stack with timber lintel, that on the ground floor being moulded and that on the first floor being carved additionally with folded-leaf ornament; in each case the mouldings are returned down the jambs. The wing must have provided a grand parlour and chamber above; perhaps the staircase, which certainly did not flank the stack, was reached through an original ground-floor doorway at the S end of the wall to E, the door from the hall range being nearer the middle, but not opposite the fireplace. Possibly the hall range was extended to W to provide such a staircase. On the first floor weathering of the W wall to S is clear; none was observed on such framing of the E wall as is exposed.

In the late 17th century a chimney-stack was built within the hall to S and an upper floor inserted; the movable screen was reset then and the present featureless partition to W built to form a narrow kitchen; the new staircase may have occupied the same position as the existing reset one. Probably at the same time the jetty to W was cut back to give a flush front, the first-floor wall being reset a little awkwardly; the walls of the hall range were heightened and the whole house reroofed uniformly. It was also extended to incorporate the stack to W; the cellar beneath the parlour was either dug then or a new doorway to it was cut immediately to S of the fireplace. No doubt the putative shop disappeared at the same time.

For illustrations, see *English Houses 1200–1800*, Figs 68 (plate), 253 (plate).

Note
1. Photograph taken in 1979, during alterations, in the possession of Mr T Colquhoun Lindsay.

(77409)
No. 105 High Street

comprises a N range parallel with the street and a wider and higher rear wing. The front range of two bays may be late medieval, with a hall open to the roof and storeyed bay to E with broad flat joists. In the late 16th century a fireplace was inserted in the hall against the partition between the bays; it has moulded timber jambs and lintel and the chimney-stack was almost certainly of timber; the upper floor in the hall bay, because it is supported by a bearer resting on the fireplace lintel, is possibly later and coeval with the rear wing. The wing is of two storeys with a fireplace at the S end and a staircase adjoining the front range; the ground-floor room probably combined the functions of hall and kitchen. Subsequently a bay, said to have been open to the roof with an earth floor, was added to W of the front range.

The external appearance of this house, with the wing roof terminating to N on a small gable above the ridge of the front roof, suggests that the original plan comprised a hall behind a front cross-wing, the hall being subsequently rebuilt; however, it is the timber fireplace, which is unlikely in a parlour, that argues to the contrary.

(77410)
No. 110 High Street (TL 265395)

was built in the third quarter of the 17th century and is of mixed construction combining ground-floor walls of brick with timber framing above. Although little evidence of alteration exists, the plan does not conform to any recognised type and may result from the rebuilding of an older house in stages. The lateral siting of the hall fireplace and staircase within the main body of the house are hard to explain otherwise; and the bearers, unusually, are midway neither between front and back walls nor between hall fireplace and front wall. The house faces S. The fireplace in the room to W (hall), perhaps originally with timber jambs and projecting 4 ft (1·2 m), makes the room unusually narrow (13 ft (4 m)). The staircase to E has been altered; it would normally face the entrance, and the use of winders instead of landings where it changes direction is a mark of alteration. To E is the parlour. In the 18th century a kitchen wing was added to NW, and to SW a low gabled addition of one storey and uncertain date looks like a waiting-room for a doctor's surgery or an office.

(77411)
Nos 39/41 Mill Street

is a small hall-house with a cross-wing, No. 41 being tall and narrow with two ground-floor rooms to S. Both hall and wing have clasped-purlin roofs and some tension-bracing is exposed. In the 17th century a chimney-stack was inserted, possibly in the former cross-passage; the hall fireplace has clunch jambs and timber lintel, and the wing fireplace, wholly of clunch, has a depressed four-centred head; an upper floor was inserted in the hall. Later enlargement of the E ground-floor room of the wing necessitated supporting the upstairs wall on a wooden classical column; at the same time a new front doorway and narrow entrance-hall were created to replace the lobby-entrance, and possibly the block to S (not examined) was added to or incorporated in the house. These changes may have been made in 1762, the date on the pargeting in the wing gable. In the 19th century the range was divided into cottages.

(77412)
The Museum, Swan Street,

formerly known as the Town House, of two storeys, jettied to S, is of *c*1500; it comprised one room on each floor, the ground floor being a shop with two unglazed openings and a narrow doorway to E; all have four-centred heads. To W two panels of close-studding correspond to the foot of the staircase, which rises to N and is lit by a small two-light window at the top; although the staircase is modern it appears to occupy the position of the original one. The crown-post roof is of two bays. To N a third bay was added in the 17th century; a lateral chimney-stack of the 18th century to W is largely within the building. In 1930 it was restored and became a museum.[1]

Note
1. Bray 1928–33, 210–11.

ASPENDEN

(77414)
Aspenden Cottage (TL 354283)
was built in the late 15th century; it had a hall, a jettied cross-wing to E and probably a service bay to W. The hall roof has crown-posts and the wing roof clasped-purlins. In the early 17th century the W bay was rebuilt as a wing and a chimney-stack and upper floor were added in the hall. To NE is an early 18th-century service range of one storey and attics; in it a room lately used as a game larder may originally have been a dairy. In a general renovation c1800 the hall chimney-stack was reduced in size; a staircase was built behind it; two chimney-stacks were added to the W wing; and new sash windows put in at the front.

(36946)
Aspenden Hall (TL 352284)
demolished in the middle of the 19th century, was a house of great size and complexity.

By the beginning of the 13th century, Aspenden was in the hands of the Tany family, at first as sub-tenants, but the most prominent of them, Peter de Tany, who was Sheriff of Essex and Herts in 1236 and died before 1255,[1] can hardly have built the medieval hall depicted in an Oldfield drawing of 1793.[2] The only medieval feature in the drawing, the hall window, appears to be of three pointed lights within a two-centred arch, with pierced spandrels, and looks like late 13th-century work. Mention of `many carved stones' found when the hall was demolished[3] confirms that it was an important medieval building. If the suggested date is correct, the hall was built either by Ralph Fitz Ralph, who was holding the manor by 1255, or his son William Fitz Ralph, who was holding it by 1303.[4] Possibly, despite Ralph Fitz Ralph's apparent forfeiture of the manor in 1266, he was the builder, for whereas he was the son of Ralph son of Fulk, his descendants adopted the surname Fitz Ralph; a conjunction of building and adoption of a surname that would be comparable to that at Almshoe Bury, Ippollitts (see page 108).

Nothing further is known about the house until it is described in a survey of 1556: `The park doth ajoin the house...it is very park-like ground to be kept as a park for the stateliness of the house which is in good estate and well repaired'.[5] Possibly the W wing extending in front of the medieval hall had been built by then; in Drapentier's engraving, made not long before 1700,[6] its two external chimney-stacks look like work of the early–mid 16th century. In 1607 the manor was sold to William and Ralph Freeman, `both Brothers and Merchants in London, who resided together, Anno 1610, 8 Jac. I in this Mannor-House'.[7] Thereafter the house must have been divided in some way because both brothers married and had family, and it may be from this circumstance that some of the peculiarities of the later house arose. Ralph, the younger brother, was Sheriff of

London in 1623, and as Lord Mayor in 1634 entertained Charles I at Merchant Taylors Hall.[8] Ralph, son of William, succeeded to the manor and was Sheriff in 1636; `He made his House neat, his Gardens pleasant...had a general insight in Architecture and Husbandry', and died in 1665.[9] His eldest son Ralph Freeman, MP for the county, `cased and adorned this Mannor House with Brick' and improved the gardens.[10] When Drapentier made his engraving, the medieval hall lay N of a main or front courtyard enclosed on all sides by buildings; to N was another courtyard flanked by a W range and probably an E range too. Although the stages of its development cannot be traced, Ralph Freeman MP is likely to have built or refronted the range to S in the 1650s, and presumably the classical W-facing loggia, its balustrade surmounted by urns, is his work. In 1662 he paid tax on 27 hearths and probably for the same number in 1673 although the second figure is defaced.[11]

In 1714 another Ralph Freeman succeeded Ralph the MP, became MP himself in 1722, Sheriff in 1736, and died in 1744. It was probably he who gave the house the appearance it had in 1832.[12] By then the S range enclosing the main courtyard had been demolished, leaving as its only trace the slight inward projection of the E and W wings at the S end; the E and W wings had been given sash windows and made symmetrical; and a W front, 14 bays long, had been built. It is not certain that there was a second entrance on this front, of equal importance with the one in the hall range, but that is what the drawing suggests. Some modest works costing about £52 were carried out in 1752 when Richard Calvert was tenant.[13] At the beginning of the 19th century this huge house was used for 11 years as a school.[14] In 1856 it was replaced by the much smaller house that still stands,[15] which was gutted for use as a farm building c1963.[16]

For illustrations, see *English Houses 1200–1800*, Figs 24 (plate), 146 (plate).

Notes
1. VCH IV, 18.
2. *A Survey of the Present State of Aspenden Church June 1793* (1796), HRO, L858, 204/100/B.
3. VCH IV, 17.
4. Ibid.
5. PRO E315/319, fo 84.
6. Chauncy 1700.
7. Chauncy I, 244.
8. Ibid, 244–8.
9. Ibid, 248–9.
10. Ibid, 249.
11. PRO E179/375/302/31.
12. Buckler Vol II, 104.
13. BL Add MS 36240, fo 20, Hamels estate accounts.
14. VCH IV, 17.
15. Cussans 1870–3, Vol I (ii), 96.
16. RCHME 1962.

Buttermilk Hall (TL 343293),
now a rambling range of buildings, has developed in ways which now have to be inferred as much from a Buckler drawing[1] as from the existing structure. It began as a late medieval house of T-plan with an open hall in the middle, a service bay to S and cross-wing to N (Fig 14). In the late 17th century an upper storey and a chimney-stack were inserted in the rather low hall; two gabled dormers were added at right-angles to the main roof to provide adequate first-floor rooms, and a chimney-stack, perhaps with rectangular shafts, was added to S. The position of the entrance at this period is not clear; the drawing, the present

plan and Buckler's convenient placing of a tree suggest that a doorway may have continued to exist at the lower end of the hall; at the other end the drawing also shows a lean-to E of the main stack which might have been a porch. The conjoined shafts of the internal stack served fireplaces in the hall and the

Fig 14 *Buttermilk Hall, Aspenden: plan*

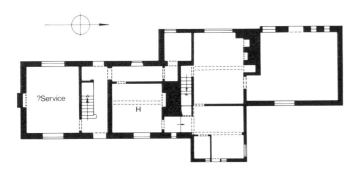

chamber over it; the space between stack and wing can never have been occupied by another fireplace and possibly the present staircase replaces an older one. A large fireplace and plain chimney-stack to W of the N wing may be later, of the 18th century, although the resemblance of plan between Buttermilk Hall and Hammond's Farm, Pirton, suggests that this plainness may be the result of the rebuilding of a 17th century stack. A single-storey building N of this stack[2] had a panelled chimney-stack and was perhaps a late 17th or early 18th-century brew-house. By 1869 the house had been altered to its present form, which is shown in outline on the enclosure map.[3]

Notes
1. Buckler Vol II, 105, undated.
2. Ibid.
3. HRO, QS, E/10.

(77416)
The Old Rectory (TL 354281)

is a late 15th or early 16th-century Wealden house. Mention in a glebe terrier of 1638 of `The parsonage house and homestall conteyning foure acres Lying betwene Aspeden strete on ye North and Woodlane on the south'[1] suggests that it may have been built as a rectory. The house is jettied to N. The square hall was separated from the cross-passage to E by a spere-truss in which short screens, now removed, terminated at a binding-beam about 7 ft (2·1 m) from the floor. At the upper (W) end of the hall were two doorways to parlour and staircase. Upstairs the N post of the spere-truss has a mortise for the rail forming the base of the cove which rose to the roof-plate; the latter is supported by the tie-beam, on which the profile of the cove is cut. In the chamber over the parlour a blocked door at the S end of the gable wall may have led to a privy. In the late 16th century an upper floor carried on a moulded binding-beam and bearers was inserted into the hall and projects to form a continuous jetty. Probably in the late 16th century a chimney-stack was built to serve the hall; the present lateral stack replaces it. Then, too, a fireplace was added in the parlour; in the brickwork above the lintel is a double trefoil-headed recess. In the early 17th century the service rooms were converted into a kitchen by the addition of a wide fireplace to E, and an E extension of two rooms and attics provided new service rooms. In 1709 the house was described as being of timber, tiled, with `3 rooms of a floor above and below, garretts over 2 parts. Kitchen floored with

paving tiles, rest boarded. Cellar. Small brew house adjoins East end...brick built one side, timber the other...thatched'.[2] A small gabled wing of two storeys was added to N in the late 17th century, and a yet smaller one to S; their functions are uncertain but the former may have incorporated a pantry.

For most of the time the Old Rectory was probably occupied by vicars or leased to tenants. In the late 16th century James Taylor, a prebendary of Ely Cathedral, was rector, and his three successors bore the same surname.[3] Next came David Rice, Dean of St Asaph Cathedral from 1696 to 1706,[4] who is unlikely to have resided here. No doubt the rectory was sometimes occupied by a vicar, of whom John Duckfield, `of Aspeden, Clerk', was one; his probate inventory, dated 18 September 1684,[5] included a library worth £90 and lists hall, parlour, pantry, kitchen, dairy and buttery, and `the passage down stairs', as well as chambers. But in 1752 Mrs Ann Pearson was tenant.[6] This situation changed in the 19th century, perhaps c1870 when the house was modernised;[7] among other alterations then the E room received a fireplace and became a brewhouse.

Notes
1. Brigg 1897, 68–70.
2. Lincolnshire RO, Terr/22.
3. Chauncy I, 249.
4. Willis 1801, Vol I, 177–8.
5. HRO, Prob 4/5151.
6. BL Add MS 36240, fo 33.
7. VCH IV, 17.

ASTON

(77417)
Aston Bury (TL 276217)

was the manor house of Aston, which belonged to Reading Abbey in the Middle Ages; it was granted to Sir Philip Boteler of Watton Woodhall in 1540 and remained with his descendants until 1778.[1] An inventory taken at Astonbury of the goods of Dame Jane Boteler on 2 October 1623[2] describes a well-appointed house of considerable size, but whether anything of it is incorporated in the present house is doubtful. One entry `In the staircase' hardly corresponds to the present house, which is remarkable for having two grand staircases, and it is difficult to see where the chapel and chapel closet, which are also mentioned, could have stood in the present building. After Dame Jane's death the house became the seat of the Cason family. Edward Cason resided at Furneux Pelham[3] and on his death in 1624 was succeeded by his son Sir Henry, who is the first member of the family to be described as `of Astonbury'.[4] Since the architectural detail of the house is more consistent with the mid 17th century the inventory must relate to an earlier house than the present one. For some hundred years after it was built, Aston Bury seems to have undergone little alteration but during the 18th century most of the windows were blocked. The Window Tax returns[5] imply that in Aston parish generally such a process was beginning in the 1730s; it probably happened when Aston Bury became a farmhouse. Drawings of 1832[6] show only the ground-floor windows still open and an engraving of the 1870s[7] shows the interior in a dilapidated state. In 1883 the house underwent considerable repair by Captain W E F O'Brien, to whom the estate descended some time after 1877.[8] In 1894 he received £500 under the Limited Owners Residences Act for drainage to the mansion and alterations to the stables.[9] More extensive restoration took place after 1907, when the house was acquired by Vernon Malcolmson.[10] In 1972 it was purchased by

Hertfordshire County Council, who carried out various alterations to adapt the house for educational use.

The house forms a two-storeyed rectangular block with a cellar, attics and two large staircase wings at the back; the ground-floor walls are of flint, banded in places with brick, and with brick dressings; the first-floor outer walls internally are of timber framing, faced and infilled with brick. It has been stated that the flintwork is medieval[11] but its continuation in the staircase wings shows that it belongs to the present house and disproves the notion. An observation in 1910 that `the whole W end is quite roughly finished'[12] was taken to imply that the house was intended to extend farther. This cannot now be confirmed and the plan argues against the inference. Dating of the house is difficult. A doorway from the hall to the E (or main)

Fig 15 *Aston Bury: early 20th-century ground and first-floor plans; second floor, as built*

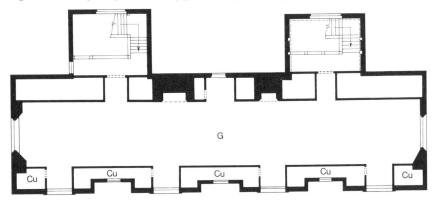

As built

Early 20th cent.

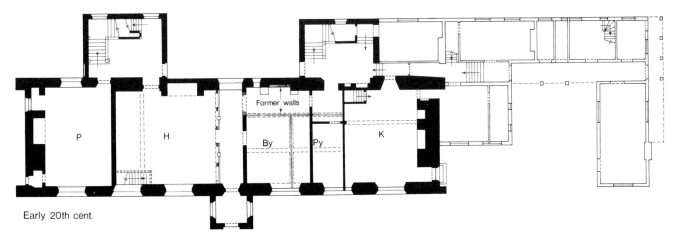

Early 20th cent.

staircase has a moulded frame, slightly recessed in the way usual in the mid 17th century, and a four-centred head with shields of arms carved in the spandrels; the arms are those of Boteler and Drury, and relate to Sir Philip Boteler, who married Elizabeth Drury and died in 1545. The spandrels, which do not fill the opening, are reset, but since they were in the house in 1877[13] must be old, despite their restored appearance; and it is on them that the ascription of the house to 1540–51[14] or the late 16th century[15] rests. All other architectural details point to the middle of the 17th century: the raised plain architraves of the front four windows; similar architraves with flat arches and lugs for the first-floor windows; a moulded cornice; curvilinear gables joined by parapets; and highly ornamented chimney-stacks, comparable to those at Rothamsted Manor (Harpenden).

The house is noteworthy for the almost perfect symmetry of all the elevations and the first-floor plan. The ground-floor plan was more conventional (Fig 15). The front door opened into a passage separated from the hall by a panelled screen in which were two openings flanked by fluted pilasters.[16] At the upper end of the hall is the doorway with heraldic spandrels and there was probably originally a door direct from hall to parlour. An unusual feature of the hall is the siting of its two windows, one large with a transom, like those of the other major rooms, and one small, without, like those of the service rooms; somewhat strangely, the small window is at the upper end of the hall. This was perhaps because, below it, was the only window in this half of the house which lit a cellar.[17] To W of the entrance rooms were two service rooms which are now defined only by bearers and mortises, although originally they were differentiated externally from the more important rooms by smaller untransomed windows. Below was a cellar, lit by the only window not on the vertical axis of the elevation.[18] A passage led past the service rooms to the kitchen.

The most remarkable feature of the house is the provision of two nearly identical spacious staircases, that to E being slightly superior in size and detail. Each was approached independently from two of the cells comprising the ground floor and each gave access to two of the principal first-floor rooms. The E staircase rises to a wide first-floor landing off which open two doorways; the W doorway opened into a large room, the fireplace of which was awkwardly placed in relation to the space to be heated. A rebate in the W jamb of the fireplace establishes that a partition, only part of which survives, once extended to the stack. The doorway on the E side of the landing gave access to a second important room, heated by another awkwardly placed fireplace set quite near the N wall. The second fireplace is of the present century and entailed the removal of a two-light window appearing in drawings by Buckler and Blore.[19] Such a disposition of fireplace and windows suggests the possibility of a partition cutting off an ante-room to the S, of which there is no other evidence. At the W end of the house there was a similar arrangement although there no evidence for a window in the chimney-stack exists. Between the principal rooms were pairs of lesser rooms, one lit from the N by a window, the other by indirect light from the staircase window through large balustraded grilles. Probably the lesser room was partitioned off from the landing and there was no doorway there, and each of these lesser rooms had two doorways leading to the adjoining major rooms. The intention underlying the whole design appears to be to eliminate passage rooms, and, by alternation of major rooms and closets intercommunicating with them, to permit the flexible use of the latter. If the dining room was upstairs it must have been approached from the W staircase, with a service room or rooms adjoining.

The second floor was a long gallery with a plastered waggon ceiling; it has two fireplaces and is lit from the gable wall as well as by four dormer windows, which form alcoves. A small cellar under the service room is approached from the W staircase and is now largely lined with modern brick; and there was formerly another cellar at the E end.

Between 1800[20] and 1832,[21] the original porch with curvilinear gable was demolished, as was a low range to NW abutting the house; the latter was supposed to have been a chapel.[22] In 1883 the upstairs windows were opened up and fitted with ovolo-moulded frames and there was a new subdivision of rooms and insertion of contemporary fireplaces to make the building a more up-to-date farmhouse;[23] the W end (parlour and room above) was subdivided to form a labourer's cottage.[24] A full-scale antiquarian restoration begun in 1909[25] included the addition of a fireplace in what had been the corridor leading to the service rooms and insertion of 'the panelling and most of the interior fittings'.[26]

For illustrations, see *English Houses 1200–1800*, Figs 116 (plate), 117, 118, 145 (plate).

Notes
1. VCH III, 56.
2. HRO, HW90.
3. VCH IV, 102.
4. *Visitations*, 37.
5. HRO LT/Misc 10.
6. Buckler Vol IV, 133,
7. Cussans 1874–8, Vol II (iii), 191.
8. VCH III, 57.
9. PRO MAF 66/12.
10. VCH III, 57; T— 1910, 450–8.
11. RCHME 1910, 42.
12. RCHME MS report.
13. Cussans 1874–8, Vol II (iii), 189.
14. Trevor Davis 1890–1, 66; VCH III, 54.
15. RCHME 1910, 42.
16. Buckler Vol IV, 135.
17. Oldfield Vol I, 278; Anderson, WCL.
18. Oldfield Vol I, 278.
19. Buckler Vol VI, 246A; BL Add MS 42040, fo 22; and see *English Houses 1200–1800*, p 187.
20. Oldfield Vol I, 278.
21. Buckler Vol IV, 135.
22. Petchey 1974–6, 179–80.
23. *The Hertfordshire Mercury and County Press*, 22 December 1888.
24. Plan as in 1908, VCH III, 54.
25. T— 1910, 457.
26. RCHME 1910, 42.

(77418)
Aston House, formerly Aston Place (TL 271225)

was demolished in recent years unrecorded and nothing about its ownership is to be found in the standard histories.[1] A schedule of writings belonging to the estate of Samuel Reeve, Gent., attached to a mortgage dated 1714[2] refers to a conveyance of lands dated 1665 from Thomas Kent to, among others, Samuel Reeve, citizen and grocer of London. Probably Reeve began building the house soon after acquiring the estate. He was a City alderman[3] who became Sheriff of Hertfordshire in 1671, when he was styled 'of Aston', and since he had acquired the advowson of the church in 1678[4] he no doubt resided at Aston House opposite. An Oldfield drawing[5] shows a late 17th-century house considerably altered in the 18th century. It had an unusual arrangement of chimney-stacks flanking the front entrance, apparently for corner fireplaces. None of the Window

Tax returns for Aston parish,[6] which range from 1715 to 1735, includes the name Reeve. In 1720 Samuel Reeve, grandson of the Sheriff, mortgaged a `capital messuage or mansion house' – presumably Aston House – to Sir John Jacob of West Wratting, so the house was evidently let to tenants then, as also in the latter part of the 18th century when it belonged to Paul Benfield.[7] During the 19th century a two-storey flat-roofed extension was added to the right of the porch and a bay window to the left.[8]

Notes
1. Miss Eileen Lynch, HRO, provided most of the information for this account.
2. HRO, D/EAB T3.
3. Chauncy II, 91.
4. HRO, D/EAS 11.
5. Oldfield Vol I, 283.
6. HRO, LT Misc 10.
7. Oldfield Vol I, 282.
8. Photographs, Stevenage Museum.

(77420)
Chells Manor (TL 267253)

comprises a hall and two cross-wings. An Oldfield drawing,[1] captioned Chells Manor House, depicts a generally similar house which is so different in detail that the caption may be wrong. The house was probably built in the late 14th or early 15th century by a member of the Wake family, who owned the manor from 1359 to 1521.[2] Only the middle range, which incorporates an open hall, is medieval; the wings were added in the 16th and 17th centuries and further alterations took place in the mid 19th century and the present century. All that remains of the original house are the N and S walls and the tie-beams; bays to E and W probably existed but have left no trace.

The heightening of the hall range, shown externally by the slight outward slope of the upper part of the wall, is confirmed by the existence of the old wall-plate in a first-floor room, just above the floor; in the same room a lath-and-plaster casing probably conceals an old tie-beam; and the roof incorporates many re-used smoke-blackened rafters. The original entrance doors were no doubt at the W end of the hall, and there was probably a further bay beyond the hall at each end.

The wing to W of the hall was built c1600; it incorporates a kitchen to N which may have had a timber chimney-stack originally; the present stack, which has two square flues[3] and weathered offsets, is of the late 17th century. Features appropriate to a kitchen are an original outside door (now blocked) and a large W window, which has been renewed and may not represent the original size, to throw light on the fireplace; there is also a smaller four-light window (blocked) to light the opposite end. The room to S has no fireplace and could have been a service room but the cellar below suggests it may have been a parlour. A smaller middle room, though now a pantry, may have accommodated a staircase for which there is no other obvious place. The E wing is somewhat later, perhaps of the second quarter of the 17th century, and has a double jetty matching the W wing. It has old fireplaces, and may, like the W wing, have combined an unheated parlour with a service room or rooms. A puzzling structural feature is that although the S gable of the wing is jettied, which appears to imply that there were ceilings (if not attics), the tie-beams flanking the short middle bay are cambered, as if this part were open at least to the height of the collar-beams.

There is no evidence to suggest that the flooring over and heightening of the hall took place before the building of its

chimney-stack, which is dated by sunk panels to c1700. The narrow stair, said to be of the early 17th century,[4] cannot be earlier than this. It may have been built because there was then no intercommunication between the W wing and the room over the hall. Its building probably marks the abandonment of the old passage entrance in favour of a new door at the E end of the hall. In the second quarter of the 19th century the E side of the house became the main entrance and was given hung-sash windows and treated nearly symmetrically. The rooms flanking the new staircase-hall were perhaps a parlour or study to N and dining room to S; both had chimney-stacks of this date. A passage prolonging the line of the entrance-hall was cut off from the old hall, which probably became a kitchen, so that the house approximated to a common kind of farmhouse plan of the period; the W wing kitchen then became a brewhouse; all windows except those to E were renewed as casements.

For illustrations, see *English Houses 1200–1800*, Figs 14 (plate), 46.

Notes
1. Oldfield Vol VI, 191.
2. VCH III, 144.
3. RCHME photograph, 1909 – now altered.
4. `evidently original', VCH III, 139; RCHME 1910, 214.

(77419)
Nos 43/45 Benington Road (TL 275227)

was built in the 17th century. It is of two storeys and attics, rendered and structurally of two bays with a short bay between them for the chimney-stack; it has a lobby-entrance and two rooms on each floor; on the first floor only the room to S has a fireplace. Such framing as is exposed is of quite large scantling; that on the ground floor appears to be close-studding; on the first floor curved braces form a pattern of Kentish framing. The first-floor fireplace has a bolection-moulded wooden surround and the downstairs fireplace formerly had a simpler one, both, apparently, of the late 17th century. In the early 19th century the house was converted into two cottages; the original staircase to E of the chimney-stack was removed and replaced by two staircases. Renovation in 1985 revealed in the first-floor room to N a painted representation of elaborate strapwork panelling, with a central diamond-shaped motif in the centre of each panel.

(77421)
Lords Farm (TL 273241)

contains no detail definitely datable before the late 17th century but its plan does not conform to any known type or familiar sequence of development. To E, and aligned N–S (correctly, to SE, and NW–SW) is a two-storey timber-framed range with 17th-century details; it is unusually wide (19 ft 6 ins (6 m)) and of two unequal bays (10 ft and 15 ft 6 ins (3 m and 4·7 m)), the larger being to S; to S is a large chimney-stack. To W is a wing of two storeys comprising one room on each floor and to N is a range of two bays, narrower than the main range but aligned with it; to N the chimney-stack, of the late 17th century or perhaps c1700, may be original. A brick range added to W c1800 incorporates a narrow entrance leading to a staircase-hall formed in the N bay of the main range.

(77422)
Yew Tree Cottage, 60 Tatlers Lane, Aston End (TL 267241),

of one storey and attics, was built in the early 16th century. It comprised an open hall of two unequal bays between two end bays (Fig 16); neither of the latter has any positive evidence of an upper floor. In the hall the only exposed timbers are in the roof,

Fig 16 *Yew Tree Cottage, No. 60 Tatlers Lane, Aston End: plan*

which has clasped-purlins and curved windbraces; the tapered end of one wall-plate is visible. In the late 17th century a chimney-stack was built in the hall and an upper storey provided throughout. In the late 18th or early 19th century the lintel of the fireplace was raised and a brick oven was added in the N jamb.

For an illustration, see *English Houses 1200–1800*, Fig 303 (plate).

AYOT ST LAWRENCE

(79341)
The Manor House (TL 195170)

is a comparatively small building of double-depth plan which was superseded by Ayot House in the early 18th century. The manor descended in 1661 to Robert Bristowe,[1] who paid for eight hearths in 1662, and in 1673 his son William paid for seven.[2] These returns must relate to the present house, which can be dated on stylistic grounds to the middle or third quarter of the 17th century. The house faces W and comprised four ground-floor rooms; the front doorway opened into the hall, behind which was the kitchen; the other room at the front was no doubt the parlour and the fourth room was perhaps originally an unheated service room. In 1724 and 1735 'Madam Bristowe' was assessed for 6s window tax for between 10 and 19 windows;[3] she had sold the manor in 1714[4] and evidently continued to live in the old house until her death. Subsequent alteration, particularly in the 19th and 20th centuries, has removed virtually all old details except the exposed bridging and common joists; and a passage was created between hall and kitchen to a N (garden) door.

For an illustration, see *English Houses 1200–1800*, Fig 129 (plate).

Notes
1. VCH III, 60.
2. PRO E179/375/30 and 31.
3. HRO, LT Misc 10.
4. VCH III, 60.

AYOT ST PETER

(77423)
Ayot Bury (TL 217153)

was probably built in the early 18th century. It was then a small house of brick and two storeys and attics comprising two ground-floor rooms, a central staircase-hall, and a back wing (Fig 17). A terracotta plaque bearing the initials and date C H/1686 and now set in a modern chimney does not relate to the present house. The rooms E and W of the entrance-hall retain an

original moulded cornice and a reeded cornice of *c*1830 respectively, but otherwise no old detail survived enlargement and alteration in the late 19th century by Sir Alfred Reynolds.[1]

Note
1. *Kelly* 1912; Newton brochure.

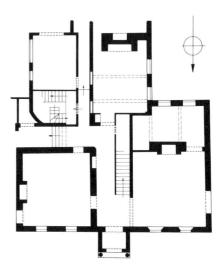

Fig 17 *Ayot Bury, Ayot St Peter: plan*

(77424)
Ayot Place (TL 211148)

appears to be the manor house of Ayot St Peter[1] and was built in the 15th century, perhaps by John Fish who was murdered in 1494.[2] The only remaining part of the original house is an open hall of two bays; the roof has an arch-braced tie-beam truss with traceried spandrels, principal rafters, cambered collar-beams, and two purlins on each side. There is no trace of the cross-passage and service rooms; they were perhaps to N. In the early 17th century a cross-wing of close-studded timber framing was added to N; it incorporated a parlour and, to W, a staircase (Fig 18). An upper floor was inserted into the hall at that time, probably at first only in the N bay; mortises cut into the tie-beam adjoining the open truss show that a partition existed here. A second adjoining beam was presumably inserted later when the S bay was floored over; it supported the studs of another partition. If the ornament on the shafts of the hall chimney has been faithfully copied, and something vaguely like it is shown by Buckler,[3] the stack and possibly the floor in the S bay also were built in the mid 17th century. Only the N bay is now of two storeys, but the Buckler drawing shows the dormer windows which still exist and which would be pointless lighting a hall still partly of one storey. In 1673 Mr William Hale paid for 12 hearths.[4] The rendering shown in Buckler's drawing was probably put on in the 18th century and removed in the 19th century during the restoration which removed part of the upper floor and the partitions in the hall. Then, presumably, a beam with ornament and cresting of Jacobean type and the date 1615 was put in. The reason for thinking this is comparatively modern work is that it masks the mortises in the beam mentioned above, which appears to have formed part of a partition. The tithe award map of 1838[5] suggests that the hall range was longer than now, although it is not certain when it was truncated. About 1916 the house was renovated and extended to the W; further

Fig 18 *Ayot Place, Ayot St Peter: plan*

alterations were made by Lady Kesteven in the 1930s.[6] On the ground floor the remaining part of the N wing and the N end of the hall now form one large room.

Notes
1. VCH III, 63–4.
2. *Cal Inq. p.m.* Hen VII, II.
3. Buckler Vol IV, 146.
4. PRO E179/375/31.
5. HRO, DSA4 10/2.
6. Inf. Mr D Cory-Wright.

BALDOCK

(77425)
`Ancient House',

demolished, location unknown, is known from a drawing of 1840.[1] It was timber framed and of three storeys, the first floor being jettied and the second flush, and comprised two distinct buildings, one set back a little behind the other. Its interest lies in a resemblance to some timber-framed buildings in London of late 17th-century appearance, Nos 273 and 413 The Strand,[2] which also had shallow pedimented bay windows and modillioned eaves cornices.

Notes
1. Buckler Vol I, 12.
2. Paul 1894, Plates XVIII and VII.

(77426)
Church Cottages, Nos 1/3 Church Street,

are adjoining houses of which No. 1 is a 15th-century timber-framed gatehouse facing E; it has one storey above the gateway and three storeys in the flanking structure to S. In the latter the ground floor is low and was probably a storeroom; the first-floor room has exposed heavy timbering; the second floor is jettied to the E and W, also S to the churchyard, and has a crown-post roof with plain four-way braces. The staircase is housed in a short W

wing jettied to S; originally it had straight flights to landings that were lit by two-light windows on the S side; one window survives and the position of another is evident; they were square-headed and of two trefoiled lights with trefoiled and quatrefoiled piercings above; the mullions have a double hollow chamfer. The chimney-stack is a later insertion and there is no sign that the building had one originally. Number 3 Church Street is not part of the gatehouse range, and although of 17th-century origin has been so completely renovated in the present century in a generally Queen Anne style as to be of little interest.

(77427)
Holford House, No. 9 High Street,

was built *c*1720–30; about a hundred years later it was enlarged to N by building over a side entrance; *c*1936 additions and alterations were made by the architects Richardson and Gill; in 1971 it was converted into offices and the original staircase sold. The original three-storey elevation was of five bays and of brick, the remaining walls being timber framed. The ground plan comprised a narrow entrance-hall between two rooms of unequal size, leading to a square staircase-hall to S of which, in a short rear wing, was the dining room. The kitchen, with a wide, shallow fireplace, was underneath it in the basement; a staircase leads up from it into a servery adjoining the dining room. A corner fireplace has been removed from the room to N of the staircase, which may have been an office or study. On the first floor were three bedrooms and a dressing room over the hall; possibly one or two of the four second-floor rooms were for family rather than servants' use.

(77428)
No. 16 High Street

(formerly Baldock Urban District Council offices, now Goldcrest Hotel) is a brick house of three storeys and was built in 1728; it incorporates a timber-framed rear wing which is probably of the 16th century, although no old features can now be seen inside or out. The 18th-century part appears to have had one large room and one smaller one on ground and first floors alike; the rear wing included a kitchen and service rooms. About the end of the 19th century the staircase and much panelling were replaced in reproduction style and a two-storey porch was added. For the prominence given to the staircase and the fewness of rooms this house may be compared to No. 107 St Peter's Street, St Albans.

(77429)
The Manor House, No. 21 High Street,

was built in the early 18th century; it is of brick and faces S (correctly SE); the ground plan comprises an entrance-hall of three bays' width with fireplace to W. To N two staircases flank a corridor leading to rear; the principal staircase to E, rising only to the first floor, has turned balusters and moulded handrail; that to W is simpler and rises to the second floor. To N of the hall and staircases is a large room, probably originally two; to S are two smaller rooms, out of which a corridor has been taken. To E a service wing was added or rebuilt *c*1830; the first-floor fireplaces are of that date, some of marble, others of wood, but all with fluted or reeded jambs; and a porch was added then. In the early 20th century the entrance-hall was fitted with reproduction panelling in early 18th-century style.

(77430)
No. 23 High Street,

now Clare House but formerly Brewery House, formed part of Simpson's Brewery until the plant was closed in the late 1960s. It is a brick building, the principal part of which, the middle block,

Fig 19 *No. 7 Hitchin Street, Baldock: first-floor plan*

is of three storeys and was built in the mid 18th century. This part comprised on the ground floor two rooms flanking an entrance-hall, with the main staircase, a small rear hall and a minor room behind them. Blocked windows show that the rear elevation was also of five bays and that no back wing existed then, although to S one bay of an earlier timber-framed building was refronted and perhaps incorporated a kitchen. In the general lines of its planning this house, although smaller, may be compared with the front range of Beechwood Park, Flamstead. Subsequent additions begin with a new kitchen block to N, followed by wings to NE and SE, and finally a large single-storey wing to S. The NE wing incorporates a large dining room on the ground floor; the wall of the original house was replaced by two columns to provide circulation and service space.

For illustrations, see *English Houses 1200–1800*, Figs 280 (plate), 281.

(77431)
No. 24 High Street, The Gates,
incorporates a large late-medieval timber gateway. The adjoining buildings were not fully investigated but the wing to W immediately behind the street range incorporates an open hall with smoke-blackened roof. This suggests that a fairly large house was arranged round a courtyard. Two phases of building are apparent: the end of the 17th century, from which a staircase with twisted balusters survives, and the early 19th century, when a general renovation, including refronting, took place.

(79347)
No. 48 High Street
comprises a 17th-century timber-framed wing aligned E–W and a brick range facing the street at right-angles to it; the latter is early Victorian with an original shop front; to N and of the same build are maltings. The rear wing has a large internal chimney-stack with two back-to-back fireplaces, lobby-entrance to N and staircase to S; the wide E fireplace and the one to the chamber above it have bolection-moulded surrounds; the staircase has turned balusters and moulded rail. This plan implies that the present street range replaces an earlier one, probably with a gateway to N leading to the rear premises.

(77432)
Houses at corner of Hitchin Street (Nos 1–5) and Bell Lane
are jettied towards both streets. They are probably of 16th-century date. The corner shop has a dragon-beam and exposed joists, all the timbers being chamfered. Not all the buildings could be examined.

(77433)
No. 7 Hitchin Street
was built *c*1500 (Fig 19); it was originally jettied and of three bays with a crown-post roof. A chimney-stack at the W end also serves a jettied S wing; both are probably of the early 17th century. In the front range a staircase and chimney-stack were inserted in the middle and E bay respectively in the early 18th century. Either then or in the early 19th century, when it received ground-floor bay windows, the house was refronted and the jetty underbuilt.

(77434)
No. 16 Hitchin Street,
of three storeys, was built in the mid 18th century (Fig 20). The symmetrical front E elevation is of five bays; the plan comprised four rooms flanking a narrow entrance-hall and a wider staircase-hall at the rear. Bay windows on the ground floor to E and a large wing to SW were added *c*1840–50; the staircase was removed then and two new ones built.

Fig 20 *No. 16 Hitchin Street, Baldock: plan*

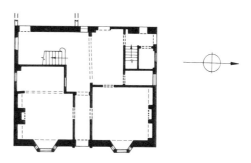

(77435)
The Bury, Nos 33/33A Hitchin Street,
is a five-bay brick house of two storeys and attics and was built *c*1700. The front (N) elevation was originally of six bays; the plan comprised three ground-floor rooms, all with a fireplace; on the first floor the room to W had no fireplace. The rear staircase turret with curvilinear gable retains the original staircase; to W is the kitchen wing. The E wing, now a separate house (No 33A), is a mid 19th-century addition of grey brick; the older house was refenestrated and otherwise altered then.

(77436)
Nos 3/5 Sun Street
stand on the N side of a street formed by the encroachment on the medieval market-place; the former was the open hall and the latter the cross-wing of a 15th-century house. The cross-wing has a crown-post roof with moulded base and caps and four-way braces, and is unusual in being jettied at both gable ends; the original staircase was in approximately the same position as the present one, in the NW corner; the landing was lit by a mullioned window.

(77437)
Oak House, No. 22 Whitehorse Street,
comprises three parts of which the rearmost, of the early 16th century, is the oldest and the front, which was rebuilt in the early 18th century, the latest. The S bay of the early 16th-century building, at right-angles to the street, was jettied to W; the two bays to N have what looks like a Wealden structure on the first floor, but are anomalous in lacking mortises and peg-holes for

braces and any housing for the wall-plate. To N is a late 16th-century block roofed E–W; it has a four-centred door-head and clasped-purlin roof and is perhaps a parlour and chamber over; if so the house stood back from the street. In the final phase two principal ground-floor rooms were added, together with a staircase and passage to the older parts of the house.

For an illustration, see *English Houses 1200–1800*, Fig 257.

BARKWAY

(77438)
Cokenach (TL 395361),
a manor, formerly the sheepfold of Royston Priory,[1] was leased to Robert Chester in 1537 and sold to him, with the priory, in 1540.[2] Chester, a gentleman-usher to Henry VIII, was knighted

Fig 21 *Cokenach, Barkway: ground and first-floor plans*

in 1551 and Sheriff in 1565 (when he was 'of Royston'), and converted the priory buildings into his principal seat but evidently built a new house at Cokenach before 1574, the date of his death. The only other possible builder of this house, his son and heir Edward, who was colonel in the Low Countries[3] and died in 1577,[4] is less likely to have engaged in building-works. After Sir Robert's death his widow resided at Cokenach, which was referred to as 'the Lady Chester's house', when it was considered as a place of call for a royal progress in 1578. Plans were then made of both floors[5] (*English Houses 1200–1800*, Fig 105). An aerial perspective engraved *c*1700 by Drapentier shows the buildings existing in 1578 substantially intact although a freestanding house had been added to them by another Sir Robert Chester, son of Edward. The new work was added after 1599, when Robert Chester 'of Royston' was Sheriff, and probably about the time he was knighted in 1603; by 1634 he was 'of Cokenach' and his eldest son Edward 'of Royston'.[6] In 1663 the executors of Sir Edward Chester paid for 22 hearths.[7]

In the early 18th century the house built by the second Sir Robert Chester was replaced by the present house, which has a rain-water head dated 1716. A plan of the estate of Robert Chester surveyed in 1728[8] shows that the new house was larger than the old one and linked the two ranges existing in 1578; the latter retained to a remarkable degree the outlines discernible in Drapentier's engraving, which in turn are essentially those of the 16th-century buildings. The 1728 plan may have been made when the estate was sold to Admiral Sir John Jennings, who had earlier purchased the adjoining Newsells Park.[9] About 1780 the house was sold to Sir John Chapman, Bart., and later descended to Sir William Clinton,[10] who in 1830, on his retirement from the army with the rank of general, and from the House of Commons as MP for Newark, came to live here.[11] His alterations are attested by a rain-water head inscribed 'W H C 1833'. About the turn of the century the house was considerably altered inside, probably by Alexander Crossman who purchased the estate in 1896,[12] and secondly, about 1925, by Douglas Crossman (Fig 21).[13] The present garden layout retains much of the overall shape of its predecessor drawn *c*1700 and some individual features, though altered, perpetuate the form of older ones; and the stableyard SE of the house is on broadly the same lines as the farmyard of which a plan was made in 1728, having been less exactly depicted in 1700.

The first Sir Robert Chester's house, which may have been built in the late 1560s, comprised two parallel ranges flanking a courtyard closed by a wall at both ends. The entrance-gate was in the N (correctly NE) wall; the hall was at the S end of the W range, and the parlour, evidently a dining room, lay between it and the pantry. Two ground-floor rooms are described as chambers; there were three good-sized and two small first-floor chambers, and over the kitchen and other offices in the E range were bedchambers, not particularised. Some of these chambers must have served the purpose of lodgings. In the early years of the 17th century a building of comparatively modest size, only two rooms and perhaps some 40 ft (12 m) in length and of unknown depth, was erected at the N end of the courtyard, unconnected with either of the existing ranges. The engraving of 1700 shows that it was of two storeys with an oversailing balustrade at the front surmounted by a tall tower-like lantern. Since the house must have been comparatively small, all service functions must have been carried out in the older buildings, which probably incorporated chambers for both the family and guests. No early 17th-century work remains even in the cellars of its successor.

The house built in 1716 joined the two parallel ranges recorded in 1578, the E of which is perpetuated by the existing wing that was probably at first incorporated as a service wing without much alteration. A drawing by Oldfield of *c*1800[14] shows a lower E range aligned with the house, either replacing or incorporating the block shown there by Drapentier in 1700. Possibly the W wing survived into the 19th century; in so far as measurements can be scaled off the plan of 1578 they suggest that this wing may have joined the 18th-century work where there is now a rain-water head of 1833 and brickwork of a slightly different character from that elsewhere. The plan of the early 18th-century work is impossible to reconstruct with any certainty and must have been altered considerably when the W wing was removed. Originally entrance was probably into a square hall with a saloon behind it. The present staircase is unsuitably located to serve the whole house, especially since the W wing is likely to have contained some of the less important bedchambers, so a second and perhaps the principal stair can be assumed to have stood W of the hall. In 1833 the creation of a new S entrance approached from the W and shown in a drawing of 1841[15] entailed the demolition of one wing. At that time the W side of the house was widened, as a wall in the basement on the old line and a slight difference in the external brickwork testify, and a W bay window was added.[16] The new upstairs rooms were served by an axial corridor leading from the E staircase, which thereafter became the only family stair. In 1842 the large room at the W end was the drawing room.[17] Interestingly, the new windows copy the style of the 1716 work, although a lodge[18] was built in Tudor style. No doubt the service rooms and kitchen were in the E wing and at the E end of the front range. The date 1833 suggested for the demolition of the W wing would fit the piecemeal rebuilding of the E wing, still incorporating a kitchen but enlarged by adding a SE wing. In the present century ground-floor additions have been made at front and back; the E end has been rebuilt; the staircase moved; and the interior so altered that scarcely any original or even old detail remains.

For illustrations, see *English Houses 1200–1800*, Figs 104 (plate), 105 (plate), 106.

Notes
1. Munby 1977, 129.
2. VCH IV, 33.
3. *Visitations*, 40.
4. VCH III, 260.
5. PRO SP 12/125.
6. *Visitations*, 40.
7. PRO E179/375/30.
8. HRO, D/E Ry P1.
9. VCH IV, 29; *DNB*.
10. VCH IV, 33.
11. *DNB*.
12. MS notes by Captain Sir Humphrey de Trafford, in possession of Mr D J Lewis.
13. Inf. Mr Olaf Kier.
14. Oldfield Vol I, 514.
15. Buckler Vol II, 113.
16. Ibid.
17. Drawing by Charlotte Bosanquet.
18. Buckler Vol II, 114.

(77439)
Nos 59/61 High Street

(only No. 61 could be visited) was built in the first quarter of the 17th century, apparently as an inn. The plan comprised a carriage entrance with service rooms to N and two rooms sharing an internal chimney-stack to S; on the first floor were three principal rooms. To S of the carriage entrance are two two-storey bay windows, emphasising the importance of the four rooms in this part of the house; to N only the chamber over the service room had a bay window.[1] The lobby-entrance to W of the stack may not be original; the main staircase lay to E with perhaps another, lit by a small high window[2] in the NW corner of the service room; how the first-floor guest rooms were reached is uncertain. The second floor has three boldly jettied dormer gables, apparently without windows; under the wall-plates are large scrolled brackets; the tie-beams are moulded and were formerly joined to give a continuous eaves-line.[3] The chimney-stacks had octagonal shafts with deep conjoined corbelled caps. The Buckler drawing suggests that the two first-floor bay windows may each have had a small fixed light to S; a larger light to N of the lobby-entrance serves no obvious purpose and may be an error. Towards the end of the 17th century a staircase wing was added to E; two wings to NE and SE may be of the same date. In the early 20th century the building was divided into two houses and narrowed to N; the wing to SE was truncated; the bay window to N was enlarged to two storeys; the chimney-stacks rebuilt with simpler caps; and the exterior rendered. The late 17th-century staircase may have been altered then.

Notes
1. Buckler Vol II, 111.
2. Ibid.
3. Ibid.

(77440)
Nos 93–97 High Street (TL 384353)

is a thatched Wealden house, and was probably built at the end of the 15th century. The exposed framing is comparatively poorly finished; at the N end of the hall are peg-holes for a bench. To N the E wall of the ground-floor room has a shutter groove and there is another upstairs, to W. The roof has crown-posts braced downwards to the tie-beams. A chimney-stack and an upper floor were inserted in the hall c1600 and painted decoration was applied in both hall and parlour. In the mid 18th century the hall was refronted in brick, leaving the plaster cove intact, and the jetties were underbuilt. The house was divided into three cottages c1800; two have been restored.

(77442)
Newsells,
also called Newsells Park (approximately TL 386371),

was burnt out and demolished in 1943. Much of its history can be reconstructed from a book of plans and other drawings made in 1805, now in the possession of Mr D J Lewis, and on which most of the following account is based.

Newsells was an important manor in the Middle Ages, the principal place (*caput*) of a barony, and was in the hands of the Scales family until the death in 1483 of Anthony Woodville, 2nd Earl Rivers,[1] to whom the estate had descended by marriage; thereafter until 1579 it belonged to the Vere earls of Oxford.[2] Despite these aristocratic connections there is nothing to suggest a house of any importance up to that time. On the evidence of the plan, the house in its earliest phase can be assumed to have had a main range flanked by two cross-wings projecting forward, and to have had two staircases; this plan has points of resemblance with Bride Hall, Wheathampstead, and the thinness of the first-floor N wall of the W wing suggests that the building was originally timber framed. This modest house was presumably built by Henry Prannell, alderman and vintner of London, who purchased the manor in 1579 and died in 1594, or by his son, also Henry, who died in 1599.[3] In the early 17th century this family was Prannell of Rushdenwells (now Rushingwells Farm, Barkway (TL 381351)), which must have been their principal seat; it is only about 1 1/4 miles (2·2 km) to S. In 1653 Sir Robert Kingsby was in possession of Newsells and in 1663 the administrator of his estates paid tax on 12 hearths.[4]

In the late 17th century, Newsells Park and demesne were purchased by William Newland, who transferred them to his son Thomas;[5] one of them, probably William, enlarged the house and refronted it in the form shown c1700 by Drapentier. To judge from the plans a N wing was added, more than doubling the floor area of the house. The principal feature was a large dining room facing N and rising through two storeys; it had a coved ceiling, carved architraves to the windows and doors and is described as being embellished with carvings in the style of Grinling Gibbons;[6] there must also have been a new staircase. The external detail was normal for the period; the principal chimney-shafts, and those of the hall range and principal wing rooms, apparently had carved shafts of the kind found at Rothamsted Manor, Harpenden; the less important shafts at the rear of the house are represented as having diagonal shafts but the distinction may not be reliable.

During the 18th century, the house was heightened to three storeys and since it also had attics it continued, rather surprisingly, to have roofs of a comparatively steep pitch which rose above a parapet. At the same time a W wing was added; although it was of a single storey it presented a two-storeyed appearance and there was certainly a somewhat wider balancing E wing; that it was only one room deep is apparent from the small break back in the E wall. All this work may have been done by Admiral Sir John Jennings,[7] who purchased Newsells Park some twenty years before his death in 1743. That he made some changes to the house is established by a rain-water head dated 1739 on the rear wing;[8] this may apply to some of the interior decoration that includes festoons and swags on the walls[9] and the staircase shown in the 1805 plans may also have been built then.

In the late 18th century the E wing was enlarged at the back, heightened to two storeys, given a new front of elliptical plan and decorated in the Adam style.[10] The ground-floor room was then, as it may well have been earlier, the library. At the same time the N wing was enlarged to the E, and as a consequence the main structure must thereafter have needed some top-lighting. Probably the flat-roofed colonnaded porch is part of the same building campaign; so, too, may be the large kitchen wing on the W side with a Venetian window. The plans of the house showing how it was used in 1805 have been redrawn in *English Houses 1200–1800*, Fig 210. Little is known of the subsequent history of the house except that in the late 19th century the porch was replaced by a single-storey garden room with mullion-and-transom windows; this in turn was removed and replaced by a pedimented doorway, and the festoons in the dining room were rearranged.[11]

For illustrations, see *English Houses 1200–1800*, Figs 149 (plate), 210, 211.

Notes
1. *DNB*.
2. VCH IV, 28–9.
3. Ibid, 29; *Visitations*, 159.
4. PRO E179/248/23.
5. Chauncy II, 203.
6. VCH IV, 26.
7. *DNB*.
8. VCH IV, 27.

9. Illustration, *CL* advertisement of early 1920s, loaned by Mr P Reid.
10. VCH IV, 26.
11. Illustration, *CL* advertisement of early 1920s, loaned by Mr P Reid.

(77443)
Newsells Bury (TL 387369)

is a small double-pile house built *c*1700, of two storeys and attics and originally of five bays; in the early 19th century the front was altered to three bays with big three-light windows flanking a new front doorway. In 1807 it was Mr Hantchet's house and the land adjoining to the S was part of his farmyard.[1]

Note
1. Plans of Newsells.

(77441)
The Want House, No. 106 High Street (TL 384355),

was built in the early 16th century and comprised a main range facing E with a cross-wing to N. The wing was originally jettied on three sides and incorporated the cross-passage and two service rooms; the open hall which adjoined it has been demolished; to S was a further bay in series with the hall. The only evidence of date is a reverse-curved brace in the wing. The hall was rebuilt *c*1600 with two storeys and a chimney-stack, and the bay to S end was replaced by a cross-wing with lofty upper storey. In the mid 17th century the stack was rebuilt with three conjoined shafts, and a staircase wing added. In the mid 19th century the house was refaced in yellow brick and a shop front put into the S wing.

BARLEY

(77444)
Lower Farm

(known as Lower Yard), of *c*1500, has a storeyed bay to W with an end-jetty towards the street. The hall to E has an upper floor and a chimney-stack of brick incorporating some clunch blocks; a possible date may be *c*1600. A first-floor fireplace to W has a shallow four-centred head, above which is a wall-painting of three vases of flowers.

(77445)
The Town House (TL 401383)

is of the early 16th century, jettied, of two storeys and four bays, the largest of which, to W, formed a separate room on the first floor. The position of the original staircase is unknown; the existing two staircases to N and W are modern.[1]

Note
1. Rigold 1973, 94–9.

BAYFORD

(77446)
Bayfordbury (TL 315104)

succeeded what is now called Bayfordbury Park Farm as the manor house of the three former manors of Bayford, all of which had been since 1678 in the possession of Israel Mayo.[1] In 1758 they were sold to the rich merchant Sir William Baker[2] who, by 1767, owned an estate of 3,000 acres (1,214 has).[3] By 1760 he was building a new house `a little above the Bury farm', which was

completed by 1762, and enclosing a park.[4] On his death in 1772 Sir William Baker was succeeded by his son William, MP for the county in all Parliaments from 1790 to 1807, who between 1809 and 1812 carried out extensive alterations to Bayfordbury[5] to the designs of Francis Aldhouse.[6]

The house of 1762 was a brick building of two storeys and seven bays, raised up on a basement; walls of the same height as the basement concealed corridors joining the main block to detached wings, that to E containing kitchens, that to W stables. In the early 19th century wings and house were connected by single-storey blocks and the exterior was stuccoed and remodelled in the Greek Doric style.

In 1939 the house was purchased by the John Innes Institute to become a horticultural research station and in 1965 was acquired by Hertfordshire County Council to form part of Hatfield Polytechnic.

The plan of the 1762 house has been altered beyond recovery. The present entrance-hall corresponds to the original one and retains the original fireplace and ceiling; the room to E has a ceiling of 1762; the room to SW is said to be the original dining room.[7] Possibly the staircase lay to E of the present one, where it could be lit by a window in the outside wall. By 1812 the present plan with long axial corridors extending from the staircase-hall had been adopted. The large room added to E was presumably both dining room and picture gallery, as it was in recent times,[8] and its counterpart to W was the Great Library. Other room uses marked on the plan are those of 1925.

For illustrations, see *English Houses 1200–1800*, Figs 198 (plate), 199.

Notes
1. VCH III, 420–2.
2. Ibid.
3. VCH III, 421; Kingsford 1971, 338–48.
4. Carrington *Diary*, 22.
5. Tipping 1925*a*, 94; 1925*b*, 124.
6. Colvin 1978, 63.
7. Tipping 1925*b*, 129.
8. Tipping 1925*a*, 94.

Fig 22 *Bayford House: plan*

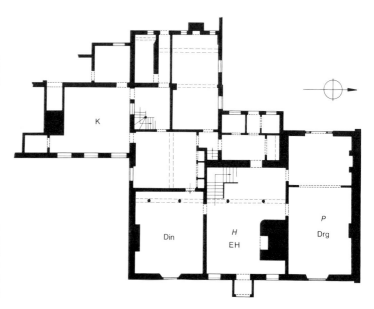

(77447)
Bayford Hall (TL 305090)

is the successor, on a different site, of one of the three pre-1678 manors of Bayford. A map of 1758[1] shows the Hall and extensive outbuildings some 300 yards (275 m) W of the parish church (approximately TL 307088), where its existence is first recorded in 1316.[2] Throughout the 14th century it was in the hands of the Scrope family; then, after a period of confused ownership, it passed to Sir John Fortescue, the Chief Justice,[3] with whose descendants it remained until 1538. The name `le Halle' or `Halle Place', which was used in the early 15th century,[4] implies that the manor house was then a building of some consequence. The map of 1758 depicts the house with an internal chimney and lobby-entrance, but the low eaves imply that it had been converted to that form in the 17th century from a medieval house with an open hall. It was perhaps comparable in size and plan to Chells Manor, Aston. In 1663 Master Ferrers was assessed for three hearths[5] and in 1678 it was sold to Israel Mayo as `the messuage or farm called Bayford Hall'.[6] When it was demolished is not known.

The present house is on the site of what was named in 1758 as Old Farm and no part of it appears to be earlier than the late 18th or early 19th century.

Notes
1. HRO, AR 626.
2. VCH III, 422.
3. *DNB.*
4. VCH III, 422.
5. PRO E179/248/23.
6. VCH III, 427.

(77448)
Bayford House (TL 305090),

although not recorded as a manor, appears to incorporate the remains of a late medieval house of manorial or equivalent status; the width of the W wing (Fig 22), its comparatively low eaves and some re-used smoke-blackened rafters in the roof suggest a hall comparable to that of Pirton Grange. There is

nothing to link this house with the appearance in the early 16th century of a third manor or capital messuage of Bayford,[1] but the documentary and architectural evidence, even though they may relate to different places within the parish, point to the same kind of development.

The subsequent evolution of the house rests on very slight evidence. The E range, ostensibly of the mid 18th century, incorporates a chimney-stack which is too large for that period and is probably part of an early 17th-century range of two storeys added to the older building. How the latter was altered then is now impossible to say; an upper floor is likely to have been inserted into the hall, and, given the L-shaped plan, there may have been a staircase where the present main staircase stands. In the mid 18th century the house was refronted, heightened to three storeys, enlarged to W and provided with a service wing to S. Subsequent alterations include the main staircase and the Doric columns screening it from the entrance-hall, which are of the early 19th century, as are the trellised porch and two front windows extending to ground level. Some of the fittings, of the late 19th or early 20th century, indicate that considerable changes took place then.

Note
1. VCH III, 422.

(77449)
Bayford Manor House (TL 312085)

(Fig 23), formerly Bayford Place, represents the most important of the three manors called Bayford.[1] It was a royal possession from the time of the Conquest until 1544 when the manor was granted to a member of the family most closely associated with it, John Knighton;[2] for as early as 1445 another John Knighton was paying for repairs to the manor, presumably as a subtenant.[3] Mention then of a chamber above the outside gate of the manor suggests a house of some consequence; and there is reference to `3,000 breke brought for the undre pynning of the same chamber'. No doubt a Knighton built the late medieval timber-framed house, part of which survives. Its precise extent is uncertain; a roof-truss of clasped-purlin type remains near the N end

Fig 23 *Bayford Manor House: plan*

of the E range and at several points on the first floor the cased-in feet of principal rafters can be seen below the ceilings.

In his will dated 1583/4 John Knighton (of the 1544 grant) reserves to the use of his wife `the chamber where she doth lie', the closet within the same, her maid's room, the brushing chamber at the stair head and the great chamber adjoining with passage to and from the house of office in the end of the same, and the little parlour with the cellar adjoining.[4] There is no documentary evidence of building-works by John or his son Sir George Knighton, but the fact that the house was called Bayford Place in 1613, when Sir George died,[5] suggests there had been some improvement. This probably took the form of rebuilding the hall with an upper floor and a wide external chimney-stack and adding another room with a comparatively low ceiling; the latter appears to have been subdivided formerly by a partition under a beam now encased and plastered. Possibly the former small room at the SW corner housed a staircase, with a parlour adjoining it. The wing to W may also be of the late 16th or early 17th century; all that can be said of it with certainty is that it must be coeval with, or earlier than, the main staircase; its thinner walls may incorporate timber framing either as a form of mixed construction or with the original infilling more or less completely rebuilt in brick.

After the death of John Knighton in 1634[6] the estate belonged to a succession of people, none of whom is likely to have done any building, until in 1655 it was bought by John Mayo.[7] Between then and 1662, the house was probably enlarged and encased in brick. The staircase is of this date; so, perhaps, is some painted panelling in a room facing the head of the stair. But the dating of the painting is open to argument: on the one hand the style has `a lingering strapwork flavour',[8] yet the panelling itself is in large squares, fits its present position, and could well be of the mid 17th century. There is no obvious sign that the partition has been reset. At Michaelmas 1662 Israel Mayo was assessed for 20 hearths,[9] and in the following March the same payment was entered in the names of John and Israel Mayo, as if the house were in joint occupation; Israel was Sheriff in 1668 and John died in 1675.[10] It was not until 1678 that Israel Mayo acquired a second house in the parish, Bayford Hall. At this period the house attained its greatest importance, and when Israel Mayo sold it in 1713 two years before his death, he was stated to be `worth £800 p.a.'.[11]

A watercolour sketch on an estate map of 1758[12] appears to depict the house as running N–S, the roof being hipped at the S end, and a large chimney-stack with shafts rising high above the roof seems to have stood somewhere N of the staircase. Possibly the sketch is inaccurate, or perhaps the angle from which it was taken is deceptive, because the hipped block may have been a detached building to W of the wing (see below). Adjoining the wing to W was another block of one storey and attics. Some parts of these two parallel ranges must have been of earlier date than the staircase. The sketch shows, in the main range, five large windows which by their proportions were of the mid 17th century; also gabled dormer windows and the roof hipped to S. After 1758, when Sir William Baker purchased the manor and proceeded to build Bayfordbury, the house was hardly more than a farmhouse and was so until the present century; but by 1912 it was the seat of Mrs Barclay[13] and had achieved substantially its present form.

By 1840[14] a second house of double-depth and of three storeys and attics, with two parallel gabled roofs, stood a few feet to W. Its distance from the wing appears to correspond to a covered passage or low building shown in the 1758 map as joining the wing to what must be the hipped block to W, from which it may be inferred that the latter had by 1848 been

enlarged, refronted as a separate house, and detached from the manor house on which it turned its back. Although it is said to have been the former rectory and its foundations are encountered in the garden,[15] its origins and function are obscure; a return to an early 18th-century Visitation noted that `By the chapel of Bayford is a House and Ground call'd ye Vicarage, £8 p.a., never in the possession of ye late or prest. Incumbt. but occupied by Mr Mayo'.[16] The date of its demolition is not known. Probably it had gone by 1851; the Census[17] enumerates Sophia Fauld, farmer, her two daughters, five sons and one house servant, and she employed eight labourers on a farm of 190 acres (77 has); but Bayford Place is listed between Bayford Hall Farm and `Joseph Stacey, farmer' with 96 acres (39 has) and there is no indication of another house nearby. In 1912 extensive alterations gave the house its present appearance.

Notes

1. VCH III, 420–2.
2. Ibid, 421.
3. HRO, Compotus Roll, 63741.
4. HRO, 1HW 41.
5. Inquisition *post mortem*, PRO C142/343/143.
6. Inquisition *post mortem*, PRO C/142/525/129.
7. VCH III, 421.
8. Rouse report.
9. PRO E179/370/30.
10. Monumental Inscription, Chauncy I, 554, correct date 553.
11. Munby 1974, 44.
12. HRO, D/EX 33 P1, 3/34.
13. *Kelly* 1912.
14. Buckler Vol III, 5.
15. Inf. Mrs S Latham.
16. Munby 1974, 44.
17. PRO HO 107/1711.

BENINGTON

(77451)
Cutting Hill Farm (TL 312221)

was built in the early 16th century and comprised an open hall flanked by two bays of one storey and semi-attics (Fig 24). The exposed framing includes the former wall-plates; the corner posts of the hall, all mortised for a rail which is well below the

Fig 24 *Cutting Hill Farm, Benington: plan*

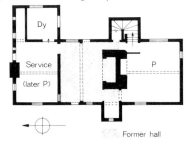

plate and was presumably intended to carry the first-floor joists of the end bays; and, in the hall, two posts with broad chamfers stopped at housings for a beam forming part of a roof truss. The ownership of the house has been traced back continuously to 1647 when, under the name of `Death's Croft in Benington' it was purchased by Henry Dixon, draper.[1] His son Henry (1625–96) of Enfield, also a draper, bequeathed the property, one of several in Benington and nearby, to the Draper's Company in 1693 in trust for apprentice boys from several parishes.[2] In the mid 17th century the house was heightened to two full storeys; the floors in the end bays were raised to be uniform with that inserted in the hall; the fireplace added in the hall has a timber lintel and, at the back, a recess with a triangular head; the fireplace in the room to S has a four-centred head in brick. It is not clear where the staircase was; the gabled stair turret appears to be an addition because a first-floor stud was removed when it was built; and since the same is true of the two-storey porch two phases of improvements may be involved, the second including the addition of the fireplace in the chamber over the hall. The staircase opens off the parlour, which was evidently the most important room in the house; the hall was also the kitchen. Later, but perhaps still in the 17th century, a dairy wing was added to N; c1800 a fireplace was added to the former service room. In the 1950s the house was extended to S to give a five-bay elevation (not shown).

Notes
1. Records of the Drapers' Company; inf. Mr M D J Chesterman.
2. Archer-Thompson 1939–40, Vol II, 157.

(77450)
The Bell PH, No. 4 Town Lane (TL 298235),

has a complicated structural development which is obscured by modern plaster and mostly has to be inferred. The oldest parts are the middle or hall range and the wing to W. The width of the main range suggests that a former open hall existed, coeval with a late medieval doorway to W which has a four-centred head. This doorway, now blocked, led into the rearmost of two rooms which were separated by a passage. The jettied E wing appears to be an addition; the principal room was at the front and a smaller room and a staircase to rear. In the mid 17th century the hall was rebuilt with two storeys and a large chimney-stack to W, backing on to a cross-passage.

The house was already an inn in 1693; it was bequeathed to the Drapers' Company and remained with them until 1910.[1] In the 18th century, perhaps c1720, a hunting scene was painted on the chimney-stack. The building was considerably altered in the mid 19th century.

Note
1. Johnson 1962, Pt 1, 40.

BERKHAMSTED

(77452)
`Ancient House',

location unknown and now demolished,[1] is of interest for the treatment of the ground-floor rooms in the wings, both of which have openings which cannot be paralleled in existing buildings; the left-hand wing has a doorway flanked by two groups of three small lights, possibly for a shop; the right-hand one has a window of quite unusual proportions with six lights. The house was no doubt timber framed but was not jettied. The right-hand wing had plaster decoration of the 1660s or 1670s; the house may have been built c1600.

For an illustration, see *English Houses 1200–1800*, Fig 263 (plate).

Note
1. Oldfield Vol II, 191.

(77453)
Ashlyns (SP 991067),

held in 1618 by Francis Wethered, was then a messuage with orchard and garden;[1] Wethered's daughter Elizabeth was the mother of Henry Guy (b.1631) of Tring Park[2] and his son Francis was Comptroller of the King's Works, 1660–8.[3] The present house, `a very pretty modern villa',[4] was built in the late 1780s by Matthew Raper Esq., who was Sheriff in 1791. The plan is nearly square overall; to S a semicircular projection of three bays is flanked to N and W by two bays; the projection forms one end of a slightly oval entrance-hall, leading to a staircase-hall to N; the latter has rounded corners to S around which rises a top-lit staircase with iron balustrade. In 1801 the house was purchased by James Smith Esq.,[5] who was Sheriff in 1808. By 1838[6] the entrance had probably been moved to W; the chosen viewpoint, from SE, and a tree combine to hide the added single-storey wing; the doorway is flanked by a pair of Tuscan columns and an outer pair of square `columns', all under one entablature. Many of the interior architraves, of semicircular section and reeded, with paterae, are of the same date, as is the conversion of a balcony around the S projection[7] into a first-floor verandah.[8] Sometime during the period between the late 19th century and the 1960s flat-roofed dormer windows were added to S.

Notes
1. PRO E315/366.
2. *DNB*.
3. *King's Works*, Vol V (1976), 469.
4. Oldfield Vol II, 179.
5. Burke's *Landed Gentry*, 565.
6. Buckler Vol I, 105.
7. Oldfield Vol II, 179.
8. Buckler Vol I, 105.

(29838)
Berkhamsted Place (SP 991088)

is the successor of the castle built in the late 11th century, probably not long after the Conquest. The castle was unoccupied after 1495 and had become ruinous by Leland's time.[1] In 1580 the manor of Berkhamsted, with which went castle and park, was leased to Sir Edward Carey who built `a large House on a different site out of the Ruins of the Castle'.[2] In 1610 the estate was granted to Henry Prince of Wales, who, on 20 December 1611, issued a warrant to pay £4,000 `due to Sir Edward Carey for erecting the house within the Prince's park at Berkhampsted'.[3] The house was sequestrated after the first Civil Wars and was occupied by Colonel Axtel, the regicide; at the Restoration it was leased to Jerome Weston, Earl of Portland, whose principal seat was at Walton-on-Thames.[4] Quite early in his tenancy much of the house was burnt. Nevertheless, `he

Fig 25 *Berkhamsted Place: plan (with room names as in 1906)*

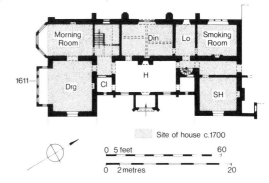

repaired the House but not above a third Part or a little more remains now standing, and yet it is a very fair large Building'.[5] In 1662 it was sub-let to John Sayer, chief cook to Charles II.[6] From 1720 to 1807 the house was tenanted by the Roper family and subsequently was purchased by John William, Earl of Bridgwater.[7] It was demolished in 1965.

Sir Edward Carey's house is stated in a Parliamentary Survey of 1650 to have been built around a courtyard and had an outer `green square court' with a porter's lodge at the entrance;[8] it must always have been approached from the E, from the direction of the town. According to the Survey, the principal elevations were built of Totternhoe stone and flint forming a chequer pattern `which doth much adorn and set forth the same'; the roofs were of slate. The `large, spacious hall' was probably to E; other ground-floor rooms included little and great parlours, the latter perhaps in the S range, and `a small room...used for a chapel'; over the parlour was the dining room, `with a fair Stone chimney-piece with the Prince's arms over same'. In the W range was `a large Gallery'; above it was a garret and below `2 lodging chambers with living and store houses belonging and a small matted room'; below the latter were `low dark rooms'. In the re-entrant angles were two newel staircases. `In another end of the buildings' a wash-house, woodhouse and chambers over formed a service range equivalent to those at Standon Lordship, Standon, or Knebworth House.

Prince Henry's alterations were probably not extensive; the gallery fireplace and a stone inscribed with the date 1611[9] are the only evidence of them. All that survived the fire of c1661 were the W range and perhaps as much as half of the N and S ranges; `that Part which escaped the Fire was the back Part of all'.[10] An engraving of c1700[11] shows that the `low room' had become an entrance-hall, reached through a pedimented classical porch and with a new staircase to S replacing one of the newel staircases. The engraving shows three tiers of windows below the garrets, in ascending order of size and importance corresponding to the rooms described in 1650; the intermediate rooms were reached from the first landing of the new staircase; a room in the N wing had a plaster overmantel of the 1660s.[12] Evidently the post-Restoration house comprised two more or less independent wings linked only through the entrance-hall and a grand first-floor room (Fig 25). To N of the N wing was an L-shaped block which appears to have comprised two distinct builds with floors at different levels;[13] possibly it incorporated the two-storey range `in another end of the building' mentioned in 1650 but if so it was heightened and enlarged c1662. Immediately after its completion the whole of the E elevation must have been rendered in order to conceal the random mixture of flint, stone and brick of which it was built. In the early 18th century the ground-floor room at the NW corner was fitted with a wooden fireplace surround having Ionic columns and pulvinated frieze and a pedimented panel above it;[14] probably then the N range was capped with a cupola.[15] In the late 18th century the two low storeys in the middle part of the W range were incorporated, making each pair of windows into one, and giving the new windows and those on the first floor false pointed heads worked in brick to give a generally Gothic appearance. By 1838 the W range had been doubled in width by the addition of a low entrance-hall and given crenellation and buttresses.[16] A fireplace to W of the new hall incorporated some late 16th-century panels in reproduction Jacobean work.[17] By 1839 the service block shown in Oliver's engraving had been rebuilt as a low two-storeyed range with a prominent kitchen chimney-stack.[18] In the mid 19th century a bay window was added to S; c1900 a square bay window was added to E and much internal refurbishing took place.

Notes
1. *King's Works*, Vol II (1963), 563.
2. Salmon 1728, 122.
3. *Cal Sp Dom* 1611–18, 101.
4. *DNB*.
5. Chauncy II, 530.
6. VCH II, 167; Chauncy II, 545.
7. VCH II, 167.
8. PRO E317/7.
9. VCH II, 170.
10. Salmon 1728, 122.
11. Chauncy II, 530.
12. Anderson, WCL 1906.
13. Oliver engraving in Chauncy 1700.
14. Anderson, WCL.
15. Oldfield Vol II, 168.
16. Buckler Vol I, 100.
17. Anderson, WCL.
18. Buckler Vol I, 101.

(77454)
Egerton House,

a large, late 16th-century house of a kind now rare in Hertfordshire, occupied the site of Nos 97–101 High Street until demolished in the 1930s. Drawings of it exist by Buckler[1] and Blore;[2] a postcard[3] and a photograph of 1910;[4] and descriptions.[5] There are discrepancies in the evidence. The house had a continuous jetty and three bay windows in each storey. Although there can be no doubt that it was timber framed and was a superior version of Nos 59/61, High Street, Barkway, chance in the form of a more selective survival of the evidence might have permitted a different conclusion to be reached. Blore shows a flush front broken only by a string course, the result of a recent underbuilding of the jetty, which conveys the impression of a brick or stone building. Although this drawing is to some degree inaccurate and certainly false to the general appearance of the building, it shows two conjoined shafts to N of the front range where Buckler shows three apparently separate diagonal shafts, and here the photographs agree with Blore. On the other hand Blore omits an internal chimney-stack, railings, and two of the four piers, all shown by Buckler and still existing in 1910; Blore's must be an idealised rendering of the subject. The underbuilding and restoration of the interior[6] probably took place before c1840, when Nos 103–109 High Street were built, replacing farm buildings adjoining to N; the porch, open in Buckler's drawing, closed in Blore's, was also altered then.

Fig 26 *No. 125 High Street, Berkhamsted: plan*

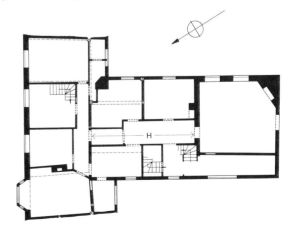

Notes
1. Buckler Vol I, 96, of 1830; Vol I, 95, of 1832.
2. BL Add MS 42020, fo 94, undated.
3. NMR.
4. RCHME.
5. RCHME 1910, 98; VCH II, 164.
6. RCHME 1910, 98.

(77455)
No. 59 Gossams Road

is a mid 17th-century house of two storeys and a two-room ground plan with an internal stack and lobby-entrance. A rear wing added c1800 no doubt replaced earlier service accommodation; the Gothick porch was added and Gothick windows inserted then.

(77456)
No. 119 High Street

is of two storeys and of brick, rendered, with a slate roof, and both inside and outside is an unremarkable early 19th-century house save for one extraordinary survival. In the first-floor rear wall of the street range are exposed a wall-post and truncated tie-beam which belong to a 16th-century or earlier building, the proportions and evidence of curved braces suggesting an open hall. This fragment is unrelated to anything else on the site.

(77457)
No. 121 High Street,

a small house of three storeys and basement, was built c1830–40. The ground-floor plan comprises a large room to W of the narrow entrance-hall, extending from front to back of the house, and a somewhat smaller one to E; possibly they were drawing room and dining room respectively. Kitchen and pantry were in the basement. The staircase, with plain balusters of square section, has on each half-landing a small room which is now, and no doubt always has been, a lavatory.

(77458)
No. 125 High Street,

the house and shop standing S of the parish church of St Peter, is of two storeys, timber-framed with a brick front, and comprises a N (properly NW) range parallel to the street and a wider wing to S (Fig 26). The wing incorporates one bay of a 14th-century open hall of raised-aisled construction. Two raised posts forming part of the E arcade and some of the braces to the plates and tie-beams are exposed; in the S truss a large brace from the W wall-post to the lower tie-beam is outlined in plaster and the peg-holes for the corresponding E brace can be seen; reversed assembly appears to have been employed for the wall-plates; the upper part of the roof has been removed entirely. The plan suggests that a second hall bay, which like the front one was 13 ft 6 ins (4 m) long, extended as far as the early 18th-century addition to S. Nothing remains to show what originally stood to N of the hall.

The N or street range is of two storeys, timber framed, and was probably built in the late 17th century; a break of alignment to W may indicate a different build. When this range was built a first floor, slightly lower than the old main tie-beams, was inserted in the hall. In the early 18th century, the wing was extended to S; it has a panelled first-floor room with a corner fireplace; the room was originally entered by a doorway (now blocked) opening from a passage which looks as if it might have had a staircase to S end; the arrangement is reminiscent of an inn although there is no evidence of that purpose here. The pilastered street front is probably of the same period. In the 19th century both floors were much altered.

(77459)
Dean Incent's House, Nos 129/131 High Street,

is so-called after John Incent, Dean of St Paul's; the connection first seems to have been first published in 1883.[1] The house is of three periods: a late medieval rear (SW) wing; the late 16th-century street range; and the SE wing of c1800 as a minor addition. The date of the SW wing is uncertain but its relation to the front range is determined by its lower first floor and by the cutting away of the N tie-beam to give access between the two parts; and although the details do not establish definitely whether the wing was of one storey or two, the latter is more likely. Its roof is not blackened by smoke so it was not part of an open hall; it may have extended N towards the street. Any such hall was replaced by a two-storeyed jettied range of three bays, entered by the doorway in the bay to E (formerly No. 127), which has a lintel of large scantling. In the hall – the middle bay – are mortises for a large bay window, probably of four lights with hollow-chamfered jambs and mullions and traceried heads, with, to W, a wide fireplace with stone jambs and probably a four-centred head; the placing of the chimney-stack to N shows that a staircase was intended to S. The E room was unheated and stands over a cellar. The upstairs rooms corresponded to those below except that there was no fireplace in the room over the hall. In recent years, early 17th-century wall-paintings have been found on the chimney-stack and staircase wall facing the hall, and in the room over the hall.

In the late 17th century, new and larger windows were inserted at the front in addition to an attic floor.

For illustrations, see *English Houses 1200–1800*, Figs 258 (plate), 259.

Note
1. Cobb 1883, 83.

(77461)
Nos 214–216 High Street

is a three-storey house of the early 18th century; the front is of brick and the remainder of timber-framing, rendered. The ground floor is now a shop; on the first floor, a room extending the full length of the four-bay front retains simply moulded panelling and ceiling cornice; a staircase with turned balusters projects into this room and the cornice is carried round it, showing that this unusual arrangement is original.

(79377)
The King's Arms, No. 147 High Street (SP 992077)

was built as an inn in the late 17th century and is first mentioned in the reign of Queen Anne;[1] the front and E walls are of brick but it is otherwise largely timber framed; the three first-floor bay windows are 19th-century replacements retaining something of the original form with a round-headed middle light. The street range facing N (correctly NE) comprised two rooms with back-to-back fireplaces, the larger room next to the covered entrance was perhaps still called the hall, with a parlour behind it; a staircase adjoining the hall was conveniently placed for arriving travellers and probably led, originally, to a gallery running to W of the rear wing. A large chimney-stack near the N end of the wing may be for a dining room, with service rooms, possibly including a bar, between it and the kitchen to S. These arrangements were much altered in the early 19th century when a third storey was added, the wing widened and corridors formed between the rooms on all floors; and a large assembly room said to be capable of accommodating 400 people was built to W of the courtyard. In its late 18th and early 19th-century heyday the King's Arms was an important place for public meetings, the petty sessions being held here.[2] A valuation of 1840 mentions a travellers' parlour, large, small and back parlours, dining room, assembly room, five bedrooms and four attics.[3]

Notes
1. Johnson 1963, Pt 2, 43–4.
2. Ibid.
3. HRO, D/ELSB 512.

(77460)
The Swan Hotel, No. 139 High Street,

incorporates a two-storey jettied range facing the street and a rear wing about 30 ft (9 m) long; the latter has had the walls removed or concealed on the ground floor and the low wall-plates, about 5 ft (1·5 m) above the first floor, provide the only hint that it had an open hall. The only datable feature is the roof of the front range which has king-struts and collar-purlins and, in the end gables, passing-braces; it is of the 14th century. The street range was extended W c1500, still jettied, with a clasped-purlin roof, and perhaps then a chimney-stack was built to W of the older part of the range. The part of the stack in the roof looks like the top of a gable wall with clunch coping in which a later brick flue has been built; perhaps originally the flue was shallow, like that of a normal medieval fireplace; this and the use of Totternhoe stone suggest it is pre-Elizabethan. In the late 16th or early 17th century an extension to E has a roof with tenoned purlins. This was accompanied by changes in the hall, probably involving the insertion of an upper floor and a chimney-stack. The painted glass formerly in the kitchen window of the Swan Inn[1] may have been put in then; it included two diamond-shaped panels with a bird (perhaps an ostrich) and the letters I B, and a third with the initials T A; but there was also a roundel with a winged ox and the inscription *Fuit vir in diebus erodie regis jude* [?] *prima capitula*,[2] perhaps early 16th century. Although the building may well have been an inn from the first, there is no definite evidence of its being so until the late 17th century, when a gallery was built to W of the hall range, returning along the front range beyond the present covered entrance. The E wing may be of the same date; it has no gallery and may have been served by a second staircase. The hall range was extended c1800 when the Swan ran its own coach to London;[3] then and later the interior has been greatly altered, especially on the ground floor.

For illustrations, see *English Houses 1200–1800*, Figs 249 (plate), 289.

Notes
1. Buckler, BL Add MS 32348, fos 132–3.
2. Vulgate, Luke 1: 5.
3. Johnson 1963, Pt 2, 45.

(77462)
The Market House

is depicted in a drawing of 1832;[1] it was a small timber-framed building of two bays comprising an open market hall on the ground floor and an upper storey jettied to S and lit by two two-light windows with four-centred heads. This is probably the building mentioned in the Parliamentary Survey of 1653 as the Corn Market, 'built with timber and lofted overhead';[2] there were also the similarly described Butter Market, which was 18 ft (5·5 m) square or thereabouts, and the butchers' shambles, 50 ft by 12ft (15·3 m x 3·7 m) and divided into several stalls. A report of 1653 by Commissioners for removing obstructions on the sale of the king's lands[3] quotes payments made in 1587 for building the church house, shamble house, cross house and market house.

Notes
1. Buckler Vol I, 97.
2. PRO.
3. In custody of the Town Clerk, Berkhamsted.

(77463)
'The residence of Peter de Noüal Esqr'

is depicted in a lithograph of 1805[1]; he was otherwise known as 'de Noil' (Land Tax). It is of interest as an extreme example of what now appear as disparate elements forming what was evidently found an acceptable elevation at the time. The architectural history of many Hertfordshire houses exemplifies the concern in the later 19th and early 20th centuries for a unified smooth Georgian appearance which has caused such irregular elevations to disappear.

For an illustration, see *English Houses 1200–1800*, Fig 142 (plate).

Note
1. HRO, among Oldfield drawings, Vol II, 171.

BISHOP'S STORTFORD

(77464)
'Ancient House',

location unknown, was drawn c1800 by Oldfield,[1] who indicated the probable date of the house and in particular of the wide four-centred arch with sunk spandrels; 'carvd on a beam under the Gateway' was the inscription 'THOM. S KYNDER. 1526', and on other timbers were two merchants' marks. There was also some painted glass; 'In a back window' was a crowned Tudor rose flanked by the initials R E and above the transom of the ground-floor window adjoining the gateway, ie probably the hall window, were four achievements of arms, two of them identifiable as the City of London and the Grocers' Company. In the two front gables to right of the arch the initials S H and the date 1601 must relate to the shallow two-storey gabled projections, like a larger kind of bay window. Chimney stacks were added in the late 17th century.

Note
1. Oldfield Vol II, 213, 215, 217.

(77465)
The Black Lion PH, No. 10 Bridge Street,

at the corner of Devoils Lane, is a two-storey block of two bays facing N to Bridge Street; the first floor is jettied to N and E and the gables are jettied to N (Fig 27). It is a building of high

Fig 27 The Black Lion PH, No. 10 Bridge Street, Bishop's Stortford: first-floor plan

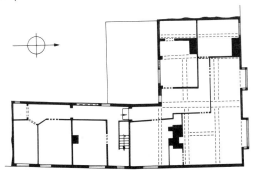

quality; the tie-beams of the gables have pendants with braces between them forming depressed four-centred arches; the first-floor bressumer is moulded and enriched with cable ornament; there is a carved corner post; and there were formerly bay windows with coved sills.[1] Nothing can now be learnt from the ground floor; on the first floor the tie-beams, in so far as they are not encased, point to there being two rooms originally. No sign of an original fireplace now exists; possibly the present stack in the SE corner of the front range replaces an earlier one. The position of the staircase is unknown. The Black Lion incorporates a jettied building of two storeys to S and also a small part of a jettied building to W, the rest of which has been demolished. The corner block is of the early–mid 16th century; the fragmentary W range may be *c*1500; the S range is perhaps mid–late 16th century although it lacks datable features.

For an illustration, see *English Houses 1200–1800*, Fig 238 (plate).

Note
1. Buckler Vol II, 15.

(77466)
Nos 2/4 Bridge Street

is jettied to N and also W towards Palmers Lane. It is of two and a half storeys with four gables on the main elevation; two have plasterwork decoration in low relief, probably mid 17th century; a dragon-beam is visible at the corner; a fireplace to rear, in the middle one of three shops into which the building is now divided, may be original. Its date is uncertain but is probably late medieval; it was heightened to two and a half storeys in the mid–late 17th century. The proportion of the present first-floor windows differs markedly from those in Buckler's view of Bridge Street in 1834.[1]

Note
1. Buckler Vol II, 15.

(77467)
No 6. Bridge Street

is a small, late medieval building of two storeys and attics (Fig 28); the upper storey is jettied to N and the roof has crown-posts with braces to the collar-purlin; the first floor apparently had no fireplace originally. The chimney-stack is probably 17th century, coeval with a short timber-framed rear wing.

Fig 28 *No. 6 Bridge Street, Bishop's Stortford: first floor plan*

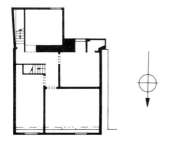

(79378)
No. 11 Bridge Street

is a timber-framed building of two storeys and of four bays which vary slightly in length. Some exposed framing on the first floor and a doorway with depressed four-centred head in the E bay suggest it is late 16th century. No evidence of a chimney-stack exists. On the ground floor the S half of the E bay has a moulded plaster ceiling of the mid 17th century, which has a Tudor rose motif comparable to a ceiling at Fiddlers Croft, Little Hadham, tentatively dated by Rouse to the early 17th century;[1] a simple incised border is like that ascribable to 1665 at Lower Bury Green Farm, Little Hadham. Early 17th-century panelling recorded in a first-floor room[2] and which still existed in the early 1960s has disappeared. In the early 18th century the roof was rebuilt with four hipped gables facing the street; they may replace vertical gables.

Notes
1. Rouse 1989, 440.
2. RCHME 1910, 65; monument no. 18.

(77468)
Church Manor House, formerly The Parsonage (TL 497218),

is a small example of the class of end-entry houses (see *English Houses 1200–1800*, pp 122–5). In 1728 Salmon spoke of the manor as `long appropriated to the Office of Precentor of St Paul's. It is let by lease of lives...to John Sandford, Esq.'.[1] The house is timber-framed but was largely encased in brick in the 19th century. It is of three-unit plan (Fig 29) and its original width (*c*22 ft (6·7 m)) suggests it may have begun as a late medieval open-hall house; it is in any case unlikely to be later than *c*1600. Two binding-beams probably indicate the position and depth of a timber chimney-stack; a lobby-entrance is likely in this place.

Fig 29 *Church Manor House, Bishop's Stortford: plan*

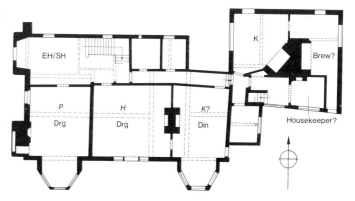

Subsequent enlargements and alterations are difficult to date; a kitchen block to NE, perhaps originally detached, is no later than the 17th century, but framing exposed internally is not closely datable. In the late 18th century the house was heightened to three storeys and rendered; a staircase and probably the adjoining rooms were added to N; and two shallow projections were added at the NW and SW corners. The plan was transformed; a new entrance to NW opened into a staircase-hall; the room adjoining it to S became a drawing room, although its doorway to W may always have been a dummy because the fireplace now blocking it corresponds to the chimney-shaft shown in 1834;[2] large bay windows were added to S to create a garden front. On the first floor a corridor from the stair head to E provided access to bedrooms and drawing rooms. Subsequently the house was refaced to W and S in brick; the parapet, platband between first and second floors, and segmental-arched window-heads with fluted keystones give a deceptively 18th-century appearance to work which cannot be before 1834 and is perhaps early Victorian.

For an illustration, see *English Houses 1200–1800*, Fig 221.

Notes
1. Salmon 1728, 271.
2. Buckler Vol II, 11.

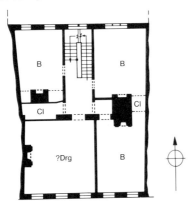

Fig 30 *No. 6 High Street, Bishop's Stortford: first-floor plan*

(77469)
No. 6 High Street

was built in the early 18th century, has three storeys and is two rooms deep (Fig 30). The ground floor is now so devoid of old features that it is impossible to be sure whether it had a narrow entrance-hall or simply two rooms, one large and one smaller, as on the first floor. The staircase appears to have been rebuilt early in the present century. Probably at that time a first-floor door-case facing the landing and opening into the larger front room was added or altered; it has the peculiarity that the elaborate cornice mouldings break forward over the pilasters and simulated keystone run underneath the ceiling cornice instead of being combined with it. The plan suggests that either the rear rooms have been extended to N or that they originally projected beyond the staircase which has itself been repositioned to N of its original position. The building is now more interesting for its c1900 work than as an example of 18th-century building.

(77470)
No. 8 High Street

was built as a small Wealden house[1] of two bays, one open and occupied by the hall and the other of two storeys; the latter incorporated the cross-passage. In the 17th century the hall was floored over and the building heightened to two storeys and attics; it was also extended to the rear (N) where one first-floor room had a painted representation of panelling. In the early 19th century the building was refronted in brick and again heightened. In 1968 it underwent careful restoration and removal of the brickwork.

Note
1. For the Wealden structure, see Gibson 1973, 127–30.

(77470)
No. 10 High Street

was built c1600; it had two storeys and was jettied to S and probably W too; the two gables to S were also jettied; the console brackets at the ends of the tie-beams survive. It was heightened to three storeys in the late 17th century; in the W gable a difference in the height of the wall-plates, the W being higher than the E, suggests that this storey may originally have been jettied to W

as well as S but was cut back subsequently; the thin framing and long thin braces of the W wall tend to confirm this. Then or earlier it was rendered. In 1976 the rendering was removed and the building restored. Little can be learned about the plan, the interior having been gutted long ago, and the principal feature of interest is the flat canopy projecting above the bow windows of the shop. In its present form this appears to be modern but it replaces one which was certainly as old as the early 19th-century shop window, perhaps older.[1]

For an illustration, see *English Houses 1200–1800*, Fig 264 (plate).

Note
1. RCHME 1910, 65 and archive photograph.

(77472)
No. 16 Market Square

is of two and a half storeys with two gables facing N to the street and was built in the early 17th century. It has been stripped of all old features but is of interest for its plan; this comprises two rooms on each floor; the slightly larger rooms to W on both ground and first floors had fireplaces discharging into a chimney-stack now destroyed but visible in an old photograph.[1]

Note
1. *Herts Country Mag*, November 1979, 40.

(77473)
The George Hotel, North Street,

at the corner of High Street, is associated with the Hawkins family `in whose name the George Inn in this town has continued about 300 years',[1] ie since c1400. Its central position in the town suggests it may have been built as an inn and it was certainly so by 1629–30 when Charles I dined there,[2] although no architectural evidence remains to establish it as such before the early 18th century. It may have been indistinguishable in plan from a private house.

The oldest part, the E range facing North Street, is probably mid 16th century; it appears to have comprised two large ground-floor rooms of equal size, each with a fireplace discharging into a chimney-stack to W, and a smaller unheated room to N; the entrance may, by analogy with Redcoats, Wymondley, have been where it is now; and the siting of the staircase adjoining the S stack suggests it may replace an older one thereabouts. Part of the W wing could be coeval with the front range; an irregularly shaped mass of brickwork incorporates part of the lintel of a large fireplace facing E to a room defined by a moulded bearer; the mouldings are mid–late 16th century (cf a similarly sited fireplace at The George Inn, Hitchin). The depth of the brickwork argues for a second fireplace facing E, in which case the E room was probably the dining room and the W room the kitchen.

Some time after 1649, Edward Hawkins purchased The George as part of the manor of Picots[3] and probably not very long afterwards the W wing was lengthened by the addition of the two shorter bays, heightened to three storeys and roofed transversely with four gables front and back. There is some conflict of evidence here. The first-floor width (22 ft 6 ins (6·7 m)) and structure of the wing show that it was designed to incorporate a gallery facing the courtyard but the balustrade, now embedded in a partition, is of the first quarter of the 18th century; perhaps the gallery was improved as part of a renovation which included refronting the main range. An addition to the NW end of the main range has a large chimney-stack, now reduced in size, which evidently served a new kitchen; this is probably mid–late 17th century work. In the early Victorian period the exterior was given its present appearance, including the channelled rustication on the ground floor of the front range and hood-moulds to the wing windows; and the W wing was widened by creating a corridor between the main bedrooms to S and the small rooms to N.

For illustrations, see *English Houses 1200–1800*, Figs 251 (plate), 252.

Notes
1. Chauncy I, 327.
2. Johnson 1962, Pt 1, 42.
3. VCH III, 301.

(77474)
No. 10 North Street

was built *c*1500 and is of two storeys, jettied to W towards the street and to E. The roof originally had a collar-purlin throughout; in the middle, about 9 ft (2·8 m) apart, are crown-posts grooved for wattle-and-daub infilling, which has since been replaced by lath and plaster. Why the crown-posts were so placed is not clear; not for a chimney-stack rising through the ridge, because the collar-purlin ran between them, as the survival of several collar-rafter couples shows, and there is no other sign of an original chimney-stack. In the mid 17th century the building was heightened by the addition of two gables to front and back and a second floor was inserted. At this time the middle space was provided with a collar-beam truss into which are tenoned purlins and on which the valley rafters for the new gables are carried. Possibly the chimney-stack to S was added then, although no feature so datable survived. Extensions to E are of the early 19th century.

(77475)
No. 17 North Street

is of three storeys with flush walls; it was built in the 17th century, and, although there are no details to refine the date, the relatively small size of the chimney-stack and the plan suggest the middle or second half of the century. The plan of the street range comprised three rooms on each floor, possibly with a lobby-entrance, and with a staircase turret W of the chimney-stack; there was a kitchen wing to N. In the early Victorian

Fig 31 Wickham Hall, Bishop's Stortford: plan

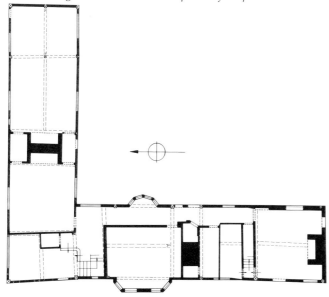

period the building was heightened and refronted and the ground-floor front wall replaced by an iron-framed shop window with nine round-headed lights grouped in threes. Then and subsequently it has been greatly enlarged at the rear.

(77476)
No. 21 North Street,

a timber-framed and rendered building of two storeys and attics, is of two unequal bays and was formerly jettied to E; it retains no closely datable internal features but is probably late medieval. At the rear (W) a timber-framed and rendered wing is an addition of uncertain date, perhaps 17th century. There are no signs of a chimney-stack in the original building; that constructed within the N bay is likely to have been added when the wing was built to serve the two principal ground-floor rooms; the stack was subsequently reduced in size. In the 18th century the building was refronted and a parapet and pediment added, and by then, if not earlier, a second floor had been inserted. In the mid 19th century, the present iron-framed shop windows and first-floor bay windows were added; a chimney-stack and first-floor fireplace were added in the S bay; and the staircase rebuilt. There is no indication where the original staircase was.

(77477)
The Guild House, No. 16 Water Lane,

was built in the late 16th century; the origin of the name is unknown. It is of two storeys with attics and cellar and was probably built to a simple, two-room plan. The larger room to N with moulded binding-beam and bearers was the hall; a chimney-stack has presumably been removed at the rear. The SE wing is probably a later addition but retains few old features. The house was refaced in the mid 18th century when a pedimented Ionic doorcase and modillioned eaves cornice were added; further alterations took place in the mid 19th century; in recent years a flat-roofed NE wing has been added and the whole building renovated.

(77478)
Stylemans (TL 492216),

of two storeys, jettied to S, has a crown-post roof and is of *c*1500. It comprises two small rooms to E which look like service rooms, the remainder being perhaps cross-passage and hall; the latter has no trace of an original chimney-stack, that to N being of *c*1700; possibly it replaces an external timber stack although no positive evidence of such was observed. Ceilings of *c*1700, inserted a little below the tie-beams, cut through arch-braces.

(77479)
Wickham Hall (TL 474230)

was described as 'the plot called Wykehams hall'[1] in January 1492 when Sir William Say leased it to Henry Freshwater for 12 years; it is first mentioned as a manor in 1641.[2] It was sold to John Gibbe in 1564 and was subsequently divided; in March 1607 Edmund Gibbe, Gent., was recorded as having held a moiety of the messuage called Wickeham Hall;[3] the other moiety appears to have gone to George, John Gibbe's grandson. In the 1630s Arthur Capell of Hadham Hall purchased the farm and manor and turned the house into a keeper's lodge.[4] The subsequent descent is uninformative, the house being always leased out. In 1786 it is the 'messuage called Hadham New Park Lodge or Wickham Hall'.[5]

Wickham Hall is now an unusually large example of an L-plan as a result of joining together what were originally two separate houses, both of which have a complicated history (Fig 31). The N range is divided by an internal chimney-stack into two parts, that to the E, which is jettied and has weathered timbers at the W end, being the older, probably of the 16th century. The apparent lack of an original fireplace might be accounted for in various ways: that there was a lateral stack to N; that the building was unheated; or that there was a much lower open hall to W. No evidence was found to decide the point. In the mid–late 17th century the chimney-stack, which has conjoined shafts, and the W part, almost identical in plan to the E, were added. The fireplaces, which are also nearly identical, have moulded jambs and depressed four-centred heads and are unlikely to have been used for cooking.

The W range has undergone greater alteration. A few indications of a 16th-century building are incorporated in the present one, which is predominantly late 17th century. In what was once the N end room the bearer is set nearer the W wall than the E, and in the E wall is a post unconnected with a bearer or truss; both suggest structural alterations of some uncertain kind. The plan does not conform to type and also appears to be the result of alteration; both stacks were built towards the end of the 17th century, that to N probably replacing an earlier timber stack. At the same time the two ranges were joined together by a short staircase-hall. Although there is insufficient evidence to establish the development of the W range it may either incorporate the remains of an open hall or owe its present form to the existence of one.

From the sizes of the fireplaces it appears that a kitchen in the E range served the whole complex (cf Walnut Tree Farm, Pirton). That the two ranges, each equal to a good-sized farmhouse, were in separate occupation by the late 17th century is hardly open to doubt, so different is the whole from anything else in the county.

For an illustration, see *English Houses 1200–1800*, Fig 186 (plate).

Notes
1. VCH III, 302.
2. Ibid.
3. Inquisition *post mortem*, PRO C142/295/89.
4. VCH III, 302.
5. HRO, D/E Cp T3.

BOVINGDON

(77480)
Nos 6/8 Church Street
form a late medieval house comprising an open hall of two bays with service rooms to E and cross-wing to W. The hall has an open cruck-truss; the end trusses have tie-beams and clasped-purlins. A timber chimney-stack was inserted in the hall c1600; the moulded lintel is incorporated in the existing brick stack of the 18th century.

(77481)
Green Farm (TL 012028),
built in the late 15th century, comprises an open hall of two bays and a storeyed bay at each end; the roof has clasped-purlins with king-struts in the partition trusses; over the hall nearly all trace of smoke-blackening has been removed. To W the chamber over the parlour is carried by an axial bearer with joists of large scantling; to E the chamber over the two service rooms originally had joists aligned E–W. In the late 16th century an upper floor and large timber chimney-stack were inserted in the hall, the stack backing on to the cross-passage; some framing remains, and a bearer in the hall is set off-axis to allow for the stack. A two-storey wing was added to W then or slightly later;

weathering is visible on the formerly exposed faces of the timbers and there is a break in the purlins at that point, but the scarf joint in the wall-plates gives the impression that the building continued; the explanation may be that the wall-plate has been replaced. The brick chimney-stack may have been built c1700 but evidence of other alterations has been almost completely swept away.

(79376)
Water Lane Cottage (TL 016025)
forms part of a late medieval timber-framed house comprising a long parlour or service room to E and the upper end bay of the open hall; the arch-braced open truss is visible in the roof. In the late 16th century an upper floor was inserted in the hall; and since the binding-beam carrying it is moulded on both sides, the hall and whatever adjoined it to W still stood and the chimney-stack necessitated by the upper floor was at the lower end of the hall. In the late 18th century the W part of the house was demolished, a new chimney-stack was built adjoining the moulded beam and the S elevation was rebuilt in brick.

(77482)
Westbrook Hay (TL 025054)
was a manor of some importance in the late 12th century; in 1238 there is reference to the court of Robert de Hagha, clerk; and in 1325 John de la Hay, Sheriff of Bedfordshire and Buckinghamshire in 1314,[1] was granted licence to have an oratory. In 1541 the estate was divided between two daughters and not until 1676 was it reunited by Joshua Lomax,[2] whose son Thomas, succeeding him in 1685, `built a very fair Mansion House of Brick there'.[3] Joshua Lomax, an attorney, `dealt much in buying and selling of lands, by which [he] obtained a fair Estate'[4] and was Sheriff in 1674; he and his heir were supporters of nonconformity, as their predecessors the Maynes had been of puritanism.[5] A drawing of c1800,[6] apparently of the N elevation, shows a two-storey house with a high basement lit by mullioned windows; the roofs, of low pitch and hidden by a parapet, look like an 18th-century alteration of the original form. A two-storey bay window to W was probably an addition. The plan of the house, though now very much changed, appears to have comprised five rooms grouped around a staircase. In the early 19th century the house was enlarged to N; large bow windows and a verandah were added to W and a two-storey block of one-room plan at the NW corner; the whole house was rendered. These additions appear on the tithe map of 1838,[7] as well as most of the three existing service wings to E; they were no doubt made by the Hon Granville Dudley Ryder, who inherited the property in 1832.[8] A drawing by J C Buckler dated 1840 and captioned Westbrook Hay[9] shows a house of seven bays with the three middle bays of three storeys breaking forward and crowned with a pediment; it is impossible to reconcile this with the architectural and map evidence.

For an illustration, see *English Houses 1200–1800*, Fig 131 (plate).

Notes
1. Viney 1965.
2. VCH II, 222–3.
3. Chauncy II, 476.
4. Ibid, 451.
5. Yaxley 1973, 252.
6. Oldfield Vol II, 230.
7. HRO, DSA 4/22.
8. VCH II 223.
9. Buckler Vol I, 107.

BRAMFIELD

(77483)
Bramfield Bury (TL 285154)

was built *c*1500. The basis for the suggestion that it is on the site of the house built by Robert Ware, bursar of St Albans Abbey from 1406 to 1420,[1] is not clear. The status of the house is uncertain. The only manor in the parish is said to correspond to Bramfield House,[2] a building of the 18th and 19th centuries, or to Bramfield Place, which in 1723 was a 16th-century or earlier timber and brick building;[3] but in 1589 James Smyth of London, Gent., leased to Thomas Glascocke of Panshanger, yeoman, the manor of Bramfieldbury and demesne lands, with provision for a dinner for the lord of the manor and his steward when they kept their courts there. In 1607 a lease refers to the manor or farm of Bramfieldbury.[4] Its claim to manorial status may have been short-lived but architecturally the house is superior to most farmhouses of the early 16th century. It comprises four cells: a storeyed parlour bay, open hall, service bay with the upper room extending over the passage, and an open kitchen bay. The roof has crown-posts. In general the carpentry is good but simple. The hall was provided with a chimney-stack and an upper floor in the 17th century; at some time unknown the house was encased in brick and divided into three cottages;[5] the brick has since been removed and the house turned back into one again.

For illustrations, see *English Houses 1200–1800*, Figs 65 (plate), 66.

Notes
1. VCH II, 343, citing *Chronica Monastici S. Albani, Ann Mon S. Albani*, Vol II, 273.
2. VCH II, 343.
3. Oldfield Vol II, 254.
4. Typescript note by O T Leslie.
5. VCH II, 343.

BRAUGHING

(77484)
Bozen Green Farmhouse (TL 411272)

is of two storeys and originally of two-cell lobby-entrance plan with a rear lean-to (Fig 32); a date in the late 17th century is indicated by chamfer stops on the bearer in the hall and the jambs of the fireplace in the room above. The hall lay to the E and an unheated parlour to the W. In the room over the parlour is a window, now blocked, of three lights with beaded square mullions. It is difficult to prove that the lean-to on the N side is original, but without it there is neither provision for a pantry nor space for a staircase, and although the latter has been altered it is still there. In the early 19th century a third room was added, a

Fig 32 *Bozen Green Farmhouse, Braughing: plan*

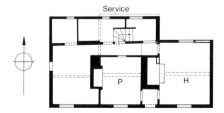

fireplace provided for the parlour and the lean-to extended. The enlargement appears on the tithe award map of 1825.[1]

Note
1. Inf. Mrs E P Wood.

(77485)
Braughing Bury (TL 395253)

belonged to the Augustinian priory of Holy Trinity, London, until the Dissolution. In 1534 the manor was granted to Sir Thomas (later Lord) Ardley, the Chancellor. Its subsequent descent, which goes some way to explaining the architectural history of the house, is presented somewhat differently by VCH and Chauncy,[1] and since the latter is based on personal inspection of court rolls it is preferred here. From Ardley Chauncy notes that it passed through the Howard family to

John Steward Esq. and Nicholas Steward, Dr. of the Civil Laws, who held a Court here on the 24th Day of October, An. 4 Eliz. from whom this Mannor was conveyed to their several sons, Humphrey Steward, and Francis Steward, who held a Court here on the 22nd of October, 8 Jac. I but upon the death of Humphrey, one Moiety of the Mannor descended to Humphrey, who was his Son and Heir...[2]

and so to William Delawood of London, merchant.[3] The other moiety, Francis Steward's, descended to Hoe Steward and on his death was sold to Delawood. It thus appears that both house and manor were held jointly from 1562 for about two generations, after which the manor was divided; the same may be true of the house although nothing definite can be inferred about it. By 1758 the Bury was divided into two tenements[4] and was still two farms early in the present century.

The oldest part of the house is late medieval and comprised a hall with crown-post roof, a cross-passage and at least one bay to E and an unheated W wing; the wing was probably of two bays and jettied to N. Drastic alterations in the early 1970s and perhaps before have removed so much of this building that its development is uncertain. Since the upper floor in the hall has a binding-beam and bearers which are probably late 16th century, a timber chimney-stack no doubt preceded the present late 17th-century one of brick, although no positive evidence of it exists. The first enlargement was the replacement of part of the E bay by a long wing (40 ft (12·2 m)) of two storeys and attics in the early 17th century; perhaps the W wing was extended to the same length at this time. Although it would have been perfectly possible for two households to coexist earlier, the two unusually long wings provide the first clear architectural indication of such an arrangement. At this stage there is no sign of separate entrances. The dating of later additions is also uncertain. The earliest is probably the gabled range parallel with the E wing, added in the late 17th century, when an independent lobby-entrance was created. In the early 18th century the W wing was enlarged to W, refronted and reroofed with two parallel ridges running E–W; it too had an independent entrance. Subsequent alterations were swept away *c*1970, when, however, one singular innovation appeared; acting on antiquarian advice that part of the house was originally open from ground to roof, the owner removed the boards of the upper floors in the E wing so that the roof timbers could indeed be seen from the ground.

Notes
1. VCH III, 308–9; Chauncy I, 440–1.
2. Chauncy I, 440–1.
3. VCH III, 309.
4. Ibid, n42.

(77486)
The Brown Bear PH, No. 14 The Street (TL 398251),

is an early 16th-century house partly of one storey and attics and partly of two storeys. The middle part was originally an open hall; the open truss has a crown-post and two-way struts. To S is a projecting and jettied cross-wing; to N was perhaps a short bay forming a separate room. The service rooms were probably in the S wing. The cross-wing on the first floor has a single large room. In the 17th century an upper storey and chimney-stack were built in the hall, the upper room of the cross-wing was divided into two and the N bay of the hall range was heightened and given the appearance of a narrow cross-wing. It is first mentioned as a public house in 1786;[1] subsequent alterations have removed or concealed most of the old features on the ground floor.

Note
1.   Johnson 1962, Pt 1, 45.

(77487)
Causeway House (TL 396252)

is of two storeys and attics and cellar; it has a three-room plan with lobby-entrance and a later and slightly lower S bay. The timber frame and the clasped-purlin roof, which has members of comparatively small scantling, appear to have been built in the early 17th century; at that time there was probably a wooden chimney-stack with two flues because, although there are no definite traces of its existence, the space between the two rooms is too large for a single flue, and the present shaft above the roof has a late 17th-century capping.

The plan (Fig 33) comprised parlour with cellar beneath, hall and kitchen; the lack of any service room argues that the present S bay replaces an older and lower structure performing that

Fig 33 *Causeway House, Braughing: plan*

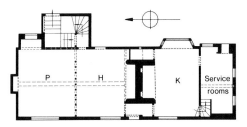

function. Possibly the parlour had a fireplace; in the cellar, which has walls of brick above some flint, is the truncated base of a corner fireplace; this presumably discharged into the chimney-stack on the E wall which has been converted into a bay window but the battering back of its N wall shows what its original purpose was. The lower part of the staircase and turret are also part of the first build. Subsequently the main chimney-stack was rebuilt in brick; a second floor and three gables were added to create attic rooms; the staircase was heightened because the doors to the attics cut through rafters, and there is a scarf joint in the newel post; and an external chimney-stack was built to N to provide a new fireplace in the parlour. The only evidence of date in this stack, which has been rebuilt from about 7 ft (2 m) above ground, is provided by two timbers built into its sides in the way usually found with internal stacks of the late 17th or early 18th centuries. The present room to S, presumed to replace an earlier one, is of c1700; the timbers of the gable which it now masks are conspicuously weathered. Similar evidence

shows that the stair turret has been enlarged to N to provide a small first-floor room.

For an illustration, see *English Houses 1200–1800*, Fig 167 (plate).

(77488)
Dassels Bury (TL 392274)

was built in the late 17th century of mixed construction which combined timber framing with brick. At the front, hall and parlour were separated by the staircase and a small entrance-hall (Fig 34). The hall still had the function of dining room; adjoining it to E was the kitchen with service rooms beyond.

Fig 34 *Dassels Bury, Braughing: plan*

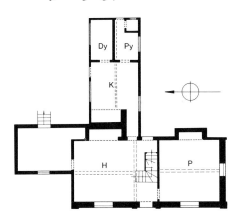

Probably the original staircase was of square plan, with winders, rising to a small landing with a lobby to N providing access to the chambers over the hall and kitchen; a door led to the chamber over the parlour; and there was no doubt a closet over the entrance-hall. The attics presumably were reached by another staircase in the wing. Originally, no doubt, the windows were of mullion-and-transom type; they were rebuilt in the early 18th century with brick architraves and hung sashes and in the early 19th century the front windows were rebuilt again as wide three-light windows. Some rise in the status of the house is indicated by mention of it in 1758 as Dassel House.[1] A wing to N is probably of c1800. The staircase was rebuilt in the 20th century.

Note
1.   Deed, PRO CP 43/700.

(77489)
The Gables, Green End (TL 393252),

is a late medieval house with hall and two cross-wings; the framing exposed in the wings has curved tension-braces. The hall is of two unequal bays, the shorter one to N probably incorporating the cross-passage; to S was the parlour wing; a cased beam in the N wing probably indicates a division into two service rooms (Fig 35). There is no proof that a chimney-stack and upper floor were inserted in the hall before the 17th century although the stack may be earlier than the three diagonally set shafts. When the stack was built the hall became a kitchen and some of its functions were transferred to the new parlour to N. To accommodate a staircase and service rooms the N wing was extended to W by two bays; exposed framing in the W wall, on the first floor, has straight tension-braces and a clasped-purlin roof. A chimney-stack was added to the S wing c1700 to provide

Fig 35 *The Gables, Green End, Braughing: plan*

fireplaces in the original parlour and chamber above. At a date rather hard to define, the S wing was more than doubled in length; a three-light diamond-mullioned window in the short bay housing the staircase suggests a date for the extension before the middle of the 17th century but the chimney-stack and staircase are probably *c*1700. The room to W of the staircase was a kitchen and the adjoining room a service room (a pantry, probably). In the late 18th or 19th century a lean-to was added at the back and the jetties and hall wall underbuilt.

(77490)
The Gatehouse, The Street (TL 397251),

is a late medieval house with hall and two cross-wings; most of the framing has been replaced by rendered brickwork; the wings are close-studded with tension-braces. The hall, which is now largely rebuilt, was of two bays; it was entered from a cross-passage within the N wing; two short screens W form a vestigial spere-truss. A blocked door at the W end of the passage has a four-centred head; adjoining it are two two-light diamond-mullioned windows separated by a stud, with a shutter groove in the plate above them. On the first floor a two-light diamond-mullioned window in the NE corner is so placed to light the head of the staircase, of which no other evidence remains. At the upper (S) end of the hall the framing incorporates stud-bracing and has peg-holes for a bench. The N wing has a collar-rafter roof; the narrower S wing has a plain crown-post roof with two-way braces.

Most of the later alterations, including the chimney-stack and part of the upper floor which were inserted into the hall, were removed in a drastic restoration of the 1950s.

(77491)
Hamels (TL 375245)

is an estate formed by Sir John Brograve, lawyer and MP, in the late 16th century, from various lands including the manors of Milkleys and Masters; his house, where manorial courts were henceforth held, was 'a neat and uniform Pile of Brick...with four Turrets in the four corners thereof',[1] and was probably built *c*1580, when Brograve was appointed *custos rotulorum* and attorney for the Duchy of Lancaster.[2] In 1613 he was succeeded by his son Simeon, during whose time Hamels was burnt. Simeon's younger brother John, 'among other works of charity', rebuilt his brother's house at his own expense,[3] leaving by will £1,000 'towards the re-edifying and finishing his house at Hamells'.[4] Nothing is known of any building-works by Sir Thomas Brograve, who was Sheriff in 1664, but his son Sir John, who inherited in 1672 and died in 1691, 'had great skill and knowledge in Building...; this inclin'd him to beautify his Seat,

and to make his House graceful and pleasant to the Eye; he...made his Rooms curious within'.[5] Only his extensive work on the porch and gardens is evident in the Drapentier engraving of *c*1700, which shows a squarish house, presumably with an internal courtyard, still substantially as rebuilt after the fire. In 1712 the estate was sold to Ralph Freeman[6] who, two years later, began rebuilding the house: 'In the Spring...the East front of the house was done; in the Summer, the North front was done; and in 1721 work was still going on in the Library and best bed-chamber.'[7] An engraving of 1722[8] shows a plain-looking front of eleven bays and three storeys with three rear wings; salient corner bays may have corresponded to the corner turrets of the Brograve house. Badeslade's engraving also shows the stable block begun in 1713, which remains. Between 1764 and 1769 over £7,000 was spent on 'beautifying Hamels',[9] but in 1772 the house was damaged by fire.[10] In 1796 the house was sold by Philip Yorke, 3rd Earl of Hardwicke, to John Mellish,[11] and on his death two years later, it passed to his infant daughter Catherine Martha Mellish. A drawing of *c*1800[12] shows the house as being of two storeys with a pediment over five bays of the E elevation. This work may have been done *c*1764 to 1772. Sir John Soane carried out alterations and designed lodges and a dairy for the Hon Philip Yorke[13] in 1781–3.[14] Sale particulars of 1795 mention that the mansion house was 'lately new roofed with slate and greatly improved'.[15]

In 1830 the entire contents of the house were sold[16] and by 1834 it had been rebuilt.[17] In certain respects the design follows the Drapentier engraving; for example, the three gables of the S elevation copy those on the entrance front of the early 17th-century house. The main entrance was transferred to W. A number of rooms received plasterwork ceilings in 17th-century style. Miss Mellish, who is shown seated in her library in a drawing dated 1842,[18] died in 1880. The only subsequent major change to the house was the addition of a range to N and internal alterations, including the opening up of the library to the staircase-hall.

The house probably incorporates parts of the 17th-century building, corresponding to thick internal walls, and the present staircase may occupy a former internal courtyard. With the exception of these and the main staircase, which was built early in the present century, what remains is the work of Miss Mellish.

Notes
1. Chauncy I, 443.
2. *DNB*.
3. Monumental Inscription, Braughing Church; Chauncy I, 447–8.
4. PRO Prob 11/146.
5. Chauncy I, 445.
6. VCH III, 314.
7. *Memoirs of Hammells* by Ralph Freeman, BL Add MS 36239.
8. Engraving, Hertford Museum; 'T. Badeslade dd., T. Harris sculpt.' A photograph of it is in NMR.
9. BL Add MS 36241.
10. Cussans 1870–3, Vol I (ii), 104 n.
11. VCH III, 314.
12. Oldfield Vol I, 369.
13. *DNB*.
14. Colvin 1978, 768; Rufinière du Prey 1979, 28–38.
15. HRO, D/EX 182.2/12.
16. CRO, 296/B/717/11, Cockett and Nash sale books.
17. Dated drawing by James Wilcox; for more detailed drawings of 1841, see Buckler Vol II, 124, 125.
18. Charlotte Bosanquet.

(77492)
The Old Rose and Crown PH,
No. 13 Church End (TL 395252),

is a continuous-jetty house built in the middle of the 16th century. It then comprised, from S to N, unheated parlour, hall, cross-passage and two service rooms. The hall fireplace discharged into a wooden chimney-stack; the parlour and the chamber over it had fireplaces connected to a big external stack of brick; the fireplace in the hall and the chamber over the parlour have similar moulded timber lintels. At each end of the house was a staircase and in the remaining studs at the S end of the hall are peg-holes for a bench. A two-storey wing incorporating an open bay for cooking (a 'smoke-bay') was added c1600 to W; it has its own staircase. A first-floor fireplace with a moulded and enriched lintel brought from elsewhere was added; the parlour chimney-stack was rebuilt with conjoined hexagonal flues; and pargeting with plaster ornament was put on. In the 19th century the house became a public house; in recent years it has been carefully restored.

For illustrations, see *English Houses 1200–1800*, Figs 152 (plate), 153.

(77493)
Turk's Cottage, Dassels (TL 392275),

derives its name from the family of Turk, which also gave its name to the manor of Turks, represented by a moated site to E (TL 401274). It is of two storeys with projecting cross-wings of unequal width. No framing is exposed outside and little but the main members inside; all the datable features are of the late 16th or early 17th century. Enigmatic evidence of an earlier building includes a first-floor post that suggests Wealden construction, although the housings and mortises for an inner plate and the wall below it are absent; breaks in the wall-plates at about the middle of the hall; and signs of alteration where the W wall of the hall meets the S wing. It looks as if a late medieval house was rebuilt piecemeal and at the same time enlarged in stages now difficult to recover in detail. The middle room of the house has an ovolo-moulded bearer that meets a similar binding-beam in front of the chimney. The stack is of 18th-century brick and perhaps replaces one of timber; the fireplace in the parlour has a moulded timber lintel. Although this lintel looks earlier than that in the hall, which is chamfered, both are probably of the same date. By c1600 the parlour was as big as the hall, with a service room to E, probably a cellar. In the hall to S mortises show a gap for a doorway to a staircase; no other door positions are traceable, perhaps because the lintels of the service-room doors were lower than that to the staircase. However, there are no mortises for a partition dividing the wing; the entrance was presumably at the S end of the hall. The staircase E of the stack rises to a landing from which opened two doors into the chambers over the parlour and adjoining service rooms. In the 19th century the house was divided into cottages.

For illustrations, see *English Houses 1200–1800*, Figs 158 (plate), 159.

(77494)
Upp Hall (TL 409241)

is of two storeys and attics, and of brick with tile roofs. After two drastic restorations its date is difficult to establish; the late 16th century[1] or early 17th century[2] have been proposed. The manor of Uphall usually went with the adjoining manor of Gatesbury; the latter was divided in the 16th century, and reunited in 1589 by Thomas Hanchett who, two years later, was Sheriff. Since nothing is known of Gatesbury manor house and it is not certain where Hanchett resided, he cannot be associated definitely with

the present Upp Hall. From 1609 until 1640 John Stone owned it; his son and heir, Richard, whose principal seat was at Stukeley (Huntingdonshire), had a son and heir John who was described as 'of Upp Hall'; they sold the manor in March, 1657, to Robert Dicer of London,[3] who was Sheriff in 1659 and created baronet in 1661. Of these, John Stone the younger is most likely to have been the builder.

The front (W) elevation has a gable over the entrance which, it has been suggested,[4] was the central one of three, one to N having disappeared when the house was truncated. Certainly to NW the string courses are cut off, the N wall is modern, and a stub of wall has a window splay; all these show that something has been removed to N, but a symmetrical front would have been inordinately long, about 110 ft (34 m), in a building which is mostly only one room deep. Perhaps the present building was added to an older one to N that was subsequently demolished (cf Salisbury Hall, Shenley). The plan[5] is difficult to interpret. It comprises to N a room with lateral stack and ovolo-moulded beams, possibly the hall, entered by a cross-passage to S; a kitchen with wide fireplace to S; and a large room to S again that had no fireplace originally and was presumably, like the wing room to E, a service room. To E of the hall stack is a former staircase wing. The only evidence of 18th-century alteration is the information that a Queen Anne fireplace existed in the N room in 1912;[6] it had an 'old fashioned wooden overmantel';[7] and in the drawing room (S end) was a white marble fireplace, probably Victorian. Both were removed in the extensive antiquarian restoration by C J Longman c1896, and subsequently the drawing room (N end) received a large early 17th-century fireplace brought from elsewhere. Little old detail of any period now survives.

Notes
1. VCH III, 312.
2. RCHME 1910, 68.
3. HRO, 43921.
4. RCHME, MS report.
5. VCH III, 312.
6. Ibid.
7. HRO, SC, 1880.

BRENT PELHAM

(77495)
Beeches (TL 304446)

was first recorded as a manor in the late 13th century, and from 1306 until the Dissolution belonged to the Augustinian priory of Thremhall (Essex).[1] Phillip Allington bought the manor in 1587 and built a 'fair House' here.[2] His descendant sold it in 1640 to Adam Washington, a lawyer and Parliamentarian, who became a member of the central committee for the Eastern Counties Association.[3] In 1662 Washington was assessed for seven hearths.[4] Following his death in 1665[5] the house was sold to Felix Calvert who, on acquiring Furneux Pelham Hall in 1677, conveyed Beeches to his son-in-law William Knight. After a short period of utter neglect and dilapidation between 1743 and 1745, vividly described by William Cole,[6] the house was renovated by Felix Knight. From the late 18th century onwards it has been successively part of the Woodhall Park and Brent Pelham Hall estates and has been occupied by tenants.

Despite Chauncy's statement it is difficult to see anything in the present house that need be of the late 16th century except, possibly, the four very shallow bay windows at the front; the framing exposed inside is not closely datable. The only hint of alteration is conveyed by a cambered beam in the middle of the long gallery, which occupies the whole roof of the main range; although shaped like a tie-beam there are no mortises to establish it as such, and, since it appears to be bolted to a beam underneath, it may have been added as strengthening in the 19th century. The stone fireplaces and brick chimney-stacks are of the mid 17th century and could well be of Washington's time, as indeed nearly all the present house may be; a drawing of 1831[7] shows a wing to W and another chimney-stack with shafts like those which remain. If these were original, and there is no reason to suppose that they were an early reproduction of an historical style, and assuming too that each ground-floor fireplace was served by two shafts, they provide the seven hearths of the 1662 assessment.

K

P   H   P

— Modern

0 5 feet   60

0 2 metres   20

Fig 36 *Beeches, Brent Pelham: plan*

The house faces S. The plan[8] (Fig 36) was dominated by a large hall in the middle; to W was a parlour, with the principal staircase to N; to E were service rooms and another parlour or study; to NE was the kitchen wing. In 1831[9] a W wing existed, more or less symmetrical with the E wing, ie looking towards a small courtyard. It is curious that this wing, which must have incorporated two quite important rooms, should, like the kitchen wing, have faced inwards. The first floor apparently comprised two groups of rooms approached from the two staircases. In the front range the roof space was occupied by a gallery, lit from both ends by two-light windows in the chimney-stacks and at the front by dormer windows; the latter had been removed by 1831.

In the 18th century, perhaps as part of Felix Knight's renovation after 1745, two bay windows were added at the front and a new doorcase and sash windows were put in the W wing.[10] By the end of the century Beeches had become a farmhouse; an insurance policy of 1797[11] in the name of John Woodley, yeoman, is for a `house and dairy under one roof'. During the 19th century some antiquarian restoration took place; a ceiling with moulded ribs forming a pattern of squares and hexagons may have extended into the added bay window and cannot have been original;[12] mention of a similar ceiling in the hall[13] is probably a mistake. The tithe map of 1839[14] depicts the house as a rectangular block with a narrow range extending to E from the E wing. Since the other projections, bay windows and chimney-stacks, are represented fairly faithfully there must have been some structure joining the wings, although it is inconceivable that the space between them was ever completely built up.

By 1851 Beeches was a farmhouse, occupied by Thomas Ashton, his wife, one child and three servants.[15] This smaller scale of occupation led to its reduction in size, the W wing and anything linking the wings being removed during the late 19th

century; in 1900, when Mr E E Barclay acquired the house, panelling and the hall fireplace were removed to Brent Pelham Hall.[16] Sometime after 1911 a new shorter W wing was built and a neo-Georgian staircase replaced the original dog-legged main staircase.

Notes
1. VCH IV, 96–7.
2. Chauncy I, 282.
3. Kingston 1894, 28.
4. PRO E179/375/20.
5. *Herts Country Mag*, November 1980, 40.
6. VCH IV, 97.
7. Buckler Vol II, 133.
8. VCH IV, 92.
9. Buckler Vol II, 133.
10. Ibid.
11. Guildhall MS 11937/2.18, 137.
12. VCH IV, 93, illustration.
13. RCHME 1910, 70.
14. HRO, DSA4/75.
15. Census.
16. VCH IV, 92.

(77496)
Brent Pelham Hall (TL 434308)

is the successor of the mansion house or manor place referred to in 1556[1] where Queen Elizabeth spent two nights in 1571;[2] this was acquired in 1597 by Edward Newport, who `built a slight but well contrived House in this Manor...and An.20th of King James I was constituted Sheriff of this County'.[3] `Slight', an unusual word for Chauncy, must imply that the house was timber framed; and the order of the sentence – first the building, then the office – may be significant. Edward's son John sold the manor in 1626[4] to Francis Floyer the elder, a former Turkey merchant who, `when he had adorned this House, he furnisht it with all things, that nothing was wanting to make it pleasant and delightful',[5] and became Sheriff in 1648. Apparently the house was leased out for a time after the Restoration; in 1662 Henry Chauncy paid for 12 hearths, in 1663 the same number are entered simply for `Brent Pelham Hall', and in 1673 Francis Floyer paid for 13.[6] Outliving all his children, Francis Floyer was succeeded in 1678 by his grandson of the same name who became Sheriff in 1686. It is curious that Chauncy does not mention any building by Francis the younger and that it should be left to Salmon[7] to state what the Drapentier engraving[8] demonstrates, that he improved the house; among other things he refronted it. The house stayed with the Floyer family, latterly by marriage, until 1839 and was little altered externally in 1831.[9] After three sales it was acquired in 1865 by Joseph Gurney Barclay,[10] with whose descendants it has remained. Considerable alterations and enlargements were undertaken in the late 19th and early 20th centuries.

Until comparatively recently the house comprised a main W range, a short wing to the N end and larger one to S; an approximately L-shaped plan which may have been established by Edward Newport. Newport's house was evidently built *c*1608, a date inscribed on a door lintel `on the north-west side of the house'[11] which was reset[12] (not seen). The only evidence for its being then of L-plan is not particularly reliable, being provided by the clasped-purlin roof of the wing and the comparatively thin (perhaps timber-framed) rear wall of the main range. Timber framing is said to have been discovered behind the late 17th-century brick walls,[13] and, although this is possible, the mixed construction found at Aston Bury (see page 17) warns

Fig 37 *Brent Pelham Hall: reconstructed ground and first-floor plans*

room, perhaps a drawing room; and opposite the stair head, but perhaps not reached from it, was a lesser room, probably a dressing room (cf Tyttenhanger House, Ridge). These dispositions appear on the reconstructed plan of the late 17th-century house. Oldfield shows the house much as it was in Chauncy's time, except that the chimney-stacks are plain and square, of mid–late 18th-century type.

By 1822 antiquarian restoration had begun; a drawing of that year[19] shows decorative chimney-shafts like those engraved by Drapentier. By 1841[20] the front entrances had been masked by a flat-roofed box-like projection with a round-headed window to W, where a door might have been expected; probably the main entrance had by then been transferred to where it is now, for there Buckler shows a second porch-like projection (Fig 38). If so, the internal stack in the W wing and perhaps the main staircase must have been modified; this was done at about the time Charlotte Bosanquet sketched the present drawing room, and shows that all the panelling and the fireplace there shown were put in by an antiquarian-minded owner. This conclusion is reinforced by another consideration: it is hardly conceivable that the principal room of an important house brought up-to-date in 1678 should have remained in the 1840s and for the next 130 years in its unaltered early 17th-century state. Probably there were extensive early Victorian alterations. The two bedrooms to N in the main range have coved ceilings of that period, and the

Fig 38 *Brent Pelham Hall: ground and first-floor plans*

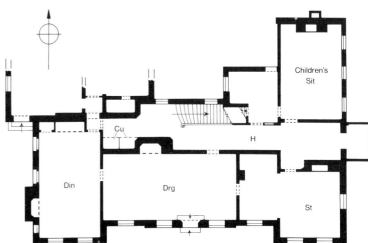

against interpreting the statement too literally. Although the Jacobean-looking overmantel in the former hall (now drawing room), together with the stone fireplace and its wooden surround, have been claimed as 17th-century work[14] the chimney-stack is of later date; the fireplace replaced one of the early 19th century[15] and the wooden jambs and lintel are suspect. Of Francis Floyer the elder's improvements, the principal evidence is the hall chimney-stack, which is capped by two mid 17th-century shafts of carved brick with moulded caps and bases.[16] The curiously sited range shown by Buckler[17] as being roofed parallel with the hall looks like an addition and may also be the elder Francis Floyer's work; it is comparable to a similarly sited range at Mackerye End, Wheathampstead. Little definite can be said about the plan of the house at this period (Fig 37). To N of the hall stack was a staircase which had a scrolled balustrade like a smaller version of the one at Tyttenhanger House, Ridge; it no doubt led to important first-floor rooms, probably including a grand chamber or dining room over the hall. It was removed in recent years unrecorded. A second staircase must have stood at the E end of the house. The chimney-stacks, with the exception of that to E of the S wing, are probably of the early 17th century, but if so it is surprising not to find evidence of an original kitchen fireplace and stack. Presumably the entrance in the early 17th century was where it was until the early 19th century, with service rooms to E, as at Aston Bury.

Francis Floyer the younger rebuilt the greater part of the external walls in brick, and gave the house an up-to-date front, which has been little altered except for the removal of the original dormer windows and the blocking of the *œil-de-bœuf* window in the pediment.[18] The building of a new staircase in the re-entrant angle between the main range and E wing corresponds to an upgrading of some rooms in the latter that is exemplified by the first-floor fireplace to E of the internal chimney-stack. The plan at the E end of the main range perpetuates the corridor leading from the screens-passage past service rooms to the little parlour – a likely arrangement in the early 17th century. On the first floor it provides for a landing giving access to a lobby leading to the wing rooms to E; to W lay the principal upstairs thoroughness of the antiquarian restoration begun in 1896 by Mr E E Barclay[21] suggests that much work in an unfashionable taste was being replaced. It continued for several years, since not until he acquired Beeches in 1900[22] was he able to transfer from that house the fireplace now in the corner bedroom to NW and most of the panelling. Most of the work was in Queen Anne style, eg the staircase, panelling and fireplace in the NW ground-floor room; and a large NW wing was added.

Notes
1. VCH IV, 94.
2. Colthorpe and Bateman 1977, 18.
3. Chauncy I, 280.
4. VCH IV, 95, n43.
5. Chauncy I, 281.
6. PRO E179/375/30, E179/248/23, E179/775/31.
7. Salmon 1728, 288.
8. Chauncy I, 276.
9. Buckler Vol II, 131.
10. VCH IV, 95.
11. Gerish 1905–7, 55.
12. VCH IV, 92.
13. Gerish 1905–7, 55.
14. VCH IV, 93; RCHME 1910, 70.
15. Drawing by Charlotte Bosanquet, 1842–3.
16. Buckler, BL Add MS 36430, fo 2103.
17. Buckler Vol II, 132.
18. Oldfield Vol II, 230; Clutterbuck.
19. Clutterbuck.
20. Buckler Vol II, 132.
21. Gerish 1905–7, 55.
22. VCH IV, 97.

(77497)
The Bury (TL 432309),

of two storeys, comprises a main range facing SW (S for description) and an E cross-wing. It is now largely a building of 1677 but incorporates parts of an earlier structure. Although no exposed timbers are definitely earlier than the late 17th century, the differences in floor heights and proportions between the wing and main range suggest that the latter may be of the early 16th century. At that time, the house was no more than an open hall with a passage adjoining a bay of two storeys to W in which was a staircase opening off the passage. In the late 17th century a wing was added to E of two storeys and attics; it provided a parlour with internal chimney-stack, a staircase in the SW corner, easily accessible from the hall, and a closet. The chimney-stack has two conjoined diagonal flues, as have the other two stacks. When the parlour wing was added a chimney-stack was built in the hall backing on to the passage and a first floor was inserted two steps higher than that of the W bay; the upstairs room is lit by two gabled dormer windows. A porch added to S has in the gable the painted date 1677. The former service room was converted into a second parlour and its function transferred to a bay of one storey and attic added to W.

(77498)
Church Cottage (TL 432307)

is a single-storey house of three rooms open to the roof throughout. The few rafters not concealed by plaster are not blackened by smoke; the present brick chimney-stack, the building of which necessitated the removal of a tie-beam, may have replaced a timber stack. The brickwork is of the 17th century and the house itself was presumably built some time in the 16th century. Subsequently an upper floor was introduced.

After a long period when it was subdivided into two cottages, the house is now in one occupation.

(77499)
Washall Green Farmhouse (TL 443302)

is a late medieval house with hall, jettied cross-wing to E end and (by inference) a service bay to W. The larger of two unequal hall bays is to E. In the 17th century the hall was heightened and an upper floor and chimney-stack inserted, the stack backing on to a cross-passage. The original service bay was replaced by a cross-wing c1700; it provides service room and staircase to N and kitchen to S and has a clasped-purlin roof.

BRICKENDON LIBERTY

(77500)
Bentleys (TL 322079)

incorporates to S the cross-wing of a late medieval house (Fig 39); to W the wing had on each floor two four-light diamond-mullioned windows; the shutter grooves remain. No division was observed on the ground floor; the first floor was one room with arch-braced cambered tie-beam and collar-rafter roof. In the mid 17th century the open hall was replaced by a two-cell internal-chimney house with lobby-entrance; the room over the hall has a fireplace of that date; some windows with moulded mullions remain. An extension to N is modern.[1]

Note
1. *Newsletter* **34**, 1974, and **35**, 1974.

Fig 39 *Bentleys, Brickendon Liberty: plan*

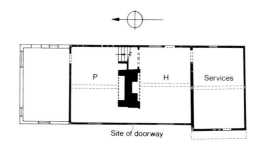

(77501)
Brickendon Bury (TL 330104)

is the house associated with the principal manor of Brickendon Liberty, the whole of which belonged to Waltham Abbey prior to the Dissolution.[1] It was then granted by Henry VIII to Thomas Knighton, together with the advowson of All Saints' Church, Hertford, with which it passed through many hands until it was conveyed to Edward Clarke in 1682;[2] the house was perhaps of no great importance then. Clarke was 'Citizen and Mercer of London', of which he was Lord Mayor in 1696, having been knighted in 1689,[3] but Chauncy does not mention his building a house. It is likely to have been built in the early years of the 18th century by Clarke's son Thomas, who succeeded to the estate in 1703.[4] Salmon thought it 'one of the delightful Seats of the Neighbourhood', mentioning particularly the 'Woods at half a Mile Distance, with Visto's all pointing to the House'.[5] On Thomas's death the house passed to relations by marriage;[6] in 1781 it was occupied by Charles Morgan, MP for Brecon, whose principal seats were Tredegar and Rhiwperra (Glamorgan)[7] and in 1842 by George Gould Morgan Esq., Sheriff in that year. It had been hardly altered externally c1800,[8] but by 1834[9] the cupola and three of the six chimney-stacks had been removed; the original six dormer windows, which had alternate segmental and triangular pediments, had been replaced by four with flat roofs; an achievement of arms had been removed from the pediment and replaced by a round window; and the segmental-headed front doorway with a crest in its pediment had been replaced by a plain porch. In 1881, when the manor was sold to Messrs Paine and Brettell of Chertsey,[10] the house lay empty;[11] then it went to Charles Gray Hill of Nottingham, who carried out extensive restorations in 1885–6;[12] sale particulars of 1893[13] state that the owner had `during the past few years spent a very large sum in modernising and beautifying it'. The house was again up for sale in June 1893[14] and went to George Pearson Esq., by whom `very extensive alterations and improvements, have been recently (1898) made'.[15] Edward E Pearson was Sheriff in 1909.

A plan of 1893[16] shows that the house had five principal ground-floor rooms. The three fireplaces of the front range correspond with the chimney-stacks drawn by Buckler but his drawing gives no hint of the parallel roof of the rear range, or the other three stacks shown by Oldfield, and must be inaccurate in these respects. The original staircase was no doubt in the same position as the present one; the turning of the bottom flight to face S must date from 1885–6. One important change to the original plan involved the reduction in size of a large stack represented by the thick wall at the NW corner of the saloon. The only hint of an early service wing is a single-storey structure to W;[17] the extensive buildings existing in 1893 were perhaps for the most part built in 1885–6. Virtually no detail of earlier date survives.

For an illustration, see *English Houses 1200–1800*, Fig 202.

Notes
1. VCH III, 410.
2. Ibid.
3. Chauncy I, 517.
4. Cussans 1874–8, Vol II (ii), 67.
5. Salmon 1728, 40.
6. VCH II, 410.
7. *Royal Kalendar* 1781, 25.
8. Oldfield Vol III, 391.
9. Buckler Vol III, 40.
10. VCH III, 410.
11. *Kelly* 1882.
12. *Kelly* 1890.
13. HRO, SC D/ELe B/18.
14. SC, Hertford Museum.
15. *Kelly* 1899.
16. SC, Hertford Museum.
17. Oldfield Vol III, 391.

BROXBOURNE

(77502) `Ancient House',
location unknown and now demolished, was drawn by Oldfield,[1] who added to the caption `date carv'd in the passage 1553'; the way the figures are drawn confirms that they were authentic. The house had a continuous jetty which was carried round both gable ends and is perhaps the only firmly dated example of this type.

Note
1. Oldfield Vol I, 419.

BUCKLAND

(77506)
Buckland House (TL 356337)
was the manor house of the jointly held manors of Buckland and Horne and belonged to a family named Watson from 1529 until 1552, when Edward Watson sold it. Subsequent owners lived elsewhere and leased the manor out, perhaps to the descendants of Edward Watson; in 1662 and 1673 another of the same name paid tax on nine hearths, the largest amount in the parish,[1] although he cannot be associated definitely with the house.

The earliest feature of the existing building is a wooden lintel about 10 ft 6 ins (3 m) long; since the mouldings were returned down the jamb at one end but have been truncated at the other it must have been slightly longer originally. Apart from this lintel, which evidently belonged to a late 16th-century house of some pretension, such datable detail as remains is of the early 18th century, including the brick front range, which may have replaced a timber-framed building.

Note
1. PRO E179/375/30 and 31.

BUNTINGFORD

(77507)
Nos 41/43 High Street,
a continuous-jetty house with crown-post roof, was rendered and had a plaster cove applied to the jetty at the beginning of the 18th century; a waggon entrance was then created, the building was divided into two tenements, and that to S (No. 41) provided with a rusticated doorcase with emphasised keystone. Only the S tenement could be examined; a chimney-stack to S has a moulded timber lintel, above which are the remains of a clunch wall with paintings of late medieval type overpainted with an early 17th-century decorative scheme. The clunch appears to be a wall because it is vertical; had it been a chimney-stack it would have sloped backwards; and the lintel is likely to be mid–late 16th century. An early 18th-century staircase is either altered or reset.

(77508)
Nos 57/59 High Street,
of two storeys and attics, comprises a main range facing E flanked by two cross-wings. A carriageway has been driven through the wing to S and the main range and wing to N were refaced in yellow brick in the 19th century; these, and extensive internal alterations, make the development of the house uncertain. It was built in the early 16th century. Little remains of the former hall but low eaves at the back suggest it was of one storey. The wing to N, which is wider than that to S, has in the E wall to N a doorway with a low head which formerly led to a cellar, and to S another of normal height. Between them are two wide openings with four-centred heads, perhaps shop windows, but if that was the original function of this room it presumably changed when a wide fireplace, of brick, plastered, with four-centred head, was built, though there is no structural evidence to show it is an addition.

(77509)
No. 66 High Street
is a small jettied house of two storeys which was built in the 16th century. It has an internal chimney-stack flanked by lobby-entrance on one side and staircase on the other; this is no doubt the original arrangement, although since the existing stack is of

the late 17th century it may replace one of timber. Although no wing or outshut coeval with the house now remains at the rear, it is likely that there was some such structure to contain a pantry and perhaps a staircase, since the existing one is cramped. In the present century the fireplaces were rebuilt, making the original room usage uncertain.

(77510)
Little Court (approx TL 364297)

is known from drawings by Drapentier and Oldfield. John Gill, whose principal seat was Wyddial Hall, refers in his will dated 25 March 1598 to `my house by me lately built called Lyttle Court';[1] both houses descended on his death in 1600 to his son George, who was knighted in 1603 and died in 1619.[2] Little Court, which faced W towards the river Rib, was of H-plan[3] with a three-storey porch, the whole standing over a basement which was reached by two doorways at the front of the wings. About the middle of the 18th century it was refronted,[4] possibly by Butler Chauncy, son of the historian, who bought it in 1760; the porch was demolished and the main body of the house heightened to provide a third storey instead of attics. After the house was acquired by Captain Henry Harman Young in 1819 it was pulled down.[5]

For an illustration, see *English Houses 1200–1800*, Fig 93 (plate).

Note
1. Cussans 1870–3, Vol I (ii), 83.
2. Chauncy I, 225; VCH IV, 80.
3. Aerial view, map of 1734, HRO, 54835.
4. Oldfield Vol I, 445.
5. VCH IV, 80.

BUSHEY

(77511)
Bushey Hall or Bushey Bury (TQ 136956)

was associated with part of the manor of Bushey[1] and its lands may have coincided with the demesne;[2] it is said to have stood within a moat, although no trace of one around the house appears in three engravings of 1700;[3] but a moated enclosure and lake with island shown to S of the mill in `The East and West Prospect...' appear to correspond to an estate map of 1799,[4] in which case the house stood to S. It was begun in 1428 by Thomas Montacute, 4th Earl of Salisbury,[5] and was described by a contemporary annalist as `a sumptuous work'.[6] The engravings are difficult to interpret and show nothing obviously medieval, but the principal storey of the W range appears to have been built above an undercroft in the manner of a first-floor hall. It was in respect of this house that Sir Walter Walker paid for 15 hearths in 1663.[7] His son George, barrister and LLD,[8] succeeded to the estate in 1674 and built `a fair House upon the River Colne';[9] this is the large double-pile range of brick, of which both the N and S prospects were drawn by Drapentier. The most unusual feature of the N front is a low window over the doorway; possibly the entrance-hall occupied two storeys, with a staircase to S. Building may have contributed to the wasting of Walter's fortune and the alienation of his estate.[10] The house was demolished in the early 19th century.

For illustrations, see *English Houses 1200–1800*, Figs 33 (plate), 148 (plate)

Notes
1. VCH II, 183.

2. Longman 1967, 3.
3. Chauncy II, 454.
4. HRO, D/P 26.29/1.
5. *DNB.*
6. *Chronica Monastici S. Albani, Ann Mon S. Albani,* Vol I, 22.
7. PRO E179/248/231.
8. Venn and Venn 1922–7; not DCL, as Chauncy II, 462.
9. Chauncy II, 462.
10. Venn and Venn 1922–7.

(77512)
Delrow (TQ 141974),

formerly Delrow House, bears the date 1669 and initials W H M[1] on rain-water heads. The house, of L-shaped plan, faces S (correctly ESE); differences of floor level and other anomalous features suggest the existence of an older house incorporated in the present one. Probably the oldest part is the middle of the main range; this has a large chimney-stack to W for the hall; the thin wall to N now forming one side of a corridor suggests that the house was timber framed; a cross-wing to W of the hall stack may be coeval. To W again is another cross-wing roofed parallel with the first; it has an internal chimney-stack with ground and first-floor fireplaces facing S; the latter, defaced, is original; the former has modern jambs and a mid 17th-century carved head. The ground floor to N of the stack has a lower ceiling than that to S; the latter was a parlour of some kind, the former perhaps a service room. Possibly the late 17th-century development of the house is to be explained by dual occupation; John Jesson Esq. and Mrs Hutchinson, also a member of the Jesson family, are rated together then.[2] A wing to E is of uncertain date, perhaps 18th century. The whole was refaced and unified between 1820 and 1840 in Tudor style, probably by Sir Adolphus Dalrymple, Bart., who succeeded his brother in the estate in 1830.[3]

Notes
1. For William Hutchinson; VCH II, 158.
2. VCH II, 158, n192.
3. Ibid, 158.

(77513)
Nos 64–68 High Street

form a late medieval house comprising an open hall and cross-wings. Little framing is exposed internally but at the upper end of the hall are peg-holes for a bench.

(77514)
Oundle, Little Bushey Lane (TL 147949)

is of two storeys and attics and ostensibly of the late 17th century. The main range, aligned N–S, is unusually wide (19 ft 6 ins (6 m)) for a house of that date; moreover it has a wide fire-place with a wooden lintel of which the small part exposed has mouldings suggesting a date in the late 16th or early 17th century. This tenuous evidence suggests that within the shell of the late medieval hall a chimney-stack was built, with staircase and lobby-entrance to W.

A transformation took place in the late 17th century; all the exposed framing is of that date; the room to N, which has to N a doorway with ovolo-moulded jambs, was widened to E; the cellar under the parlour is of the same period. The staircase was built in the mid 18th century; in the early 19th century pointed Gothick windows were put in, together with a Tudor-style grate in a first-floor room. Early in the present century the house was enlarged to N and W.

(77515)
Patchetts Green Farm (TQ 138976)

was built in the 15th century as a Wealden house. The hall is of two bays with a rebated crown-post roof; the S bay is of two storeys and jettied; there are slight indications that the house originally had a N bay too, now demolished. Whether the N end continued the Wealden form is uncertain, and a development like that of Yew Tree Farm, Much Hadham, is a possibility. A floor, supported by an ovolo-moulded bearer, was inserted in the hall in the early 17th century; it implies the existence of a timber chimney-stack. A kitchen wing and stables were added at the rear. The present chimney-stack was built in the late 17th century. Externally the house was refaced in brick or rendered in the 18th and 19th centuries.[1]

Note
1. Isometric drawing in Dulley 1978, 85.

BYGRAVE

(77516)
The Manor House (TL 264360)

was of considerable importance in the 13th century when it belonged to the Somery family; it was presumably there that Edward I stopped in 1299 and 1302.[1] In 1383 Sir John Thornbury purchased the manor and in 1386 had licence to crenellate his two houses; earthworks suggest the existence of a second house (the `Palace' (TL 265360)) adjoining the present manor house. The estate was sold successively to Francis Cleaver in 1651, whose son Charles paid for 11 hearths in 1662,[2] and to the Earl of Salisbury in 1682; since then it has been at lease. Captain Taylor, who paid £2 9s 0d tax on 24 windows in 1783,[3] presumably lived here. The oldest part of the existing house is a cross-wing to N (correctly NE), of uncertain date but perhaps 16th century. To S, at right-angles to it, the hall range may be a later replacement of an earlier construction. A wing to S of the hall may be coeval but, like the rest of the house, has no pre-19th-century features. Extensions to E and W of c1700 produced a square double-pile plan (excluding the N wing); it was then re-roofed with two parallel hipped roofs running E–W. The house was greatly altered c1830; a first-floor fireplace of that date survives in the S wing and to S and E are iron verandahs of that date.

Notes
1. VCH III, 215.
2. PRO E179/375/30.
3. HRO, Land Tax, Misc Bundle 10.

CALDECOTE

(77517)
Caldecote Manor (TL 236384),

formerly a possession of the monastery of St Albans,[1] is a much altered Wealden house built c1500. None of the framing is exposed outside and little inside but two doors at the W end of the hall perpetuate the screens doors, and the staircase in the W bay corresponds more or less to the original one but has been turned round. The hall had a crown-post roof. In the 17th century a wing was added to E; a chimney-stack and upper floor were put in to the hall; a lobby-entrance replaced the cross-passage; and the roof-plate cut back to give light to the chamber over the hall. The house was enlarged in polychrome brick c1900 and a new entrance created to S.

Note
1. VCH III, 218.

CHESHUNT

(33632)
Elm Arches, Turners Hill, Cheshunt,

is of brick, of four bays and three storeys, and was built c1730–50; it was enlarged in the 19th century and early in the present century, and now presents the appearance of having two two-storey wings, although the one to N is of only one storey with a screen wall simulating a second storey. The entrance and staircase-hall occupied the bay to S; the remaining three bays formed one large room on each floor. Apart from its plan the house is now of little interest. It was given to Cheshunt Urban District Council in 1913.[1]

Note
1. Edwards 1974, 107.

(77518)
The Four Swans Inn, Waltham Cross (TL 360004)

had, when Buckler drew it in 1830,[1] a jettied range facing the yard with a first-floor gallery lit by 13 openings with four-centred heads. It was entered by a doorway also with a four-centred head reached from the yard by a straight flight of wooden stairs. When the building was demolished is uncertain; the whole site was redeveloped in the 1960s.

Note
1. Buckler Vol IV, 38.

(29842)
The Great House (TL 345027),

of brick and of two storeys with basement and attics, was built in the mid or late 15th century by one of two people: either the John Walsh who, having acquired in 1440 a moiety of the manor of Le Mote, united it with a manor called Andrews, the two becoming henceforth Andrews or Andrews Le Mote; or his son, also John Walsh, whose tenure was from some time after the death of his widowed mother, still living in 1474, to 1500.[1] Architectural detail makes the former more likely.

The 15th-century house comprised a hall open to the roof with a two-storeyed cross-wing to N and probably another to S; the whole stood above undercrofts, of which only the part under the hall was vaulted, perhaps in order to support an open hearth. The cross-passage was to S; at the N end of the hall was an oriel to E, spanned by a wide arch with a depressed four-centred head. The hall roof had close-spaced arch-braced trusses with tenoned purlins and wind-braces; the arch-braces were tenoned into wall-posts resting on corbels carved with human heads or angels holding shields. One angel had a `corkscrew' hairstyle, which is unlikely to be any later than the 15th century;[2] this and the mouldings of the corbel refine the date to the later 15th century. To N was the parlour wing and the service rooms were presumably to S, although the demolition of the latter and the existence of the undercroft make the location of service functions rather uncertain.

In the early 17th century the house was enlarged to N; this part had a three-light mullioned window and a chimney-stack with three diagonal flues.[3] The basement was a kitchen; above it was a parlour and above that a great chamber; to W was a staircase. This work is probably attributable to Sir Thomas Dacres, Sheriff in 1614. To SW a wing of two storeys and attics with an `inverted W' roof was added in the mid–late 17th century.[4] By then the house was *c*130 ft (40 m) long and divided into two storeyed parts by an open hall, which provided the only communication between them (a duality found in some other 17th-century houses). By 1700, after three sales in 25 years, what was by then a large, rambling house came into the possession of Sir John Shaw, 2nd Baronet, who may have undertaken a general renovation. The date 1750 which has been suggested for this work[5] appears too late for the architectural detail, although Cussans[6] specifically says that `in 1750 it was modernised and encased with brick'. `Encased' is certainly wrong; the basis for the date is not known. The E or garden front, from which the N wing certainly and the S wing probably projected, was refaced flush with the former, ie the oriel was demolished and a new wall added about 7 ft (2 m) in front of the old hall to produce an imposing elevation of 18 bays; above the basement, which was treated as a podium, the two principal storeys were of equal height, divided by a moulded platband, with sash windows, and the whole was finished by a cornice and parapet with sunk panels corresponding to the bays. The W or entrance front was not altered equally thoroughly, only as much as the internal dispositions permitted. It was largely refaced; the hall was given tall windows with segmental heads (cf Knebworth House), above which was a moulded band and sunk panels; the remainder was given sash windows uniform in size and spacing with those to E, and the whole was capped uniformly with cornice and parapet. A general renovation of the interior included an imposing staircase at the N end of the house (cf Salisbury Hall, Shenley); the rooms opening off it to E were panelled and given new fireplaces, the one in the ground-floor room being of high quality; the hall was paved with square stones with small `marble' squares set diagonally at the intersections, fitted with fielded panelling to a height of 9 ft (2·8 m), and a fireplace to N.

In the early 19th century so inconvenient a plan was drastically altered by lopping off everything to S of the hall and creating an end-entrance plan with a symmetrical S front. This is said to have taken place in 1801;[7] the new work had Gothick detail. In 1965 the house was demolished.

The Great House is of particular interest because of the way it developed, beginning with an open hall with storeyed ends; in the late 17th century the ends had become more or less independent blocks of rooms, with the hall as link and passage room; in the early 18th century a complete refacing stressed the importance of the garden front and provided better communication between the two ends; finally one of the two end blocks was removed entirely to unify the house. It is remarkable that the open hall should have survived throughout.

For an illustration, see *English Houses 1200–1800*, Fig 34.

Notes
1. VCH III, 453; Gover, Mawer and Stenton 1938, 221.
2. Inf. Professor G Zarnecki.
3. VCH III, 442.
4. Hughson 1805–9, Vol VI, engraving opposite p 138.
5. VCH III, 453; `recased in brick'.
6. Cussans 1874–8, Vol II (ii), 217.
7. VCH IV, 442, following Cussans.

(77519)
The Old Parsonage (TL 349024),

of the late 15th century, has a hall with service wing to W and parlour wing to E, both jettied. In the hall the two principal posts of the open truss can be seen on the ground floor but have been entirely removed above the ceiling; the post to N has

a few big peg-holes, perhaps for an applied moulding; in the partition at the upper end are peg-holes for a bench and, to N, a chamfered doorway formerly opening on to a staircase, the head of which was lit by a two-light window; before its heightening the hall probably had a crown-post roof. In the 17th century an upper floor was built in the hall; and a wing was added to N, with a common chimney-stack providing fireplaces for hall and kitchen; to N of the latter was a dairy or pantry. At this period the original staircases in the E and W wings presumably remained in use, with another, perhaps to W of the chimney-stack, serving the N wing. In the 18th century the W wing was converted into a parlour by the addition of a fireplace and a larger staircase was built to N. In the 19th century the outside of the house was embellished in Tudor style, and at the same time the rail and newels of the main staircase were altered.

(77520)
Theobalds (TL 355011),

demolished, was one of the most important Elizabethan houses. Reference is made to it in *English Houses 1200–1800* only for the purposes of comparison with other houses of the period.[1]

Note
1. For the fully documented study see Summerson 1959*a*, 107–26; and for the wall-paintings, Nichols 1821–3, Vol II, 10–11.

CHIPPERFIELD

(77521)
Manor House (TL 048013)

was formerly Pingelsgate, a farm built up by piecemeal purchase. John and Thomas Carter of Pingelsgate are mentioned in a survey of Kings Langley manor in 1556,[1] but the house is said to have been built by Thomas Galston, clerk, before 1591 and was described in the early 17th century as a beautiful tenement.[2] William Over purchased it in 1637; in 1663 he paid for three hearths.[3] In 1673 the probate inventory[4] lists hall, parlour, kitchen; chamber and one other room over hall, chamber over parlour, chamber and closet over kitchen, closet over porch; garret, brewhouse, cellar. It passed by marriage *c*1700 to John Marriott, who refronted the house in brick in 1714.[5] In 1850 the house, together with the manor of Kings Langley, descended to Robert Blackwell who, in 1852, demolished the medieval manor house in Kings Langley High Street[6] and transferred the name to Pingelsgate. In 1911–12 his nephew Samuel enlarged the house by adding wings to N and S of the seven-bay front.[7] The present house contains fragmentary evidence of late medieval origin; it had an open hall with cross-wing to S; the latter, probably jettied, has heavy plain joists and a plain crown-post roof with four-way struts; a wing to N has been largely gutted. In the 17th century a floor carried on an ovolo-moulded binding-beam was inserted in the hall, as was a chimney-stack with diagonally set shafts; the hall fireplace has a four-centred head and simply moulded surround; a gabled staircase wing was added to E. The refronting included windows with flat arches of rubbed brick, which were intended to have a central mullion and casement lights,[8] and the parapet was to be plain. When sash windows were put in and the present parapet with sunk panels built is not clear; they represent a change of design in 1714 but the parapet could equally well belong to the same restoration as the staircase, which is of early 18th-century style, and may have been reset. Wall-paintings of uncertain date were discovered in 1850.[9]

Notes
1. Blackwell Papers, HRO, 20754/57.
2. Munby 1963, *xiii*, 64–7, 105.
3. PRO E179/248/23.
4. PRO Prob 4/5074.
5. HRO, 20251, agreement with Cock of Watford, bricklayer, with drawing of front elevation.
6. Oldfield Vol IV, 381.
7. Munby 1963, *xiii*.
8. HRO, 20251, drawing of front elevation, 1714.
9. VCH II, 235.

CHORLEYWOOD

(77522)
Nos 4/5 Chorleywood Bottom (TQ 028957)
is a two-bay house of *c*1600. It comprised a hall and an inner room to N which may have been a parlour; mortises in the wall to E indicate a structure of some kind there, possibly a pantry with a lean-to roof. The lack of a window on this side of the hall may be why a small window was sited in an unusual position beside the entrance. The staircase was in the NE corner of the inner room.[1]

Note
1. Plan and original details recorded by Mr C F Stell during restoration in 1964.

(77523)
Dell Cottages, Quickley Lane (TL 011953),
was perhaps built in the 17th century, although its dating presents difficulties. The house comprised a hall entered through the N gable wall, and two unequally sized inner rooms, the larger being the parlour and the smaller a pantry or general service room (Fig 40). The staircase was probably always in much the same position, as a chamfer stop on the bearer shows: the need for doorways from hall to inner rooms indicates that it must have been a steep, ladder-like stair originally. One slight indication that at first the house may have been of one storey and attics is that on the first floor the E wall, particularly in the S bay, leans outwards markedly (cf High Tree Farm, Ardeley), as if it had been heightened. The plan belongs to the class of long-house derivatives.

Fig 40 *Dell Cottages, Quickley Lane, Chorleywood: plan*

(77524)
King John's Farm (TQ 028953)
comprises an early 16th-century range which suffered drastic restoration *c*1910 when wings were added to E and W and the name was changed from King's Farm;[1] it derives from Philip

Kynge, mentioned in 1556.[2] A photograph taken on 11 September 1894[3] shows how great the changes were. Structurally the old house is of two nearly equal bays with a shorter one between them; it was divided into two ground-floor rooms, the joists being chamfered and stopped throughout (Fig 41). The hall fireplace is probably of the 18th century and the simply treated cap of the comparatively small chimney-stack[4] confirms this date; but

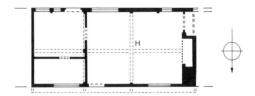

Fig 41 *King John's Farm, Chorleywood: plan*

presumably this stack replaced an earlier one. The position of the staircase is unknown; in the room to E marks on nearly all the joists of laths for a plaster ceiling make it difficult to suppose the staircase was there; if it was in a rear turret the complete rebuilding of the S wall has destroyed all traces. Upstairs each bay forms a room; the partitions appear to be original. The comparative smallness of these rooms compared with those of, eg, John O'Gaddesden's House, Little Gaddesden, or the Town House, Barley, rules out the possibility that this was ever a communal building. An unusual feature is the existence of an apparently original ceiling over the whole of the upper storey; the joists and bearers are flush on the soffit as if for plaster ceilings, and the beams appear to be tenoned into the tie-beams.

Notes
1. *CL* Supplement, 7 October 1911, 8*–12*; made available by Mr C F Stell.
2. Gover, Mawer and Stenton 1938, 83.
3. Anderson, WCL, 1093.
4. Photograph in Summer 1904; a reference owed to Mr C F Stell.

(77525)
The Retreat (TQ 028956)
is a small house of two storeys and two bays, which appear to have comprised only one room on each floor. On the ground floor the binding-beam shows no peg-holes for a studded partition, and where the soffit is exposed it has no peg-holes or groove for infilling; and on the first floor a cambered tie-beam, chamfered and stopped, has no mortises or peg-holes for a partition. Although the timbers are weathered at both ends the house must once have been larger; the low wooden building to S, through which the house is entered, may replace an older structure because there is no sign now of any other entrance into the house, although alteration has obscured much evidence. A large S chimney-stack may once have backed on to a cross-passage. The house is unusually wide (18 ft 10 ins (5·7 m)) for its modest length.

CLOTHALL

(77526)
The Old Ram and Hurdle PH, Luffenhall (TL 292287)
incorporates to W the wing of a 16th-century house; it can be inferred that the mid 17th-century main range replaces an open

hall. Whether the wing had two ground-floor rooms is uncertain; the only binding-beam is plastered, perhaps to conceal the empty mortises of an original partition. The staircase does not seem to have opened directly out of the hall, but was probably a straight flight rising to a landing near which is a two-light window now blocked. Probably the staircase was not partitioned from the chamber over the service rooms, which is spanned in the middle by an open arch-braced truss with clasped-purlins. Surprisingly, the wing is not jettied.

The main range was completely rebuilt in the late 17th century, the date indicated by a notched chamfer stop on the bearer in the hall. The chimney-stack, at the upper end of the hall, has two ground-floor fireplaces, one in the parlour to E and the other in the hall; to S is a staircase; lodging-plates carry the ends of the joists. The late medieval cross-passage entrance was perpetuated. In the late 18th or early 19th century a chimney-stack was built in the wing, perhaps when the farmhouse was turned into a public house; a lean-to added at the same period to N of the main range had a copper with its own chimney; a bread oven (since removed) beside the hall fireplace was probably of that date.

(77529)
Quickswood (TL 275328),

the house associated with the manors of Clothall, Hanvills and Botteles,[1] is first mentioned in the `latter End of the Reign of H.VIII'.[2] In February 1592, when Dorothy Burgoyne was said to be in possession of the capital messuage called Quickswood House, Thomas Burgoyne and others broke into the said mansion.[3] It was purchased c1600 by Nicholas Trott Esq., who was Sheriff in 1608; he built `a fair House'[4] and sold it in 1617 to William, second Earl of Salisbury, who immediately set about enlarging it.[5] The work was not very extensive; an inventory of 1620[6] includes `my lords's new bedchamber and closet and the women's new chamber' in a house of about forty-five rooms. Other additions and alterations `according to a plot drawn by Robert Liming' in 1623–4 comprised a new kitchen above a cellar, with provision for lodgings in the roof if required;[7] there is also a `plat' showing the division of the gallery into chambers.[8] A fireplace removed to Hatfield House is the only relic of the house, which was completely demolished c1790 by the 1st Marquess of Salisbury.

The existing house is no doubt the messuage `near the Earl's mansion house called Quickswood House' which, in 1671, was leased to John Greene;[9] its function in relation to the mansion is unclear. It comprises a range to W and N, of double depth, making an L-shaped plan. The former incorporates an internal-chimney timber-framed house of two rooms with lobby-entrance; the chimney-stack has conjoined shafts; on the first floor a principal post supports a plastered tie-beam; the thickened head of the post has a simple 17th-century moulding; the roof has clasped-purlins. Any service rooms forming part of this house have disappeared. The development of the N range, which is of brick, is uncertain. In the late 17th century it was built to about half its present length, the termination being marked by a straight joint; to S was an entrance-hall with staircase to W and to N a parlour with corner fireplace backing on to that of the hall; possibly the W range was extended to S to provide a large service room. The N side of the N range has purlins supported by struts. Not many years later the N range was extended to E; to S is a large unheated room, to N another parlour with corner fireplace backing on to the first; this room is now and perhaps always was a kitchen; to E are service rooms and a servants' staircase. In the late 18th century the W range was refaced in brick; in the 19th century the staircase and some

fireplaces were renewed. Sale particulars of 1885[10] mention entrance-hall, dining room, drawing room, kitchen, dairy, pantry, scullery, seven bedrooms and underground cellar.

For an illustration, see *English Houses 1200–1800*, Fig 107 (plate).

Notes
1. VCH III, 222–5.
2. Chauncy I, 101.
3. Hatfield MSS, Deeds 47.
4. Chauncy I, 101.
5. Hatfield MSS, General 7/21, account of works, September 1617.
6. Hatfield MSS, Box C32.
7. Hatfield MSS, General 3/2, 43/6.
8. Ibid.
9. Hatfield MSS, Legal, Box 1/13.
10. Ibid, Box 2/96.

(77527)
Walnut Tree Farm, Luffenhall (TL 292285)

is a small, late medieval house comprising a low main range in which were the open hall and service rooms, and a wing to S of two storeys. In a cupboard beside the inserted chimney-stack can be seen the principal post supporting the open truss of the former hall, a moulding on the post having been cut away; the roof has clasped-purlins and is blackened by smoke. The cross-wing, jettied to E, has one room on each floor; the middle truss has a cambered tie-beam and a crown-post roof with high collar-purlin and thin two-way braces. Some close-studding is exposed at the front (E) on the first floor. The service room to N, formerly used as a dairy, has a staircase in the original position rising from the cross-passage (cf Tenements Farm, St Stephen). The chimney-stack, which backs on to the passage, was inserted in the hall c1600 together with an upper floor and staircase. A single-storey kitchen wing was added to W c1700; and during the early 19th century the hall chimney-stack was rebuilt.

(77528)
Whitehall, Luffenhall (TL 292286),

was built towards the end of the 15th century; it then comprised an open hall with a two-storeyed jettied cross-wing to W, and a service room to E. In the wing, which has exposed close-studding, the ground-floor room was the parlour and originally had no fireplace; the binding-beam has a double hollow chamfer; and two studs in the wall to N have housings for a large window, whose shutter groove extends the whole length of the wall. The site of the wing staircase is uncertain. Upstairs is one room, spanned by an arch-braced tie-beam and having a clasped-purlin roof. The hall extended about 21 ft 6 ins (6·6 m) to N and had at 16 ft (5 m) a roof truss, perhaps only partially open, marking off the cross-passage; an upper chamber over the passage may have extended to this truss. The service bay to N retains little old detail. A chimney-stack was built c1600 at the S end of the hall. The moulded lintel of the hall fireplace has been shortened to S and was raised when the existing chimney-stack was built; the lack of any brickwork coeval with the lintel suggests that the chimney-stack was of timber. In the late 17th century a timber-framed bay, possibly a dairy and room above, was added to E and the hall chimney-stack with conjoined diagonal flues was built. Then, or possibly somewhat earlier, a fireplace was added to the parlour, and a staircase to S of the stack replaced an earlier one. In the 18th century a large kitchen wing was added to S.

CODICOTE

(77530)
Codicote Bury (TL 218185),

belonging to St Albans Abbey until the Dissolution, passed through several hands before being sold in 1659 to George Poyner; `Citizen and Merchant of London, he built a fair House...with convenient Stables and Out-houses, and died about the year 1670'.[1] The house is square in plan, and of two storeys with basement and attics. The front (S) elevation forms an unusual composition dominated by a pilastered and pedimented centrepiece of two storeys with niches in the side bays,[2] so that part of the front range must have been rather dark inside. On each floor and on each side of the centrepiece were three recesses; probably all had three-centred heads with a mullion-and-transom window originally. This arrangement suggests that the present two rooms to S, which are of unusually elongated proportions, each had two closets originally. The fireplace to SW is likely to have been enlarged; that to NW is probably of the original width and is appropriate to the kitchen. To E and W of the chimney-stacks were lobbies, the former leading to the garden and the latter to stables (cf Mackerye End, Wheathampstead). The basement provided cellarage, the equivalent of the medieval buttery, and was reached by a staircase from the kitchen. The original arrangement of the first floor is not altogether certain. Probably the principal room was to SE, its entrance facing the head of the staircase; it may have been the drawing room. A blocked doorway with a mid 17th-century frame led to a smaller room to W. The lobby from the landing to the SW bedroom is probably original. To N two bedrooms have proportions which suggest some subdivision to N of the kind existing in the room to E. On the top floor the two rooms to S have good-sized fireplaces (blocked), with depressed four-centred heads and high stops to the chamfered jambs (a similar fireplace in the room to NE is a modern copy); the rooms to N were unheated. The main roof covers the front half of the house, and there are three roofs at right-angles to it; wherever necessary door-jambs are tenoned to the collar-beams. In the late 18th century hung sashes replaced the original windows; parapeted elevations were built on all four sides; and the chimney-stacks were rebuilt. Most of the fireplaces seem to have been replaced and in the NE room both the fireplace and panelling are modern, no doubt part of the alterations undertaken for J L Hunter Esq.[3]

For illustrations, see *English Houses 1200–1800*, Figs 127 (plate), 128.

Notes
1. Chauncy II, 408.
2. Buckler Vol IV, 154.
3. Newton brochure; *Kelly* 1912.

COLNEY HEATH

(77531)
Hill End Farm (TL 184060)

incorporates a two-storey range of two 10 ft (3 m) bays, which may be of the 15th century. The comparatively low ground-floor rooms and the fact that the chimney-stack is clearly an addition argue that this range is the cross-wing of an open hall that was demolished and replaced by brick buildings of the 18th century and later, which themselves form cross-wings to the older fragment. This was probably done not long before the drawing of 1832 entitled `Hill End Farm...belonging to Wm. Knight Esq.'.[1]

Note
1. Buckler Vol III, 152.

(77532)
Oaklands (TL 182076),

said to have been built in 1782 and enlarged in 1844,[1] is the subject of five drawings[2] that suggest a rather different development. Two, done in 1835 before enlargement, are dated 1835 and captioned `the seat of William Knight Esq[re].'; they show it in the Tudor style favoured in the first quarter of the 19th century. Had there been anything of earlier date it was by then completely obscured to E, W and S, whereas the recession of the narrower middle bay of the frontage suggests that the whole may have been of one build.

The three drawings of 1844 show enlargements including the tower to SW and wing to NE. Since 1920 the house has been put to educational use as an agricultural college.[3] Removal of the original gables and chimney-stacks has destroyed much of its picturesque appearance.

Notes
1. Pelham 1971, 12.
2. Buckler Vol III, 147–51.
3. Pelham 1971, 13.

(77533)
Popefield Farm (TL 200080)

is a lobby-entrance house of two-room plan and of two storeys and semi-attics, except for the part to the S (correctly SE) end, which is of only two storeys. It was built mostly in the mid 17th century but appears to incorporate parts of an older house; some of the framing exposed internally shows straight braces and original window openings. Peg-holes in pairs, for a bench, can be seen in the hall to S of the stack, and a bench would be unusual as late as the mid 17th century. The framing in the room to S again joins the main block in a clumsy way, which suggests that it is a relic of an earlier house; it was provided with a fireplace in the late 17th or early 18th century. When this happened the rooms to E, which retain little evidence of date, were no doubt added as service rooms. In 1980 the house was carefully restored.

COTTERED

(77534)
Broadfield (TL 324310)

was the only manor in the parish of that name and belonged, at the beginning of the 17th century, to Edward Pulter, from whom it descended in 1608 to his grandson Arthur, then aged four.[1] Arthur Pulter was JP, captain in the militia and, in 1641, Sheriff; but on the outbreak of the Civil War `declin'd all publick Imployment, liv'd a retir'd Life, and thro' the Importunity of his Wife, began to build a very fair House of Brick upon this Mannor, but dying he never finish'd it'.[2]

It is difficult to be sure in which years he was building; probably not much before 1650, but hardly much after, to judge by the style. Chauncy states that Pulter was succeeded in 1689 by his grandson James Forrester, who

repaired the Mannor-house, which was much decay'd thro' the want of finishing it at the time it was built; made a new Roof, with a fair Gallery and Lodging-Chambers on the West side thereof, pav'd the Hall with Stone, erected a fair Screen, beautify'd the House, made a fair Garden, enclos'd it with a Brick Wall...[3]

but he died in 1696, aged 36, before the work was finished.[4] Hawksmoor was the architect[5] and he may have been responsible for the modillioned eaves cornice, dormer windows, panelled chimney-stacks and perhaps the doorways.[6] The mullion-and-transom windows are clearly the work of Arthur Pulter, who seems to have built a rather advanced house of double-pile plan with the principal rooms on the first floor. It is impossible to reconstruct it with any certainty but the reference to a screen suggests that the hall was large and perhaps lit by the two windows to the left of the front doorway. Probably there was a basement storey originally; the terrace shown by Buckler is likely to be of the 18th or early 19th century. The stable block, which survives, may be by Hawksmoor.[7] In the early 19th century the house was in the possession of Richard Forrester French, who died in 1843;[8] it was being offered for sale in 1844[9] and again in 1851, when it was said to be `out of repair'.[10] It was pulled down in the 1870s and a new house built in 1882, which in turn was rebuilt in the 1930s.[11]

For an illustration, see *English Houses 1200–1800*, Fig 123 (plate).

Notes
1. VCH III, 210.
2. Chauncy I, 145.
3. Ibid, 147.
4. Ibid.
5. Colvin 1978, 402, citing Hine 1951.
6. Buckler Vol II, 148.
7. Downes 1969, 27.
8. VCH III, 211.
9. *Lincoln, Rutland & Stamford Mercury*, 8 November 1844.
10. *The Hertfordshire Mercury and County Press*, 23 September 1851.
11. Hine 1951, 8.

(77535)
Hall Farm, Broadfield (TL 324310)

was built in the late 17th century. It has an unusually elongated plan; the room to S, with a fireplace of *c*1700, is a parlour; a service room and staircase separate it from what was probably the kitchen; the fireplace jambs and a doorway to W suggest this function. The room to N of the chimney-stack may have been the hall, with service rooms beyond. The unusual sequence of rooms may reflect the difficulty of enlarging the traditional three-cell plan without resorting to a double-depth plan. To E a wing was added in the early 19th century.

For illustrations, see *English Houses 1200–1800*, Figs 172 (plate), 173.

(77536)
The Lordship (TL 318291)

was the manor house of Cottered; formerly it stood within a moat, of which only the NE and SE arms remain. The architectural detail of the house suggests it was built while the manor was in the possession of John Fray, who was holding it by 1428; he became chief baron of the Exchequer in 1435 and died in 1461.[1] Alterations made *c*1600 are dated by wall-paintings; they were undertaken by a member of the Pulter family, possibly Edward Pulter, who may have lived here after handing over his principal seat of Broadfield Manor to his eldest son Litton in 1600 and before the latter's death in 1608, when he seems to have moved back.[2] After Arthur Pulter sold it in 1624–5,[3] The Lordship became a farmhouse.

The open hall, excluding the passage, was approximately square and of two bays, of which only the lower one, about 12 ft

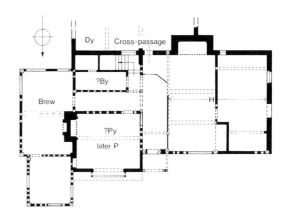

Fig 42 *The Lordship, Cottered: plan*

6 ins (3·8 m) long, remains fairly complete; the upper end bay is slightly longer (Fig 42). A spere-truss divides hall from passage; the upper part of each screen is open with, originally, an arched head, mortises for which are clear to S. Three adjacent doorways with four-centred heads open into the cross-wing; the middle one is higher than the others and leads to a passage looking like the way through, between buttery and pantry, to a former detached kitchen.[4] However it is strange for a kitchen passage to have had the most important doorway; the framing to N is unlike that to S; the joists are tenoned into a binding-beam to S and run over the N head-beam; the binding-beam in the front room is placed in relation to the S wall, not the N wall of the passage; these points suggest that the N wall is a 17th-century insertion. Probably a staircase rising directly into the great chamber was reached through the middle doorway, the head of which was higher to emphasise its importance; at the top of the staircase is a door into the smaller (S) chamber. It follows that the kitchen was a detached structure S of the house. The wing formerly had a crown-post roof.

The first change may have been the flooring over the W end of the hall, reducing it to one bay, but still with an open hearth and screens-passage; there is nothing to date this work, which is inferred from the form taken by the late 17th-century alterations. In the early 17th century the wing was remodelled. A chimney-stack with two diagonal shafts was added to E and was sited to provide a fireplace in the middle of the long wall of the great chamber; the fireplace has a four-centred head and its slight projection into the room argues that the stack is not, as might be expected, original. On the S wall, paintings adapted to close-studding survive; the panels have elaborate classical scroll-work with grotesque heads or profile masks and the studs have a triangular motif forming vertical divisions; on the plates are fragments of a leaf scroll. The room below, which has a similar fireplace with carved and moulded overmantel, is lined with panelling in small squares, and was reduced in size when the passage was formed; the original doorway was then blocked, perhaps because it was thought inconvenient opposite the fireplace, and the present one made. The passage led to a two-storey block with two interconnecting ground-floor rooms of uncertain purpose; one was probably a pantry. A staircase was built, probably in the same position as the present one. In 1909 the upper floor contained `a good deal of plain Jacobean panelling', behind which, as recent repairs had shown, `the partitions had been...lined with boarding...and...decorated with painted work'.[5]

It is difficult to say exactly what this signifies; perhaps the covering-up of Jacobean wall-painting by somewhat later panelling. A jettied two-storey porch was added.

The last important building phase saw the flooring-over of the screens-passage and of the E bay of the hall, the joists of which are carried, at the E end, on a beam with a double-ovolo moulding; the addition of the chimney-stack which is dated 1699; the creation in the former screens-passage of an entrance and staircase-hall; and the S extension of the wing, which has purlins supported on queen-posts. The hall by this time had become the kitchen; then or in the 18th century one of the E rooms was fitted with a large brewing copper,[6] and a room was added to N either as a fuel store or farm entrance. In recent years the house has been carefully restored.

For an illustration, see *English Houses 1200–1800*, Fig 70 (plate).

Notes
1. VCH III, 229.
2. Chauncy I, 134.
3. VCH III, 229.
4. RCHME 1910, 84.
5. RCHME, MS report, 1909.
6. VCH III, 227, plan.

(77537)
Rumbolds (TL 325284)

is a small, late medieval house comprising an open hall and a jettied cross-wing to S. The wing originally had two ground-floor rooms entered by adjacent doorways; a staircase rising beside the back wall is probably in the same position as the original one. In the late 17th century a two-storey bay was added to N; a chimney-stack with conjoined diagonal flues was built, serving fireplaces in the hall and the new ground-floor room; and an upper floor, carried on a moulded bearer, was inserted in the hall. The staircase is in the same position as the original one. The room to N appears to have been a kitchen; although the bread oven is an addition of the late 18th century, the square plan of the fireplace contrasts with the splayed plan of the fireplace in the former hall and suggests that there was some change in the latter's function.

For illustrations, see *English Houses 1200–1800*, Figs 53 (plate), 54.

(77538)
Throcking Hall (TL 338300)

was a late 17th-century moated house which had a very short life. George Hyde, who held the manor and died in 1549, mentions his mansion house in his will and in 1663 Sir Thomas Soame paid for 16 hearths.[1] Subsequently it descended in 1683 to Robert Elwes[2] who in 1692[3] began to build `a curious and neat Fabrick for the Manner-house'.[4] It was a large double-pile house of orthodox late 17th-century appearance, except for having at each end two flat-roofed bays with parapets contrasting oddly with the high hipped roof on the main block of nine bays; this contrast may have been the result of enlargement some few years after the original design was completed. As a result of a family quarrel the house was pulled down in 1744.[5]

Notes
1. PRO E179/248/24/9.
2. VCH IV, 112.
3. Cussans 1870–3, Vol I (ii), 109, n.
4. Chauncy I, 238.
5. VCH IV, 113.

DATCHWORTH

(77539)
Bulls Green Farm (TL 272174)

is of two storeys and attics and has a two-room plan with lobby-entrance. Built in the 17th century, its datable features are the chimney-stack, much of the brickwork of the two ground-floor fireplaces, and some exposed first-floor framing to E, probably of the last quarter. The hall fireplace may be earlier because it appears originally to have been of timber; the lintel has two peg-holes for wooden jambs, and one in the middle for a post to support a bearer, suggesting an original timber chimney-stack. The lintel is the only feature to suggest a date as early as the time of William Spencer of Bulls Green, yeoman, who probably lived here and whose Inquisition *post mortem* is dated 15 August 1625.[1] The larger room to S was the hall and that to N the parlour; its fireplace may be a later addition. A lean-to bay to S is comparatively modern but the timbers of the gable wall, seen during restoration, are said never to have been exposed to the weather,[2] so a service room may always have been here. A narrow wing to E was added in the late 18th century. In recent years the house has been enlarged and renovated.

Notes
1. PRO C142/590/12.
2. Inf. Mrs Osman.

(77540)
Hawkin's Hall Farm (TL 273184),

the house of a reputed manor first recorded in 1564, belonged to a branch of the Bardolf family whose principal manor was Crowborough, Watton-at-Stone.[1] The estate was sold in 1591 to Edward FitzJohn and in 1673 to Edmund Knight.[2] Since the house incorporates an open hall some 21 ft (6·4 m) wide, the reputed manor was of some importance long before 1564. Of the late medieval house some studs and part of the S wall-plate remain, and, to W, the cambered tie-beam and an arch-brace of the open truss. It had a crown-post roof with four-way struts; a W cross-wing jettied to S was probably original.[3] The house is unlikely to be as early as the William Haukyn mentioned in 1365;[4] it is probably of the early 15th century. In the 17th century a chimney-stack was inserted in the hall, serving two back-to-back fireplaces; the one to E had a moulded timber lintel, subsequently raised; the stack now has a plain cap. The first floor is of the same date. In the early 19th century the house was divided into cottages, rendered, and its roof given a half-hip to E. After a fire in the 1920s the part to W of the stack was demolished.

Notes
1. VCH III, 162.
2. Ibid, 79–80.
3. Old photograph in possession of Mrs P Adrian.
4. Gover, Mawer and Stenton 1938, 123.

(77541)
Hoppers Hall

is of two storeys and attics and has a three-room plan with two-storey porch to W and staircase wing to E; it was built in the mid 17th century. From N to S the ground-floor rooms are parlour, hall and kitchen; the location of the pantry is uncertain. A wing to SE, which probably included both pantry and dairy, is apparently a later addition; possibly the original pantry formed part of the staircase wing. The staircase, to judge by the profile of the handrail, was rebuilt in the early 18th century. In the early 19th century a bakehouse was added to E.

A painted panel over the hall fireplace depicting a hunting scene, and probably original,[1] has disappeared. In recent years the house has been altered considerably.

Note
1. RCHME 1910, 85.

(77542)
The Horns PH, Bulls Green (TL 271174),

of one storey and attics, was built in the early 16th century and comprises a hall of two bays with a further bay, probably lofted over, at each end. The bay to E was probably the service end. In the early 17th century an upper floor was built within the hall by inserting two chamfered posts with a housing for a binding-beam; the chimney-stack was perhaps of timber and was rebuilt in the 18th century. The bay to E has a brick floor and is said to have been a dairy. The building was an inn or alehouse in 1789.[1]

Note
1. Johnson 1962, Pt 1, 55.

(77543)
Old Pound House (TL 269182)

is of two storeys and of two-cell plan with lobby-entrance. To S of the chimney-stack a binding-beam has, in front of the fire-place jambs, two mortises for posts, and the fireplace lintel has peg-holes for wooden jambs and other peg-holes for posts above it, suggesting that a wooden chimney-stack, probably of the 16th century, preceded the present one; in the first-floor wall to W the two principal bays have Kentish framing and may be of the same date. The remaining exposed framing is probably of the late 17th century. An ovolo-moulded bearer in the larger room to S, and the chimney-stack with three conjoined square flues and moulded coping, are of the late 17th century, and other details are consistent with that date. The room to S of the stack was the hall, that to N the parlour, and the chamber over the hall also had a fireplace. The roof has clasped-purlins and a ceiling at collar level. To S and E are modern additions.

EASTWICK

(77544)
Culverts (TL 434118),

of two storeys and attics, is a brick house of the early 18th century. It comprises from E to W a large room which was the principal living room; an entrance-hall with staircase partly in a shallow projection to S; and a smaller room which originally had a passage to S leading to the W room; these two rooms have fire-places set towards the front of the house, perhaps to provide for a pantry adjoining the W room. The house has been consider-ably altered in recent years.

ELSTREE

(78458)
The Hollybush PH (TQ 178954) [1]

is a mid 15th-century house which had an open hall approxi-mately square in plan, the roof having a crown-post of cruciform section; a two-storey wing to S was jettied to E; and there was a service bay to N. The wing room to E, probably the parlour, has a chamfered binding-beam with two-centred arch-braces; to W a straight late 17th-century staircase with splat balusters occupies the site of the original one; the roof has clasped-purlins. The

wing had a chimney-stack inserted in the late 17th century and was extended by three bays. The W bay was of two storeys and perhaps accommodated a pantry, while the next bay is a kitchen. In the roof one 15th-century tie-beam is re-used; nearly all the rafters come from a collar-purlin roof. In the present century the N end of the building was demolished.

Note
1. This account incorporates information from Mr S C Castle.

(77545)
Nicoll Farm (TQ 183960),

of c1500, comprised an open hall of two bays and a third bay to W, which also appears to have been open; the roof, which has clasped-purlins, provides almost the only evidence of the first build. The first addition, of c1600, was a bay to E, roofed as a cross-wing and probably jettied to S; it has a clasped-purlin roof. In the mid 17th century a chimney-stack with conjoined square flues was added to NE; a first floor carried on ovolo-moulded beams was inserted throughout the original house; a chimney-stack with diagonal flues was added to the former service room; and a room was added to W. The house then comprised, from W to E, pantry, kitchen, hall (apparently unheated) and parlour wing. The siting of the parlour fireplace suggests that a space was partitioned off for a stair and closet to S. In the early 18th century, perhaps in the second quarter, a chimney-stack was added to N of the hall; a staircase was inserted to W; and the N and S sides of the house were refronted in brick. In the mid 19th century a wall was built to divide house and garden from the farmyard, and the windows facing the garden were enlarged.

(77546)
Schopwick Place (TQ 178954),[1]

a double-pile house of two storeys and attics, is spanned by a wide roof of comparatively steep pitch. It was probably built in the early 18th century, but has a complicated development obscured by much reproduction work copying detail from the 16th and 18th centuries. A difference of level between the W (front) and E (rear) ground-floor rooms suggests that the former correspond to the principal part of the original house, which may have had a square staircase turret opposite the front doorway. The entrance-passage may always have been narrow, as now, otherwise the staircase has to be envisaged as projecting within the hall. Probably the kitchen was in a wing to SE, and if so, the unusual arrangement of a small room between it and the parlour at the front may be original, intended to provide one or more service rooms including a pantry. It is difficult to detect straight joints between the main five-bay elevation and the single-storey flanking wings, which are perhaps original. An early 19th-century print[2] shows these wings joining single-storey ranges, running at right-angles and each with a circular window in the gable, so that at the front they presented the appearance of pavilions; they are of uncertain date but appear on the enclosure map of 1803. When the room to NE was added is uncertain; an early 19th-century grate may be original to it, and since the fireplace and doors in the SE room are also of this date, the present kitchen was probably added then. In the latter part of the 19th century the house was occupied by the Second Master and some pupils of Elstree School;[3] it may have been used in that way earlier since the print cited above is inscribed in pencil `a school near Elstree'. The house underwent extensive antiquarian restoration c1900, when fireplaces and doorcases were altered and a large bay window was added at the rear. In 1912 it was a private house.[4]

Notes

1. Mr S C Castle provided some of the information for this account.
2. BL ADD MS 32349, fo 78.
3. Truman Press, `Elstree: the school and village', *Herts Illustrated Review* 1893, 290–5.
4. *Kelly* 1912.

ESSENDON

(39610)
Bedwell Park (TL 276076)

is a manor house first recorded in 1388, when it was granted to John Norbury, and is so called from the park of 800 acres (323·8 has), which Norbury was granted licence to make in 1406. In 1466 Sir John Say acquired the estate as well as other lands in Essendon and Hatfield[1] and soon began rebuilding or altering the house, for the `tiles called brick' that were brought from Hatfield in 1470[2] can hardly have been intended for any other house than Bedwell Park. The park, the use of brick and a visit by Mary Tudor in 1522 imply a house of importance. Subsequently it passed by marriage to Henry Courtenay, Marquis of Exeter,[3] and on his attainder to the Crown.[4] After 1547 the park and part of the demesne were separated from the manor and passed through several hands until sold in 1648 to Edward Dacres,[5] who in 1651 settled them on Thomas Atkins, the natural son of Dame Annabelle Atkins.[6] Lady Atkins paid tax on 15 hearths in 1666 and 14 in 1673.[7] She was succeeded by Thomas Atkins, the dedicatee of Drapentier's engraving of *c*1700, who `much adorned this seat with pleasant Gardens'[8] and may have improved the house; he died in 1701. By his will, dated 10 October 1699,[9] he bequeathed certain fittings and furnishings to his nephew Sir Henry Atkins, among them the iron backs to the chimneys and the `locks to my dwelling house'; `my cousin Goodfellowe's chamber' is also mentioned. For a time, before the house was sold to Richard Wynne, it lay empty[10] and, as an estate map of 1765 shows,[11] little alteration had taken place by that date except for some enlargement at the service (N) end and possibly the addition of a NW wing. In that year the house was acquired by Samuel Whitbread, who in 1767 was Sheriff; he refronted the house,[12] retaining the tripartite division. In 1807, when the house was sold to Sir Culling Smith, Bart.,[13] it was described as `not modern, but...convenient', and `kept in a state of perfect Repair'.[14] It comprised, on the ground floor, `An Entrance Hall, Good Staircase, and Four Principal Rooms'; on the first floor, `a handsome drawing room, five principal chambers, several smaller Apartments, and a Water Closet'; and, on the upper storey, numerous servants' rooms and closets. It appears that at the time the 1st Baronet died[15] the house was leased out because in that year John Currie Esq., styled of Bedwell Park,[16] was Sheriff. Subsequently Sir Culling Smith, 2nd Baronet, occupied the house himself; in February 1827 he and his son Culling Eardley Smith agreed to spend £2,000, part of the proceeds of sales at Spalding, on repairs at Bedwell Park. In 1828 Culling Smith was Sheriff. Sir Culling Eardley Smith, 3rd Baronet, carried out an extensive rebuilding in 1861.[17] A tower on the W front which abuts a gable and window of 1861 very awkwardly must be still later and was probably added by Robert Culling-Hanbury after 1865.[18]

The house of *c*1700 had an unusual appearance; the wide gables were high enough to accommodate small windows lighting (presumably) the space over the attic rooms and, unless Drapentier was much less careful than usual in depicting an elevation, the apex of each gable was considerably higher than

the roof ridge. Such a discrepancy in proportion would be explicable if the main range were somewhat lower than was usual at the time the gables were added, and suggests the possibility that a late medieval house had been refronted; and it is of some interest that an outbuilding to the right of the house incorporates a feature hardly paralleled in the Drapentier engravings, a two-light Gothic window. Some alteration of the front had taken place in the late 17th century; the doorway, cupola, diagonal chimney-shafts and the small circular windows (whose function is not certain but may have been to light closets) were all of that date, but they modify an earlier bay-windowed frontage. Adjoining the house to the right is what looks like a staircase wing, crowned by a pedimented curvilinear gable. (Mackerye End, Wheathampstead, has a staircase in a somewhat similar position.) The gable of a wing to SW is clearly visible. In relating the present house to the old drawings the starting point must be that Drapentier and the 1765 map show the house facing E; probably it still did so after Whitbread's alterations, but in the 19th century, probably in 1861, was turned round to face W. The three-storey E elevation drawn by Oldfield is still discernible under its heavy mid-Victorian disguise but it is difficult to reconcile the two chimney-stacks and three-gabled N end with the existing remains, which suggest that the front range of the three was stepped back, as in Drapentier and no doubt for the same reason, to give light to a staircase. Although all trace of the little medieval building that existed in 1700 has vanished, a much longer range, featureless but of several periods, preserves the old alignment oblique to the house.

Notes

1. VCH III, 460–1.
2. *Hatfield and its People*, Book 10, 7.
3. *DNB*.
4. VCH III, 460.
5. HRO, F409.
6. HRO, F412, F439; not as Chauncy I, 544.
7. PRO E179/375/31.
8. Chauncy I, 544.
9. HRO, F418.
10. Munby 1974, 44.
11. HRO, 54333.
12. Oldfield Vol III, 82.
13. VCH III, 460.
14. SC, HRO.
15. October 1812; Cussans 1874–8, Vol II (ii), 157.
16. VCH III, 459.
17. Inscribed stone tablet.
18. VCH III, 461.

(77547)
Camfield Place (TL 268069)

was not a manor house. When the estate was built up is not clear,[1] but by 1600 the mansion house and farm called Camfield was sold to William Potter.[2] By 1627 it was in the possession of William Priestley, who died in 1664;[3] in March 1666 `Mrs Prisly' paid for 10 hearths;[4] and by 1668 the house was owned by Thomas Priestly Esq. who, four years later, was Sheriff. His house is unique among those depicted by Drapentier[5] in being timber framed, and this and its several phases of construction give it a remarkably old-fashioned air by comparison with the other engravings in Chauncy`s book. A glimpse of the garden through the rear door shows that there was a cross-passage; the lower windows to W (left) suggest the converted hall of a late medieval house, both ends of which had been rebuilt. The continuous lines of small windows to E must be of the early 17th century but the roof line, and what looks like an inserted dormer window, point to the alteration of a service end, the length of which suggests that the E cross-wing was an addition to it. At the W end a projecting cross-wing with an oriel window was perhaps a late 16th-century addition, and beyond that, and lying somewhat back, is what was probably a kitchen block, with a jettied-out staircase connecting its upper storey to the higher first floor of the main house. The only post-Restoration features are the two-storey porch with a simple classical door architrave and a three-light mullioned window above it; these, and the sundial, all fit a date close to 1672, when Priestley was Sheriff.

The subsequent architectural history of the house is poorly documented. It was owned successively by Thomas Browne, who bought it in 1760 from a nephew of the last Priestley owner, and his son William, who was living in 1815, on the death of whose widow it was sold in 1832;[6] but a drawing captioned `Camfield Place'[7] which should relate to the Browne ownership, shows the same house as that drawn by Oldfield,[8] where the caption `Clamfield Place' [sic] has been struck out and `Bird's Place' substituted; moreover the outline of the house deducible from the drawings differs materially from that on a map of 1806.[9] This map shows that Drapentier drew the SE elevation, and that in 1806 the square block at the W corner of the house still existed, enlarged; it can be observed on a map of 1838.[10] Sometime after the death of William Browne in 1815 the house was leased to Thomas Robert, 4th Baron Dimsdale, who was styled of Bedwell Park when Sheriff in 1831. In 1866 the house was sold to Edmund Potter, the father of the author Beatrix Potter; he altered it extensively,[11] and there is a detailed outline plan of 1891.[12]

Notes
1. VCH III, 461.
2. HRO, F405.
3. Monumental Inscription, Chauncy I, 546.
4. PRO E179/248/28.
5. Chauncy I, 544.
6. VCH III, 461.
7. Charnock.
8. Oldfield Vol III, 74.
9. HRO, Sessions Records, Highways, 177–9.
10. HRO, D/EX 234, 11.
11. Inf. Mrs Barbara Cartland.
12. SC, HRO, D/ERy B211.

(77548)
Essendon Place (TL 273079)

was built mostly in the early 19th century, perhaps during the 1830s, but incorporates earlier work; a building which preceded or forms part of the present house appears on a map of 1822.[1] Not long after 1865 it was purchased by Charles John, 5th Baron Dimsdale, who may have resided there since being made Sheriff in 1843.

The house faces S (correctly SE), the principal part, of the 1830s, being to E; the latter is of rectangular plan with projecting wings and a loggia of the Ionic order between them; entrance is through the loggia into a staircase-hall, to N of which is a large lounge with a canted bay window facing the garden. A lower service wing to S incorporates an older building, for which the principal evidence is an encased binding-beam and a bearer. There are Victorian and Edwardian additions. By 1922 the house was owned by Sir Frederick William Lewis, Bart., who enlarged it at both ends and drastically altered the interior.[2]

Notes
1. OS 1-inch, repr Newton Abbot 1969.
2. Inf. Mr G Higgott.

FLAMSTEAD

(39611)
Beechwood Park (TL 045144)

is a large country house built at three principal periods in the 17th and 18th centuries. It occupies the site of the small Benedictine nunnery of St Giles in the Wood, which was dissolved in 1537;[1] shortly afterwards it passed into the hands of John Tregonwell, one of the Commissioners for the Dissolution of the monasteries. He immediately set about creating a house for himself but appears to have done little building; when ordered by Henry VIII to hand over the property to Sir Richard Page, he had spent `£120 in necessaries for husbandry, hedging, marking the ground, etc.'.[2] Chauncy records a tradition that the infant Edward VI was at Beechwood for his health's sake;[3] no doubt at that period the monastic buildings had been adapted as a residence. In 1574–5 the manor was sold to Richard and Thomas Smith and there are certificates of residence for Richard Smyth, Gent., in 1587 and 1591 and for his widow Margaret in 1592.[4] The certificate for 1592 refers to Richard's widow Margaret Smyth, assessed for £15 in goods at Beechwood, and also his son Thomas, assessed for £12 in lands, who, with his wife Margaret and their household and family, was resident at Beechwood.[5] Thomas Smith sold it in 1628 to Thomas Saunders of Puttenham, on whose death in 1664 his grandson Thomas inherited and held it until his death in 1693.[6] Chauncy remarks that `There are no Remains of the old House, Cloysters, Chappell, etc, but the Mannor-House is a fair Brick House, of the Figure of a Roman H'; it was evidently built by the second Thomas, who `made this Mannor an excellent Seat' not long after his grandfather's death in 1664. There is no reason to suppose that this house, which is incorporated in the present building, is Elizabethan.[7] Nearby was an old farmhouse, referred to in the caption to an 18th-century drawing (see below). Thomas Saunders, whose building ambitions also extended to almshouses in Flamstead[8] and a splendid church monument,[9] paid for 13 hearths in 1673;[10] his grandfather paid for only 9 in 1663.[11] On his death the house passed by marriage to Sir Edward Sebright, Bart., who enlarged it; its subsequent history is well documented by plans and drawings in the possession of Beechwood School, and others known only through a typescript catalogue.[12]

One drawing shows the front elevation of Thomas Saunders' house and another the block added by Sebright in front of it to form a closed courtyard. The first major addition was the only part of an undated design for rebuilding the W front that was actually executed; it was a Great Room, now the library, and is attributed to Roger Morris.[13] No drawing of it earlier than 1841[14] is now available; its tall pedimented windows are consistent with the early 18th century. A new west front was also proposed.[15] It would be in keeping with the Sebright family's building habits for Sir John, who succeeded in 1738 at the age of 13,[16] to have added a `great room' on attaining his majority in 1744; and Morris died in 1749. In 1754 `Capability' Brown prepared plans for the addition of two matching wings to N and S of Thomas Saunders' house;[17] the wings are `closely comparable to present wings but with central cupola and clock in pediment'. Brown's plans also included `an Ice House to be built...in the Cellar of Old Farm House'[18] (the ice house still remains about 30 yds (27 m) to W of the N wing) and a Gothick folly like the W end of a church,[19] inscribed: `This front is to stand obliquely in order to show its side in perspective to the windows of the House'. This is said to have been a bath-house.[20] A major rebuild entailing demolition of the library was in prospect by 1759, when Matthew Brettingham was paid £100 by Sir Thomas Sebright, 5th Baronet, for plans and an elevation `for the intended alteration of his house';[21] these intentions, which would have reduced the house to a compact Palladian three-storey block,[22] were not executed. About the middle of the 18th century, a covered passage was built (or proposed) to link the front block to the old house[23] – a clear indication of the inconvenience caused by the courtyard. Some time between 1755, when he set up in practice, and 1770, when he was knighted, William Chambers produced a `Plan of Stair Cave to the New Nursery in the Garrots', which is said to relate exactly to the N stairs from first to second floors.[24] In 1794 the house passed to another man of building ambition, Sir John Saunders Sebright, 6th Baronet, who built a school and almshouses but appears to have done little more than alter the interior of the house; there are proposals to alter the first floor of the c1700 block in minor ways; and a drawing[25] shows that by c1800 the cupola had been removed. Designs for remodelling the library were made by Sir John Soane[26] and Alexandre-Louis de Labrière;[27] Thomas Cundy finally designed and executed the work in 1804.[28] Sir John was Sheriff in 1797. His son, Sir Thomas Gage Saunders Sebright, undertook further improvements a few years after inheriting the house in 1846.[29] An unsigned `perspective sketch of proposed Saloon', dated 1 September 1851 at 6 Stratton Street, shows the courtyard roofed over as now, and a plumbing and heating plan of 19 February 1853 shows the saloon as either in progress or finished; plans dated May 1851 show considerable extension to the offices on the S side, and a drawing, the date of which is illegible but which includes the `New Saloon', shows Tudor-style exterior details to be added to the W elevation. Sir John Gage Saunders Sebright succeeded his father in 1864;[30] drawings of 1866 show a new billiard room and stables grouped around a court to N. In 1874 he was Sheriff. On 1 December 1879 Sir John Saunders Sebright received £1,650 under the Limited Owners Residences Act for `additions to mansion house'[31] and a further payment of £400 was made on 26 July 1882 `for improvement of water supply'. In the early years of the present century the house was leased to G G McCorquodale.[32] Plans dated February 1905, by Mark H Judge and Sons, Architects and Sanitary Surveyors, deal mainly with new drainage but show the conversion of the former billiard room into a coach-house and – significant conjunction – the Chapel into a `Motor House'. Finally Sir Giles Sebright, 12th Baronet, succeeding to the title in 1933, undertook the restoration of the late 17th-century front block,[33] albeit in a way not at all faithful to the original. In recent years the house has been used as a school.

The 1660s' house had a main range flanked by two wings which projected more to E (correctly NE) – the front – than to W. The original front elevation is shown in a drawing of c1695, which may embody some intended alterations; the quoins of the wings were revealed a few years ago when the plaster was stripped from the walls of the saloon; in the wing to N two windows with hollow-chamfered mullions remain; and in the wing to S are the upper flights of a staircase with moulded handrail and newel post with simple finial. The rear elevation is dominated by two external chimney-stacks, symmetrically designed and positioned. A drawing of 1839[34] shows what appear to be moulded string courses rather than the platband used at the front, and those above the windows of the first-floor wing suggest that originally large mullion-and-transom windows, perhaps of five lights, were intended. A surprising feature is that all the chimney-shafts are diagonal, whereas those of the 1695 drawing are rectangular and plain; either the 1695 drawing was simplified or the shafts had been rebuilt before 1835. In the late 17th century the porch probably led directly into the house; an 18th-century drawing[35] shows it leading into a passage into the hall to N. Possibly the room to S of the porch was the parlour; the wing to N incorporated the kitchen. In the middle of each wing was a staircase.

The new block to E added between c1695 and 1702 is of half-H shape. Although its general appearance is preserved, details have been altered and the original plan is by no means certain. Initially the windows had plain surrounds with keystones and stone sills; some of those in walls to N and S were blind in the late 18th century,[36] but whether they were so from the first is uncertain. Inside hardly any old detail remains. The principal feature of the plan was the large entrance-hall, with a fireplace to S; very little else is certain. To N and S are two large rooms, each of which originally formed a squarish room, and a small room or closet at the corner of the house; plans of proposed alterations show this arrangement on the ground floor to S,[37] with no indication that it was an innovation, and on the first floor to N (cf. Bonningtons, Stanstead Abbots);[38] the latter plan shows a different partitioning of the S side as an intended alteration. Behind the entrance-hall, and reached from it only by a doorway, was the main staircase; adjoining the latter to N was a comparatively small room, marked `Pantrey' on a late 18th-century plan;[39] this usage suggests that what looks like a corner fireplace may have been a cupboard, although the corresponding room upstairs certainly had a fireplace then.[40]

Exactly how the grand new enlargement related to the old house is obscure; if the kitchen was in the S wing of the latter, the dining room may have been on that side of the new block, perhaps near the kitchen. How the old house then functioned is uncertain but probably the wing to N remained in use as a parlour looking on to the garden, and possibly a study; these rooms would provide a suitable approach to the later library. Only one first-floor plan[41] of the 18th century shows the wings extending to meet those of the older building; in the N wing is what looks like a servants' staircase, and it is shown as an existing feature. So frequently did the Sebrights alter the house that the first-floor arrangements shown in this plan may not be original; but they imply that in the 18th century there were five principal bedrooms, each with its dressing room. Access to the attics was at the N end only.

Of the library, the first alteration in the 18th century, nothing can be said save that it had tall pedimented windows and a parapet. A few years later the owner, perhaps Sir Thomas Sebright, showed an interest in the Gothick; a folly (see above) was considered and perhaps built; Hill Farm, Flamstead, dated by a drawing to 1761, was built as an `eyecatcher', and possibly the barge-boards and quatrefoils in the gables were added to the house.[42] A plan to reduce the house to a compact rectangular block having been rejected, flanking blocks linked by short arcades were added. In the block to S the two largest rooms were kitchen and scullery, the former flanked by scullery and servants' hall, the latter by dairy and wash-house; above were bedrooms. To N in 1853 was a chapel, there, perhaps, from the first. Both blocks have been completely altered inside. The library was evidently altered in the early years of the 19th century; Soane's drawings show round-headed doorways or recesses at the ends whereas the corners are now rounded, with doorways in the middle of each end wall. This is presumably Cundy's arrangement, although some of the details look like reproduction work. At the time of the 1851 Census the house was occupied by Sir Thomas Sebright, his wife and young son, his sister and 14 servants. Subsequent alterations, all after 1850, are shown in the plan. Three arches opening from the entrance-hall to the staircase, which is a renewal of the original, were built in 1863.[43] Drawings of that year show that the pitch roof of the library was replaced by the present lean-to roof, retaining the parapet.

For illustrations, see *English Houses 1200–1800*, Figs 136 (plate), 137, 200 (plate).

Notes
1. VCH IV, 432–3.
2. PRO L&P Henry VIII, XIII, 2, No. 74, VCH II, 196.
3. Chauncy I, 514.
4. PRO E115/362/82/97.
5. PRO E115/347/118.
6. VCH II, 196; Chauncy II, 511–13.
7. Oswald 1938a, 476.
8. VCH II, 196.
9. Chauncy II, 513.
10. PRO E179/375/31.
11. PRO E179/248/23.
12. Colvin and Harris nd. The numbers cited in the Notes refer to the catalogue entries.
13. Colvin and Harris nd, describing 2A, 2B; Fischer Fine Art Ltd 1981, No. 52. Lees-Milne 1970, 263.
14. Buckler Vol III, 360B.
15. Fischer Fine Art Ltd 1981, No. 54.
16. VCH II, 196.
17. Colvin and Harris nd, describing 3B.
18. Ibid, describing 3F.
19. Ibid, describing 3G.
20. Stroud 1975, 71.
21. Brettingham accounts, PRO C108/362.
22. Colvin and Harris nd, describing 4A, 4B, 4C.
23. Ibid, describing 8A.
24. Ibid, describing 7C.
25. Oldfield Vol III, 120.
26. Fischer Fine Art Ltd 1981, Nos 77–80.
27. Ibid, Nos 38–9.
28. Colvin 1978, 245.
29. VCH II, 196.
30. Ibid.
31. PRO MAF 66/12.
32. VCH II, 196; *Kelly* 1908.
33. Oswald 1938a, 476.
34. Buckler Vol IV, 10.
35. Colvin and Harris nd, describing 8A.
36. Ibid, describing plans 4B, 5.
37. Ibid, describing 5.
38. Ibid, describing 8B.
39. Ibid, describing 8A.
40. Ibid, describing 8B.
41. Ibid.
42. Buckler, not numbered.
43. Not c1700 as stated in Oswald 1938a.

(77549)
Cheverells Park (TL 055153)

seems always to have been part of the Beechwood estate[1] and is said to have been built as a dower house c1695;[2] a brick outside the Pine Room at the SW corner of the house is inscribed `Wm Willingdon 1706'.[3] The elevation to W, of the early 18th century, has segmental-headed windows and a parapet surmounted with urns. To S two semi-octagonal bay windows would appear to be additions, as the brickwork is not fully bonded to the front wall.

No original detail remains inside on the ground floor and little on the first floor. To N a long service wing, mainly Victorian, incorporates earlier outbuildings. Extensive alterations took place in 1911;[4] Sir Edgar Saunders-Sebright, who owned the house early in the present century, was Sheriff in 1904.

Notes
1. VCH II, 193.
2. Typescript notes compiled by Mr Sugden in 1959.
3. Sugden; not seen
4. Sugden.

(77550)
Delmerend Farmhouse (TL 083143),

now entirely encased in brick, was timber framed in the late 16th century; it is not certain that it was all of one build. The plan comprises three rooms of which only the middle one, backing on to the cross-passage, was definitely heated originally. At the gable end of the room to W a smoke or chimney-bay (cf that at the Old Rose and Crown, Braughing) occupies an unusual position as for a kitchen; to E is the parlour, with gable-end fireplace flanked by a staircase of the late 17th century. These arrangements suggest that from E to W the house comprised parlour, entrance-passage, hall and kitchen; a reversal of the order normal in Hertfordshire but one that is quite common among longhouse derivatives. Attics were created in the late 17th century and in the late 18th century the whole house was refaced in brick. The N side is now roughcast.

(79462)
Spring Cottage, Roe End (TL 048156)

is said to have been called Shepherd's Cottage, for the shepherd of the Beechwood estate, until recent years. It is timber framed with brick front to N and bears the carefully incised date 1777 on the binding-beam in the kitchen or living room to E. To W are the staircase, opening off the kitchen and aligned N–S, and two rooms without fireplaces.

FLAUNDEN

(77551)
Hollins Hall (TL 002016),

of brick and of three storeys, facing S, is dated by a brick in the gable wall to W adjoining a doorway, which is inscribed I B 1808. The plan comprises a passage entrance-hall with staircase and room to W and a room to E, off which is a narrow kitchen wing to E.

(77552)
Oak Cottage (TL 016008)

was built in two phases, the earlier one, of the late 15th century, being apparently incomplete in itself. This first phase comprises a hall open to the roof and measuring about 30 ft x 19 ft 6 ins (9·2 m x 6·0 m); the roof is of two bays divided by open trusses, which have hollow chamfers running continuously through wall-posts, arch-braces and soffit; the wall-plates and other principal members are also moulded to create an unusually rich effect. The rafters are smoke blackened throughout, with no trace of a louvre, and evidently any partitions dividing up the floor area did not extend into the roof; the only trace of such a partition is a short length of beam with mortises suggesting the existence of a screen where now the hall is entered.[1] A third truss marks the end of the hall to E; it is moulded to the W side, plain to E, and has no mortises or peg-holes for a studded partition. The wall-plates and the middle rail to S extend beyond the third truss for approximately the width of a cross-passage and terminate abruptly at the later E wing; the length of the N middle rail is uncertain because a modern tile roof over the front doorway masks part of it, but it may extend the full width of the wing and, as a cut-through mortise at the NE corner suggests, formerly somewhat farther. Apart from this the original end of the house to E has been lost.

It was replaced in the second phase by a cross-wing higher than the older part, its tie-beam being at present eaves level. No closely datable features remain except for the close-studding at the front, which is probably of the mid–late 16th century; the fact that the studs are not pegged into the rail may strengthen the suggestion that the latter is part of the earlier phase. The ends of the joists rest on the rail, which indicates either an inferior mode of construction or possibly the removal of a jettied upper storey to produce a flush front, although nothing was observed which might confirm the latter. The wing appears to have comprised only one room on each floor. At the same time a wooden chimney-stack was built in the former passage; only the moulded lintel for the fireplace remains. Probably an upper floor was built at the same time although nothing about it is closely datable; the disposition of the beams suggests that the hall was still a single room. In the late 17th century, the hall chimney-stack was rebuilt in brick and two smaller fireplaces were added to N, implying a subdivision of the E parlour. Then and probably earlier a staircase adjoined the stack to N. Probably the hall was divided into the present two rooms in the late 17th century. Subsequent changes are minor. A chimney-stack was added to W bearing the date 1747 on a brick;[2] it may have served the corner fireplace of a subdivided room; probably then the house was rendered; and if the supposed jetty existed, this was when it was cut off and the eaves of the hall range were raised without providing attics, solely to provide a more regular appearance. In 1838 the owner was Elizabeth Hudson, the occupiers Thomas Slade and four others, and it comprised house, yard, garden, stable, barns, and sheds, and five cottages and gardens.[3] In the early 20th century the rendering was removed and in the wing, planks were used to simulate the heightening of the hall and so maintain some regularity in the stripped-down elevation. A SW wing was added in recent years.

The following interpretation is suggested. Initially it was a longhouse, with a detached structure containing kitchen and service rooms; the latter remained in use when the byre was rebuilt as a large parlour and chamber over; in the late 17th century the former hall also served as a kitchen, the W end of it was partitioned off as a service room, and the parlour was divided into two heated rooms; in the 18th century part of the room to W became a parlour or study, with perhaps some change to a service function of one of the E rooms.

For illustrations, see *English Houses 1200–1800*, Figs 76 (plate), 77, 299 (plate).

Notes
1. For parallels, see Alcock and Laithwaite 1973, 109–11.
2. Inf. Mrs R Liversedge.
3. HRO, Tithe Award.

FURNEUX PELHAM

(77553)
Furneux Pelham Hall (TL 427279)

was an important manor house. Between 1237 and 1241 Simon de Furnell was granted licence by the Dean and Chapter of St Paul's, who then owned the manor, to build a chapel at his house (*curia*) there.[1] Robert Newport, who acquired it in 1406, twice represented Hertfordshire as MP, as did his son William three times, and another Robert was Sheriff in 1496. Subsequently it passed by marriage to Sir Henry Parker, who was Sheriff in 1536. Early in the 17th century the manor house was separated from the manor and sold to Richard Mead;[2] `he pulled down the greatest Part of it, because `twas too large for his Estate, sold the Materials [and] converted the remaining Part into a convenient Habitation'.[3] It was sold in 1614 to Edward Cason, who paid for 13 hearths in 1663.[4] By 1677 the house was in the hands of Felix Calvert, who is said to have made considerable alterations.[5] After the death of William Calvert in 1749 the Calverts resided either at Hunsdon House or in London, and the house was let out to tenants. In the present century considerable restoration took place.

The existing plan[6] clearly results from piecemeal alteration, and an early 19th-century drawing[7] reveals a complicated history not easily discernible in the existing fabric. The principal part is a rectangular double-pile house (*c*58 ft x 45 ft (17·7 m x 13·7 m)) facing S. It comprises, from E to W, three parts: a former cross-wing (*c*20 ft x 45 ft (6·1 m x 13·7 m)) with two external chimney-stacks on the E wall; the hall for entrance and staircase, in the N part of which a service room has been contrived; and two large rooms sharing an internal chimney. To N of the third part, a N wing was first truncated,[8] then largely rebuilt in the present century. The cross-wing, with two rooms on each floor, may be of the 16th century; the open hall presumptively lying to W of it was probably earlier (cf Chells Manor, Aston, or Aspenden Hall), and must have been quite wide perhaps 25–30 ft (7·6–9·2 m); it has been removed, probably by Mead; whether there was a second wing to W is unknown. Chauncy's statement may refer to the demolition of a courtyard. The N or kitchen wing is comparable in position to that at Rothamsted Manor and must have been added to the hall range; an exposed close-studded roof truss,[9] probably related to a partition-wall, suggests it was always of two storeys; either Sir Henry Parker or Richard Mead is the likely builder. In the mid or late 17th century the S and W elevations were rebuilt with curvilinear gables and probably mullion-and-transom windows; the chimney-stacks[10] appear to have had paired or clustered shafts. The present staircase was inserted *c*1700; it appears to have replaced one occupying the space to W of the chimney-stack in the W block and another that may have been in the former E wing. Then, or early in the 18th century, hung sash windows were introduced and perhaps a round-headed first-floor window above the entrance too.

The undated Buckler drawing is unusual in showing the rear of the house; the impressive E elevation to the kitchen wing, with a curious combination of stepped and round gables, and the stepped gables of the main block, one of which is asymmetrical to accommodate a probable heightening of the E wing, suggest that the artist was interested in a comparatively recent antiquarian restoration. A further restoration took place in the late 19th century, when mullion-and-transom windows were fitted to S and W. Probably then the two ground-floor rooms of the E wing were united to form a large drawing room; the two E windows of the S room were blocked and concealed by reproduction panelling differing slightly from the original.

Notes
1. D&C St P, Lib A, fo 29.
2. VCH IV, 102.
3. Chauncy I, 286.
4. PRO E179/248/24/8.

5.	VCH IV, 102.
6.	Ibid, 100.
7.	Buckler Vol II, 34; nd.
8.	Ibid.
9.	Ibid.
10.	Clutterbuck.

GILSTON

(77554)
Gilston Park, formerly New Place, (TL 441129)

replaces a large house standing to E, of which only a fragment remains in the park. The earlier house, `a fair Structure',[1] was built by Henry Chauncy (d.1587) in the 1570s, and since the land attached to it did not correspond to any existing manor but was taken from three adjoining manors, it was called New Place. In 1639 the then owner, John Gore of Sacombe, was Sheriff and `did not only beautifie but also enlarge the Dwelling-house';[2] knighted in 1641 he became Sheriff for a second time in 1654, when he is styled Sir John Gore of Sacombe, so his work at New Place was probably done before 1639. His son Humphrey Gore, knighted at the Restoration and assessed for 25 hearths in 1662,[3] `did much adorn the House with Walk and Gardens [and] made a pretty Park to the same';[4] he died in 1699. In that year his son Henry Gore, who for the previous four years had paid tithe on the house,[5] was Sheriff. Two years later he sold New Place to John Plumer of Blakesware, for whom the Gilston estate provided a second house which was probably leased out. One lessee may have been the John Turvin Esq. of Gilston, Sheriff in 1729 and 1756, for whom no other residence is known; and New Place is the only seat shown in the parish in 1766.[6] When in 1767 William Plumer, grandson of John Plumer, succeeded to his father's estates, he chose to live at New Place, not Blakesware; he made extensive additions and alterations. On his death in 1822 the house and estate passed to his widow who, in 1830, took as her second husband Robert Ward, the politician and novelist;[7] she died in 1831, he was Sheriff in the following year. The statement that the house remained empty after her death[8] is contradicted by Buckler drawings of 1830 and 1836, which show that considerable changes had been made between those years. Ward died in 1846; the house was up for sale in 1849;[9] and in 1851 the new owner, John Hodgson, pulled it down and built the present house.

The house built by Henry Chauncy and embellished by John Gore was engraved by Drapentier,[10] and later drawings confirm the general correctness of the engraving so far as the W elevation is concerned, although the absence of chimney-stacks is disconcerting; the S elevation may correspond to Henry Chauncy's work. The rhythm of small windows flanking the doorways and larger ones beyond appears at Pishiobury Park, Sawbridgeworth, and elsewhere. In Drapentier's view of the E elevation, what look like a wide band below the gables and a narrow one at the first floor in fact were moulded cornice and string respectively,[11] and what look like drainpipes are pilasters. Gore appears to have rebuilt the garden (E) front below the attics, but to N contented himself with a new entrance doorway. By c1800 the windows to N had mostly been replaced by upright openings[12] and two-storey bay windows had been added to E. To W a tower with clock had been added and behind the entrance front was a large `Octagonal Hall'; the resemblance between the latter and similar additions to Pishiobury Park and Great Hyde Hall, Sawbridgeworth, and other known courtyard houses is the only reason for supposing that New Place was also built around a small courtyard. The octagonal hall must have been built by William Plumer some time after he inherited his

father's estate in 1767, and the tower is likely to be his too. Later alterations include large service rooms to W and a bow-fronted wing with curious pinnacles on the coping of the parapet. Only the early 19th-century porch survives, rebuilt, in the park.

Notes
1.	Chauncy I, 370.
2.	Ibid, 373.
3.	PRO E179/248/27.
4.	Chauncy I, 373.
5.	*Home Counties Mag* 1901, 3, 270.
6.	Dury and Andrews 1766.
7.	*DNB*.
8.	VCH III, 321.
9.	Sale Catalogue, HRO D/P41 29/3.
10.	Chauncy I, 372.
11.	Buckler Vol II, 41.
12.	Oldfield Vol III, 302.

GRAVELEY

(77555)
Chesfield Manor Farm (TL 247279)

was owned with the manor of Graveley from the 14th century onwards. In 1566 both came into the hands of William Clarke,[1] whose grandson of the same name was the representative of the family of Clarke of Chesfield in 1634.[2] Presumably the nine hearths on which the latter's son, also William, paid tax in 1662 and 1663[3] relate to Chesfield manor house; his widow's benefactions to Chesfield church[4] suggest that she lived there until her death, when the manor descended by marriage to George Throckmorton.[5] On Throckmorton's death in 1696 his inventory[6] included the following rooms: hall, kitchen, larder, brewhouse, dairy house, men's chamber, stair-head chamber, maids' chamber, closet, chamber over the parlour, hall chamber, study (with `his library of books, £70'), Holufers chamber, the red chamber, perhaps a second stair, since one is mentioned here; and the blue chamber. `Holufers' probably refers to wall-paintings depicting the story of Judith and Holufernes in the Apocryphal Old Testament Book of Judith. Clearly it was a large house. Both Chauncy[7] and Salmon[8] describe the Throckmorton arms in the hall window, and if the family went to the trouble to do that they made other alterations too. This house must have been one of the three in the parish on which tax for 30 or more windows was assessed in 1715[9] when, by a process of elimination, it appears that a Mr Goodwin occupied Chesfield. By the end of the century more drastic changes had taken place. The caption to a drawing of c1800[10] states: `There was about 20 years ago the large Old Hall remaining but about that time it underwent an alteration to its present form, and I presume at that time the Coats of Arms of the Throckmorton family were taken away'. This information is hard to reconcile with the existing buildings. Oldfield chose a viewpoint to depict the present E range and exclude that to N, although the latter certainly existed then. The range to E is shown much as now, and is generally regarded as having incorporated the hall.[11] These two ranges are joined corner to corner and the brickwork appears to be bonded; both were built in the late 17th century and a single-storey structure in the corner between them was the only means of intercommunication. Lower down the social scale a parallel for such an arrangement is Leggatt's Farm, King's Walden (see page 111). Comparable problems of reconciling architectural and record evidence are presented by Skimpans Farm, North Mymms, and Temple Dinsley, Preston.

Notes
1. VCH III, 87.
2. *Visitations*, 42.
3. PRO E179/375/30; E179/248/23.
4. Chauncy II, 126.
5. VCH III, 87.
6. PRO Prob/4/5206.
7. Chauncy II, 123.
8. Salmon 1728, 187.
9. HRO, Lt Misc 10.
10. Oldfield Vol III, 223.
11. RCHME 1910, 93; plan, VCH III, 86.

GREAT AMWELL

(77556)
Amwellbury,

a manor house, was owned by Westminster Abbey from 1270 until the Dissolution; a hall is mentioned in 1289 but by 1600 any house had probably disappeared.[1] Nor is anything now visible of the house occupied by the Filmer family to whom Celia Fiennes was related and where she several times stayed; that can perhaps be equated with Amwell Hall, which had eight hearths in 1666.[2] A late 17th-century dovecote stands to W. In 1776 `the new erected messuage in Great Amwell whereon Amwellbury House lately stood' was leased by Bibye James of St Margarets, Esq., to Haughton James of St George's Hanover Square, who had taken down the old house and built the new one. A drawing of *c*1800[3] shows a house facing E comprising two bays flanked by three-sided bay windows of two storeys, with parapet; it was then the seat of Major Brown. By 1817 the bay window to N had been removed and the house may have been truncated at that end; it then had a mansard roof; and what looks like a separate small house stood at right-angles and a little distance to N.[4] In 1840 Amwellbury had dining and drawing rooms, and five best and two secondary chambers.[5] By 1907 the house formed the E wing of an L-shaped block, with the wing to N forming the domestic offices.[6] In 1955 the N wing was demolished; the bay window to E, another to S, probably of the early 19th century, and the mansard roof were removed; and the house became a rectangular block, partly rendered, with hipped roof and extensions to N.

Notes
1. VCH III, 416–17.
2. PRO E179/248/28.
3. Oldfield Vol I, 214.
4. Aquatint by L Hassell, 1817, in Hertford Museum.
5. *Herts and Beds Reformer*, 16 May 1840.
6. HRO, sale catalogue.

(77557)
Amwell Grove (TL 371126)

is a small villa built in 1794–7 by the architect Robert Mylne for himself.[1] It was of two storeys with a chimney-stack in each corner. The principal part of the house comprised breakfast room, dining room and drawing room, of which only the first was reached directly from the combined entrance and staircase-hall; the two latter were gained from a common lobby. To S a courtyard of the same size as the house was flanked by the library to W and combined kitchen and scullery to E; the yard had pump and well in the middle and was surrounded by elegantly arranged service rooms. In the first phase of alteration, prior to *c*1840, the dining room and drawing room were made

into one and a bay window added to E; the former library was enlarged to S and became the dining room; the kitchen became the new library, a study and WC were added to S. The kitchen's function was transferred to the room underneath in the basement; servants' rooms were contrived in the basement; and the courtyard was rebuilt with larger service rooms and a greenhouse, the latter having a wing to S forming a garden approach. In the mid 19th century, the courtyard was completely rebuilt as a two-storey extension to the house; the function of the ground-floor rooms, one large, facing the garden, and one small is not known; there was also a staircase; the original staircase was rebuilt and the entrance transferred to N. Later in the century the house was heightened by one storey. The dates of these alterations are unknown but all are probably pre-1860. In the present century the entrance was removed to S, further alterations were made there, and the interior has been embellished with reproduction Georgian detail.

Note
1. Colvin 1978, 573.

(77558)
The Flint House (TL 371123),

built in 1842–4 by the architect William Chadwell Mylne for himself,[1] is of brick faced with untrimmed flints and of two storeys with cellars. In planning the house symmetry was sacrificed to compactness; the former was achieved in the longer garden (W, correctly NW) front of five bays but not in that to E; in the combined entrance and staircase-hall the staircase winds back over the entrance and precludes a narrow window to N of the porch matching that to S which lights a closet; this disposition is repeated on the first floor. The dining room to W of the hall has to N the kitchen and to S the drawing room; the rooms to N and S of the hall were probably breakfast room and library respectively. The staircase and some of the original fittings remain. In the late 19th century, the drawing room was enlarged to take in the library and attic bedrooms were created in the low-pitch roof.

Note
1. Colvin 1978, 578.

GREAT GADDESDEN

(77559)
Ballingdon Cottage (TL 038139)

was built in the late 15th or early 16th century and was probably wholly open from ground to roof (*English Houses 1200–1800*, Fig 78). It appears to have had a hall with an inner room to S; to N, presumably, were the cross-passage and a further bay. In the 17th century upper floors were inserted and the house was heightened to two storeys; a chimney-stack was built in the hall, leaving space for a cross-passage behind it; and the N bay was completely rebuilt. The staircase may always have adjoined the stack to N, no other position being visible; and heightening has produced the characteristic lean in the upper part of the wall (*English Houses 1200–1800*, pp 43-4).

For an illustration, see *English Houses 1200–1800*, Fig 78 (plate).

(77560)
Gaddesden Hall (TL 042096)

is the successor of the manor variously called Southall, Gatesden or Oliver's Place. The most relevant parts of its descent are that in 1448 the manor fell to co-heirs; in 1614 it came to three brothers; and in 1658 it was sold to John Halsey of Great Gaddesden and Thomas Bamford of Ashridge.[1]

The building has two distinct parts, the main range to S and a range to E. Each comprises a two-storey hall block and a slightly narrower and lower cross-wing; the cross-wings abut one another. They intercommunicate now and perhaps always did, but functionally Gaddesden Hall comprised, in the 17th century, two contiguous houses. Their separation was emphasised by the position of the two-storey porch[2] at the W end of the S range; originally the E range was probably entered to N, the two door-ways shown in 1832 being evidently later insertions. Both houses were originally timber framed in part and perhaps wholly; Buckler[3] depicts the cross-wing of the E range as framed and jettied to E; the wing of the S range has been underbuilt but was originally jettied to N; the porch of the S range also had the appearance of underbuilding and had a timber-framed gable; and the present walls of flint may not be original.

The two ranges were built at different times and each is of more than one period of construction. In the main (S) range, the greater height of the hall compared with the wing suggests that the former has been rebuilt and heightened; and if the hall were once lower it is likely to have been open to the roof, of late medieval type. No datable feature remains from the first phase, which appears to be of the late 15th or early 16th century. In the last quarter of the 16th century the hall was rebuilt in flint with two storeys; the chimney-stack projecting to S has fireplaces on the ground and first floors; a continuous plinth shows that stack and staircase turret are contemporary; a fireplace with carved spandrels was inserted in the previously unheated parlour; and a timber-framed porch was added. This phase corresponds to ownership of the manor by Martha Jermyn, who held it from her husband Edmund's death in 1557 until she died in 1593;[4] her successor, Henry Clerke of Westminster, is a less likely builder on grounds of date and non-residence. In the late 17th century the porch was rebuilt in brick; an attic storey with a large dormer to S was built, and the stair turret heightened; probably the wing jetty was underbuilt. Sash windows were inserted in the hall range before 1832[5] but thereafter little happened until careful restoration took place in recent years.

The E range seems to have been of similar origin. The low wing and the taller hall range suggest that the latter represents the rebuilding of a single-storey timber-framed open hall, and the double ovolo-moulding of a binding-beam argues that this was comparatively late, perhaps the mid-17th century; the fact that the hall chimney-stack has splayed offsets whereas the stack of the main range rises flush to the top may confirm this, although both have diagonal shafts. An entrance bay to N can be presumed. By 1832 the building was apparently a pair of cottages. In 1851 Gaddesden Hall Farm, as it then was called, was occupied by Joseph Hill, farmer, his wife, seven children, a house servant and three farm labourers. No doubt the servant and labourers lived in the E range.

Fig 43 *Golden Parsonage, Great Gaddesden: block plan as in 1717*

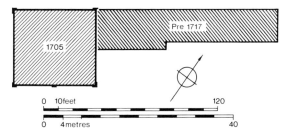

Notes
1. VCH II, 204.
2. Buckler Vol I, 120, of 1832; demolished.
3. Ibid, 123.
4. VCH II, 204.
5. Buckler Vol I, 120.

(77561)
Glebe House (TL 027111)

is remarkable for combining a hall open to a smoke-blackened roof with a two-storey jettied bay, of which the upper storey rather than the lower one is flush with the hall (*English Houses 1200–1800*, Fig 64). The two are coeval because the middle rail in the S wall of the hall has a housing for the plate of the ground-floor wall of the storeyed bay. The W ground-floor wall in the S bay was completely occupied by a four-light diamond-mullioned window and a wattle-and-daub panel of which the wattle-holes are visible; there are no mortises for door jambs. By analogy, the hall is likely to have been approximately square in plan; if so, the only place for the original cross-passage is in a long-demolished bay to N. Thus from N to S the house will have comprised service and entrance bay (perhaps of two storeys); hall; and upper end or solar bay. The subsequent development is consistent with the conjectural plan in so far as the chimney-stack built in the hall backed on to the putative passage. In the late 16th century a block of one storey and semi-attics was added to S; a jettied porch provided a new entrance and was combined, unusually, with a chimney-stack as a mode of display. The new block appears not to have been jettied, although recasing in brick and renovation of the interior may have removed the evidence. In the early 17th century the hall was divided into two storeys and a chimney-stack built. Perhaps at the same time the wing to W was built; originally it had no chimney-stack and was presumably for service and farm purposes, eg a dairy.

For illustrations, see *English Houses 1200–1800*, Figs 63 (plate), 64.

(77562)
Golden Parsonage (TL 051126)

was the rectory manor and belonged to the priory of Dartford up to the Dissolution. In 1544 it was granted by the Crown, together with the advowson, to William Halsey, with whose descendants it remained until 1804; it then passed by marriage to Joseph Thompson Whately, who thereupon adopted the name of Halsey and whose descendants still own it.[1] It was a large house in the time of Charles II, when John Halsey Esq. paid tax on 15 hearths in 1662 and 1666;[2] Thomas Halsey, who inherited in 1670, paid for the same number in 1673.[3] He built the present house, which is dated to 1705 by the weathercock, and died in 1715.[4] He was Sheriff in 1679 and several times MP for the county. The house, remarkable for the high quality of the brickwork, was never complete in itself. An estate map of 1717[5] shows the square block of the present house adjoining a long range to SE, which was no doubt the old house or part of it; this was pulled down *c*1774.[6] Its orientation is difficult to reconcile with the fact that the SE elevation is the most impor-tant one; presumably the surveyor was mistaken and it was really to NW (Fig 43). There is architectural evidence of alter-ations in the early 19th century; photographs taken prior to changes in 1935 show that the whole house was predominantly of that period. Later additions include a block to NE bearing a terracotta plaque with a crest, the initials T F H and the date 1874. In 1885 the house was leased to the brothers C B L and H G Tylecote as a preparatory school and was so used for nearly fifty years.[7] Its reversion to private occupation led to extensive internal alterations which were undertaken by Messrs Waring and Gillow for Sir Arthur Cory-Wright; all the rooms on the ground and first floors were stripped of their fittings and refurbished in the Queen Anne style.

The plan is approximately square with service ranges to N (correctly NE) (Fig 44). All the other elevations have Roman Doric pilasters and a moulded cornice below the parapet. The elevation to W, of four bays, is the plainest; that to S, of five bays, has the parapet treated as an entablature, with triglyphs, and the windows have keystones and shaped aprons; and that to E, of six bays, is divided by a pilaster in the middle and its windows have keystones. Clearly the present position of the entrance to W is not original, and the S side is precluded by the proportions of the rooms, unless they have been totally altered. With that proviso the obvious place is in one of the two bays flanking the middle pilaster to E; but this breaks the symmetry so clearly sought after, and looks clumsy in an otherwise rather sophisticated exterior. Nevertheless the front door was probably immediately to N of the middle pilaster, opening into a large

hall (c33 ft x 26 ft (10·1 m x 7·9 m)); ie a square living area with the addition of the space between the entrance and main staircase. The stair has been rebuilt; originally it will have faced the entrance and was lit by a window now blocked; the window, below which was a doorway, broke the regular bay intervals to W for some reason not now obvious. A reconstruction of the original plans of the ground and first floor has been attempted in Fig 45. Difficulties arise from the apparent lack of load-bearing walls running from one side of the house to the other. The first floor presents particular problems because no old detail now remains to show which partitions are original.

During the 18th century the service range to NW was rebuilt, no doubt to provide a new kitchen. A beam in the main span of the roof (running N–S) dated 1766[8] probably corresponds to a lowering of the pitch and the removal of attics. Alterations of the early 19th century are now illustrated principally by a fireplace in the bedroom to NW; the corner fireplace in the drawing room to E was probably added then; in 1836 the house was advertised as having 12 principal and secondary bedchambers in all, dining room, large library and ladies' morning room. A long list of

Fig 44 *Golden Parsonage, Great Gaddesden: plans*

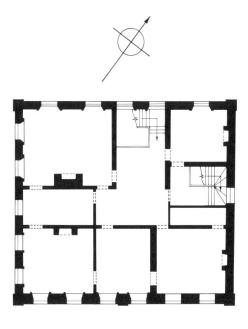

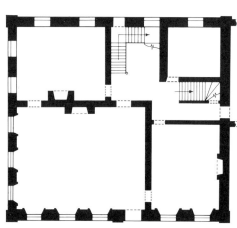

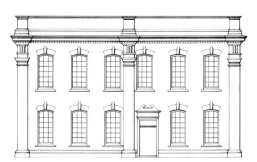

Fig 45 *Golden Parsonage, Great Gaddesden: reconstructed elevation and plans of 1705*

domestic offices includes housekeeper's room with two closet beds and butler's pantry with closet bed.[9] The only later addition of any importance, the block to NE built in 1874, was a billiards room in the 1930s and may have been so earlier. The plans and reconstructions are based on drawings made in 1935 in connection with renovation.

For an illustration, see *English Houses 1200–1800*, Fig 188 (plate).

Notes

1. VCH II, 204, 207.
2. PRO E179/375/30; E179/248/25.
3. PRO E179/375/31.
4. VCH II, 206.
5. HRO 15595.
6. VCH II, 205.
7. Inf. Mr G M Halsey.
8. Inf. Mr N G Halsey.
9. *The Times*, 8 September 1836; transcripts, Mr N G Halsey.

(77563)
The Hoo (TL 037128) [1]

is now largely modern, but incorporates to W the wing of a house of half-H plan drawn in 1838,[2] plans of which were prepared in 1946. Differences of proportion and window levels suggest that the middle, or hall range was the oldest part and was probably timber framed originally; it comprised a hall and a further bay to E, and is likely to have been built in the early 16th century. The position of the chimney-stack suggests that the entrance-passage lay to W of it. The first addition, in the 17th century, was the wing to E and probably at the same time a cupola was added to the hall range. At the end of the 17th century a wing was added to W, the hall range refronted with a parapet, and the whole of the older part refenestrated. In the ground-floor room to N of the wing a wooden fireplace surround of that date exists. According to notes compiled by a former owner, the house belonged to the Welles family[3] until in 1683 it passed by the marriage of Elizabeth Welles to Dr Edward Greene of St Bartholomew's Hospital, London, who may have been responsible for the late 17th-century work. In 1904, when a new house called The Hoo was built in the park (TL 032123), the old house was largely rebuilt and subsequently, when the 1904 house was demolished, resumed its former name.

Notes

1. The Old Hoo, OS 1:25 000 map 1963.
2. Buckler Vol I, 123.
3. Inf. Mrs S Wood; Chauncy II, 500.

(77564)
Lovatts Cottage (TL 039139)

was built in the early 16th century and comprised an open hall between storeyed end bays. The hall was unusual in having a timber chimney-stack, the existence of which can be inferred from the absence of smoke-blackening in the roof and the slightly higher level of the first floor in the long hall bay. The bay to W comprised pantry, buttery and staircase; that to E was the parlour, entered through a room which was larger than was needed purely for a staircase. The beaded joists in the hall suggest that the insertion of the floor is contemporary with wall-paintings in the hall and parlour that are dated to the third quarter of the 16th century. Facing the hall was a series of pairs of three-quarters-length nude female figures, each flanking or forming part of a fantastic column; between them was scroll-work with foliage or flowers, the whole in black and white. In the parlour, below a frieze, were framed text panels in good quality black letter; the inscriptions, in English, were no longer legible. About the end of the 17th century the present brick chimney-stack was built; in the early 19th century, when the house was turned into cottages, some walls were rebuilt or infilled with brick.

(77565)
Moor Cottage (TL 039102)

is a late medieval cruck-trussed house of three bays, the middle one – the hall – and the one to S being open to the roof; that to N contains the cross-passage and two service rooms with a chamber above them; the upper floor is reflected in the external framing; the staircase was probably beside the wall to W. In the truss separating cross-passage from hall the upper part, from a beam a little above first-floor level to the apex, was filled by a wattle-and-daub partition (cf Arne Cottage, Northchurch); it did not form the wall of a room over the passage because the bearer of the upper floor inserted in the hall spans the passage. To S the hall framing has peg-holes for a bench and bench-end. To E the

Fig 46 Moor Cottage, Great Gaddesden: section showing cruck frame

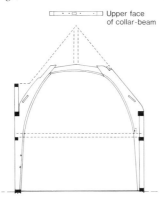

Upper face of collar-beam

framing of the hall provides for a large casement window of much the same size as the present one, flanked by higher windows with fixed glazing (Fig 46); the whole is probably of the late 16th century, but since the pegging-through of the joints is not completely traceable, it is difficult to establish whether the present arrangement is of that date or original. No window of this size existed opposite it to W, but one, of which only the rectangular mortises for the N jamb and one mullion can be seen in the soffit of the corresponding rail, stood nearer the upper end; it must be original, having been removed when the fireplace was built, and was probably intended to light the space in the front of the bench. The bay to S was presumably the parlour, although no positive indication of function remains. All the cruck blades terminate just above the collar-beams.[1] The addition of a lateral stack is unusual; it is of the late 17th century, when a floor was inserted in the hall, a wing built to W and a gabled dormer added to the bedroom over the hall. Subsequently a fireplace was provided in the latter.

Note
1. Type W, Alcock 1981, 7.

(77566)
No. 3 The Moor, Water End (TL 039101),

comprises two bays of a house of late medieval type; the E (correctly SE) bay, the hall, was originally open to the roof and that to W was of one and a half storeys. The wall-plates corresponded to the height of the present ground-floor rooms. In the W bay a rail to S at mid height of the wall has a shutter groove for a two-light window; the rail appears to have been intended to carry floor joists, hence the inner room had a sunken floor; and to confirm this, a blocked doorway in the partition (now demolished) separating the bays had a low lintel.[1] A third bay incorporating the cross-passage originally stood to E. Towards

the end of the 17th century a chimney-stack was built backing on to the passage; the house was heightened to two full storeys; both ground and first floors were altered to be level throughout, the latter being at the height of the old wall-plates; and a staircase and service room with bedroom above were added to S. Later a narrow lean-to was added. In the late 18th century, when the house was divided into two cottages, the chimney-stack to W, a second staircase and two adjoining front doorways were added; the trap for the staircase is visible in the W bay. The modern timber lean-to to E replaces an older one.

Note
1. Inf. Mr G Benningfield.

(77567)
Stagsend (TL 068120)[1]

is an early Victorian seat and was called Gaddesden Bury in the 1851 Census. Some comparatively small additions were made in the late 19th century. In 1907 a new oak staircase was built and sundry alterations made to the interior and in 1920 a kitchen wing was added, all designed by W B Hopkins, architect, for Frederick Braund Esq.[2]

Notes
1. Tags End, tithe map 1838, HRO DSA/3/40/2.
2. Inf. Mrs S Wood.

GREAT MUNDEN

(77568)
Brockholds Farm (TL 228365),

a moated site, was a small manor. Geoffrey Brokhole was Sheriff in 1385, and after his death in 1397 the manor descended in moieties until reunited in 1452 by Ralph Holt;[1] the open hall and bay to N, which are incorporated in the main range of the present house, are probably of the mid–late 15th century although no datable detail remains. In size they correspond closely to Stebbing Farm, Stevenage, built in 1442–3.

The only late medieval framing now exposed is to S of the hall; two posts, thickened at the top, have housings for beams, now removed, which carried the upper floor of a structure preceding the present wing. Little can be said about the hall except that the tile-cladding may correspond to a heightening. No old detail is visible to N of the internal chimney-stack, which was inserted in the late 17th century together with a first floor; the stack had a lobby-entrance to W and probably had a staircase to E. One of its fireplaces served the hall, the other to N the parlour. The wings are of uncertain date. The one to N may be of the 16th century; the foot of the staircase appears to have been in a square projection at the upper end of the hall and has subsequently been turned to rise in the opposite direction; the chimney-stack to N is of *c*1700, when the wing was widened to N with low eaves and a larger dormer added. In the wing to S a staircase in the NW corner was probably turned round when rebuilt in the 19th century. An unusual feature of this wing is that its gabled roof does not extend as far as the rear (E) of the main range; instead it terminates with a long lean-to roof. The house acquired its present appearance in the late 19th century when tile-hanging was applied to the upper storey and the upper parts of the chimney-stacks were rebuilt; inside, a general renovation included a new staircase in the former hall.

Note
1. VCH III, 127.

(77569)
Bugby's Farm (TL 347238)

comprises three parts: a gabled wing to W, a hall range, and what was originally a wing to E but is now roofed continuously with the hall. The E wing, perhaps of the 16th century, was not jettied; its W wall has been removed on the ground floor and only one cambered tie-beam of the roof remains. This wing, too, is not jettied; it has a clasped-purlin roof of two bays with windbraces, and is of c1600. The middle range, formerly an open hall, has to E one clean roof truss without any trace of smoke-blackening; it is later than the wing to E. Framing exposed on the ground floor to E, despite its early appearance, incorporates re-used timbers and is coeval with the hall, probably mid 17th century. The framing has no signs of a pair of service doors, so this was the upper end of the hall. In the late 18th or early 19th century a fireplace was added to the E wing to make a kitchen; sash windows were put in; and the exterior was clad in weather boarding. In recent years the weather boarding has been replaced by rendering.

(77570)
Cold Harbour (approximately TL 352200)

was 'fitted up' by Timothy Caswall about 1783 to replace the old house at Sacombe Park that he had inherited, and was demolished c1806 when the present Sacombe Park (see page 152) was completed. It was a long low range of two storeys and attics[1] quite unlike the country seats of the period but resembling Old Ashridge, Little Gaddesden.[2]

Notes
1. Oldfield Vol II, 470.
2. Buckler Vol I, 137.

(77571)
High Trees (TL 354219)

comprises a range to W of two storeys and a somewhat lower range to S, forming an L-shaped plan. The W range, jettied in the middle and with the bays to N and S flush with the first floor, resembled the Old Manor House, Aldbury, although the jetty is unusually high (c8 ft 6 ins (2·6 m)); the roofs have clasped-purlins; that to N may be older than that over the remainder of the house, which has thin curved windbraces. The jetty is the one visible feature earlier than the early–mid 17th century. Little framing is exposed internally; binding-beams and bearers in the hall are chamfered and stopped. The plan comprises hall with rooms to N and S; all three have fireplaces to E; the S wing, much altered, has a passage to N (cf Rooks Nest Farm, Walkern) and appears to have been service rooms with kitchen to E. In the hall a remarkable screen to S, of the early–mid 17th century,[1] has heavy ovolo-moulded stiles and rails and a frieze with triglyphs and dentilled cornice; the space between the latter and the ceiling is filled with 19th-century plaster and boards; that and the position of the only opening, which is not in the middle but nearer the entrance to W, are the only reasons for supposing it reset from elsewhere; on the other hand the panels and the spacing of the triglyphs fit the room.

Note
1. Pevsner and Cherry 1977, 195.

(77572)
Old Farm (TL 340251),

a moated house now demolished, was comparable in size to Pirton Grange, and its appearance[1] suggests that it had a similar development.

Note
1. Anderson, WCL; engraved, VCH III, 125.

HARPENDEN

(77573)
Cross Farm (TL 150129)

takes its name from the High or Hill Cross that Thomas Cowper alias Berkeley directed the executors of his will to build in 1485.[1] From 1065 it was owned by Westminster Abbey, except for the years 1650–60 when it passed into the hands of Sir John Wittewronge of Rothamsted.[2] Its next known occupiers are Thomas and Robert Carpenter who, before 1592, surrendered a moiety of the messuage called le Crosse to the use of John Neale. In 1651 William Elleys surrendered his messuage adjoining on the lands of the Crosse Farm to the use of a member of an important local family, Thomas Kentish of Burston, St Stephen parish,[3] who may have entered on the farm on coming of age; a man of the same name who died in 1712 at the age of 81[4] made a charge of 10 shillings yearly upon his farm called Cross Farm for the benefit of the parish.[5]

The earliest part of the house, a late medieval hall of two bays with a two-storeyed bay at each end, may have been Thomas Cowper's. The reference of 1592 shows that the house was divided by then although no architectural details remain to confirm this; the chamfer stop at the S (correctly SW) end of the bearer inserted in the hall may be somewhat earlier and the framing of the wing to S, which was exposed in 1840,[6] is probably Elizabethan. The principal changes took place in the late 17th century and are to be associated with Thomas Kentish. A wing was added to N and the whole of the medieval house refaced in brick, probably in the 1660s or 1670s; a date after 1668, when Thomas's father William died – he was the second son[7] – would suit the details. By then the house was divided into two parts at the former open truss; the original entrance was masked by a two-storey porch and another doorway adjoined it to S of the partition. The smaller part to N has the better internal finish – fireplaces, staircase and chamfer stops. In 1840 each of the three chimney-stacks had three rectangular flues with moulded cappings. It is not possible to establish when the S of the two entrance doorways was blocked and the house unified from the architectural evidence.

For illustrations, see *English Houses 1200–1800*, Figs 181 (plate), 182.

Notes
1. HRO, ASA/AR2, fo 55; VCH II, 298.
2. VCH II, 297.
3. WAM 14049, 14051.
4. Monumental Inscription, Oldfield Vol III, 321.
5. VCH II, 313.
6. Buckler Vol III, 194.
7. Oldfield Vol III, 301.

(77574)
Harpenden Hall (TL 135142)

was formerly known as Blakesleys. Its earliest recorded owner is William Cressy Esq., who died in 1559 leaving to his wife 'my messuage or mansion called Blakeslyes in Harpden', of which the cross-wing of the present house formed a part. In 1642 it was sold to Godman Jenkyn, a domestic servant of James I and Charles I, who died in 1670. He left the house in trust for his grandson, also Godman Jenkyn, who attained majority in 1678 and rebuilt the former hall range in brick. After passing through several hands it was used in the 19th century successively as a Dissenting grammar-school, surgery, private lunatic asylum, girls' school, convent and school, and finally urban district council offices.[1]

The late medieval house, which was timber framed, comprised a hall range and jettied cross-wing to N. The wing incorporated the cross-passage and comprised two rooms on each floor and a staircase between them; there is no evidence of original fireplaces. If the late 17th-century hall corresponds to the earlier hall, the latter was about 18 ft (5·5 m) wide, with a fireplace to E. Possibly the S end of the house represents the rebuilding of an earlier wing. In the 16th century the wing jetty was underbuilt in chequered brick and flint. In the mid 17th century the upper storey was refronted in brick and a two-storeyed porch added, no doubt by Godman Jenkyn senior. Fireplaces were provided in the two rooms to W and the porch chamber provided a dressing room to the principal bedroom. Some reset balusters of a contemporary staircase remain. Soon after 1678 the hall range was refashioned. To E was a large fire-place, next to which was the foot of the staircase.[2] To E of the hall and sharing the same chimney-stack was the kitchen, with a pantry to N.[3] Whether the kitchen was added c1678 or existed earlier is uncertain. The dining room may have been on the first floor over the hall. To S on the first floor a second important suite comprising a chamber with a dressing room opening off it was added to the earlier one to N; and there were three lesser chambers over the service rooms, served by a staircase to E of the kitchen.[4]

During the 18th century windows with hung sashes were inserted and then, probably, a room to S of the kitchen, perhaps a large drawing room or library, was built. At the end of the 19th century the main chimney-stack was reduced in size and the foot of the stair turned to S, to provide the axial passage characteristic of the period.

In 1931, when the house was converted for use as local government offices, the principal first-floor room and that to S were made into one and lined with reproduction bolection-moulded panelling.

Notes
1. Busby 1933.
2. As shown on a plan of 1847, HRO, QS Misc, Bdle 9.
3. Ibid.
4. Ibid.

(77575)
No. 27 Leyton Road, formerly the Old Bull Inn (TL 135139),
was built in the late 16th century; its owners and lessees in the 17th century have been traced in some detail.[1] The name is first recorded in 1586 (in the parish register) and was probably in general use; legal documents were more conservative, describing the building in 1613 as `that Messuage or Tenement called Woodwards, otherwise the Angell'; and again in 1639 and 1649 it was the `tenement anciently called...the Angell and now the Black Bull'.[2] The house is of T-plan, jettied to E, and was designed as an inn. The main range has an internal chimney-stack of timber with two ground-floor fireplaces; to E were two rooms, not intercommunicating; to W the former hall has a moulded binding-beam, which is housed awkwardly on the post to N so that it looks like a later insertion; to W again the division into two rooms is not provably old. To S was the kitchen wing and space for a small service room between it and the main range, although a plaster ceiling conceals any evidence of such a room. Upstairs on each side of the timber stack were two rooms; they were served by staircases to NE and SW and to N of the

stack; a fourth staircase was in the kitchen wing, perhaps to S of the stack. A probate inventory of 1719[3] (see Appendix) shows that these arrangements had been modified, no doubt when the late 17th-century brick stack was built within the timber frame. On the ground floor the two rooms to E had become the parlour, although no contents are listed; a beam was inserted beside the original one, to give extra strength when the partition was removed. Mention of `the Stare Case' may imply the removal of others. Ceilings at collar-beam level are likely to be of the late 17th century, as is the cellar. Subsequent changes include the addition of an early Victorian wing in the re-entrant angle to SE incorporating an entrance-hall and bow-fronted parlour, and the lengthening of the kitchen wing in the present century.[4]

For illustrations, see *English Houses 1200–1800*, Figs 285 (plate), 286, 306.

Notes
1. Scattergood 1933–5, 282–92.
2. Ibid, 286–7.
3. HRO, 38 HW 38.
4. Photograph c1900, opposite p 276, Scattergood 1933–5.

(77576)
No. 2 Southdown Road (TL 134142)
is a late medieval house, of which most of the hall and one cross-wing remain. The hall has been truncated to N; the proportions of the existing part suggest it was of two bays, with the chimney-stack built against the cross-passage; the crown-post roof had two-way struts. The wing was jettied to W (front) and had only one large room on each floor; the staircase was in the corner to SE.[1] At the lower end of the hall there was probably a service bay. An upper floor was built in the hall c1600; since the bearer is stopped against the present early 19th-century chimney-stack, it is likely that the latter replaces an earlier stack of brick or timber. The hall was then embellished with wall-paintings now too fragmentary to be interpreted; they preclude the continuance of a bench at the upper end of the hall. In the late 17th or early 18th century the wing was divided into two rooms on each floor; a fireplace was added in the room to W, and a new staircase built in the corner to SW. In the early 19th century the house was divided into two cottages; the chimney-stack to N rebuilt; the wing underbuilt and a bay window added; and rooms added to E.

Note
1. Inf Mr N F Mable.

HARPENDEN RURAL

(77577)
Faulkners End Farm (TL 111151)
was built in the late 15th century and comprised an open hall with cross-wing to W; the chimney-stack in the hall to E was probably built backing on to a cross-passage, with service rooms beyond. The width of the hall (19 ft 6 ins (6 m)) suggests the house was of some consequence. Peg-holes for bench and bench-end are visible. Above them, and antedating the insertion of the first floor, are late 16th-century paintings, perhaps of c1560–80; a timber chimney-stack probably existed by then. The probate inventory of George Carpenter, dated 1571, lists hall, chamber next the hall, buttery, larder; a new chamber where he died, another chamber, and a chamber over the larder.[1] It is not clear where the new chamber was, but it was not over the hall; the bearer for the upper floor cuts into the painting. In the late 17th

century the hall was heightened, a brick chimney-stack was built and all to E of it demolished; the wing was largely rebuilt, heightened to two storeys and attics, and the first floor raised; a chimney-stack added to W has a rectangular shaft with diagonal fillet and the fireplaces have curved corners. Some blackened rafters remain in the hall roof.

Note

1. *Wheathampstead and Harpenden* Part 2, 70, 71.

(39613)
Rothamsted Manor (TL 125131)

is the most important mid 17th-century house in the county. Its history has been confused by the misapplication of documents referring to a different house.

The manor, first recorded in the early 13th century, passed by marriage to the family of Bardolph in 1525; in 1611 it was mortgaged by Edward Bardolph to Jacob Wittewronge;[1] and in 1623, the year after Jacob's death, his widow Anne bought it for £5,400 in trust for her son John.[2] A `Particular of the Manor'[3] made about the time of her purchase, taken in conjunction with some timber framing in the house, suggests that the Bardolphs, who continued in occupation for some years, had by then largely rebuilt a late medieval house. Attached to the trust deed is a lease of the manor for nine years from the trustees to Edward Bardolph, who held a manorial court in 1624.[4] The first hint of alteration to the house occurs in the year the lease expired, when, presumably, Anne Wittewronge began to reside at Rothamsted.

In December 1638 her son (Sir) John Wittewronge married and may have begun to reside intermittently at Rothamsted;[5] he also began building, and his memoranda in a diary and account-books refer to work done both there and at his Buckinghamshire house, Stanton Bury, so that it is not always easy to allot entries to the right house. In September 1667 he noted: `I had an oak growing in the warren which I caused to be felled when I began to repair my house at Rothamsted about 1638 or 1639';[6] and 18 March 1640, `Sent to Rothamsted to pay some workmen £10'.[7] Another memorandum[8] makes it clear that the work of 1640 was all joinery – boards in the dining room and gallery, wainscoting in the hall chamber, and `the portall in the hall chamber'. By then he was living at Rothamsted, for on 1 June 1641 he paid `£12 in lands, assessed in Harpenden where he was resident with his family for most part of the year last past'.[9] Not until 1647 does building begin again, with modest sums paid to brick-makers; in 1648 payments are made for plastering in various rooms and the `new stairs'; but the most significant entry follows 1 March 1649: `There was burnt 184000 of brick this year, 385 quarters of lime'.[10] Most of the bricks must have been used in refronting the house, although there were some extensions; payment was made, 22 June 1649, for `setting up the wainscot in one of the new rooms'.[11] In July and September 1653 payments are recorded for a further 32,000 bricks, and 2 May 1655 Mr Gregory was paid `for the chimney piece for the room over the hall'.[12] It is likely that the payment made on 28 May 1659 to `the Luton waggoners for bringing down 300 ft of Purbeck stone for the arched walk'[13] applies to Rothamsted because the major works at Wittewronge's other house seem to have begun only on 1 April 1663, with a payment `for making the ground and digging the kiln at Stanton'.[14] However, in June 1679 the masons were paid (in part) `for carriage of the stone for paving my hall from Olney to Rothamsted, being in all 6 loads £5'.[15] That appears to be the final entry concerning Sir John Wittewronge's house. Everything in the diary and accounts suggests piecemeal alteration without any very fixed idea of completion. The entries

accord perfectly with the date 1654 at the base of the main (W) chimney-shafts, and with Wittewronge's becoming Sheriff in 1658.

There is now no evidence in the house of any work done in either the late 17th or the 18th centuries. The diary of Jacob Wittewronge,[16] who inherited the estate in 1721 and died in 1728,[17] covers the years 1721–5 and mentions only repairs and (December 1722) `new glasing front of the house'. There was formerly a rain-water head bearing the date 1722 on the W front. In 1748 the house passed to Jacob's younger son Thomas, who was Sheriff in 1750, and on his death in 1763 descended to his cousin John Bennet, who was the first owner of architectural ambition since the Commonwealth sheriff. His intention, never carried out, was to transform totally the S, W and perhaps the E elevations, bringing them to the height of fashion yet retaining withal the essential relations of the old plan and as much as possible of its structure (*English Houses 1200–1800*, Fig 201). No further work is recorded until 1863, when the house was enlarged by the addition of a big drawing room, to which, two years later, a small staircase was added; the latter was replaced by a large library in 1900. In that year a general antiquarian restoration of the house began, in the course of which three fire-places from Rawdon House, Hoddesdon were imported.[18]

The little evidence of a late medieval house that now remains is principally a wall incorporated in a first-floor partition; it has close-studding, so was intended to be exposed; the wall-plate is lower than the present plates; and all the timbers are flush to E, with possible traces of weathering. It may be one bay of the wall of a cross-wing, although this is difficult to reconcile with the supposed weathering; the date of the framing is uncertain.

The only other close-studding, to W of the hall facing into the bay window, shows neither signs of weathering nor any discontinuity with the adjoining timbering in large panels. It has been suggested that panels of this size were intended to frame wall-paintings, yet this is unlikely; paintings are usually continuous over stud and panel alike. Under the reproduction panelling can still be seen fragments of the paintings found in 1901. These were of two phases, the earlier being simulated timber framing and the later a design in two registers, the upper with fruits and swags, the lower with an archer and what may be mermen.[19] Such framing as can be seen to N of the hall and on the first floor above the hall to W is of the same large-panel kind, the former being associated with a painted frieze of a repeat pierced strapwork design. The probable association with it of paintings confirms the general impression that the framing is of c1600 and suggests that the bay window is integral with the hall. Whether the hall is of the same date as the adjoining parlour is uncertain. The only relevant evidence is that the posts to W of the hall are flush on the exposed side and project some 3 ins (7·5 cm) beyond the plaster infilling at the back.[20] Wall-paintings in the parlour – of battle scenes, and of animals in an architectural frame – are on a structurally separate timber frame, hence the hall may be of a different date from the W as well as the E wing; probably not very different but corresponding to piecemeal rebuilding and enlargement. By 1623 Rothamsted was a manor-house of considerable size and up-to-date in its planning (Fig 47). It is described in the Particular as follows:

two storeys high, an indifferent large Hall, two parlours whereof one of them is a verie fair and large Roome, both of them being to the face of the house: one lodging chamber belowe staires on the back parte of the house, one reasonable fair Kitchin; a larder, a Bakehouse with two faire ovens, a Brewhouse, one little closet by the parlour. Butterie between the Hall and the lesser Parlour. A small Cellar being verie shallow within the Earth, a little Butterie by the Cellar. Over the Hall a very fair dineing room, over the parlour a verie faire lodging chamber, a Chamber over the lower lodging Chamber, a faire Chamber over the lesser parlour. A Chamber between the chamber over the Parlour and the dining Chamber. Over the Porch a closset. Over the Kitchin, Brewhouse, and Bakehouse, lodging chambers for servants. A Garrett or Cockloft over the Chambers, on the topp of the house, but most part of it is shutt upp and made of no use.[21]

This suggests that the plan was much the same as now, and tallies with a contemporary sketch of the house 'drawn on a half membrane of a court roll of 1624 subsequently used as the Cover for a rental of 1636'.[22] One difference is that to E is a gabled single-storey building now removed. This was not the kitchen, which had lodging chambers over it, and may therefore be the small cellar which had a little buttery by it. At the opposite end of the house the very fair and large parlour presents a problem. It cannot correspond exactly to the existing room, which the chimneys dated 1654 show was then divided into two, each with its own fireplace; if the drawing of 1624 shows correctly a chimney on the axis of the wing and not to W, the parlour had either an internal stack flush with the rear of the hall or an external stack. The location of the rooms connected with the storage and preparation of food and drink, ie, kitchen, larder, bakehouse and brewhouse, is uncertain. Possibly the first two were situated much as they had been from the end of the 18th to the early 20th century, but the other two, and perhaps all four, could equally well have been in the timber-framed range to N of the courtyard.

The expiry of the 1623 lease corresponds to the date 1632 scratched on a panel in the parlour, which may be when the paintings were covered up; and the date 1635 'neatly scratched' on the hall fireplace has been held to date it.[23] These are the only alterations definitely known to have been made before Sir John Wittewronge took up residence and transformed the appearance of the house. Wittewronge seems not to have altered the essentials of the plan if the rooms of the 1623 Particular have been correctly identified. He lengthened the house to W, adding a loggia, the small room to N, and perhaps another room to N of the parlour; and to E by replacing the little building of 1624 with a two-storey block of two-room plan. Although the functions of the E addition are unknown, one room may have been the housekeeper's as it was in the early 20th century. To W the small room adjoining the loggia, possibly a parlour, must have been reached through a lobby while the arches were still open. The main staircase has been attributed to Sir John Wittewronge[24] and dated 1678 on the basis of diary entries[25] which are primarily to do with work at Stanton; an entry 'End of these accounts 1678' is followed by the words 'Dealboard for wainscot of great parlour. For new Staircase', and then comes a memorandum relating to Rothamsted in 1640. Stylistically neither main nor secondary staircase will fit 1678 in a gentry house; the former is comparable to that of *c*1660 at Codicote Bury and both are of the early 1650s. Wittewronge rebuilt the kitchen wing; the first-floor walls are of comparatively thin brickwork which relies on timber framing to give load-bearing strength. The pattern of circulation appears to have been as follows: the hall was still both point of entrance and principal room, from which three rooms to W, all with fireplaces, were reached; a passage led between service rooms to a secondary stair, another parlour, perhaps a butler's or housekeeper's room and a servants' hall; any other rooms were presumably for service purposes. From the hall the main staircase rose to a first-floor dining room and a suite of three important chambers to W, but the present doorway, which is too narrow and awkward to be original, establishes that there was no access originally to N. Access to first-floor rooms to N and E was from the secondary staircase, and the servants may well have used a third and architecturally very minor stair to N of the kitchen wing. Both stairs rose up to the attics, where too little detail remains to say what the room arrangement was.

Fig 47 *Rothamsted Manor, Harpenden Rural: reconstruction of 1624 plan*

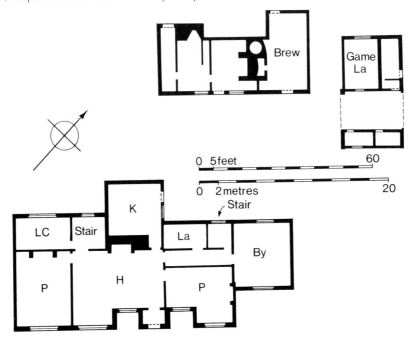

By the 1760s the house was old-fashioned. The uses assigned to ground-floor rooms (*English Houses 1200–1800*, Fig 122) are surprising only in so far as there is no mention of a dining room; and it is of some interest for social history that, firstly, the very large room above the `Long Parlour' was the Billiard Room now Library' and, secondly, that the proposed new house made no provision for billiards. It would be interesting to know more about John Bennet. The plans show the remarkable survival of the large mid 17th-century windows, none of which were replaced by hung sashes, so that it can safely be said that the present windows, though heavily repaired, correspond to the originals and are not antiquarian replacements of an 18th-century phase. The work of *c*1900 included the characteristic alteration of the staircase to provide one riser below the newel post; consequently the treads fit the string awkwardly.

For illustrations, see *English Houses 1200–1800*, Figs 122, 143 (plate), 201.

Notes

1. VCH II, 303.
2. HRO, D/ELW T12.
3. HRO, D/ELW E17.
4. HRO, D/ELW M10.
5. Boalch 1978, 9.
6. HRO, D/ELW F20.
7. HRO, D/ELW F18.
8. HRO, D/ELW F22.
9. PRO, E115/399/24; cf Boalch 1978, 10.
10. HRO D/ELW F23.
11. Ibid.
12. HRO, D/ELW F18.
13. HRO, D/ELW F20.
14. Ibid.
15. HRO, D/ELW F21.
16. HRO, D/ELW F42.
17. Boalch 1978, 18–19.
18 Dr J Carpenter and Mr T Cawley of Rothamsted Research Station have provided information incorporated in this description.
19. Hodgson 1902, 378–84.
20. Ibid, 382.
21. HRO, D/ELW E17.
22. Letter, P Walne, 14 January 1981, RCHME file; sketch now in HRO; redrawn, VCH II, 304.
23. VCH II, 306.
24. Ibid; RCHME 1910, 108.
25. HRO, D/ELW F21.

HATFIELD

(33636)
Brocket Hall (TL 214130)

is a large house of three storeys built *c*1760–5 by James Paine for Sir Matthew Lamb, Bart., and Sir Penistone Lamb, Bart., later 1st Lord Melbourne; it was not examined, but the plan throws light on the house the present one replaced. A recent study of Brocket Hall[1] establishes that its peculiarities arise from the piecemeal reconstruction of a courtyard house range by range, and this point is confirmed by a block plan of the house dated 1752,[2] showing buildings around three sides of a courtyard. The plan of 1752 shows wings extending to E and W of the courtyard house; they were probably additions.

The lands associated with the house were called Watership or Durantshide, and by 1477 had come into the possession of Thomas Brocket; they are not referred to as a manor before 1532.[3] In 1531, John Brocket Esq., and in 1566 and 1581 his son, also John, served as Sheriff. After the younger John's death in 1598 the estate was divided among five daughters and a grandson; and before 1637 it had been reunited and came by marriage to Sir Thomas Read.[4]

The courtyard house is likely to have been completed before 1598 and Sir John Brocket may well have been responsible for much of it. In 1580 there is a reference to `the manor of Durrants Hide now Brockett Hall' and a brief description:

The mansion house called Brocket Hall with the little park being on the West side of the mansion house and on both sides of the water 94 acres. The ground before the court gate with the bowling alley lying on the East side of the mansion house, 14 acres 1 rood. [5]

Chauncy does not state that the house was of brick, although it was `enclosed with a brick Wall on the West side of the Road, for the length of a Mile'.[6] Paine's work began with the N and E ranges;[7] no doubt it was convenient to add a new range to N before beginning to rebuild the rest. The S range, in which were the entrance and the principal rooms flanking it, was the last to be completed.

Notes

1. P Leach, `The life and work of James Paine', unpublished D Phil thesis, University of Oxford 1975, 239–41.
2. HRO, D/EP P9.
3. VCH II, 101–2.
4. Ibid, 101.
5. BL Add MS 29438, fo 5.
6. Chauncy II, 16.
7. Paine 1783, Vol II, 15.

(77578)
Great Nast Hyde (TL 078104)

is of the mid 17th century but appears to be the result of piecemeal rebuilding. Although described as `formerly an ancient Manor House'[1] the estate may have been built up not long before the house was first built. In 1642 Nast Hyde was owned by Philip Oxton, Gent., a member of a family of maltsters and a Parliamentarian;[2] he paid tax on nine hearths in 1663[3] and probably built the house. It then had large mullion-and-transom windows and three curvilinear gables; the two-storey porch had a stepped gable; the roof was crowned by a cupola. The plan comprises a hall range with E and W cross-wings which project slightly to the S (front) and considerably more to N. Several features of it are anomalous in a mid 17th-century house. The width of the hall range (19 ft 6 ins (6 m)) would be appropriate to a late-medieval manor house or reputed manor, and is greater than that of, for example, Rothamsted Manor (Harpenden) and Bride Hall (Wheathampstead); unusually for a gentry house, the hall chimney-stack is placed axially to W and not laterally; behind the stack is what looks like a cross-passage; and the small forward projection of the wings is no more than would result from replacing a jetty. All these features are intelligible if the house is assumed to be a piecemeal reconstruction of a late medieval open-hall house; this would also account for the clumsy way in which the entrance, so placed for symmetry, leads directly in front of the hall fireplace. The E wing is divided between the parlour and, to N, the main staircase,[4] which occupies nearly half of the E wing and is comparable to that at Rothamsted Manor, Harpenden; it suggests that an important room, perhaps the dining room, was above the hall. The W wing is occupied mainly by a kitchen with a small service room (a scullery in 1907) to N; in the NE corner of the wing is a small secondary staircase reached from the hall by a modern renewal of what probably had been an original lobby. The former cross-passage may have become a pantry, with a cellar added beneath it.

Philip Oxton died in 1665 and was succeeded by his eldest son of the same name, who, in the following year, was assessed for only eight hearths;[5] (an instance, perhaps, of the errors complained about in the first assessment of the tax). By 1690 the estate had come into the possession of Robert Kentish, in whose family it remained throughout the 18th century, and, perhaps because it was let to tenants latterly, little alteration is discernible in Oldfield's drawing. Early in the 19th century William Cannon acquired the property; he put in bay windows on the ground floor and sash windows on the first floor and gave all the gables a straight coping. Somewhat surprisingly the cupola remained. In the early years of the 20th century Great Nast Hyde ceased to be a farmhouse and was enlarged and restored as an `Elizabethan' residence.

Notes
1. Oldfield Vol III, 329; VCH II, 417.
2. The subsequent history is taken for the most part from an unsigned typescript, based on documentary sources and apparently reliable, in the possession of Hawker Siddeley Aviation Ltd.
3. PRO E179/248/24/1.
4. Godfrey 1911, Plate 8.
5. PRO E179/248/25.

(77579)
Hatfield House (TL 236084)

was begun by Robert Cecil, Earl of Salisbury, in 1607 and finished shortly after his death in May 1612. Although the house is one of the best documented in England resources were not available to examine all the relevant family papers; moreover, Lawrence Stone has studied its building in detail.[1] In these circumstances two series of manuscript excerpts[2] made early in the present century were utilised. In addition, several inventories,[3] excerpts from which appear in the Appendix, elucidate the original plan and later architectural history of the house. Information communicated by the Marquess of Salisbury's librarian and archivist has also been incorporated into the following account.[4]

Although the exterior of the house was less austere in 1612 than now,[5] its shape and general appearance have changed little in recent years and the interior hardly at all; consequently descriptions published many years ago are still relevant and do not need repeating.[6] Prior to achieving its present state the interior underwent a transformation in the late 18th century as well as a number of lesser changes, and only by combining inferences from the inventories with the drawings made in connection with those alterations can the disposition of rooms in the early 17th century be understood.

In 1612 the house comprised a main or north range and east and west wings forming a half-H plan, the whole being of three storeys and basements. The fabric of the building was finished when the earliest inventory, dated 30 September 1611, was compiled, but how much remained to be done, and the changes of intention that could occur before it was occupied, are shown by a memorandum dated January 1612:

[the carpenters] have taken down the partission of the pallet room adjoyning to his L's lodging on E side and are setting it up again for a passage and have taken out some part of the roome adjoyning

to it for presses. Also the carpenters have yet to alter the lobbyes adjoyning to the Kings lodgings on the E side. And they are to make two slite partissions in the 2 pallet roomes fronting to the south. More they are to make one false floore in the lodging fronting to the north which roome is now 16 ft high. And they are to alter the lobby with a partission and a dore throw the back wall adjoyning to the Queens lodging on the W side of the house and two partissions in the pallet roomes adjoyning.[7]

The external aspect of the house as completed in 1612 may have differed in one important respect from its present state, the N elevation perhaps then being finished with a row of gables resembling those to S. Evidence of this is provided by the principals of the roof trusses, which stand on tie-beams at second-floor level and have mortises for windbraces. This would have heightened the contrast between the hall range and the terminal blocks, which have flat roofs of lead. A feature of the N elevation for which no explanation can be offered is that the first-floor windows to W of the porch are set about two courses of brickwork higher than those to E.

A schematic reconstruction of the plan (*English Houses 1200–1800*, Fig 102) is based on inventories of 1611 to 1646, with all documented alterations removed. The numbers on the plans relate to the inventories (Appendix, pp 220–3). The principal differences between the reconstructions and the plans published in 1910[8] are, on the ground floor: (1) W of the hall the screens-passage, service rooms and corridor to the Adam and Eve staircase have been restored; (2) the colonnade now known as the Armoury is closed off from the lobbies at each end; (3) what was called in 1910 the Maple Room[9] but is properly the Birch Room, does not exist; and (4) there are no internal staircases in the E and W wings (as already indicated by Girouard,[10] this is apparent on the first floor too); also (5) the present library in the W wing is subdivided; (6) W of the hall the present Winter Dining Room is shown as three rooms; and (7) the mezzanine in the W wing is absent. As appears below, the changes made in the early 1780s and continual alterations between 1823 and 1868 make the positions of original doorways and fireplaces so uncertain that they have been omitted.

The planning of Hatfield House was governed by the need to provide accommodation for King James I and his queen during the visits which Robert Cecil hoped they would make. This entailed providing suites of interrelated rooms of a size and number appropriate to the respective needs of the royal couple and equipped with furniture destined exclusively for royal use. In the event Cecil died before he could entertain the king and queen at Hatfield, and because of the unfitness of his son for public life – `a man of no words, except in hawking and hunting, in which he only knew how to behave himself'[11] – the house was never used as intended. That an alternative purpose was envisaged for the royal apartments is shown by the provision of a second, less splendid set of furniture for those rooms destined for the personal use of royalty; whether this was for visitors a little below the pinnacle of society or for the Cecils themselves[12] is not perfectly clear.

The N range was planned on conventional lines with a hall, screens-passage, steward's room and probably a pantry. The pantry does not appear in inventories in its appropriate position but mention of a chamber over the pantry (14) in 1629 implies that the latter was next to the steward's room (37); in the light of the 1611 inventory this may have been a matter of accounting since the closing entry is `In the Kitchen Larder and Butteries in Mr Shaw's keeping'. The colonnade in front of the hall is called the Open Gallery in 1612, when two seats were set up there; it led nowhere and was presumably intended for show, exercise and the support of the gallery above. A corridor led past the pantry and steward's room to the W staircase and kitchen; to S a window corresponded to each bay of the colonnade; those to W lit the corridor; some, and perhaps all, of those to E on the house side must always have been blind. The hall has been refurbished at various times without significant alteration of its form; the only slight uncertainty relates to the narrow first-floor Minstrels Gallery to E, which is neither mentioned in any inventory (perhaps because it contained no furniture or fittings) nor listed by the 2nd Marquess among his numerous works. The hall range terminates in two large and nearly square blocks, each containing a principal staircase and the principal upstairs rooms of state adjoining them. These terminal blocks and adjoining wings differed in plan: the E or king's side has the grander staircase and rooms whereas the state rooms on the W or queen's side were restricted in number and size by the presence of the chapel and large kitchen. The outer parts of the E and W wings were similar to one another and each was identical except for minor details on ground and first floors. Each floor had to N, adjoining the courtyard, one large room through which those to S were reached; in the W wing this was the chapel, from which corridors were perhaps partitioned off, at least by screens of less than storey height.

The galleries to N and S appear to have been shorter than now; slight differences in the pilasters and the key blocks of the arches, and breaks in the horizontal timbers, suggest they have been lengthened by about 10 ft (3 m), which would have left space originally for both a family pew and passage to W. Adjoining each of these two large rooms to S, and surrounded by five other rooms, was a dark chamber, entered, as comparison of the room order in the inventories suggests, from E and W and probably N too. The combination of dark chamber and two minor staircases to SE and SW appears to have had two purposes, one being the provision of closets and stool houses and the other a mode of circulation which reduced the need to enter one room through another. Since a gallery connected the two royal suites on the first floor, the hall appears to have been the principal and perhaps only passage room. On the second floor two suites of rooms to NE and NW were reached from the polygonal staircase turrets; the description in 1611 of those to NE as antechamber, bedchamber and pallet chamber, and of those to NW as being for the son and heir, Lord Cranborne, shows that they were good rooms. Later inventories suggest that to each chamber belonged an outer chamber, separated from it by the N–S corridor flanking the massive block of masonry formed by the chimney-breasts rising from the lower floors. Probably the corridors continued to S on something like the present lines, with rooms to E and W, to reach the corner turrets on the courtyard side. Somewhere on this storey were the Wardrobe and Armoury, the former perhaps in the W part of the hall range and the latter to E. Possibly a staircase from the first to second floor adjoined the gallery but had no connection with it, since it was reached only from the room of which the porch formed part.

Of the many subsidiary buildings little is known. The house had 'Three courts below; the First contains the Stablings and other Conveniences for Poultry, etc';[13] this is no doubt the courtyard of which the Old Palace, converted into stables by the hunting Earl c1628, formed part. 'When you come through the Chief Avenue to the Park Side, and when the Gates of the lower Courts are open, there are Walls...to the farther end of the Park'; the two 'lower Courts' were presumably directly N of the house.

Inventories indicate that the house underwent little alteration for about fifty years. In 1629 four turrets are mentioned and in 1638 six; in 1646 four closets 'on the leads at the top of the house'

were presumably among the small rooms at the top of the four staircase turrets to S and the two to N. No doubt these rooms were in existence by 1612 and the numbers mentioned in inventories varied as their more or less permanent allocation to individuals changed. At one or more points staircases gave access to the balustraded 'leads' which appear in an engraving of 1700; on the E side a window above the round-headed doorway opening on to the gallery leads may indicate the site of one such staircase. The basement was also inhabited; how many people lived there is uncertain. The first definite mention occurs in 1683 when an entry, 'the usher of the Hall his Chamber underground', is followed by 'the next chamber' and four more chambers not specifically located but probably in the basement. These were for the principal servants, the key members of the household; lesser servants lived around the courtyards.

The significance of the changes of use and occupier for the rooms needs to be assessed in the light of the changes in the household, but, broadly speaking, the structure of the house made alteration in their relative importance difficult. Two imposing rows of chimney-stacks in the square blocks to E and W of the hall and two more aligned E–W in the wings limited the possibilities of major internal change; the two principal and six minor staircases, being sufficiently numerous and conveniently placed, further limited the possibility of external change; consequently, short of an almost complete rebuilding, little could be done to the house except improve its internal facilities. Even then the width and outline of the wings reduced the scope for alteration to a minimum. At the south end, since each wing was three rooms in depth, alternatives to passage rooms had to be contrived to avoid the inconveniences of the latter. This was done on ground and first floors by means of lobbies and on the second floor, and also in the basement, where size and dignity of rooms were of no account, by L-shaped corridors. At the top and bottom of the house the corridors have remained in use, with slight modifications, to the present day, but on the two principal floors staircases replaced the lobbies (except for a brief period in the E wing). If, as Stone argues, the expansion of the wings was an afterthought (and not a very happy one at that)[14] it proved sufficiently convenient in practice to ensure that the only alternative, the kind of fate that befell Knebworth House, never overtook Hatfield.

The first recorded changes in Hatfield House appear to have been the result of a fire. On 28 March 1666, Denton, the bailiff, wrote to Sir Ralph Verney that 'Hatfield House was half burned Monday was sennight', that is to say on 22 March. This was an exaggeration; later that year an account for 'Repairs to that part of the House that was burnt', and of which no details are given, amounted to £463, a comparatively small sum in relation to the size of Hatfield.[15] The cost of repairs may be compared with £200 paid for carpenters' work at the quite modest Ryston Hall in 1670–1, or £1,500 for that at Horseheath in 1663-6.[16] The surveyor who carried out these repairs was Captain Richard Ryder, who was normally employed by Lord Salisbury for architectural work in London and at Cranborne. To locate the fire with certainty after so much later change is impossible but the one part apparently of that date is the secondary or Adam and Eve staircase, which, perhaps because of confusion over dating such work, survived the 19th-century attempt to recreate the Jacobean house. At the head of the stairs going into the gallery is a wide doorway with a segmentally pedimented head. In the tympanum is an achievement-of-arms of the 2nd Marquess, but the doorway itself is either late 17th century-work or a copy. No new building is mentioned in 1666 and the '3 new rooms on the top of the house' listed in an inventory of 1685, which must be on the top floor of the west wing, were probably added before

Fig 48 *Hatfield House: ground and first-floor plans c1785*

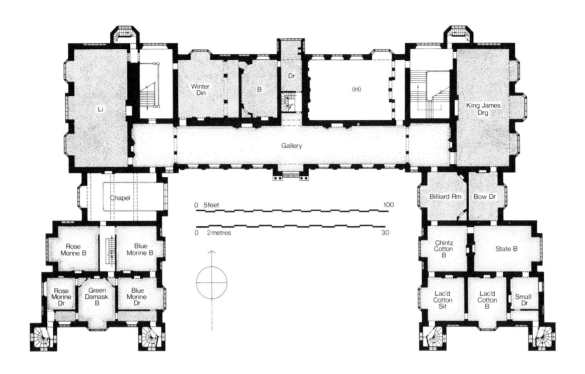

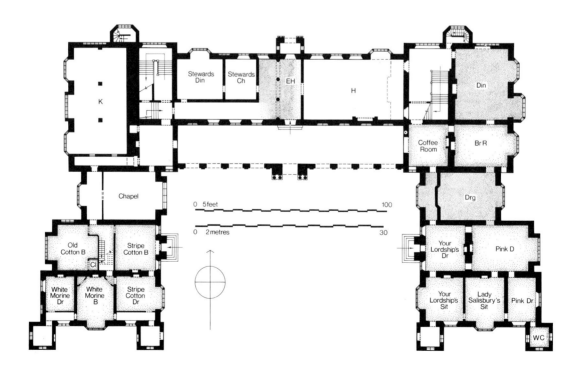

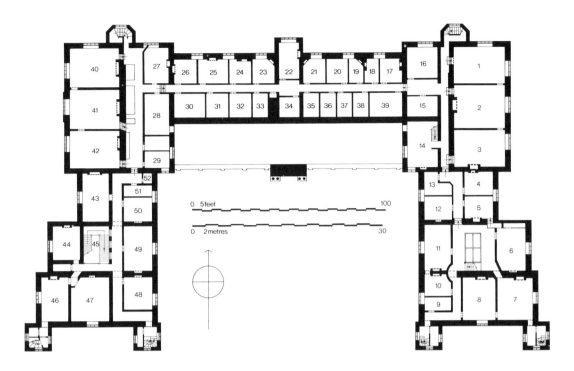

Fig 49 *Hatfield House: attic plan* c1860

1680 when `the farther new roome' appears in an inventory. No mention of the turrets is made thereafter. In 1710–11 new doorways were opened in the Upper Dining Room and `next the King's room', but, attics and minor works apart, most expenditure on the house was for routine maintenance. Thus payment in 1678 for `building the kitchen chimneys'[17] is unsurprising in view of the wear they suffered. Equally the payment of £222 in 1691 for 2,223 yards of plastering and finishing walls in imitation of stone `at 2 shillings', also described as `white finishing', is presumably a renewal of some part of the original exterior treatment. In the time of the 6th Earl, 1734–80, no money seems to have been spent on the house, and most of his last thirty years were spent at Quickswood (Clothall).

James, 7th Earl and 1st Marquess of Salisbury (in 1789) inherited the Cecil estate in 1780; he called in the architect John Donowell[18] to make Hatfield fit to be his principal residence, and in the course of three years spent nearly £25,000 on house, park and gardens. The courtyards to N were swept away and the two principal floors thoroughly refurbished with comparatively little change in the plan; and it is extraordinary that the two wings were still approached in the late 18th century as they had been in the totally different circumstances of the early 17th century. Internal alterations are shown on the plans (Fig 48). Little was done to the exterior apart from inserting sash windows in the private rooms of the Marquess and Marchioness and lengthening the windows of the two big rooms to E down-

wards. Had the E elevation been straight it would no doubt have been refronted like North Mymms Park, but, since removal of its recessions and projections would have necessitated total rebuilding, Hatfield's unusual plan ensured that at this critical moment in its history its external appearance was preserved save for the removal of paint from the brickwork.[19] One of the principal alterations was the creation of a new entrance-hall about twice the width of the former screens-passage; probably the double doors in the old screen, which have fielded panels to W and carving in slightly lower relief than the four original, are of this date. Another was the suppression of the dark rooms in the middle of the wings, those to W being replaced by a top-lit staircase and those to E by passages. The complete refitting of the E wing, except for the great parlour, great chamber and great staircase, is recorded in Donowell's drawings and led to the removal of all original fittings and the opening of some new doorways. A general renovation of the W wing at the same time is not recorded in detail, and what happened to the second floor chambers, if anything, has not been traced. Room names, not always informative about function, appear on a plan reconstructed c1785 (Fig 48), with an indication of the extent of the work done by Donowell.

All the 1st Marquess's work of the 1780s in the N and E ranges was ripped out by his heir. Although no precise dates are available the 2nd Marquess, also James, must have begun a restoration of the principal rooms in the Jacobean style soon after succeeding to the estates in 1823, and by 1833 a published plan of the first floor shows that his intentions had been largely fulfilled. On the ground floor the passage to S of the steward's room and pantry was suppressed, and the colonnade, which in the 1st Marquess's time had been closed in, fitted with hot-house lights and turned into a conservatory in winter, and otherwise used only to shelter the dogs at night, was enlarged by uniting the lobbies into it, glazed and made into the Armoury. On the first floor the Winter Dining Room was created out of the two rooms into which the 1st Marquess had formed the original three, and the transept or aisle running north from the gallery (now called the North Gallery) was opened up by removing a staircase to the second floor. In the E wing, on both ground and first floors, a staircase replaced the dark passages. During the renovation of the Billiard Room after a fire at some date unstated, but before 1833, a corner fireplace and a matching corner cupboard were removed. The appearance of the interior dates largely from the 2nd Marquess's time. The gallery was enlarged by the incorporation of the former lobbies and its panelling and chimney-pieces renewed `in the old style'; but in fact, whereas the chimney-pieces appear to be entirely of the period, much of the panelling, at least below the lower cornice, is original. The fluted pilasters which form part of the original

work have a less regular appearance than the machine-cut copies at the ends and some show traces of paint in the deepest cutting of the fluting. Elsewhere one chimney-piece was brought from a house in Hertford and eight more were `renewed' or built entirely from `fragments of shrines' bought on the continent.[20] One further change that took place in the 2nd Marquess's time was the reconstruction of the second storey to provide a large number of bedrooms for both visitors' servants and those of the household (Fig 49); this was done before 1848, when 23 servants' bedrooms are listed along the North Passage.

On 27 November 1835, a fire that started in the rooms of the Dowager Marchioness burned all the W wing as far as the chapel, the ceiling and floor of which were destroyed, and caused sections of the E and W walls to collapse. The walls were subsequently made good, even to conserving the old windows; the whole interior was reconstructed in contemporary taste.

In 1868 Hatfield passed to Robert, the 3rd Marquess, who was three times Prime Minister.[21] Apart from alterations to the chapel in 1869, when new seating, reading desk, screen and a stone altar were put in, his principal concern was to make the house more efficient; gas lighting was installed in 1868, electric bells and new arrangements for water in 1869, electric light in 1881 and fire hydrants in 1887–9; a general renewal of the

Fig 50 *Hatfield House: ground plan c1870*

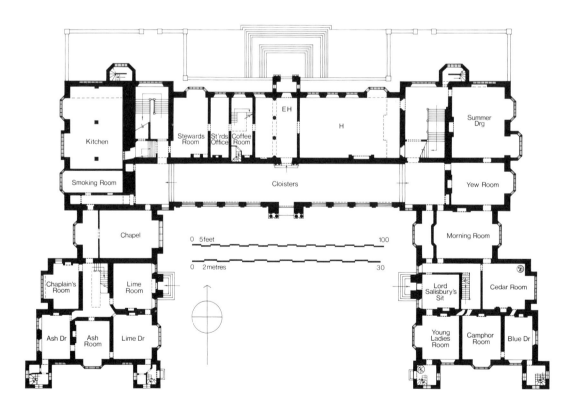

sewage system took place in 1891. In 1870–1 what is now known as the Birch Room was built as a smoking room, occupying part of the kitchen to S (Fig 50); and the number of rooms on the second floor was reduced to create larger ones. In 1897–8 some windows in the W wing that had survived the fire needed repair.[22] The many minor internal alterations made during the 3rd Marquess's time and subsequently have not affected the plan materially. The N front was refaced in 1959.

For illustrations, see *English Houses 1200–1800*, Figs 101 (plate), 102.

Notes
1. Stone 1955, 100–28.
2. *BHH, HH & G.*
3. Transcribed by Mr R T Gunton, private secretary to the 3rd Marquess, and available in typescript.
4. The Commission is indebted to Mr R H Harcourt-Williams for his assistance.
5. Stone 1955, 124.
6. RCHME 1910, 53–8; VCH III, 95–9; Tipping 1920–37, Vol II, 305–52.
7. *BHH*, 89.
8. RCHME 1910, 54, 56.
9. Ibid, 54.
10. Girouard 1978, 115 (plan).
11. Clarendon Vol II, 596.
12. Girouard 1978, 115.
13. de Sorbière 1667, 64.
14. Stone 1955, 113.
15. *HH & G*, 291, 297.
16. Gunther 1928, 185, 129.
17. *HH & G*, 297.
18. Colvin 1978, 270.
19. Oldfield Vol III, 306, 309.
20. *Notes on Hatfield House.*
21. *DNB.*
22. Butterfield 1908.

(77581)
Howe Dell, formerly The Rectory or Parsonage (TL 227082),

is a large, rambling building of two storeys and attics, and is predominantly of roughcasted timber framing with some brick. Hardly any old detail is now visible. It is a well-documented house: the principal sources are a survey for repairs *c*1534, a more detailed survey of 1606–7, and a plan drawn about 1607[1] and a Buckler drawing of 1839.[2] Comparison of the plan of 1607 with that of the present building[3] shows that it is accurate enough to permit deductions about the early development of the Rectory. The hall, mentioned in the survey of 1534 as having `an high or open roof', appears in the plan of 1607 to have been about 35 ft x 36 ft (10.8 x 11 m). Whether `the entrance between the hall and kitchen' (1534) was included in the 36 ft (11 m) length of the former hall appears doubtful in view of the fact that the living-space in a hall was normally square; perhaps it was N of the hall and was demolished before 1607. The 1534 survey does not mention a pantry or buttery at the lower end of the hall, only a kitchen, and no doubt the bakehouse and malthouse were not far away. Except for the hall, the house was `contrived for the most part in two storeys'. A parlour is mentioned, presumably the `Stone Parlour' S of the hall. In its size and complexity, Howe Dell may be compared with the Old Rectory, Therfield.

In the late 16th century whatever lay N of the hall was for the most part rebuilt or, as the 1607 plan suggests, incorporated in a large group of buildings arranged around three small court-yards; some of the buildings still exist.

Notes
1. Hatfield House MSS; reproduced in *Hatfield and its People, Book 10*, 9.
2. Buckler Vol III, 20.
3. *Hatfield and its People, Book 10*, 9.

(77580)
The Old Palace (TL 235086),

the manor house of Hatfield, was an important residence of the bishops of Ely by the early 13th century, and several times accommodated the king in the 13th and 14th centuries.[1] All that remains today is the main or W range rebuilt by Bishop John Morton, *c*1480, and the small gatehouse to NW. It has been fully described[2] and is included here for the plan drawn *c*1608, which is of interest for comparison with other 16th-century courtyard houses. When the other three wings were built is uncertain, but to judge by the size of the staircases in the corners and the complete absence of octagonal stair turrets of the kind found in other Hertfordshire houses of this type, the courtyard plan was not completed until well into the second half of the 16th century. The view has been expressed that these wings were never built, and that the plan must represent an abortive project for a new house for Robert Cecil on the old site rather than a survey of the royal house as it stood in 1607.[3] If this were so it would imply an intention to preserve the medieval hall, to W of which is shown the distinctive porch with adjoining staircase that survives in the Old Palace today, and it is hard to believe that a man of Cecil's building ambition did not intend to rebuild so important a part of this new house; moreover a reference in 1608 to taking down the great stairs by the old hall[4] is compatible with the plan. But even if it is an unexecuted design it throws some light on the planning of large houses. The disposition of the rooms in the main (W) range is clear: the hall lay to S of the cross-passage and the pantries and buttery and the kitchen to N. Above the service quarters was a large solar or great chamber, but how it was reached is not quite clear; the newel stair within the main range may only have led to a cellar, and a more likely approach was via the newel staircase beside the W porch and a gallery over the passage. The N range appears to have comprised three sets of chambers, each with one heated room and a smaller unheated one; staircases in the re-entrant angles of the E and W ranges probably led to three more sets of chambers on the first floor (cf Hadham Hall). At the S end of the main range, adjoining the hall, was an apparently unheated room, either a parlour or an antechamber to a parlour in the S range. Possibly the staircase in the SW corner of the courtyard, the largest of the four, led to a parlour on the first floor, because the existence of a wing running S from the S range makes a ground-floor parlour less likely. The E or entrance range abutted the N and S ranges corner-to-corner and was linked to them only by the staircases; it too presumably provided suites of lodgings. In 1628–9 the hall range was converted into stables. In the gatehouse to NW is a wall-painting depicting a lion hunt.[5]

For an illustration, see *English Houses 1200–1800*, Fig 90.

Notes
1. VCH III, 94–5.
2. RCHME 1910, 58–62; VCH III, 94–5.
3. *King's Works*, Vol IV (1963), 149–50.
4. *HH & G*, 305.
5. RCHME 1910, 62.

(77582)
Ponsbourne (TL 304050),

a manor, belonged in the 15th century to Sir John Fortescue, the Chief Justice;[1] he died in 1476 and was succeeded by his son of the same name, who was Sheriff of Essex and Hertfordshire in 1481 and 1486. At this period Ponsbourne must have been a sizeable house. A park, mentioned as being disparked in 1640, may have been made in the Fortescues' time. From 1553 until the early 17th century the house belonged successively to Sir John Cocke and Sir Henry Cocke his son;[2] their arms and others' were still in the hall window in the early 18th century.[3] It was no doubt this house which Paris Slaughter, `Citizen and Factor of Blackwell Hall in London', `repaired and beautified'[4] in the late 17th century, perhaps in 1684.[5] In 1718 Samuel Strode bought the house and is said to have rebuilt it;[6] this must be a mistake, if only of emphasis, because a somewhat later engraving shows what looks like a refaced 16th-century house with pedimented mullion-and-transom windows like those of Knebworth House.[7] Rustication was applied to the whole building, probably by Paris Slaughter. The plan comprised a hall range of six bays entered by a two-storey porch and flanked by two boldly jutting wings, with projections, probably staircases, in the re-entrant angles. The brick foundations confirming the form of the house were dug up in 1875.[8] Lawrence Sullivan, who pulled the old house down after buying it in 1761, built a new one on a higher site. His son Stephen may have altered it because a drawing of c1800[9] shows a quite up-to-date house. After 1875, when the house was sold to James William Carlile, it was refaced and incorporated in a much larger building. Carlile was sheriff in 1882. Cussans' statement[10] that the house was pulled down and rebuilt is incorrect. The house is now divided into flats.

Notes
1. *DNB*.
2. VCH III, 105.
3. Salmon 1728, 212.
4. Chauncy II, 14.
5. C[arlile] nd, 11.
6. Cussans 1879–81, Vol III (i), 290.
7. C[arlile] nd, 3.
8. Ibid.
9. Oldfield Vol III, 316.
10. Cussans 1874–8, Vol II (iii), 271.

(77583)
Popes (approximately TL 259077)

was the manor house of Holbeaches in the 14th century and is mentioned as the manor house of Popes Park in 1542.[1] Its subsequent history is uncertain, although excavation revealed fragments of a 17th-century building;[2] it was burnt in 1746[3] but was rebuilt before 1760.[4] A drawing of c1800[5] shows a house of seven bays spaced 2:3:2; a somewhat earlier and perhaps less accurate drawing[6] shows regularly spaced bays. Both show the house flanked to E by a stable block and to W by a matching service block. Up for sale in 1815, it was bought in 1817 by Lord Salisbury, who had demolished it by 1820.[7] The estate maps of 1785 and 1814 show the house.[8] The present Pope's Farm appears to be a stable block or other special-purpose building converted into a house.

Notes
1. VCH III, 103.
2. Fletcher 1972, 83–6.
3. *Hatfield and its People, Book 7*, 9.
4. Daniell 1923–7, 155.
5. Oldfield Vol III, 720.
6. Charnock.
7. Daniell 1923–7, 158.
8. Hatfield MSS.

HEMEL HEMPSTEAD

(77584)
Boxmoor Place or Hall (TL 037056)

`was originally a Farm House but increased to a little Villa by Mr Almon once Editor of the General Advertizer',[1] ie John Alman, 1737–1805, journalist, imprisoned for supporting John Wilkes.[2] Oldfield's drawing[3] shows a house of three bays with balustrade capped by urns and joined by low wings to single-storey pedimented pavilions, each with a Venetian window. The position of the entrance is uncertain; it was not in the principal elevation. By 1840[4] the balustrade had been removed and the house had a hipped roof; a view entitled `Remains of the Offices'[5] shows the house with a timber-framed gable to rear and a brick range of two storeys, which is perhaps of c1700.

Notes
1. Oldfield Vol III, 349.
2. *DNB*.
3. Oldfield Vol III, 348.
4. Buckler Vol I, 108.
5. Ibid, 109.

(81803)
No. 25 High Street,

of the late 16th century, is a narrow building originally of two storeys and now of three, and of three bays. To rear a chimney-stack with clustered shafts has, above a blocked fireplace to W, a painted representation of a panelled and carved overmantel, probably of the second quarter of the 17th century. In the early 19th century the building was refronted in brick and given Corinthian pilasters.

(77586)
Nos 33–39 (odd) High Street

are of brick and of three storeys. The front is of eight bays; the two in the middle break forward very slightly and between them is a downpipe capped by a rain-water head bearing the date 1728 and the initials W S S; below the two second-floor windows are aprons moulded with an unusual relief pattern. Numbers 33 and 35, which may incorporate an older building, were not examined. Number 37 is a narrow tenement two rooms in depth with a staircase between them, both with corner fireplaces; that in the rear room has been removed. The second floor of Number 39 suggested a similar development.

(77587)
No. 63 High Street

began as a 16th-century timber-framed building of two storeys. What remains is a bay about 16 ft (4·9 m) square with a jettied upper floor (Fig 51); to rear (E) the chimney-stack incorporates flintwork and the stone jambs of a fireplace; the roof, at right-angles to the street, has clasped-purlins and wind braces. Possibly the building had a second bay to N (see below). The position of the staircase is not known. In the mid 17th century the jetty was underbuilt in timber to give a flush front and the first floor was raised and supported on inserted posts and a moulded binding-beam. A wing was added to E comprising on each floor a narrow room leading to a wider one; there is no evidence to show that this replaced an earlier wing. At the same time the original chimney-stack was rebuilt with four diagonal shafts, one serving a fireplace in the narrow room; a relieving timber over the front ground-floor fireplace belongs to this phase and shows that virtually the whole stack was rebuilt. An attic storey was created; the wing roof has raking struts carrying

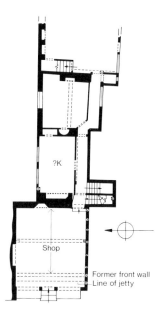

Fig 51 *No. 63 High Street, Hemel Hempstead: plan*

purlins. In the early decades of the 18th century the house was refronted in brick with segmental-headed windows, and a new staircase with moulded balusters and a handrail was built beside the main chimney-stack; presumably it replaced an earlier one in much the same position. Then or perhaps in the late 17th century the N ground-floor wall was completely rebuilt, so as to leave no trace of jettied construction; this may be an indication that the building originally extended in that direction, although there is nothing to confirm this in the adjoining building. In the early 19th century further rooms were added to E and a corridor was formed to S; the present round-topped front to the attic wall was also added. Early in this century a fragment of glass with the date 1620 scratched on it was found somewhere in the house.[1] A rain-water head dated 1736[2] is of doubtful relevance to this building because it is actually on the adjoining property to S.

Notes
1.   RCHME 1910, 111; VCH II, 215.
2.   DoE List.

(77588)
Nos 65/67 High Street,
built *c*1700, formed one house of timber framing with a brick front. A lack of correspondence between the decorative bay system of the front (W) elevation and the structural system behind it, the former having five bays and the latter three, has the consequences that the binding-beams terminate at the front above windows and therefore cannot have been related to partitions, and that chamfers and stops no longer reveal where partitions stood. The plan comprised a wide street (W) range and to rear two wings flanking and projecting slightly beyond the staircase. On the ground floor the kitchen was probably in the longer SE wing; the rest is gutted. On the first floor were two front rooms, the larger of which can be assumed to have been a reception room and perhaps the smaller one too; in the wings were bedrooms with adjoining closets. In the 19th century the building was divided and the adjoining carriageway to N was built over to enlarge No. 67; the height required for vehicles to pass necessitated a flight of steps from the lower first-floor level of the 18th-century house.

For an illustration, see *English Houses 1200–1800*, Fig 304 (plate).

(77589)
Nos 70/72 High Street
are of two bays and two storeys and attics, with internal chimney-stack and lobby-entrance; the houses were not examined but are of interest because they have a pent roof carried on brackets, which is of the kind used above shop fronts of the 17th and 18th centuries.

(29839)
Nos 75/77 High Street
was built in the mid–late 16th century. It was of three unequal bays aligned N–S, the middle one being the smallest, and was of two storeys with a flush front wall; the roof has clasped-purlins. The N and S bays have bearers of quite large scantling and were always floored; the middle bay has a slighter chamfered bearer markedly off-centre, suggesting that a timber chimney-stack adjoining the street front had fireplaces for one or two ground-floor rooms. The building does not conform to any known domestic plan; possibly it was a small inn (cf 27 Leyton Road, Harpenden) not needing the lobby-entrance that might be expected. To S of the S bay chamfering on the bearer extends 4 ft (1·2 m) and stops at the mortise for a post; the purpose and form of this subdivided part (which had no windows, so far as the soffits of the rails show) is uncertain. A wing was added to SE *c*1600 and extended in the late 17th century at the same time as a wing was built to NE. Minor extensions were made *c*1800 and in the 19th century the building was divided into three tenements.

(77590)
Nos 76–80 High Street
form a late 16th-century building with continuous jetty and lobby-entrance; the trusses of the clasped-purlin roof are incorporated in later partitions. The block was raised to three storeys and refronted in brick. The new front is of six bays; the second-floor windows have simple aprons; the fourth first-floor window from S has a shaped head and keystone, probably indicating that it stood above the original entrance to the refronted building. This work is dated by a rain-water head inscribed 1719/T S (No. 78), when the chimney-stack was rebuilt. To W are 19th-century additions, including a kitchen wing to N (No. 80). Numbers 76/78 were formerly the Brewers' Arms PH.

(77591)
Nos 81/83 High Street,
of brick, are of three storeys with cellars and were built *c*1700 (Fig 52). On the ground floor each house occupies two bays of a

Fig 52 *Nos 81/83 High Street, Hemel Hempstead: first-floor plan*

five-bay frontage; in the middle is a carriageway, the bay above it and most of the cellar beneath forming part of No. 81 to S. Number 83 has two rooms with corner fireplaces on each floor, with a staircase between; No. 81 has to W (front) a large first-floor room and two second-floor bedrooms; the rear rooms have fireplaces at the gable end.

(77592)
Lockers (TL 050076)

was owned by John Howe in 1544[1] and remained with his descendants until the mid 17th century; the family built the larger of two gabled wings to S, probably of c1600, which adjoined a hall range at right-angles to N; to N again was prob-

Fig 53 *Lockers, Hemel Hempstead: development plans*

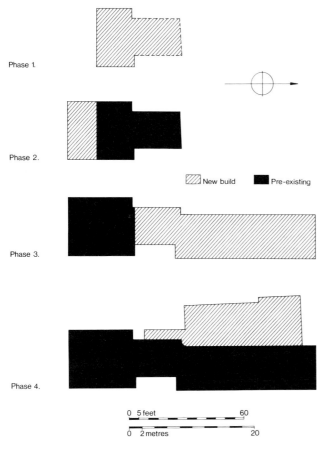

Phase 1.

Phase 2.

New build   Pre-existing

Phase 3.

Phase 4.

0 5 feet   60

0 2 metres   20

ably a bay containing service rooms (Fig 53). A ground-floor room has a plaster ceiling with royal arms, lion, unicorn, griffins and masks in several panels; a first-floor fireplace with four-centred head bears painted initials, one an M, the other indistinct, in the spandrels. In the 17th century a narrower gabled wing was built parallel to the first. In the 18th century the hall range was demolished and a two-storey range of eight bays built. Bills and letters indicate that minor building-works were in progress c1747–50.[2] In the early 19th century this range was rendered and doubled in depth to W.

Notes
1. Subsidy Roll, PRO E179/121/156.
2. HRO, 19960B, 19961, 19964.

(77593)
Manor House, SW of church,

of uncertain date, was demolished c1790,[1] leaving only a mid 17th-century two-storey porch of stone standing. Formerly the arms of Richard Combe were visible[2] but are now defaced. Sir Richard Combe paid for 17 hearths in 1663.[3] The house was replaced on a different site by The Bury (TL 054676), which is of five bays, rendered, with shallower pediment. The staircase, in early 18th-century style, appears to be reproduction work of the present century.

Notes
1. VCH II, 220.
2. Ibid; Buckler Vol I, 159.
3. PRO E179/248/23.

(77594)
The Market House and ancillary buildings (TL 055078)

stood on the E side of the churchyard; their appearance is known from early 19th-century drawings.[1] They comprised principally a long timber-framed range of corn lofts and court room at the N end, the whole above a market-place open to E; in 1825 a town hall with brick end walls gabled E and W was built, probably replacing a gatehouse mentioned in a terrier of 1708.[2] Open-fronted sheds extended N to provide further space for stalls. The terrier mentions the women's market house of three bays, a shop and fifteen butcher's stalls. All the buildings were demolished in stages between 1851 and 1888 and replaced by a market-place and corn exchange built of brick.[3]

Notes
1. Buckler Vol I, 154; BL Add MS 32350, fo 5
2. *HGA* III, 115–17.
3. VCH II, 218–19.

(77595)
68 Piccotts End

was probably a late medieval guest-house for pilgrims; see Rigold and Rouse 1973.

(77596)
Piccotts End Farm (TL 051092)

has an L-shaped plan; the longer arm has, to S, a bay with a lower roof forming the cross-wing of a small open-hall house extending to W. To N the main range incorporates some timber framing, which is all that remains of a building, probably a house, of the same order of size as that to S. This was an example of the unit-system c1500 (see *English Houses 1200–1800*, p 107); c1600 one house was entirely removed except the bay to N and replaced by a block of two-room plan and two storeys and attics, with a lobby-entrance to W. The new house presumably had a wooden chimney-stack because the present brick stack is of the late 17th century, perhaps as late as c1700; to E is a rail about 2 ft (0·6 m) below the wall-plate running the entire length of the elevation, providing for fixed side lights flanking the principal windows, which are of four lights with transoms. Since few if any studs above or below the rail appear to be pegged into it, it is not clear how many of these minor windows were actually built; where one of them should be in the room to N of the stack is an original wall-painting: this room has several other fragmentary wall-paintings; an elaborate all-over classical scheme of foliage and lions' masks was interspersed with three or four black-letter texts, including Proverbs Chapter 10, 27 and Chapter 25, 2. Over the fireplace is a hare hunt.

The principal alteration occurred c1800, when the early

building at the N end was largely destroyed; hence the spindly timber framing of the present N and W walls.

(77597)
Three Gables, Lawn Lane (TL 057059),

of two storeys and attics, was built in the early 17th century and appears to have been added as a N cross-wing to an earlier hall to S. On the first floor the original timber framing survives; it is close-studded, with a rail about two-thirds of the storey height forming a sill for small windows with fixed lights flanking larger ones with casements. Originally it was jettied to N and E. In the late 17th century a wing was built to SW, probably parallel to and sharing a chimney-stack with the old hall, which no doubt served as a kitchen; the new block provided a dining room on the ground floor to W; it has two gabled roofs placed transversely. By then the house approximated to a double-pile plan. A rain-water head dated 1719 may refer to improvement in roof drainage rather than to any addition. In the middle or third quarter of the 19th century the hall was replaced by the present kitchen; the main staircase is of the same date; and the entrance was moved from E to W.

(77598)
The Vicarage

(demolished) to SE of the parish church was timber framed and rendered; it was described in a terrier of 1638 as `lately new built by the present vicar Mr John Taylor',[1] perhaps soon after his induction in 1628.[2] His work must have included three jettied gables of unequal size; they are the only ones of their kind to be even approximately dated.

Notes
1. *HGA* III, 114.
2. Yaxley 1973, 238.

(77599)
`Mr Ginger's villa'

(location unknown) is illustrated in an early 19th-century engraving[1] (*English Houses 1200–1800*, Fig 193).

Note
1. BL Add MS 9063, fo 254.

(77600)
`Mr White's new built house at Two Waters'

was a small late 18th-century villa flanked by pavilions; it is known only from a drawing of *c*1800.[1] The circumstances under which it was built are of interest:

this mansion has been created since the Cutting [of] the Grand Junction Canal (near which it stands) the House and grounds were open fields before that time; not far from this pleasant residence Mr White has established a Timber Yard on a very extensive scale. The situation is well adapted for inland traffick.[2]

Notes
1. Oldfield Vol II, 345.
2. Ibid.

HERTFORD

(39616)
Balls Park (TL 335119)

belonged to Hertford priory and after the Dissolution passed into the hands of the Willis family.[1] In 1637 their mansion house was sold to John Harrison of London, one of the Farmers of the Customs in 1640–1 and MP for Lancaster; he was knighted in 1640.[2] He

built a very fair stately Fabrick of Brick in the Middle of a Warren consisting of a square Pile with a Court in the Middle thereof, every side equally fronted and exactly uniform; the Ceilings within the House wrought with several and distinct Patterns of Fretwork, the steps in the great Staircase wainscotted in Pares, the Hall paved with black and white Marble, the inward Court with Freestone...[3]

In 1643 John Evelyn, visiting the house, described it as `new built',[4] so it was presumably complete by then. For his support of Charles I, Harrison's estates were sequestered and the house lay empty for some years,[5] and only after compounding was he able to reoccupy it. He died in 1669. His son Richard, who did not inherit the house until his mother died in 1705, does not appear to have done any building; but `In his Time this beautiful Seat has been greatly augmented and improved, and the land about it, laid into a Park, by Edward Harison, Esq., his son'.[6] Presumably father and son were sharing the house. Edward Harrison, who acquired a fortune in the service of the East India Company,[7] added long, low wings connected to the existing house by curving colonnades, and altered the house itself considerably. On Edward Harrison's death in 1732 the house descended to his daughter Audrey, wife of Charles, 3rd Viscount Townshend, but not until the death in 1759 of her uncle, who had been living there, did she occupy it.[8] Towards the end of her life she evidently intended to alter the house and may have done so; the only remaining evidence of this is a drawing of the front elevation by the Revd Backhouse dated *c*1800.[9] The wings appear in a drawing of *c*1800[10] but had gone by 1805,[11] removed by Lord John Townshend, who may even have instigated the proposals of 1786. His conversion of the inner courtyard into a vast saloon, lit from the top, must be before 1827.[12] In the late 19th century Balls Park became one of the principal seats of the 5th Marquess Townshend[13] who, in September 1884, was granted £400 for additions to the mansion under the Limited Owners Residences Act; the money was probably for service quarters to W and NW. From the late 1880s the house was leased by Sir George Faudel-Phillips, who was Sheriff in 1900 and purchased it in 1901. Probably he renovated the house extensively, although neither he nor his son Benjamin, who was Sheriff in 1907, are mentioned as builders; the latter is expressly said to have been concerned with the gardens.[14] Further alterations were made *c*1925 by the Scottish architect Robert Lorimer.[15] In 1946 it was purchased by Hertfordshire County Council for a training college.

Balls Park retains hardly any original detail inside and the outside has been considerably altered. Drapentier's engraving[16] shows the house before Edward Harrison began his alterations and something of the original plan can be conjectured from that of 1901[17] (Fig 54). The principal change compared with earlier courtyard houses was the transfer of the hall range from back to front (N). How closely the emphasis given to certain of the symmetrically disposed windows in the N elevation reflected internal arrangements is difficult to say; on the ground floor one of two segmental-headed windows distinguished by a keystone lit the upper end of the hall, and the other appears to have lit a parlour at the W end; between these rooms was probably the pantry. The principal staircase, reached through an ante-room E of the hall, no doubt extended into the re-entrant angle of the N and E ranges. Opposite the staircase was a garden door. The E room is occupied by what is now called the Oak Room, which has preserved its original coffered ceiling. In the S range the fire-

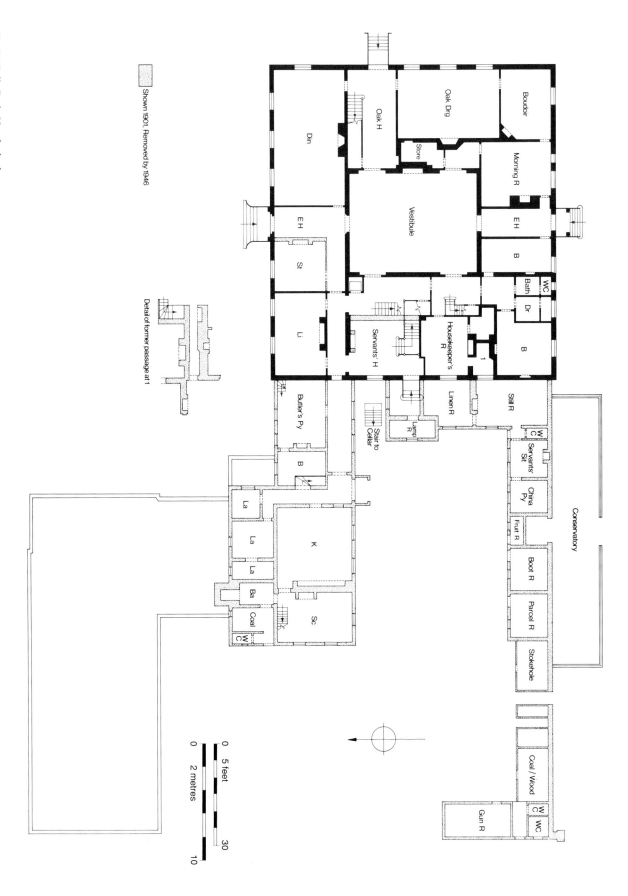

Fig 54 *Balls Park, Hertford: plan*

Shown 1901, Removed by 1946

Detail of former passage at 1

Din

Oak H

Oak Drg

Boudoir

Store

Morning R

Vestibule

E H

E H

B

B

WC

Bath

Dr

St

Li

Servants' H

Housekeeper's R

1

B

Butler's Py

Stair to Cellar

Lamp R

Linen R

Still R

W

C

Servants' Si

China Py

Fruit R

Boot R

Parcel R

Stokehole

Conservatory

B

La

La

La

Ba

Coal

C W

K

Sc

Coal / Wood

W

C

WC

Gun R

0   5 feet   30

0   2 metres   10

place in the morning room allows for a corridor to N, returning along the W range, which may have been an original feature (cf Pishiobury Park, Sawbridgeworth, plan). Room use in the S range is unknown. Service rooms with cellars underneath were in the W range, the kitchen being perhaps in the SW corner; this room, like the Oak Room, once had a large chimney-stack that was subsequently hollowed out to create small rooms. Little can be said about the first floor: two major rooms over the hall and Oak Room were reached from the principal staircase; two other staircases, one at each end of the W range and corresponding approximately to those existing, are likely; with corridors or lobbies to N and S they would be sufficient. A first-floor room in the middle of the S range has a simple plaster ceiling and was perhaps a lodging chamber.

Edward Harrison's work can be dated between his return to England from India, which was perhaps not long before he became MP for Hertford in 1722, and 1728.[18] The wings he added were of one storey and attics, raised on a basement, and the colonnades were capped with urns. At the front of the house he replaced the top of the frontispiece by a pediment; removed the pediments of the ground-floor windows; replaced the original dormers by fewer and larger ones, pedimented and with more restrained detail; and probably rebuilt the main staircase. Lord John Townshend's work early in the 19th century included painted perspectives in the saloon or hall, which were replaced early in the present century by reproduction Jacobean panelling,[19] and the cutting of a passage through the large SW chimney-stack to give easy access to the service wing. Townshend probably rebuilt all the chimney-stacks.[20] By 1901 the house had attained more or less its present form. The principal change in the plan, one probably due to Sir George Faudel-Phillips, was the creation of a first-floor gallery running the full length of the E range.

Notes
1. *Visitations* 1634, 104.
2. VCH III, 412–13.
3. Chauncy I, 520–1.
4. Evelyn *Diary*: 15 April 1643.
5. *Cal Cttee for Compounding* ii, 1523.
6. Salmon 1728, 71.
7. *Gent Mag*, November 1732, 1083.
8. VCH III, 413.
9. Illustration, RIBA Catalogue of Drawings.
10. Oldfield Vol III, 422.
11. Clutterbuck Vol II, 158.
12. Dated sketch, Luppino.
13. VCH III, 413.
14. W— 1912, 587.
15. Sangster 1972, 41.
16. Chauncy I, 520.
17. Plan in sale catalogue, Hertford Museum.
18. Salmon 1728, 71.
19. W— 1912, 587.
20. Buckler Vol III, 39.

(77601)
Bayley Hall (TL 325126)

was referred to in 1621 as `the manor of Bayly-hall'.[1] The present house dates from the early years of the 18th century; it was described in 1721 as being lately in the tenure of Edward Blackmore, Gent.,[2] who was mayor of Hertford in 1713 and may possibly have built it. By *c*1800 it was in the possession of Henry Allington Esq. `who is Coroner for the County and has several times served in the office of Under-Sheriff'.[3] It was

described as the residence of Henry Allington when advertised for sale in 1845.[4]

Apart from the removal of a large segmental pediment over the three middle bays,[5] the house is still well preserved; the staircase, several of the fireplaces and much of the panelling of *c*1700 remain. The ground-floor plan (Fig 55) comprised four rooms on either side of the hall and staircase; the service rooms were in the basement, the kitchen being beneath the dining room and the pantry beneath the hall. On the first floor the two principal front bedrooms had unheated dressing rooms. The second floor had a similar plan.

In 1900 the house was purchased for use by the headmaster of Hertford School and for boarding pupils;[6] no doubt then the E extension with its separate entrance was built. The whole is now used as offices.

For an illustration, see *English Houses 1200–1800*, Fig 220 (plate).

Notes
1. VCH III, 493.
2. HRO, Hertford Borough Records, lease 9 September 1721.
3. Oldfield Vol III, 395.
4. *The Hertfordshire Mercury and County Press*, 26 April 1845.
5. Oldfield Vol III, 394.
6. VCH II, 93.

Fig 55 *Bayley Hall, Hertford: ground and first-floor plans*

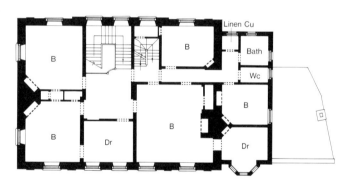

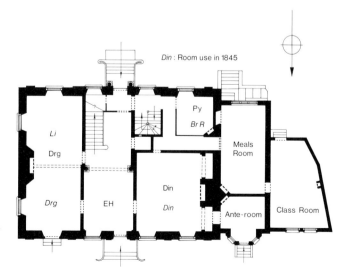

(39618)
The Castle (TL 324126)

formerly incorporated an aisled hall known only from a plan of 1587;[1] the plan was first published and the significance of the aisled hall brought out by Sir Alfred Clapham.[2] It may well have been of the 12th century. In 1236 'the aisle of the King's hall towards the East which is covered with straw was ordered to be covered with shingles'.[3] A survey of the castle in 1327 states that 'the King's great hall with 2 chambers attached' are almost ruined.[4] Later, when a large fireplace was added to S, the high table was presumably moved to one side of the hall, perhaps facing the oriel; a comparable arrangement, of the late 14th century, existed at Dartington Hall (Devon).

The only medieval building still standing within the castle wall is the gatehouse built by Edward IV between 1460 and 1465. It is of three storeys and of locally made brick with dressings of stone from Merstham (Surrey) for most purposes, but from Ashwell for chimney-pieces and from Kent for those parts where hardness was most needed, ie the treads of the newel staircase and the corbels supporting the machicoulis.[5] Timber mouldings, joints and carpenters' marks were recorded during restoration in 1971.[6] All the buildings except the gatehouse were demolished c1608.[7]

Notes
1. PRO MPF 161.
2. Clapham and Godfrey nd, 41–5; also *King's Works* Vol II, 678–9.
3. Cal Lib 1267-72, 288, No. 2429.
4. PRO E101/465/15.
5. *King's Works* Vol II, 680–1.
6. *Newsletter* **30**, 1971.
7. *King's Works* Vol III, 257.

(77602)
Epcombs, Hertingfordbury (TL 317122),

originated as a pre-Conquest farm;[1] its descent after 1606 is uncertain.[2] It is of brick and appears to incorporate a comparatively small house of the 17th century with hall range and cross-wings to E and W, that to E extending farther to N; the earliest datable features are brick bands on the N gable wall of the E wing, which are stepped up over the windows of the ground and first floors as if they were part of a refacing of an earlier building, but there is nothing to confirm this idea. The siting of the principal chimney-stack, serving fireplaces in the hall range and W wing, is characteristic of vernacular rather than gentry practice. In the early 18th century the hall range was refronted and made almost flush with the wings; then or somewhat later a range was added to N, partly overlapping the E wing, to create a double-pile. In the early 19th century a new entrance was created to W, with an entrance-hall traversing the wing to reach a new staircase, perhaps sited near to its predecessor, to N of the principal chimney-stack; this change created in effect an end-entrance. The W wing was either rebuilt or refaced then; the first floor is higher than in the remainder of the house. In 1902 a wing was added to SE in a style matching the existing work; it comprised a large smoking room with bedrooms above and a single-storey servants' hall at the rear. The work was carried out by Wood & Ainslie, architects, for Mr C F H Leslie.[3]

Notes
1. Hoskins 1955, 46.
2. VCH III, 467.
3. Plan in possession of Mr H L Thompson-McCausland.

(39617)
Goldings, Bengeo (TL 310142),

of the late 17th century, was the centre of an estate corresponding to the manors of Waterford Hall and Half Hyde;[1] separation of land from manorial rights may account for confusion about the builder of the house. Humphrey Hall, who paid for 11 hearths in 1663 and 1673,[2] 'had a fair House in the Parish, called Thomsons, where he lately died';[3] that was in 1695 and he is said to have built Goldings in the 1680s;[4] but 1650–60 is more likely. An alternative builder, it has been suggested, is Thomas Hall who owned the house from 1695 to 1748.[5] The earliest drawings show Goldings much as it was when occupied by the Dowager Lady St John prior to its sale in 1770 to Robert Emmott, who was Sheriff in 1775; it was still the house of 'Emmott Esq' c1800.[6]

The main body of the house was a rectangle about 82 x 55 ft (25·0 m x 16·8 m) with an L-shaped service range and stables extending to NE;[7] the S (correctly SE) elevation, of seven bays and of two storeys and attics and cellars, had a wide pediment over the three middle bays;[8] the N elevation, of the same length, was of nine bays and had a pediment of the same width as that to N extending over the middle five bays;[9] the roof was hipped to E and W. The sale particulars of 1770 describe the interior in considerable detail. In the attic storey were seven servants' bedrooms and two large bedchambers with Portland chimney-pieces and closets, and, on the first floor, five large bedchambers 'neatly wainscoted' with marble chimney-pieces, a dressing room and four closets. The Hall, 'large, lofty and elegant' had 'a dome ceiling stuccoed in compartments...[and] the floor is paved with Portland'; the architectural details were 'all whitened and gilt'. The staircase, of mahogany, had stuccoed wall panels with festoons, and stuccoed cornice and ceiling; a 'Breakfasting Parlour' had a purple marble chimney-piece and 'the mantle and tabernacle frame are carved and particoloured'; the drawing room had a veined marble chimney-piece, its carved overmantel being supported by 'trusses' (possibly console brackets). In the dining parlour the wooden details were of mahogany and the walls were stuccoed with enriched panels. A large stable block to E was of c1700.

Robert Smith inherited the estate in 1861, was Sheriff in 1869[10] and commissioned a new house from George Devey;[11] it was built between 1871 and 1877 a short distance to W.[12]

For an illustration, see *English Houses 1200–1800*, Fig 144 (plate).

Notes
1. Sale particulars, 1770, HRO, 75080.
2. PRO E179/248/23; E179/375/31.
3. Chauncy I, 529.
4. Hertford Civic Society *Newsletter* 1978, 2.
5. *Newsletter* **9**, 1958.
6. Oldfield Vol III, 426.
7. Tithe Map 1843, HRO, DSA 4/16.
8. Oldfield Vol III, 424; Charnock; Edward Dayes, BM Prints and Drawings, 1870-5-14-3063.
9. Late 18th-century drawing, Ashmolean Museum, Gough Maps 11 fo 586; Luppino, early 19th century.
10. *Newsletter* **9**, 1958.
11. Girouard 1973, 54, 81.
12. Cussans 1874–8, Vol II (ii), 36.

(77603)
Dimsdale House, No. 16 Bull Plain,

is of brick and of two storeys with cellars and attics. A release dated 16 March 1704 states that this property had on it 'the Case Shell or Outside' of 'a new Messuage or Dwelling House which is not yet finished';[1] one of the releasors was Richard Hoddy, bricklayer. The new owners were John Dimsdale the younger and John Dimsdale the elder, the former being a doctor, Mayor of Hertford in 1706 and 1711 and knighted in 1725; he died in 1726 leaving a son Thomas, a physician famous for the discovery of inoculation.[2] The house is symmetrical, of five bays; a sixth to S was added *c*1706, when `Mr Dimsdale' was granted a lease for 99 years of ground on which to build part of his house.[3] Originally the central part of the roof was flat, covered with lead and surrounded by a balustrade. The ground plan comprises four rooms around an entrance-hall and staircase-hall[4] and the first floor will have been similar. The first-floor rooms matched each other until those at the front were made into one, with a fireplace to N; this may have been done in 1843 when the building was taken over by the Literary and Scientific Institution, which had its library on the first floor.[5] Subsequently it was turned to industrial use until restored in 1973.[6]

For an illustration, see *English Houses 1200–1800*, Fig 275 (plate).

Notes
1. *Newsletter* **6**, 1955.
2. *DNB*.
3. HRO, Hertford Borough Records, Vol 47.
4. Staircase details are drawn in *Newsletter* **39**, 1975.
5. Lutyens and Andrews 1945–9, 41.
6. Kirby 1974, 29–32.

(77604)
The Old Vicarage, Church Street,

is dated 1631 on the front door (reset in a late 18th-century door-case; the date may refer to the greater part of the house, although earlier and later work is incorporated. The late medieval S wing, the oldest part, has a crown-post roof and is of two bays jettied to E; it has mortises for brackets at the ends of the middle binding-beam; the joists, of large scantling, were painted with chevrons and roundels alternately and there may have been extensive painted decoration on the walls. This wing implies the existence of a hall range earlier than the present one of two storeys – presumably an open hall. The hall is heated by a fireplace (somewhat altered) which is small in relation to the size of the room and shows no definite signs of early 17th-century origins; the arched opening has quite a high head and only a continuous chamfer with no stops. In the N wing the principal room, with a fireplace on a cross-wall, has unusual proportions for the early 17th century, suggesting the incorporation of a small room to E, as at Bride Hall (Wheathampstead), where kitchen and service room were together. This wing may be coeval with the hall, although the chamfer stops could be thirty years later. The chronology remains uncertain, but the date on the door is possibly misleading and may apply to the N wing, rebuilt before the middle of the 17th century as the size of the internal stack suggests; the shallower hall stack is of the late 17th century. In the early decades of the 18th century a staircase turret and some small rooms were added at the rear of the hall, the staircase off the NW corner of the hall was rebuilt and probably the exterior rendering was added. A terrier of 1709 lists five rooms on a floor, two storeys, one cellar, two butteries and four closets.[1]

Note
1. Lincolnshire RO, Terr/22/541.

(77606)
No. 7 Cowbridge

is an early 17th-century house of two storeys and attics, standing at right-angles to the street; the attic storey has a jettied gable; in the rear gable is an ovolo-moulded staircase window. The staircase was rebuilt in the early 18th century.[1]

Note
1. Moodey drawing, HRO.

(77607)
House on S side of Fore Street

(demolished) is known from a Luppino drawing; it was of two bays with a square bay window on the first floor and two boldly jettied gables in which were attic windows. It was probably built in the early 17th century.

(79519)
The Salisbury Arms, Fore Street,

was The Bell until 1820; early 17th-century surveys describe it as being between Church Lane to E, Cow (now Bell) Lane to W, the Market Place to N and the vicarage garden to S; it can probably be identified with an inn called The Bell mentioned in 1431.[1] In 1756 it had 25 beds and stabling for 20 horses.[2] The N range facing the Market Place has a first-floor jetty, now underbuilt, which returns to E and W; the plan (Fig 56) may have comprised two ground-floor rooms, one to N and one to S, on each side of

Fig 56 *The Salisbury Arms, Fore Street, Hertford: first-floor plan prior to partial demolition*

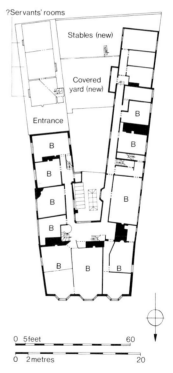

the entrance, although if this were so, only the latter had a fireplace. There were perhaps five rooms upstairs and the main roofs ran N–S. Probably each wing had a staircase adjoining the courtyard. The timber frame of this part of the building may be of the early 15th century as the simple brackets suggest. During the 16th century both wings were extended, that to the E being perhaps the earlier; it comprised no more than two rooms on each floor and was jettied to E. The extension of the W wing is jettied on both sides to provide a gallery facing the courtyard and is of *c*1600, when the front range was altered considerably. Much rebuilding took place *c*1600; an early 19th-century sketch[3] shows a jettied semi-attic storey roofed as two cross-wings to a short middle range and three three-sided bay windows on the first floor; an ovolo-moulded window was observed when exposed briefly in 1973.[4] The next major improvement, in the mid 17th century, entailed reorganising the plan around a new staircase in the E wing; it served the principal first-floor rooms overlooking Market Street and, by a gallery over the courtyard, those in the W wing too. This staircase does not now rise to the second floor and perhaps never did, in which case another staircase served the quite important rooms on the second floor; but the position of the main staircase implies that by then the middle part of the front range had been extended to S and the chimney-stack built. In the early 19th century the front jetty was underbuilt; the top storey heightened and made flush with the storey below; new bay windows put in; and stables and outhouses to the S end rebuilt. All this is probably early Victorian work. During the 19th century the main staircase was considerably altered; the present pargeting and the date 1570 were applied towards the end of the century. Recently much of the E wing and the buildings at the S end of the yard were rebuilt.

Notes
1. Johnson 1962, Pt 1, 65–6.
2. PRO WO 30/49.
3. Luppino.
4. G E Moodey, HRO, Box 12, 192.

(77605)
House in Cowbridge

(demolished),[1] probably of *c*1600, was of two bays with internal chimney-stack; its principal interest is the two jettied gables, a feature now rarely to be seen in the town (cf the Vicarage, Hemel Hempstead).

Note
1. Luppino drawing, 1829.

(77608)
Nos 3–13 Fore Street

form a range of timber-framed buildings of three storeys and attics; No. 13 has its principal front facing the Market Place. The front walls are flush and are still largely covered by the original boldly scrolled plasterwork. The whole range was built in the third quarter of the 17th century and perhaps can be identified with an entry in the Hearth Tax returns for Michaelmas 1662, when John Holywell, Gent., paid for 11 hearths in his own house and for 36 in five of his houses untenanted.[1] If this return is correctly applied to Nos 3–13 Fore Street, the discrepancies between the number of houses and the number of hearths may be due to the difficulties of assessment in the first collection of Hearth Tax, especially as related to empty houses.[2] Each house had two rooms on each floor, all with fireplaces except those in the attics. It is possible to reconstruct the original plan of the second floor with reasonable certainty. Why one tenement should be smaller than the others is not known; no evidence of any reduction in size was noticed. Of the remaining five tenements those to E and W were larger than the others; all had two principal rooms, both heated, on each floor; and there were two smaller unheated rooms. The first floor no doubt followed the same plan while the ground floor was modified to the extent that a shop occupied the front room, or part of it; and there was no doubt a passage to the staircase at one side. All rooms were

approached from the staircase through a lobby. A Rowlandson drawing of *c*1800[3] shows the return facing the Market Place with a boldly projecting cove of plaster, roofed with tile, protecting the shop fronts; no doubt all were like that as built.

For illustrations, see *English Houses 1200–1800*, Figs 261 (plate), 262, 265 (plate).

Notes
1. PRO E179/248/24/1.
2. Walker 1957, *xiii*.
3. Hertford Museum.

(77609)
Nos 25–31 Fore Street

form a range of timber-framed and plastered buildings of two storeys and attics; they were probably built in the late 17th century although the only evidence for this lies in their materials, proportions and some corner fireplaces now blocked.

(79521)
Nos 28/30 Fore Street, and No. 5 Church Street,

formed the principal part of the White Swan Inn, which appears to have been built around a long narrow courtyard like the adjoining Salisbury Arms. It shows three principal phases of construction, the earliest part (No. 5 Church Street) being a jettied building, which has on the first floor exposed framing of *c*1500. This continues to S as a long range in which very few old features can be seen; No. 5 has to E what may have been a gallery, providing the only hint of an inn before the late 17th century. The next phase, probably late 16th century, is the W range, some 36 ft (11·0 m) long and running parallel with Church Street; it was jettied to N and W originally and may have been the cross-wing of a range extending E along Fore Street, one of the two ranges flanking the principal pedestrian entrance to the inn. On the first floor were two rooms; the larger, to S, was about 20 ft by 24ft (6·1 m x 7·3 m) and, if the chimney-stack is coeval, may have been entered from a staircase in about the same position as the present one, while the smaller room perhaps opened off the larger one and was subsidiary to it. There is nothing in the architectural evidence to establish that this part of the building was used as an inn at this period; that cannot be shown to have happened until the middle of the 17th century. The E part fronting Fore Street was built, anything older on the site being swept away; it must have required a new staircase from which the rooms were reached; and a second new stair was provided to serve the older range in which a corridor was formed. Possibly the present staircase is a replacement in much the same position as the original one, leading directly from the yard. When Church Street was widened *c*1800 the W side of the building was cut back.

For illustrations, see *English Houses 1200–1800*, Figs 247 (plate), 248.

(77610)
No. 42 Fore Street,

of brick, rendered, and of three storeys, was built as a shop with living accommodation above and is one of the few examples of the Egyptian style. It was built shortly after 1824 when the previous building on the site, the Turk's Head inn, was pulled down.[1] The original shop front remains but inside the building is destitute of old features.

Note
1. G E Moodey, letter, *CL* **127**, 26 May 1960, 1201, with photograph and woodcut of *c*1850.

(77611)
Nos 88–96 Fore Street,

a brick house of the early 18th century, was heightened to three storeys in the early 19th century. Nearly all old internal features have been removed and the chief interest is the plan of the first floor (Fig 57). Two principal rooms were to N, probably with an unheated room between them. On both first and second floors the room to E is entered by a slightly inset door; this suggests that when the building was heightened a corridor provided access to all front rooms; but the setting-back of the stair head to

Fig 57 *Nos 88–96 Fore Street, Hertford: first-floor plan*

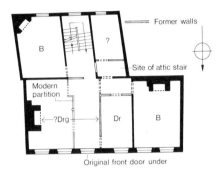

S, leaving a wide landing, argues that this was not the original arrangement. That is tentatively suggested in Fig 57: a drawing room to E, a principal bedroom to W, and a dressing room or closet interconnecting with one or both. Possibly a dressing room or closet was partitioned off the bedroom to SE, both being reached from the staircase via a lobby.

(77612)
Nos 99/101 Fore Street

occupy a brick house built at the end of the 17th century; No. 99 is a separate shop to W. The front doorway, originally pedimented, opens into a panelled passage between two rooms, the slightly larger one to left (W) being entered from the passage and the other from a door to N. The staircase, which has twisted and turned balusters up to the first floor and plainer turned ones above, has been altered; probably the ascent has been made gentler, especially the first flight. In the staircase-hall were arches with keystones breaking forward from the ceiling cornice (cf Thorley Hall). In the 18th century the eaves cornice was replaced by a parapet. In the mid 19th century a shop front was inserted in the front room to W; a small doorway replaced the original entrance; a wing was added to N and the adjoining room altered; and the staircase rebuilt with chamfered newel posts.

For an illustration, see *English Houses 1200–1800*, Fig 276.

(77613)
No. 130 Fore Street,

of brick and of two storeys and attics, was built in the mid 17th century; it is dated by moulded beams, raked balusters (reset), and the chimney-stack to E which has six octagonal flues. The plan comprised a main range parallel with the street and two rear wings separated by a narrow yard. It can perhaps be identified with one of three houses built by John Kelinge, probably just before 1649.[1] All four ground-floor rooms have fireplaces; the location of the pantry is unknown. The wings were extended c1900; the house was privately occupied until the late 1920s.

For an illustration, see *English Houses 1200–1800*, Fig 260.

Note
1.   M[anchester] 1945–9, 135–6.

(77614)
House, possibly now Nos 7–9 Market Place,

appears in the background of a Rowlandson drawing (*English Houses 1200–1800*, Fig 265) and is the subject of an anonymous drawing in Hertford Museum. The building is of interest for its decorative external treatment. Most of the drawn details are of the third quarter of the 17th century: the panelled effect of the plasterwork, possibly bolection moulded; the mullion-and-transom bay windows; the pediments of door and windows; and the gabled top storey. The panelled chimney-stack has a somewhat later appearance; the four large ground-floor windows are late 18th or early 19th centuries; the second-floor windows are alterations of the similar; and the casement window on the first floor probably replaced a small two-light pediment window. The plain flat termination at the bottom of the bay windows suggests that they originally stood on a flat shop canopy. If the building is correctly identified it has been gutted of all old features.

(77615)
No. 14 Market Place

was built in the 16th century; it was of two storeys, probably jettied and may not have had a chimney-stack. In the late 17th century it was doubled in depth and heightened to three storeys; the corner fireplaces are presumptive evidence of date although little original detail survives. Subsequent alterations include the present staircase, subdivision of the larger rear room, and an addition at the rear; most of these took place in the 19th century.

(77616)
No. 3 Old Cross,

now much altered, is known from a ground plan made in 1860[1] which shows what the smallest kind of house and shop was like. The position of the fireplaces, which are on the long walls, unlike No. 5 Old Cross (see below), suggests that it was built in the 18th or early 19th century.

Note
1.   Hertford Museum.

(77617)
No. 5 Old Cross,

an interesting example of a small house and shop (Fig 58), was built in the early 18th century, apparently by the subdivision of an older timber-framed building, because there is evidence that

Fig 58 *No. 5 Old Cross, Hertford: plan*

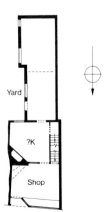

a jetty has been underbuilt. The evidence for the shop is the absence of a fireplace in the front room and the existence of a large coved brick support for the corner fireplace of the room above. It is not absolutely certain that this coved support is coeval with the subdivision of the property, although no parallel for it has been found in those cases where a fireplace has been removed. Behind the shop was the living room, with a corner fireplace; presumably cooking was done there. Two narrow rooms flanking the back yard are later additions and contain nothing to show what their original functions were; perhaps scullery and wash-house. The two bedrooms each have a corner fireplace; there are attics.

(77618)
Nos 10/12 Old Cross

incorporate the jettied cross-wing of an open-hall house of c1500; it has Kentish framing; the doorway from hall to wing had an ogee head. In the late 17th century the hall range was rebuilt with two storeys in thin timber framing with straight braces; a chimney-stack with four conjoined octagonal shafts backs on to the cross-passage. The hall range was refronted in brick in the early 19th century.[1]

Note
1. Drawings by G E Moodey of details now concealed, HRO.

(77619)
No. 23 Old Cross,

of two storeys and attics, is timber framed with a brick front and was built in the early–mid 18th century. It has a central staircase and two rooms on each floor (Fig 59), heated by fireplaces at the gable ends. The original staircase remains; the sash windows with thin glazing bars and the shop window are early Victorian.

Fig 59 *No. 23 Old Cross, Hertford: plan*

Ground floor: Entrance   Shop front

(77620)
No. 27 Railway Street

comprises a squarish jettied block to S, facing the street, and an adjoining part which once had an open arcade to E. (A similar arcade, infilled, exists at the White Hart, Salisbury Square – not examined.) Despite the jetty, which suggests an earlier date, the corner fireplaces and lofty first-floor rooms are unlikely to have been built before the Restoration. A long N wing jettied to E has mid–late 17th-century fittings probably coeval with the front range. In Hertford Museum are nine painted panels removed from a room to the front of the building in the late 19th century; the panels are of the late 17th century and the paintings of the early 18th century.[1] Subjects are mostly classical: Diana, Mars, Venus and Cupid; Flora and Pomona; Venus and Cupid; Mars; Ceres; the Judgement of Paris; one still life and possibly a second. A tenth panel is now lost.[2] A curious feature of the S elevation is the central jettied projection for a staircase, its

lowness being necessary to accommodate the first landing; since the staircase, ostensibly of c1700, cuts across panelling of that date, the projection must have been built when the staircase was moved, probably c1900.

Notes
1. Rouse report.
2. Inf. Mr Gordon Davies.

(77621)
No. 2 St Andrew's Street,

of three storeys, is ostensibly of the early 18th century with nothing of earlier date inside, but can best be explained by

Fig 60 *No. 3 St Andrew's Street, Hertford: reconstructed east floored bay (top); reconstructed plans and section of beam (showing the building before alteration, based on a drawing by Mr A C Carter of East Herts District Council) (bottom)*

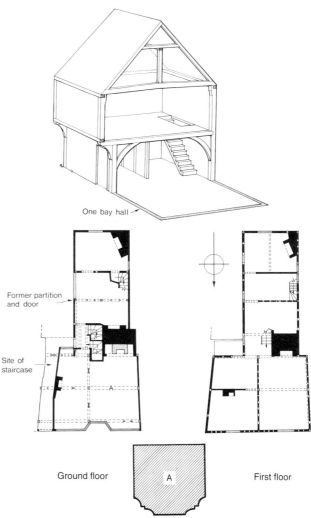

One bay hall

Former partition and door

Site of staircase

Ground floor   A   First floor

postulating piecemeal rebuilding of an older structure. The entrance is in an unusual position, at the W end instead of in the middle of the front; but since the staircase is in the customary relation to the entrance-hall, at the rear, and no other position is possible, this must be the original arrangement. Presumably either the whole of the ground floor or at least the E room was in commercial use, perhaps, as now, as a shop. The staircase led to the two most important first-floor rooms; that to S has a smaller intercommunicating room to W and may have been a drawing room; that to N was possibly the dining room and the room below it the kitchen. The corridor is a later alteration and if any communication existed between the principal front room and the E end of the house it was by a low door past the secondary staircase; but quite possibly there was none, and the E end of the house was connected with a ground-floor shop. An anomalous feature in an 18th-century house is the internal stack; its position, and that of the principal staircase, suggest the rebuilding of a three-cell lobby-entrance house of *c*1600. In the early 19th century a wing was added to N, blocking the staircase window; the present shop was built at the end of the 19th century.

(77622)
No. 3 St Andrew's Street

was built *c*1500 as a small single-ended Wealden house. The W bay formed the hall; the sawn-off ends of the inner wall-plate forming the original top of the hall wall are visible but since the posts supporting them show no trace of the usual cove (cf The Old Rectory, Aspenden) or any brackets the exterior may have been finished more simply than usual. The service bay was divided into two rooms, apparently not partitioned from the hall (Fig 60); possibly the front room was a shop. To S of the cross-wall is a first-floor doorway, perhaps original, as if the upper room had been approached from the hall. The range to N has a crown-post roof with braces to the collar-purlin. A wing added to S in the late 16th century has a chimney-stack which is now of 18th-century and later brickwork but originally was probably of timber, with fireplaces to N and S, the latter room being the kitchen. On each floor of the wing were three rooms, with no indication of use. The jetty was underbuilt, the hall refronted, and a chimney-stack and corner fireplace added to S *c*1700. In 1976 the whole building was carefully restored.

(77623)
Nos 4/6 St Andrew's Street,

originally one, are timber framed with a brick front, of two storeys and attics, and were built in the late 17th century. The ground floor was considerably altered by the division of the property, but some bolection-moulded panelling remains. Division into two shops has made the position of the entrance uncertain; probably it was in the third bay from W. The plan comprised two large rooms facing an entrance-hall; behind the latter, in a short wing, is the staircase, which has moulded balusters. On the first floor to S were three rooms with fireplaces; some bolection-moulded fireplaces remain. In the early 19th century conversion into two shops with living accommodation entailed either building a new staircase or rebuilding an existing secondary stair towards the E end.

(77624)
Nos 22/24 St Andrew's Street

was built in the early 17th century; the first floor is jettied but not the two gables of the attic storey, unlike some other houses in Hertford (cf No. 7 Cowbridge). The ground plan, approximately square, comprised four rooms; to W a passage from street to rear may be original; the room to SE (Fig 61) appears to have been a shop with a passage to W, a door to N and probably another to E; neither this room nor that to SW has a fireplace. The two rooms to N have back-to-back fireplaces; the late 18th-century staircase probably occupies the site of the original one. On the first floor are four rooms each of the same size as its counterpart below; the addition of a fireplace in that to SE closed

the original access to the NE room and made the former a passage room; it also necessitated building a lobby in the adjoining room to W.

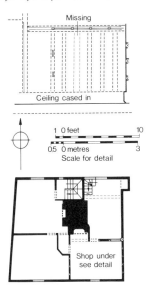

Fig 61 *Nos 22/24 St Andrew's Street, Hertford: detail of shop on ground floor (top); first-floor plan (bottom)*

(77625)
No. 23 St Andrew's Street

is a small, late-medieval Wealden house with a storeyed bay to W; two doorways (blocked) can be seen at that end of the hall. The hall was floored over in the 17th century and a chimney-stack inserted; a fireplace with three-centred head is exposed on the first floor. Then or later the building was heightened slightly, rendered, and divided.

(77626)
No. 28 St Andrew's Street,

a small house of the early 18th century, is remarkable for the high quality of the brick detailing.[1] The rooms are arranged on either side of a central staircase-hall, a large one to W and two smaller ones to E, all with fireplaces; the service rooms, including the kitchen, were possibly in a now demolished range to S. The upper floors correspond exactly in plan to the ground floor, with the addition of a square closet to N over the entrance. A mature tree makes it impossible to improve on the photograph published by Lloyd.

For an illustration, see *English Houses 1200–1800*, Fig 277 (plate).

Note
1. Lloyd 1925, 225, 280.

(77627)
Cawthorne, No. 51 St Andrew's Street,

timber framed and of two storeys and attics with a small cellar, is of the early years of the 18th century. The front is now rendered and plain except for a narrow wooden band joining the ground-floor window lintels, but an early 19th-century drawing[1] shows other such bands joining the sills and lintels of the first-floor windows, and vertical strips running from ground to eaves and framing the mullion-and-transom windows. These, with the pilaster-like boards at each end of the front, produced a panelled effect in the whole elevation and must have been the last attempt to represent framing externally as a decorative treatment. The plan comprises a large room with fireplace to E (correctly SE) – the hall, in 17th-century terminology; an unheated entrance-hall off which opened a small room with fireplace which may have been an office for a professional man; and a smaller room to W, probably the dining room near the rear kitchen. Although the original first-floor dispositions are less certain they may have been largely preserved except for a rearrangement in the S wing. About the beginning of the present century the interior underwent extensive refitting.

Note
1. Luppino.

(77628)
No. 52 St Andrew's Street,

of brick and of three storeys, was built in the late 18th century. The plan comprises four rooms around a central staircase-hall. In a rear wing to NE is the kitchen; the room above it has a re-used ovolo-moulded bearer.

(77629)
Nos 19–23 West Street

are a range of houses of two storeys, cellars and attics, built c1700; only No. 21 was examined. It comprises on each floor a large room to W (front) and a smaller one to E. The construction of the chimney-stack is of interest (see *English Houses 1200–1800*, p 189).

For an illustration, see *English Houses 1200–1800*, Fig 311 (plate).

(77630)
Bridgeman House, Nos 37a–37d West Street,

takes its name from an organist at All Saints' church who died c1874. It is an unusually well-built internal-chimney house of two storeys and attics and of lobby-entrance plan. It has an arcaded front and chimney-stack with arched sunk panels and was built in the mid 17th century. To W was the parlour, to E the hall-kitchen, and to E or S of the latter there was probably a service room. It is surprising that the staircase, which has heavy splat balusters, is not in a wing or turret; it may have been reset in its present position although until the balusters were concealed by boarding in the 19th century they could have been seen to advantage. Additions were made to E, W and S in the 18th and 19th centuries and it is now four dwellings.

For illustrations, see *English Houses 1200–1800*, Figs 267 (plate), 268.

(77631)
Amores, Hertingfordbury (TL 307119)

was held by copyhold of the manor of Hertingfordbury, which belonged to the Duchy of Lancaster.[1] The name derives from the family name `at More' and was described in 1540 as a tenement formerly called John Amores. For most of its history it appears to have been leased out by the copyhold tenants. A rental of c1560[2] describes the property as being in the holding of William North, who described himself as of Shephall in his will dated 21 December 1563.[3] In the period between 1630 and 1680 it appears to have been in the hands of a considerable number of tenants. Although the house has a complicated history it has hardly any closely datable features except an inscribed fireplace.

The oldest part appears to be the cross-wing to S, which is presumably late medieval; the coeval or earlier hall was replaced by the present main range in the mid 16th century, the latter being dated by the first-floor fireplace to N inscribed in black-letter characters `1563/wyllyam northe'.[4] The plan is unusual in detail. To N was the parlour with a fireplace much like the one on the first floor, with moulded jambs terminating in a quatrefoil stop and four-centred head with carved spandrels. The hall has a lateral fireplace placed very close to the parlour partition, presumably to allow for a large window lighting the lower end of the hall; two doors (blocked) led to the cross-passage.

The wing rooms are large for service rooms; possibly that to E was always a parlour. The first-floor rooms of the hall range were open to the roof; the tie-beams are cambered. In the mid 17th century two identical part-octagonal staircase turrets were added to W and S and attic rooms were created; a large kitchen fireplace was inserted in the wing to W, backing on to the cross-passage. Two staircases of good quality imply separate suites (cf Aston Bury). Mullion-and-transom windows replaced older ones with ovolo-moulded mullions, one of which is exposed in the gable wall to N. Probably the rendering seen in old photographs was applied at that time. In the late 19th century bay windows were added and gabled dormer windows replaced the original segmental-headed ones. In 1959 the whole house was carefully restored.

Notes
1. Mr H J Secker supplied details of occupation.
2. Inf. Mr Secker, citing HRO, D/Ept T 640.
3. Inf. Mr Secker.
4. *Newsletter* **14**, 1963.

(79532)
Hertingfordbury Park (approx TL 313118)

takes its name from a park created before 1285.[1] In the reign of Charles I it was acquired by Sir William Harrington `who converted the Lodge into a good House fit for his own Habitation, where he lived sometime'.[2] From him it had passed to Thomas Keightley (1580–1663)[3] by 1643, when his cousin John Evelyn visited him.[4] Keightley's grandson, also Thomas, sold the house in 1681 to John Cullinge[5] who built `a very fair House' before his death in 1687[6] and, to judge from its appearance in the Drapentier engraving, rebuilding was extensive, if not complete. Thenceforth its appearance was unaltered prior to its demolition in 1816.[7] The house was built on a high basement lit by two-light mullioned windows, which were the only old-fashioned feature of an otherwise very up-to-date front; other windows had flat arches and hung sashes. The emphasis given to the middle window suggests it lit a dining room and the large round-headed window above it implies that the middle attic room was specially important. Some repairs were undertaken and a drain was made in 1799 when the house was found to be suffering from damp.[8]

For an illustration, see *English Houses 1200–1800*, Fig 151 (plate).

Notes
1. VCH III, 464.
2. Chauncy I, 535.
3. *DNB*.
4. Evelyn *Diary*: 3 March 1643.
5. VCH III, 465.
6. Chauncy I, 535.
7. VCH III, 465; Oldfield Vol III, 488; Charnock.
8. HRO, Panshanger Papers, Box 52; agent to Lord Cowper, 24 January 1799.

(77633)
Little Manor, Hertingfordbury (TL 307120)

is of brick and largely of the 17th century but its L-shaped plan, with front range to W and kitchen wing to S, implies a complicated development.

The W range may originally have been of three-cell plan with service rooms (now demolished) to N. The middle room had a chimney-stack to N, the evidence for which is brickwork in the cellar corbelled out for a hearthstone and, in the roof, a break in the purlins at approximately the same point, although no change was noted in the external brickwork; possibly the stack backed on to a cross-passage; the room to S, lacking a fireplace, was presumably an unheated parlour. In the late 17th century the wing was added to E in order to centralise the plan; it incorporates a large chimney-stack with six diagonal shafts for two large ground-floor fireplaces and two smaller first-floor fireplaces. The unheated parlour became a dining parlour, with a wider fireplace than now; to E were, successively, hall-kitchen and service room, probably with a staircase to NE where a two-light window may have lit the stair head; a cellar was dug beneath the former hall, which became a second parlour (cf Hyde Farm, Abbots Langley); to N a small room, presumed to replace a larger subdivided bay, may have provided closets and similarly on the first floor. At this time the walls of the W range were rebuilt in brick. The entrance may have been screened off from the parlour to S, providing an approximately symmetrical front to W; the staircase positions are unknown but a two-light brick window above the present front entrance may have lit one. The subsequent total removal of the hall stack and its replacement about 6 ft 6 ins (2·0 m) to N suggest that it was of timber.

In the 19th century the front to W was refenestrated and rendered.

HERTINGFORDBURY

(77634)
The Old Curatage, Birch Green (TL 294116),

was built in the middle of the 17th century with two storeys and attics. It has two principal ground-floor rooms, the hall (to N) and parlour (to S); an internal chimney-stack and (originally) lobby-entrance; a gabled stair turret to E and lean-to pantry adjoining the hall to E. The lean-to is contemporary with the hall, its framing being tenoned and pegged in at its N end. The ground-floor rooms were lit only by windows to W. A curious feature of the hall is that the bearer, chamfered and stopped, terminates on a shaped bracket of brick which is corbelled-out in front of the chimney-breast; this was perhaps to avoid either the need to provide a binding-beam on which to terminate it, or the risk of fire in carrying it to the stack. Neither of the upstairs rooms originally had a fireplace. Early 19th-century additions included an oven (and the fireplace to N was rebuilt); first-floor fireplaces and a room to S of the staircase. These together with a narrow entrance-hall formed then give the house an early Victorian appearance.

HIGH WYCH

(77635)
Bursteads (TL 476172)

was associated with the manor of Chamberlains, alias Burstead, which is first recorded as having manorial status in 1524 and is so called from the family of that name.[1] The width of the house,

about 23 ft 6 ins (7·2 m)[2] suggests it may have been built in the late 14th or early 15th century (cf Chells, Stevenage). Access was not permitted.

Notes
1. VCH III, 342.
2. Ibid, plan.

HINXWORTH

(77636)
Cantlowbury, later Harvey House (TL 237408),

took its names from two of the families who owned it, the former, derived from Cantilupe, in the 12th and the latter in the 18th century.[1] The only record of the house is a brief description of it as being `built round a court' and of stone, with mullioned windows.[2] It is shown, without any indication of a courtyard, on the enclosure map of 1802[3] and was demolished in the mid 1860s.[4] The mistaken identification of the site with Hinxworth House[5] is corrected by Lucas.[6]

Notes
1. VCH III, 236.
2. Lucas 1908–11c, 161.
3. HRO, QS/E 36.
4. Lucas 1908–11c, 161.
5. Cussans 1870–3, Vol I (iii), 11.
6. Lucas 1908–11c, 161.

(77637)
Hinxworth Place (TL 238396)

can be equated with the reputed manor of Pulters,[1] named `from one Pulter, who was the Owner hereof in the time of Edw IV and held it of the King by the yearly Rent of 10s 8d'.[2] The reference may be to John Pulter Esq. of Hitchin, sometime Sheriff of Bedfordshire, who died in 1485.[3] Subsequently it came into the possession of Andrew Gray, who died in 1614;[4] his arms, depicted among several coats in glass now gone,[5] confirm the otherwise uncertain identification of Pulters with Hinxworth Place. These details of the tenurial history may help to explain a rather unusual building.

The house comprises a main range facing E and built of local stone in the late 15th century, which is unusual for its date in being of two storeys throughout; and a wing to S of mixed construction in stone and timber which was added in the 16th century. A drawing of c1800[6] shows the S wing extending to E of the main range.

To E the original doorway, square-headed with moulded jambs and two-centred arched opening, has a label with head stops; in the sunk spandrels are two shields on which are scratched the date 1870 and the initials E S and J S, the latter for John Sales who bought the manor in 1881[7] and before then was doubtless tenant. It must have been on one of those shields that Salmon noted in 1728, `In Stone over the House Door, Gray's Arms quartered with three more'.[8] In the W wall opposite the front door is its plainer counterpart, the two together defining the screens-passage. To the S was the hall, heated by a wide fireplace (now blocked) of which the jambs and lintel are traceable; the latter is flat, with a sharply cambered top. Adjoining the entrance doors and forming the N end of the hall is a timber-framed partition, in which are two doorways with four-centred heads opening into the former service rooms; the partition between the latter has been removed, as has a third doorway opening off the passage to a staircase. The head-beam of the partition is moulded towards the hall, and since the mouldings are returned along an axial bearer and also along two binding-beams there must always have been an upper storey throughout the house. The moulded beams and the position of the fireplace establish that for a manor house that is late medieval, the hall had somewhat unusual proportions, the ratio of length to width being about 2:1 (39 ft 6 ins:20 ft (12·1 m: 6·1 m)); equally uncharacteristic of the period is the predominance of the hall over all other ground-floor rooms, which are comparatively unimportant. To E, near the S end, was probably a bay window; the only original windows, to E and W in the service rooms, are of two cinquefoiled lights in a square head.

To W a doorway N of the fireplace led to a staircase (now removed) and up to a first-floor doorway that lacks any old detail; the latter opened in to a great chamber, probably as big as the hall, which has, to W, a fireplace with moulded jambs and a four-centred opening within a square head; it is comparatively shallow and has a tiled back. A smaller room to N has a fireplace (blocked) with depressed four-centred head; since it has a relieving arch of squarish clunch blocks exactly like that over the other fireplace it is likely to be original, although the mouldings of the jambs are stopped well above hearth level in a way commonly taken to indicate the 17th century. Above the fireplace is a single wall-painting of c1500. Presumably the two first-floor rooms did not intercommunicate; a doorway to W in the N room, with a two-centred head and a broad chamfer to E, is unlike any other original detail but can hardly be of any later period; probably it was at the head of the second staircase (cf Redcoats, Wymondley); an original window in the wall to N lit the top of the minor staircase. The smaller upper room has a window to W, of a single pointed cinquefoiled light, rebated for a shutter. The roof has been completely rebuilt.

The parlour wing to S is an addition of the mid 16th century; it masks a shallow buttress aligned with the W wall of the main range which can be seen internally on the first floor. The existing part of the wing provided a principal ground-floor room or parlour which has moulded binding-beams and bearers, and a fireplace with some classical detail; in the early years of the present century the window to W still had some of the armorial glass recorded in the 18th century. The demolished E part of the wing had a chimney-stack to S. Wall-paintings in the N first-floor room of the main range are of the late 16th century.

In the early–mid 17th century the main range was refenestrated with mullion-and-transom windows, of four lights on the ground floor and three on the first floor, and one of five lights was put in to W of the parlour. Three of the removed windows, two of three and one of four lights, were re-used in the lean-to block to W which was added to provide service rooms and perhaps a dairy. Although the masonry of this part of the house is eroded and so concealed at crucial points that it is difficult to be certain, the suggestion that it is of two builds[9] appears to be unfounded. If the interpretation of the lean-to is correct the manor house was by then no more than a large farmhouse, with the hall used as a kitchen. The present internal chimney-stack does not appear in Oldfield's drawing, and although on general grounds it is hard to believe it can be as late as the early 19th century, it may be part of a general renovation of the house at that time which included demolition of the E half of the wing; the removal of the buttress at the front, where the new masonry bears the scratched date 1826; and the insertion of some sash windows and staircases. Whatever the date of the internal stack may be, the old lateral stack will have been demolished then. In 1912 it was said that sixty years previously the then entrance-hall and kitchen were separated only by the brick stack, without

any partition between them.[10] A scratching on a door-head in the wing `T Instrip (Shefford) 1832' may be connected with this phase of alteration.

Apart from some minor alterations in the late 19th century that is how the house remained until a thorough and systematic restoration c1970.

For illustrations, see *English Houses 1200–1800*, Figs 30 (plate), 43.

Notes
1. VCH III, 233, n5; Oldfield Vol III, 365.
2. Chauncy I, 64.
3. Chauncy II, 174.
4. VCH III, 237.
5. Oldfield Vol III, 237–375; *Gent Mag* 1784 (ii), 745–6.
6. Oldfield Vol III, 364.
7. VCH III, 236, 237.
8. Salmon 1728, 341.
9. Lucas 1908–11c, 159, plan.
10. VCH Vol III, 233.

HITCHIN

(82743)
House, location unknown,[1]
is of interest for a two-storey timber-framed porch projecting boldly out into the street and supported on wooden pillars, an architectural feature that has now disappeared from Hertfordshire towns; the whole front and porch were treated with plaster rustication; that, and the hipped roof and absence of a jetty to the porch suggest the late 17th century. The date of the house is unknown.

Note
1. Oldfield Vol IV, 151.

(77638)
The Brotherhood, Nos 3–5 Bancroft (TL 184292),
is generally identified[1] with the hall of the Guild of Our Lady, which was founded by royal licence in 1475.[2] It was originally jettied to E. No old work can now be seen on the ground floor, which was divided by partitions; a photograph[3] taken during restoration establishes only one as being original. The first floor formed a large hall (48 ft x 21 ft (14·6 m x 6·4 m)) open to the roof; the roof of five bays has trusses with cambered and arch-braced tie-beams, above which are queen-struts and arch-braced and cambered collar-beams; all the trusses, wall-posts, purlins and windbraces are moulded. Its subsequent development is impossible to trace in its present condition, split up into offices and shops. A SW wing is an addition; it bears the painted and not necessarily authentic date 1588. In 1815 the building was said to have a `porch, hall, entry and great parlour Much painted glass, but destroyed when this gentleman [either the occupier, Charles Nicholas, or the owner, George Beaver] sashed it'.[4] In 1879 it was said to have been `lately so *improved* that nothing but the massiveness of the walls remains to indicate its age'.[5]

Notes
1. VCH III, 37.
2. Ibid, 18.
3. Hitchin Museum.
4. Dunnage 1815.
5. Cussans 1874–8, Vol II (i), 56.

(29843)
The Croft, Bancroft,

was demolished in 1964–5.[1] New windows and details were added to the front and the garden elevation was rebuilt in polychrome brick c1866.[2]

Notes
1. Mercer 1975, 169; *Newsletter* **16**, 1965.
2. Photographs of 1866 in Poole and Fleck 1976, Plates 51 and 52; garden view, painted 1873, in Hine 1927–9, Vol II, opposite p 162.

(77639)
The Hermitage, Bancroft

comprised a group of rendered timber-framed buildings of various dates. The garden elevation was refronted in the 18th century; the three middle bays were flanked by pilasters and had a pediment; the two flanking bays on each side were capped with urns.[1] This elevation was rendered and refenestrated in the late 18th century.[2] Part of the house and garden were removed in 1874 to make Hermitage Road; the remainder disappeared in 1927.[3]

For an illustration, see *English Houses 1200–1800*, Fig 274 (plate).

Notes
1. Drawing dated 1789, BL.
2. Poole and Fleck 1976, Plate 50.
3. Hine 1927–9, Vol II, 431, 436.

(77640)
Nos 23/24 Bancroft

form a two-storeyed jettied range of four bays which was built in the 16th century. Both houses were extended to W; the wing to N is of c1700. The two chimney-stacks to W of the two N bays (No. 24) do not appear to be earlier than the early 18th-century eared architraves of the first-floor fireplaces. The first floor to E was rendered and refenestrated with paired hung sash windows in the 18th century and somewhat later the roof was rebuilt with a double pitch to provide a second floor. (Only No. 24 to S was examined.)

(77641)
Nos 31/33 Bancroft,

of c1500, formed a pair of single-ended Wealden houses with the respective storeyed bays to E; the clasped-purlin roof over the former hall is heavily sooted. Number 31 (to S) has an inserted first floor with ovolo-moulded beams of c1600; it probably had a timber chimney-stack which was rebuilt in the 18th century; it was refronted c1966 with a flush wall, preserving the plastered coved eaves of the hall inside. To N No. 33 was refaced in brick in the early 18th century.

(77642)
No. 34 Bancroft,

called Bancroft House, is of mid 18th-century appearance and of five bays, the middle one projecting slightly and emphasised by the ramping-up of the parapet. An earlier building is incorporated; the ground-floor room to S has chamfered beams, probably 16th century, and on the first floor are slight indications of an old roof. The plan comprised a large room to S and a smaller one to N; the latter incorporated originally the present narrow entrance-hall; and a third room to N was enlarged, probably incorporating part of a wide covered entrance, in the 19th century, when the building underwent great alteration, as it did again in the 1960s.

(77643)
No. 87 Bancroft,

built during the late 16th century, is of two storeys, jettied, and two bays. No traces of an original chimney-stack can be seen. The existing stack and staircase are of the late 17th century, the former having been heightened in the 18th century. To E are later extensions; part of the adjoining 16th-century building to N is now incorporated.

(77644)
No. 105 Bancroft,

built c1500, is of interest for the way a compact street frontage was used; its development is not very clear because little internal timbering is exposed. It comprises a covered carriageway to N, a very short open-hall range (now occupied by an entrance-hall to N and chimney-stack) and a jettied cross-wing; it is close-studded. The wing, of two bays with one room on each floor, has a moulded binding-beam spanning the ground floor; the first-floor framing is not jointed to the adjacent principal post to N, as if the wing were a rebuilding of part of the hall. In the late 16th century the hall range was truncated by the covered way which is almost as high as the hall eaves; the room over it has close-studding and a clasped-purlin roof. To E 18th-century and later extensions have been added.

(32290)
Nos 114/116, Bancroft;

For a description of this house, see Mercer 1975, No. 189.

(77645)
No. 32 Bridge Street

has a two-storeyed W wing, jettied to N and W, which is probably of the late 15th century; no doubt an open hall stood to E. In the late 16th century the latter was rebuilt as a jettied range of two storeys; a chimney-stack to W provided fireplaces in the ground-floor hall and the principal room of the wing; its siting to S within the range suggests that a staircase and lobby-entrance were to N; a doorway was here until 1970. To E of the hall a covered carriageway is equivalent to the cross-passage of the normal late-medieval hall; in the jettied E bay two ground-floor rooms corresponding to buttery and pantry existed until recently. If the E bay is coeval with that to W the plan resembled that of the simpler kind of inn by c1800, if not earlier. In the early 19th century the building was converted into cottages and in 1970–1, after a long period of neglect, was restored for use as offices.

(77646)
The George Inn, Bucklersbury,

an inn of some importance in the 17th and 18th centuries, comprises a timber-framed range of late medieval origin fronting the street and a courtyard to E flanked by wings to N and S. The oldest portion comprises part of one of the long walls of the hall in which is a mutilated three-light window, with hollow-chamfered wall-plate and mullions; the moulded principal post of the open truss and part of the tie-beam and an arch-brace; and to N of the covered carriageway, two adjoining doorways for a pair of service rooms. The open hall was about 22 ft by 19 ft (6·7 m x 5·8 m). To S was a two-storey block apparently jettied towards the hall, and forming a kind of canopy; the ground floor was divided by a partition into two rooms and on the first floor the wall to W has close-studding. The only element of the ground plan to suggest that the building was designed for an inn is the wide carriageway defined by hollow-chamfered posts and with twin doorways to N (cf No. 19 High Street,

Puckeridge, Standon). A short wing to SW may be coeval with the front range; its only datable feature is a chimney-stack built of tile and incorporating a tile relieving arch; the fireplace, which has been rebuilt, may originally have been like those at Redcoats, Wymondley. This wing was probably jettied although the joists are concealed at the relevant point; to E is a stair trap which may have served both the first-floor room above and the adjoining one to S of the hall.

In the late 16th or early 17th century the hall was rebuilt with a jettied upper storey and attics, and probably the S wing was extended to W. There is no sign of an inn gallery at this period so presumably the enlarged wing had its own staircase. The wing to N may be in part of the same date. Towards the end of the 17th century an open first-floor gallery was added to S of the courtyard, with turned balusters and moulded handrail; it may have been necessitated by the building of the wide first-floor room to which it leads and which now has no datable features (cf No. 3 High Street, Puckeridge, Standon). A short timber-framed range to W, probably also of the late 17th century, shows little finish in its construction and may not have provided inn rooms on the first floor. Subsequent changes include the gutting of much of the ground floor and some rebuilding in brick. The use of much of the lower storey of the wings as stables well into the present century is probably of very long standing. (Considerable parts of this building could not be examined.)

For an illustration, see *English Houses 1200–1800*, Fig 310 (plate).

(77647)
No. 15 Bucklersbury

incorporates to S a jettied range at right-angles to the street, and of the 15th century; it is of two storeys and two bays, has close-studding and shows no definite signs of being a house or part of one; such studs as are traceable to N and S, and the position of the staircase, virtually rule out the possibility that it was a wing attached to an open hall. It was presumably a shop with a large storeroom upstairs (cf No. 2 Market Place, St Albans); the stair-case is in the position of the original one because the first-floor joists are otherwise complete throughout, and the position of a small upstairs window to W is governed by it; the window is off-centre to the gabled roof but central to the room space excluding the staircase. On the ground floor the binding-beam and wall-posts dividing the two bays have a double chamfer so that except for the staircase, the foot of which was partitioned off, the ground floor was one room. A mortise in the one surviving front post may be for some kind of fixed counter.

The building was extended by a two-storey addition of one bay to E which has flush walls and crown-post roof; another to N is jettied and has a clasped-purlin roof.

(77648)
No. 9 Churchyard

is timber framed and rendered and is only of interest for the evidence, visible on a modern staircase from the first to the second floor, that it was built with two storeys and semi-attics; at the front, where the cutting-through of the wall-plate can be seen, it was heightened to three storeys. The original build is probably late 16th century; a rear wing is perhaps late 17th century; the heightening took place in the early 18th century.

(77649)
Nos 10/11 Churchyard,

of two and a half storeys originally, were built in the late 16th century as separate buildings. They were heightened in the late 17th century and refronted in the 19th century.

(77650)
No. 4 High Street

was built in the late 16th century; it is of two bays and was origi-nally of two storeys and semi-attics, both the upper floors being jettied; there is a wing to W. A chimney-stack to N of the street range[1] was originally external, projecting into a wide carriage entrance; it has been removed completely, leaving as its only trace a large blank space in the first-floor framing of the wall to N. In the rear wing the principal first-floor room has a bay window with ovolo-moulded mullions and casement lights; immediately to E is the frame of a small window which no doubt had fixed lights. To W the framing is open on the first floor, implying that the range beyond it, which is of a different build, is coeval or earlier. In the late 17th century the wide entrance was made into a covered gateway; *c*1800 the street front was raised to three storeys, made flush and refenestrated, including first-floor bay windows; the wing was also height-ened. In the present century the covered entrance was incorpo-rated into the adjoining shop.

For an illustration, see *English Houses 1200–1800*, Fig 256 (plate).

Note
1. Hitchin Museum, photograph 52/14.

(77651)
Nos 2/2a Market Place

surround a small courtyard on all sides and are in several occu-pations. The front (S) range incorporates a timber-framed building of two storeys, perhaps of the late 16th century, of which some evidence remains on the first floor to NE. An internal chimney-stack may be coeval but has no definite evidence of date. To E of the courtyard a short timber-framed range was probably built in the late 16th century and incorpo-rates a chimney-stack of that date; in the late 17th century a first-floor fireplace was added which has a clay fireback bearing at the top the initials I H M and a date which is probably to be read as 1670; otherwise the surface is covered somewhat irregularly with devices of various kinds.[1] Above the fireplace are several embossed plaster devices: fleur-de-lys, thistles, a Tudor rose, a crown and stars. In the mid 18th century the S range was height-ened to three storeys and refaced in red brick with blue headers.

For an illustration, see *English Houses 1200–1800*, Fig 255 (plate).

Note
1. Smith, J T 1978, 127–8.

(77652)
No. 4 Market Place

(formerly The Red Cow PH) is of brick, of three storeys and semi-attics with a gabled street front, and was built in 1676; the date is cut in a riser of the staircase going up to the second floor. It is an internal-chimney house set at right-angles to the street, both rooms on each floor having a fireplace; the only unusual feature of the plan is the length of the front rooms, which may be connected with the use of the ground floor as a shop (Fig 62). The precisely dated simple architectural details include chamfer stops, two-light windows with chamfered mullion lighting the staircase, a plain mullion-and-transom window on the first floor to N and some cupboard doors and part of the moulded shelf over a fireplace on the second floor. The semi-attics have always been used as warehouse space. The principal alteration was the addition, in the mid 18th century, of a small block to NW, the original purpose of which is not known.

For an illustration, see *English Houses 1200–1800*, Fig 255 (plate).

Fig 62 *No. 4 Market Place, Hitchin: first-floor plan*

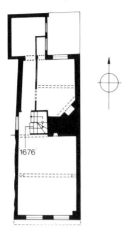

1676

(77653)
Nos 8–12 Market Place,

once The Artichoke inn, formed the W, S and E sides of a court-yard; that to N had disappeared before 1912;[1] that to E was demolished and that to S altered in 1970–1. The two-storeyed range to W, probably late 15th century, is jettied and has a crown-post roof with two-way braces; the front (W) had close-studding but elsewhere the studs were more widely spaced; there is no trace of an original chimney-stack. On the first floor a gabled projection replaces wall framing and must be a later addition; it stands over a wide doorway with shouldered lintel; a gateway forming part of The Artichoke is shown here on a plan of 1812.[2] A chimney-stack was inserted *c*1600; a first-floor fireplace has moulded jambs and four-centred head. To rear (E) are indications of an inn gallery, apparently an addition, but such timbers as remain are plastered over. To E of the courtyard was a four-bay range of two storeys and attics, built towards the end of the 17th century, with a staircase wing to E. Then or subsequently the W range was refronted and doubled in depth. To N of the W range what is now a single-storey shop was prob-ably a late 17th-century row of cottages, of one storey and attics.

Notes
1. RCHME 1910, 122.
2. Trinity College, Cambridge, Archives, *Plan of the Impropriate Estate...belonging to Trinity College, Cambridge*, 1822.

(77654)
No. 20 Market Place,

a three-storey timber-framed building, has no datable features but the boldness of the jetties (over 2 ft (0·6 m) for the first floor) may denote the early 15th century; brackets from posts to bearers on both ground and first floors are unusual and may also be an early feature. In the 16th century a carriageway was created to W. A taller block of three storeys, cellar and attics, originally a separate house and (presumably) shop, was added to E in the late 17th century; it appears to have had a lobby-entrance to E towards Sun Street and retains a few original features, including a ground-floor fireplace carried on a coved support visible in the cellar (cf. No. 5 Old Cross, Hertford), and

windows on the first and second floors which have four lights with a big cased mullion dividing two pairs of casements. In the late 17th or early 18th century the building was refronted on a line about 7 ft 6 ins (2·3 m) in advance of the original front, which may represent either an encroachment on the Market Place or the incorporation of the site of a stall.

(77655)
No. 23 Market Place

was built *c*1500 as a narrow and apparently unheated range, jettied, with a moulded fascia beam, and probably of two storeys. On the first floor the front wall was largely occupied by a window of which the rectangular mortises for the mullions are exposed. The second floor is also jettied; no timberwork is exposed, which suggests that it is a heightening of the 18th century; however, the first-floor posts are not thickened as might be expected if they had originally supported tie-beams.

(77656)
Nos 103/104 Queen Street

(demolished) formed a late medieval house comprising an open hall with a wing to S; the N end of the hall range and a wing to N had disappeared by 1910. The hammer-beam roof, about 19 ft (5·8 m) in span, was moulded with a double ogee;[1] an old photo-graph of it has been redrawn (Fig 63). The building is claimed, on inconclusive grounds, to have been the Tanners' Guildhall.[2]

Notes
1. RCHME 1910, 125.
2. Hine 1923–7, 302–3.

Fig 63 *Nos 103/104 Queen Street, Hitchin: hammer-beam roof*

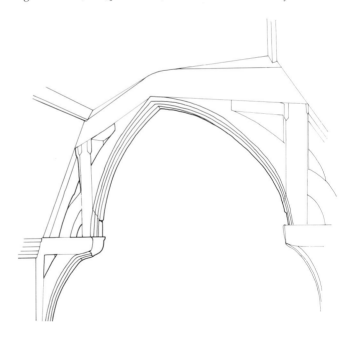

(77657)
The Sun Hotel, 3/4 Sun Street,

developed in several phases during the 17th and 18th centuries into a large inn on three sides of a courtyard. The inn is first referred to in 1575[1] and by 1600 was the meeting-place for the borough sessions;[2] a two-storey range to SE is of about that period and implies the existence of a building facing the street, so that the inn by then was of considerable size. The first-floor corridor in the SE range shows no positive sign of being original but, if not, separate staircases must have given access to groups of rooms. Later phases of development are shown on the first-floor plan; hardly any old details remain. The range fronting the street is of the early 18th century and has plat bands dividing the elevation into three storeys; the first-floor band is stepped up over the wide carriage entrance. A large assembly room was added to E of the N range in 1770, the ground floor being used to stable six horses and to house open chaises.[3] Other rooms listed then in a survey of the college properties[4] are: best parlour, travellers' room, second-best parlour, two sleeping rooms, smoking room, laundry, pantry, bar, kitchen, scullery, club room, excise office – all, presumably, on the ground floor; four bedrooms in front (one being subdivided later to form the narrow room to S), two small ones (to N, one being over the bar and the other over the kitchen), ostlers' room, soldiers' room, assembly room and market dining room on the same floor; four attics in front, three lumber rooms over the kitchen used occasionally as soldiers' rooms; followed by a list of cellars, service rooms, stables and barns. In the late 19th and early 20th centuries the buildings on the W and N sides of the yard were greatly altered.

Notes
1. Hine nd (Sun Hotel), 3.
2. Ibid, 4.
3. Trinity College, Cambridge, Archives, *Plan of the Impropriate Estate...belonging to Trinity College, Cambridge*, 1822.
4. Trinity College, Cambridge, Archives.

(77658)
No. 5 Sun Street,

of brick and of the mid 18th century, has two storeys and attics and a basement lit at the front by an `area'; the three middle bays of five break forward and are pedimented. The plan is square; to NE was the kitchen, with a wide fireplace; it has perhaps been enlarged to incorporate a service room to S. The use to which the other rooms were put is uncertain; the large room at the front (to NW) may have been a dining room and the smaller one to SW an office. The large first-floor front room was probably a drawing room.

In the present century the house has on two occasions been greatly altered.

(77659)
No. 7 Sun Street,

of three storeys, is timber framed and rendered and jettied on the first floor. It contains no datable features earlier than the mid–late 17th century but the part to S fronting the street was probably built in the 16th century. It has two ground-floor rooms; that to W has a fireplace, probably original. A mid–late 17th-century addition to N included a staircase and kitchen; *c*1830–40 the whole was heightened by one storey and bay windows were added on the ground floor and round-headed windows on the first floor; a further enlargement including a new entrance encroached on the house to E.

(77660)
No. 13 Tilehouse Street,

of two storeys with cellar and attics, was built in the second quarter of the 18th century; it is of six bays, the first-floor windows having shaped aprons and the brickwork being generally of good quality. Originally there were three ground-floor rooms with a stair projection to S (correctly SE). The front doorway, sash windows with thin glazing bars, and wing to W with Mansard roof can all be dated to 1789 (rain-water head). Somewhat later a SE block was added, followed *c*1830 by the large bow-windowed room called the ballroom. Extensive additions and alterations have been made to adapt the building as offices; little old detail survives.

(77661)
No. 19 Tilehouse Street

incorporates a small cross-wing that by inference was joined to an open hall to E. The wing, which has a clasped-purlin roof, comprises one room on each floor and has to S (rear) a blocked first-floor window; the staircase is modern but occupies the same position as the original one. Subsequent developments took an unusual course and are not easy to put in sequence. In the mid 17th century a chimney-stack was built in the hall; it has a fireplace for the ground-floor room of the wing but there is no sign of a fireplace backing on to it to serve the hall, which seems to have declined in importance then. At much the same time the wing was extended to S, with a large room on each floor; a chimney-stack to E has some moulded brickwork; above it the large modern shaft probably replaces some form of conjoined shafts. In the early 18th century the hall was rebuilt; the bay to W became an entrance-hall and perhaps in part a service room; that to E became a kitchen by the addition of a wide fireplace S. In the early 19th century the W bay was refronted in brick and bay windows were added here and to E.

(77662)
No. 42 Tilehouse Street,

a plain-looking house of brick and of three storeys, was built in the late 18th century by the Revd Lynch Salusbury; originally it was flanked by detached single-storey pavilions[1] giving it the appearance of a small country house (cf Bleak House, St Albans). The pavilion and courtyard to W were replaced by an early Victorian wing of two storeys; the pavilion to E may have been heightened and joined to the house at that time to form a service wing; it is considerably lower than the rest of the house. An extension of the E wing to N has neo-Georgian details and is probably of *c*1900. In recent years the house has been divided into flats.

Note
1. Oldfield Vol IV, 153.

(77663)
Nos 76/77 Tilehouse Street

is a small, late medieval, open hall with some timber framing exposed externally; the roof has a cambered tie-beam with queen-struts and clasped-purlins. There is no sign of a storeyed end bay or wing and the hall has comparatively low walls.

(77664)
The Coopers Arms, Nos 81/82 Tilehouse Street,

probably of *c*1500–20, comprises a hall originally open to the roof and cross-wings to E and W, the former being jettied to N and S; the setting-out is unusually irregular. The idea that it was the guildhall of the tilers and masons, in part based on misconceptions about its original form,[1] is unfounded. The hall was comparatively small and was entered from a cross-passage within the wing to E, but it was enriched with mouldings to an unusual degree; the tie-beams are moulded and crenellated towards the hall and plain towards the wings; and the principals and tenoned purlins are moulded. The jettied service wing to E retains few old features. The wing to W is of stone on the ground floor and has timber framing, not jettied, above. To N and S are windows of nine cinquefoiled lights grouped under three depressed four-centred heads; that to S is treated as a bay window with returns of one light; doorways to E and W have depressed four-centred heads and moulded jambs. There is nothing to show that this wing had a fireplace originally. The building is quite unlike any known guildhall and no other special purpose suggests itself so it was presumably the house of an important burgess. In the 17th century a floor with ovolo-moulded bearers was inserted in the hall, a staircase turret was added to N, and then, presumably, a chimney-stack was built in the wing to E; these changes can perhaps be linked to the date 1614 formerly visible in one of the upper rooms.[2] In the late 17th century the chimney-stack was rebuilt with four clustered shafts[3] all with deep corbelled caps (cf Brookmans, North Mymms, *English Houses 1200–1800*, p 188); they provided for fireplaces in the hall and on both floors in the wing. A brick-fronted wing of one storey and attics was added to W *c*1700,[4] perhaps as part of the conversion of the house into cottages. When the wing to W became a public house *c*1800[5] the stone windows were mutilated. Then or later the clustered chimney shafts were rebuilt as a single rectangular stack.

Notes
1. Aylott 1912–14, 78–81; VCH III, 5; RCHME 1910, 121.
2. Aylott 1912–14, 81.
3. Buckler Vol III, 59, 60.
4. Ibid.
5. Aylott 1912–14, 81.

(77655)
No. 85 Tilehouse Street

incorporates to E a boldly jettied cross-wing, which originally stood at the end of an open hall; it has a roof of two bays with a moulded crown-post and a ground-floor doorway with four-centred head and sunk spandrels. The present street range may occupy the position of wing or bay to W.

(77666)
No. 95 Tilehouse Street

presents the appearance of a continuous jetty but incorporates two, separate late medieval buildings, each of two bays with a crown-post roof.[1] The part to N has timbers of comparatively large scantling, binding-beams thickened at the ends and a crown-post with four-way struts; that to S has much slighter timbers and the crown-post has a reverse-curved brace. There is no trace of an original chimney-stack or staircase.

Note
1. Cf houses in Bridgefoot Street, Ware; Mercer 1975, 170–1.

(82742)
Former inn, location unknown,[1]

was unusual in having, in a jettied front of two bays, a gateway with a wide four-centred arch, rather like a gatehouse; nothing comparable appears to survive in Hertfordshire. The other bay had, on the ground floor, a three-sided bay window, probably lighting the hall.

Note
1. Oldfield Vol IV, 151.

HODDESDON

(77503)
Broxbourne Bury (TL 353071),

the most important 16th-century house in the county, is of brick with stone dressings; the roofs are mostly of tile with some Welsh slate, and in general appearance it is a late Victorian version of the Elizabethan style.

The complex architectural development of the house has little documentary or graphic evidence to elucidate it. In 1544 the manor of Broxbourne, which had belonged to the Knights Hospitallers prior to the Dissolution, was granted by the Crown to John Cock or Cokke, a lawyer who, in Queen Mary's reign, became Master of Requests. Cock, who was Sheriff in 1548, no doubt built an appropriate house for himself, but it is not certain that any part of the present fabric antedates his death in 1557.[1] After his widow's death, manor and house passed to his son Henry, who was Cofferer to Queen Elizabeth, Sheriff in 1574, knighted in 1590 and died in 1610. The courtyard plan was no doubt complete by 1603 when James I stayed for a night on his journey to London, for it was at this house that `the lord keeper of the great seale, the lord treasurer, the lord admirall, with most of the nobility of the land, and councell of state...were favourably received' on 2 May.[2] In 1667 the house descended by marriage to Sir John Monson KB, who in February 1670 had licence to empark 320 acres, which he stocked with deer.[3] His grandson and successor Sir Henry Monson, who died in 1718, probably enlarged and improved the house. In 1790 it was sold to Jacob Bosanquet, who refronted the E and S elevation, added two-storeyed bow windows and made internal alterations which prompted the remark in the 1840s that `Great part of the present building is modern'.[4] It can be dated between *c*1793,[5] and 1799 when Elizabeth, wife of Jacob Bosanquet, died;[6] her funeral hatchment, placed above the front door, is shown in the Oldfield drawing[7] together with one of the bow windows in side elevation. This work was swept away in 1878 in a general restoration of the house by Horace Smith-Bosanquet to the designs of John Livock.[8] In recent years additions have been made to W by Hertfordshire County Council to adapt the house as a special school.

The elevations to E and W are entirely Victorian; that to S has three 16th-century stepped gables; and that to N, though partly masked by modern additions, has an old chimney-stack and a semi-octagonal stair turret. The walls facing the courtyard incorporate patches of 16th or early 17th-century brickwork but are mostly of later periods, and all the windows and doorways are of the late 18th century or the 19th century. Since hardly any 16th-century work can be seen inside except, possibly, the roof timbers, the development of the house has to be inferred from the plan. It can be difficult to decide whether a feature in 16th-century style is a Victorian renewal of something which existed at the time of the restoration or an embellishment by the architect. However, one consideration may limit speculation of this kind: the Victorian replacement of unfashionable details with others in keeping with the Elizabethan house was not complete, and not only permitted the survival of 18th and early 19th-century features in the less important elevations but even the preservation, unchanged, of a late 17th-century addition to the otherwise Elizabethanised W elevation. Evidently the architect was principally concerned to alter the unfashionable late Georgian stuccoed appearance of the house.

The earliest architectural features now visible are as follows: the W range has three stepped gables to W; a fourth at the end of the W range is Victorian. They could be as early as John Cock's time but can more probably be ascribed to Henry Cock, and are unlikely to be later in a house of this importance. The only 16th-century feature of this W range is a fireplace in the chamber over the hall, which is of clunch with moulded jambs and depressed four-centred head within a square frame. The hall door is aligned on the gateway in the E range; the passage led, not to an outside door, but into a squarish room of uncertain purpose, presumably a parlour. To S were service rooms and (probably) a kitchen. All that can be said about arrangements to S of the hall is that the present staircase probably replaces an earlier one; it led to the chambers over the hall and the W parlour. To N of the hall was a large parlour; if a blocked fireplace to N was in the middle, the room was about 28 ft (8·5 m) long, extending to a partition screening off an ante-room and a newel staircase; the room was lit by two windows flanking the stack. Both chimney-stack and staircase-projection, though much altered, incorporate undisturbed 16th-century brickwork.

Whether the other three ranges surrounding the courtyard are all contemporary with the hall is impossible to tell, for although there is nothing to suggest they are not, most other courtyard houses in Hertfordshire are of two or more builds. How the E range was originally divided is unknown; the gateway was flanked by semi-octagonal turrets and chimney-stacks like those at Standon Lordship; the roof originally had two ranges of purlins, the lower ones tenoned into the principals, the upper ones clasped by collars since removed. The N range is devoid of old features except for a similar roof; to E is half of a semi-octagonal stair turret, faced in Victorian brick, which perhaps conceals or replaces 16th-century work. Above the roof near the S end rises a stepped gable entirely in modern brick. It corresponds to a change in roof height to E of the stair turret but on the courtyard side any break in the brickwork is completely masked; a second coping to W is plain and corresponds with the end wall of the presumed great parlour, hence the N range may have been the last to be completed. The S range does not preserve any pre-1878 details. A drawing of c1812[9] shows a curiously asymmetrical S elevation; that part of it W of the E range has seven tall round-headed windows apparently rising almost from ground level, although the first and second floors only have three square-headed windows.

The first alterations took place in the late 17th century when a short parlour wing was added to W of the hall; it has a hipped roof and a modillioned eaves cornice; it may be after 1683 because Chauncy, who mentions Sir John Monson's creation of a deer park,[10] makes no reference to the house. In the mid 18th century the gateway range was altered to become the principal part of the house. The elevation to S was certainly refronted and may have acquired the shallow and apparently solid projections on both ground and first floors which appear in Oldfield's drawing of 1799 and still exist; a cornice and parapet with sunk panels were added (for the date cf The Grove, Sarratt). With the addition of a large staircase the gateway became a wide entrance-hall, and the flanking rooms became more important than formerly. Passages behind these rooms led from the foot of the stair to the N and S ranges, and there were corresponding first-floor passages. On the first floor a large room about 33 ft (10 m) long in the N range was given a coved plaster ceiling, part of which remains; the chamber over the parlour was split into two rooms, one of which has the cut-back remains of a corner fireplace, whose chimney-shaft remains in the roof. The great parlour was probably split up at this time, although no detail of the period remains; if so the corridor next to the courtyard and a staircase preceding the present one were coeval with it. In the N range attic rooms were created or improved; one pedimented dormer window faces the courtyard and the parapet which capped the additions to the E range was continued along the N and W sides.

In the form it had reached by c1600 the house had a second courtyard around which stables, brewhouse and other work-places were grouped (cf Hatfield House). By 1742 this had changed and, although the house itself was in `the old Gothick style there are also new Offices, in a Quadrangle...They are placed behind a large Plantation of Trees, so that they do not appear until you are upon them, yet at a convenient Distance from the Mansion house, which I was informed his lordship also proposes to rebuild.'[11]

In the 1790s Jacob Bosanquet refaced the S elevation with stucco; added a two-storey bow window at the S end of the front range; created a row of tall round-headed windows on the ground floor; and refenestrated and remodelled the rooms above it. The drawing room sketched in 1842[12] probably formed part of this range. His work may include a new staircase and the ogee-headed Gothick window shown in the view of the inner hall;[13] a simpler window with interlacing tracery survives on the first floor, facing the courtyard. Livock drastically altered the E and S ranges; refaced the N range; added a N wing with provision for servants' quarters; and generally gutted the house of its 18th-century fittings.

For an illustration, see *English Houses 1200–1800*, Fig 91.

Notes
1. VCH III, 432.
2. `The True Narrative of the Entertainment of His Royal Majestie...', 20, in Nichols 1821–3, Vol III.
3. PRO Warrant Books 1670474 (IND 6753); VCH III, 432.
4. *Bosanquettina*.
5. Plan, HRO, B1441.
6. Cussans 1874–8, Vol II (ii), 176.
7. Oldfield Vol I, 412.
8. HRO, D/EBb P1; reference due to J Brushe.
9. *Bosanquettina*.
10. Chauncy I, 567.
11. Defoe *Tour*, Vol II, 200.
12. Charlotte Bosanquet.
13. Ibid.

(77504)
Rawdon House, High Street, (TL 084373)
and
(77505)
The Grange, No. 15 High Street, Hoddesdon (TL 083372),

both of which are said to have been built by the Rawdon family, have a very confused history, not least because so many of the members of the family were named Marmaduke. The relevant evidence is contained in the `Life of Marmaduke Rawdon of York'[1] and the manuscript `Breife Relation of...the Rawdons',[2] which is dated 1667.

Sir Marmaduke Rawdon (1582–1646) was a merchant, a member of the City Council and alderman (in 1639) who received `diverse favours' from James I and Charles I – `& King James would often call at his house at Hoddesdon...& there had pleasant communication together';[3] a certificate of residence of 1628 states that he `hath byn of longe tyme there resident'[4] and in 1638 he entertained the Earl and Countess of Salisbury and other notable personages there.[5] This was Hoddesdon House[6] and was presumably large, although Sir Marmaduke was only one of four Hoddesdon men assessed at £7 in the subsidy of March 1626.[7] By 1641 he was paying £10.[8] The tenement he is mentioned as holding in 1618 formerly called Rawlins and another called Lathers in 1628[9] cannot be identified with any existing house. He is said to have built the present Rawdon House,[10] which bears the date 1622. This date appears on a panel in the middle gable of the front and also, with the initials M R E, in a cartouche set above the rear doorway in the stair turret. Two early 19th-century drawings of the front elevation[11] do not show the date, and slightly earlier drawings of the rear elevation[12] lack the cartouche. A statement that the date 1622 appears in one of the panels of the staircase[13] is unfounded; no date appears in the drawings, made at the time of restoration, of the balustrading,[14] nor is one there now. The first definite appearance of the date 1622 is in the front as restored by Ernest George and Peto in 1879;[15] the architects are said to have copied old rain-water heads so dated.[16]

If this evidence is discounted the only information about building-works is given in the family history. In 1657 Sir Marmaduke's fifth son, also named Marmaduke (the third), `over against his Mothers, built a faire brick house furnished wth ponds, fountaines, gardens...& something of those

Curiosities that belong to a noble house';[17] in 1660 he married, and on 17 October he and `his yonge lady, with their servants, came to Hodsdon to live in a faire new bricke house which...he had made an end of buildinge that summer';[18] and in a passage referring to the year 1665 the town of Hoddesdon is said to have been `much adorned of late by the fameley of the Rawdons, who have built here tow faire bricke howses, and Sir Marmaduke Rawdon did, att his owne proper cost and charges, much beautifie it with a conduit of water'.[19] The Grange is identified with the house of 1657–60[20] because it stands at the corner of Cock Lane, named from the Cock Inn which belonged to Elizabeth Thorowgood when she married (Sir) Marmaduke Rawdon in 1611; and since Marmaduke the third (son of Lawrence Rawdon of York and nephew of Sir Marmaduke) lived, on his return to England in 1656, with his mother,[21] this is taken to mean that she lived at the present Rawdon House. Apart from this the only

Fig 64 *Rawdon House, Hoddesdon: ground, first (top left) and second-floor (top right) plans*

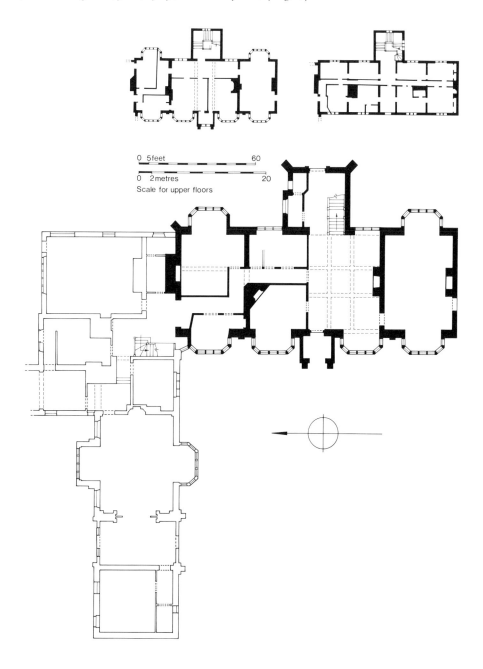

97

evidence to link Rawdon House with the Rawdons is its being so named on a map of 1830.[22] Against this is the impossibility of identifying the present building with one having the 27 hearths for which Lady Rawdon paid in 1673[23] and which imply a house comparable in size to Aspenden Hall, also with 27, or Hertingfordbury Park or Gilston, each with 25 hearths. Most unfortunately the entry for Marmaduke Rawdon Esq. (the third) is damaged and the number of hearths unknown.

Rawdon House has to be dated by the following features: the classical detail, ie Ionic pilasters; ground-floor frieze with triglyphs; moulded first-floor frieze; curvilinear gables and the middle pedimented gable; the bay windows and especially the crenellation at the top; and the fact that it is of three storeys. Some antiquarian features can be disregarded, eg the chimney-stacks, which were built by Ernest George and Peto and do not appear in that form in any of the older drawings, and the ceilings, fireplaces, panelling and `Jacobean' pilasters, all of them 19th-century work. Much of the staircase must have been early Victorian. The newel posts with their finials and distinctive rustication resemble others of 1637 at Stanborough House, Hoddesdon,[24] and are genuine, but the carved balustrade, contrary to 16th and 17th-century practice, is plain on the staircase side; the treads on the middle flight from ground to first floor cut across the carving; and the newel at the foot of the second-floor stairs and the arch over the stairs meet very clumsily. Removal of the half figures from the newels at the foot of the staircase showed that they had been applied against rustication; and were work of 1842–3.[25] Probably the antiquarian inspiration for the staircase stemmed from the tenancy in 1777–8 of John Dymoke, hereditary Champion of England,[26] whence the caption `Champion House' beneath Oldfield's drawing and later the Queen's Beasts forming carved finials to the newels. A series of photographs taken in 1891[27] show much more reproduction Jacobean work than now exists, and it was this which was sold off by the Roman Catholic diocesan authorities c1896. Once the Ernest George work is discounted, the remaining detail is consistent with the period c1630–50.

The house (Fig 64) is in part of double depth, which puts it in the middle of the 17th century rather than earlier. Entrance is through the porch to what must have been the hall, which had, as usual, an imposing staircase at the back; but in that case the hall, which cannot have been larger than at present unless one or more of the windows or the door were in awkward places, was set transversely, another unlikely feature in the early 17th century. The N room was either subdivided or unusually large in relation to the hall. To S of the hall the present rooms may correspond to the original service rooms; a cellar below is entered from outside. To S again was presumably a kitchen. It is more difficult to explain the arrangement of the first-floor rooms and the reconstruction proposed is largely founded on Aston Bury. The staircase rose up to a first-floor landing within the turret; a longitudinal corridor opened off the landing and led to two principal rooms to N and S. Each of the first and second-floor chambers is assumed to have had a dressing room and two of those on the first floor to have had an adjoining closet as well. The second-floor corridor is comparable to that at The Bury, Rickmansworth. At the S end a mutilated roof truss, probably originally of clasped-purlin type, survives.

A small bay-windowed projection of two storeys, probably comprising one room on each floor with a corner fireplace, was added c1700 to N;[28] then or a little later pairs of sash windows replaced the original mullion-and-transom windows lighting the principal rooms to E;[29] and perhaps then the exterior was rendered. In 1842–3 the house underwent an antiquarian restoration which included remodelling the staircase with plaster figures and details;[30] in 1879–80 it was restored for Henry Ricardo by Ernest George and Peto, who added a wing to W on the site of `a recent badly-built extension'.[31] On its becoming St Monica's Priory, the property of canonesses of the Augustinian order, in 1897 many fittings were sold and a galvanised iron chapel was built;[32] in 1971 it underwent further changes to adapt it as flats and offices.

For illustrations, see *English Houses 1200–1800*, Figs 15 (plate), 124 (plate), 125, 126.

Notes
1. Davies 1863.
2. HRO, 79959X.
3. `Breife Relation of the...Rawdons', 3, HRO, 79959X.
4. PRO E115/327/44.
5. Davies 1863,24.
6. `Breife Relation of the...Rawdons', 3, 25, HRO 79959X.
7. PRO E179/270/55.
8. PRO E115/320/150.
9. Hatfield MSS, Acc 57/1.
10. RCHME 1910, 125; VCH III, 431; Hunt, J A 1902–4, 11–17.
11. Buckler Vol IV, 46; Clutterbuck.
12. Oldfield Vol IV, 170; BL Add MS 9062, fo 287.
13. Godfrey 1911, 28, 36, 37; Plates 20, 21.
14. *Building News*, 12 November 1880.
15. Drawing, Hunt, J A 1902–4, 11.
16. Hunt, J A 1902–4, 13.
17. `Breife Relation of the...Rawdons', 24–5, HRO 79959X.
18. Davies 1863, 92.
19. Ibid, 157.
20. Tregelles 1908, 117.
21. `Breife Relation of the...Rawdons', 25, HRO, 79959X.
22. HRO, B 1460.
23. PRO E179/375/31.
24. RCHME 1910, 125–6; Godfrey 1911, Plate 12.
25. Hunt, J A 1902–4, 14.
26. Tregelles 1908, 146.
27. By Bedford Lemere; NMR.
28. Clutterbuck.
29. Oldfield Vol IV, 170.
30. Hunt, J A 1902–4, 15.
31. *Building News*, 2 July 1880.
32. RCHME 1910, 125 and Ms report.

(77505)
The Grange (TL 083372)

has at the front some brickwork which may be of the late 17th century, but after being rubbed down, coloured and given false pointing its date is uncertain, and although there is more narrow brick to the E end of the N wall there is no obvious break of joint between it and the rest of the building. The only other features likely to be of the late 17th century are the two parallel roofs with tenoned purlins. If the plan, incorporating a spine wall in which the chimney-stacks are placed, is of 1657–60 it is of an advanced kind, although Tyttenhanger, Ridge, provides a model for this; and for the first floor Aston Bury is comparable in having two large staircases and an alternation of major and minor rooms. A reconstruction of the ground-floor plan has been attempted, and for the first floor the suggested room division and use has been superimposed on the modern plan (*English Houses 1200–1800*, Fig 133). Some alterations may have taken place in the early 18th century when a gateway bearing the date 1725 and the initials A O (for Lady Arabella Oxenden) was built.[1] A drastic late 19th-century restoration in the style of this period has obscured the date and development of the house.

Some early 17th-century panelling is reset but otherwise all the internal detail and fittings, all the rubbed brick window surrounds at the front and the plastered or composition surrounds at the back are of the late 19th century. This was undertaken after the house had been occupied between 1854 and 1872 as a school.[2]

When The Grange was converted into offices in 1979 and the roof timbers and those of the first floor and attics were exposed, a high proportion of them proved to be re-used roof and floor members from a late medieval house, including some smoke-blackened rafters of considerable size. To S of the house, building operations showed that the W wall was on a substantial foundation, and there was something similar about 25 ft (7·6 m) to E, whereas the E wall had a much slighter foundation.[3]

Clearly neither Rawdon House nor The Grange corresponds to Lady Rawdon's house of 1673 with its 27 hearths and there is no architectural evidence to suggest that Sir Marmaduke Rawdon built either of them; indeed, the literary evidence does not say he built anything more than a conduit. Until further evidence is forthcoming about the ownership of these two houses in the later 17th century, it is impossible to relate the references to them correctly. The only tenuous link with Sir Marmaduke's time is provided by the re-used timbers at The Grange, which may have come from the large house where he entertained his sovereign.

For illustrations, see *English Houses 1200–1800*, Figs 132 (plate), 133.

Notes
1. Tregelles 1908, 119; Paddick 1971, 77.
2. Paddick 1971, 77.
3. Inf. Mr P Devlin.

HOLWELL

(77667)
Church Farm (TL 165334)

shows an unusual development. The oldest part, the cross-wing, is of *c*1500; all exposed framing is close-studded; to E a three-light window on the ground floor proves that there was no adjoining structure on that side originally; the roof has clasped-purlins and curved windbraces. To W there was doubtless an open hall.

In the late 16th century a two-storey range, jettied to N and S, was added to E; the plan comprised two rooms entered by a front doorway adjoining the wing. Consequently, unless the original entrance to the hall was suppressed, the house had two front doorways and may have resembled Walnut Tree Farm, Pirton. Originally there was a wooden chimney-stack between the rooms with one fireplace to W. To S of the stack was a lobby between the two rooms and a stair turret; the studs blocking the presumed site of the stair doorway are insertions, not being pegged to the plate; upstairs a blocked doorway with four-centred head is probably connected with a stair turret. Since the date when the presumed open hall was pulled down is not known, the function of the storeyed range is uncertain. The E room was perhaps an unheated parlour; it has close-studding and diamond-mullioned windows. The room to W was probably a new hall, leaving the old one as a kitchen; in the wing were service rooms. In the E range both upstairs rooms have fragmentary wall-paintings; that in the W room consists of a repeated representation of panelling, the panels being enclosed in strap-work; the central motif is a diamond enclosed within an oval; there is a dado and an elaborate frieze. The room to E had a

large-scale repeat pattern, in black and white, of sixteen-petalled roses enclosing an eight-petalled centre. Stylistically the paintings are of *c*1600 plus or minus 10 but perhaps earlier rather than later;[1] this agrees with the architectural evidence.

In the 18th century the presumed wooden chimney was replaced by a brick stack with two fireplaces heating both the ground-floor rooms. By the middle of the 19th century the medieval hall had been replaced by a brick block W of the wing, comprising a narrow staircase-hall and four large rooms each with a fireplace discharging into an internal stack.

Note
1. Rouse 1989, 439.

(77668)
Gurneys (TL 165334; formerly North Farm),

of two storeys, comprises a main range with cross-wings to E and W. The E wing of *c*1500 has close-studding on the first floor and a clasped-purlin roof; a staircase to N is probably in the same position as the original one. The former open hall to W was rebuilt with two storeys in the 17th century; the fireplace to W perhaps backed on to a cross-passage; the roof has clasped-purlins. The W wing, no doubt replacing an earlier service bay, was built in the late 17th century; a fireplace was added to rear of that in the hall, blocking the passage and creating a lobby-entrance; a staircase to NE probably had a small service room to W; the roof has clasped-purlins with long, straight windbraces. Subsequently a chimney-stack was added to W, presumably when the wing was subdivided; the purpose of this is not clear. In recent years the house has been carefully restored.

HORMEAD

(77669)
Bell House, formerly The Bell PH (TL 389297),

incorporates to N the cross-wing, approximately square in plan, of an early 16th-century house; it was of one and a half storeys and no doubt adjoined a small open hall to S. In the mid 17th century everything but the walls and first floor of the wing was demolished and, from the completeness of the rebuilding and the incorporation of the wing into the new work despite the need to heighten it, it appears possible that the hall was of earth-fast construction (cf Yew Tree Farm, Much Hadham). The hall range is of two storeys; the chimney-stack has fireplaces in hall and wing, lobby-entrance to E and a small stair turret to W. Access to the staircase was only from the parlour; it led to the chamber over the parlour and possibly over the hall as well, although entrance to the latter was awkward. In the W or kitchen wing, also of the late 17th century, is a smaller staircase to the chambers over kitchen, service rooms and probably hall. A range of buildings to S connected with the inn was added in the 18th century. In 1851 the Bell Inn was occupied by William Lawrence, carpenter, a master employing two men.[1] In 1975 it was restored after a considerable period of dereliction.

Note
1. Census.

(77670)
Brick House (TL 412310)

was probably built in the early 1570s by Thomas Brand of Lambeth, yeoman,[1] who in November 1576 enfeoffed his sons Thomas and Michael with `all the messuage called Le Newe brick house'.[2] Licence was granted on 1 September 1579 to

Michael to sell the reversion of his portion,[3] and again on 2 September 1586 to James Grymshawe to sell the Brick House and some land.[4] Nothing is known of its subsequent ownership and occupation. It was in poor condition c1900, with settlement cracks and several blocked windows[5] and so remained until restored in 1954–8.

The house is unique in Hertfordshire in combining the rooms appropriate to a prosperous yeoman – albeit in an unusual

Fig 65 *Brick House, Hormead: plan*

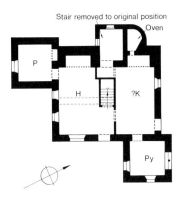

Stair removed to original position

arrangement – with brick, a walling material then unknown at vernacular level (Fig 65). The largest ground-floor room, the hall, faces E; the front doorway was to E opposite the newel staircase. Although the hall had the larger of the two ground-floor fireplaces the lack of a second outer doorway suggests that this room was not the kitchen; that was probably the smaller room to N which has, in the NE corner, an outer doorway, and was certainly the kitchen in the 19th century; yet its proportions are quite extraordinary for a kitchen and the fireplace is comparatively small. Possibly the E end of the N room was partitioned off as a passage linking hall, kitchen and pantry and outer door, almost like a conventional cross-passage. On the first floor it is not certain that either of the principal rooms had fireplaces; that in the hall chamber is Victorian, perhaps replacing an earlier one; that in the kitchen chamber is of c1700. There were in addition two small first-floor rooms and at least four second-floor rooms. Several small windows on the second floor provided light when the larger casement windows were closed; there are also two in the stair turret. In the 19th century the old staircase was removed and a new one built in the living room (hall).

Notes
1. VCH IV, 74.
2. HRO, H482.
3. PRO C66/1180, m 30.
4. PRO C66/1283, m 40.
5. Gerish 1901, 113.

(77671)
Great Hormead Dane (TL 405301)
is a three-cell continuous-jetty house of the late 16th century; it faces S and has a thatched roof. In plan and structure it resembles Tudor Cottage, Albury, except that the close-studding is of poor quality as if intended for plaster, and the joists under the jetty, which have squared-off ends, look unfinished, as if a moulded fascia were intended. In the service bay the bearer is

mortised for a partition; mortises for the four-centred heads of twin doorways are exposed. A beam embedded in the N side of the internal chimney-stack suggests there may have been a wooden stack originally, probably set to S with the staircase and way through from cross-passage to hall to N. On the first floor a doorway to the chamber over the service rooms has a four-centred head facing the presumed stair head. In the late 17th century a wide fireplace was added to N, altering the service rooms into a kitchen, and the internal chimney-stack was rebuilt in brick; a wing added to N has a staircase replacing an older one nearby, and originally accommodated a service room and dairy. In the early 19th century attics were created and a fireplace was added in the ground-floor room to N.

(77672)
Judd's Farm (TL 402300)
incorporates the jettied cross-wing of a late medieval house, the open hall of which (to E) has been rebuilt. The wing was divided into two ground-floor rooms with paired doorways to the cross-passage. Perhaps the house declined subsequently; there is a striking absence of heated rooms in a house of this size, the only fireplace in the main range being the one serving the hall, where normally back-to-back fireplaces would be expected. The hall range was rebuilt in 1724 (date painted over former lobby-entrance) and possibly the bay to the E also. The kitchen wing to S may also be of 1724; its roof is entirely of re-used timber. In the 19th century the principal staircase was added, no doubt replacing an older one at the E end of the house.

For an illustration, see *English Houses 1200–1800*, Fig 55 (plate).

(77673)
Old Swan Cottage, Hare Street (TL 390294)
is a small house of the early 16th century which comprised an open hall and two jettied cross-wings. The hall was about 16 ft 6 ins (5 m) square and by analogy such a space would have excluded the cross-passage, which was probably in the wing to N because the ground-floor window is set to N as if to allow for a doorway adjoining the hall. The hall was of two equal bays, divided by an open truss which has an almost flat tie-beam with comparatively small curved braces, one of which remains. No original partitions can be detected in either wing; the roofs have clasped-purlins.

In the late 16th century an upper floor and fireplace with moulded lintel were built in the hall, leaving space for a passage behind the stack. If the original site of the cross-passage was correctly conjectured, the new site argues a completely new disposition of the house, perhaps with the old passage now cut off from the hall; and the size of the new room, only about 9 ft (2·6 m) in depth, is more appropriate to a kitchen than a hall. It was perhaps at this time that the wing to S was extended by one bay. About the beginning of the 18th century the passage was blocked by the building of a second fireplace backing on to the first and a narrow staircase was built beside the stack. A cellar was built under the parlour; the steps approaching it blocked the way through from hall to parlour and necessitated the building of a lean-to passage. In 1725 the messuage called `The Sign of the Swan' is mentioned, and in December 1796 it passed to John Phillips of Royston, `common brewer'.[1] In 1821 his two nephews were each admitted to a moiety of the messuage called The Swan; this may be when the house became cottages; in recent years it has been restored to one occupation.

Note
1. Copy of court roll in possession of owner.

(77674)
Old Tudor Cottage,

of the late 15th century, comprised an open hall with service bay to S and jettied cross-wing to N; both bay and wing have heavy joists and staircases to E. The opposite doorways in the hall and another into the service bay survive; the wing was originally divided on the ground floor into two rooms by a framed partition, near the middle of which was a doorway. An upper floor and chimney-stack were inserted in the hall *c*1600; the stack was rebuilt in brick in the 18th century.

(77675)
Nos 1/2 Thatched Cottages (TL 402290)

formed a small single-storey house of three rooms, all open to the roof originally. Two rooms had back-to-back fireplaces discharging into a tapering chimney-stack made of timber with an infilling of clay, chalk and straw. The plan, single storey, timber chimney, and exposed studding suggest the late 17th or even the first quarter of the 18th century. It is one of the smallest houses with this kind of plan (cf. Church Cottage, Brent Pelham) and presumably belonged to the lowest level of farmer or a labourer with some land. A fourth room was added to S *c*1800.

HUNSDON

(81466)
Brick House Farm (TL 421118),

of two storeys with basement and attics, is only explicable as the result of several successive phases of rebuilding. It comprises a symmetrical front range facing S and a wider range to N forming a T-plan (Fig 66); a straight joint shows that the former was enlarged by a bay to W, but the thin wall between the two

Fig 66 *Brick House Farm, Hunsdon: plan*

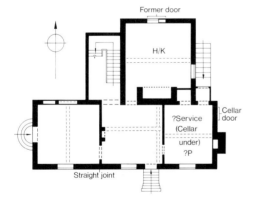

parts must be of timber. The oldest datable feature is the large chimney-stack backing on to the S range; it has three diagonally set shafts of the 17th century, two for the large kitchen fireplace and one for the bedroom above. The phases of rebuilding are suggested in Fig 67; the one feature not satisfactorily accounted for is the high basement, which is unusual in a farmhouse.

(77677)
Briggens (TL 413111)

replaced two messuages called Great and Little Briggens or Over and Nether Bredens;[1] these had evidently been united in one estate and must have been of some importance by the late 17th century when Briggens was occupied by William Crowley,

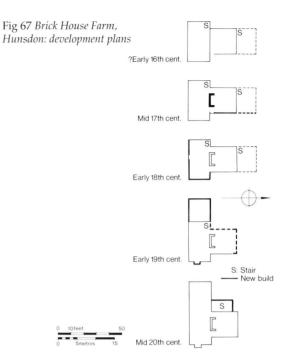

Fig 67 *Brick House Farm, Hunsdon: development plans*

Gent.[2] He paid tax on five hearths in 1662.[3] This and other property was bought in 1706 by Robert Chester,[4] goldsmith and West India merchant, and son of Edward Chester of Royston who was Sheriff in 1675. Robert Chester became a director of the South Sea Company in February 1715[5] and must shortly afterwards have begun building a completely new house. An annotated design for the chimney-piece of the hall signed `J Thornhill 1720' shows that the fireplace surround was to be of statuary marble and the trophies of arms above were `to be green Gold', ie presumably painted.[6] Payments to building craftsmen, including glaziers, plasterers and other finishing trades, were being made between July 1720 and March 1721.[7] These dates accord with Salmon's statement in 1728 that `Robert Chester, Esq hath within a few Years built a Seat in this Parish and enclosed it with a Park';[8] Bridgeman was working on the gardens *c*1720.[9] An inventory dated 23–5 February 1720/1 includes the following rooms: `Common Parlour, Hall and passage, Best Parlour and closets, Saloon, Drawing Room and Closet; Kitchen and Scullery, Storeroom, Dairy, Servants Hall and Buttery office; Chamber, Chamber backwards [with] dressing room and closet, Chamber and closet, Gallery; six chambers and Gallery'. The general appearance of Chester's house has been conjectured (Fig 68) from later plans and discoveries recorded during the work of enlargement in 1908.[10]

Robert Chester died in 1732 and in 1740 the estate was sold to Thomas Blackmore of London. No alteration to the house can definitely be ascribed to this Thomas, who died in 1763, or to his cousin and successor of the same name who was Sheriff in 1778 and died in 1783, although a lead cistern inscribed T B 1751 and a bell in the stables dated 1770 show that both undertook some works, if only of a minor nature.[11] It was no doubt the cousin's son, another Thomas, who had succeeded to the estate as an infant, of whom it was remarked *c*1800 that he `has rebuilt the house in a very handsome manner' and laid out the gardens `in the more modern style'.[12] Just what the rebuilding entailed is not recorded but the proportions of the attic storey windows compared with the others suggest that the house was heightened and that the two-bay end blocks were added (Fig 68). In 1824 the estate passed by marriage to Charles Phelips[13] who, five years later, was Sheriff, and remained with his family until 1907. Latterly the house was on lease, in 1900–1 to John Oakley Maund and subsequently to Arnold Friedlander;[14] the alter-

ations made by Maund are shown in the plans and drawing (Figs 69 and 68). In 1907 the house was sold to H C Gibbs[15] who proceeded immediately to enlarge it and alter the interior. In

Fig 68 *Briggens, Hunsdon: development perspectives*

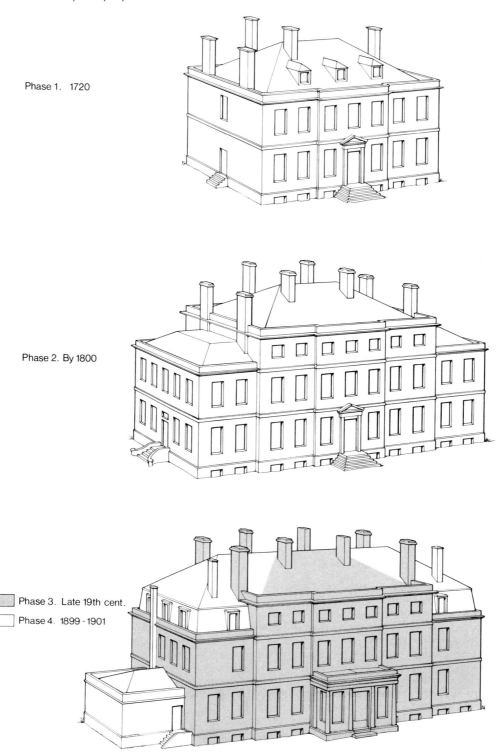

Phase 1. 1720

Phase 2. By 1800

Phase 3. Late 19th cent.

Phase 4. 1899 - 1901

recent years it was a company hotel; the room uses shown on the plans (Fig 70) are of that period but are probably the same as between the two world wars or even earlier.

Notes
1. Lease 1740, HRO D/EB 1630 T41.
2. Gibbs, H C 1915, 22–3.

Fig 69 *Briggens, Hunsdon: 1901 plans*

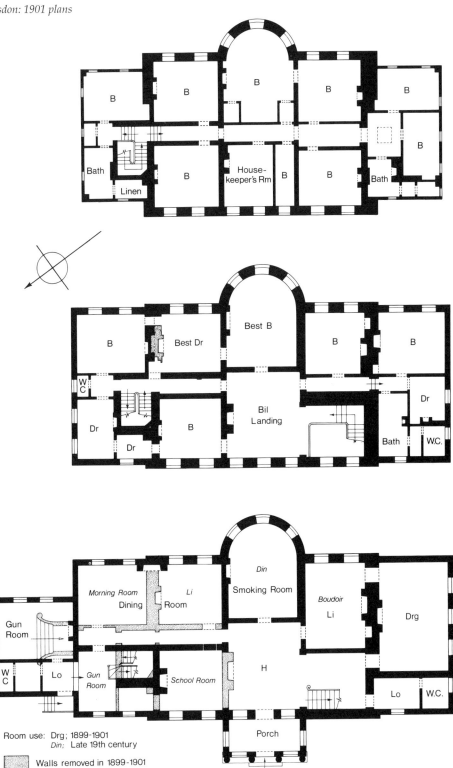

Room use: Drg; 1899-1901
Din; Late 19th century

Walls removed in 1899-1901

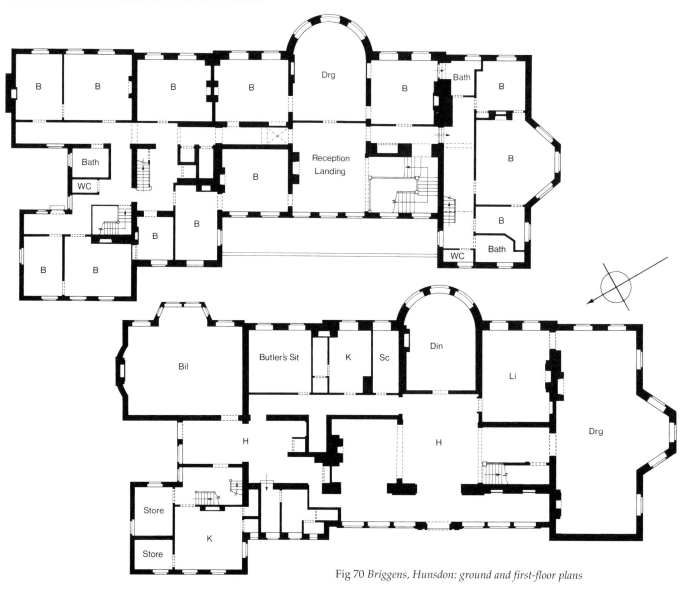

Fig 70 *Briggens, Hunsdon: ground and first-floor plans*

3.   PRO E179/375/30.
4.   Gibbs, H C 1915, 22–4.
5.   Carswell 1960, 276.
6.   Private collection; inf. Mr J Newman.
7.   *Particulars* 1721, Vol I.
8.   Salmon 1728, 253.
9.   Willis 1977, 59.
10. Gibbs, H C 1908.
11. Gibbs, H C 1915, 25–6.
12. Oldfield Vol IV, 61.
13. VCH III, 236.
14. Gibbs, H C 1908.
15. Gibbs, H C 1915, 26.

(77678)

Briggens Home Farm (TL 396124),

built in the late 16th century, has a lobby-entrance plan comprising three rooms, that to W being an unheated service room; the framing exposed inside includes long slightly curved braces; the roof has clasped-purlins. The present chimney-stack is of the late 17th century, presumably replacing one of timber; it incorporates a fireplace, now blocked, in the first-floor room to

E. A bay was added to E, perhaps *c*1800 when the house was refronted with a high parapet and large Gothick bay windows, and the staircase rebuilt. In the 19th century single-storey wings were added for farm purposes.

(77679)

Hunsdon House (TL 419127)

incorporates part of a mid 15th-century tower house of brick but otherwise is of *c*1804–10. The following account is provisional and will need revision in the light of recent archaeological excavations.

By 1445 the manor of Hunsdon was in the possession of Michael, Duke of York, who, in 1447, was granted licence to build and embattle a tower of stones.[1] In that year the manor came into the possession of Sir William Oldhall,[2] who built a large house described by William Worcestre thus:

The tower of the manor of Hunsdon...with other buildings and stables made of brick, about 80 of my steps or paces long, cost in building...7000 marks 8s. 2 1/2d. [£4667 1s. 6 1/2d.]. The breadth of each side of the said tower is 80 feet, and on each side of the said tower are seven very thick buttresses. The height of the said tower with the upper storey called an Oriel...is as is said more than 100 feet from the base of the said tower. Also the length of the great hall of the said tower is 80 feet and its breadth 24 feet.[3]

A tower of this size must have been comparable to that at Tattershall (Lincolnshire), built by Lord Cromwell.

The brick structure incorporated in the E end of the house appears to be of the 1450s. Its original extent can best be judged in the basement (Fig 71): a long barrel-vaulted cellar, lit at the N and S ends and with a hexagonal shaft for a hoist in the NW corner, has three smaller cellars at right-angles to E; the middle one projects beyond those in the re-entrant angles; the two latter are inaccessible. Opening off the NE corner of the middle cellar is a staircase; the original stone newel remains. To W of the long cellar are the stubs of walls of other structures now demolished. Externally the brickwork above these cellars has a diaper pattern in blue bricks; to NE and SE are shaped angle buttresses; the only original openings are narrow loops of stone, some of which are in the angles formed by buttresses and walls. The internal dispositions of the ground floor (Fig 72) are best preserved to SE, where a vaulted room has moulded ribs springing from head-corbels; the vault is supported by thick walls but at the SE corner these are reduced to provide a very small room with a complex brick vault, lit originally by the loops in the buttress angles. The middle room to E, has to N a staircase with timber newel and stairs, and of uncertain date; blocked openings show that the turret itself is original. No trace of vaulting exists in the room to NE, although loops visible externally like those to SE suggest that a similar small vaulted room once existed. On the first storey the mutilated brick vault of a small room like the one below adjoins the buttress to SE. Original brickwork rises to about the middle of the second storey but no old details remain.

This large structure is a very early example of double or even triple-pile building. Above what was no doubt a wine cellar must have been a long room with windows to N and S and perhaps to E if there was any point where other structures did not mask it; and there was a similar first-floor room.

Sometime before July 1471 the house was bought by Edward IV,[4] and in 1514 was granted to Thomas Howard, on his creation as Duke of Norfolk, who was succeeded by his son and heir in 1524. `Thomas duke of Norfolk, suspecting that a tower of the house would fall by reason of the height, took downe a part thereof'.[5] Although a `Commentarie or Exposition' to a late 16th-century poem is not the most likely source of reliable information, the statement accords with both Worcestre's description and the surviving remains and may well be correct. By 1527 the house was in the possession of Henry VIII, who, by February 1534, had carried out extensive building-works costing £2,900.[6] Accounts include payments for clamps of brick; freestone for the chimneys in the King's watching chamber, pallet chamber and privy chamber and in the chambers beneath them; carpenters' work at the end of the great gallery with two chambers above the same; and new lodgings, gallery and closets. It was a highly decorated building; payments were made to painters working upon chimneys and other external parts, and for gilding and leadwork. Henry VIII's palace is said to be depicted in the background of a portrait of Edward VI painted *c*1546,[7] although it presents certain difficulties, especially in the apparent lack of a moat. A reference in 1543[8] to a new bridge over the moat from the inner court into the king's lodgings suggests that one arm of the moat was within the area of the palace.

In March 1559 the house and manor of Hunsdon were granted by Queen Elizabeth to her cousin Sir Henry Carey (lately created

Fig 71 *Hunsdon House: basement plan*

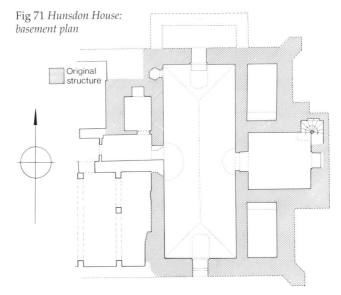

Original structure

Fig 72 *Hunsdon House: ground-floor plan*

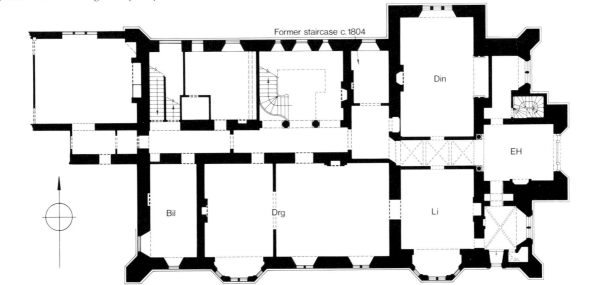

Former staircase c.1804

Din

EH

Bil

Drg

Li

Lord Hunsdon); Henry, the 4th Baron, inherited the estate in 1617.[9] By then, probably, much of Henry VIII's work had been pulled down, and the 4th Baron may have carried out the refronting depicted in Drapentier's engraving, which shows the principal elevation with a two-storey porch and two wings projecting forward. Lord Hunsdon, whose estates were sequestered following the Civil War, sold Hunsdon in 1653 to William Willoughby. He, in 1662, paid for 22 hearths and Lord Francis Willoughby for 8;[10] by 1664 all 30 hearths were paid for by William Willoughby.[11] Presumably the house was in dual occupation for a few years. In 1671 it was purchased by Matthew Bluck Esq., one of the Six Clerks in Chancery, to whom Drapentier dedicated his engraving of c1700 and from whom it descended to his son Matthew.

By 1743 the house was described as 'a very large old building capable of accommodating a family of 100, but in so ruinous a condition that it would never be worth any gentleman's while to repair'.[12] Demolition of part of the house was by then foreseen: 'The wainscotts, hangings and floors of all the West appartments have already been taken down'. The remaining wainscot and flooring would sell for £30, but the bricks were not worth the trouble of cleaning, 'especially as it must be scaffold on account of the moat'. In 1745 Josias Nicolson of Clapham purchased the manor and pulled down the wings.[13] The mid 18th-century appearance of the house is recorded in four views dated 1758,[14] after drawings then in the possession of Nicolson Calvert. They show the house as adapted by Josias Nicolson. The main entrance front was still to W but was by then symmetrical, unlike its predecessor, which had an extra bay to N of the entrance. The E view shows the second of the 'two bridges of communication, one in the front, the other at the back of the house';[15] the E front in 1758 was generally similar to its present appearance. The other views are from NW and SE; the former shows the church and the garden wall outside the moat, the latter the outbuildings and the entrance gates corresponding exactly with Drapentier's view of c1700.

The next illustration is a view from S in 1773[16] and shows the W bridge. A later 18th-century drawing[17] made c1788 and engraved[18] shows the house from W. At about this time the moat was filled in.[19] This drawing and Oldfield's[20] show minor discrepancies, the latter being probably the more accurate; but clearly little work was done in the late 18th century.

The estate descended to Nicholson Calvert, great-grandson of Josias Nicolson, who undertook the building of a new house at Hunsdon, possibly to the designs of William Leach.[21] The work is referred to in Mrs Calvert's letters:

> [6 August 1805] We find building the new house so dreadfully expensive a job, that we meditate giving the matter up, though we have completed cellars, etc. We think of adding to, and repairing the old house instead, which we fortunately as yet, have not pulled down...
> [16 April 1806] I hear there is hardly a bit of old Hunsdon House standing...it will be nearly a new house. [22]

Calvert

> ...judiciously restored the whole in the castellated form of the original edifice, the identical front of which, now remains, and the windows, which had been modernised, have resumed their ancient mullions; the entrance alone has been altered from the west to the east end, and the offices vice versa. [23]

The Calverts moved to Hunsdonbury c1840 and left Hunsdon House empty so long that it fell 'into an almost ruinous state'.[24] It was sold in 1858 to James S Walker and in 1861 to James Wylie (or Wyllie),[25] who put in new fenestration; added hexagonal turrets with steep-pitched roofs above the corner buttresses; and

built an elaborate verandah to S and created a new staircase-hall dominated by large marbled columns with capitals of vaguely Egyptian appearance. These alterations appear in a lithograph of 1869.[26] In 1983 careful repair of the house was begun, in the course of which much 15th-century brickwork was revealed.

Notes

1. *Cal Pat* 1446–52, 77.
2. VCH III, 321.
3. Worcester *Itineraries*, 51.
4. Roskell 1957, 112.
5. Vallans 1590, *xviii*.
6. *Cal L&P* Henry VIII, 250.
7. Colvin 1971, 210 and Plate 52.
8. *King's Works* Vol IV, 156.
9. VCH III, 328.
10. PRO E179/375/30.
11. PRO E149/248/27.
12. HRO, Particular, D/EB 1630 Tb.
13. Cussans 1870–3, Vol I (i), 46–7.
14. Clutterbuck, D/EC1, 5, 184.
15. Neale 1819–29, Vol III.
16. Gough, Herts, 18.
17. Bodl, Gough Maps, 11.
18. Nichols 1821–3, Vol I, 10.
19. Neale 1819–29, Vol III.
20. Oldfield Vol IV, 196.
21. Colvin 1978, 508.
22. Blake 1911, 49, 66.
23. Neale 1819–29, Vol II.
24. Cussans 1870–3, Vol I (i), 47.
25. Gibbs, H C 1915, 21.
26. Cussans 1870–3, Vol I (i), 47.

(77680)
The Pump House (TL 141418)

has a main range (Fig 73) flanked by two slightly lower cross-wings which may be of different dates, that to S being slightly wider than that to N. The wings may be earlier than the main range because their roof ridges are lower; this would usually imply that they were associated with a medieval hall (cf Pirton Grange) that has been replaced by the existing range, yet the distance between them, nearly 34 ft (10·4 m), is too great for a hall alone, and requires a different explanation; possibly there was a hall and further bay, ie a service room or parlour. The main range now comprises two rooms with lobby-entrance; the room to N, with the larger fireplace, was the hall, and the other probably the parlour. Behind the chimney a staircase projection

Fig 73 *The Pump House, Hunsdon: plan*

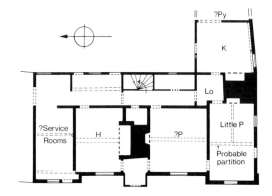

rises above an outshut containing a corridor which joins extensions of the two wings, all of which are part of a late 17th-century rebuilding. The provision of corridors suggests that the building was an inn, a function consistent with the two ground-floor rooms in the middle range. In a first-floor cupboard beside the chimney-stack is a two-light window with ovolo-moulded mullion; on the first floor the openings to the staircase have four-centred heads. To E the S wing incorporated a kitchen, probably with a pantry adjoining. In the early 18th century the lobby-entrance was embellished with panelling and a doorway with egg-and-dart surround, and then or in the early 19th century the front gables of the wings were altered to give a continuous roof line, and the upper storeys were underbuilt.

(77681)
No. 6 Widford Road (TL 420160)

is of late medieval origin and comprises a hall formerly open to the roof and a cross-wing to S of two storeys; some timber framing is exposed. In its first phase the house had a comparatively small hall, only 16 ft (4·9 m) wide, open to the roof, and of uncertain length, and a cross-wing with cambered tie-beams having peg-holes compatible with a crown-post roof. Much of the framing, including the straight braces and roof construction, appears to be of the same date as the chimney-stack and the lintel of the parlour fireplace, in which is cut the date 1681. At that time a fireplace and an upper floor were built within the hall, and a stair wing added to E. The plan then comprised a kitchen (formerly the hall) and a parlour in the wing, both reached from the lobby-entrance. The other ground-floor room in the wing was an unheated service room. In the early 19th century the house was fitted with sash windows.

ICKLEFORD

(77682)
The Manor House (TL 179311; demolished)

was a double-pile building of three storeys and seven bays; an estate map of 1771[1] shows the house flanked to E by a stable range to S and service court to N. A drawing of c1800[2] showing brick bands dividing the storeys, suggests that the house may have been built in the late 17th century; in 1743 Thomas Ansell Esq., who then owned the house, was Sheriff. By c1800 the hipped roof had eaves gutters and symmetrically placed drainpipes. A semi-octagonal ground-floor extension covering the three middle bays was added to W c1830–50, and then or later a two-storey block was added to N.[3] The house was for sale in 1919,[4] when it was flanked to E by two single-storey wings.

Notes
1. HRO, D/E Ha P1.
2. Oldfield Vol IV, 223.
3. Western 1975, un-numbered Plate.
4. *CL* Supplement, 8 February 1919, *vi*.

(77683)
Old Ramerick (TL 171350)

incorporates the shell of the medieval manor house of Ramerick; neither the structure itself nor the descent of the manor give much indication of its date. It is first recorded in the 13th century and by 1303 was in the hands of Gerard de Braybroke[1] who, in 1339, leased the manor to three people, presumably trustees, reserving to himself and his heirs the hall with all the chambers annexed to the hall and the kitchen with the stables.[2] The existence of an open hall can be inferred from the width of the present entrance-hall (22 ft (6·7 m)), which is too great for a post-medieval farmhouse, and the fact that the rear wall-plate is only 4 ft (1·2 m) above the first floor, which is too low for a house of two storeys. The hall was about 27 ft (8·2 m) long and if this included the screens-passage the living-space was apparently square. E of the hall a 16th-century cross-wing probably incorporates part of a late medieval structure. That the medieval building was timber framed is suggested by the breaking-down of part of its walls during its seizure by Lord Cobham in 1530.[3] The earliest discernible alterations, perhaps of the late 16th century, may include the reroofing of the E end as a wing which incorporated a parlour at the front and kitchen behind. By 1625 the house had become the `farm place or site of the manor of Ramerick'.[4] In 1663 Thomas Hanscombe, yeoman, paid for six hearths.[5] In the late 17th century the NE block, probably a granary, was added; it is of two storeys and of clunch rubble with brick dressings, its upper floor being carried on what was originally an independent timber frame within the rubble wall. It is not certain that the old open hall had been completely floored over by this time. Part of the first floor, a stretch 11 ft (3·5 m) long over the W half of the entrance-hall, is one step higher than the rest, as if one bay of the medieval hall had been floored over later than the other to the E. Although there is no positive evidence to date these two operations, the flooring-over of the E bay may be connected with the provision of a stair to the E wing, in which there is otherwise no space for one, and of the W bay with the building of a chimney-stack there, which appears to go with the refronting and the building of a new staircase wing in the early years of the 18th century. The symmetrical front then created extended W of the medieval hall, where a new room was added – possibly a parlour or drawing room – with some inferior room behind it; some of the lean-to extensions at the back are probably of the early 18th century. The status of the house at about that time is indicated by its having a coach-house.[6] In the 19th century a new W block was added in brick; it provided a kitchen at the front with perhaps a dairy or pantry behind it; a cellar, down a flight of three steps, and a secondary staircase were also added. All this can be dated by the tablet over the doorway in the W wall dated R E/1829; the College Rental for 1830 mentions the expenditure of £899 on new buildings. Probably the old kitchen at the E end went out of use at this time, and the ground floor of the NE block was given a fireplace with a crudely finished cambered lintel; possibly the latter room, then, as now, was the farm office.

Notes
1. VCH III, 22.
2. St John's College, Cambridge, deeds, 19.
3. See *English Houses 1200–1800*, p 21; Sta. Cha./2/8/66; VCH III, 23.
4. St John's College, Cambridge, deeds, 16, 14.
5. PRO E179/248/23.
6. Sale particulars 1760, St John's College, Cambridge.

(77684)
The Parsonage (demolished),

lay to NE of the church[1] and incorporated part of a medieval stone building including a doorway with two-centred head.[2] This cannot have been part of the church.[3]

Notes
1. Estate map, 1771, HRO, D/E Ha P1.
2. Oldfield Vol IV, 221.
3. As stated in Western 1975, 44; cf estate map of 1771, HRO, D/E Ha P1.

IPPOLLITTS

(77685)
Almshoe Bury (TL 206254)

was built in the 13th century, probably by Simon Fitz Adam, who held the manor of Almshoe of the tenants-in-chief, the Fitz Walters, and who settled it on his wife in 1241;[1] henceforth the family took the surname Fitz Simon. The house, as the successor of the small settlement which is recorded in 1086 and which shrank as Ippollitts grew, had a chapel, the site of which is unknown. An account roll[2] records under the date 26 July 1358 expenses incurred by `the Queen and the Queen of Scotland, in the Park of Almeshoe', that is, by Isabella, wife of Edward II, and her daughter Joan, wife of David Bruce, King of Scotland. This event probably occurred in the lifetime of Hugh Fitz Simon, who was Sheriff in 1354; his son Edward, who held the same office in 1374, is styled `of Hatfield', where the family had held, since Simon Fitz Adam's day, the important manor of Symonshyde.[3] The distinction thus made may mark the abandonment of Almshoe Bury as the family's principal manor, because the architectural development and quality of the house towards the end of the Middle Ages are more appropriate to an important farmhouse than to the residence of a county magnate, and it is no doubt to this early decline in status that the survival of so interesting a timber structure is due. No subsequent occupier had any pretensions to the office of sheriff, nor do subsequent changes of ownership[4] throw light on the architectural history of the house.

The house is timber framed and plastered and roofs are of tile; some brick refacing, a complete refenestration and minor additions at the back give it in detail an early 19th-century appearance, which is belied by the proportions and low eaves of the main range as well as by the flanking gabled wings. In the 13th century the plan comprised an aisled hall of two bays divided by a spere-truss from the half-bay occupied by the screens-passage; in this part are visible the capital of the post in the N arcade which forms part of the open truss; the corresponding post, of quatrefoil section, to S; and, above the latter, springing from the top of the capital, a fragment of the arch-brace from post to tie-beam which is carved with dog-tooth ornament to E and is moulded to W. In the present kitchen the S post of the spere-truss is now freestanding but upstairs both posts can be seen, as can the arch-braces joining them to the tie-beams; the braces have filled spandrels. In the attic 22 rafter couples of the 13th century survive, heavily blackened by smoke from the open hearth; the open truss and the end truss to W incorporated passing-braces; the spere-truss did not, and at this

Fig 74 *Almshoe Bury, Ippollitts: plan*

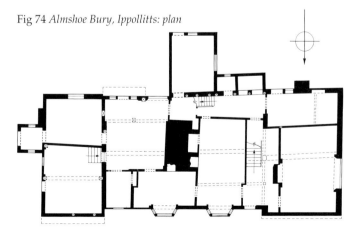

Fig 75 *Almshoe Bury, Ippollitts: development perspectives*

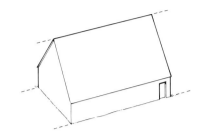

Phase 1. 1241

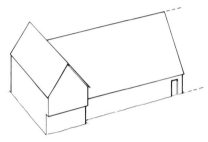

Phase 2. Mid 15th cent.

Phase 3. Early 16th cent.

Phases 4&5. Mid 17th cent., pre-1663

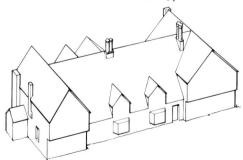

Phase 6. 19th cent.

point the rafters are not seated on the tie-beam; and the end truss to E has been removed. Since there is no trace of an original partition to E of the hall there was presumably another bay, and to W a similar conclusion can be drawn from the fact that the bracing timbers form a flush face towards the hall but not to W. Such end bays may or may not have had an upper floor.

The first alteration (Figs 74 and 75) was the building of a cross-wing to E; the crown-post roof, of three bays with thin four-way braces, is of the mid 15th century. The wing was probably jettied to N and divided into two rooms on each floor; it appears not to have had a fireplace when built. In the early 16th century a parlour was added to W. Thereafter the development of the house is difficult to follow. The central chimney-stack was built in the 17th century; its two diagonal shafts are not closely datable but must be before 1663, when John Love was occupying the house[5] and paid tax on eight hearths.[6] Space was left to N of the stack for a lobby-entrance and staircase. An upper storey was inserted at the same time. In the 18th century a wing, possibly a dairy, was added to S. In the 19th century there was some refacing in brick, a general renewal of windows and a reorganisation of the plan at the W end of the middle range; this included a staircase and entrance-hall and a new chimney-stack in the parlour. By this time the original staircases in the wings had been removed; the present two staircases, designed to segregate family and servants, are a 19th-century arrangement.

For illustrations, see *English Houses 1200–1800*, Figs 20 (plate), 22.

Notes
1. VCH III, 26.
2. BL Cotton MS Galba E XIV, fo 22.
3. Chauncy II, 15–16; *Cal Pat* 1247–58, 388.
4. VCH III, 26–7.
5. HRO, D/E B513 T48.
6. PRO E179/248/23.

KELSHALL

(77686)
The Maltings (TL 328362)

incorporates a 15th-century cross-wing which, by inference, was attached to an open hall to W; the latter was demolished in the 17th century and rebuilt with two storeys and an internal chimney-stack; subsequently it was converted into four cottages, probably after the Enclosure Award of 1797.[1]

The wing, jettied to N, comprised two service rooms entered by paired doorways with four-centred heads, and two chambers upstairs. To S a trimmer joist shows that the present stair occupies the site of the original one; on the first floor a four-light window with diamond mullions gave light to the stair and the small top landing. A blocked doorway at the foot of the stair was no doubt entered from a cross-passage to E and implies that the medieval hall was wider than its successor; a total width of between 22 ft and 23 ft (7·0 m) implies manorial status or pretensions to it. The wing has a crown-post roof with two-way struts. The hall range was rebuilt in the mid 17th century; the framing is divided at first-floor height by a middle rail; the braces are straight and of small scantling; and the roof is of clasped-purlin type, with ceilings at collar-beam height. Only the bay farthest from the wing had timberwork of any quality, the first-floor joists being set upright, not flat, and chamfered and stopped, so this room was of some importance and may have been a parlour. Surprisingly, neither here nor in the hall did a 17th-century

chimney-stack survive; the existing stacks are of the late 18th or early 19th century.

Note
1. Tate 1945–9, 24.

KIMPTON

(77687)
Nos 26/28 High Street, The Old White House (TL 176183),

has an open hall of two bays with a cross-wing to E. Its small size – the hall is about 18 ft 6 ins by 14 ft 6 ins (5·6 m x 4·4 m) – suggests it was built not earlier than the 16th century. In the wall to S is the principal post of the open truss, the tie-beam of which has been cut away. In the early 17th century the hall was divided into two storeys; the binding-beam is chamfered and stopped in the middle to E where the bearer meets it; its W side, where there is now no bearer, is treated in the same way. Presumably the existing chimney-stack replaces a timber chimney-stack; the lintel of the existing brick fireplace has two peg-holes, as if to secure the tenons of wooden jambs. During the 17th century a two-bay structure was added to W, with two rooms on each floor, that to E being a parlour. In the early 19th century bay windows and sash windows were put in and the stair was rebuilt to make it wider and give it a gentler rise. Subsequent additions at the back doubled the size of the house.

(77688)
Kimpton Grange (TL 165182),

a brick house of the mid 19th century, replaces a timber-framed house which must originally have had an open hall and two cross-wings and is shown in a `View of Kimpton Park' of 1840.[1] It appears to have been of about the same size as Nos 59/61 Collier's End, Standon.

Note
1. Buckler Vol IV, 168.

(79569)
Kimpton Hall (TL 173176)

appears to be the manor house corresponding to that part of the large pre-Conquest manor of Kimpton known in the middle ages as Hockinghanger.[1] From 1235–6 until 1493 it belonged to the Northamptonshire family de Vere; it was then divided between heiresses until reunited in 1582 by Lewis, Lord Mordaunt. He sold the manor in 1596 to Thomas Hoo of St Paul's Walden, after which it became a minor part of the Hoo

Fig 76 *Kimpton Hall, Kimpton: reconstruction*

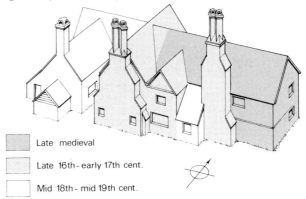

Late medieval

Late 16th – early 17th cent.

Mid 18th – mid 19th cent.

estates. A drawing of 1834[2] enables the development of the house to be understood more fully than would otherwise be possible (Fig 76). The oldest part to E was the hall; the roof incorporates many re-used smoke-blackened rafters of good quality and scantling but otherwise nothing medieval is observable. The large cross-wing to W, jettied to N, has no closely datable features but the clasped-purlin roof may be of the 16th century and suggests that the wing may have been added to an existing upper end bay; the latter was subsequently enlarged to S by the addition of a small gabled block of two storeys. The jettied range to W and the range to S of that appear to be successive additions. In the mid 17th century the hall was rebuilt; the stops on the chamfered bearers and the chimney-stack[3] are of that period. So too is the large stack added to the cross-wing, which is so wide as to suggest it was for a kitchen. The function of the other ground-floor rooms is uncertain. In the bay at the upper end of the hall a modern staircase may succeed an original one; and the unusual arrangement of binder and stops at the W end of the hall may represent the position of the seat of honour.

Notes
1. VCH III, 29–30; Gover, Mawer and Stenton 1938, 16.
2. Buckler Vol IV, 170.
3. Ibid.

(77690)
Ramridge (TL 152182)

is a late medieval timber-framed house which originally comprised an open hall between two-storeyed ends, a cross-wing at the service end and a parlour bay at the other. In the late 16th century the hall was floored over and a timber chimney-stack built backing on to the cross-passage; the hall fireplace has a lintel with rich mouldings which originally returned down the

Fig 77 Ramridge, Kimpton: plan

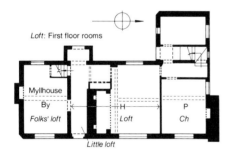

jambs. The probate inventory of William Davy of `Ramridges', yeoman, proved 19 March 1611/12,[1] lists the following rooms: hall, with andirons, bacon in the chimney and painted cloths; parlour, with two bedsteads and bedding, also painted cloths; chamber over the parlour, with two beds and bedding and painted cloths; loft over the hall, with two beds and bedding; the little loft, with one bed; `the folks' loft', with one bed and bedding; `the myll house', with a quern and mustard mill; the buttery; the kitchen. These room names have been indicated on the plan (Fig 77) as far as possible although it is difficult to be sure that the mill house was one of the service rooms. Presumably the kitchen was detached; it is the one room which clearly was not located in the house. The total valuation of the inventory was £290 2s 4d.

In the late 18th century the house was refaced in brick, a fireplace provided for the parlour and a wing added to W. In the 19th century a fireplace was added in the service bay.

Note
1. HRO, 32 HW3.

(77691)
Tallents (TL 160178)

was built in the late 16th or early 17th century; restoration has made its interpretation uncertain. It has an L-shaped plan with the main range running E–W and a wing, which is slightly narrower and has a slightly lower ridge, to NE. The main range originally had to E a chimney-stack with back-to-back fireplaces and a lobby-entrance; the disposition of the bearers and their chamfer stops shows that the size of this presumed stack was appropriate to a timber or early brick chimney. From W to E the ground-floor rooms were: service, hall-kitchen, parlour; there are some indications that another room adjoined the parlour to N. The staircase position is not known. A timber-framed lean-to in the re-entrant angle, apparently an addition, may have incorporated another service room. The present kitchen was added to N in the 18th century; subsequently the ground floor was rebuilt in brick. All the chimney-stacks were rebuilt and the existing entrance-hall created in the course of restoration work undertaken in the present century.

KINGS LANGLEY

(77692)
Langley Lodge (TL 064014)

stands in the former royal park of Langley and was perhaps the house of the keeper or some other officer. The oldest part is a close-studded timber building of two storeys, probably the late 15th-century cross-wing of a medieval hall which lay to E; of the latter nothing remains, although its successor incorporates one post re-used from an aisled building and dated by a notched lap joint to the 13th or 14th century. The wing was about 30 ft by 14 ft (9.2 m x 4.3 m) and unusually lofty, being 23 ft (7.0 m) from ground to wall-plate; there is no evidence of an original chimney-stack. The ground floor has been much altered. On each floor were two rooms with a bay between them for the staircase; the newel post remains. The large first-floor room to N is spanned by the chamfered collar-beam truss of the clasped-purlin roof; the room has a high four-light window to W lighting the doorway from the staircase. The room to S has lost most of its original timberwork and its length is uncertain but was at least 11 ft (3.4 m). It was probably lit by large windows in the gable-end walls. In the 17th century a wing was added to W incorporating a kitchen, and subsequently the hall was replaced by a two-storey block. In the early 18th century the house was enlarged slightly to E and refronted to S; a chimney-stack was added to W of the 17th-century wing; and a new staircase, with turned balusters and moulded handrail, was built. In the entrance-hall is a recessed cupboard of the same date; on its coved head is a painted classical subject: a rider on a winged horse (possibly Pegasus) leans over to lead another horse by the bridle. An early 19th-century tenant named Newman Hatley is mentioned by Arthur Young as a particularly progressive farmer,[1] and he may have been responsible for refacing and enlarging the wing to W.

Note
1. Young 1804, 16, 97, 111.

KINGS WALDEN

(77693)
Nos 38–42 Chapel Road, Breachwood Green (TL 150219)

has a late-medieval open hall of two bays with cross-wing to N and storeyed bay to S. In the early 17th century a chimney-stack and first floor were inserted in the hall; the partition at the upper end of the hall has a painted representation of panelling in deep red and a yellow/brown background, the centre of each panel bearing a floral device; it is drawn freehand and is of the early 17th century.[1] There are other fragmentary paintings above the first-floor fireplace which was added to S; the stack has diagonally set square shafts.

Note
1. Rouse 1989, 440.

(77694)
Heath Farm (TL 149225),

built in the late 15th century, comprised a hall and two cross-wings flush with it; the wing to E is jettied, that to W not, and they may not be coeval. All three hall trusses are moulded; the open truss has moulded capitals; the roof has clasped-purlins. A fireplace was inserted in the hall in the late 16th century; at one end of its moulded lintel is a peg-hole suggesting that the jambs, now of 18th or 19th-century brick, were originally wooden.

(39628)
Kings Walden Bury or Park (TL 161235)

was the house of a manor first recorded in the early 13th century. It passed through many hands until bought by Richard Hale in 1576, and remained with his family until 1884. The house was evidently important in the 17th century; William Hale was Sheriff in 1621, Richard Hale in 1631 and Rowland Hale in 1647; Rowland paid for 17 hearths in 1663[1] and William Hale for the same number in 1673.[2] A drawing of 1832[3] and several late Victorian photographs showing the principal elevations suggest that the exterior to S was largely of the late 17th century. The larger part to W was symmetrical with three shallow projections, two gabled and the middle one with a parapet; to E was a symmetrical block three bays in width, the middle one projecting and with a parapet; and joining them was what had presumably once been an entrance, recessed very slightly behind the other two blocks and bearing the Hale coat-of-arms. The roof line confirms the division into two blocks. The Buckler drawing of 1832 shows that the N elevation was equal to five bays and had two large gables and a smaller one, concealed by a shallow parapeted projection in the middle. The E elevation, shown in an old photograph, was six bays in width; two to N were under a gabled roof, the next had a parapet, the next two formed a shallow parapeted projection like those to S and W, and the S bay was parapeted. Evidently the whole exterior had been treated as uniformly as possible but the general impression is of two distinct parts, like some other late 17th-century houses. Some of the chimney-stacks drawn by Buckler may have been of that date. The history of the house cannot be traced in detail, but probably William Hale, who was Sheriff in 1830, gave it the end-entrance with Gothic doorway and oriel window over, the two pinnacles crowning each of the square projections, and the large window reaching to the ground. A curious feature of the E elevation is that it comprised two storeys almost equivalent in height to the three storeys to S; some windows in the latter may have been dummies.

For an illustration, see *English Houses 1200–1800*, Fig 208 (plate).

Notes
1. PRO E179/248/23.
2. PRO E179/375/31.
3. Buckler Vol III, 69.

(77695)
Leggatt's Farm (TL 165245),

comprising two houses joined by a short connecting block of one storey, is an example of the unit system. Both houses are timber framed, comprise a hall range and one cross-wing, and have lost most of their original detail. The house to W appears to have had an open hall; an upper floor and chimney-stack were added in the last quarter of the 17th century, as was, in a rear turret, a staircase with heavy moulded handrail. The house to E (which was not examined) was much altered in the middle of the 19th century; the cross-wing may be earlier (perhaps 16th century) than the main range, and, if so, implies that the hall is of late medieval origin.

For an illustration, see *English Houses 1200–1800*, Fig 177 (plate).

KNEBWORTH

(79579)
Knebworth House (TL 230307),

now a large stuccoed building in late 19th-century romantic Gothic style, incorporates the shell of a 16th-century courtyard house. Drawings made before extensive demolitions in 1811[1] suggest that the oldest part was a three-storey gatehouse block forming part of the E range; it was of brick with stone dressings, the entrance-arches were four-centred and moulded, and the windows were generally of two lights with four-centred heads; to E (correctly NE) were two salient square corner turrets to N and S; to W the gateway arch had a two-storey oriel window above and a part-octagonal staircase tower to S. The date is uncertain but its proportions, resembling those of the gatehouse of Hertford Castle, suggest it was built by William Lytton, who was Sheriff of Essex and Hertfordshire in 1511 and died in 1517.[2] His heir Robert was a minor who did not come of age until 1534, which is rather late for such a bare, fortress-like exterior. No building-works can definitely be ascribed to Robert, who was Sheriff in 1546 and died in 1551. A tablet bearing the date 1563 and the arms of Rowland Lytton,[3] who was Sheriff in 1568, denotes when the old hall range, probably timber framed, was pulled down and the courtyard plan, incorporating the gatehouse, was completed uniformly in mid 16th-century style. Work of this period, visible in the hall, comprises pedimented mullion-and-transom windows and diaper-patterned brickwork in the W wall; similar windows are exposed in the SE return of the great parlour; remains of another such window have been revealed on the first floor adjoining the S wing at the rear. These details confirm two drawings of the courtyard dated 1805.[4] In 1988 a first-floor timber-framed partition painted with bold foliage patterns was exposed; it adjoins the W part of the S wing and has been truncated to S. This and the mutilated window nearby, coupled with the lack of a thick internal longitudinal wall, show that the range extending from the entrance to the S wing must have been two rooms deep as built. Presumably there was an axial corridor with indirect light from both sides (cf, much later, Rickmansworth Bury). The blocked windows of the hall show that the room existing to N c1800 was an addition but the plan suggests that the great staircase and the vestibule to S were original, since it is difficult to envisage any alternative position. A second large staircase to S of the entrance, of uncertain

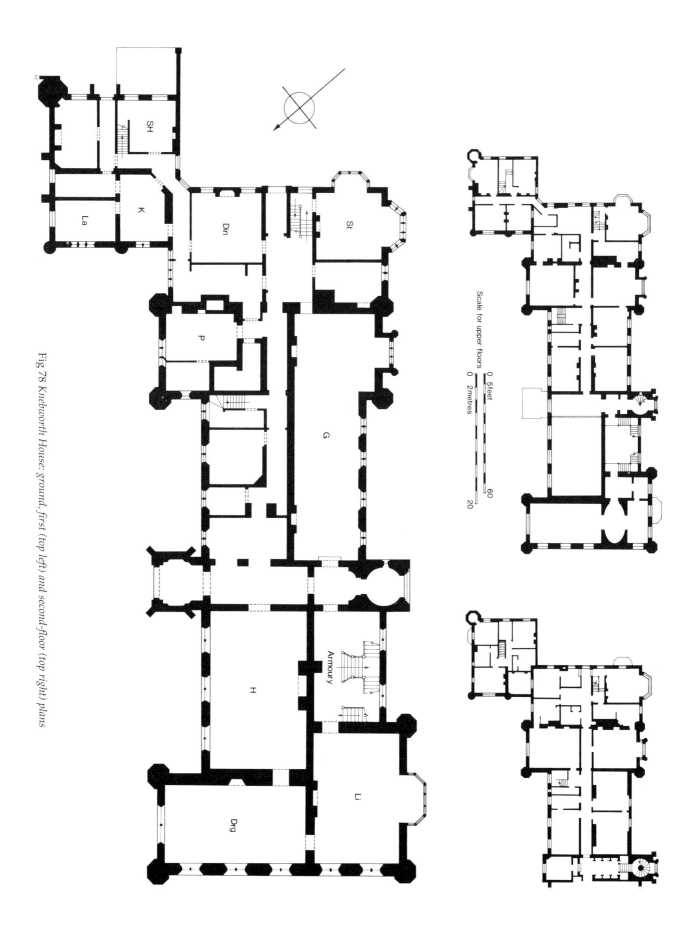

Fig 78 Knebworth House: ground, first (top left) and second-floor (top right) plans

Scale for upper floors

0   5feet
0   2metres

20   60

date but perhaps built in the 1560s, indicates that there was a set of important rooms at either end of the hall, in principle like the arrangement at Hatfield House. These conclusions are incorporated in a reconstruction of the house in the early 17th century (*English Houses 1200–1800*, Fig 83).

An engraving of 1700[5] shows that the E elevation had been heightened by the addition of an attic storey, and the S elevation had been treated similarly;[6] the lack of pediments suggests that the windows had been altered to conform to late 17th-century style. This refacing is ascribable to Sir William Lytton, who inherited in 1674, was knighted in 1677, became Sheriff in the following year, and died in 1705. He probably added the rooms to N of the hall; that on the ground floor was described as Sir William Lytton's closet in an inventory of 1707. Tall windows on the E side of the hall with round heads, emphasised keystones and sunk panels above in the parapet may be somewhat later, perhaps by William Robinson Lytton, who was Sheriff in 1710. In the late 17th or early 18th century a long stable block of two storeys with cupola was built to N of the house.[7] In 1790 it was noted that `at the west end of this colonnade [ie the N range] is a suite of rooms with modern sashes';[8] similar windows had been inserted in the S and E elevations.[9] Some of these alterations may have been made by John Robinson-Lytton, who owned the house from 1732,[10] came of age in 1745,[11] was Sheriff in 1758 and died in 1762. William Skinner's remark in 1805 that `After Haddon Hall I think it the most perfect specimen of the hospitable habitations of our ancestors I have seen in the country'[12] suggests that the house had changed comparatively little. The plans, based on Skinner's drawings, are shown in *English Houses 1200–1800*, Fig 213 and the external appearance is reconstructed in Fig 83. By 1810, when Elizabeth Bulwer inherited it, the need for alteration was apparent. The first intention (*English Houses 1200–1800*, Fig 214) was to retain the gatehouse while demolishing or reducing to one storey the remainder of the E and much of the N and W ranges, but to minimise its inconvenience by building a new colonnade with passage above to join it to the house (cf Beechwood, Flamstead); the principal fronts would be to N and E (*English Houses 1200–1800*, Fig 216).[13] This plan is interesting for the respect shown for the oldest part of the house, and as providing the long cloister-like approach desired in other houses (cf Cassiobury, Watford, and Munden, Aldenham). It was not adopted, and in 1813 the W or hall range was extensively altered, the remainder of the courtyard plan with stables and service wing demolished, and new service and stable courts were added to S.[14] All the new work was in Tudor style. On the W side of the park a lodge incorporating details from the gatehouse provided a vague reminiscence of it,[15] as an inscription dated 1816 over the gateway testifies. The architect for this work was John Biagio Rebecca.[16] On inheriting in 1844 Edward Bulwer-Lytton altered the house to designs by H E Kendall jnr,[17] including a staircase modelled on the Great Staircase at Hatfield House, with royal beasts on the newel posts.[18] In 1878 his son Robert Bulwer-Lytton added a third storey to that part of the house S of the entrance and embellished the whole with profuse Gothic detail to the designs of John Lee; and at about the same time George Devey enlarged and rebuilt the service wing and stable court.[19] Subsequently Sir Edwin Lutyens altered the Great Hall and remodelled the gardens,[20] and further modifications were made by Philip Tilden in 1948.[21] Plans of the house as it is today appear as Fig 78.

For illustrations, see *English Houses 1200–1800*, Figs 81 (plate), 82 (plate), 83, 85 (plate), 92 (plate), 213, 214, 215, 216 (plate).

Notes

1. VCH III, 112.
2. Ibid, 115.
3. Ibid, 112.
4. The Revd W Skinner, BL Add MS 33641, fos 208–9.
5. Chauncy II, 92.
6. BL Add MS 33641, fo 206.
7. Baskerfield drawing, BL Add MS 9063, fo 63.
8. *Gent Mag* 1790 (ii), 983–6.
9. BL Add MS 33641, fo 206 and comment fo 212v.
10. VCH III, 116.
11. *Knebworth House* 1974, 23.
12. BL Add MS 33641, fo 212v.
13. Reconstructed from elevational drawings, HRO, K 522–9.
14. Buckler Vol III, 174.
15. Buckler Vol IV, 175.
16. Colvin 1978, 673–4.
17. Ibid, 487n.
18. NMR DD60/111.
19. *Knebworth House* 1974, 21.
20. Weaver 1925, 318.
21. Tilden 1954, 170.

LANGLEY

(77696)
The Forge (TL 215222),

of the early 16th century, comprised a hall formerly open to the roof and a further bay to S. In the hall peg-holes may denote a bench to S; if so, the cross-passage was to N. The two-storey bay to S is unheated and may always have had two ground-floor rooms, one of which may have been a shop, as at Yew Tree Farm, Much Hadham. The bay to N, somewhat taller than that to S, shows no clear sign of heightening and may have been completely rebuilt *c*1600; the structural break with the hall leaves the usual squarish living-space for the latter. A first floor was inserted in the hall *c*1600 and probably a timber chimney-stack added at the same time; a post now embedded in the brick chimney-stack to W may be a relic of the latter; possibly both hall and N bay had fireplaces. In the 18th century the chimney-stack was rebuilt in brick and the first floor in the N bay raised; the lobby-entrance was retained and a staircase built to E of the chimney-stack.

LETCHWORTH

(77697)
Letchworth Hall Hotel (TL 217308),

a manor house, belonged to Thomas Hanchet of Bedford by the middle of the 15th century. His son William, who succeeded him in 1474,[1] probably built the late medieval timber-framed house of which the cross-wing survives (Fig 79a). This service wing, to S of the hall, has a crown-post roof with four-way struts; the projection of the wing beyond the hall suggests that a jetty has been underbuilt to E and possibly also to W (Fig 80). Until about 1905 a wing `of massive timber-framing' with a jetty projecting about 2 ft (0·6 m) and with rounded ends to the joists stood to N of the hall.[2] One other possibly late medieval part of the building is what was originally a detached structure to S of the S wing. It was timber framed, partly plastered and partly weatherboarded, and gabled and possibly jettied to E;[3] it has to S some blocks of chalk and flint incorporated in what was described as `a small disused porch'[4] and is now a stair turret. Although modern alterations have removed all old features except the chalk and flint blocks, its small size (14 ft x 12 ft (4·3 m x 3·7 m)

Fig 79 *Letchworth Hall Hotel: development perspectives*

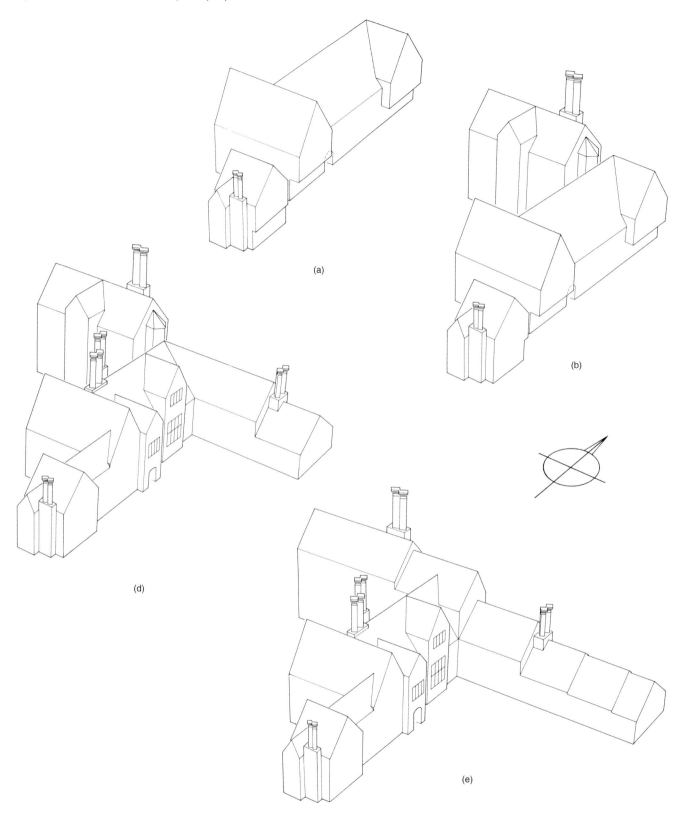

internally) suggests it might have been a detached kitchen and the blocks part of a 17th-century chimney-stack and staircase.

In 1597 Sir Rowland Lytton acquired the manor[5] and added to NW a parlour wing of two storeys and attics (Fig 79b) almost completely detached from the earlier building; his arms and crest were `in the parlour window'.[6] Originally it had two ground-floor rooms; in the parlour is a stone fireplace with four-centred head within a square outer moulding; it has an oak over-mantel divided into two compartments with scalloped surrounds flanked by demi-figures. Over the parlour was an important room with another and more ornate stone fireplace, flanked by female herms which support a moulded and enriched entablature; and above it is a large plaster panel in high relief depicting the Judgement of Paris. On stylistic grounds the panel may be a generation later than the fireplace. Formerly the attic storey had another important room above the chamber; and the wing had a wide gable facing S, apparently projecting well beyond the present S wall, as if each of the three principal rooms was nearly square as built; the projection probably formed a bay window on ground and first floors;[7] the newel staircase serving these rooms was in a polygonal and apparently timber-framed turret to E (cf Amores, Hertingfordbury, Hertford); it probably occupied the position of the original cross-wing staircase. The

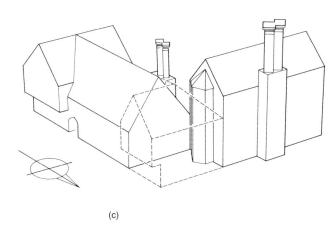

(c)

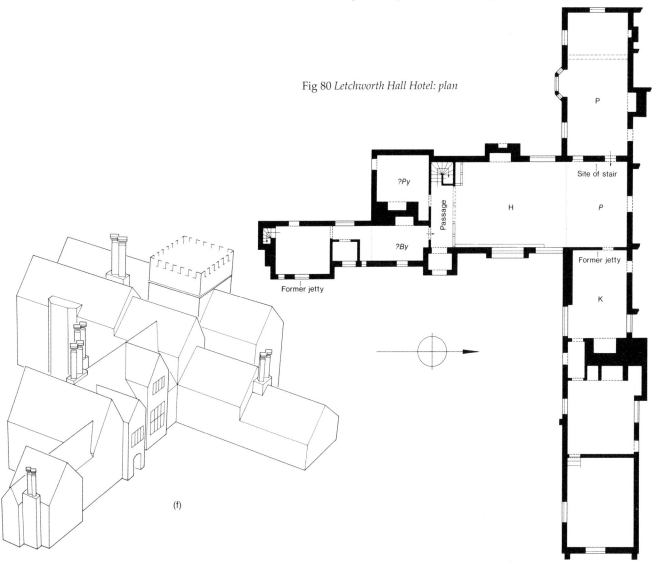

Fig 80 *Letchworth Hall Hotel: plan*

(f)

problem of the relation of Lytton's parlour wing to any earlier cross-wing is shown in Fig 79c; and cf Amores, Hertford, for such a staircase within an existing structure. The hall, originally open to the roof, apparently was not provided with a chimney-stack and an upper storey before the mid 17th century (Fig 79d). A shallow bay window of four lights was added to E and carried up to provide a large dormer to the first-floor room; rustication was applied to the brickwork between the windows. At the same time a two-storeyed porch in rusticated brickwork was added[8] and the passage was separated from the hall by a panelled screen with two wide doors flanking a column with a Doric capital; the service rooms were refaced in brick and joined to the presumed kitchen by a passage.[9] A short block to E of the N cross-wing, of one storey and attics, may be coeval; it has, to E, a chimney-stack with diagonal shafts; it was a kitchen in 1908.[10] A single-storey wing to E of this new kitchen was built by 1800 (Fig 79d).[11]

In the early 17th century the house comprised two distinct blocks of rooms, of two or three storeys, separated by the open hall; the NW wing faced S, the hall range to E. In the mid 17th century the rooms to S of the hall were improved but still faced S, and no attempt was made to centralise the house by providing a new main staircase; that to N remained in use, that to S was rebuilt.[12]

Little change took place in the 18th century, but by 1840 the original cross-wing had been heightened to match the NW wing; the little block to SE refaced; and a single-storey outhouse built and joined to the latter by a crenellated wall (Fig 79e).[13] About 1845 the Revd John Alington, who owned the house from 1830 to 1863, built a large block to E of and parallel with the NW wing, refacing the latter and eliminating the original bay windows; he also made the ground-floor rooms into one, put in the corridor which masks the first-floor fireplace[14] and moved the principal entrance to N (Fig 79f). Considerable alterations were made about 1905 to convert the house into a hotel, when the former cross-wing was incorporated into the hall. At some time after 1910 the first floor was removed to recreate an open hall.

Notes
1. VCH III, 120–2.
2. Aylott nd.
3. Oldfield Vol IV, 479.
4. VCH III, 118.
5. Ibid, 121.
6. Oldfield Vol IV, 481.
7. Ibid, 479.
8. Ibid, now much rebuilt.
9. Ibid.
10. VCH III, 119, plan.
11. Oldfield Vol IV, 479.
12. VCH III, 120, engraving after A Whitworth Anderson photograph.
13. Buckler Vol III, 73.
14. Aylott nd.

(77698)
Puncharden Hall, Willian (TL 225308)

takes its name from Robert de Pentcarden who held land here in 1086 and whose descendants were tenants of some importance in the 13th century.[1] Who built the present house, which is of modest size relative to the status of the earlier tenants, does not appear from the descent of the manor; it is of the early 16th century and comprises an open hall flanked by cross-wings. The hall has been rebuilt except for some original roof trusses. Probably the wings were jettied originally; no evidence of this remains but it would explain why, when refronting took place,

the hall was widened by 2 ft (0·6 m). In the early 17th century a floor was inserted into the hall and a square chimney-stack with diagonal fillets[2] was built to serve fireplaces in the hall and parlour and probably in the two chambers above them. Apparently the stack was placed at the upper end of the old hall and a lobby-entrance replaced the former cross-passage at the W end. Perhaps somewhat later a chimney-stack with two diagonal shafts[3] was built to serve a fireplace in the former service rooms; the new room may have been a kitchen. In 1625 the `capital messuage called Puncherdownes'[4] belonged to Edward Wilson, lord of the manor of Willian, who was living in 1634[5] and in his lifetime settled Puncharden on his son Ralph who died in 1637. In the Hearth Tax return of 25 March 1663[6] Mrs Wilson – presumably the widow of `Wilson Gent.' who in Michaelmas 1662, paid for eight hearths – paid for eight and Mr Luke Wilson for seven. This suggests either a house divided into two occupancies, like Hunsdon House (see page 106) or, more likely, two adjoining houses like Temple Dinsley, Preston, or Leggatt's Farm, Kings Walden. In the early 18th century a brick front and rear staircase wing were added and a fireplace with three-centred head and keystone was put in the chamber over the hall; this may be the work of John Priest who paid six shillings (for between 10 and 20 windows) in various Window Tax returns between 1724 and 1735.[7] Subsequently a large wing containing service rooms was built to NW, incorporating to N an older timber-framed building. Puncharden Hall is depicted in a drawing of c1800, but not the one so captioned in the Oldfield drawings;[8] it is identical with the `House in the village of Willian...formerly the property and residence of Mr Priest',[9] so that if ever two houses had existed here, one had been demolished by then, as happened at Temple Dinsley, Preston. In the mid 19th century the front door was moved and two bay windows were added; a fireplace was added to make the lobby into a small room and the main stack was rebuilt with five shafts. Recent alterations revealed a wallpaper with Gothic architectural motifs of 1830–50[10] in the ground-floor room of the W wing and if this room had ever been a kitchen it ceased to be so then.

Notes
1. VCH III, 179.
2. Oldfield Vol VII, 327.
3. Ibid.
4. VCH III, 179.
5. *Visitations*, 105.
6. PRO E179/248/23.
7. HRO, LT Misc 10.
8. Oldfield Vol VII, 327.
9. Ibid, 325.
10. Inf. Miss J Hamilton, V&A.

LILLEY

(77699)
Ward's Farm (TL 115271)

is of brick and mostly of two storeys and attics. It has an L-shaped plan; the main range, running N–S, was built in the mid 18th century, and a wing was added to E in the early 19th century. The former has a central staircase-hall; the parlour is to S with a cellar under it, and the principal living room or kitchen to N; to N again are two unheated service rooms, one a pantry. This range lacked symmetry both of elevation and plan, and there is a step up from the entrance-hall to the principal room, yet there is nothing else to suggest that the house is of more than one build. The wing, which subsequently combined a large kitchen with a pantry and staircase, may originally have been unheated because, in the roof space, the chimney-stack appears to be an addition.

LITTLE BERKHAMSTED

(77700)
Epping House (TL 293067)

is first mentioned as a farmhouse in 1658.[1] Sir William Horne, Attorney-General 1832–4,[2] built the present house not many years before 1838, when it appears on the tithe map.[3] In the 1851 Census it was occupied by Charles Lowther, fundholder, his wife, two children, five nieces, a preceptor (Robert Davies, incumbent of Hatfield), two preceptresses, six indoor servants and a groom.[4]

The map shows two not quite symmetrical bow windows to E, one of which remains today, with a smaller square projection between them, perhaps a porch for the garden doorway. The house was approached from S; a pediment corresponds to the width of the entrance-hall; to N is the main staircase; there are four principal ground-floor rooms. A drive appears to have run under a covered way between the house and the service wing to W.[5] The house underwent extensive internal renovation c1900 and hardly any of the earlier fittings remain. It is now a Special School.

Notes
1. Millington 1981, 23.
2. *DNB.*
3. HRO, DSA 4/20/2.
4. PRO HO 107/1711.
5. Estate map, 1844; HRO D/EL/P5.

(77701)
The Old Manor (TL 294080)

is timber framed and of two storeys and attics. Definite evidence of late medieval work is lacking; in the rear (W) wall a chamfered post rises to the ceiling as if for the roof truss of an open hall but is not traceable upstairs; a re-used beam to N, with mortises for joists, and a beam cutting across the E bay window at a considerably lower level than the ceiling are evidence of alteration. On balance the house was probably always of two storeys and was built in the late 16th century. It is thus earlier than the chimney-stack drawn in 1839, which had square shafts of the last quarter of the 17th century;[1] an earlier stack must have existed and can only have been of timber; this is confirmed by the fact that the binding-beams are placed clear of the existing brickwork as if to allow for one. The only other 16th-century feature is the clasped-purlin roof. The plan comprised a lobby-entrance with hall to N and parlour to S; the hall is unlikely to have been as big as the present drawing room, the proportions of the latter suggesting it incorporates a small service room to N. The porch and the two-storey bay window with ovolo-moulded mullions were added in the mid 17th century. Probably the first-floor room over the hall was then divided by a partition carried into the bay window and extending the roof apex; this partition replaced any earlier division corresponding to the hall/service room partition below. A two-bay outhouse some 14 ft (3·3 m) to N, perhaps of c1700 and probably a brewhouse, was originally open to the roof; in the mid 19th century the internal chimney-stack was rebuilt with diagonal shafts; in the ground-floor room to S is a fireplace surround inscribed 1657.

Note
1. Buckler Vol III, 10.

LITTLE GADDESDEN

(77702)
John O'Gaddesden's House (SP 998127),

so called from a spurious connection with the 14th-century physician,[1] is of c1500 and is of the same architectural type as a guildhall. There is no evidence that a guild existed and besides, the building is extraordinarily richly finished for such a purpose. It is of two storeys, has a very bold jetty (4 ft (1·2 m)) to E and S, and originally had no fireplaces. Further evidence that its use was not domestic is provided by four wide arched openings to S and two to N, resembling shop windows, which show that only the bay to N and possibly that to W were partitioned off from the principal ground-floor room. The entrance was possibly where it is now (cf the Town House, Barley) but the staircase was probably to N in a narrow structure roofed continuously with the main span and apparently original.[2] The first floor, except for a short bay to W, formed one large room which is hardly equalled among Hertfordshire vernacular buildings for the quality and profusion of its ornament. The middle truss of the clasped-purlin roof is identical, above the tie-beam, with the two intermediate trusses; all have cambered collar-beams and solid arch-braces with carved spandrels; the stub tie-beams of the intermediate trusses are carved with human heads.

In the late 17th century the building was converted into a house. The wide ground-floor openings were filled by windows or infilling, a brick chimney-stack was added to W, and a lobby-entrance formed. A panelled ground-floor room was created to W by taking in part of the lean-to to N. Probably the first floor was divided into two rooms by a partition at the middle truss; this would account for the considerable repairs needed after the partition had been removed. Perhaps at this time a cross-wing was added to W; its N wall is of brick, the first floor being corbelled out slightly on three moulded courses; the ground floor room was the kitchen.

In the present century the house was restored and greatly enlarged in various antiquarian styles, including the stepped gable to N of the wing which is entirely modern; its earlier form is unknown.

Notes
1. *DNB.*
2. Anderson drawing, 1907, HM.

(77703)
The Manor House (SP 997128)

is associated with a manor first recorded in the late 12th century and known alternatively, from its long possession until 1466 by the Lucy family, as Lucies. By the middle of the 16th century it was owned by the Dormers; Sir Robert Dormer, who inherited in 1574, commemorated his rebuilding or enlargement of the house by a tablet bearing the date 1576 and the initials A R D and E B [?] (third initial indistinct), for himself and his wife Elizabeth Browne. In 1606 the manor was sold to Thomas, Lord Ellesmere and John Egerton his son;[1] nobody of that surname appears in the Hearth Tax return for 1662 but a member of the family commemorated some building work by a rain-water head bearing the date and initials 1684 I E M. The considerable antiquarian restoration in the Tudor style that had taken place by 1811[2] may have been undertaken by Francis Henry Egerton,

8th Earl of Bridgewater,[3] who succeeded his brother in 1823 and died in 1829; or possibly by his brother's wife Charlotte, who held the estate from then until her death in 1849. The house was enlarged in 1890 by the 3rd Earl Brownlow.[4] A statement[5] that after a fire the house was largely unoccupied for about a hundred years prior to 1890, only one wing being inhabited as two cottages, appears to be untrue.

The 16th-century work in the house as it stands at present amounts to no more than two rooms, one on each floor; their proportions suggest they may originally have been partitioned. Far from being a house appropriate to Sir Robert Dormer it may well have been merely an addition to an older building which has since disappeared. Matters are further complicated by the early 19th-century alterations, which were so extensive that most of the apparently Elizabethan features are suspect.

Notes
1. VCH II, 211–12.
2. Buckler Vol I, 129.
3. *DNB*.
4. *Manor House*, guidebook.
5. Ibid.

(39612)
Old Ashridge (SP 992114),
sometimes called the Lodge, is the name given to a two-storey mid 18th-century house to NE of the gatehouse leading to Ashridge itself – the courtyard house which incorporated the medieval college of Bonhommes. It was completely detached in 1762,[1] having been built because the old house was out of repair,[2] but had been joined to the gatehouse by 1814.[3] A drawing of the rear elevation[4] suggests it had been considerably altered and two semi-octagonal conservatories added. It was demolished in the 19th century and the orangery built on the site. (Cf Cold Harbour, Great Munden.)

Notes
1. Estate map, HRO, AH 2770.
2. *Gent Mag* 1802 (ii), 611–12.
3. Buckler Vol I, 138.
4. Ibid, 137.

LITTLE HADHAM

(77705)
Acremore Cottage (TL 413211),
of two storeys and with a three-cell plan, has some exposed framing of fairly closely spaced studs and is thatched. Slight evidence suggests it was built *c*1500 and was open to the roof with a timber chimney-stack and fireplace in the hall: the ceilings of the ground-floor rooms are progressively higher from W to E; the bearer in the E room is neither supported by nor tenoned into wall studs nearby; and the bearer in the hall is supported on a short post above the lintel, as if inserted. In the late 17th century a brick chimney-stack with conjoined diagonal flues was built, with staircase and lobby-entrance to S; the inserted chamfered bearer in the hall has bar-and-lozenge stops; and the bearer in the bay to E is grooved for a boarded partition. In the 19th century a narrow N wing, accommodating a kitchen and dairy, was added.

(77706)
Ashmeads (TL 435216),
of two storeys, comprises a main range, probably replacing a late-medieval open hall, and, to S, a cross-wing of *c*1600 which

may replace an earlier bay. The wing, formerly jettied to E, has close-studding; each floor forms one room, with fireplace to S; the ground-floor room has, to N adjoining the hall to E, a moulded doorway with four-centred head and a pellet ornament in each of the hollowed spandrels and, to W, a four-light window with ovolo mullions; in the first-floor room a three-light diamond-mullion window with shutter groove has been replaced by a bay window with ovolo mouldings. The position of the fireplace suggests some original subdivision to E of this room, as if for a staircase of which no definite evidence remains; peg-holes for close-studding appear to preclude a doorway to the staircase; however, a blocked doorway, adjoining to E the one described and having a lower lintel with a short stud above it, could have led to the parlour, whilst the existing doorway opened directly on to a staircase. In the hall range the fireplace has a moulded lintel of *c*1600; the stack probably backed on to a cross-passage and if so the postulated staircase perpetuates the position of one that might be expected in the storeyed service-end bay of a late-medieval open hall. The significance of the wing is that although the ground-floor room may formally have been called the parlour, it had taken over some important functions of the hall and had perhaps reduced the latter to a kitchen. To N the house has been rebuilt and alterations of the 18th and 19th centuries were removed during restoration in recent years.

For an illustration, see *English Houses 1200–1800*, Fig 163 (plate).

(77707)
Att House Farm, Green Street (TL 456219)
is a double-pile house of brick with pilastered front and rear elevations; it was built about the beginning of the 18th century but a chamfered and stopped beam unrelated to the present plan suggests that part of an older building is incorporated. The plan is square; originally it comprised, to S, hall and (to E) parlour; to N were the staircase and two unheated service rooms. In the early 19th century the hall was reduced in size to make a narrow entrance-hall; a fireplace was added in a room to NE to make a new kitchen; various additions to N and W may replace older wings but now contain no old features.

(77708)
Bridge End
and
(77708)
The Whare (TL 439226),
at the cross-roads in the middle of the village, are so close and in such an unusual relationship to one another as to suggest that they formed an example of the unit system; the alternative explanation, that their closeness arises from their being in a village, hardly holds good in so small a settlement.

Bridge End is a much altered house of late medieval origin. The existence of an open hall is established by the low eaves and a tie-beam, which has been cut through to provide access between rooms after a first floor had been inserted; a bay to S may have been floored over originally. The inserted floor has chamfered bearers and the stair rail has moulded balusters and a heavy rail with a rounded top grip, all consistent with the first half of the 17th century, but the chimney-stack and ground-floor fireplace are considerably later, perhaps of the date painted, with the owner/builder's initials, outside: I N M 1732. The practice of building lateral rather than axial chimney-stacks within former open halls seems to belong to the late 17th and early 18th centuries. The W wing may have been added in the early 18th century.

The Whare was built *c*1500 with an open hall between the E wing and the bay to W of the chimney-stack; this is established by the low eaves; the posts of a truss and the sawn-off ends of a tie-beam near the E end of the main range; and another truss which was probably open. In the bay to W the lighter colour of the rafters shows that this was not part of the hall; it may have been of two storeys. The E cross-wing is a later addition incorporating many re-used timbers; it comprises two rooms on each floor, and may be coeval with the upper floor and chimney-stack inserted in the hall in the 17th century. The ground-floor rooms were then, from W to E: parlour; kitchen/hall, the proportions suggesting that the first function was the more important; and two unheated rooms, one of which must have been a pantry and the other perhaps a dairy or an unheated parlour.

For an illustration, see *English Houses 1200–1800*, Fig 178 (plate).

(77709)
Bury Green Farm (TL 452209)

incorporates a late medieval house of which a clasped-purlin roof truss with smoke-blackened rafters to S, over the open hall, is the only evidence. The bay to N was perhaps of two storeys; probably a similar bay existed to S but has left no trace. In the late 17th century a brick chimney-stack with diagonal shafts was built to heat hall and parlour, and a lobby-entrance was created to E; the hall then became the kitchen. In the early 19th century a wing was added to W, to form a new kitchen with an oven to S of the fireplace; the original service bay was probably demolished then and a new front entrance, with a lobby at the foot of the staircase, was created to S.

For an illustration, see *English Houses 1200–1800*, Fig 56 (plate).

(77710)
Clintons, Bury Green (TL 449209),

is a manor house named from Henry Clynton who possessed it in 1396;[1] a successor of the same name is mentioned in 1464.[2] The hall and cross-wing to E are of the early 15th century and were probably built by one or other Henry Clynton; the resemblance between the tracery in the spandrels of the open truss and that in Westminster Hall roof of 1396-7 makes a date as early as *c*1420 not impossible; cf also tracery, not closely dated, in St John's chapel, Berkhamsted church.[3] The former open hall comprises two unequal bays spanned by an arch-braced tie-beam truss. To N of the E bay a four-centred arch originally opened into a bay window; the mouchette in a spandrel, like the cinquefoiled tracery of the open truss, suggests the early 15th century. Another indication of comparatively early date is the fact that the structural posts are flush with the wall-plates and lack the jowls usually found in late medieval buildings. To W a roof truss may have marked the cross-passage; possibly there was some kind of spere-truss. The tie-beam of the open truss is more elaborately moulded to E, facing the upper end of the hall, than to W (cf Almshoe Bury, Ippollitts). The roof has principal rafters with tenoned purlins and wind braces, all hollow chamfered; since it is devoid of smoke-blackening the hall must originally have been heated by a lateral fireplace located in the usual position opposite the bay window. To E the hall framing appears to have formed a decorative pattern although it is not certain how faithfully this was reproduced during restoration. The wing to E is structurally separate from the hall and was not jettied, because the framing to N of the first floor is flush with that of the hall. Although the building of two chimney-stacks has removed the

E and W walls, the transverse bearer and heavy, plain joists carrying the first floor appear to be original; if so, the ground floor was undivided. A first-floor doorway to S with hollow-chamfered four-centred head and jambs stood at the head of an external staircase approached from the E end of the hall through a doorway where now is a window. Probably the upper storey was divided by a partition, the larger room being to N; this would account for the siting of the bearer in the room below.

In the early 16th century a two-storey wing of brick was added to E, possibly by Henry Patmore, who held the manors of Clintons and Joyces between 1513 and 1520;[4] it comprises parlour and first-floor chamber, both with fireplaces. Little original detail survives: in the E wall, which is of somewhat irregular bond, a Latin cross is worked in blue headers; both fireplaces retain relieving arches and a large patch of tile at the back of the hearth, but not the original jambs and heads; the roof is of collar-rafter type, with ashlar pieces standing on an inner plate which has a double hollow-chamfer. It is not clear why the fireplaces are off-centre to the N wall. To E, on each floor, is a window; neither is datable but the need for light near the fireplace suggests they are original. In the mid 16th century a floor, with moulded binding-beam and bearer, was inserted into the hall.

The most difficult problem presented by Clintons concerns the relative dates of the two principal chimney-stacks, neither of which can be closely dated; it is hard to see why they were not built back-to-back. The point is of historical as well as architectural importance because their building appears to connote a change of status from manor house to farmhouse. Both were built within existing structures, the hall stack in the cross-wing and the stack to E in the E wing. The stack to E may have been built first, *c*1600, perhaps to make a kitchen; if so, the latter may have taken over some of the functions of the hall. Probably a new staircase was built then, replacing the external flight to S; a possible site is suggested by the splay to SE, which may provide for a stair winding over the way through to the end room. These changes may have taken place after 1558, when the house came into the possession of Roland Baugh, and before his death in 1612.[5]

In the 17th century lateral chimney-stacks fell into disfavour in houses of declining status (cf Hinxworth Place) and the original hall stack was replaced by one to W *c*1600–70; the room then became a parlour, and the cellar customarily associated with it was provided underneath. Plaster ornament in the ceiling is comparable to that of 1665 at Lower Farm, Bury Green, Little Hadham. The cross-wing was reroofed in series with the buildings to E and W, the new roof having tenoned purlins into which the rafters are tenoned. In the 18th century the W end of the medieval house, including the cross-passage, was demolished; a wing providing a new entrance and staircase opposite was added to N; and a minor room to E provided for access from the yard.

For illustrations, see *English Houses 1200–1800*, Figs 38 (plate), 39, 295 (plate).

Notes
1. VCH IV, 54.
2. *Cal Pat* 1461-7, 338.
3. *TSPES* 1881–5, opposite p *xxv*.
4. VCH IV, 55.
5. Ibid.

(77711)
Gouldburns and May Cottage at Hadham Ford (TL 435216)

correspond respectively to a small, late medieval two-cell house and a later bay to N. The house to S (Gouldburns) formerly had an open hall; an arch-braced tie-beam truss may mark off the hall from the cross-passage, which is presumed to have been occupied by the inserted chimney-stack; a second bay to S may have been of two storeys. The N frame of this structure can be seen in May Cottage, where the roof with clasped-purlins, and first-floor framing are clearly later.

Fig 81 Green Street Cottage, Little Hadham: plan

(77712)
Green Street Cottage (TL 454220)

was built in the early 16th century, when it comprised a small open hall and a cross-wing to W of two storeys (Fig 81); it is thatched. In the hall roof three pairs of smoke-blackened collar-rafters remain in position. The wing now has two ground-floor rooms but may originally have been undivided because exposed framing shows that the two adjacent doors usual in a service wing did not exist; the staircase, probably to S, has left no traces; upstairs was one room, spanned by an open truss with arch-braced tie-beam. The cross-passage was no doubt where the chimney-stack now is, because a stud in the N wall precludes its having been at the W end of the hall. A service room to E was replaced in the 17th century by a two-storey parlour block with close-studding; since no stair trap is visible in the exposed joists the staircase must always have been in its present position. To N, S and W the parlour has wall-paintings of the first quarter of the 17th century; the design consists of a series of arches joined by strips and interwoven by a trellis in which is a flower-like motif; just below the ceiling is a scrollwork frieze.[1] The E block has a diamond-shaped painted panel with the initials and date S I E 1660, which appears too late for the parlour and its paintings but could refer to alterations to the hall; a chimney-stack and upper floor and a three-light window with ovolo-moulded mullions to S, lighting the hearth area, were inserted. In the 18th or 19th centuries the W wing and hall were reroofed continuously, probably because the rafters of the latter were racking badly; the attics there, which have floorboards, then fell into disuse.

Note
1.   Rouse 1989, 440.

(79597)
Cottage at Hadham Hall (TL 451227),

of two storeys and thatched, formed the cross-wing to an open hall now demolished. It is of two principal bays with a short staircase bay to S and has a crown-post roof; the open truss dividing the principal bays has a very short crown-post standing on a collar-beam, formerly arch-braced; the shortness of the crown-post necessitated two-way brackets of four-centred profile to the collar-purlin. In the mid 17th century the putative hall was demolished and the walls to W and N were refaced in brick; a first-floor window of four lights has ovolo mullions and the chimney-stack to E has two octagonal flues.

(79598)
Hadham Hall (TL 452227),

of brick with tile roofs, comprises the W range and part of the S range of a large courtyard house. The house was of several periods of construction, and although most of it was demolished in the late 17th century and is known only through excavation, the records of the restoration in 1902–3 permit certain deductions about the important additions which were made in the 16th century.

The manor of Hadham Hall was in the possession of the Baud family from the 12th century, and perhaps from the Conquest; William Baud, who was Sheriff for Hertfordshire and Essex in 1371, MP for the county in 1373, and was subsequently knighted, is said to have been the first of his family to reside at Hadham[1] and is likely to have built a suitable residence; Chauncy says specifically that he `died at this Mannor-house' in 1375.[2] All that can safely be said about the medieval house is that part lay to SE of the present building.[3] In 1505 the manor was sold to Sir William Capell but not until the late 16th century did Hadham Hall become the family's principal residence; the likely builder of what remains of the house is Henry Capell, who in 1572 was still living at Rayne (Essex) and in 1578 entertained Queen Elizabeth at Little Hadham.[4] A banqueting hall was added c1634 by Arthur Capell,[5] who was beheaded in 1649 for his participation in the second Civil War. His son Arthur, created Earl of Essex in 1661, moved to Cassiobury c1668. About that time Hadham Hall was much reduced in size to adapt it as a farmhouse of a superior kind; in 1723 it was occupied by James Green, Gent.[6] In 1900 it was bought and restored by William Minet. In 1950 it was sold to Hertfordshire County Council for a school.

The best preserved part of Henry Capell's house is the gateway range (Fig 82), where the brickwork and many details of the W elevation are substantially intact. A manuscript account of the restoration[7] states that `The West front had probably never been altered, except by the insertion of the small door to the south of the main entrance'; and `the front door is unchanged'.[8] Two semi-octagonal turrets flank the archway; the latter is round-headed with a classical entablature breaking forward over flanking pilasters which had been removed before 1832.[9] The windows have moulded pediments; over the entrance is a gable with moulded coping and a low four-light window above; to N and S were matching gables originally.[10] The courtyard elevation has no turrets; the windows do not have pediments; and there are two blocked doorways with four-centred heads. The original arrangement of this range was perhaps as follows: on each side of the entrance was a narrow room; adjoining it was a doorway into the courtyard, and near it a staircase – presumably a newel stair and leading to a first-floor corridor; beyond this was an unheated room, and beyond again a room with a fireplace in the gable wall. The placing of the fireplace off-centre to the room suggests that there may have been a passage through to the adjoining range. No doubt the staircases led to other sets of chambers, with the whole forming a lodgings range but incorporating also a room or rooms for a porter.[11]

Of the S range less than half remains, greatly altered. Minet noted that to N `On the ground floor there is no trace of any...mullioned windows having existed', and further `On the south side the eight original windows of the ground floor are all circular headed'.[12] No evidence remained of any original partitions and by 1819, when all the ground-floor windows were blocked[13] the E half of the part still surviving was used as a brewhouse. The chimney-stack serving the brewing copper is described as massive and square and of plain character with two shafts;[14] the shafts appear from slight indications in drawings[15] to have been set diagonally.

The lack of old partitions coupled with the existence of eight round-headed openings permit the interpretation of the ground floor as an open gallery, resembling the colonnade at Knebworth and almost exactly equal in length; but here the round-headed openings were definitely windows and were interrupted in the middle by a wide arched gateway with four-centred head. A cellar extended the full length of this gallery, while above it was perhaps an unheated long gallery, again like the one at Knebworth. Whatever its purpose the upper storey was of some consequence, having large mullion-and-transom windows; one, to W, appears in a drawing,[16] and Minet noted two to N.[17] The long gallery was heated by a fireplace to S; the chimney-stack surmounting the W gable presumably served an attic room.

About the N wing nothing is known. The E or hall range appears in the somewhat schematic plans resulting from Minet's excavations to have been of two rooms deep throughout, an arrangement that can hardly be of the 1570s and is more likely to have resulted from later additions, possibly c1634. More buildings, said to be the foundations of the earlier house, lay to SE. About 1634, a banqueting hall was added to E of the hall range, thereby enclosing a second, inner courtyard.[18]

The greater part of the house was demolished c1668, and alterations made then are, according to Minet,[19] difficult to distinguish from others made c1720. However, since the W range became the principal part of the new house, most of the following changes must have occurred c1668: the gateway became an entrance-hall, equivalent to a wide cross-passage; a chimney-stack was built backing on to it to serve a fireplace in the principal room to S; probably the room to N of the entrance was also provided with a fireplace and combined the functions of hall and kitchen; and a new staircase was built. All later alterations are of minor importance.

For illustrations, see *English Houses 1200–1800*, Figs 17 (plate), 18 (plate), 84.

Notes
1. VCH IV, 52.
2. Chauncy I, 304.
3. Minet 1914, 61–2.
4. VCH IV, 52.
5. Minet 1914, 68–70.
6. Guildhall, Insurance MS 11936/17, 35.
7. Minet MS, [1].
8. Minet MS, [2]; RCHME 1910, 145 describes it as 'modern'.
9. Buckler Vol II, 59.
10. Minet 1914, 65 and Plate 7.
11. Ibid, 66.
12. Ibid, 67.
13. Luppino drawing; Minet MS [2].
14. Minet 1914, 67.
15. Luppino; Buckler Vol II, 59.
16. Buckler Vol II, 58.
17. Minet 1914, 66.
18. Minet 1914, 68–70.
19. Ibid, 73.

Fig 82 *Hadham Hall, Little Hadham: first-floor plan*

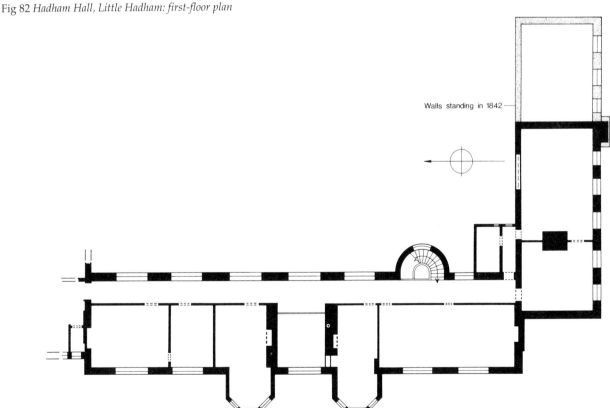

Walls standing in 1842

(77713)
Hollands Close and No. 2 Ford Hill (TL 435215)

comprise a low range to W and a tall cross-wing to E; the former is timber framed, largely refaced in brick, and of one storey and attics; the latter is of brick and of two storeys and attics. The taller part bears a strong but perhaps deceptive resemblance to the `Old House, Little Hadham Ford',[1] and the drawing cannot safely be identified with the existing house. The timber-framed range has no positive dating evidence but is probably of the 16th century; it appears to have comprised an open hall; a shorter bay probably of two storeys to E, in which is a staircase to S preceding the present one; and perhaps a bay to W. The roof has clasped-purlins. In the mid or late 17th century the E wing was added; the principal room or parlour took over some of the functions of the hall and has a wide fireplace with a four-centred brick arch so depressed as to be nearly flat. Stops on a chamfered bearer show that to S of the parlour was a small room off which the newel staircase opened. The chamber over the parlour has a smaller fireplace with a depressed four-centred head and hollowed spandrels within a simple moulded surround. The chimney-stack has two octagonal shafts. When the wing was added an upper floor and fireplace were put into the hall; the floor is carried on an ovolo-moulded bearer and binding-beam; and possibly the W bay was added then. In the late 18th century a fireplace was added in the E bay.

For an illustration, see *English Houses 1200–1800*, Fig 164 (plate).

Note
1.   Buckler Vol II, 60.

(77714)
Home Farm (TL 434218)

has the general appearance of a late medieval house with a hall and two-storeyed cross-wing, but every vestige of antiquity is now concealed both inside and outside.

(77715)
Westfield (TL 423215)

was built in three phases (Fig 83). The first, between the two principal chimney-stacks, was probably a late-medieval open hall of two bays; a pair of principal posts with mortises for arch-braces suggests this, but the roof space was not accessible to check it. Since there is no evidence of a bay to E the hall either stood alone or formed the first stage in the replacement of a two-roomed and presumably earthfast structure (cf Yew Tree

Farm, Much Hadham, for alternate development in the opposite order). The chimney-stack is coeval with the rooms to W of the hall because both E and W faces of the stack batter inwards, implying two ground-floor fireplaces. The hall fireplace, if renovated accurately, dates the W room to the late 17th century; the stack itself has been rebuilt. The E wing, of the same period, was intended for plaster externally; it includes a parlour and staircase-hall above a basement; the new approach from E gave the house the appearance of a gentleman's residence rather than a farmhouse (cf Rooks Nest Farm, Walkern). Two rooms on the top floor have a painted representation of panelling on the wall plaster.[1] In the hall four oak panels formed into a door are painted with a central motif of a red ovoid surrounded by arabesques; they may be late 17th century but could be somewhat earlier. A schedule dated 1772,[2] when the farm was on lease from Samuel Rush, jeweller, of Ludgate Hill, London, to John Bradshaw, husbandman, records room names. In the 19th century, when the staircase was turned round, a window to W was blocked and the existing one to N put in; the E entrance was probably blocked in the present century, when Westfield ceased to be a farmhouse and was restored.

Notes
1.   Rouse 1989, 441.
2.   In possession of Mr A J Hill.

LITTLE MUNDEN

(77716)
Burnside Cottage and Hunt's Cottage at Dane End (TL 332213)

originally comprised an open hall, a cross-wing to N and possibly one to S. In the hall the posts of the open truss are exposed; the cambered tie-beam is of two orders, the outer chamfered, the inner with a quarter-round moulding; there is a crown-post braced laterally to the tie-beam; the collar-purlin has been removed. The quarter-round moulding of the tie-beam suggests the 14th century but is not a certain criterion of date, and the comparatively modest size of the house and its plan-form point to the 15th century. The N wing was originally jettied, with quite closely spaced studs and tension-bracing; the wall facing the hall has a pattern of curved braces. The wing to S is probably a 17th-century addition but has no datable detail; it may be coeval with the chimney-stack with lobby-entrance to E and the upper floor, carried on a chamfered bearer with pyramid stops, which were inserted in the hall. The existence of

Fig 83 Westfield, Little Hadham: plan

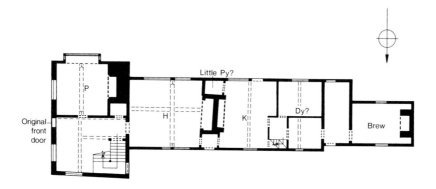

two fireplaces necessitated the removal on the ground floor of the S wall of the N wing; the tie-beam was cut through for the chimney-stack and the removed portion was then re-used as a fireplace lintel. In the early 19th century the house was divided into two cottages.

(77717)
Dane End House (TL 334213)

was built in the early 19th century, probably by John Corrie Esq., whose seat it was in 1817,[1] as a quite small rectangular house facing N with four rooms on each floor, planned around a central hall and staircase. It was enlarged in two phases. In the mid 19th century a bow-fronted dining room and what was presumably a very large drawing room, both facing W, were added to S, together with most of the service rooms; early in the present century two large rooms were added to E and W of the original house.[2] The house is no longer in private occupation.

Notes
1. *Gent Mag, Lib Eng Topog*, 210.
2. Inf. Mr C Marshall.

(77718)
Green End House or Green Elms (TL 330223)

was probably built *c*1825 by Nathaniel Chauncy Snell Esq. Purchases of wallpaper in 1827 for several rooms[1] show that the house was nearly ready for occupation. In 1840 Snell was Sheriff; four years later the house was advertised for sale;[2] mention is made of the morning or gentlemen's room, dining room 26 ft 6 ins by 18 ft (8·1 m x 5.5 m), and drawing room 46 ft by 18 ft (14·0 m x 5·5 m) with folding doors and library. At the time of the 1851 Census it was inhabited by Henry Allen Harrison, retired from the East India Company Service, with his wife, eleven children, French governess, nursery governess, and eight servants. Considerable internal alteration has taken place since then.

Notes
1. V&A, Wallpaper Book, 412.
2. *The Hertfordshire Mercury and County Press*, 27 July 1844.

(77719)
Potters Hall Farm (TL 351207)

was built in the late 17th century and is of two storeys and attics. It has virtually no old details and its date is inferred from the internal-chimney plan and general appearance. Slight irregularities in the plan suggest that it may represent a piecemeal rebuilding of an earlier house. A rear wing and the staircase projection in the re-entrant angle are additions or replacements of the 18th century.

(77720)
Whitehill, Dane End (TL 342213),

having few datable features and with rendering and additions obscuring almost all original wall surfaces, is difficult to explain without postulating the rebuilding of a small, late medieval house with a jettied cross-wing to W and an open hall to which a longer cross-wing to E was added. The plan comprises a short range flanked by cross-wings, that to E projecting boldly to S, that to W very slightly. The external walls are of brick except that to N which is thinner and must be timber framed; the only exposed posts, though re-used, flank and are flush with the chimney-breast in the hall and must be coeval with it. Although this combination of brick and timber occurs in the mid 17th century (cf Aston Bury) the stack lacks the horizontal timber usual above the opening at that period, having instead a triangular-headed relieving arch of perhaps *c*1600. The fireplace in the wing to E has a generally similar stack but since the wing stands at a slightly obtuse angle to the middle room it is presumably an addition to or rebuilding of the original house; posts beside the stack establish that the walls were timber framed. To W the house has a cellar with brickwork possibly of the 17th century; the room above originally had no fireplace; its slight projection to S (1 ft 6 ins (0·5 m)) is consistent with the underbuilding of a jetty. In the 17th century the E wing formed two rooms; the binding-beam to S of the stack is cased, as if to conceal the mortises of a partition cutting off a service room or closet. The entrance-passage was to W of the hall, within the wing; the site of the staircase is unknown but was possibly in a turret to N. On the first floor are two fireplaces with plastered four-centred heads; the attic rooms are of the same period. The house was extended to N in the 18th century, when the fireplace in the room to W was added. In 1862 Whitehill Farm, `recently altered and repaired', comprised three attics, four bedrooms, dressing room, dining and drawing rooms, kitchen, cellar, pantry, brewhouse, dairy and WC.[1] In the early 20th century the house was extended and altered, including provision of a new entrance-hall to W and staircase to N.

Note
1. Sale Catalogue, HRO.

LONDON COLNEY

(77721)
Colney Park or Colney Chapel House (TL 175028)

was built by Philip Champion de Crespigny Esq., MP for Aldborough (Suffolk) and King's Proctor;[1] he bought the site in 1775 when it was a farm.[2] It came *c*1783 into the possession of Charles Bouchier, Governor of Madras, who spent £53,000 on improving the house and grounds prior to serving as Sheriff in 1788. It was sold successively to the Margrave of Anspach, the Earl of Kingston and, in 1804, George Anderson. Anderson evidently intended to demolish the house, for in *The Times* of 7 November, 1805, was advertised the sale of the building materials of `Colney Mansion, an elegant mansion built and furnished within the last thirty years at an immense expense'.[3] The intention was not carried though and by 1824 the house was in the possession of Patrick Hadow Esq., who was Sheriff in that year. Towards the end of the 19th century it was burnt; how much the rebuilt house resembled the old one is not known. It had a short life, being sold to the community known as the All Saints Sisters, who pulled it down to erect a convent in 1899.[4] The plan in 1887[5] is of interest for its combination of a compact main block and wings terminating in pavilions; `The House itself is not large, but perfectly commodious'.[6] The NE pavilion included the kitchen; the other offices `which are rather extensive, being connected by an underground passage, are concealed from sight by the Plantation' lying NE of the house.

For an illustration, see *English Houses 1200–1800*, Fig 195 (plate).

Notes
1. *Royal Kalendar* 1781, 22.
2. Oldfield Vol II, 259.
3. Quoted in *Middx and Herts N & Q*, 149–50.
4. VCH II, 269.
5. MS date on sale catalogue plan, Andrews Collection.
6. Neale 1819–29, Vol II.

MARKYATE

(77722)
Caddington Hall (TL 067172)

was an estate owned by the dean and chapter of St Paul's until 1804, when they exchanged it with the Pedley family for Zouches Farm, Caddington, Bedfordshire (TL 040212). The Pedleys pulled down the existing small house and built a modest country seat. This became an old people's home about 1948 and was demolished, unrecorded, in 1975; plans were made available by Bedfordshire County Council.

The house was a rectangular double-pile, the room to rear (N; correctly NW) being slightly larger than those at the front. To S the entrance-hall contained a staircase of semicircular plan; the drawing room was to W and the dining room to E. An axial corridor separated the dining room from the kitchen to N; a large rear hall had a semicircular portico leading to the garden; to S was the breakfast room. Both first and second floors had an axial corridor running the full length of the house; the former had five principal bedrooms, each with dressing room. To NE was an L-shaped service block with wings to N and E.

(77723)
Markyate Cell (TL 057174)

is the successor to a priory of Benedictine nuns founded in 1145 and dissolved in 1537.[1] The site was granted in 1539 to Humphrey Bourchier of the King's household, who `did much cost in translating of the priory into a manor place, but he left it nothing endid'.[2] On his death in 1540 his widow married George Ferrers, to whom the site of the late monastery was granted in 1548;[3] Ferrers, a poet and politician, who served

Fig 84 *Markyate Cell: reconstruction of 1657 plan*

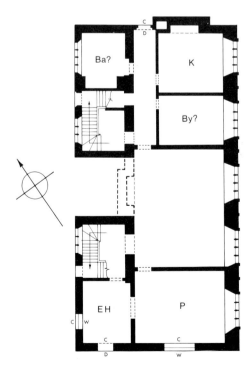

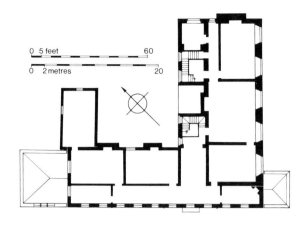

Fig 85 *Markyate Cell: first-floor plan, c1800, partly conjectural*

successive monarchs and was MP in several parliaments,[4] must have completed the house. Part of Bourchier's work is said to be the short wing in chequered stone and flint at the E (correctly NE) end of the present house;[5] it appears to have been a service block roofed at right-angles to the main or hall range; it could equally well be Ferrers' work. After the latter's death in 1579 the estate descended to his son Julius and, in 1596, to his grandson Sir John Ferrers,[6] one of whom is likely to have added the W wing before c1600. In 1648 Sir Thomas Fanshawe of Ware Park acquired the property by marriage;[7] his estates being sequestrated, he is unlikely to have done any building before selling Markyate in 1655. By 1657 it was in the hands of Thomas Coppin who died in 1663 and was succeeded by his son John. An engraving of 1805 by Thomas Fisher FSA[8] and a nearly contemporary watercolour[9] show that much building took place in the mid 17th century, probably by Thomas Coppin, the most likely person. He built a new S elevation with five gables[10] and added two large staircases in the manner of Aston Bury,[11] so that the middle range must have been virtually rebuilt; some of the chimney-shafts shown in the 1805 view may be of the same date. Thomas Coppin's grandson John, who in 1734 built a chapel at Markyate Cell,[12] may previously have refaced the W elevation.[13] A single-storey building with a Venetian window,[14] probably a library, was added to N of the W wing, perhaps by the Revd John Pittman-Coppin, who owned Markyate Cell from 1781 to 1794;[15] it looks too early to be the work of Joseph Howell, who repaired and enlarged the chapel after purchasing the house c1800.[16] Howell opened up the W front by removing a terrace and yew trees which had masked it.[17] In 1825 the house was sold to Daniel Goodson Adey of St Albans, JP, who employed the architect Robert Lugar to transform it in Elizabethan style;[18] after extensive demolition the new house is said to have had 35 rooms fewer than its predecessor.[19] A drawing of 1832[20] shows elaborately carved chimney-stacks, whereas Lugar's own drawing of 1825 shows them plain and square; this change was probably made during building. Even after the drastic change of the late 1820s the house still retained much of the shell of the old main block and E wing, including the two staircase projections,[21] which appear in a drawing of 1839,[22] although the E staircase was removed. Cussans says that this rebuilding, dated to 1840, followed a fire, the last of three. In the present century the house was owned by Sir John Pennefather, who altered it extensively, imported panelling and other features and made the present courtyard. When, about

1925, he moved to Eastwell Park (Kent) he rebuilt the latter in imitation of, and with panelling and other fittings from, Markyate Cell.[23]

The architectural development of the house, though full of problems, is summarised up to 1825 in Figs 84–7. It was built on sloping ground to E of the church, on a new site unrelated to the buildings of the monastery; it had a basement which, to W, rose well above the ground surface and was more like an undercroft. Little is known about the rest of the house except that it had a narrow cross-wing to N and adjoining it was the hall, lit by 'windows of Perpendicular Pointed architecture'[24] and with a lateral fireplace still evident in Lugar's ground-floor plan; and probably there was a cross-wing. With a plan of this kind the entrance ought to have been on the S side up a flight of steps; if that were so the house as left by Bourchier and Ferrers may have been comparable in its general arrangement to the earlier Wyddial Hall, modified, no doubt, by having a hall range of two storeys. Some material from the monastery was re-used, including, in the kitchen, a beam on which a shield was carved.[25] A long NW wing shown in a drawing of 1805[26] was probably, despite some similarities of style such as drip moulds, an addition to the main body of the house because of the great differences of levels; the first floor of the new building corresponded to the ground floor of the old. The 1805 engraving shows a first-floor window of this wing as being rather taller than the one below it, hence the principal rooms were on the same level as those of the building to which it was added; and, if that is correct, the entrance may have remained on the S side. A minor addition of one storey and attics with a timber-framed E gable was built in the early 17th century at the NE corner of the W range.

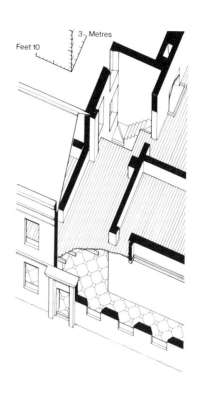

Fig 86 *Markyate Cell: conjectural axonometric reconstruction of 18th-century entrance*

Fig 87 *Markyate Cell: Lugar's plans, 1825*

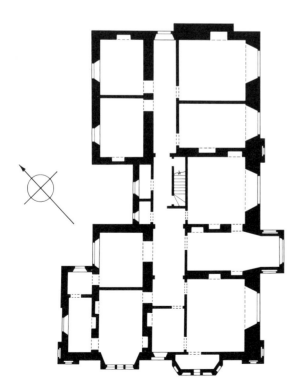

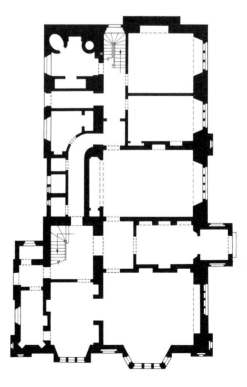

The transformation presumed to have been wrought by Thomas Coppin made Markyate Cell a quite extraordinary house. The general intention to produce a plan based on two staircases of almost equal importance is clear enough, but the early 19th-century drawing of the S elevation, showing no trace of a principal entrance, demonstrates that the result was achieved in an unusual way. Since the drawing gives no hint of the removal of a mid 17th-century S doorway through antiquarian restoration, the entrance must have been on the W side at approximately the same point as in the early 18th

Fig 88 *Markyate Cell: ground and first-floor plans*

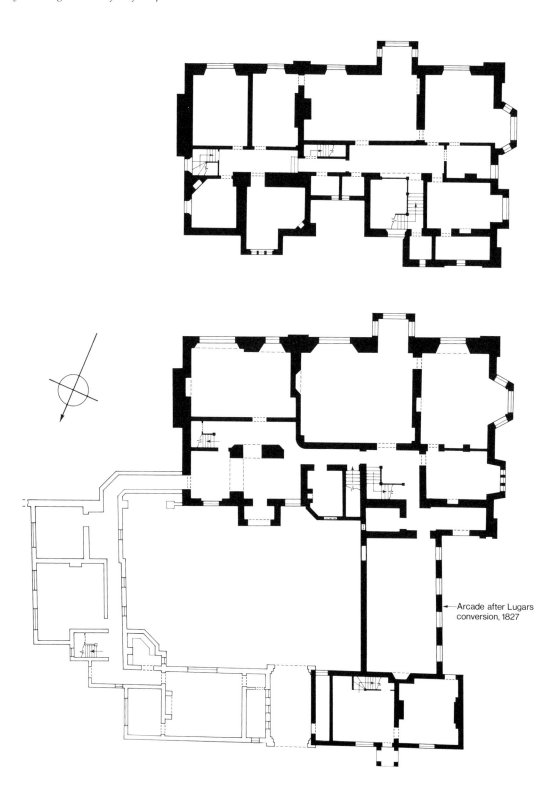

Arcade after Lugars conversion, 1827

century. A two-storeyed porch is likely in the mid 17th century, with the front doorway facing the foot of the W staircase which led up to the hall on the principal floor; a reconstruction of this arrangement has been attempted (Fig 86). From the hall a passage presumably led to the E staircase and the small room adjoining it; the E room was perhaps subdivided. How the other rooms at this level were used is uncertain.

However extraordinary this conjectural arrangement appears, it makes the subsequent refronting and widening of the house intelligible. The W range, shown in 1805 as about 30 ft (9·2 m) wide overall, was more than one room in depth; probably it had been doubled in width to W when it was refronted in the early 18th century.

Whatever way the plan of the 18th-century house (Fig 85) is reconstructed it must have been inconvenient, and this no doubt led to Lugar's drastic remodelling of it as a compact rectangular house in Tudor style (Fig 87). An arcade provided a covered way to an outbuilding, possibly a brewhouse or laundry.[27] Later the arcade was made into a room and an enlarged courtyard created but these alterations have not materially altered the plan and general appearance of the house as Lugar left it (Fig 88).

Notes

1. VCH Beds I, 359–60.
2. Leland *Itinerary*, Pt 1, 104.
3. VCH II, 189.
4. *DNB*.
5. RCHME 1910; VCH II, 190.
6. VCH II, 190.
7. *DNB*; Chauncy I, 408.
8. *Gent Mag* 1846 (ii), 467–70.
9. V&A, Dept Prints and Drawings, 93 A 9; possibly the source of drawing No. 3, *Gent Mag* 1846 (ii), 470.
10. Oldfield Vol IV, 502.
11. Engraving, 1805, by Thomas Fisher, *Gent Mag* 1846 (ii), 467–70.
12. VCH II, 190; Buckler Vol IV, 18.
13. Watercolour painted soon after 1811, in possession of Mr A E Sursham.
14. Oldfield Vol IV, 502.
15. VCH II, 190.
16. *Gent Mag* 1846 (ii), 467–70.
17. Clutterbuck; Sursham watercolour.
18. Colvin 1978, 527.
19. Cussans 1879–81, Vol III (i), 115.
20. Buckler Vol IV, 18.
21. Plan, Lugar 1828, Plate 40.
22. Buckler Vol IV, 20.
23. Inf. Mr P M Reid.
24. *Gent Mag* 1846 (ii), 470.
25. BL Add MS 32349 fo 6.
26. Engraved for *Gent Mag* 1846 (ii), 467–70.
27. Buckler Vol IV, 18; BL Add MS 32349, fo 4.

MUCH HADHAM

(77724)
Bull Cottage and Campden Cottage (TL 427193)

is a small, late medieval house comprising an open hall and cross-wing to N. The service rooms to S may originally have been of one storey. The hall range has been gutted. The wing is unusual in being boldly jettied to E and W; the rear jetty modified the location of the staircase; instead of rising parallel with the W wall it is placed against the N wall with the top

landing on the jetty. Probably the ground floor of the wing was one large room; the upper storey, over 20 ft (6·1 m) long, may have been partitioned, but any evidence of this was lost with the removal of the middle tie-beam. The wing-framing visible within the hall formed a simple decorative pattern. In the 17th century a chimney-stack and upper floor were probably inserted into the hall. There was only one fireplace, to N of the stack; the staircase W of the stack was added because there is no first-floor access from the wing.

For illustrations, see *English Houses 1200–1800*, Figs 72 (plate), 73.

(77725)
Camwell Hall Farm (TL 417174),

of two storeys, comprises a comparatively short main range between two gabled cross-wings; the S wing is jettied but the N wing, which projects equally far forward, is not. The house was built in the mid–late 15th century, and had an open hall; at the S end the binding-beam, which projects to form the wing, was moulded towards the hall; a small part of the moulding is exposed, terminating to E where the beam is chamfered as a door lintel; the open truss has a cambered tie-beam and octagonal crown-post with moulded capital and base. The room S of the hall was probably the parlour. The siting of the later chimney-stack suggests that there was a staircase at the rear. The proportions of the hall, about 20 ft (6·1 m) square, suggest that the cross-passage lay to N; probably a further bay contained service rooms. In the late 16th century an upper floor and a chimney-stack with a moulded wooden lintel were built within the hall; the stack adjoins the open truss and, if the conjecture above is correct, will have backed on to the cross-passage. The high lintel suggests that the stack may originally have been of timber, there being no trace of 16th-century brickwork. In the middle or second half of the 17th century the presumed N bay was demolished and replaced by a wing, the ground floor of which was a single large room; at the back, in a narrow service wing, is a staircase. At the same time the present brick chimney-stacks were built, and the size of the new parlour makes it likely that the former hall and the new parlour had to a large extent exchanged functions. A mullion-and-transom bay window in the former hall is of the same date; the S end stack is probably later, of the early 18th century. In the 19th century greater privacy was achieved by creating corridors in the principal rooms.

(77726)
Gaytons (TL 427193),

of the late 17th century and of brick, has a lobby-entrance in the middle of the E elevation, which is surmounted by three wide

Fig 89 *Gaytons, Much Hadham: plan*

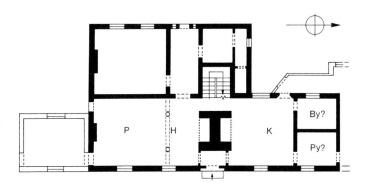

gables. The plan (Fig 89) comprises four cells: that to N is divided into two service rooms; next to S is the kitchen; to S of the stack what was probably the hall has a wide fireplace with depressed four-centred head; the partition between hall and the parlour to S, has been removed. To W of the chimney-stack is the staircase, in a timber-framed turret. Much alteration took place in the 18th and 19th centuries. Service rooms and a dining room were added to W; the front was refenestrated, rendered and painted white, so that the original size and shape of the windows is not now clear; and on the first floor corridors were formed to W, leading from the staircase.

For illustrations, see *English Houses 1200–1800*, Figs 174 (plate), 175 (plate), 314 (plate).

(77727)
Green Tye Farm (TL 446186)

has a continuous jetty to S and was built in two parts, neither at all closely datable; the earlier part to E appears to be of the early 16th century, the part to W late 16th century. The principal interest of the house lies in the existence, formerly, of two front doors side by side (Fig 90), as if for a unit-system arrangement like New Hall, Ware Rural; this notion receives some support from the descent of the property.[1] A William Hampton `at Grene' is recorded in 1525 and in 1543 he was `of Grene Tye'. He

Fig 90 *Green Tye Farm, Much Hadham: plan*

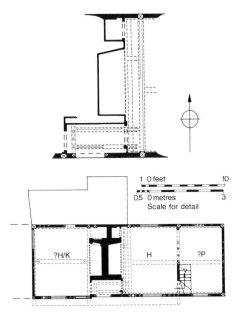

1 0 feet 10
0.5 0 metres 3
Scale for detail

?H/K   H   ?P

surrendered Green Tye and other lands to his son William in April 1570 and in 1577 there is reference to William and Robert Hampton of Green Tye, from which it appears that father and son then occupied the house jointly. William Hampton either built or rebuilt the E part of the house, which comprised two rooms on each floor and has indications of an original timber chimney. The beams and joists in the principal room are chamfered, those in the E end room not, but there is nothing to show that the latter was a service room; the door into it is in the position customary for a parlour door and there is no subdivision into buttery and pantry as might be expected. If this interpretation is correct there must have been a service room elsewhere, presumably to W, although mortises for studs show

that it was not reached from the lobby-entrance. The original arrangement in this part of the house is difficult to reconstruct in detail and is perhaps explained in a general way by alternate rebuilding (cf Walnut Tree Farm, Pirton).

The W part is built against the end of the earlier structure and had a separate entrance, now blocked, alongside the earlier one. The W end wall has been reconstructed to give a flush face to W, the rooms beyond it having been demolished; originally it was an internal wall with its flush face to E. The roof over this part is of collar-rafter construction without purlins.

Note
1. Rickman 1928–33, 288–312.

(77728)
Kimbolton, Maltings Lane (TL 428186),

is a small three-cell house only 12 ft (3·7 m) wide, of one storey and attics; little of the framing is exposed, there is no closely datable detail, and consequently its date and development are uncertain. Two slight indications that it may originally have been wholly or partly open to the roof are the dormer windows built on the wall-plate, and two staircases, one in each end bay; it was probably built in the 16th century, perhaps as late as c1600. The chimney-stack was added in the late 17th or early 18th century and a bay to W, with a ground-floor fireplace, may be of the same date. In the 19th century the house became two cottages.

(77729)
Hoglands (TL 438174)

is a late medieval house which comprised an open hall flanked by a cross-wing to W and a bay to E, which was probably of two storeys. Many of the structural relations between the various parts of the building are now obscured by plaster or furnishings, so that its development is somewhat uncertain. The only definitely medieval feature in the hall is the crown-post roof. In the E wall of the house, a post is mortised for the head-beam of the partition between pantry and buttery and rebated for two adjacent windows. No medieval detail can be seen in the W wing.

In the early 17th century a chimney-stack was built backing on to the cross-passage; the hall fireplace has a moulded lintel. Possibly the original stack was of timber, occupying a larger area than the present stack, which is probably of the 18th century. The wing, which is unusually tall in proportion to the hall, may have been altered or rebuilt in the late 17th century. A chimney-stack with two conjoined diagonal flues was added then, and a staircase-projection, incorporating a small room, to S. The roof has clasped-purlins; the N gable has barge-boards with an ovolo moulding. In the 19th century a narrow S wing, perhaps a bakehouse or brewhouse, was added.

(77730)
Mingers (TL 437166)

is timber framed; the ground floor is rendered and the first floor weatherboarded. The main range incorporates to S the cross-wing of a medieval house; the wing was jettied and on the first floor part of the wall-plate, with dovetail housing for a tie-beam, can be seen; it is considerably lower than the present plate. In the SW corner of the ground-floor room the framing for the original stair opening remains. To N of the main range the existence of a jetty suggests that a second original wing is incorporated in an otherwise featureless part of the house. If both wings are original the hall between them was about 17 ft by 21 ft (5·2 m x 6·4 m). In the late 16th century the hall was completely rebuilt with a jettied upper storey and a chimney-stack backing on to the cross-passage; the siting of the stack suggests that a staircase adjoined it, facing the hall and rising against the N wall. The hall has a clasped-purlin roof. In the mid 17th century the SW wing was added, with a wide fireplace in the ground-floor room. Probably the staircase was added at the same time; originally it must have faced the hall and has subsequently been turned round. To provide better upstairs rooms the S wing and hall including the passage were heightened and re-roofed in two transverse spans, in profile like an inverted W; this provided for attic rooms to which the new stair extended. Presumably the SW wing was a kitchen, the original parlour being by then a pantry; the hall remained the principal room; then or in the 18th century the NE room became a dairy. In the early 19th century a single-storey wing was added to provide a brewhouse and bakehouse. The house has recently been carefully renovated.

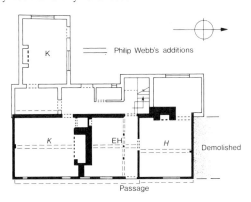

Fig 91 *Morris Cottage, Much Hadham: plan*

(79620)
Moat Farmhouse, Kettle Green (TL 416182)

comprises two distinct parts, neither complete in itself, and is an example of alternate rebuilding; a mid 17th-century cross-wing of brick was added to W of an earlier range, which was itself rebuilt not long afterwards. The cross-wing, of two storeys and attics, has two ground-floor rooms, each with a fireplace having a four-centred arched head. A newel staircase to S of the entrance-passage is coeval with the hall; the subsequent need to adapt its winding treads to give access to other first-floor rooms argues that the hall range was still open to the roof when the wing was built. This stair leads to a lobby over the entrance-passage from which the two principal bedrooms are reached, and to the attics. The generally awkward relation of the two parts of the house suggests that they are of slightly different dates, despite having similar conjoined chimney-shafts. In the hall range a chimney-stack backs on to the former cross-passage; an early 19th-century staircase to SE may perpetuate an older one in a storeyed bay to E of the hall. When the wing was added the hall probably became a kitchen in which only the farm and indoor servants ate. The remainder of this range was turned into a large dairy and pantry.

(77731)
Moor Place, formerly Mores Place (TL 422187),

an estate of the bishops of London, was held in the 15th century by a family called More. By 1550 it was in the possession of Mary Dalton, widow, whose descendants held it until 1620.[1] A member of the Dalton family may have built the house in the late 16th century;[2] this may be so but the row of five gables shown by Drapentier[3] look like mid 17th-century work, as do the mullioned windows, each with two transoms; anything done then can be ascribed to Sir Richard Atkin, who acquired the estate in 1650,[4] made a small park[5] and was created baronet in 1660. The house was replaced by the present one, built between 1777 and 1779, on a new site about 50 yds (45 m) to N.

It was designed for James Garden by Robert Mitchell,[6] who published plans and a view of the N and W (entrance) fronts;[7] Oldfield and Buckler drew the E and N fronts.[8] There is a curious discrepancy between, on the one hand, Mitchell's view and the house as it is today, and, on the other, Oldfield's and Buckler's views; the latter do not show the chimneys which are so prominent on the N front. A wing was added to S in the early 1860s by Mr Morey Wigram and a wing to N, designed by Norman Shaw and containing the kitchen, in 1887 by Mr F H Norman;[9] that to S was enlarged in 1907 to the designs of Sir Ernest Newton.[10]

Notes
1. VCH IV, 62–3.
2. Nares 1956*a*, 157.
3. Chauncy I, 317.
4. VCH IV, 63.
5. Chauncy I, 316.
6. Colvin 1978, 554.
7. Mitchell 1801.
8. Oldfield Vol III, 236; Buckler Vol II, 52.
9. Norman 1902–4, 146.
10. Nares 1956*b*, 206.

(77732)
Morris Cottage (TL 427193)

takes its name from William Morris's sister, Henrietta, who lived nearby at The Lordship with her mother until the latter's death early in 1895; on 4 February of that year William Morris recorded in his diary: 'To Hadham to see house for Henry. Webb with me'.[1] Philip Webb's drawings for alterations[2] are dated July 1895.

The house is of Wealden type and was built in the late 15th or early 16th century with hall and two-storeyed bay to S (Fig 91); the framing of the latter includes tension-bracing. At the N end of the hall are a straight tie-beam and one rib of the original cove to the roof-plate; the open truss has been removed but at the corresponding point in the collar-purlin is a mortise for a crown-post. The cross-passage was to S, the lower part of the wall separating passage and hall being treated as a spere-truss; the infilling of the partition between the passage and the room to S has been removed and the studs show no sign of the usual service doors, nor does the bearer have mortises for an axial partition. The N gable end is completely plastered so there is nothing to show whether the house had a second storeyed bay.

In the early 17th century a two-storeyed bay and chimney-stack were added to S; because this bay has no stair trap, access to the upstairs room must have been from the adjoining bay. A jettied upper storey was inserted into the hall *c*1600 and a chimney-stack built to W of the hall; the stack was later reduced in size. A drawing of 1835[3] shows this bay as a separate cottage and establishes that the framing has always been exposed. In 1895 Philip Webb enlarged the house at the back in a plain, dignified style; in the wing he added to W the kitchen has been altered but otherwise his work largely remains.

For an illustration, see *English Houses 1200–1800*, Fig 16 (plate).

Notes
1. BL Add MS 45410.
2. RIBA Drawings Collection.
3. Buckler Vol II, 51.

(77733)
The Palace (TL 430197)

was the manor house of Much Hadham which belonged to the bishop of London from before the Conquest until its sequestration in 1647. After being in lay possession during the Interregnum it reverted at the Restoration to the bishop, who reserved the right of residence and leased it out to tenants.[1] Evidently this right was no longer exercised by the time the palace became a private lunatic asylum, to which the earliest recorded admission was in 1817;[2] the building was still so used in 1863.[3] In 1868 it passed to the Ecclesiastical Commissioners who, in 1888, sold it as a private house.

The house was built in the early 16th century with a hall range and cross-wing to W, but it is now difficult to reconstruct in detail the form and plan of a somewhat unusual building. The main range is of five bays; the roof trusses have flat tie-beams and had large curved braces springing from the wall-post just above the present first floor. The hall was of three bays; mortises in tie-beams show that the bays to E and W were partitioned off from it; the partitions have been completely destroyed. No evidence remains to show how the wings were used. To NE about 12 ft (3·7 m) away from the main range is a square two-storeyed building, originally freestanding. The lower storey is of brick except to S where the wall has long been removed; inside the N wall are the remains of a four-centred arch nearly 9 ft (2·8 m) wide, evidently a doorway. The large close-spaced joists carrying the upper floor are plain. In the upper rooms the only old features are moulded wall-plates and tie-beams, the latter being embattled. The plastered wall to S is only 6 ins (15 cms) thick and must be timber framed, but no signs of a partition appear in the roof truss above. To S the truss is weathered. This small, unheated, yet very well-finished building may have been a gatehouse; its closeness to the house is matched at West Bromwich Old Hall, Staffordshire[4] but its alignment on the E bay of the hall is difficult to explain. How the upper room was reached is unknown. That some structure antedated the late 17th-century staircase which now links porch to house is suggested by a single rafter, apparently the sole relic of a roof with a lower apex than the present one, which is incorporated to W. The early 16th-century buildings of the palace lack any evidence of an original hearth or chimney; a

lateral stack may have been removed from the hall; and since a wing as large as that to W can hardly have been unheated, original chimney-stacks may have been demolished when the W elevation was refronted in the 18th century.

In the late 16th century a two-storeyed wing of brick was added to E. The thick wall between it and the hall range is unusual, normal practice being to begin the brickwork at the existing outer walls (cf The Old Hall, Pirton); possibly, in this rather early example of a kitchen wing incorporated in the house, the danger of fire was in mind. In the large kitchen to N, at about 4 ft (1·2 m) from the present brick chimney, a binding-beam is chamfered towards the room but plain towards the stack and indicates some functional difference between the two parts of the room. A beam at the corresponding point in the room above suggests the possibility of a large flue above an open hearth, like a medieval kitchen. To N is a smaller room with hollow-chamfered beams; it may have been no more than a pantry or buttery although its better finish might suggest a dining parlour. The hall may still have been open to the roof when the Civil War broke out although the description in the 1647 Parliamentary Survey[5] – 'The manor of Hadham consisteth of a hall, 2 parlours wainscotted, a kitchen, buttery, a larder with 7 chambers over them, besides garrets' – is indecisive on this point.

When the palace reverted to the See of London in 1660 and was divided into a house for a tenant and occasional accommodation for the bishop, a second porch was added at the W end of the hall and the old porch refaced to match. The E porch led to a staircase-hall and so, in all probability, did that to W; it is likely that at this period the open hall was floored over and the chimney-stack built, the position of the latter being more appropriate to a house in dual occupation than to its former status. In the bedroom to W of the stack a stone fireplace with chamfered jambs and four-centred head has the characteristic relieving timber of the late 17th century. At this time the house was refaced in brick; a gable was added to light attics over the hall;[6] and the presumed wooden chimney in the kitchen replaced by one of brick.

In the mid 18th century, when the elevation was refenestrated and a parapet added, it became the principal entrance to that part of the house. A narrow entrance-hall was

Fig 92 *The Palace, Much Hadham: plan based on 1829 plan, showing layout as private asylum*

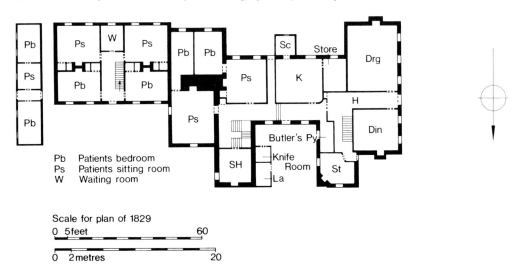

Pb Patients bedroom
Ps Patients sitting room
W   Waiting room

Scale for plan of 1829

0   5feet   60

0   2metres   20

formed, with a large dining room to S and a smaller drawing room to N; to E of the latter and opening off the entrance-hall was a new staircase. The large room occupying the W part of the medieval hall was by then a kitchen and had perhaps been so earlier. These dispositions appear in plans drawn in 1829 (Fig 92) which show the whole building in one occupation, the part to W accommodating Mr James Smith, surgeon and apothecary, and the remainder as intended for the use of `15 lunatic Patients'. In the early 19th century what was virtually an independent house, of brick and of two storeys with a slate roof of low pitch, was added to E of the old house. Only the lack of kitchen and service rooms show that this conventional-looking plan was a special-purpose building designed to house mentally ill people.

Later alterations include the replacement of the 18th-century staircase in the W part by one which occupies the presumed site of the 17th-century stair; the addition of service rooms to N, some of which have recently been removed; and the reopening of the porch to W when the 18th-century entrance became no more than a garden door. The S wall was rebuilt and a three-sided bay window added in the 1920s and then or later gabled attics, matching the older house in style, were added to the early 19th-century building to E.

For an illustration, see *English Houses 1200–1800*, Fig 114.

Notes
1. VCH IV, 62.
2. HRO, Notes and Extracts from the Session Rolls, 2, 419.
3. HRO, Guide, 129.
4. Jones, S R 1975–6, 1–63, especially Fig 1*a*.
5. Guildhall MS 10464 A.
6. Buckler Vol II, 50.

(79614)
The former Red Lion Inn (TL 428196)

is a late medieval building which had an open hall and crown-post roof. Possibly it was built as an inn; the former hall is approximately square and the covered way leading to the yard at the rear served as a cross-passage; these correspond to the common domestic formula of square hall plus cross-passage, between storeyed ends (cf Thorpe House, No. 19 High Street, Puckeridge, Standon). In 1577 it was the Angel; *c*1720 it had become the Red Lion.[1] Alterations in the late 17th century establish that the building was by then definitely an inn; the principal staircase opens off a passage but is easily reached from both hall and entrance; and the first-floor corridor gave access to six bedrooms, four of which had fireplaces; only the rear two were unheated. In the early 19th century a large first-floor bedroom (over storerooms) was added to W.

Note
1. Johnson 1962, Pt 1, 59.

(77734)
Yew Tree Farm, Hadham Cross (TL 426185),]

a Wealden house, was built in the late 15th or early 16th century; it has much exposed framing externally and a roof of thatch with verge tiles, and, although the original structure is generally well preserved, restoration early in the present century has removed some evidence of its subsequent development. The hall is of two bays; to W is a tall mullion-and-transom window of which two diamond mullions and the lintel, about 2 ft (0.6 m) below the wall-plate, remain; opposite it to E the transom of a matching window has mortises for two three-light openings with diamond mullions separated by a king-

mullion of rectangular section. The open truss had a rebated crown-post. To S the house departs from the Wealden norm; a wing, jettied to E, projects about 1 ft (0.3 m) to W; it was originally divided into two rooms, probably pantry and buttery because the other important service room, the kitchen, always appears to have been at this end; in the W room was a staircase; originally the roof was gabled at both ends. The hall range was added to the wing; the wing wall adjoining the hall is studded and plastered throughout. This sequence implies the existence of an earlier hall which was improved by the addition of a two-storey wing (never an independent structure) and was subsequently itself replaced by the Wealden hall. The upper end was also divided into two rooms; the small room to E is too wide for a staircase, which is usually placed at the rear of the house. It may have been a craftsman's shop with the parlour behind it. Incorporated in the later SW wing, about 31 ft (9.5 m) from the house, is a single-storey timber-framed building which has a collar-rafter roof with some smoke-blackened rafters; it may be of the 16th century and was no doubt a kitchen. The hall was reduced *c*1600 to one bay with an open hearth when the S bay was floored over at the same level as the cross-wing. The flooring-over was completed *c*1700, to give the external appearance of a continuous-jetty house. At the same time a brick chimney-stack with a large rectangular shaft having a square fillet on each face was added at the S end of the hall. This entailed changes in the plan. The former service rooms were made into one and a fireplace added; the N bay of the former hall became an entrance-hall; in it was a new staircase replacing the two earlier ones; the two rooms at the N end of the house became one and a fireplace was installed. This work is dated by the addition of attics over the hall, lit by a gabled window on which are painted the date and initials 1697 T W S. A lean-to to W with no datable features is no doubt coeval; it provided service rooms including a cellar and probably a dairy. A single-storey link to the old kitchen probably existed by this time, if not earlier; the present range is of the mid 19th century. In the present century the house was restored and enlarged to W.

For illustrations, see *English Houses 1200–1800*, Figs 50 (plate), 51, 52, 301 (plate).

NETTLEDEN WITH POTTEN END

(77735)
Holly Bush Farm, Frithsden (TL 015099),

has developed in three phases into a lobby-entrance plan (Fig 93). The oldest part, to E, comprised a late medieval hall and an inner room, the former being open to the roof, the latter storeyed. No doubt the hall had an open hearth but a complete reconstruction of the roof precludes confirmation of this. The chimney-stack, which has a heavy corbelled capping, was built in the late 17th century, and the cross-wing to W may be

Fig 93 *Holly Bush Farm, Nettleden with Potten End: plan*

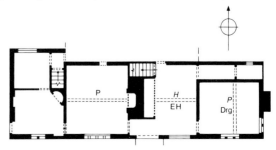

contemporary because it appears to have had an attic storey from the first. The room to W of the stack is interpreted formally as the parlour, but being larger than the hall it must have been more important and have taken over some of the latter's functions; the hall became primarily a kitchen. In the early 19th century a second cross-wing, of brick, was added to W and service rooms were added to N.

(77736)
Nos 1–3 Frithsden Gardens (TL 103003)

was probably built in the 16th century; its oldest part comprised a hall of two bays with an open hearth and a storeyed bay to W; a staircase in the NW corner may replace an original one in that position. The house was probably entered by a cross-passage at the E end of the oldest part, ie in the same position as now; the lower range to E may have had no upper floor originally, since the joists at their outer ends merely rest on the rails, which are not continuous. This end, which is a later build and probably of the 17th century, is said locally to have been a byre; whether this is a genuine tradition or an antiquarian assertion is uncertain but possible positions for doorways exist. Other 17th-century alterations include the building of a chimney-stack backing on to the cross-passage; it has three diagonal flues and is no doubt coeval with the upper floor inserted in the hall and the upper chamber lit by a gabled dormer window inscribed with the date 1632. A cross-wing to W of two storeys and attics was probably added in the third quarter of the 17th century to provide a new heated parlour and chamber over; the ground floor has a plastered chimney-breast and a wide fireplace with three-centred head and moulded jambs. At this time the former inner room was no doubt wholly a service room; a lateral fireplace and chimney-stack were built within it in the late 18th century, perhaps when the house was turned into three cottages.

(77737)
Nos 7/8 (Corner Cottage) Nettleden (TL 020105)

is in two distinct parts. The W range comprised originally a hall and unheated inner room and chambers over; the hall chimney-stack has been removed in this century. Adjoining it to E is a one-bay block, jettied to front and rear, in which were presumably the parlour and principal bedchamber. Both parts are difficult to date; both may fall in the late 16th century, the jettied bay being perhaps a later addition, and a process of alternate rebuilding is likely.

(77738)
No. 13 Frithsden (TL 016098)

was built in the late 16th or early 17th century and is of two storeys. Its plan comprises hall and subdivided inner room with a vestigial cross-passage behind the hall chimney-stack; later extensions were added on at both ends. Formally it is a longhouse derivative.

NEWNHAM

(77739)
Newnham Hall (TL 247375),

formerly known as Church Farm,[1] is of red brick and was built in the early 18th century; in the mid 19th century it was enlarged at the rear in white brick and most of the interior fittings were removed. It has no connection with the moated manor house (TL 242347) rebuilt by William Dyer after he succeeded to the estate in 1680 and before he became Sheriff in 1694;[2] this was pulled down early in the 19th century.

Notes
1. VCH II, 355.
2. Chauncy II, 423; illustrated, *Apollo*, July 1978, 5.

NORTHAW

(77740)
Northaw Place (TL 270024)

(Fig 94) was built c1690 by Sir George Hutchins, King's Serjeant and one of the Commissioners of the Great Seal 1690–3;[1] he died in 1705 and was succeeded by his son Leman Hutchins, to whose time the paintings on the staircase have been ascribed.[2] The first addition was made in the 18th century immediately to N; the proportions of ground and first-floor windows suggest it was of one storey originally. By the early 19th century the house

Fig 94 *Northaw Place: ground and first-floor plans*

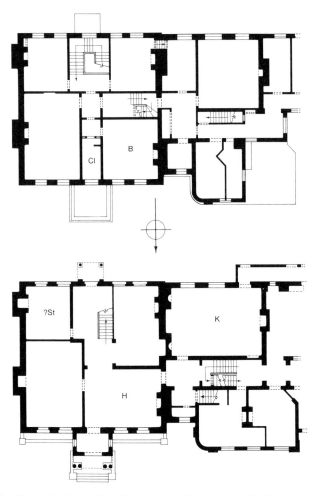

had been heightened to three storeys from the original two and attics, and had a parapet; the extension to N had been heightened to two storeys; and a single-storey building, perhaps corresponding to the present kitchen, had been added to N again; farther to N a single-storey structure, apparently detached, had a central chimney-stack and hipped roof; all these buildings had slate roofs and to E the brickwork of the house had been rendered.[3] Subsequently the detached building was replaced by two carriage arches with a storey above on each side, rather like a gatehouse; it antedates the heightening of the kitchen block and the adjoining scullery and may be contemporary with the Italianate refronting of the house. In 1868 the house was purchased by John Mounsey Esq., who `enlarged and restored the house, without...structural alteration in the original building';[4] this may refer to the refacing and heightening of the kitchen and scullery among other things. At this time the paintings on the staircase were discovered; the following remarks are relevant:

> On the ceiling and walls of the principal staircase were some old paintings, apparently of little merit and in some places partly obliterated. On carefully cleaning them, it was found that many years ago an attempt had been made to remove the thick coat of discoloured varnish...The operator was unsuccessful and contented himself with repainting certain portions with more energy than discretion, [adding] a liberal coat of copal varnish.[5]

In 1868 the second painting and the successive coats of varnish were carefully removed and the original paintings, `in an almost perfect state of preservation, were brought to light';[6] but they include the Mounsey arms.[7] In the present century further restoration of the house was undertaken. Some of the bolection-moulded panelling, in very tall narrow panels, is probably of this date; so is a panel painting over a fireplace which is alleged to be of c1690 and to depict the original house.[8] Towards the end of the 19th century the house became a school; in 1928 it was reoccupied by Sir Philip Devitt as a private house;[9] and in the 1950s it became an assessment centre for children.

The plan of the house, being governed by the position of the entrance, staircase and chimney-stacks, cannot have been much altered in its essentials; no doubt there was always a service block to W; probably a servants' staircase on the W side of the house, now represented only on the first floor, has been removed. Perhaps the kitchen was originally in the basement. On the first floor a large room to NE corresponds to one below. The first addition to W was probably a library; it contains no datable features but is of the first half of the 18th century.

Notes
1. Binyon MS, 26–7, HRO, D/P73 29/3; *DNB*.
2. Croft-Murray 1962–70, Vol II, 302; the paintings are dated to c1728–32.
3. Jones illustrating grangerised Clutterbuck, Vol III, fo 158.
4. Cussans 1879–81, Vol III (ii), 13.
5. Ibid.
6. Ibid.
7. Croft-Murray 1962–70, Vol II, 302.
8. Croft-Murray 1962–70, Vol I, 225.
9. *Kelly* 1928.

(77741)
Northaw House (TL 274024),
called Nyn Lodge in the early 19th century, was built in 1698 with a front (N) of five bays and a double-pile plan comprising four rooms with a staircase-hall to rear; entrance was no doubt directly into the principal room, the hall (Fig 95). To E and W were detached blocks, the former being stables and the latter kitchen and services (cf Langleybury, Abbots Langley). In the late 18th century and certainly before 1805[1] the front was enlarged to seven bays; the wings were probably extended too although this may have taken place somewhat later (Fig 96). During the ownership of J B Joel c1899–1910[2] the house was greatly altered in the Queen Anne style. Subsequently it became a preparatory school for boys[3] and is now offices.

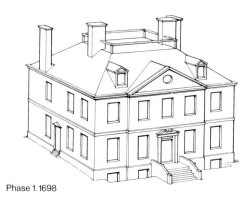

Phase 1. 1698

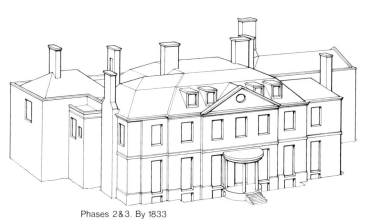

Phases 2 & 3. By 1833

Fig 95 *Northaw House: development perspectives*

The plan (Fig 97) originally comprised a large hall to NW and three other rooms; the kitchen was possibly in the basement. An unusual feature is the use of internal chimney-stacks to heat the front rooms and lateral stacks to E and W for the wings; a drawing of 1833[4] shows a recessed panel in that to E. The extension of the front range was probably intended to provide a large dining room to NW because a kitchen added to W of the W wing appears to be coeval; the dining room has a rococo plaster ceiling. The entrance-hall was reduced to a passage, and to E a room with external chimney-stack was added. By 1805 the ground floor front windows were lengthened, cutting the plinth; those in the dining room have reeded architraves. A room to SE and facing S may also have been added by then, because something depicted indistinctly appears there in the engraving; a conservatory to E of it was

Fig 96 *Northaw House: block plan*

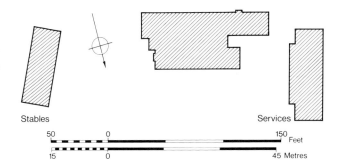

Stables

Services

50   0   150 Feet

15   0   45 Metres

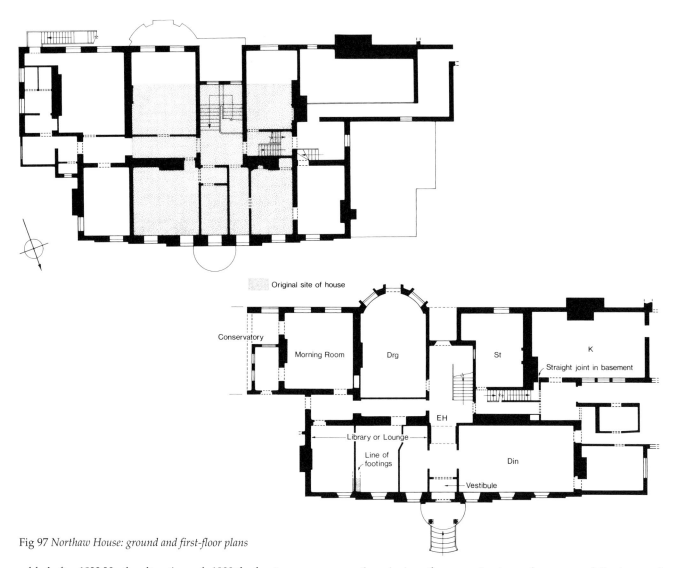

Fig 97 *Northaw House: ground and first-floor plans*

added after 1833.[5] In the alterations of *c*1900 the front range was provided with a Mansard roof and quoins were added to the E and W extensions to make their appearance uniform with the original five bays.

Notes
1. Engraving by L P Malcolm, Andrews Collection, Hertford Museum.
2. *Kelly* 1912; notes by H C Butcher in HRO.
3. SC, October 1943, in NMR.
4. Buckler Vol I, 76.
5. Ibid.

(77742)
Nyn or Ninn Hall (TL 279031),
the exact site of which is not known, stood somewhere near a 19th-century house, Nyn Park, which was itself demolished in the 1960s. It is known from an early 19th-century engraving from a printed source not traced; another etching `from a sketch in possession of the Revd John Heathfield of Northaw 1796'; an 18th century drawing;[1] and an early 19th-century etching[2] showing only the medieval part of the house. This last etching, which appears to indicate that for a time the medieval part of the house was left standing, is probably the product of inaccurate

antiquarianism; the engraving is much more carefully done and is the source for what follows.

Nyn was the manor house of Northaw which belonged to St Albans Abbey from the 11th century until the Dissolution. The medieval hall of five bays may have been built in the time of Abbot Hugh (1308–76), who leased out the manor for six years for £60; each bay had a gabled window of three cusped ogee-headed lights (four in the early 19th-century etching) with a crocketed label; in one of the end walls was a pair of windows with pointed heads, perhaps with a circular opening above, and all blocked when drawn; no doorway is shown. Soon after the Dissolution the manor was granted to William Cavendish and after being sold back to the Crown in 1552 was leased to William, Earl of Pembroke.[3] In 1556 it was said that the house was `in much decay and will not be repaired under £66 13s 4d', a state of affairs ascribable, no doubt, to `the often shifting of tenants' which had also caused depredations in the brewhouse, bakehouse and kitchen.[4] In 1576 the estate was granted to Ambrose Dudley, Earl of Warwick,[5] who `raised here a stately House from the Ground, and contrived it in a very beautiful Order, gracing it with delightful Gardens and Walks, and sundry other Pleasant and necessary Devices'.[6] Dudley will certainly have built the main range, the principal feature of which was a lofty hall, standing over cellars or a basement and probably, like Knebworth House and similar halls, open to a ceiling at the level of the tie-beams of the roof; the existence of such a hall can be inferred from four mullioned windows, each of four lights with four transoms, arranged as two pairs flanking the entrance. The doorway opened into the middle of the hall and despite its 18th-century pedimented porch may have been the original entrance, in the same position as at Sutton Place (Surrey). Two-storeyed bays stood at each end of the hall, and a block at right-angles to this range, linking it with the medieval hall, had a window even taller than those of the 16th-century hall, perhaps for a staircase. Facing it at the opposite end of the hall range was a squarish or L-shaped range apparently added in the early or mid 17th century; it was probably then that the gabled dormer windows, rising from a parapet, which look original to this one block, were added to the other ranges, and a lantern or cupola added. The 17th-century work can be ascribed to William Leman, woollen draper of London, who purchased the manor in 1632;[7] and since he was Sheriff in 1635 the work may well be between those years. Stylistically it fits that period better than after the Restoration. In May 1641 Leman was certified as abiding with his family for the most part of the year in Northaw and being taxed £12 on his lands.[8] Leman was created baronet in 1665. No major changes took place after his occupation except for the porch already mentioned and the insertion during the 18th century of a Venetian window in the left-hand block.

A description of Nyn Hall was written by John Hickman Binyon,[9] who lived in Northaw for over fifty years prior to his death in 1879, and although the account is obviously second-hand some details can only have been learned from someone who had seen the house. The hall was

paved with Marble Compleat in the form of a College Hall with a platform of oak for the Upper Table, and every appearance of a Buttery Hatch at the lower end of the Hall, with the painting of the Arms of the Knights of the Garter in Queen Elizth's time in the Windows and a variety of Stags' Horns in the Walls. It had likewise a Gallery of ninety feet in length, and library of Considerable Size at the end of it.

The house was demolished in 1774.[10]

For an illustration, see *English Houses 1200–1800*, Fig 25 (plate).

Notes
1. Bodl, Gough Maps 11, fo 57v.
2. The engraving and etchings are in the Andrews Collection, Hertford Museum.
3. VCH II, 358.
4. PRO E315/391 (Misc BR), fo 21.
5. VCH II, 358; *DNB*.
6. Chauncy II, 385.
7. VCH II, 358.
8. PRO E115/248/155.
9. Binyon MS, HRO, D/P73 29/3.
10. VCH II, 358.

NORTHCHURCH

(77743)
Arne Cottage, Dudswell (SP 965097),

is of L-shaped plan, the E (correctly SE) wing being late medieval and the N wing late 16th or early 17th century. Two bays of the original house remain, both open to the roof originally because the middle tie-beam was too low for a first-floor doorway. The wall height, equivalent to one and a half storeys, suggests that at least the inner (E) room or bay had an upper floor, but the bearers and joists in both bays are similar in appearance and scantling, and the former rest awkwardly on their supporting posts. The bay to E may have been both parlour and storeroom; that to W was the hall. To W of the inserted chimney-stack is a truss which, in part at least, was closed to form a partition or gable wall, because it has auger holes for a wattle-and-daub infilling. To W this truss shows some weathering, but not as pronounced as that on the external face of the wall-post to N; probably, as the plan suggests, the house formerly extended to W, although that part may not have been of the same build as the rest. The chimney-stack, of clunch, was built in the early 17th century and the first floor was probably inserted then; bearers and joists are uniform throughout. When the presumed W bay was demolished is uncertain, but it was not before the N wing, of brick, was added in the 18th century; the site of the original cross-passage was preserved to form a storeroom. The wing has been largely modernised.

For illustrations, see *English Houses 1200–1800*, Figs 79 (plate), 80.

(77744)
Marlin Chapel Farm (SP 963071)

is depicted in an early 19th-century drawing[1] as a timber-framed main range with a jettied cross-wing; possibly it was late medieval. All that remain are brick footings and, on the long wall of the cross-wing, the outer face of a chimney-stack (now reduced to the lower courses) built of chequer-work in stone and flint. The stack of the 16th century is possibly original to the house, and in a house of modest size is unusually early.

Note
1. Buckler Vol I, 169.

(77745)
Shootersway Farm (SP 961083)

was built in the 16th century; it comprised a hall with chimney-stack to N (correctly NE); behind the stack lay the cross-passage, and beyond that a quite large unheated room with no definite indication of its original purpose; a staircase may have stood to W of the stack. The bay to S, with staircase and lobby-entrance, appears to be a later addition; the first-floor partition dividing it from the room over the hall has no doorway in it. In the early 19th century the timber framing was infilled with brick, a gable was added to the S bay, giving the appearance of a cross-wing; a chimney-stack and fireplaces were added, and the main chimney-stack was rebuilt and reduced in size.

NORTH MYMMS

(77746)
Brookmans (TL 253048),

a manor house, took its name from John Brookman who held it in 1400. Probably Thomas Faldo, who owned the manor from 1621 to 1638, built the house described in a particular,[1] undated but evidently drawn up for a sale in 1638;[2] it was

A faire house new built with brick with all convenient and well-contrived rooms, as a faire hall, 2 parlors, kitchin, buttery, milk house, divers convenient cellars with faire upper chambers, most of the rooms well wainscoted, strongly built and costing about £1500'.

It was on a new site because rent was still being paid for `the old mansion house'. When the particular was written Paul Pinder, the purchaser, was already occupying the house, paying rent of £36 per annum. In 1666 his descendants sold the manor to Andrew Fountain Esq., of Saul (Norfolk), who `built a very fair House upon this Mannor in the Year 1682';[3] there were rain-water heads dated 1680.[4] An undated sketch[5] shows a chimney-stack of that period but probably Fountain only altered and enlarged the earlier work. In 1702 he sold it to John, Lord Somers, the former Lord Chancellor, who evidently acquired it as a place of retirement after his impeachment and subsequent exclusion from office in 1701.[6] In the mid 18th century the house was refronted with new doorcase, sash windows and parapet;[7] it was by then a large double-pile facing NE[8] and six bays in depth.[9] Samuel Robert Gaussen, a London merchant, purchased the estate in 1786[10] and was Sheriff in 1790; Humphrey Repton was remodelling the park for him before 1795.[11] A descendant, Robert William Gaussen, was Sheriff in 1841, just when the park of Brookmans was enlarged to incorporate Gobions; probably then a new end-entrance with semicircular porch was created to SE.[12] This did not affect the overall size of the house, about 80 ft by 62 ft (24·4 m x 18·9 m), which remained the same from 1820 and probably much earlier, until 1844.[13] The house was burnt out in 1891;[14] some of the walls remained standing until c1910;[15] the stables were converted into a house and subsequently became a golf clubhouse.

Notes
1. PRO SP/16/408 fo 142.
2. VCH II, 256.
3. Chauncy II, 441.
4. *Home Counties Magazine* 1902, 4, 125.
5. Buckler, BL Add MS 36430, fo 2057.
6. *DNB*.
7. Oldfield Vol V, 70.
8. HRO, DSA4, 69.
9. Photograph of 1864, Colville, nd, opposite page 80.
10. VCH II, 256.
11. Stroud 1962, 166.
12. Photograph of 1864, Colville nd, opposite page 80.
13. HRO, maps 80231; DSA4, 69.
14. Colville nd, 77.
15. RCHME 1910, 159, and unpublished photographs.

(77747)
Gobions or Gubbins (approximately TL 252039),
known as the manor of More Hall in 1300 when it belonged to the Knights Hospitallers, was held by John More in 1390 and remained with the family for three hundred years.[1] `Mr Moore, a Papist', said in 1645 to have money and goods in his house `near Gubbins',[2] is presumably the Basil More, whose `great losses...sustain'd by reason of his loyalty to his Prince caused him to sell this Mannor'[3] in 1693 to Sir Edward Des Bouverie, a London merchant.[4] The house may have been leased out for many years since the name More is not attached to a house of any size in the Hearth Tax returns of 1663 and 1673. In 1694 Sir Edward conveyed it to a trustee for his son Jacob and died in 1695. Jacob lived here with his brother William[5] before selling the house in 1697.

With the house so long at lease it is impossible to ascribe any building-works to a particular person but plasterwork and a staircase with alternately twisted and symmetrically turned balusters[6] may have been of c1700. To NE a range of 10 bays with pediment and cupola was perhaps of the same date; the pediment spans four bays, not the usual three or five. The first

recorded owner of architectural ambition was Sir Jeremy Sambrooke, Bart., who purchased the house before 1728;[7] James Gibbs, who was his architect, `added a large room';[8] he is unlikely to have executed the plasterwork and staircase drawn by Buckler. It was said that Sambrooke `for the Beauty of its Gardens, as well as the House ...made the Place one of the most remarkable Curiosities in *England*'.[9] John Hunter, `who by long success in trade as a free Merchant in the East Indies had raised a very ample Fortune, upwards of £100,000, and arrived to a seat in the East India Direction',[10] bought Gobions in 1777 and is likely to have engaged in building. After 1802, when he left the property to Thomas Holmes (who assumed the name of Hunter), and before 1840[11] two semicircular bow windows of the `East View' were added. Perhaps then the main elevations were refaced with round-arched recesses and the whole rambling house was unified by, among other things, balustrades to the roofs. Who did this work, and when, are uncertain; in 1819 part of the house had been lately rebuilt and was then the residence of Thomas Kemble Esq.[12] On Thomas Hunter's death in 1836 the property was sold to R W Gaussen of Brookmans Park; the depiction of the house on an estate map attached to an indenture of that date[13] corresponds quite closely with the Buckler drawings, with the addition of a long wing to NE, evidently a service wing, which was hidden from view by trees. Gaussen, unike many earlier Hertfordshire landowners, did not need two large houses only half a mile apart (see *English Houses 1200–1800*, p 63) and by 1840 the building materials of this `celebrated mansion' were being offered for sale.[14] A large-scale estate map, dated 1841,[15] shows only the rectangular N range of the house, with a porch to NE; all was demolished shortly afterwards.

Notes
1. VCH II, 256–7.
2. *Cal Cttee for Money* i, 47.
3. Chauncy II, 448.
4. VCH II, 257.
5. Chauncy II, 448.
6. Buckler Vol I, 68.
7. Salmon 1728, 66.
8. Colvin 1978, 342.
9. Defoe *Tour*, Vol II, 184.
10. Oldfield Vol III, 65.
11. Buckler Vol I, 67.
12. Neale 1819-29, Vol II.
13. HRO, 34188.
14. *Herts and Beds Reformer*, 1 February 1840.
15. HRO, 41151.

(77748)
Lower Farm, Bell Lane (TL 252053)
was formerly the Swan Inn; in 1756 it had eight beds and stabling for twenty horses[1] but by c1812 was described as a dwelling house.[2] It is a large timber-framed house of three main phases of construction. The main range, which faces E and is of three cells with lobby-entrance, was built in the late 16th century; it is not certain that the room to N was heated originally, its fireplace being much smaller than that in the hall, which occupies the whole width of the building except for the doorway from the lobby; this suggests a timber chimney-stack and possibly a cross-passage originally (cf The Old Rose and Crown, Braughing). The only surviving detail of this phase is the entrance, which has ovolo-moulded jambs. In the mid 17th century a kitchen wing and staircase were added to W; it was probably then that a fireplace with somewhat indeterminate

mouldings was inserted in the room at the corner of the L-plan. This was evidently the dining room, conveniently accessible from the kitchen, and adjoining a pantry and staircase to W. Probably the internal chimney-stack was rebuilt in brick and a fireplace added in the parlour to N; this left the hall as a passage room, although if the building was already an inn this would not have mattered; access from hall to wing was through a lobby, one feature of 17th-century planning to survive. These changes appear to have been made to convert the building into an inn. The rooms over hall and kitchen had fireplaces. Towards the end of the 17th century a range was added parallel to the original house; it has no fireplaces so the ground floor was presumably occupied by store rooms, with two unheated bedrooms above. An extension to W of the kitchen wing, of one storey and attics, is of the same date; it incorporated a brewhouse. In the 1970s the house was restored.

Notes
1. Victuallers Building Return, PRO.
2. SC, HRO, D/EL B584, nd.

(61271)
North Mymms Park (TL 217042)

is the manor house of North Mymms. The manor, important before the Norman Conquest, was divided into two or more parts from the middle of the 13th century until reunited by John Coningsby in 1529–30; he was Sheriff in 1547. A house of some size must have been in existence then. After John's death his son Henry settled the manor on his mother Elizabeth and her second husband William Dodds for their lives.[1] Dodds was Sheriff in 1570 and although no place appears beside his name in the list of Sheriffs, North Mymms appears to have been his principal manor and residence; Henry Coningsby, who was Sheriff in 1569, may then have been living at Randolphs in Aldenham.[2] After the manor reverted to Coningsby he was again Sheriff (and knighted) in 1582,[3] and on his death in 1590 it passed to his son Sir Ralph Coningsby. The present house was built in all probability by Ralph before he was Sheriff in 1596 although the basis for the definite assertion[4] to that effect is not clear. A fireplace in the house dated 1563 must be imported. The estate descended to Thomas Coningsby, who forfeited it for supporting Charles I; in 1650 his son Henry, seeking a lease of the sequestered property, alleged that `The Manor house which cost £10,000 is falling into ruins.[5] A View and Examination of the manor 9 March 1650 was more precise: `The manor house is much decayed in lead and gutters about the house which do let in the water upon every rain upon the ceilings and brickwork of the house which is much decayed.' The house was further stated to be `out of repair in the tilings and lathings, glassing and walling, in the coping of the brickwork about the house...[it] will cost £50 to repair, but if not timely repaired may cost a far greater sum'.[6] In 1658 house and manor were sold to Sir Thomas Hyde of Aldbury[7] who, in 1663, paid tax for 24 hearths.[8] In 1733 Thomas, Duke of Leeds, inherited the estate; by 1742 he was said to have put `a great Part of the House and Gardens in good Repair'.[9] A drawing dated 26 August 1799 shows that his work included refurbishing the E elevation.[10] Another drawing of c1800 by Oldfield[11] shows windows of two lights in the hall and parlour to E of it; these do not appear in the 1799 drawing.

In 1800 the estate was bought by Henry Browne Esq.,[12] who may already have had the house on lease; the 1799 drawing is captioned `Duke of Leeds now Mr Browne's'. The new owner, who was Sheriff in 1803, restored the hall and parlour windows and gave the house a stuccoed and generally Tudor appearance.[13] The name of the architect is unknown, although W H Ashpitel[14] worked here. About 1824 it was sold to the trustees of Fulke Southwell Greville, who was then a minor; he made some alterations prior to 1843[15] and in 1844–6 Edward Blore was working there.[16] In 1850 Greville was Sheriff. His household in 1851 comprised himself, his wife and four children, a cousin in the Artillery, a tutor in classics and fifteen indoor servants. In 1893 the house was sold to Mr Walter H Burns, who employed Ernest George and Alfred B Yeates to restore the exterior of the house in the Elizabethan style and to add a large block to SW.

The original plan of the main (N) range, though now much altered, seems to have been conventional. The porch led into a screens-passage or the lower end of the hall; the hall had a lateral fireplace; in the E wing was the parlour. To W of the hall were service rooms and in the W wing probably another parlour, with the kitchen beyond. In the re-entrant angles of the long rear wings were two staircases. The E wing, which had two chimney-stacks backing on to the courtyard, may have served sets of lodgings. Although there is now no indication where other staircases were, there was probably one at the end of each range, not unlike the two stair towers built in the mid 19th century. Hardly any original internal detail survives.

For an illustration, see *English Houses 1200–1800*, Fig 212 (plate).

Notes
1. VCH II, 254.
2. Chauncy II, 309–10.
3. Ibid, 310.
4. VCH II, 254.
5. *Cal Cttee for Compounding*, 1643–1660 ii, 854; see a similar complaint in respect of Balls Park, Hertford.
6. *Cttee for Compounding*, sp 23/g77.
7. VCH II, 254.
8. PRO E179/248/24/19.
9. Defoe *Tour*, Vol II, 183.
10. Meynell Collection.
11. Oldfield Vol V, 60.
12. VCH II, 254.
13. Buckler Vol I, 62; *Middlesex and Herts N & Q* 1895, Vol I, 73.
14. 1776–1852; Colvin 1978, 71-2.
15. Sale advertisement, *Northampton Mercury*, 29 April 1843.
16. Colvin 1978, 118.

(60013)
Potterells (TL 236046)

was a manor in the 15th century, described as appurtenant to Brookmans. In 1632 it was sold to Thomas Coningsby of North Mymms Park and, after 1658, became the family seat[1] and a house of importance. The present building incorporates brickwork which may be of the late 17th century; it rises to the height of the first-floor window lintels, has wide mortar joints, was subsequently painted red and tuck pointed, and formed a large house of nine bays. Originally it faced W, probably with a large hall occupying three bays in the middle; the hall chimney-stack was to E; service rooms were to S. To E, at the N end, is a wing, and, towards the S end, a three-bay block which may have contained a large dining room. Probably there were two staircases. This plan, narrower in the middle, is comparable to Rothamsted, Harpenden, or Brent Pelham Hall, although the stages by which it developed are beyond recovery. In 1792 the house came by descent to Justinian Casamajor, who `added to the building and embellished that which was before standing'.[2] Casamajor was Sheriff in 1800. He changed the entrance from W to E; added a third storey throughout and a large bow window to W of the former hall; enlarged an existing service wing to S; and located, between wing and dining room, a portico *in antis* with the top storey carried over it. Oldfield shows, erroneously, a symmetrical front with the portico flanked by three bays to left and right, whereas Buckler's drawing of 1840 shows the house as it is today, with only two bays to the right of the portico.

In 1912 and 1929 the house was in the ownership of Hugh Francis Seymour,[3] who appears to have rebuilt the three internal walls and the wooden columns of the portico, perhaps in the 1920s; his initials appear on a rain-water head at the NE corner. At the same time the interior detail, except for the S staircase which is of *c*1800, was extensively renewed.

Notes
1. VCH II, 254–5.
2. Caption to Oldfield Vol V, 57.
3. *Kelly* 1912, 1929.

NUTHAMPSTEAD

(77750)
Bury Farm (TL 400349)

is a manor house. In 1422, when it became part of the dower of Queen Katherine, widow of Henry V, a hall and chambers were built,[1] and although the house is now entirely devoid of medieval detail it appears to incorporate the shell of those buildings. It passed as dower to Elizabeth, Edward IV's queen, who was deprived of it by Richard III in 1483.[2] In the succeeding sixty years it was leased out by the Crown until bought in 1545 by Robert Chester of Royston; thereafter it was always a minor part of a large estate.

That the E part of the present house is a remodelling of the 15th-century hall can be inferred from its width (24 ft (7·3 m)), but its length and the location of the screens-passage are uncertain. The oldest structural features now visible are in the two-storeyed jettied block built to W in series with the hall; this is probably of the mid 16th century and appears to have comprised a parlour with chamber above, both rooms having fireplaces. In the early 17th century a small wing, jettied to N, was added to the W block; in the late 17th century the hall had an upper floor inserted and was heightened to two storeys and attics, the shaped heads of two posts providing the only evidence of date. The chimney-stack and staircase were built then, also a belvedere (since removed); the roof timbers which supported it remain. In the late 18th century the house was refronted in brick.

Notes
1. PRO Ministers' Accounts, DL 29/42/820.
2. VCH IV, 31.

OFFLEY

(77751)
Little Offley House (TL 285129)

bears the name of a manor and deserted village[1] that descended with the manor of Welles.[2] It is unlikely that there was a manor house of any consequence before 1557 when the manor was conveyed to Richard Spicer alias Helder, who disposed of it to William Crawley in 1569;[3] the present house incorporates fragments and much of the plan of a timber-framed house built in the late 16th century, probably either by Spicer or Crawley.

From this time no record appears of the manor until 1704;[4] but Chauncy[5] purports to show that Richard Helder Esq. was holding one part of it *c*1700, and since he is the person to whom Drapentier's engraving of Little Offley is presented he must have lived there. Since William Helder and Widow Helder paid for eight and six hearths respectively in 1663[6] the house was perhaps divided then. Certainly a little later the manor itself was 'the Mannor House and chiefest Part of it being in the possession of Mr Henry Bolderne "the present owner"'.[7] Either Henry Bolderne or Richard Helder must have refronted Little Offley Hall in 1695.[8]

The house was originally timber framed and of H-plan with the main range facing S. The hall, with chimney-stack to N, occupied the W part of the main range; the present narrow entrance-hall in the middle perpetuates the cross-passage; two service rooms lay to E, with a passage to rear of them leading to the kitchen at the front of the E wing; the parlour was in the W wing. The positions of staircases are uncertain.

In 1695 the house was refaced in brick; the E wing enlarged; a two-storey porch and cupola added; the roof rebuilt as an attic storey; and a staircase added, rising from the passage behind the former service rooms and leading to new principal rooms. The use of sash windows in the first-floor wing rooms rather than the mullion-and-transom windows found elsewhere[9] indicates that they were especially important; the external indication that the opposite ends of the house were equally important is an example of the duality found in so many late 17th-century houses in Hertfordshire. Consequently the staircase, turning anti-clockwise, gave access, from the upper of its two landings, to a short flight and passage added behind the hall chimney-stack, and so to an ante-room and principal rooms in the W wing; the main flight, continuing from the upper landing, led to a passage corresponding to that on the ground floor, from which the chambers over the hall and new parlour and those in the E wing were reached without any being a passage room. The attics were reached by a continuation of the main staircase and probably also by a secondary staircase to E, which has been entirely removed. How rooms were used is less clear. The hall continued to be a combined entrance and living room; the old service rooms were made into a parlour or study and fitted with a fireplace; their function was transferred to an extension of the E wing, where the larder, butler's pantry and servants' hall were situated in recent years; and the kitchen retained its old position. Upstairs the dining room and withdrawing room were probably in the middle range, with the wing rooms to S being bedchambers.

Subsequent alterations are difficult to date. A map of 1807[10] shows farm buildings at the front of the house and on the site of the gardens; the house was owned by one Sheppard and had descended to Charles Sheppard Marsh by 1912.[11] He or a subsequent owner added small outer wings, extended the existing E wing further and renovated the house in the Queen Anne style.

For an illustration, see *English Houses 1200–1800*, Fig 115.

Notes
1. Chauncy II, 197.
2. VCH III, 41–2.
3. Ibid, 42.
4. Ibid.
5. Chauncy II, 199.
6. PRO E179/248/23.
7. Chauncy II 199 (as Dolderne); but cf VCH III, 42.
8. Dated rain-water head; RCHME 1910, 161.
9. Cf also the pairs of triangular pediments giving

emphasis to the wings at Tyttenhanger, Ridge.
10. HRO, D/56 C2/52.
11. *Kelly* 1912; not as VCH III, 42.

(79639)
Offley Hoo (TL 261148)

is of brick and was built in the early 18th century. The plan was L-shaped with a central staircase-hall between hall and parlour in the front range and a kitchen in the rear (E) wing. The wing was probably always subdivided to provide a pantry, although it is not clear exactly how this was arranged; the outside door needed in a kitchen is beside the fireplace in the E wall and the pantry must have left space for access to it. The main staircase, which has turned balusters, rises only to the first floor; the attics were reached by a staircase with splat balusters which is situated in the wing. In the mid 19th century a block with two E-facing gables was added in the angle of the L; a room with a small corner fireplace may have been the farm office.

(39632)
Offley Place (TL 145270)

was the manor house of Offley St Ledgers which, c1554, came into the possession of Sir John Spencer of Althorpe (Northamptonshire). He died in 1586, leaving it to his fourth son Richard, who became Sheriff in 1597, was knighted in 1603 and died in 1624.[1] It was probably Richard Spencer who gave the principal part of the house engraved by Drapentier[2] its appearance, although differences in window levels suggest a complicated history. An addition at the right-hand side, perhaps a long wing giving the house a T-plan, was probably made by Sir Brockett Spencer, who held the manor from 1633 to 1668 and was created baronet in 1642.[3]

The mullion-and-transom windows and two groups of chimney-shafts appear in a drawing of c1800[4] of the NE or garden elevation. By then the main body of the house was of three storeys and its long garden front was punctuated by three semi-octagonal bay windows, one or two of which may have occupied the sites of chimney-stacks shown in the Drapentier engraving. The enclosure map of 1807[5] shows that the earlier range had by then largely disappeared, although the entrance must have been to N. Stylistically the three bay windows to S look to be of the mid 18th century and might have been added by Sir Thomas Salusbury, who owned the estate from about 1745 until 1773.[6] During his time Mrs Thrale, friend of Samuel Johnson,[7] lived for a while at Offley Park and was inspired by its grounds and associations to write two poems.[8]

In 1806 the house passed to the Revd Lynch Salusbury (later Burroughs) who, over the next four years, engaged Sir Robert Smirke to rebuild it.[9] `His rage for building' here and elsewhere `caused him to employ many workmen',[10] and he built what was virtually a new house, incorporating to E a small part, refaced and refenestrated, of the old one. A sketch plan of c1810 shows the uses of the principal rooms.[11] Some of the early 19th-century fireplaces, doorcases and cornices remain; the principal alteration was the removal of the tower in 1929 by Colonel Acland, who had purchased the house in the previous year.[12] Since 1943 it has been used for educational purposes.

For an illustration, see *English Houses 1200–1800*, Fig 134 (plate).

Notes
1. VCH III, 407.
2. Chauncy II, 192.
3. Ibid, 193.
4. Oldfield Vol V, 204.

5. HRO, QS/E 56.
6. VCH III, 41.
7. Hester Lynch Piozzi; *DNB*.
8. *Thraliana*, 74–7, 85–91.
9. Colvin 1978, 744.
10. Lucas *Diary*, Vol I, 109.
11. GLC Collection, in mixed collection bought at Sothebys; inf. Mr A F Kelsall.
12. Fraser nd, 7.

(77753)
The Old Post Office
(recently renamed The Court House) (TL 142270),

of the late 14th century, comprises a range of two storeys facing the street to W (correctly NW) and jettied, with an open hall of two bays to rear (E). The hall has a base-cruck truss with crown-post roof; service rooms to N have been removed. The street range comprised two chambers on the first floor, the ground floor perhaps being divided into parlour and shop, as its location suggests (cf Yew Tree Farm, Much Hadham).[1]

Note
1. Gibson 1974–6, 153–7.

PIRTON

(77754)
Burge End Farm (TL 144323),

of two storeys, was built in the mid 17th century on a two-cell lobby-entrance plan and staircase turret to W; to S of the turret was a lean-to forming a pantry. To S of the stack was the hall; its fireplace has a defaced moulded lintel re-used from elsewhere. The exposed framing has fairly closely spaced studs with long straight braces; the windbraces in the roof are straight; the staircase has symmetrical balusters. In the late 18th century the house was refaced in brick and extended at both ends; at the same time, internal alterations were also made.

(77755)
No. 2 Bury End (TL 148317),

a late medieval house, comprised an open hall with cross-wing at the upper (W) end; only the W bay of the hall remains, the passage and service end having been destroyed; the open truss of the hall has a cambered tie-beam and rebated crown-post. The cross-wing, narrow and relatively tall, has a two-bay crown-post roof with two-way braces; originally it was jettied to N; the roof extends to S over the present staircase but although the S gable wall has been rebuilt the wing was probably no larger than now, the half-bay being for the original staircase. An upper floor was put into the hall in the 17th century; the existing brick chimney-stack is later, perhaps of the 18th century, and was probably built when the E end of the hall was demolished. The wing chimney-stack was added in the early 19th century; the hall range heightened from one storey and attics to two storeys; and thatch replaced by slate, early in the present century.

(77756)
Hammond's Farm (TL 145319)

derives its name from a family prominent in the parish from the early 16th century until 1695.[1] It incorporates evidence of a late medieval house, most of which was replaced in the 17th century, probably in stages and ending in the third quarter of the century. The only sign of late medieval work is in the former hall, where the framing to W (correctly SW) end has peg-holes for a bench; and the bearer carrying the first floor is an insertion, showing that this room was originally open to the roof. If the hall was square the cross-passage would have been in the same position as the present entrance, with service rooms beyond. The first alteration was probably the building of a timber chimney-stack on the site of the cross-passage; the evidence for this comprises peg-holes in the present fireplace lintel and more definite ones in a tie-beam at the corresponding position on the first floor. In the second quarter of the 17th century the house was heightened and rebuilt with a cross-wing to E and a two-storey porch and staircase on opposite sides of the internal chimney-stack. The E wing was a kitchen and may have taken over some of the functions of the hall; the hall then became more like a parlour; and service rooms were added to W. Not long afterwards the internal stack was rebuilt; it has a large rectangular shaft of later appearance than the three diagonal shafts of the E stack but both stacks have the same mouldings at the base of the shafts. Part of this rebuilding may have been done by John Hammond, whose will is dated 1641.[2]

The cross-wing provided one large room on each floor; the upstairs room has an open truss which originally may have had a shaped pendant like the external ones on the S gable. Both wing and porch have original simply moulded barge-boards and there are mortises for a flat-roofed bay window to S of the hall. In 1908 the first-floor fireplace over the kitchen had an elaborate surround said to be Jacobean;[3] what remains now is reproduction work.

For illustrations, see *English Houses 1200–1800*, Figs 165 (plate), 166.

Notes
1. Andrews 1908–9, 27–31.
2. Ibid, 29.
3. Ibid, illustration opposite page 30.

(77757)
High Down (TL 144345)

was the manor house of one half of the manor of Pirton. It appears to have come into the possession of the Docwra family during the 16th century, as a stone panel bearing the arms of Sir Thomas Docwra[1] and the date 1504,[2] which is reset in the NE gable of the stable range, suggests; and by 1599 it was in the possession of another Thomas Docwra, who in that year settled it on his son, also Thomas, on his marriage to Jane Periam.[3] Part of the house is of that date. Thomas the younger received a grant of free warren at Pirton in 1616 and after his death in 1620 house and manor descended successively to his son Periam, who died in 1642, and the latter's son Thomas. The house was considerably enlarged before it passed to Martha, daughter and heir of the last Thomas Docwra, on whose marriage to Sir Peter Warburton of Arley (Cheshire) it ceased for a time to be a seat. On Martha's death in 1726 it was sold to Ralph Radcliffe, one of whose descendants in the late 18th century proposed to rebuild the house as a large Palladian mansion.[4] High Down has undergone comparatively little alteration since then.

The house is difficult to understand and the following account must be regarded as provisional. It is of square chalk rubble which is almost entirely concealed by rendering, and has tile roofs. Although regarded as being of the early 17th century[5] or as having been begun in 1599[6] the anomalous plan and elevations suggest the house is not of one build. A drawing captioned High Down[7] is of some other house.

The oldest element appears to be the E wing (Fig 98), part of which and perhaps the whole is of c1600. The first-floor walls are quite thin despite being of clunch; both wall-plates are of broad flat section oversailing the walls inside; the few peg-holes

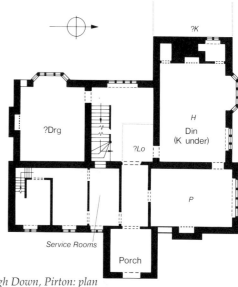

Fig 98 *High Down, Pirton: plan*

do not correspond to regular framing, and no mortises are visible. On the ground floor the walls are of stone with no trace of framing, hence this may have been a form of mixed construction akin to that at Aston Bury. The disposition of rooms on the ground floor is unknown; upstairs was a principal room about 23 ft long (7·0 m) of two bays divided by an open truss with braced and slightly cambered tie-beam, and separated from a smaller room at the W end by a close-studded partition. This wing appears to have incorporated service rooms and a good-sized chamber, without a fireplace, above; and the 19th-century staircase may be in the same position as the original one. The hall associated with this range was in the NW wing and is unusual in having a wooden floor over a basement. Above the hall the great chamber, spanned by an arch-braced collar-beam truss, probably always had a ceiling at collar level. The fireplaces, chimney-shafts and roof truss are consistent with a date of c1600 and date this part of the house to the marriage settlement of 1599,[8] but the chimney-shafts have been renewed, a 19th-century drawing in the house showing them as diagonal shafts. If this reconstruction of the first phase is correct the hall may have been entered by a door in the re-entrant angle. This range extended farther to W, as shown in an early 19th-century sketch on an estate map.[9]

In the early 17th century a gateway to N bearing the arms and names of Thomas Docwra and Jane Periam and the date 1613 was added; it was possibly the first stage in forming a courtyard,[10] although not opposite the hall doorway, and provided an approach not unlike that at Standon Lordship. The small E wing which is now a porch must be of the same date as the wing since only a light partition separates them; it is unlikely to have been a porch originally because the doorway into the porch, rather than from porch into house, is anomalous; it may have been a staircase turret; possibly an internal lobby in the SW corner of the parlour led to a passage, from which the staircase and other ground-floor rooms were reached. In the late 17th century a double-pile plan was created. It appears to have involved turning the house round to face E. The putative staircase became a porch, a function for which it is really much too large. The wing was doubled in depth to provide a staircase-hall and a room to S which was perhaps a drawing room. The dining room has unusual proportions because the fireplace is at the gable end rather than on a long wall; such proportions are not uncommon around the middle of the 17th century and suggest some subdivision at the S end of the room, perhaps for an ante-room. An old partition in the basement may correspond to the suggested division of the principal floor, and would give a square room above. The brick arch of the kitchen fireplace and the large relieving timber above it are of the mid-late 17th century. The turned balusters of the main staircase are of this date but the staircase itself has probably been altered.

In the porch the upper armorial panel (Docwra impaling Hales) is a later insertion, being surrounded by brickwork, and is of uncertain significance, there being no mention of Hales in the county histories; the 1599 date panel is presumed to be reset; the three-light window over the front door is likely to be coeval with it.

In the 18th century some remodelling of the ground-floor rooms took place and three windows replaced older ones to S of the porch. A late 18th-century painting of an Arab stallion shows in the background the house more or less as it is today, although the estate-map sketch mentioned above shows no porch.

In the early 19th century the staircase was altered: the flight to the basement was concealed by panelling and a door of that period, and in the main flight the handrail and newel post and probably the string were renewed. On the E side of the house the windows, by their unusual proportions, appear to have been altered, and possibly the rendering was put on in the 19th century to conceal patches of brickwork. This may have been done before 1842 when William Lucas of Hitchin recorded visiting `Wm Brown in his new and romantic residence at Highdown'.[11]

Notes
1. *DNB*.
2. VCH III, 46.
3. Ibid, 48–9.
4. Inf. Mr Spencer-Smith; drawings in the house.
5. RCHME 1910, 163–4.
6. VCH III, 45–6.
7. Oldfield Vol IV, 141.
8. VCH III, 48–9.
9. HRO, D/E 564A.
10. Plan, VCH III, 45.
11. Lucas *Diary*, Vol II, 279.

(77758)
Pirton Grange (TL 122329)

is a moated house of the 15th century of which only the S wing survives; an open hall stood to N. In the E gable of the S wing are a king-strut, mortised for a collar-purlin, and several original rafter couples; although the roof establishes that the S wing is medieval it is strange that there is no sign of a jetty, the existence of an axial bearer precluding one. The hall extended to the present N wing; the tie-beam of the open truss, chamfered only to N, is embedded in a partition and relates to the wall-plate, now cut by the upstairs windows, which is visible outside. Some re-used smoke-blackened rafters in this range no doubt come from the medieval hall. No medieval work remains to N of the hall although a bay in series probably existed. The earliest addition may be the narrow jettied block to S of the S wing (cf the small detached building at the S end of Letchworh Hall); the fireplace was once larger although alteration has made its original size uncertain. A fireplace was doubtless added in the ground-floor room to N but no evidence of it is visible. Access from the kitchen may have been to W, by a pentise. Upstairs a great chamber was created, having a fireplace above which was painted an improving inscription.[1] Since the room over the

kitchen can only have been reached from the adjoining chamber it may have been a pallet room or closet.

The development of the hall and N cross-wing has been obscured by heavy-handed restoration in the late 19th century. Probably an upper floor and a chimney-stack were inserted in the hall c1600; if so, the N wing with its clasped-purlin roof is coeval; as in the S wing, an axial bearer precludes an original jetty. The original function of the wing rooms is uncertain; the wide fireplace in the room to W suggests it may always have been a kitchen, as in recent times, with a service room to E; the lobby within the latter probably perpetuates the original arrangement, as does the staircase. In the early 17th century a short wing was added at right-angles to the S kitchen wing as a dairy or service room, and a bay window was added to the room over the kitchen, providing a second well-finished chamber at this end of the house. If room use has been interpreted correctly the two kitchens suggest a family organisation akin to that at Walnut Tree Farm, Pirton and other examples of the unit system. In about 1700 the hall roof was raised and three tall windows inserted; the new roof has a modillioned cornice and the walls were rendered; a shell-hood doorcase was added. Inside, an imposing staircase was added to W of the S wing. The hall and chamber above it and the room to S were lined with bolection-moulded panelling and given new fireplaces; only the fireplace in the last-mentioned room remains, the others having been replaced by early Victorian fireplaces with simply moulded jambs and paterae. In the late 19th century the house underwent extensive alteration; timbers were repaired and exposed; new fireplaces were put in; and the S kitchen became a sitting room. A single-storey vaulted cellar, perhaps a dairy, was added to W of the NW wing.

For an illustration, see *English Houses 1200–1800*, Fig 11.

Note
1. Rouse 1989, Plate XXVII c.

(77759)
The Old Hall, now called Docwra Manor (TL 313145),

of two storeys, is of flint and rubble formerly plastered,[1] with brick dressings and tile roofs. It is dated by a plaque which was formerly in the SW wall (W for description) and is now reset over the principal ground-floor fireplace; it bears the arms of Thomas Docwra and the inscription '1609/ EN DIEV EST TOVT'. The stone end walls return along the E side for only a few feet and the remaining space of about 34 ft (10·4 m) is filled by timber framing, from which it appears that the existing structure was a parlour cross-wing added to an earlier timber-framed structure. If the width of this structure was 34 ft (10·4 m) it must have been aisled; the alternative suggestion of a conventional 17th-century plan[2] does not explain why the stone walls terminate as they do.

Few old features have survived the conversion of the wing into a public house in the 19th century and drastic alterations in recent years. An original chimney-stack on the W front has sloping offsets, a cross worked on its face in flint and a brick cornice with simple moulding; it serves a ground-floor fireplace, with moulded stone jambs and depressed four-centred head. In 1909 this fireplace had an 18th-century surround.[3] A smaller chimney-stack is of brick and probably of the 18th century. The ground-floor plan comprised two large rooms, that to N having a fireplace with moulded jambs and depressed four-centred head; between them was a lobby, to W of which was a staircase, its existence attested by a two-light window lower than the two windows lighting the upstairs rooms.[4] The two large first-floor rooms each had a three-light ovolo-mullioned window in the gable end wall; the lintels are higher than the wall-plates and imply that there were ceilings at the level of the collar-beams. The N room probably had a fireplace from the first.

Notes
1. RCHME 1910, 104.
2. Lucas 1908–11a, 31–3.
3. RCHME 1910, 165.
4. Anderson WCL, 1898.

(77760)
No. 28 Shillington Road (TL 144320)

comprises part of the open hall of a late medieval house and a cross-wing of two rooms on each floor. It is not quite certain at which end of the hall they stood; the upper end is more likely. The large wing chimney-stack, partly rebuilt, is probably of the early 17th century; the hall has a clasped-purlin roof. The framing is generally of indifferent quality.

(77761)
Walnut Tree Farm (TL 148314)

is one of the most interesting examples of the unit system in Hertfordshire. The oldest part of the present building is a late medieval timber-framed house at the E end; it comprised originally an E wing of two storeys (with, surprisingly, no evidence of an original jetty), a low hall with an open hearth and, presumably, a service bay (Fig 99). In the late 17th century an internal-chimney house of brick with lobby-entrance and of two storeys and attics was added to W; it has a two-storey porch and the staircase was probably N of the chimney-stack. Not long afterwards the presumed service bay of the original house was rebuilt in brick; a chimney-stack with a wide kitchen-type fireplace was built on the site of the cross-passage, converting it to a lobby-entrance; and a staircase turret and a gabled rear bay were added. At the front the new brickwork was bonded in with the old. After

Fig 99 *Walnut Tree Farm, Pirton: plans*

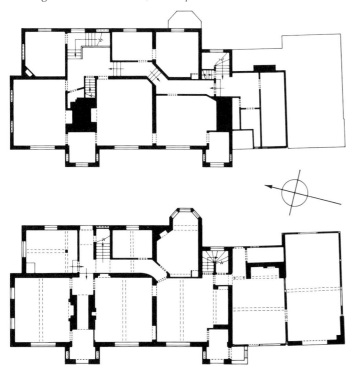

another comparatively short interval the internal-chimney house was converted into a house of double depth by the addition of a three-bay rear range with gables of slightly steeper pitch than the one at the E end; in the middle was a staircase, approached through a new doorway from the room E of the stack; W of the stair was a small parlour and E of it a pantry or other service room. By this time the house was in two distinct parts, each with a separate entrance; the E part was smaller and inferior to the W part. In the attics there has been intercommunication between the two parts of the house but the doorway is now blocked and may not be original; on the first floor there is still a doorway which, too, is not necessarily an original feature.

There is no evidence of 18th-century alteration. In the late 19th century a passage was tunnelled through the W stack; passages were created on ground and first floors to unify the house; a new main staircase, requiring the opening of new windows and the blocking of the old, was built; six wide segmental-headed windows replaced twelve upright ones at the front; and then or subsequently the cross-wing was gutted completely, even to the removal of the first floor.

For illustrations, see *English Houses 1200–1800*, Figs 183 (plate), 184.

POTTERS BAR

(77762)
Nos 62–68 Blanche Lane, the Old Post Office (TL 222010),

is mainly of the mid 17th century but incorporates some earlier work. It has an internal chimney-stack with lobby-entrance; to S is the service bay and to N a cross-wing jettied to E and W. The first-floor framing of the wing, one of the few approximately datable features, is of the mid 17th century; this is unusually late for jetties and these may be part of an earlier building.

(77763)
Clare Hall, South Mimms (TL 002219)

was described as newly erected c1745; it was built by Thomas Roberts, linendraper, who formed the estate between 1730 and 1745 and died bankrupt c1747.[1] It incorporates a low and originally timber-framed range to N, which was built in the 17th century and may have had a central chimney-stack and two-room plan. It became the service quarters of the double-pile brick house added to S. The new block had a central front doorway and narrow entrance-hall; to W was the principal room, and to E probably the dining room. The staircase-hall had to W a smaller room with a fireplace (parlour or study) and to E an unheated service room. The present staircase, with coarse detail and altered wall-panelling, may not be original; it leads to a landing off which four rooms, corresponding to those on the ground floor, opened (Fig 100). The bedroom to SE was probably the principal one, with a square dressing-room adjoining to N; the SW bedroom had a narrow dressing-room corresponding to the entrance-hall and was reached through a lobby cut out of the least important bedroom on this floor. The size of all these rooms except the narrow dressing-room is established by plaster cornices. The attics were presumably reached by a continuation of the main staircase.

A square block, added to E in the early 19th century during the ownership of Catherine Sharp from 1797 to 1842, has at the front (E) three semicircular arches of rubbed orange brick and there were three similar arches, probably for windows lighting a new end-entrance hall, to N; and on the partition wall cutting off the remaining space as one large room were matching arches. On the first floor were three bedrooms, two large and

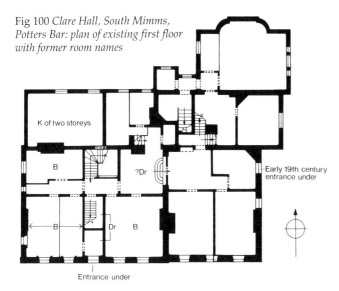

Fig 100 *Clare Hall, South Mimms, Potters Bar: plan of existing first floor with former room names*

one small, all reached from a square passage-room; and the addition of the new block made the former square dressing-room into a passage. Subsequently the house was twice enlarged to NE, the second time probably by Edward Knight, stockbroker, who owned it from *c*1874 to 1886.[2] Thereafter it was a convent and from 1896 to *c*1976 a hospital.

Notes
1. VCH *Middlesex*, Vol V, 289.
2. Ibid.

(77764)
Knightsland Farm, South Mimms (TL 233985)

was formerly a timber-framed building comprising an open hall with cross-wing to W; the latter has no closely datable features but is probably of the early 16th century because the first floor is slightly lower than that of the adjoining range. The wing, unusually long (46 ft (14·0 m)), may have been enlarged to S. The main range is dated to *c*1600 by wall-paintings;[1] of the same date is a semi-octagonal stair turret in the re-entrant angle to S, which has small square timber-framed newels and, at the top, a doorway with moulded jambs and two-centred head (cf Queen Hoo Hall, Tewin, and Stanstead Bury). On the ground floor the main range is of four approximately equal bays; the W bay was partitioned off with one doorway adjoining the staircase and another towards the N wall. The other binding-beams have mortises for braces – an unusually late appearance of this feature. Presumably the two middle bays formed the hall, which must have had either a lateral chimney-stack to N or an internal stack to E. Where the house was entered and what the function of the bays to E and W of the hall were are not clear. On the first floor the main range comprises two rooms; that to E has, on the partition wall, paintings dated to *c*1590–1610 depicting the parable of the Prodigal Son.[2] In the S room of the wing the partition is largely occupied by wall-paintings of 1610–20: a brocade pattern interspersed with pomegranates or other devices, with a frieze of five-petalled flowers between bands of various colours. The rebuilding of the hall range may be attributable to William Crowley, who owned the estate in 1618.[3] In the late 17th century the outer walls were rebuilt in brick except for the N and W walls of the wing. Then, as probably earlier, the entrance was to S; over what is now the garden door a platband is stepped up seven courses to accommodate a cartouche or achievement of arms. The octagonal stair-turret was

made square externally and the foot of the staircase turned to face N instead of W. Some of the panelling in the house may be genuine work of this period but some of it is certainly of the late 19th century in Queen Anne style. In the 18th and 19th centuries new windows were inserted and the entrance transferred to N.

Notes
1. Rouse 1989, 442; RCHME 1937, 95–6.
2. RCHME 1937, 95–6, Plate 172.
3. VCH *Middlesex*, Vol V, 287.

(77765)
Salisbury House, No. 81 High Street,

is of brick and of two storeys, cellar and attics, and was built in the mid 18th century; it appears to be the tenement or dwelling house erected on a piece of land, formerly a gravel pit, held by John Fennel from 1740 to 1756.[1] It faces W and originally had a front elevation of five bays. The ground plan comprises four rooms, all now (and perhaps originally) with fireplaces, arranged around entrance and staircase-halls to W and E respectively; the rooms to S of the halls are slightly larger than the others; the SE room, which has a bigger chimney-breast, was probably the kitchen. A NE wing shown on an estate map of 1769[2] was replaced in the early 19th century by a two-storey structure of yellow brick with orange dressings, the ground-floor windows being set in round-headed recesses giving an arcaded effect; it may have been intended to provide accommodation for the boys' boarding school which was established here *c*1805–55.[3] Service rooms to S of the kitchen may be of *c*1800; and later in the 19th century a prominent bay window of two storeys was added to the SW room. Subsequent alteration removed nearly all of the old fittings. In 1975 the additions to the original rectangular plan were demolished and new wings added to convert the whole into offices.

Notes
1. Inf. Mrs H Baker, citing Enfield manor court roll.
2. Inf. Mrs H Baker.
3. VCH *Middlesex*, Vol V, 306.

(77766)
Wrotham Park (TQ 247991)

is built on land purchased in 1750 by Admiral John Byng,[1] who employed Isaac Ware as architect of a house –'a Stareabout Pile near Barnet'[2] – with a central block flanked by wings terminating in pavilions. It was altered repeatedly: before 1771; *c*1810, when the wings were heightened; and in 1854.[3] In 1860 tenders for alterations were sought.[4] In 1883, following a fire which virtually destroyed the interior, the central block was heightened.[5] Only the plan remains virtually intact.

For an illustration, see *English Houses 1200–1800*, Fig 197 (plate).

Notes
1. *DNB*.
2. Andrews 1936, 4, 149.
3. VCH *Middlesex*, Vol V, 289.
4. *The Builder* 1860, 18 (i), 208; the architect was Henry Clutton.
5. *Vitruvius Britannicus* Vol V, Plates 45, 46.

(32256)
Wyllyots Manor (TL 249013)

incorporates an aisled barn of the 15th or 16th centuries, at one end of which has been added a small double-pile house of *c*1800 built largely of re-used timbers and originally stuccoed. The house was extensively restored in 1925, when the stucco was removed; subsequently it was converted successively into offices and a restaurant.

PRESTON

(77767)
Preston Castle (or Hunsdon House) (TL 175251)

is a house about which very little information is available. The name Preston Castle derives from Captain Robert Hinde, who built earthwork fortifications in the grounds and is said to be the original of Lawrence Sterne's Uncle Toby.[1] An early 19th-century engraving[2] shows that the house comprised two wings, one facing E and the other S. The older E wing had details of about the middle of the 17th century, including pilasters on the first floor (cf Drapentier engraving of Stagenhoe, St Pauls Walden) and in what had evidently been built as gables (cf Rothamsted, Harpenden); these suggest a building with two cross-wings and possibly curvilinear gables. Behind this range and overlapping it was added a taller early 18th-century wing of six bays. Hinde provided the entire house with battlemented parapets of uniform height and cross-loops like those of a medieval castle. The whole was demolished in the 19th century.

Notes
1. Dunnage 1815; Hine 1927, Vol I, 119.
2. Andrews Collection.

(77768)
Temple Dinsley (TL 181248)

was a manor successively of the Knights Templar and Hospitallers. Although nothing is definitely known about their buildings, one of them may be the buttressed two-storey structure with a pointed doorway – perhaps a granary – drawn by Drapentier.[1] At the Dissolution the manor was granted to Sir Ralph Sadleir and remained with his descendants until 1712.[2] In 1661 Edwin Sadleir of Temple Dinsley was created baronet; he died in 1672, having, probably, altered the front of the house to the form shown by Drapentier. In 1663 he was charged for 10 hearths and in 1673 for 12,[3] and the change may correspond to one or both of the panelled chimney-stacks at the ends of the house which were certainly post-Restoration in style. 'A Particular of the Mannor...to be sold by Act of Parliament' of c1705[4] describes the house as 'a substantiall brick building wth a large court yard and garden wall'd in...now lett to Richd Shephard gent at £56 per Annm, lease expired'; a description which agrees with Drapentier. Although it is difficult to see how the house drawn by Drapentier relates to that drawn by Oldfield[5] and captioned 'Temple Dinsley partly pulled down', the two must be the same because the caption is confirmed by a statement made in 1815: that the mansion house was left by the sisters and co-heirs of Benedict Ithell to Thomas Harwood, who gave it to Joseph Darton, whose son, also Joseph, 'finding the house too large as a residence for himself, pulled down the two wings which has reduced it considerably'.[6] It was Benedict Ithell who purchased the manor in 1712[7] and built a new house immediately E of the old one;[8] he was Sheriff in 1727. A drawing dated 1832 and captioned 'Temple Dinsley the Seat of Mrs Darton'[9] shows Ithell's early 18th-century house; this is the one which survives today, the older one presumably standing beside it until demolished between 1815 and 1832. A fireplace now in the music room, with 16th-century detail and four blank shields on the lintel, may be a relic of the older house. Drastic alteration in this century makes it difficult to reconstruct the plan of the early 18th-century house with certainty (Fig 101). Its most remarkable feature was the staircase, lit by two tall windows;[10] the latter still exist but the disposition of the stair itself has been slightly altered.[11] The placing of the chimney-stacks in the middle of the E and W walls suggests that there may have been corner fireplaces originally, at least in the staircase-hall. There were probably three ground-floor rooms; the kitchen and other service rooms appear to have been in another building. Thomas Harwood Esq., who lived here when Sheriff in 1776, is not known to have done any building. In the early 19th century a kitchen was added to E;[12] by 1840 the W end of the roof had been reconstructed with a half hip,[13] but this particular drawing is not sufficiently accurate to be reliable in other respects. The drawing room to W[14] and the large bay window to N were added later and possibly the kitchen was rebuilt to give a more or less symmetrical façade. Some or all of the work may have been carried out in the early 1870s, when 'several thousand pounds' were spent on the house[15] by Joseph Weeks, to whom W H Darton granted a full repair lease in 1869.[16] In 1908–11 the house was greatly enlarged and altered by Lutyens.[17] It now forms part of the Princess Helena College.

Fig 101 *Temple Dinsley, Preston: plan*

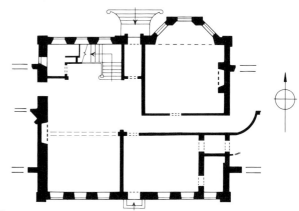

Notes
1. Chauncy II, 176.
2. VCH III, 10.
3. PRO E179/248/23; E179/375/31.
4. HRO, 65072.
5. Oldfield Vol IV, 159.
6. Dunnage, 1815.
7. VCH III, 10.
8. W— 1911, 568.
9. Buckler Vol III, 62.
10. Ibid.
11. W— 1911, 568.
12. Buckler Vol III, 62.
13. Ibid.
14. W— 1911, 568.
15. *The Hertfordshire Mercury and County Press*, 8 June 1872.
16. HRO, 67116.
17. Butler 1950, Vol I, 39–41; Vol III, plan 37, Plates 82–8.

RADWELL

(77769)
Radwell Grange (TL 235371)

is predominantly of the mid 17th century but extensive mid 19th-century alteration obscures its development, which may result from piecemeal rebuilding of an earlier house. The exterior is wholly rendered except for the external chimney-stack and gable-end wall to W. The L-shaped plan comprises a main range facing N and a rear wing to E; in the N range is the hall with a cellar beneath to E and a parlour to W; the hall and room to S, probably a parlour rather than a kitchen, because it has a cellar beneath, shared a common chimney-stack; adjoining the stack to W, in the re-entrant angle, is a staircase turret leading to first floor and attics. To S again is a wider and lower block of square plan, with indications in the S wall to E of a fireplace wider than the present one, as if for a kitchen; possibly it had only a partial upper floor; exposed framing is of mid 17th-century appearance. The only other datable details are the first-floor windows in the gable wall to W, of two lights, and the chimney-stacks and shafts; all are compatible with the payment for nine hearths by John Paine 'in the Grange house', 23 April 1663,[1] although one hearth is unaccounted for. Hints of piecemeal rebuilding are: the brick W gable appears to be added to earlier framing because it has a higher plinth and the first-floor windows are slightly above the eaves; the attic floors of the main range are at different heights; to E, for about 6 ft 6 ins (2·0 m) the roof of the main range has lower eaves and pitch than to W, its N slope rising as a lean-to against the N end of the wing roof; and the battering-back of the S face of the internal chimney-stack, which suggests a date c1600 or earlier. Conjecturally a three-cell medieval house, represented only by the low eaves to E, had a wing added to S with a chimney-stack serving both hall and wing – hence the battering stack. The mid 17th-century rebuilding created a house with three parlours, one of them the former hall, so necessitating a new kitchen to S; the chimney-stack to W was added and the upper part of the internal stack rebuilt.

In the 19th century windows were renewed throughout; a wide staircase with an entrance-lobby at its foot and rising to the first-floor landing in the turret, was inserted between the hall and the parlour to W; and the end block to S became a scullery and pantry.

Note
1.   PRO E179/248/23.

REDBOURN

(77770)
Nos 1/2 Beech Hyde (TL 112088)

incorporates a late-medieval aisled hall aligned E–W. Only one bay, 15 ft (4·9 m) long remains, with the open truss to E; the N arcade-post is complete and has a curved brace and part of a passing-brace rising to the tie-beam (Fig 102); the two arch-braces from posts to arcade-plate remain; and in the truss to W of the bay all the timbers were flush to W, hence the building probably ended there. It is much the smallest aisled hall in Hertfordshire, having a clear span of only 12 ft (3·7 m) in the nave; this suggests a comparatively late date, perhaps the early 15th century. In the late 16th century a two-storey wing of two bays was added to S of the aisled hall, forming a T-plan (a rare arrangement; cf Hole Farm, Albury); the wing incorporated two fireplaces back-to-back. A bay is set to W of the middle axis, aligned with the W jamb of the fireplace and is chamfered to E; possibly the larger part of this room was open to the roof, as for a kitchen (cf The Palace, Much Hadham), the part to W being floored and screened off for a predecessor of the present staircase and landing. To S is a four-light window with diamond mullions, blocked when the narrower end bay, perhaps a pantry

or dairy, was added in the 17th century. In the late 17th century the existing chimney-stack and possibly the first floor were inserted in the hall, which may have remained open until then; the N aisle was removed to enable the upstairs rooms to be adequately lit; and a staircase, having a newel with a shaped finial, was added. Until recently there was no access between the two ranges on the first floor. The E end of the hall was completely rebuilt at this time, and this range apparently comprised a parlour at the E end and a hall or kitchen at the W end, ie it had the same functions as the S range. In the 18th century the E-facing parlour was refaced in brick, and in the early 19th century a small independent brick house, like a terrace house, was added to N.

Fig 102 Nos 1/2 Beech Hyde, Redbourn: cross-section

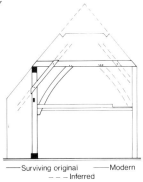

—— Surviving original —— Modern
- - - Inferred

(77771)
Hogg End (TL 115090)

comprises a late 16th-century range to W and a somewhat taller one of the late 17th century to E forming a T-plan. The W range is of two storeys with a clasped-purlin roof; a lateral chimney-stack to N is probably of the early 18th century; the range has been truncated by the building of that to E. The latter has an internal chimney-stack with four conjoined diagonal shafts; the ground-floor fireplaces suggest that the room to S was in the nature of a hall and that to N a parlour. It is not clear where the original entrance to either range was, and the lack of direct entry to the supposed hall is unusual.

(77772)
Redbournbury (TL 120107)

was the house of Redbourn manor, which belonged to St Albans Abbey from before the Conquest until the Dissolution.[1] At the N end of Redbourn village was a small priory (TL 107124), to which the building-works of Abbot Thomas refer;[2] Redbournbury itself is not documented. The present farmhouse (*English Houses 1200–1800*, Fig 26) incorporates a large hall, which is built either of stone or, more likely, flint with stone dressings, and is wholly rendered; this is not closely datable but could be as early as c1400; to W is a cross-wing, timber framed and rendered, and apparently contemporary with the hall.

The hall (c36 ft x 20 ft (11·0 m x 6·1 m)) has a roof of three bays divided by arch-braced collar-beam trusses with principal rafters, tenoned purlins and curved wind braces, and in the middle bay, slightly nearer the upper (E) end, are the trimmers which supported a louvre (Fig 103). It is impossible to distinguish any of the original openings with certainty; even the wide gap now filled by the front bay window, which looks like the position of a large hall window, relates awkwardly to the site of the hearth and one of the roof trusses. A stone doorway in the SE corner may have led to a wing or other continuation. A door near the high seat is by no means rare and in a transverse wall almost invariably leads to a parlour or great chamber, of which there is no sign in the existing building to E. A coeval door at the SW corner of the hall led to some structure which has disappeared without trace. Since the hall extended beyond the truss to W, which is chamfered on both sides and has no mortises for a partition, it is probable that the chimney-stack was built on the site of the entrance-passage, so that the absence of a thick wall at the back of the stack argues that wing and hall are of one build – a point not otherwise provable because the junction of the two ranges is now masked by later work. The cross-wing was probably divided into two ground-floor rooms because the transverse bearer is cased as if for mortises; the first floor was divided at the same point. Only its position indicates that this was the service wing, and how it was used is quite uncertain. The unequal sizes of the rooms as indicated by the beams suggests something different from the usual buttery and pantry division; perhaps the room to N included a staircase; there is no sign either of the central passage from hall to kitchen or of an original chimney-stack.

In the mid 16th century a stone fireplace was built in the cross-passage; it is nearly 9 ft (2·8 m) wide and has moulded jambs and depressed four-centred head. A stone wall and doorway were built flush with the jambs of the fireplace; the hall must have been reduced in size at this time and perhaps ended at the cased beam E of the old hearth; presumably an upper storey was built then but since no beams are exposed it is undatable. In the mid–late 17th century a fireplace of brick with timber lintel was built to E of the hall, probably for a kitchen, and the timber-framed rooms there are probably coeval. The position of the entrance is uncertain; perhaps where it is now. A staircase wing to SW is of the late 17th century. In the early 19th century casement windows were inserted throughout; a bay window was added to N to make the former kitchen into a dining room; the service rooms to E were cased in flint with brick dressings and converted into a kitchen, with an oven; a large drawing room over a cellar was added on the S side; and the exterior was rendered.

For illustrations, see *English Houses 1200–1800*, Figs 26 (plate), 27, 296 (plate).

Notes
1. VCH II, 365–6.
2. 1349–96; *Chronica Monastici S. Albani, Gesta Abbat*, Vol III, 258, 399.

REED

(77773)
Reed Hall (TL 360356),

a manor house, belonged to the de Scales family, whose last representative John Scales had it from 1443 to 1467[1] and may have built it. John's daughter Anne, to whom the manor descended and who died in March 1494, married twice, but since `both her husbands suffered from financial embarrassment'[2] they are less likely. The house retains very little datable detail but its plan and proportions are late medieval; a Buckler drawing shows that the exterior has changed little since 1832.[3]

It is of H-plan. The hall, *c*20 ft (6·1 m) wide, was approximately square without the screens-passage; the latter was to E. The W wing is jettied to N and W; the crown-post roof has curved braces to the collar-purlin, straight braces from rafters to collars, and ashlar-pieces standing on a moulded plate; it has had a plaster ceiling. This, and the siting of what appears to be an original chimney-stack to W against the jetty (cf Redcoats, Wymondley) suggest the wing is of *c*1500. The ground floor has a lofty parlour (*c*11 ft (3·4 m)) with a fireplace to W; the staircase has always been in the smaller room to S. The larger first-floor chamber also had a fireplace. The E wing may replace a bay in series with the hall; it has a clasped-purlin roof of *c*1600; otherwise all old detail has been concealed; the room arrangement is of the mid 19th century. A jetty to N[4] has been cut back flush with the ground-floor wall. Extensive alterations took place in the late 17th century; the N elevation of the W wing was rebuilt with the sparse framing and large plaster panels of the period,[5] probably when the hall was heightened and the wing roofs hipped; a staircase with symmetrical turned balusters and moulded rail was built in the W wing. Before 1832 (before Buckler's drawing) an entrance-hall with fireplace was formed (cf Old Ramerick, Ickleford). Later the E wing was enlarged with kitchen and service room.

Notes
1. VCH III, 249.
2. Ibid.
3. Buckler Vol II, 173.
4. Ibid.
5. Ibid.

Fig 103 *Redbournbury, Redbourn: sections*

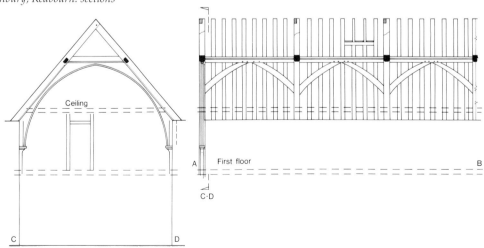

RICKMANSWORTH

(77774)
The Bury (TQ 060941)

was the manor house of Rickmansworth until, in 1741, it came into the possession of Henry Fotherley Whitfield, who built the mansion of Rickmansworth Park.[1] The manor belonged to St Albans Abbey from before the Conquest until the Dissolution and after passing through several owners was sold in 1632 to Sir Thomas Fotherley;[2] his father, Thomas Fotherly, Gent., died in 1624 and, since he was buried in Rickmansworth church,[3] was perhaps a tenant of The Bury. Sir Thomas was succeeded by his son John Fotherley Esq., who was Sheriff in 1652 and probably enlarged the house considerably, paying for 20 hearths in 1673.[4] After his death in 1703[5] there is little evidence of building-works or of any owner likely to have done anything extensive. In 1830[6] the house was still in good order but by the mid 19th century was in disrepair and partly used as a warehouse; its restoration was undertaken during the ownership of John Saunders Gilliatt, director and sometime governor of the Bank of England, who bought it in 1868 but did not reside there.[7]

The oldest part of the house, the parlour wing to N, may have been built in the late 16th century; it has two chimney-stacks with stepped copings and diagonal shafts, the E stack having some diaper patterning; the roof has clasped-purlins. There were two rooms on each floor, all with a fireplace; the spacing of the tie-beams in the roof suggests that a larger room to E may have been separated from a smaller one by a narrow bay containing a staircase. Of the hall that coexisted with it no direct evidence remains, but the large internal chimney-stack facing E, which fits clumsily into the rooms behind it and looks on plan as if it were originally external, may have been connected with it. The SE wing may be coeval with the N wing because it too is spanned, for two thirds of its width to N, by a clasped-purlin roof; nothing else is definitely as old as the roof, and the original disposition of rooms is lost.

In the mid 17th century the main range connecting these wings was rebuilt with two parallel roofs and the W end of the N wing roof was cut back to give a uniform appearance. The E elevation preserved the gable of the N wing and a second gable was added over the entrance in the middle of the new range; above this doorway was a bay window which, like the other windows, was of mullion-and-transom type; most were of three lights, some of four. The former hall appears to have remained in use as both principal room and entrance. To S were service rooms, not now serving the old hall but a large room to W which was perhaps called a great parlour and was probably the dining room; the kitchen is to S, and to N, accessible from the great parlour as well as the hall, was the staircase, some parts of which have been re-used in the present one. The room to E of the kitchen, which was the `Servants' Sitting Room' in 1938,[8] may well have been a servants' hall since the 17th century. On the first floor the rooms in the main range were reached from the staircase by an axial corridor; two rooms, one with its original doorway blocked, lie to W and two to E, one of which corresponds to the service rooms below and the other to the greater part of the hall; only the rooms to E had fireplaces. The corridor probably led to a room over the kitchen. In the N wing were two rooms with a smaller one, perhaps an antechamber or dressing room, to E of the main stair. To S of the main range was formerly a second 17th-century staircase[9] to give access to the room E of the kitchen chamber and to the E wing.

The date, plan and function of the E wing present difficulties. If the development of the house has been conjectured correctly, the wing must have joined the service rooms corner to corner, unless they were uncommonly long; even if they were, the size and position of the original wing suggest it was a virtually independent structure of two storeys. The first alteration involved a widening to S, which had four parallel gabled roofs; the sawn-off stubs of their wall-plates can be seen; an early 19th-century drawing[10] shows the roof at the E end as built. The wing is too wide for any room to have occupied the full width, and it is likely that the present modern loggia restores something of the original arrangement, with a first-floor gallery above it. There are slight indications that the roof of the E range continued farther to W than at present, and since further piers spaced like those that remain would terminate exactly on the small projecting block at the SW corner, it is possible that the whole S elevation once presented a uniformly regular arcaded and galleried appearance, with a winding staircase to W. The function and date of such an arrangement is uncertain. A gallery suggests a lodging range; it may be of the early 17th century.

Subsequent alterations prior to the late 19th-century restoration affected the plan comparatively little. The SE wing was given two-light mullion-and-transom windows[11] probably c1700, and it may have been then that the putative loggia was walled up and made at least partly into rooms; one of the piers has the remains of a fireplace. The chamber over the hall was partitioned into two rooms, each with a corner fireplace discharging into the existing stack, and a bay window was added to the N wing before 1800.[12] In the 18th century the small room over the N end of the hall may have been formed; it has a cornice of moulded plaster. Fireplaces were inserted in the two first-floor rooms to S of the main stair; the W elevation was refenestrated symmetrically. Refurbishing of the house in the late 19th century entailed the removal of the front door to its present position; a reconstruction of the main staircase re-using some of the old material, notably the handrails and newel posts; and the rebuilding of the loggia. So extensive is the alteration in the E wing that this is likely to have been the part of the house used as a warehouse for coal and grain.[13] Subsequently the building has been used as offices.

For illustrations, see *English Houses 1200–1800*, Figs 119 (plate), 120, 121 (plate).

Notes
1. VCH II, 374.
2. Ibid, 373.
3. Chauncy II, 349.
4. PRO E179/375/31.
5. VCH II, 373.
6. Buckler Vol IV, 113.
7. VCH II, 374; *Kelly* 1911.
8. Hertfordshire County Council plan, Architects' Department.
9. VCH II, 374; RCHME 1910, 171.
10. Clutterbuck, fo 203.
11. Oldfield Vol V, 387.
12. Ibid.
13. VCH II, 373.

(77775)
Nos 7/9 Church Street

incorporate to N (in No. 9) one bay, perhaps of a late-medieval open hall, with a crown-post roof. The adjoining house, No. 7, has to S a clasped-purlin roof truss apparently of a single-storey building; a chimney-stack was built within it, c1600, to serve a south-facing ground-floor fireplace, ie serving No. 9.

(77776)
Nos 29–33 Church Street

is a timber-framed building refaced in brick; it is now of one and a half storeys with three gables at the front. It is of three bays, of which the middle bay and probably the N bay too were open from ground to roof; the tie-beams originally precluded access from one bay to another. The roof has clasped-purlins and curved windbraces.

(77777)
No. 36 Church Street,

The Feathers PH, incorporates the late 15th-century cross-wing of a hall house. The framing in the W wall towards the hall has curved bracing which forms decorative patterns. The hall was rebuilt in the late 16th century and subsequently enlarged and refaced in brick.

(77778)
The More (TQ 082940)

was a moated manor house, first recorded c1182, which became important in the 15th century when a crenellated house was built. For a full account of its history see Biddle, Barfield and Millard 1959, 136–99.

For an illustration, see *English Houses 1200–1800*, Fig 37.

(77779)
The Priory (TQ 061942)

is an early 16th-century building of two storeys and four bays, the long walls to N and S being jettied. It comprises, on each floor, three rooms, the middle one being of two bays; wattle-holes in the soffit of an axial beam show that the ground-floor room to E was subdivided as if for pantry and buttery. Its position at the edge of the churchyard and the lack of any definitely original chimney-stack suggest it was a church house or marriage-feast house originally. In the principal ground-floor room is a fireplace with cambered lintel and wooden jambs; it is unlike any comparable 16th-century fireplace in being placed well inside the lateral wall instead of flush with it, hence it is a later insertion. The original position of the staircase is not known. The building had a general resemblance to John O'Gaddesden's House, Little Gaddesden, and The Old Farmhouse, Bury Farm, Wheathampstead.

Conversion to a house probably took place about the end of the 17th century but antiquarian restoration early in the present century has removed most of the evidence.

RIDGE

(77780)
Tyttenhanger House (TL 191047)

was a manor, otherwise known as Ridge, belonging to St Albans Abbey from before the Conquest. In the early 15th century a mansion house was built as a place of resort for the abbots and for the entertainment of guests; it was sufficiently large to permit Henry VIII and his queen to stay for a fortnight in 1528.[1] In 1547 Sir Thomas Pope, who had received the surrender of the monastery in 1539, was granted the manor.[2] In 1620 part of the house was demolished[3] and in 1654 it descended to Sir Henry Pope Blount, author and traveller.[4] He proceeded to demolish the remainder of the house and build `a fair structure of brick',[5] which has been ascribed to the architect Peter Mills.[6] Blount was Sheriff in 1661 and after 1669 lived in retirement at Tyttenhanger. The estate passed first to his wife and then to his son Sir Thomas Pope Blount, created baronet in 1680 and several

times MP.[7] In the mid 18th century the house is said to have fallen into decay. In 1757 it passed by marriage to Charles Yorke, second son of the 1st Earl of Hardwicke, for whom Sir John Soane undertook repairs in 1783 and 1789.[8] In 1834 it came into the possession of the Earl of Caledon, with whose descendants it remained until 1973, when it was converted for use as offices.

Externally the house achieved an almost perfect symmetry, which was broken only in two minor ways: to N by the two extra windows needed to light the former cellar at the NW corner; and to W by a doorway, now blocked. Inside, although hardly any original detail remains and probably none is in its original place, the room plan appears to have changed little; nevertheless it is difficult to account for the 31 hearths on which Sir Lawrence Blount paid tax in 1673;[9] some were presumably in outbuildings. The entrance to S was probably separated from the hall by short screens. To E of the hall was probably a pantry and to N a rear hall which may not, originally, have had a fireplace. To E was the kitchen and two subsidiary rooms, the partition forming the smaller one, a storeroom, to S being marked by the exposed binder; it is not certain that the larger N room originally had a fireplace but if it did it was probably the pantry, with ovens. How the W wing was arranged is less certain. The larger room has, opposite the fireplace, a doorway (blocked) into the garden. This room was no doubt a parlour, and had a fireplace; the smaller room to N, originally a mezzanine above cellars, was possibly a pantry well placed to serve an upstairs dining chamber.

The very slightly larger windows and the main staircase reflect the importance of the first floor. Scrolled architraves mark the position of the two most important rooms, the dining room probably being over the hall. There has been considerable alteration on the landing; it seems likely that two of the four doorcases must be modern (*English Houses 1200–1800*, pp 68–70); and the width and finish of the present opening from the landing suggest that a steel girder is concealed. Originally an arched opening may have led from the landing into a lobby with doors to E into the dining chamber and withdrawing room beyond and to W perhaps into a grand bedchamber. Conjectural room uses are set out in *English Houses 1200–1800*, Fig 109. In the E wing the S part probably accommodated a bedchamber and closet, and on the second floor the same is true of both wings. Some of the doorways on the upper floors may be later, eg the one from the putative drawing room to the E wing. The attic storey is largely taken up by a gallery; the awkwardness of approach from either stair is remarkable. In February 1783 Sir John Soane was attending to the paving of the kitchen[10] but by 1798 Tyttenhanger was considerably in need of repair, and the main stair was so sunk that orders were given to support it.[11] In 1834 Lady Caledon, in carrying out a general renovation, transferred the entrance to N[12] and added porches to N and S.[13] Much careful restoration took place towards the end of the 19th century, when two of the elaborate first-floor doorcases appear to have been made. Much of the panelling, some linenfold and some in small squares, is reproduction work and none is demonstrably in its original position. The existing S door-head must be work of the late 19th or early 20th century and betrays its date by being slightly more elaborate than the original, which is shown in a drawing of 1832.[14]

For illustrations, see *English Houses 1200–1800*, Figs 108 (plate), 109, 110 (plate) and cover.

Notes
1.   PRO L&P Henry VIII, IV 2, No. 4428.
2.   VCH II, 387–8.

3. *Gent Mag*, 1797 (i), 10.
4. *DNB*.
5. Chauncy II, 388.
6. Colvin 1978, 551.
7. *DNB*.
8. Colvin 1978, 768.
9. PRO E179/375/31.
10. Soane Note Books 6, Sir John Soane's Museum.
11. BL Add MS 35699.
12. van Koughnet 1895, 141.
13. HRO, tithe map, DSA4, 81/2.
14. Buckler Vol III, 157.

ROYSTON

(77781)
The Bull Hotel

is timber framed, in two parts marked by different floor levels, and has no visible features older than the late 17th century; the two internal chimney-stacks have fireplaces of that date. A ballroom was added at the rear *c*1830, when a general remodelling of the interior took place and the whole building was refronted; on the ground floor the brickwork has channelled rustication.

(77782)
Nos 17/19 High Street

is of two storeys and attics and of brick; the timbers of a clasped-purlin roof exposed in the N gable suggest that the building may have been timber framed but there is nothing inside to confirm this; the front (E) elevation is rendered and later additions obscure the rear. The oldest datable feature is the staircase in a turret which originally projected to W; it has flat, shaped balusters and a moulded rail and is probably of *c*1700. All fireplaces and nearly all traces of the chimney-stacks have been removed; the first-floor plan may have comprised a large room to S with a lateral stack, a drawing room opposite the staircase landing and a N room with a fireplace in the NW corner. It is not clear why the four front windows are irregularly spaced.

In 1712 the house, then described as 'a messuage now used as two tenements in Middle Row',[1] was sold by Robert Chester of Bygrave to John Wells of Royston, plumber; the tenements were then at lease but in 1742 when Mary Wells, widow, sold, only one messuage is mentioned.[2]

Notes
1. Deeds in possession of Curwen Jessop and James.
2. Ibid.

(77783)
No. 41 High Street,

of two storeys with cellar and attics, has a four-bay E front of brick but is otherwise timber framed; it was built in the first quarter of the 18th century. The plan is L-shaped, the wing being to N. The entrance seems always to have been to N, not in the main elevation facing High Street; a former doorway in the S bay is now a window and its awkward position in relation to the fireplace suggests it was originally such. The plan comprised three ground-floor rooms, all with fireplaces; the smaller front room to E of the entrance may have been an office, corresponding to the similar rooms found in some double-fronted houses; probably the original staircase was in the re-entrant angle and lit from S and W. A room was added to W of the wing in the 19th century.

(77784)
Nos 59/61 High Street,

of two storeys, form the earliest infilling of the south market-place. Number 61 (to S) is the earlier of the two; it is jettied to N and E with dragon-beam and carved corner post. To S on both floors is a doorway with four-centred head, as if this building either extended to S or adjoined an earlier structure. There is no evidence of an original fireplace, the chimney-stack to N being an insertion. To N, No. 59, of the late 16th century, was built against No. 61 and conceals its jetty. The first floor of No. 59, which is jettied to E and W, was made level with that of No. 61; consequently the ground floor is unusually lofty because it is on ground falling away to N. A chimney-stack to S is probably a later insertion.

For an illustration, see *English Houses 1200–1800*, Fig 239 (plate).

(77786)
No. 9 Kneesworth Street,

part of James I's hunting lodge (or palace), was the cross-wing of an open hall to S (Fig 104). It was built in the late 15th century and is jettied to W (front) and E; the rear jetty is remarkable for the projection of four joists for a distance of 4 ft (1·2 m), apparently to form a bridge to a two-storey range to E, which is jettied to S and has been truncated. The existence of the bridge suggests that there was a way through to the buildings to N (No. 11), ie these buildings were linked long before the hunting lodge was established.

(77786)
No. 11 Kneesworth Street

is a jettied building of two storeys and of three bays and a fourth very short bay to N (Fig 104). Chamfers on the binding-beam and bearers in the short N bay suggest there was originally a timber chimney there; to W the N bay has a window of two pointed lights with flush spandrels; traces of other such windows exist on ground and first floors. The first floor was divided into a large room of two bays to N and a small one to S, distinguished by the treatment of the truss between them which is moulded to N and plain to S. In the early 18th century the exterior was faced with lath and plaster, casement windows were inserted and the chimney-stack rebuilt in brick. The original entrance must have been from either one of the adjoining buildings to N and S or to E. A doorway at the S end of the street front, now blocked, is not original.

For an illustration, see *English Houses 1200–1800*, Fig 245 (plate).

Fig 104 *Nos 9 and 11 (left) Kneesworth Street, Royston: plans*

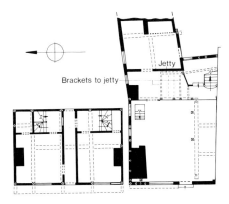

(77787)

No. 18 Melbourn Street, known as Thurnalls (TL 357407),
is of c1600. It is named from Harry Joseph Thurnall, an artist,[1] who lived there early in the present century and who appears to have improved some of the paintings and added to others to make the house celebrated for its profusion of painted decoration.[2] How much of the painting is original is uncertain and the judgements expressed below, as about several of the fittings, are tentative.

The plan (Fig 105) c1600 appears to have been L-shaped, with a street range to S and a wing to W; the middle room of three in the S range was the hall, with a wide fireplace to E and staircase to N of the stack; to E was an unheated service room and to W the parlour, its fireplace back-to-back with that in the kitchen to N. In the mid 17th century a large room, with ovolo-moulded bearer and jettied to N was added some 8 ft (2·4 m) to N of the hall; the intervening space was probably occupied by a staircase to E and chimney-stack and fireplace to W; this was presumably a dining room and the room above a drawing room. In the semi-attic storey the principal rooms are those above hall, parlour and kitchen, all of which have fireplaces with chamfered four-centred heads, plastered. Nowhere is it possible to examine the

Fig 105 *No. 18 Melbourn Street, Royston: plan*

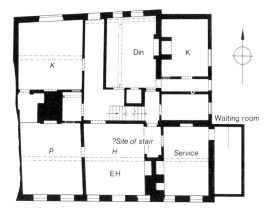

junction between the wings and the main range but the similarity of detail suggests they are of one build. In the 18th century the house was refronted with a symmetrical elevation which clashes with the internal chimney-stack; a rectangular light over the entrance incorporates the initials J A B, for Joseph and Ann Beldam, who are said to have bought the house in 1767.[3] A staircase, of somewhat old-fashioned appearance for that date, was put in; the middle rooms became an entrance-hall with staircase-hall to N; the chimney-stack was rebuilt to accommodate a fireplace to E. In the mid 19th century the S elevation was altered by raising the middle of the parapet and rebuilding the chimney-stack; an addition to E contains scullery and china-pantry; the kitchen was transferred to the room N of the hall; the former kitchen became the dining room. In the late 19th century the garden (N) elevation was refaced in brick. A lean-to addition to the main range is said to have been a doctor's waiting-room.[4] The panelling in the room to W of the front range was put in early in the present century.

The paintings, all in first-floor rooms, have to be considered against the architectural development of the house. The only one of undoubted authenticity is in the room to E in the front range; a brick fireplace with four-centred head, plastered, is painted and has above it a panel probably representing Abraham and Sarah and the Angels, and on a frieze is a female figure apparently

leading an animal among grotesque. The room over the hall has a painted imitation of plaster fretwork filled by grotesque, with four roundels containing representations of the Four Elements: nude female, back view, with fruit, vegetables and corn-stalk, for Earth; nude female emptying large water pot, for Water; nude female with flying hair and clouds, for Air; male figure with flaming hair, on a salamander in fire, for Fire. Despite some repainting the ceiling appears authentic; the fireplace, with chamfered four-centred head, has painted swags of fruit or flowers. In the wing room to W the fireplace is modern and the overmantel is divided by columns into a wide middle panel and narrower flanking panels, with cameo-like panels depicting the Five Senses; the overmantel, which bears the date 1635, has been partly repainted and its connection with the house is suspect. In the W room of the street range is a brick fireplace with chamfered four-centred head; above it is a modern overmantel of Jacobean style; the panelling in the same style is mostly modern; a ceiling, like that in the room over the hall but with ten roundels containing putti or cupids holding sprigs, is probably modern because it fits the fireplace surround. An elaborately painted chimney-piece over a late 19th-century fireplace in the room over the parlour is of uncertain antiquity; it bears initials and date T A M 1635, which have been identified with Thomas and Mary Archer[5] and whose connection with the house has no other foundation. In a small attic room which may originally have been the head of a staircase are some long, narrow painted panels of late 16th-century style having female caryatid torsos with bunches of fruit and pairs of birds; the studs have a continued strapwork pattern. When these paintings were first noticed early this century[6] they were said to be `somewhat obliterated' and the pattern was put together with some difficulty; they are now virtually complete. Similar patterns on the main staircase are modern copies.

Notes
1. He was resident in Royston Street in 1898 and in 18 Melbourn Street in 1902 (*Kelly*, 1898, 1902).
2. RCHME 1910, 175; Croft-Murray 1962–70, Vol I, 212; Cornforth 1963, 676–9.
3. Cornforth 1963, 678.
4. Inf. Mrs B Aitchison.
5. Cornforth 1963, 677; Croft Murray 1962–70, Vol I, 212.
6. Kinneir Tarte 1902, 385–6.

(77788)

Royston Priory (TL 357406)
is the former manor house of Royston. The manor comprised lands granted to the Augustinian priory when it was founded sometime after 1163[1] and after the Dissolution in 1537 was first leased to and later acquired by Robert Chester.[2] Chester converted part of the priory buildings into his principal residence and entertained Mary of Guise here on her journey from Scotland to France in 1551.[3] He was knighted in that year, was Sheriff in 1565 and died in 1574. When, in 1578, his house was considered as a stopping-place on a royal progress, it was dismissed as `A very unnecessary hows for receipt of her Ma`ty yt stands adioyninge to the Church over the Sowth syde thereof not haveing any pleasant prospects any way'.[4] It was referred to as `Mr Chesters hows at Royston', although the owner by this time was Robert, aged 12, the son and heir of Edward Chester, who died 25 November 1577.[5] Plans prepared at that time show buildings around three sides of a courtyard, with the principal rooms above cellars. By c1600 Robert Chester had made Cokenach his principal residence. In 1628 a payment of £450 was made to Sir Robert Chester `for houses and land bought of

him...and for rent due by the late King for the use of Sir Robert's house for one year'.[6] By 1634 his son and heir Edward, `of Royston',[7] was living at the Priory and a younger son, Henry Chester, is also `of Royston'. Edward, who died in 1640, probably built a timber-framed house, part of which survives, and possibly demolished the converted priory buildings. His grandson Edward was Sheriff in 1675, dying during his term of office.[8] The house was occupied by tenants before Edward Chester's grandson sold the property in 1759.

The buildings depicted in the 1578 plans are difficult to relate to the church but were evidently part of the claustral buildings; the present house is sited to W. To N it incorporates three unequal timber-framed bays of two storeys, perhaps of c1600; the truss to S is weathered. The only exposed framing is a large post to S which is mortised, as if for a window. An addition to N, with a lateral stack and probably a staircase to W and terminating at an exposed pargeted gable, was built in the mid 17th century. Excluding whatever remained of the house of 1578 the Priory was by c1650 comparable in size to Queen Hoo, Tewin. A timber-framed addition to S, perhaps a service room, is of the late 17th century. In the early 18th century the E elevation, excluding the latest addition to S, was refaced in brick with chamfered quoins, and the present entrance-hall was probably created. Later in the century a single-storeyed wing was added to SW; a corridor and staircase to W of the main range were built; the wing to SW was heightened to two storeys, and pilasters and a pediment were added to E. Two bay windows to E, although both of late 19th-century appearance, have different wall thicknesses, and probably that to S is of the 18th century, refaced. In the late 19th century a wing was added to N. The portico was built in the present century.

For an illustration, see *English Houses 1200–1800*, Fig 103 (plate).

Notes
1. Knowles and Hadcock 1953, 151; VCH III, 260.
2. VCH III, 260.
3. PRO Acts P C 1550–2, 406.
4. PRO SP 12/125.
5. VCH III, 260.
6. *Cal SP Dom* 1628–9, 31.
7. *Visitations*, 40.
8. VCH III, 261; Chauncy I, 182.

RUSHDEN

(39634)
Julians (TL 307323)

was a messuage or farmhouse, the centre of a small estate in Rushden and the adjoining parishes of Cottered and Broadfield. In the 16th century it belonged to Edward Newport and in 1603 was bought by John Stone, who immediately transferred it to his `infant sons', Richard and William.[1] William Stone may have built the house in the early 17th century;[2] Richard is also said to be the builder.[3] No work of that date can now be seen although in 1909 much oak panelling `in small squares with stopped mouldings, and a carved chimney-piece with arabesque ornament and turned columns' existed; it was ascribed to the late 16th century.[4] An engraving of c1700[5] shows a house with shallow wings and a two-storey porch capped by curvilinear gables, the main range having plain gables; a curious feature is that the cornice mouldings, presumably of moulded brick, are drawn in profile. The curvilinear gables and the rusticated brickwork of the porch suggest that an earlier house had been

altered in the mid 17th century, perhaps in the time of Sir Richard Stone, whose principal seat was at Great Stukeley (Huntingdonshire).[6] In 1663 `The Lady Stone' paid tax on seven hearths.[7] Sir Richard's son and heir Thomas inherited in 1696 and when he died not long afterwards Julians was at lease.[8]

Fig 106 *Julians, Rushden: ground and first-floor plans*

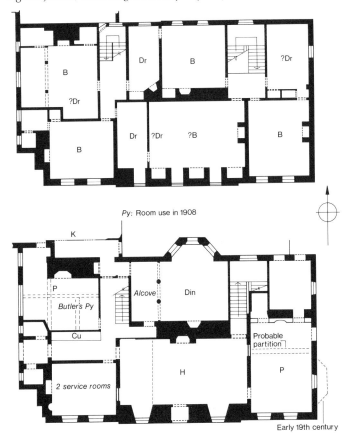

After his death the house was occupied by his widow Penelope, who in 1699 married Adolphus Meetkerke, and it was he who undertook refronting and other alterations. Although minor works were undertaken in the 19th century the house seems to have changed comparatively little until the drastic alterations of 1937–9.[9] The wings of the 17th-century house corresponded to the recessed flanking bays of the existing frontage and until the 1930s the old front wall of the middle range still existed, separated by cupboards and very narrow corridors from the present early 18th-century front.[10]

Little can be said about the plan (Fig 106). In 1908 `the beam across the hall' was taken to suggest `the old arrangement of screens';[11] the beam was probably W of the front door and may have been for a partition enclosing a pantry, with a passage behind the latter to a room with a fireplace, a parlour probably, over cellars. Presumably the staircases were comparatively unimportant since they were swept away soon after 1699. Adolphus Meetkerke, as well as refronting the house, contrived a hall corresponding to the pedimented projection and added behind it a large room flanked by two staircases. The kitchen may have been to N of the W wing (not shown on plan) where cupboards now occupy what appears to have been a large fireplace; if so, its position suggests there may have been an upstairs dining room over the hall. The only certain later additions, prior to the work of the 1930s, are two bay windows, of the first decade of the 19th century; one was added to the present dining room (N of the hall) the other to the E wing; the latter is not shown in a drawing of c1800[12] but appears in an early 19th-century sketch.[13]

For an illustration, see *English Houses 1200–1800*, Fig 219 (plate).

Notes
1. Winterton 1969, 33–40.
2. Chauncy I, 159; Cussans 1870–3, Vol I (iii), 165; VCH III, 268.
3. Winterton 1969, 34.
4. RCHME 1910, 176.
5. Chauncy I, 160.
6. Winterton 1969, 34; VCH *Hunts*, Vol II, 232.
7. PRO E179/248/24/1.
8. Winterton 1969, 34.
9. Hussey 1947, 1160–3.
10. Lucas 1908–11b, 78.
11. Ibid.
12. Oldfield Vol V, 409.
13. Clutterbuck.

SACOMBE

(39635)
Sacombe Park (TL 339190)

is the successor of a manor house of some architectural importance in the middle ages. From the early 13th century it belonged to the Comyn family and in 1334 Eufemia Comyn received licence to have an oratory in her house. In 1420, when it was bought by Robert Basthorpe, the house comprised a hall and `five chambers high and low'.[1] By the time of Charles I it was in the hands of John, later Lord Belasis, a Royalist, whose financial straits compelled him to sell Sacombe to Sir John Gore; Gore was Sheriff in 1654 and in 1662 was assessed for 13 hearths.[2] He sold the house and manor in 1688 to Sir Thomas Rolt, formerly president of the East India Company and Governor of Bombay, who, in 1695, was Sheriff. Rolt's son Edward succeeded him in 1710. He was MP for Chippenham (Wiltshire), became rich through the South Sea Company and intended to rebuild the house. Initially this was to be by Vanbrugh[3] but subsequently a design was produced by James Gibbs.[4] Charles Bridgeman first laid out the gardens on a monumental scale[5] but the second stage, the new house, was abandoned following Rolt's death in 1722. A probate inventory of January 1724[6] listing nine principal rooms, nursery, gallery, three garrets and some service rooms, gives the impression that the existing house was not particularly large. The old house, which stood a little to W of the present one (approx TL 338189), came by marriage to Timothy Caswall who, c1783, pulled it down,[7] and went to live at Coldharbour, Great Munden. When his son George inherited in 1802 a fortunate marriage enabled him to build the present house. Building was still in progress in October 1805[8] and Caswall was Sheriff in 1807. After George Caswall's death in 1825 the estate was sold to William Abel Smith of Watton Woodhall and thereafter the house was leased out. An early 19th-century drawing[9] shows the six columns of the S elevation as Corinthian; they were later altered to Doric columns, probably when William Gambier added the W porch in that style in the late 1830s.[10] There is no record of anything else being done to the house in the 19th century. It was occupied by Sir Richard FitzWygram, Bart., and eight servants in 1851. A

fire in January 1911 destroyed all the interior except the N wing.[11] It was rebuilt faithfully to the original except that the pitch roof and attics were replaced by a flat fireproof roof with a balustrade. Since 1951 much of the house has been converted into offices.

Notes
1. VCH III, 137.
2. PRO E179/375/30.
3. Mr E S D Medlicott, typescript notes citing Decker diary (not now to be found) at Wilton House.
4. Gibbs 1728, Plate 53.
5. Willis 1977, 60; Salmon 1728, 225.
6. PRO Prob 3/23/8.
7. Carrington *Diary*, 93, n11; Clutterbuck says that George Caswall demolished the old house.
8. Carrington *Diary*, 121.
9. Clutterbuck.
10. Buckler, BL Add MS 36364, fo 199v.
11. *The Hertfordshire Mercury and County Press*, 28 January 1911, photograph.

ST ALBANS

(60044)
Bleak House, Catherine Street,

was formerly Dalton's Folly, `which name it had from the original builder'.[1] As built in the early 18th century it had two storeys with basement and attics and was of a nearly square plan with four ground-floor rooms set around a narrow entrance-hall and staircase-hall to rear (N). In the late 18th century wings of one storey were added and the house was given a Mansard roof. This work may not have been very recent otherwise the caption to Oldfield's drawing would probably have mentioned it; at that time the proprietor was a Mr Emmot. Where the wing fireplaces were is not apparent; perhaps flues were led from them into the backs of the original stacks. In the mid 19th century the wings were doubled in depth and the whole house refurbished with new ceiling cornices, fireplaces, etc; a bow window and rear porch may be somewhat earlier. In the early 20th century the wing to E was heightened to two storeys. In the 1950s the house was acquired by Hertfordshire County Council as offices.

Note
1. Oldfield Vol VII, 523, caption.

(77789)
Nos 13/15 Fishpool Street

are part of the former Crow Inn. Number 13, to E of the covered gateway, is of three storeys, the upper two originally being jettied; it was probably built c1500. The ground-floor room was originally about 18 ft (5·5 m) square and has hollow-chamfered beams; a chimney-stack to S does not appear to be original. The roof, of two bays, has clasped-purlins and queen-struts. In the 18th century the first floor was underbuilt and provided with sash windows. The W part of the inn, now No. 15, was not examined fully.

(77790)
Nos 38/40 Fishpool Street,

built c1500, has a crown-post roof of three bays, one truss to SE (in No. 40) being closed; all the crown-posts are plain with curved braces to the collar-purlin and are devoid of smoke blackening. On the ground floor a doorway with four-centred head may have led to one of two service rooms. Although the building was presumably domestic there is no evidence that originally there was any form of heating.

(77791)
Nos 57/59 Fishpool Street

illustrate the problems of town-house development. The oldest part of No. 57 is the front range facing N; a plastered beam, perhaps a tie-beam, can be seen in the wall to E; on the ground floor is a mid–late 17th-century bearer, probably secondary; the timber-framed front wall was apparently flush; and this slender evidence points to an open-hall house, which may have included the older part of No. 59 to W, where hardly any timbers are exposed except a clasped-purlin roof. To S of No. 57 a wing of two storeys and attics was added c1600; it has been truncated but retains about half of a quite elaborate plaster ceiling; a coeval chimney-stack serving both front range and wing has been reduced in size by subsequent rebuilding. That part of No. 59 to E was built in the early 18th century and probably then the hall-house was divided and heightened; additions to S contain no datable features except a late 18th-century fanlight over the garden doorway. Both houses were refronted in the early 19th century.

(77792)
No. 137 Fishpool Street,

a small Wealden house, was built c1500. Few timbers are exposed inside; they include the post to W of the hall which has a mortise for the rail forming the base of the plaster cove to the outer roof-plate; the outline of the cove is visible. The hall was floored over in the mid 17th century and a new staircase built to W in the same position as the original one, which served the storeyed W bay; the balusters remain, reset. In the 18th century the house was refronted in brick and then or later it was enlarged to S.

For an illustration, see *English Houses 1200–1800*, Fig 244 (plate).

(77793)
Nos 3–9, French Row,

formerly the Christopher Inn, is a complex building of several periods. For perhaps a hundred years it was divided into tenements and fell into bad condition before being bought by the City Council in 1949 and restored in 1953–4. P K Baillie-Reynolds, writing an analysis of the building made from inadequate observations made during restoration, remarked somewhat complacently: `I do not think that anyone now is in a position to contradict me';[1] nevertheless a few conjectures can be made.

Baillie-Reynolds assigned the first period of construction to c1480–1500, whereas a drawing not known to him[2] of a doorway which had disappeared by the 1950s suggests that some part of the building was of the early 15th century. Probably the present two-storey range, which faces E, replaces an open hall of that date and the S wing, which has an exceptionally bold jetty carried on two large hollow-chamfered brackets with solid spandrels, may be coeval; the N wing has an only slightly less bold jetty and if not of the same date is late medieval. At some time in the 16th century the hall was replaced by a two-storey jettied range which, on the ground floor, extends to S into the wing, so that the jetty of the latter appears to wrap round that end of the hall. At this time a carriageway existed at the S end of the building, within the wing; the possibility that it is an alteration is suggested by the close-studded wall between it and the hall which, at the E end, abuts the post into which is tenoned

one of the large brackets mentioned above. In the close-studded wall is a doorway, now blocked, by which the hall was entered. By this time the building was certainly an inn and may well have been so from the first, although that is not demonstrable architecturally. The internal arrangements cannot now be reconstructed but at the N end of the hall is a fireplace with moulded jambs and depressed four-centred head of the late 16th century; and since the chimney-stack has been built within the N wing and there is no evidence of a timber predecessor the hall itself may be of that date.

At the rear of the building a NW wing was added to provide a kitchen on the ground floor; it now has at the W end a brick chimney-stack which probably replaces a flue of the kind found at The Palace, Much Hadham, extending the full width of the wing; the evidence for this is a binding-beam about 2 ft 6 ins (0·8 m) from the face of the stack. The axial bearer from this beam terminates on another about 4 ft (1·2 m) from the front range, as if providing for a corridor on both floors. Another addition was made to SW, parallel with the older building; it extends over the carriageway and is dated by fluted pilasters and a bracket in the form of a crouching figure to c1600; the fireplaces serving it discharge into a chimney-stack built within the hall range. As built, this wing was probably of two storeys with cellars and attics and was roofed, as it still is, parallel to the street range. Presumably the putative corridor in the NW wing, the line of which is continued by a beam to S, was intended to give access to the SW wing and consequently the wings must be coeval; the alternative, that the NW wing is later, is unlikely, given the existence and likely date of the kitchen fire-hood. Access to the first-floor rooms from the inn yard was probably by a straight flight of stairs adjoining the SW wing.

At the N end of the building (No. 9) is a two-storey jettied block, narrower than the hall range, originally of one room on each floor and with a large rear fireplace on the ground floor. It was added to provide extra important rooms, presumably before the kitchen wing was built because intercommunication between the two is so awkward.

The NW wing was heightened to three storeys and the adjacent staircase rebuilt c1700. Another staircase in the corridor at the S end of the kitchen wing may have been added at the same time, no doubt replacing an earlier one hereabouts. A wing to W of the northernmost block is of the late 17th or early 18th century. Many minor alterations were made to convert the inn into tenements in the 19th century.

Notes
1. Moody 1961, 59.
2. Buckler, BL Add MS 36432, fo 945.

(77794)
No. 6 George Street

is a small jettied building of two storeys and two bays, and is probably of the 15th century. The exposed first-floor timbers approximate to Kentish framing; the end posts do not have the peg-holes or brace mortises which would be expected if it had been built as part of a Wealden house. The exposed joists show that the ground floor was divided by a light partition near the middle of the building.

(77795)
No. 12 George Street

is of two storeys, rendered, with very little timber-framing exposed internally, but in a passage to E the joists of an end-jetty are visible; these are probably late medieval. Originally this jettied elevation faced Romeland.

(77796)
No. 18 George Street

was built as part of a galleried inn, probably in the mid 15th century. A view of the inn courtyard in 1824[1] was engraved for the *Gentleman's Magazine*.[2] One side of the inn fronted Spicer Street; this is depicted in a painting of the Abbey by Cornelius Varley. It is difficult to relate the two views to one another or to what now exists with any certainty. The only entrance to the inn for carts or carriages appears to have been from Spicer Street, there being no sign of a covered way on the George Street side. Comparison of roof heights suggests that Buckler drew the rear range. Both views show that the inn was of several builds, the rear range being the earliest part, the W range being plainer and presumably later, while the E range, which had mullion-and-transom windows, was built or altered in the second half of the 17th century. The front range, of the early 15th century, has what appears to have been a gallery, long wall braces of squarish scantling and a crown-post roof.

Notes
1. Buckler Vol III, 144.
2. *Gent Mag* September 1845, 261.

(77797)
Nos 26–26B George Street,

formerly the George Inn, comprise a S range fronting the street and two wings flanking the courtyard to N. A drawing of *c*1800[1] shows that the ground floor had been rebuilt in brick but the first floor was still timber framed and jettied, with three bay windows with canted sides; the middle window was above the carriageway. To N a gallery spanned the carriageway; it was probably reached from a staircase in the re-entrant angle of the wing to W. In the early 19th century, perhaps after the building had ceased in part to be an inn, it was refronted in brick, forming six bays; the ground-floor rooms then or subsequently became shops.

Note
1. Oldfield Vol VIII, 471.

(77798)
Nos 27/28 (`Tudor Tavern') George Street

comprises three ranges, one facing the street to S (correctly SSW), another to NE of it, and one to W of to the latter (here called the rear range). The NE range is of the 15th century and appears to have been truncated to S; it is of two storeys, the first floor being carried on binding-beams with heavy braces, one of which remains; the upper storey is lofty and has a crown-post roof of three bays. There is no sign of an original fireplace, the present chimney-stack being definitely a later insertion, nor of smoke blackening; this and the absence of mouldings on the tie-beam, braces and wall-posts suggest the wing was never an open hall.[1] Perhaps an open hall stood to either W, antedating the street range, or to N, antedating the present rear range. In the 15th century the S range, of two storeys, jettied, was added; the entrance was wide originally but has been widened subsequently; a staircase was probably at the N end; and since the range has no chimney-stacks it may have comprised only inn chambers on both floors. In the late 16th century a chimney-stack was built in the NE wing serving a first-floor fireplace with moulded stone jambs and cambered wooden lintel; another fireplace formerly existed on the ground floor. In the late 17th century the first-floor framing to S of the street range was altered to provide larger windows; and the staircase and putative hall range may have been rebuilt then. Evidence of this

and subsequent changes has been entirely swept away in two restorations, of *c*1935 and *c*1960.

(For details with plans and cross-section see Wood 1936–8, 99–104).

Note
1. Wood 1936–8, 101–2.

(77799)
No. 3 High Street,

of brick and originally of two storeys and attics, was built *c*1700; it is of five bays with giant pilasters at the ends of the front elevation, and a moulded cornice. It was heightened by a storey in the early 19th century, the pilasters being extended to a plain frieze below the bold flat eaves. Only a few Victorian fittings have survived conversion to bank premises.

(77800)
No. 14 High Street

was probably built in the 15th century although no exposed features are definitely of that date. It was a narrow shop (about 10 ft x 20 ft (3·0 m x 6·1 m)) with a room above, but without a chimney-stack (cf No. 2, Market Place). In the late 17th century, perhaps *c*1670–80, it was heightened to three storeys; a chimney-stack with fireplace on ground and first floors was inserted; and a staircase with moulded balusters was added to N. The gabled roof is of collar-rafter type.

(77801)
No. 17 High Street,

of three storeys and jettied, was probably built *c*1500, although strictly all that can be said of its date is that it antedates the plasterwork of the front. It had no chimney-stack. In 1665, the date embossed in a cartouche in the gable, plasterwork was applied to the front (N) and a staircase with moulded balusters was added to S. Enlargement has been by encroachment on the plot to E, and since there is little sign that the original building was intended for domestic use the encroachment may have been designed to create living-quarters attached to the original shop premises.

(77802)
No. 33 High Street

was examined after severe fire damage in October 1975. It was of *c*1600 and of two storeys and attics; the plan is uncertain but may have comprised a front range with a wing to S. The fire revealed early 17th-century wall-paintings (now in the Verulamium Museum) behind panelling in a first-floor room facing the street; four female figures holding, from left to right, a small trumpet or pipe, a pair of compasses, a lyre and a book, formed part of a larger series representing the Muses, Liberal Arts, or Fashionable and Polite Accomplishments. In the early 18th century the house was heightened to three storeys, the front being of brick and the rest timber; a moulded brick cornice runs at second-floor level; there was no doubt another one at first-floor level and a similar eaves cornice. Subsequently a carriage entrance was driven through the two bays to W and the rear wing extended over it, making the upper floors two rooms deep throughout. The whole was given a hipped roof of low pitch, with boarded eaves on paired brackets; this work is probably early Victorian. Rebuilding in 1979 left only the brick front.[1]

Note
1. *Herts Country Mag* May 1979, 27–8.

(77803)
The White Hart Hotel

comprises two adjacent buildings (Nos 23/25 Holywell Hill), that to S (No. 25) being the principal part of an inn established *c*1500 called the Hartshorn.[1] The early stages in the development of the inn are uncertain. Part of the E wing, which adjoins the street range, may be of 16th-century origin but no framing of that date is exposed; it appears definitely to antedate the late 17th-century street range. The latter replaces a building of the 16th century or earlier; it has flush framing with thin studs of storey height and a minimum of larger structural members; it was intended to be rendered, as it was *c*1800;[2] with the wing it forms an inverted T-plan. The adjoining property to N (No. 23) is of the late 16th century; of two storeys, jettied; and generally rendered but with exposed framing and a bay window to W above the entrance to the yard. Wall-paintings discovered in the first-floor room *c*1890 and in 1901 were large-scale compositions in black and white, with `inhabited' pillars, putti, animals and foliage; they are now remounted and framed. A gallery formerly to E is now incorporated in this room. In a ground-floor room of No. 23 another painting,[3] probably depicting the death of Adonis, was found. The gallery may be of the late 16th or late 17th century; the addition to No. 23 of a semi-attic storey continuous with that of No. 25 establishes that both buildings formed part of the inn. The E wing of No. 25 was extended to E in brick *c*1700, the new block, of L-shaped plan, sitting, as it were, on the stem of the T. It was probably entered directly from the courtyard to N by an entrance-hall adjoining the older wing and leading to a staircase-hall; it comprised, on the ground floor, a room with corner fireplace, kitchen and service rooms; on the first floor three large and two small rooms opened off the staircase. The plan of the older part of No. 25 may have comprised, to W (the street range), two rooms with corner fireplaces; to E, two rooms with internal chimney-stack and lobby-entrance facing the yard; and an entrance and staircase of *c*1700 in the re-entrant angle to N, providing access from the yard. A corridor to S of the staircase landing gives access to the first-floor rooms of the W range; from it another corridor to N led to two large rooms to E and W of the internal stack; and there was formerly a gallery leading N to No. 23. Oldfield's drawing does not show a doorway in the street front of either No. 23 or No. 25. (The range to N of the yard, to E of No. 23, was not examined.)

Notes
1. Kitton 1895–1902, 239–41.
2. Oldfield Vol VIII, 488.
3. Kitton 1895–1902, 240.

(77804)
No. 37 Holywell Hill,

formerly the Crown and Anchor, is perhaps the best-preserved 16th-century inn in Hertfordshire. A range of nine bays extends to E along Sopwell Lane and is jettied to N and W, with a boldly jettied first-floor gallery to S. The bay to W is of an earlier build than the remainder. On the ground floor the unheated room to W, at the street corner, was perhaps a bar or a parlour; to E the hall, entered from the courtyard by a doorway adjoining the parlour, has a fireplace to E; originally the staircase was to S of the hall chimney-stack; the remaining bays to E appear to have been unheated and are plainly finished. On the first floor the staircase rises to the gallery, off which opened a series of chambers, each lit by windows to N and S. The exact number of chambers is not certain; at the E end of the range two bays show no sign of an original partition and may have formed one room;

the next two bays to W may always have formed two smaller rooms; to W again a larger bay forms another room, with that part of the adjoining bay to W not occupied by the chimney-stack and staircase forming a small inner room; W of the stack two bays appear originally to have been one room; finally there is the large corner room. Given the elements of doubt, the correct interpretation may be three large chambers, each of two bays; a chamber and inner chamber; and the corner chamber. Some of the uncertainty is caused by later subdivision of the large chamber, that to E, probably in the late 17th century, when fireplaces were added to the supposed bar and the corner chamber above; the chimney-stack backs on to the carriageway to S leading to the courtyard. In the late 18th century the rooms over and to S of the carriageway, which were probably once part of the inn, went into separate occupation. In recent years the building has been carefully restored and most of the later alterations removed.[1]

For an illustration, see *English Houses 1200–1800*, Fig 284 (plate).

Note
1. Weaver and Poole 1961, 43–9, with plans and isometric drawing; *Newsletter* **14**, 1963, drawing of hall fireplace head and moulding.

(77805)
No. 18 Lower Dagnall Street,

of two storeys and two bays and jettied to S, was the cross-wing at the upper end of a 15th-century house, the open hall, long demolished, being to W. It was not examined for the present survey, but having been fully photographed[1] and drawn[2] is mentioned for comparison with the formally similar unheated buildings found in market-places, eg No. 2 Market Place, St Albans. The principal differences are that the staircase rose from the NE corner of the hall and was not related to an entrance from the street; to N a first-floor doorway probably led to a garderobe; and there was evidence of a bench and bench-end. Each floor comprised two rooms. Some curvilinear window tracery could be of the late 14th century but the hollow mouldings of the jambs and of the doorway, coupled with the thin plank-like braces to the crown-posts, favour the early 15th century.

Notes
1. Verulamium Museum, St Albans.
2. *Newsletter* **37**, 1975.

(77806)
No. 2 Market Place,

of three storeys and cellars, was built in the 15th century as a permanent encroachment on the market-place. It has two rooms on each storey with the original staircase in the corner to SE. Two partitions in the ground-floor front room are difficult to interpret; one may have formed a passage from the front to the staircase; the remaining part was perhaps mostly a shop with either a small room or a separate entrance beside it. There is no evidence that the two bays of the ground floor formed two rooms although that was so on both the upper floors; nor of an original chimney-stack, whether of timber or brick.

For an illustration, see *English Houses 1200–1800*, Fig 236.

(77807)
No. 25 Market Place and Nos 2-8 Upper Dagnall Street,

a jettied building of two storeys, is commonly called the `Moot Hall'; this is based on a misapprehension. The position of the

Moot Hall is known from references to two shops standing between another shop to S and 'le Stokhous', otherwise the Moot Hall, to N, and abutting at one end on the king's highway and at the other on Bothelstrete;[1] this must have been an island site within the market-place and cannot refer to a building which faces Dagnall Street to S. In 1540–1 a tenement 'situated at le Mothall' (distinct from one near the Moot Hall) was 'vacant, unoccupied and defective';[2] the fate of the building is not recorded. The Moot Hall has with no good reason been equated with the hall of the fraternity of All Saints, otherwise known as the Charnel Brotherhood,[3] the location of which does not seem to be specifically recorded. In 1546 the Brotherhood house was 'not letten' and certified by the Chantry Commissioners as a decayed tenement.[4] It was this building 'a certain house...called in the vulgar tongue the Charnell House otherwise called The Towne House'[5] which was designated as the Common Hall and house of the mayor and burgesses. But the present building has on the first floor principal posts datable by mouldings to the third quarter of the 16th century and, moreover, it is designed with an original ceiling to the first-floor room, something unknown in medieval vernacular buildings. This evidence implies that a new town hall was built not many years after 1553.

No old features are visible on the ground floor. The principal room on the first floor (c40 ft x 18 ft 6 ins (12.2 m x 5.6 m)) was to W, and of four bays divided by moulded posts. How the other first-floor rooms, occupying six bays, were used is not clear.

The subsequent history of the building, which was known in the 17th century as 'the Counter', is one of repairs and minor alterations. In 1717 the pillory stalls in the butchers' shambles were ordered to be taken down to repair the Counter House.[6] In 1756 the Town Hall was ordered to be repaired but by 1762 was sufficiently out of repair for the Court of aldermen and assistants to adjourn to the White Hart.[7] In 1772 an estimate of £61 2s 3d for taking down the kitchen was accepted; in 1773 the Council Chamber was ordered to be wainscoted to chair height and papered, the beams to be cased, a Portland stone chimney-piece to be put in, and windows of the Venetian order inserted to make the Council Chamber uniform with the Town Hall; and in 1781 the penthouse around the Town Hall was ordered to be taken down.[8] Possibly the plaster ceiling near the corner of the building was built then. Guttering and spouts to carry rainwater off the roof were not provided until 1804.[9] These improvements were not enough; by 1825 the Corporation was thinking of selling the Town Hall and in 1831 did so, by auction.[10]

Notes
1. Briggs 1895, 93–5.
2. Ibid.
3. VCH II, 480 and n129.
4. Brown 1909, 24.
5. MS translation of Letters Patent of Edward VI, 12 May 1553, St Albans City Library.
6. Gibbs, A E 1890, 108.
7. Ibid, 130, 133.
8. Ibid, 138, 139, 147.
9. Ibid, 157.
10. Ibid, 174, 183.

(77808)
New Barns, now Sopwell House Hotel (approximately TL 161063),

was described as 'lately built' in 1603.[1] An Oldfield drawing[2] shows a house of 18th-century appearance, partly of three storeys and five bays and partly of two storeys and two bays;

the front doorway is off-centre, being in the end bay of the taller part next to the lower part, so that it can be interpreted in the light of Salisbury Hall, Shenley, as the rebuilding in two phases of the late 16th-century house. Edward Strong, the master mason principally concerned with the building of St Paul's Cathedral and Blenheim Palace, bought New Barns, probably c1714–16 when he acquired other Hertfordshire estates, and died there in 1724;[3] he may have been responsible for the five-bay part. The house was enlarged in the 19th century, and after its conversion to a hotel is almost entirely devoid of old detail.

Notes
1. Gover, Mawer and Stenton 1938, 100.
2. Oldfield Vol VIII, 546.
3. Colvin 1978, 791–2.

(77809)
Nos 61/63 Park Street (TL 148040)

comprised two distinct parts both roofed N–S, a lower range to N and a taller range to S, which is jettied to W. The N part appears to have been originally a late-medieval open hall; the S part, comprising a parlour and chamber above, but without chimney-stack or fireplace, was added in the late 16th century. Both parts have clasped-purlin roofs. The existing chimney-stack and floor may have been inserted in the hall as late as the 18th century; the parlour stack is earlier. The building was extensively restored in 1973.

For an illustration, see *English Houses 1200–1800*, Fig 57 (plate).

(77810)
Romeland House, Romeland Hill,

was built in the mid 18th century by Frederick Vandermeulen who, being elected Mayor in 1762, successfully pleaded exemption from that office on the grounds of his not being of English parentage.[1] It is an unusually large town house, facing S (Fig 107); the entrance-hall extends the full width of the house with E and W wings projecting slightly to N; to S are the two principal ground-floor rooms, presumably the drawing room

Fig 107 *Romeland House, St Albans: plan*

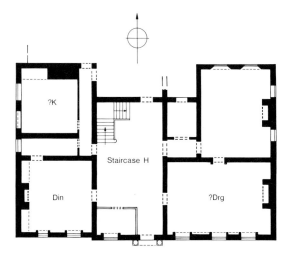

(with a rococo ceiling) and dining room, and a small room which was perhaps a butler's pantry; to N one of two somewhat smaller rooms was perhaps an office. The staircase is notable. The building has been greatly enlarged to N and is now offices.

Notes
1. Gibbs, A E 1890, 133.

(77811)
St Julians (TL 142055),

long demolished, occupied the site of a leper hospital suppressed in 1505.[1] After the Dissolution the land was granted to Sir Richard Lee and in the late 16th century was described as the site of two barns.[2] In 1649 it was sold to John Ellis Esq., a draper of London, who `built a fair House there',[3] and was Sheriff in 1667.

Notes
1. VCH IV, 464–7.
2. PRO SP 12/288/47.
3. Chauncy II, 305.

(77812)
`In St Peter's Street Mr Kentish has a mansion'

which had, in the garden wall, a gateway of c1600;[1] it had a round-headed arch flanked by fluted pilasters and with pediment; in the spandrels were shields bearing a fess nebuly between six fleurs-de-lys. A map[2] suggests it may correspond to No. 1, St Peter's Street, which incorporates timber framing and has binding-beams and bearers with a double-ogee moulding, but the creation of Spencer Street in the 19th century makes precise identification difficult.

Notes
1. Oldfield Vol VIII, 468.
2. Ibid, 6.

(77813)
No. 6 St Peter's Street,

has, to SE of the street range, a narrow wing (14 ft (4·3 m)) of two bays which is probably of the 16th century. The bay to W has, on the ground floor, a chamfered binding-beam with pyramidal stops. The wing roof has clasped-purlins; the bay to W is of re-used timber and that to E has curved windbraces and is blackened by smoke; possibly the E bay was a kitchen rather than a hall. The wing wall-plates are oversailed by the rear plate of the front (W) range, which is of the early 17th century; an internal chimney-stack serves both ranges; the W range has a clasped-purlin roof with straight windbraces; panelling in the first-floor room to S is of the early 17th century and may be largely in its original position. A first-floor fireplace in the front range is of the late 17th century; the staircase, of the same date, retains twisted and turned balusters. The lower flights of the staircase were rebuilt in the mid–late 19th century, perhaps when the building first became a solicitor's office.

(77814)
The Grange, No. 16 St Peter's Street,

of brick, was built by John Osborne in 1764;[1] it is now of interest principally for the plan. To N of the central entrance and staircase-hall is the principal and largest room; to S are a smaller room and a passage to the former garden to S; and to E a second room faces the garden. The coeval service wing to E blocks the obvious point from which the main staircase might be lit; presumably there was a top light, with some light on the first floor from a window to S. Some late 18th-century and Victorian detail remains; the staircase has very attenuated balusters and a ramped moulded handrail, and at the foot has been turned to S.

Note
1. Inf. the late Miss B V Entwistle, Town Clerk.

(77815)
No. 32 St Peter's Street

was built in the 17th century and has an internal-chimney, lobby-entrance plan; no details remain. In the early–mid 18th century it was refronted and a parallel range, also with an internal chimney and with a new principal staircase to S, was added. It was considerably altered c1830 when a tunnel was cut through the front internal stack to provide a passage-hall leading to the staircase-hall; two fireplaces are of that date.

Sopwell (TL 150063),

a small priory of Benedictine nuns dependent on St Albans Abbey,[1] was dissolved in 1537; there were then five nuns, and an inventory of that year mentions only hall, kitchen, napery, church and choir.[2] In 1540 the site was granted to a military engineer, Sir Richard Lee[3] who, in 1548, retired to Sopwell for about ten years and proceeded to build.[4] This accords with the coin evidence produced by archaeological excavation, which establishes that work was in progress c1550.[5] Evidently Lee made use of the foundations of the cloister for the courtyard[6] but apart from this little is known about the house, not even the location of the hall. By January 1562, when he was proposing to enclose a road in order to form a park,[7] work was no doubt complete. `Sir Richard Lee's house at St Albans' was one of several in which Queen Elizabeth stayed during a progress in 1564.[8] After 1560 house and park were separated from the manor, the latter being leased out.[9] At some time not yet established by excavation, but perhaps before the end of the 16th century, all but the W range of the courtyard was demolished and a new N range incorporating a hall was built on the site of the church. It is suggested[10] that this work antedates Lee's death in 1575, on the grounds that his heiresses married into families whose principal seats were elsewhere.[11] It has not so far been possible to link the second house with a mid 17th-century drawing of Sopwell[12] made during the occupancy (1624 to c1663) of Robert Sadler. The drawing shows the house as a straight range, gabled at the front and with two cupolas to rear; the latter suggest two staircases, rather like Aston Bury. In 1669 the estate was sold to Sir Harbottle Grimston[13] who, by 1673, was using materials from the house for the alterations at Gorhambury.[14] Since then the house has been a ruin.

Notes
1. VCH IV, 422–6.
2. PRO E117/12/30.
3. VCH II, 413.
4. *DNB*.
5. Johnson and Weaver 1962–3, 5.
6. Platt 1978, 216, plan.
7. VCH II, 470, 15.
8. PRO E351/3202.
9. VCH II, 413.
10. Johnson and Weaver 1962–3, 5.
11. Cf VCH II, 413, n28.
12. Ibid, 415.
13. Ibid, 413.
14. Rogers 1933–5, 73.

ST MICHAEL

(77817)

Childwick Bury (TL 140102),

formerly Childwick House, belonged to St Albans Abbey from the late 10th century.[1] A large barn and other necessary buildings were erected in the time of Abbot John De la Moote (1396–1401) but there is no specific reference to a house.[2] After the Dissolution the manor passed through several hands until c1666 when it was bought by Joshua Lomax, who probably built the nucleus of the present house; he was Sheriff in 1674 and died in 1685.[3] The house was of two storeys and attics and had a pediment over the three middle bays of seven. Drawings,[4] from which a heightening to three storeys can be inferred to have taken place by c1800, show that all the chimney-stacks were on outside walls, and since this mode of planning is characteristic of a later period and rare or non-existent before 1700 it argues major alterations during the 18th century, perhaps by Caleb Lomax who was Sheriff in 1753; a mid-century date would fit the enlarged attic storey and parapeted roof. The house in 1840[5] differed little from its appearance in c1800,[6] save for the addition to S of a large detached structure surmounted by a tall cupola, probably a stable block.

In 1852 the house was advertised as a genteel residence with dining, drawing and breakfast rooms, eight bedrooms, and stabling and a double coach house.[7] A sale catalogue of 1854 mentions the enrichment to the Drawing Room, Ladies' Morning Room and staircase as `executed by the celebrated Gibbons, and of a very elegant description'.[8] In that year it was acquired by Henry Heyman Toulmin, who transformed it into a large country house. Additions included two projecting single-storey wings to W;[9] a two-storey range to N in which were an entrance-hall and flanking rooms; and large service wings to E. A new drainage system was installed[10] and a roof balustrade was added to unify the whole house. A carved pediment is said to have been removed and reset on the George Inn, St Albans;[11] it is no longer there.

Toulmin was Sheriff in 1866. On his death in 1871 his son succeeded him and c1883 sold the house to Sir John Blundell Maple, son of the founder of the furnishing firm, of whom it was noted:

Since [he] bought the house and estate some nine years ago...great and continuous improvements have been carried out...money has been spent with a truly prodigal hand. No estate in the kingdom could be kept up with greater thoroughness and completeness.[12]

Much of the interior, including the fine main staircase, is of his time, and he probably added the billiard room as a wing to NE. A fireplace, overmantel and plaster ceiling in what is now called the Chinese Room have been dated to c1760;[13] they are, however, incompatible with an entrance-hall of the width implied by drawings[14] and must be late 19th-century work. Another elaborate fireplace surround and overmantel, said to be of c1760[15] or by Grinling Gibbons,[16] was in the drawing room (possibly the present library); it is now in the Pine Room, minus the overmantel. Maple died in 1903 and in 1906 his widow sold Childwick Bury to J B Joel, whose son H J Joel sold it in 1978; their work continued Maple's standards, including that done in the 1960s by O N Bateman Brown.[17]

For an illustration, see *English Houses 1200–1800*, Fig 130 (plate).

Notes

1. VCH II, 397.

2. *Chronica Monastici S. Albani, Gesta Abbat* Vol III, 445.
3. Cussans 1879–81, Vol III (ii), 256–7.
4. Oldfield Vol II, 262; Buckler Vol III, 153.
5. Buckler Vol III, 153.
6. Oldfield Vol II, 262.
7. *Herts Guardian*, 15 May 1852.
8. HRO, BH6 /36.
9. Cussans 1879–81, Vol III (ii), 257.
10. Plan dated February 1856 in Estate Office.
11. Kitton 1895–1902, 257.
12. Kitton 1892, 182.
13. L— 1909, 918–19.
14. Oldfield Vol II, 262; Buckler Vol III, 153.
15. L— 1909, 919.
16. SC 1906, NMR 477.
17. Obituary, *The Times*, 18 September 1978.

(39636)

Gorhambury (TL 113081)

corresponds to the pre-Conquest manor of Westwick which, in 996, was granted by King Ethelred to St Albans Abbey. Its name derives from the building here of a hall by Geoffrey de Gorham, who was abbot from 1119 to 1146,[1] and ever since that time the place has been an important residence, albeit with at least two changes of site. After the Dissolution the manor was granted by the Crown in 1541 to Ralph Rowlett of St Albans, who was Sheriff in 1542 and died in the following year. It is not clear exactly where Rowlett lived; if at Gorhambury, he must have used the medieval manor house. The next owner of importance was Sir Nicholas Bacon, Lord Keeper of the Great Seal, who purchased the estate in 1559[2] or 1561[3] and built a courtyard house on a new site (TL 110077) between 1563 and 1568. This was the house visited by Queen Elizabeth in 1572, of which she is supposed to have said `My Lord Keeper, what a little house you have gotten';[4] a remark which caused Bacon to add the long two-storeyed W `cloister' before her second visit in 1577. On Bacon's death in 1579 Gorhambury passed to his elder son (by his second marriage) Anthony, who died in 1601, leaving it to his younger brother Sir Francis, later Lord Verulam. Anthony Bacon is unlikely to have had the means[5] to do much in the way of building; his brother, who had both the means and the ambition, certainly embellished the house with painted glass[6] and may have added the N courtyard.[7] After Francis Bacon's death in 1626, the house entered on a period of neglect lasting until its purchase in 1652 by Sir Harbottle Grimston, whose principal recorded work was the enlargement of the chapel; but the attention given to furnishings[8] shows that the house must have been generally improved, partly to the designs of Captain Ryder. His successor Sir Samuel Grimston continued to improve the house by, among other things, putting in sash windows.[9] On his death in 1700 Gorhambury descended to his nephew William Luckyn, provided the latter changed his name to Grimston and paid Sir Samuel's grand daughter £70,000; and it was the second provision that necessitated dividing the house for a number of years and leasing one part of it to tenants. Throughout the 18th century work continued to be done on the house by William, created Viscount Grimston in 1719, who is the probable builder of a ballroom to SE of the main courtyard, and his son James, 2nd Viscount, who succeeded him in 1756 and died in 1773.[10] An engraving which can hardly be earlier than c1760[11] shows that a Venetian window had been inserted in the centrepiece of the gallery and the ballroom either demolished or discreetly hidden by trees (by the engraver). By 1775 the 3rd Viscount was considering plans for a new house, which eventually was designed by Sir Robert Taylor and built between 1777 and 1784. This is the present Gorhambury House (TL 113078), which was not seen in connection with the present survey. Demolition of Nathaniel Bacon's house took place in stages. A watercolour dated 1787[12] shows that the front half of the main courtyard had been removed and the ends of the truncated wings made good, that to E incorporating what looks like a reset pedimented door architrave; the cloister and gallery were in an advanced state of demolition. Subsequently the house was reduced to the hall and porch.

For illustrations, see *English Houses 1200–1800*, Figs 86 (plate), 87 (plate), 95 (plate), 196 (plate).

Notes
1. VCH II, 393; IV, 414.
2. Rogers 1933–5, 38.
3. VCH II, 394.
4. Mercer 1962, 14, citing D Lloyd, *State Worthies*, 1766, 355.
5. *DNB*.
6. Archer 1976, 1451–4, 1562–4
7. Rogers 1933–5, 53.
8. Ibid, 68–71.
9. Ibid, 78–9.
10. Ibid, 83–5.
11. Bodl, Gough Maps 11, fo 36*r*.
12. Ibid, 36.

(77818)
Verulam House (approximately TL 085125),
built by Sir Francis Bacon (Lord Verulam) *c*1610,[1] is known only from Aubrey's description[2] and sketch drawn from memory.[3] The sketch suggests the house was square or nearly so, one side being of three bays and the adjoining one of five; Aubrey's accompanying note says `I doe not well remember...whether the number of windowes on the East side were 5, or 7; to my best remembrance but 5; the parallel sides answer one another'; and it had bay windows to E. The plan is difficult to reconstruct. There was a single chimney-stack which apparently incorporated nine flues, although in March 1663 Sir Harbottle Grimston was noted as having had eleven hearths `in the house called Verulam house now demolished'.[4] The roof was leaded, with a balustrade and seats around the stack; all the service rooms including the kitchen were in a basement. Excerpts from letters relating to the demolition of the house appear in *Hertfordshire Countryside Magazine*.[5]

Notes
1. Archer 1976, 1564
2. Aubrey, *Brief Lives*, 194–5.
3. Bodl, MS Aubrey 6, fo 72; Archer 1976, 1564; *Middlesex and Herts N & Q* 1897, Vol III, 132 and Plate.
4. PRO E179/248/23.
5. *Herts Country Mag* January 1981, 22–5.

(77819)
Viccars House (TL 140106),
of brick with stone dressings and of two storeys and attics, incorporates the walls of a ruinous house drawn in 1839.[1] As drawn it appears to have been of one-room ground plan, facing SW, with chimney-stack to NW and probably a lobby-entrance. Later in the 19th century it was enlarged and much restored and was subsequently taken to be wholly of the 16th century.[2] The moulded stone band at first-floor level and moulded cornice suggest a later date, perhaps mid 17th century. The principal interest of the house lies in the combination of good quality with a one-room plan. It is not clear what the social position of its

owner or occupier was; possibly it was built for its present purpose, as a bailiff's house for Childwickbury. Buckler's exaggeration of height in his drawing is relevant to others of his drawings (cf. Baldock, `Ancient House').

Notes
1. Buckler Vol III, 154.
2. RCHME 1910, 193.

(77820)
Westwick Row Farm (TL 093065)
faces S and is in two distinct parts, that to W of the internal chimney-stack being of two storeys and that to E of one storey and attics. The latter is a late-medieval cruck house with a bay to E, which has an original upper floor, and an open hall of two bays. In the 17th century a chimney-stack and an upper floor were inserted in the hall, the stack, which was perhaps of timber, virtually filling the W bay; a new hall and parlour with chambers over were added to W; and the cross-passage was abandoned and a lobby-entrance created. It appears that two staircases were in use, one original to the cruck house and another in the added W bay. The present brick chimney-stack has three conjoined square shafts of different sizes; the brickwork need not be older than the mid–late 18th century, which is perhaps when the timber stack was replaced, an upstairs fireplace added to W, and a staircase built opposite the entrance.

ST PAUL'S WALDEN

(77821)
The Bury (TL 187217)
was a manor of of St Albans Abbey from *c*900 until 1539 and in 1544 passed by exchange to the dean and chapter of St Paul's, London.[1] The house was separated from the manor and sold to Edward Gilbert,[2] who died in 1724;[3] he probably rebuilt the house and his son Edward laid out the garden *c*1725–30.[4] The house faces N (correctly NNE) and is of three storeys and five bays; the top storey is treated as an attic; two brick bands divide the storeys to SE;[5] the windows had segmental heads; and a large second-floor lunette to E lights the upper flights of the staircase, which was probably always in its present position to SE. The plan at this period is otherwise uncertain; the proportions suggest it comprised to N two rooms, that to E being both a reception room and entrance-hall; a range, probably the older house, and including the services, lay to S. Edward Gilbert the second died in 1762[6] and the house descended by 1767 to his granddaughter Mary Bowes who, in that year, married John Lyon, 9th Earl of Strathmore[7] and enlarged and altered the house. Two flanking two-storey semi-octagonal pavilions were added, projecting to N; the E pavilion also has semi-octagonal bays to E and S; and a giant dentilled pediment extending the full width of the old house was added. This work is dated by rain-water heads. Exactly how the old house was altered is uncertain. A stone band above the first floor of the pavilions extends across the five-bay front and meets the tall windows awkwardly at about one-third of their height from the sill; but the position of this band is not determined by the older platbands to SE, which are at quite different heights. The plan of the middle range was altered to provide a wide but shallow entrance-hall, with columns forming small lobby-like spaces to E and W at the entrance to the pavilion rooms. By this time the house had a hybrid form of plan, resembling the end-entrance type in so far as the entrance

was on the same axis as the long service block. The range to S was subsequently rebuilt; it was of at least seven bays and by 1887 was rendered.[8] In 1887 this range was completely rebuilt, the entrance moved to E, and much alteration took place in the remainder of the house, including a new staircase.

For an illustration, see *English Houses 1200–1800*, Fig 207 (plate).

Notes
1. VCH II, 405.
2. Ibid, 406.
3. Monumental Inscription, Oldfield Vol VI, 295.
4. Hussey 1956, 475.
5. Photograph, pre-1887, in possession of Mr Simon Bowes-Lyon.
6. Monumental Inscription, Oldfield Vol VI, 295.
7. Hussey 1956, 472.
8. Photograph, pre-1887, in possession of Mr Simon Bowes-Lyon.

(32423)
The Hoo (TL 187195)

was an important manor house in the early 13th century, when William de Trumpington, Abbot of St Albans 1214–35, permitted Richard del Hoo to establish an oratory in his court `del Ho'.[1] The only member of the family to be Sheriff was William Hoo in 1629. After the death of Thomas Hoo in 1650 the manor came to his daughter Susan and so by marriage to Jonathan Keate.[2] Keate was created baronet in 1660 while he was rebuilding the house, which had rain-water heads bearing the date 1661 and the initials I K S.[3] A reconstruction of the original plan has been attempted (Fig 108) on the basis of plans made prior to demolition. The house must have been of advanced design if, as seems to have been the case, the services were all in the basement, but many features were destroyed or obscured by alterations (Fig 109). On each floor the three-bay N projection probably corresponds to a single room behind it, the one on the ground floor being the entrance-hall. An engraving of c1700[4] shows that the chimney-stacks were grouped in four blocks and Buckler confirms the modern plan in showing those in the N range as being aligned E–W and those in the S range N–S; this makes the customary large fireplace at the rear of the hall unlikely, and fireplaces at each end of the hall, discharging into the two main stacks, are a possibility. The use of two fireplaces can only be paralleled in a much smaller house, Abercynrig (Llanfynach);[5] alternatively the hall had no fireplace

Fig 108 *The Hoo, St Paul's Walden: reconstruction of ground-floor plan as built*

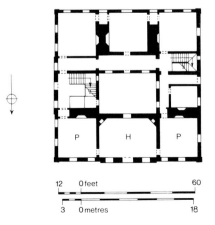

Fig 109 *The Hoo, St Paul's Walden: development perspectives*

Phase 1: 1661

Phase 2: early 18th century

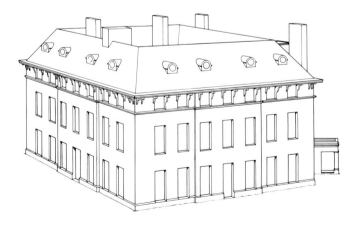

Phase 3: late 19th century

(cf Coleshill, Berks). E of the hall is a parlour or ante-room and beyond it the Great Staircase, leading, it is assumed, to the Great Dining Chamber on the first floor. The staircase had been altered; a photograph[6] shows the different rake of the handrail in the short middle flight, and the lower flight, extending beyond the newel post, must be an arrangement dating to the late 19th or 20th century; they are drawn in the reconstruction with a wall 8 ft (2·4 m) square allowing for a doorway to the room to S. The first alterations to the house occurred in the early 18th century (Fig 109). A two-storey kitchen block to W can be dated by a reset staircase to c1710–20;[7] perhaps then mullion-and-transom windows were replaced by hung sashes and the shaped gables by parapets and dormer windows; whilst the cellars, following the removal of the kitchen, were reduced in size, the windows to E blocked, and a Venetian window inserted at the W end of the N range. The position of this large window, markedly off-centre to the room, may be connected with the addition nearby of a secondary staircase in its own turret, although at the time of demolition a 19th-century staircase was there. A reason for adding the secondary stair may be that the entrance was transferred from N to E, entailing removal of the architrave and balustrade of the window over the old front door. These works were probably for Sir Henry Hoo Keate, who owned the estate from 1705 to 1732. Thomas Brand, on inheriting the house from his mother, who had bought it, made further alterations in the 1760s. Work was certainly in progress by July 1764 when he wrote to his architect, Sir William Chambers, complaining of a mason's unsatisfactory workmanship.[8] Chambers supplied designs for chimney-pieces, ceilings and bookcases as well as for stables, offices and garden buildings;[9] he probably replaced the original stable court to W by a new service block adjoining the house. The most interesting feature of this work is the conscious reversion to the past expressed in a fireplace executed in the style of Charles II.[10] Chambers may have been responsible for adding the part-octagonal three-storeyed bay to S, incorporating a garden doorway and two windows above; the bay is shown in an engraving of 1829.[11]

Subsequent changes included the insertion, in the late 18th century, of three-light sash windows on the ground floor to E.[12] A low gabled range to W,[13] added after the kitchen because it blocked a casement window in the latter,[14] is given special prominence in one view,[15] perhaps because it had what must have been comparatively recent Gothic windows. Possibly Thomas Brand, who succeeded to the estate in 1794, became Baron Dacre in 1819,[16] and died in 1851,[17] added this range, broadly following the lines of a range shown in the engraving of c1700 but putting in fashionable antiquarian detail. A general early-Victorian renovation of the second floor gave all the fireplaces plain marble surrounds, and probably then the courtyard received a glass roof. In the late 19th century a new entrance porch was provided and bold bracketed eaves replaced the parapets (Fig 109); and in the present century the central hall, the former courtyard, was enlarged to S and a 17th-century fireplace imported to heat it. The house was demolished in 1958.

For an illustration, see *English Houses 1200–1800*, Fig 135 (plate).

Notes
1. BL Cotton MS Julius Diii, fos 65v–66.
2. VCH II, 407.
3. RCHME 1962 and report.
4. Chauncy Vol II, 402.
5. Jones and Smith 1965, 36–8.
6. Photograph, NMR.
7. MS report, NMR.
8. RIBA Cha 2/22.
9. Harris 1970, 54, 211; RIBA Drawings Catalogue.
10. Harris 1970, 210–11.
11. Neale 1819–29, Vol V.
12. Ibid.
13. Buckler Vol IV, 166–7.
14. MS report, NMR.
15. Buckler Vol III, 90.
16. Neale 1819–29, Vol V.
17. VCH II, 408.

(77822)
Hoo End Farm (TL 180197)
incorporates a late medieval hall (c22 ft 6 ins x 18 ft 6 ins (6·9 m x 5·6 m)) and a jettied cross-wing to W; the hall roof, with clasped-purlins, has smoke-blackened rafters. In the late 16th century an upper floor, carried on a moulded bearer, was inserted in the hall; at its W end the bearer is tenoned into a defaced binding-beam, from which a chamfered bearer runs into the chimney-stack. The difference between the bearers may indicate that the original stack was of timber but the evidence is tenuous. Another late 16th-century insertion is the large window with two small flanking lights to S of the W wing. In the 17th century the house was doubled in size to E; the extension has two wide gables to S and one to N (rear), and the attic floor over the hall was provided with similar gables to N and S, giving a four-gabled front elevation characteristic of the mid 17th century. The rear gable over the hall has an ovolo-moulded tie-beam. To E of the hall is the kitchen, with a wide lateral chimney-stack to N, and to E again were service rooms. The probate inventory of John Hill of Hoo End, yeoman, dated 9 July 1662, lists (not in order) hall, little parlour, kitchen, milk house, buttery, bolting-house, meat house; chambers over hall, parlour, kitchen, and 'Folkes chamber'.[1] In 1673 Thomas Hill paid tax on six hearths.[2] In the late 17th century a fireplace with bolection-moulded wooden surround was added in the first-floor room of the W cross-wing.

Notes
1. PRO Prob 4/5017.
2. PRO E179/375/31.

(77823)
Hoo End Grange (TL 180198),
formerly Leggats' End, was the 'manor or messuage called Leggats'[1] and was so-called from a family holding it in the 14th and 15th centuries. In 1430 it was acquired by St Albans Abbey; Abbot John Whethamstede spent £35 in repairs during his first abbacy, which ended in 1440.[2] This sum probably paid for the building of the existing house, which comprises a comparatively long hall range of one storey and attics flanked by gabled cross-wings of two storeys, and incorporates two roofs of the early 15th century.

Externally the low eaves of the hall are the only sign of its medieval origin; in the wing to E framing with tension-braces forming a decorative pattern is exposed on the first floor; the only other 15th-century work visible is the roof, which originally had crown-posts; these, the tie-beams on which they stood, and the wall-plates have been removed; each rafter couple has a collar-beam. The wing to E is coeval with the hall; its projection about 2 ft (0·6 m) to N indicates that a jetty has been underbuilt; the roof has a down-braced crown-post; the tie-beam had arch-braces. The end of the collar-purlin of the hall roof is halved where it meets the rafter of the wing roof, suggesting that the two are coeval: the service wing to W is probably of the 16th century, replacing an earlier service bay; it has a doorway with four-centred head opening into the hall, and clasped-purlin roof.

After the Dissolution Hoo End passed to the Crown and in 1544 was granted to the dean and chapter of St Paul's. In the late 17th century the manor was leased to Nathaniel Younge;[3] for most of the 18th and 19th centuries the house was owned and occupied by the Wellington family.[4] In the early 17th century the large open hall (c35 ft x 24 ft (10·7 m x 7·3 m)) was divided into two rooms with chambers above; a chimney-stack with clustered shafts was built centrally; a drawing of 1781[5] shows a lobby-entrance. The room to W of the stack was probably the kitchen, that to E the hall, in which some contemporary panelling remains; the chamber over the hall has a large dormer window whereas that over the kitchen had in 1781 a much smaller one. A third dormer window between the first two, and intermediate in size, may have lit a closet; the staircase was probably to S of the stack. A cellar in the W wing may also be of the 17th century. In a small room added at the NW corner of the old hall a mid 18th-century fireplace is now the only work of that date in the house. In the late 19th century the house was widened to S, the internal chimney-stack reduced in size,[6] a staircase built to S, and fireplaces and windows were generally renewed; a new dormer window over the former kitchen matched that over the hall.

Notes
1. *Chronica Monastici S. Albani*, Ann Mon S. Albani, Vol II, 167.
2. Ibid, 263.
3. VCH II, 408.
4. *EHAST* 1912–14, 217.
5. Estate map, HRO 26911.
6. *EHAST* 1912–14, 217.

(77824)
Stagenhoe or Stagenhoe Park (TL 185227),

a manor, was purchased in 1595 by Richard Hale, from whom it passed eventually to his grandson John,[1] who built a new house about 1650, was knighted in 1660 and became Sheriff in 1663.[2] The house he built `about the year 1650'[3] is known from an engraving of c1700;[4] it was of seven bays and was raised above a basement; had a two-storey porch; and resembled Balls Park in having large carved brackets beneath the eaves. In the cellars wall-cupboards with shaped heads appear to mark the ends of the mid 17th-century house, which was about 60 ft (18·3 m) long. It was probably more than a single straight range, with either a wing or a staircase-projection to rear (W), the form and appearance of which are unknown. Building accounts for this house have been alleged to exist.[5] On Sir John Hale's death in 1672 the house passed to his daughter Rose, who married Sir John Austen, Bart., to whom Drapentier's engraving[6] is dedicated; his son sold it in 1703 to Robert Heystone Esq., MP successively for Lancaster and London, who died in 1722.[7] In 1737 the house was burnt in a fire caused by building operations; it was rebuilt c1740[8] as a Palladian house with a frontage of 11 bays, and by then was probably of double depth almost throughout. The main entrance was removed c1800 from the middle of the E front to the S end and has remained in that position to the present day. In the late 1830s the house belonged to Captain Arthur Duncombe[9] who, c1838, `employed one of the first artists in building to remodel and nearly rebuild' it.[10] Henry Rogers Esq. purchased it in 1843 and in 1852 the house is depicted with the roof balustraded and a conservatory to N.[11] Subsequently[12] the house was bought by the 4th Earl of

Caithness, who enlarged it,[13] heightened the middle bays of the E front to three storeys and added his coat of arms and motto `Commit Thy Work to God'.[14] Considerable sums of money were spent by the next owner, William Bailey Hawkins;[15] his successor, Sir Henry Whitehead, a wool magnate, is said to have spent a quarter of a million pounds on the estate before his death in 1928. After 1940, with one brief intermission, the house ceased to be in private occupation. Alterations from 1893 onwards have left virtually no old fittings or ornament.

For an illustration, see *English Houses 1200–1800*, Fig 150 (plate).

Notes
1. VCH II, 407.
2. Chauncy II, 211.
3. Ibid, 212.
4. Ibid.
5. Hine nd (Stagenhoe), paragraph 22 (quoted, *Herts Country Mag*, January 1969, 32–3); they are merely isolated bills not definitely related to Stagenhoe (inf. Miss E Lynch).
6. Chauncy.
7. *Gent Mag*, 1798 (ii), 758.
8. VCH II, 407.
9. Ibid.
10. Sale advertisement, *Northampton Mercury*, 10 April 1841.
11. Engraving, Hertford Museum, Andrews Collection.
12. In 1866, Sale Catalogue of 1893, Hertford Museum; or in 1869, VCH II, 407.
13. Cussans 1874–8, Vol II (i), 128, n.
14. Sale catalogue 1893, Hertford Museum.
15. *Kelly* 1912.

ST STEPHEN

(77825)
Burston Manor (TL 135037),

formerly moated, was a possession of St Albans Abbey from before the Conquest until 1539; it is an aisled hall of the late 12th century and the earliest surviving domestic building in the county. Who built it is not known: possibly that Hamo who is known only through the name of his son, Robert Fitz Hamo, the earliest recorded tenant, who enlarged the manor by a grant of land to the Abbey in 1225.[1] In 1340 it was alleged that the tenant, William de Brok, who was said to be insane, was tied by his groom, John Golefre, and two of his servants to a post in his own hall for four days.[2] Of the original hall only the middle or

Fig 110 *Burston Manor, St Stephen: plan*

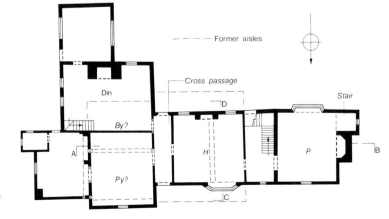

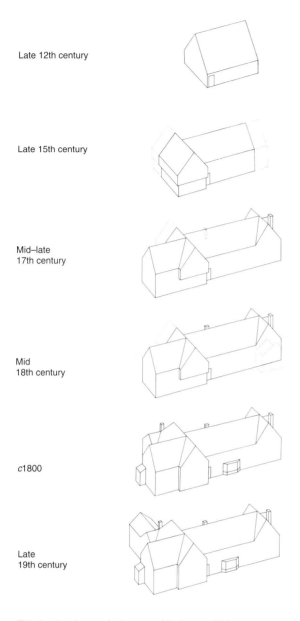

Late 12th century

Late 15th century

Mid–late
17th century

Mid
18th century

c1800

Late
19th century

This drawing shows only the parts of the house which survive, not those parts implied by the existing structure or known only from documentary sources.

Fig 111 *Burston Manor, St Stephen: development perspectives*

open truss and the N side of the nave roof remain. Although both aisles have been destroyed their existence is implied by the proportions of the structure, and by the small exposed portion of the N post of the open truss. The lower part of this post is shaped as a column with a scalloped capital, which provides the principal dating evidence. Above the capital the post is of square section; from it and its fellow to S spring passing-braces of unusually large scantling which were halved across the flat tie-beam and a collar-beam – the latter now removed – and terminated a little distance below the ridge. The roof was of collar-rafter type and a considerable number of rafters have peg-holes as if for rafter-braces which have since been removed, although not all the peg-holes are easy to explain in this way. All original timbers are heavily blackened with smoke. Although the

roof trusses at both ends have been destroyed, the surviving structure suggests that the hall incorporated two bays each about 16 ft (4·9 m) long so that below the wall-plate each nave bay formed approximately a cube with sides 16 ft (4·9 m) in length.

The building was originally larger than this. The end rafter to W is grooved for a partition which has been wholly removed; on the hall side this rafter is encrusted with soot whereas on the other side it is not weathered but merely stained by smoke, showing that smoke had leaked into the roof extending to W. To E the sooted rafters extend beyond the hall and have been truncated by the wing roof; evidently there was originally either a third bay or a short bay separated from the rest of the hall by a spere-truss.

The subsequent development of the house is unusual (Fig 110). To E a wing jettied to N and E was built in the late 15th century; it comprised two service rooms each entered by doorways with hollow-chamfered jambs and four-centred head; a third doorway between them, now blocked, has housings for a similar head and probably led to a staircase. Upstairs were two rooms open to the roof, which has clasped-purlins. This wing may have been built in the time of William Skipwith, who held the manor sometime before 1518 (Fig 111). To N the wing does not extend as far as the presumed position of the N aisle wall, so it is likely that the hall underwent alteration at the time the wing was built, either by a narrowing of the aisles, or, less likely, by their complete removal, which would have produced an extraordinarily lofty and narrow hall. Surprisingly, there is no evidence c1600 of the usual process of insertion of an upper floor and the building of a chimney-stack within the hall. To W a wing was added in the third quarter of the 17th century, possibly by William Kentish who held the manor from 1642[3] to 1668;[4] the ground-floor room, no doubt a parlour, has a stone fireplace with moulded jambs and high stops; the chimney-stack is flanked by a brick turret which probably housed a staircase originally. After 1668 the house may have been neglected. It descended to Sarah, one of the co-heiresses of William Kentish and wife of Godman Jenkyn; the latter died in 1746 aged 91 and was described as `of Harpenden',[5] where he occupied the Hall. The hall is spanned by a plain transverse beam, which, like the existing fireplace and chimney-stack, need not be earlier than the mid 18th century. In the early 19th century Burston Manor was a farmhouse.[6] An estate map of 1793[7] shows a wing to NW which must have been added to the present W wing and was later removed. Considerable alterations took place in the 19th century when the S part of the E wing was replaced by the present dining room; the main staircase was built; the block to E was added; and the house was weather boarded to N.

For illustrations, see *English Houses 1200–1800*, Figs 19 (plate), 290.

Notes
1. VCH II, 425.
2. PRO JI 337.
3. VCH II, 425–6.
4. Monumental Inscription, Oldfield Vol VIII, 315.
5. Ibid.
6. Oldfield Vol VIII, 20.
7. HRO, 63791/11.

(77826)
Holt Farm (TL 121036)

is first mentioned in 1314[1] and in 1368 Joan atte Holte was presented in the manor court of Windridge for not repairing her house.[2] The present house comprises two timber-framed buildings, both apparently houses, which abutted only at one

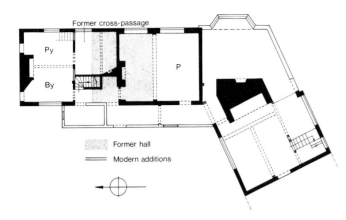

Fig 112 *Holt Farm, St Stephen: plan*

corner but were made into a unified whole in the 19th century (Fig 112). Both were originally open in part from ground to roof, with an open hearth. The N house is of four bays, the middle two being the former hall; in the middle of the hall roof was a closed truss, the tie-beam having been cut off subsequently; the wattle-holes of a partition are visible in the collar-beam. Possibly the division corresponds to one open bay next to the service room, with a hearth, and one floored bay. The N bay still has the depressed four-centred heads of two doorways leading to buttery and pantry; in the latter is a stair trap. In the S gable the timbers are clearly weathered. The W house was also open in the NE bay, in which the roof is heavily sooted; the second bay has an original floor; this building may have been used as a kitchen. In both houses a chimney-stack subsequently replaced the open hearth; this probably took place in the late 17th century in the W house, and somewhat later in the N house.

Holt Farm is of interest as an example of dual occupancy; the division of functions is similar to that at Walnut Tree Farm, Pirton. A series of deeds[3] ranging from 1508 to 1796 does not throw any light on this.

For an illustration, see *English Houses 1200–1800*, Fig 12 (plate).

Notes
1. Gover, Mawer and Stenton 1938, 99.
2. HRO, typescript, excerpt from Court Rolls.
3. HRO, D/EB 1622 T31.

Fig 114 *Tenements Farm, St Stephen: sections*

(77827)
Searches (TL 113034)
incorporates to S (correctly SW) two pairs of crucks which perhaps correspond to the hall of a late medieval house; the apexes have been removed and the tops of the blades roughly jointed to tie-beams of the later storeyed house. The hall and a small room to S are approximately coeval with the tenure of either John Smith or John Wydesore, who held the tenement and 60 acres of land called Searches in 1493 and 1503 respectively.[1] Probably between 1577 and 1598, when it was held by William and Alice Flye, the house was rebuilt with an internal chimney-stack of timber and lobby-entrance on the site of the former cross-passage, and a kitchen or parlour to N. Thus rebuilt the house conforms to a plan-type, common on the west fringe of Hertfordshire, which can be interpreted as being derived from the longhouse; from S to N it has inner room, hall, passage and parlour converted from a byre (cf Westwick Row Farm, St Michaels). The chimney-stack was rebuilt in brick in the late 17th century; the house was refronted in brick in the late 18th century; and an extension to S, including a parlour and combined entrance and staircase-hall was added *c*1840.

Note
1. HRO; W le Hardy, letter of 5 January 1925, with extracts from rentals at Gorhambury.

(77828)
Tenements Farm (TL 105031)
was built in the late 15th century as a range of four bays, the middle two being occupied by an open hall (Fig 113). To N (correctly NE) the service bay had an end-jetty and possibly the demolished bay to S was similar. The hall has an open tie-beam truss (Fig 114); the posts and tie-beam have a chamfer and an

Fig 113 *Tenements Farm, St Stephen: plan*

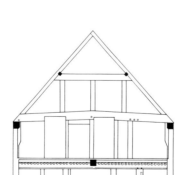

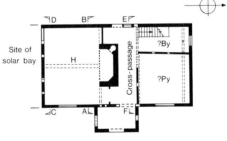

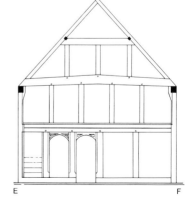

inner hollow chamfer. To E the front doorway has a four-centred head and hollowed spandrels. To S a wide stud forming the jamb of the door leading to the demolished parlour bay and staircase has mortises for a bench-end; other studs have pegs for the bench; the middle rail is battlemented. To N two doorways like the one to E imply an unusual disposition of service rooms; the large room to E, perhaps a pantry, is separated by a studded partition from a small room to W which appears to have incorporated both staircase and buttery. The staircase ascends directly from the passage but there is no definite indication of the shaped doorhead that might be expected if the opening were original. The W room has to N housings for the diamond mullions of a shuttered four-light window. In the early–mid 17th century a chimney-stack and first floor were built in the hall; the stack, with three diagonal shafts, backs on to the cross-passage and the hall fireplace has stone jambs and chamfered wooden lintel; the floor has an ovolo-moulded bearer and beaded joists; all but the three joists to S are incised with a St Andrew's cross where they meet the bearer. A two-storey porch was added in the late 17th century. During the 18th century the house was refenestrated, the roof half-hipped, and the S bay demolished.

SANDON

(77829)
Hyde Hall (TL 342327)

originated as the tenement called Olivers, first called a manor in 1506, which in 1522 was conveyed to George Hyde of Throcking and eventually passed to William Hyde, who was buying other lands in Hertfordshire in the mid 1550s.[1] Chauncy merely notes that `it was called Hyde Hall from the Hydes, who built a fair House or Seat',[2] but Salmon remarks, in connection with the passing of the estate in 1561 to William Hyde, that `About this Time the House was built'.[3] An engraving by Drapentier of *c*1700 depicts the house as being of brick, with a hall rising the height of two storeys to attics[4] and the architectural detail, notably the pedimented windows, corresponds to a late 16th-century date. It also establishes that a not particularly large manor house might still at that date have a lofty hall, although it was probably no longer open to the roof; and the classical frontispiece and doorway may well be coeval despite their advanced style for the 1560s. The less likely alternative is that the house was built or greatly altered by Sir Leonard Hyde, who was knighted by James I in 1603,[5] was Sheriff and `of Throcking' in 1606, and sold the manor in 1607.[6] In the reign of Charles II the house descended to Sir Nicholas Miller, who was Sheriff in 1681. The insertion of dormer windows to light the attics and the addition of pediments to the bay windows and of parapets were possibly his work. At what date the house was pulled down is not known.

Nothing in the present house, which is of two storeys and of timber framing and brick, with tile roofs, can be definitely identified with William Hyde's house.[7] A large brick barn nearby, of L-shaped plan, is probably of the late 16th century; the gable wall facing the present house has mullioned windows lighting the unheated rooms at that end, which is of two storeys and attics, as if to incorporate an agricultural building into an architectural composition with the house. Strangely, nothing of this is shown by Drapentier.

Notes
1. VCH III, 249.
2. Chauncy I, 162.

3. Salmon 1728, 352.
4. Chauncy I, 160.
5. Ibid, 162.
6. VCH III, 274.
7. Despite VCH III, 274.

(77830)
Old Sextons (TL 321345),

built in the mid 16th century, is jettied on both long walls and to W (Fig 115). Both fireplaces in the internal chimney-stack have moulded timber lintels; that in the hall has peg-holes as if the jambs and no doubt the whole stack were originally of wood. To SE of the hall a moulded door jamb probably marks the site of an original cross-passage; a small room to N of the E service bay may be the site of the original staircase. In the 18th century the present staircase was built, with a short entrance-passage to S; this encroachment on the hall entailed relocating the stack to W, while rebuilding it in brick; evidence of this is that the W fireplace protrudes into the room and batters back to the ceiling where it masks a binding-beam, and the fireplace to E stands clear of the binding-beam with which it may once have stood flush. The brickwork of the chimney-stack dates these changes to the 18th century.

Fig 115 *Old Sextons, Sandon: plan*

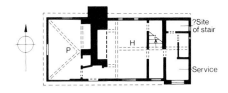

(77831)
Sandon Bury (TL 322344),

a manor house, belonged to the canons of St Paul's from the time of Athelstan until 1863, with an intermission under the Commonwealth. In the middle ages the dean and chapter built a stone house, part of which is depicted in a drawing of *c*1800;[1] it had a two-light window and vertical tracery and was perhaps of the 15th century. In 1649[2] the mansion house comprised hall, parlour, kitchen, pantry, two butteries, cellar, milk house and six chambers over them. After the Restoration the dean `granted a new lease thereof to Sir John Nicholas, Kt., who has built a very fair House of Brick'.[3] As built the house was a double-pile of two storeys and attics and of five bays with a symmetrically placed entrance to S leading into the hall; to E is a parlour lined with bolection-moulded panelling. The staircase faces the entrance; the kitchen is to N of the hall, with pantry to E, over the cellar. The front of the house was raised to a full storey *c*1800 `within these few years'.[4] In the early 19th century the medieval building was replaced by one of brick and of two storeys which provided a large drawing room on the ground floor; the parlour became both entrance and staircase-hall, and the hall the dining room; the old staircase was enclosed by partitions, enlarging the kitchen; and the front attics were improved bedrooms.

Notes
1. Oldfield Vol V, 481.
2. Survey, Guildhall MS 11816.
3. Chauncy I, 161.
4. Oldfield Vol V, 481.

SANDRIDGE

(77832)
Pound Farm (TL 169107),

now a large double-pile house, incorporates a late medieval house of four bays; these are, from N to S, *c*13 ft 6 ins (4·1 m); 13 ft (4·0 m) and 9 ft 6 ins (2·9 m) forming the hall; 10 ft 6 ins (3·2 m); the first three are blackened by smoke, the truss separating the first two bays incorporating a wattle-and-daub partition which is blackened on both sides. If both hall and room to N (possibly a parlour) were open to the roof, and nowhere is there any evidence of an original upper floor, there is perhaps no reason why an open fire should not have been used in both. Probably the cross-passage was in the shorter bay of the hall. In the early 17th century a room was added to N, probably with a large gable-end chimney-stack which has since been removed; the hall can be inferred to have been floored over, because the roof has had laths for a three-sided ceiling below the collar-beams; and a chimney-stack, possibly of timber, must have been built. In the 19th century the house was enlarged to W and N and completely refaced in brick. The room to S of the original house was heightened and a big Venetian window inserted; the date of this is uncertain and may be late 19th century.

SARRATT

(77833)
Chandler's Farm (TG 068981)

was built in the 15th century with an open hall and a cross-wing to E. In the hall the only original details are the open truss of the crown-post roof and the S wall-plate, which appears to have been cut off to W. The E wing probably had a jetty to S; the partitions are modern but may perpetuate an original division into two rooms on each floor, perhaps with a staircase to N. The W wing, added in the 17th century, is not jettied; it has a clasped-purlin roof with windbraces; the chimney-stack to N had a staircase to E. When the open hall received an upper floor and a chimney-stack is not clear, but the comparatively uncommon lateral position of the stack and its form, in so far as rebuilding has not destroyed it, suggest the late 17th century. Then each wing had a staircase; that in the hall is part of an early Victorian renovation which includes a chimney-stack added to the E wing and underbuilding the jetty. In the present century the house has been greatly enlarged and altered.

(39638)
Goldingtons (TQ 038984)

is a manor first recorded in the 13th century. By the late 17th century it was in the possession of Matthew Williams,[1] one of whose descendants rebuilt or at least refronted the house in the middle decades of the 18th century.[2] David Williams Esq. was Sheriff in 1764. Oldfield's drawing shows a symmetrical seven-bay frontage with a service range to S; high garden walls joined it to outbuildings of classical design. In the early 19th century, perhaps *c*1820–40, it was heightened to three storeys, stuccoed, reroofed in slate at a low pitch,[3] and much altered internally; it then had a long service range to W.[4]

Notes
1. VCH II, 440.
2. Oldfield Vol V, 502.
3. Photograph, NMR.
4. HRO, tithe map, DSA4/92/2.

(77834)
The Grove (TQ 081987)

was a manor in the old parish of Watford and in the 16th century was held by the family of Heydon, of whom Francis Heydon, Sheriff in 1583, was an important member. He is the likely builder of a house, the existence of which has to be inferred from much later drawings. During the ownership of Clement Scudamore from 1602 to 1631 certificates of residence dated 1610 and 1611 show that the house was then leased to Lady Anne Waller.[1] By 1703 The Grove was in the hands of Sir William Buck, and either he or his son Charles, who succeeded his father in 1717 and sold the estate in 1728, is said to have rebuilt the main range and W wing. Sir William's probate inventory, taken on 21 October 1717,[2] is difficult to relate to the present house, and its old-fashioned terminology, beginning with hall, great parlour and little parlour, suggests that much of the Elizabethan house remained unaltered. In 1753 it was sold to the Hon Thomas Villers, created Baron Hyde in 1756 and Earl of Clarendon in 1776,[3] who employed Sir Robert Taylor to alter the house.[4] Building-work, not specified in detail, was going on from 1754 to 1761.[5] Payments made between May 1754 and December 1757 include £169 to brickmakers and £214 to bricklayers, and (in 1755) £58 to John Cuenot, carver. In 1760 two payments totalling £49 3s 2d were made to the sculptor John Cheere. The 4th Earl, who was four times Foreign Secretary, employed Edward Blore in 1841–2 to heighten and enlarge the house.[6] Cussans, ascribing the heightening to *c*1780, remarked that 'the late Earl made further additions to the mansion, but so cleverly were they made that it is impossible to designate them'.[7] Further alterations to give the house an early 18th-century appearance are the work of the 5th Earl, who succeeded to the estate in 1870 and died in 1914. In 1939 the house was purchased by the London, Midland and Scottish Railway for use as offices in the event of war,[8] and has been so used ever since.

To make the known development of the house intelligible it is necessary to postulate the existence of an earlier structure which was rebuilt piecemeal. The earliest known illustration[9] shows the house after the alterations of 1754–61 and gives prominence to what was evidently the principal (E) elevation, which is likely to be the work of Sir Robert Taylor. A break of joint in the S elevation, corresponding to the use of blue headers to W and their absence to E, shows that Taylor enlarged an older house of T-plan; and since, given a main entrance to S, such a plan is unusual, particularly in the early 18th century, it is possible to suppose that what Taylor altered was a 16th-century house comparable to Cassiobury Park, Watford, in being built on an imperfect H-plan (⊢). If so, the sequence of events appears to be: (1) in the early 18th century the main range, of seven bays was rebuilt, the three middle bays being framed by pilasters which cut across a first-floor platband and rose to the moulded cornice, and the whole having a parapet with sunk panels ramped up over the doorway; (2) later the W wing was refaced in similar style, with pilasters framing the three-bay centrepiece of the W elevation; (3) probably between 1754 and 1761 the E wing was demolished and rebuilt; the cornice and parapet were returned along the new entrance front to E, the parapet still with sunk panels corresponding to the windows flanking the pedimented frontispiece.

How the principal rooms were disposed is now difficult to understand, all original detail having been removed. In the early 18th century the door in the middle of the S elevation led into a large hall flanked by two important rooms, the principal staircase to N being reached through a lobby rather like one at Cassiobury Park, Watford. The W wing may have included a dining room; the kitchen probably lay to N of the courtyard and the curved passage may be a comparatively early feature of the plan. When the E wing was built the entrance was transferred to that side of the house, so providing an early example of the end-entrance plan. Since the new entrance-hall had a kitchen to E, the room to W was probably the new dining room. Such an arrangement implies the existence of the right-angled corridor connecting kitchen and dining room and either a new and larger staircase where the present one stands – the likely solution – or a long first-floor corridor running E from the main staircase of the early 18th-century house. By c1800[10] a semicircular projection, with two windows on each floor, had been added in the re-entrant angle formed by the main range and W wing. Blore's work in 1841–2 included the addition of an attic storey capped by a balustrade with urns, and probably an extension to N of the W wing. A range to NE running obliquely to the rest of the house is probably Blore's work, as also are extensive service rooms S of it. No attempt was made to work out the development of this part of the house in detail.

For illustrations, see *English Houses 1200–1800*, Figs 205 (plate), 206.

Notes
1. PRO E115/408/24; E115/416/6.
2. PRO Prob 3/20 84.
3. VCH II, 462.
4. Colvin 1978, 817.
5. Bodl, MS Clarendon dep c 350–6; subsequently reclaimed by Lord Clarendon.
6. Colvin 1978, 118.
7. Cussans 1879–81, Vol III (ii), 170.
8. PRO British Transport Historical Records, L M and S R Board Minute 3926.
9. Oldfield Vol VII, 80.
10. Ibid.

(77835)
Redheath (TQ 066970),

now York House School, is connected with an estate of that name which belonged to the Baldwin family from the early 16th century.[1] In 1666 Henry Baldwin paid tax on eight hearths;[2] in 1709 his son Thomas died and the estate descended to his nephew Charles Finch Esq., who in 1712 (date-panel) added to W an imposing block one room deep and of three storeys (Fig 116).

Fig 116 *Redheath, Sarratt: block plan of existing 1712 house and demolished wings*

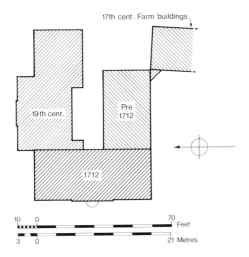

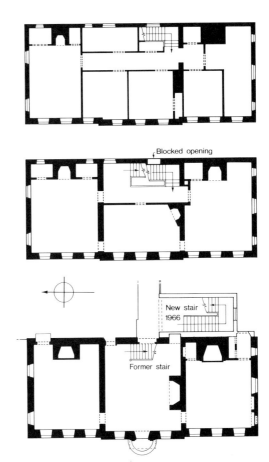

Fig 117 *Redheath, Sarratt: existing ground-floor plan; reconstruction of first and second-floor plans*

Minor works were undertaken in the 1740s and in 1866 the house was enlarged to N and altered inside by Henry Charles Finch.[3] After c1900 the house passed through several hands[4] until it became a school in 1966; whatever remained of the pre-1712 house was replaced by extensive buildings, mostly single-storeyed, to E. The 1712 block comprises three rooms on the two principal floors and four on the second floor (Fig 117); the large room at each end (one now subdivided) had fireplaces, the two small ones at the front of the house were unheated. On the ground floor the middle room is both entrance and staircase-hall; cellars extend throughout. Kitchen and service rooms were evidently in the old house, the only remains of which are two double-ovolo moulded beams re-used in the cellars. The cupola may have been added in 1743, the date inscribed `George Clarke, Whitechapple', on the clock mechanism (now removed). A pane of glass, also removed, is inscribed `John King blummer/and Glasier from Watford/in Hartford Shire 1747/ Wm Crawley Labbour'; it may indicate some renewal of the windows then. A single-storey NE wing, said to be a 19th-century addition, may correspond to the work of 1866, but if so it has been refaced in brick comparatively recently, when additions to S were removed. Some original panelling survives but much is modern.

Notes
1. VCH II, 461.
2. PRO E179/248/25.
3. Cussans, 1879–81, Vol III (ii), 182–3.
4. *Rickmansworth Historian* Spring 1963, **5** 94–5.

SAWBRIDGEWORTH

(77836)
Nos 1/3 Church Street (TL 484148)

are of the 16th century, being dated by moulded beams, and formed a special-purpose building such as a town or church house. The ground floor was divided into a large middle room with a smaller room at each end; the disposition of the first floor is less certain but may have comprised only two rooms, the smaller one to E being of the same size as the one below and the large one corresponding to the hall of other such buildings (cf Guildhall, Nos 57–61 High Street, Ashwell). There is no sign of an original chimney-stack. The first addition, a timber-framed wing to NE, is of the early 17th century. In the late 17th century the street (S) front was provided with three-light windows with moulded mullions and transoms and was pargeted in a simple wavy pattern.

(77837)
The Elms Health Centre, Bell Street (TL 481148),

timber framed, of two storeys and attics and of c1700, has a plastered front to N which is divided into panels by incised lines (cf Cawthorne, 51 St Andrew Street, Hertford). The plan comprises a wide entrance-hall lit by two windows flanking the entrance; the room to E is lit by one window, that to W by two, producing an asymmetrical elevation. Little original detail now remains.

(77838)
Great Hyde Hall (TL 496154)

was a manor belonging to the family of Jocelyn from the early 13th to the mid 20th century but was not always their principal seat; Thomas Jocelyn, who was created Knight of the Bath in 1547, was styled 'of High Roding', Essex.[1] Probably the present house was begun in the lifetime of Thomas's son Richard, who was described as 'of Hyde Hall' in 1572[2] and who died in 1605. He was succeeded by Robert, Sheriff in 1645, whose eldest surviving son, also Robert, inherited in 1664, was created baronet in 1665 and was Sheriff in 1677; he is likely to have built or altered the house engraved by Drapentier c1700.[3] The next

member of the family to be Sheriff was Sir Conyers Jocelyn in 1745, who owned the house from 1741 to 1778 and probably refaced it.[4] In 1797, Hyde Hall came by collateral descent to Robert, 3rd Viscount Jocelyn and Auditor-General of the exchequer, for whom Jeffrey Wyatt (later Sir Jeffrey Wyattville) produced designs in 1803[5] and rebuilt the house in 1806–7.[6] Soon afterwards the house was leased out, first to Alexander Annesley[7] and then to Admiral Sir Thomas Williams.[8] In 1869 H L Bischoffstein Esq., of London, 'thoroughly renovated the interior',[9] and further alterations were undertaken for William Henry Jocelyn, 6th Earl of Roden, some time between 1897 and 1904.[10] The staircase is said to have been rebuilt in 1920.[11] No architectural detail earlier than Wyatt's now survives in the house but from the evidence of old illustrations coupled with that of the plan the earlier development can be inferred (Fig 118).

The house originally faced S; its asymmetrical appearance c1700[12] suggests that the rusticated brickwork, flat-arch window-heads and alternating segmental-headed and pedimented gables, all of the mid–late 17th century, represent the refronting of an earlier house in which a large hall was flanked by parlours to E and W; the hall clearly had a large external chimney-stack and another stack otherwise unaccounted for may imply the existence of a wing to W. All traces of 17th-century work in the S range have disappeared except for the low ceilings. In the early 18th century this range was heightened to three storeys and refaced[13] as an imposing garden front of nine bays; it appears to have had three shallow projections, those at the ends being of two bays, that in the middle of three, like a more restrained version of the W elevation of The Grove, Sarratt. The projection to W was repeated on the W elevation, giving the appearance of a corner tower; this was balanced to N by a similar projection which, in the top storey, was no more than a façade.[14] Between them a two-storey range of five bays must antedate the N projection; it has in the middle a two-storey porch which is likely to be of the 17th century, the doorway and pediment forming part of the general refurbishment of this elevation. This reconstruction presents difficulties: either the L-shaped 17th-century house had two entrances or the W porch is of much later date than others of the kind. No evidence has been found to show that the plan was quadrangular.[15] In 1803–6 Wyatt refaced the S and W elevations in a uniform classical manner, lowering the middle bays of the S front to create another corner tower to E. In the re-entrant angle of the S and W ranges he built a large saloon, perhaps with top lighting, and to E of it added a large and lofty dining room with lobbies at each end. Service rooms may have stood to N of the saloon; if so they were subsequently removed.

Notes

1. VCH III, 341.
2. *Visitations*, 14.
3. Chauncy I, 358.
4. Oldfield Vol V, 448.
5. Linstrum 1972, 238.
6. Clutterbuck Vol III, 203.
7. *DNB*.
8. Neale 1819–29, Vol II; *DNB*.
9. Cussans 1870–3, Vol I (i), 82.
10. Morris 1902–4, 207.
11. Pevsner and Cherry 1977, 271.
12. Chauncy I, 357.
13. Oldfield Vol II, 75.
14. Ibid.
15. Linstrum 1972, 78.

Fig 118 *Great Hyde Hall, Sawbridgeworth: development of ground-floor plan*

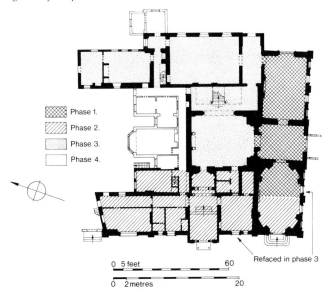

Phase 1.
Phase 2.
Phase 3.
Phase 4.

Refaced in phase 3

0 5 feet   60

0 2 metres   20

(77839)
The Parsonage (TL 485147)

was built `at his great Cost and Charges' in 1685 by John Ward, vicar 1678–92, and was described as `a fair House of Timber, on the South Side of the Church-yard'.[1] It replaced the one described in a parliamentary survey of 1649,[2] which had `a fair gatehouse' combined with a lodging chamber for servants and a small pigeon-house over it; hall, two wainscot parlours, two kitchens, four butteries, two milk houses, five lodging chambers and some dozen other rooms. The point of most interest is the duplication of kitchen and butteries, which is comparable to that at Place House, Ware, in the late 17th century.

Notes
1. Chauncy I, 361.
2. Lambeth Palace Archives, x11a/16.

(77840)
Pishiobury Park (TL 480134),

formerly the manor of Sawbridgeworth,[1] had in 1304 a hall with chapel and chambers[2] and by 1534 a large park.[3] Acquired in 1555 by Thomas Mildmay it descended in 1567 to his second son Walter Mildmay,[4] who built `a very neat and fair pile of building, for the Mannor-house',[5] perhaps not long after he inherited the estate and no doubt before he became Sheriff in

Fig 119 *Pishiobury Park, Sawbridgeworth: ground and first-floor plans*

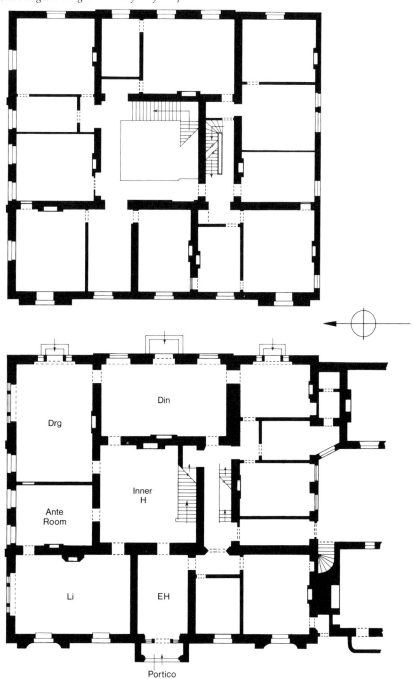

1590. Early 17th-century `Particulars' speak of `a fair well built house in perfect good repair'.[6] In 1614 the manor was purchased by its most famous owner, Lionel Cranfield,[7] who, in the following year, caused a new porch to be built; the bills include payments to Peter Thornton for `carving work about the porch' and mention six hanging pieces, three pendants `between the hanging pieces', three fluted columns and ten balusters. Where the porch was made is not stated; its carriage to the house cost £9 10s.[8] Cranfield owned the house for 10 years and in 1622, when he was created Earl of Middlesex, an inventory was compiled of `all such household stuff remaining at Pishobury'.[9] These words tend to confirm that Cranfield's main concerns there were the farms and gardens;[10] nevertheless the study contained `36 great books with white covers' as well as two bibles and nine other books.

After an interval in royal possession the manor was acquired in 1635 by Thomas Hewett who, at the Restoration, was created baronet and made Sheriff (1660). At Michaelmas 1662 Sir Thomas Hewett paid for 20 hearths[11] and not long afterwards carried out some work which included adding to the porch a sundial bearing the date 1664. Drapentier's engraving[12] and Salmon's remark in 1728 that `the present house...tho' of so long standing, is remarkable for its strength and lofty Rooms',[13] both suggest that the house had even then been comparatively little altered except for the porch.

In 1782 the house was burnt out and was subsequently rebuilt by James Wyatt;[14] four years later the then owner, Jeremiah Milles Esq., became Sheriff. In the early years of the present century, probably c1904 (dated rain-water head on outbuilding), much of the internal detail was renewed and the stucco put on by Wyatt was removed. In a suitable light it can be seen that Wyatt, who is said to have `utilised some of the old material',[15] did more than that, for in fact all four corners incorporate undisturbed 16th-century brickwork and the plan suggests that more remains inside. The Drapentier engraving, an inventory of 1662,[16] and comparative material from the Thorpe drawings[17] make a possible conjectural reconstruction of the plan at that date (*English Houses 1200–1800*, Fig 99); changes of nomenclature apart, it may not have altered in essentials since the house was built. The inventory lists the following rooms which are indicated on the plans, some by numbers (in brackets):

Three garrets, 1 with a closet, on the right hand and 3 on the left;

first-floor chamber over the kitchen, closet near this room (1), *a little room by this closet* (2);

the Red Chamber, closet and room at the red chamber door (3);

chamber over the little parlour, closet, room to this chamber (4);

room over the porch (5);

the Great Chamber, the hole within this room (6);

the great stairs;

Ground floor, *the wrought chamber, room within this chamber* (7), *Great Parlour, Drawing Room, closet at the back stairs foot* (8), *Sir Thomas Hewytt's own closet* (9), *the Little Parlour, Hall, porch* (10), *buttery;*

basement, *beer cellar, wine cellar, entry at the great stairs foot, room under the great stairs, entry by the kitchen, pantry, wet and dry larders.*

On the ground floor the precise position of the Great Parlour, which might have been expected in the NE corner, and the Drawing Room, are uncertain; so too, on the first floor, is the location of the small rooms around the Chamber over the Kitchen. The new work proclaimed by the sundial of 1664 certainly included the pediments above the bay windows and the garden wall with its gatepiers.

In the reconstruction after 1782 the ranges to W, N and E became a series of grand rooms, and the courtyard was roofed over and made into a staircase-hall with a `Statuary Marble Chimney piece Elaborately carved by the Celebrated John Bacon [the elder]';[18] the identifiable rooms are indicated on the modern plan (Fig 119).

For illustrations, see *English Houses 1200–1800*, Figs 98 (plate), 99, 100 (plate).

Notes

1. VCH III, 336.
2. PRO S C 12/8/43.
3. Munby 1977, 135.
4. VCH III, 338, n2.
5. Chauncy I, 351.
6. Kent RO, Pishiobury U 269/E286, 2–3.
7. *DNB*.
8. Kent RO, Pishiobury, U 269/A512.
9. Ibid, U269/E277.
10. Tawney 1958, 277–8.
11. PRO E179/248/27; E179/75/31.
12. Chauncy I, 348.
13. Salmon 1728, 262.
14. VCH III, 338.
15. Ibid.
16. PRO Prob 4/5021.
17. Summerson 1966, eg Plates T111, 118, 211.
18. SC 1865, HRO, D/P41 29/3.

SHENLEY

(77841)
Salisbury Hall (TL 028195)

is the house of the manor formerly known as Shenley Hall; it acquired the name in the late 14th century after coming to John Montagu, 3rd Earl of Salisbury (1350?–1400)[1] by his marriage to the widow of Sir Alan Buxhull (d.1372). A `Curia well built' is mentioned in an extent of 1276[2] and armorial tiles dated to c1380 which were found during excavations[3] indicate that Montagu did some building. In 1507 two of the four parts into which ownership of the manor was then divided were bought by Sir John Cutte, Under-Treasurer to Henry VII and Henry VIII,[4] who subsequently obtained the other two. `Old Cutte buildid Horeham-haule a very sumptuus house...by Thaxstede...buildid at Childerley in Cambridgeshir...[at Salisbury Parke] by S Alban's';[5] he was Sheriff in 1519. His work or part of it was drawn c1800.[6] What difference `buildid' and `buildid at' implies, if any, is uncertain: it may imply a distinction between Cutte's activities at his principal and minor seats; also, in the light of the architectural history of Salisbury Hall, between altering an existing building and putting up a completely new one. What may be involved here is the principle of alternate rebuilding. The ground plan of the late 17th-century house is so traditional, with the entrance-passage at one end of the hall and the parlour at the other, as to make it certain that it perpetuates an older building in a new architectural guise. If so, the Tudor work to N drawn in 1800 is likely to have included the service quarters and perhaps a parlour too. A probate inventory dated 24 January 1620 of Henry Hull[7] implies that the house was of no great size: the rooms comprise hall, parlour, kitchen, chamber over kitchen, chamber over the buttery and milk house, and `over the porche'. Only the hall and parlour were necessarily to S of the cross-passage, and the lack of reference to a chamber over the hall suggests it was still open to the roof. This accords with the completeness of the late 17th-century rebuilding of that end. All that survive of the earlier work are a few blackened rafters incorporated in the present roof. Later in the 17th century the house was in the possession of Richard, son of Thomas Cole, `one of the gent'n that followed the Erle of Lester, and, after, the Queen's Servant'; the herald's uncertainty about his rank is shown by the note: `Respit the Armes...To be disclaymed'.[8] Nevertheless this Richard Cole may be the man of that name who was Sheriff in 1640, although his monument (he died in 1653) does not mention his holding the office.[9] In 1663 his son William paid for 12 hearths.[10]

In 1668 the manor was bought by William and John Snell as trustees for their relative Sir Jeremiah Snow, goldsmith,[11] to whom is ascribed the rebuilding of the upper end of the house,

Fig 120 *Salisbury Hall, Shenley: ground and first-floor plans*

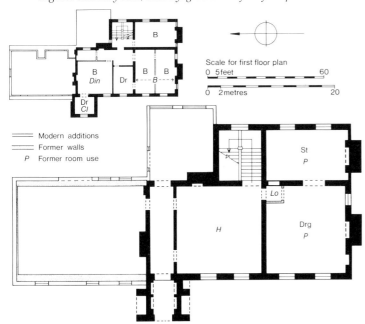

including the passage; it looks like the first stage towards a large symmetrical house of nine bays. Snow's chequered financial career no doubt accounts for the unfinished appearance of the house.[12] How much he lived there prior to his death in 1702[13] is uncertain, for his nephew Robert Snow, who was described in a memorial inscription as `Lord of this Manor of Shenley'[14] and paid for 17 and 4 hearths in 1673,[15] presumably resided at Salisbury Hall until his death, aged 32, in 1684. By 1699, when Sir Jeremiah Snow is listed as a freeholder in Shenley,[16] he was no doubt living at the Hall, because other freeholders not residing permanently in the county are described as merchants in London.[17] The hall has a series of stone medallions with profile busts in low relief depicting Julius Caesar, Augustus, Trajan, Marcus Aurelius, Mark Antony, Zenobia and Cleopatra;[18] they were brought from Sopwell, St Albans (demolished 1669–73). To E is the principal staircase and to S the principal parlour (Fig 120). A lobby in the parlour ensured

access to a secondary parlour or study without making the former a passage room. Upstairs the room over the hall was perhaps the dining room, reached from the kitchen by a secondary stair to N; the fireplace, like that in the hall, looks earlier than Jeremiah Snow's time but the latter is certainly original, and both are stylistically somewhat retarded. The remainder of the first floor was occupied by one large and one small bedroom, both with fireplaces; and there were attic bedrooms. All service rooms were in the earlier block. In 1702 the property reverted to the Snells and remained with them until 1831.[19] That part of the house to N of the passage was demolished in 1819[20] and replaced by a rectangular block.[21] This range was rebuilt in 1884 and again c1955.

For illustrations, see *English Houses 1200–1800*, Figs 36 (plate), 313 (plate).

Notes
1. *DNB*.
2. PRO SC 11/Roll 296.
3. Inf. Mr W J Goldsmith.
4. VCH II, 267.
5. Leland *Itinerary*, Vol IV, 30–1.
6. Oldfield Vol VI, 38.
7. HRO, H22/542.
8. *Visitations*, 42.
9. Chauncy II, 453.
10. PRO E179/248/24/19.
11. VCH II, 276.
12. Girouard 1959b, 709.
13. VCH II, 267.
14. Chauncy II, 453.
15. PRO E179/375/31.
16. VCH *Herts Families*, 175.
17. Ibid, 277, Great Hormead.
18. Girouard 1959b, 711.
19. VCH II, 267.
20. Ibid.
21. Plan in conveyance dated 1830, HRO, 71217.

STANDON

(77842)
Nos 59/61 Collier's End (TL 371207),

built in the early 16th century, had an open hall and two jettied cross-wings (Fig 121). The wing to N is also jettied to E; possibly the original staircase rose to a landing on the rear jetty. The service wing to S has a crown-post roof of two bays, the open truss being slightly to W as if to allow for a staircase at the rear. In the 17th century a chimney-stack and first floor were inserted

Fig 121 *Nos 59/61 Collier's End, Standon: plan*

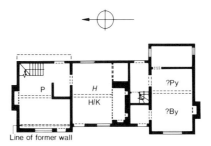

in the hall. In the late 18th or early 19th century the house was divided into two cottages and the front jetties underbuilt; much of the existing detail is of that date.

For illustrations, see *English Houses 1200–1800*, Figs 74 (plate), 75 (plate).

(77843)
Fabdens (TL 372172)

was built *c*1500, the first reference to it being in the will of John Kyrkeby of Standon, proved 22 January 1522/3, who bequeathed to his son Nicholas `my place called Fabydons'.[1] It is a Wealden house with a hall of two unequal bays (Fig 122); the open truss has hollow-chamfered posts, cambered tie-beam and moulded crown-post. The studded partition to E of the hall has peg-holes for a bench, with mortises for a bench-end on the N jamb of the door leading to parlour and staircase. To W the

Fig 122 *Fabdens, Standon: plan*

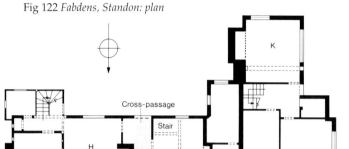

two four-centred heads of the service doors are exposed; there was formerly a third door which led to a staircase, the stair trap being exposed in the adjoining bay. The bearer in the W bay is mortised and grooved for a stud-and-plank partition, the studs being placed further apart than is usual. In the chamber over the service rooms is a three-light diamond-mullioned window near the middle of the W wall. This bay is spanned axially to the house by a tie-beam intended to resist the thrust of the hipped roof. In the roof to E is a smoke vent formed of boards laid upon the collar-beams and a low wattle-and-daub partition immediately below the roof gablet; this was intended to remove through the gabled vent of the first-floor chamber the smoke rising over the partitions at the end of the hall, which terminated at the collar-beams. To SW is a kitchen, formerly detached; though greatly altered it retains part of an old chimney-stack; no datable features remain but having apparently always been lofted over it is probably of the mid or late 16th century. In the 17th century a chimney-stack serving ground and first-floor fireplaces was built in the hall, backing on to the cross-passage; an upper floor was put in and a staircase was added to S of the E wing. Early in the 18th century the service rooms were converted into a parlour or dining room, and a pantry was added to the kitchen. The chimney-stack of the E wing is probably of the late 18th century. In the present century the kitchen and service block were enlarged and greatly altered, and in the 1940s and 1950s the house underwent a careful restoration.

For illustrations, see *English Houses 1200–1800*, Figs 49 (plate), 305 (plate).

Note
1. PCC wills, 1522/3, I Bodefelde.

(77844)
Fisher's Farm, Collier's End (TL 371207)

comprises a main range with low eaves and two gabled cross-wings of two storeys. The main range comprised a late-medieval open hall about 20 ft 6 ins by 16 ft (6 m x 5 m), ie a square living-space and a cross-passage. A coeval bay to S may have had an upper storey; the evidence is insufficient. The wing to N, of *c*1600, has close-studding; the first floor has chamfered and stopped joists and is carried on an axial bearer; there is no jetty and no evidence of a fireplace. The wing to S is of the mid 17th century; the chimney-stack has three diagonal shafts; the room to E was probably the kitchen, with an unheated service room to W; the first-floor room to E has a fireplace. The building of a fireplace and an upper floor within the hall is dated to the late 17th century by the square chimney-shafts. Surprisingly, there is insufficient space beside the stack for a lobby-entrance, and perhaps the length of the house necessitated placing the entrance where it now is, in the S bay of the middle range. In the early 19th century this bay became a staircase-hall.

(77845)
Green End Farm (TL 359199)

comprises a main range, and a cross-wing to W. Rendering and internal concealment of timbers make its history uncertain. The cross-wing is of the early 16th century and was probably jettied to S, though no evidence can be seen; a cased beam on the ground floor may represent an original division into two rooms, the smaller one, containing the staircase, being to N; the roof has clasped-purlins. A small open hall coeval with the wing can be inferred; it was replaced in the mid 17th century by a two-storey main range comprising a hall with wide fireplace, a staircase projection to N of the latter and an unheated bay to E incorporating two service rooms. In the wing a fireplace was added and the original two rooms made into a large parlour; to N a service room, perhaps a dairy with bedroom above, was added. Alterations in the 19th century included adding a lean-to to E and putting a fireplace in the former dairy to make a kitchen.

(77846)
Hangingwood Cottage (TL 387201)

comprises the upper end bay of a two-bay open hall and the adjoining storeyed bay; it has a crown-post roof and was built *c*1500 (Fig 123). The partition between the rooms has a feature which can rarely be seen: all but one of the studs are kept firm by a combination of tongue-and-groove joints with wedging. A chimney-stack and upper floor were added in the hall in the 17th century; and a small fireplace was provided in the parlour in the 19th century, by which time the lower end of the house had been pulled down.

(77847)
The Old Waggon, High Cross (TL 362185)

is late medieval and comprises an open hall with crown-post roof and a jettied cross-wing to N; it is partly rendered and partly weather-boarded. A fireplace inserted in the hall can be dated to the first quarter of the 17th century by a floral scroll painted on it; the scroll, on a reddish-brown ground, and the flowers and leaves, are outlined in black; the leaves are blue-green and the flower centres are red or brown.

(77848)
Plashes (TL 379203)

has a plan which does not conform to any known type and is apparently the result of a complicated development (Fig 124; and cf Brick House Farm, Hunsdon). Its oldest parts are a cross-

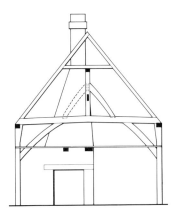

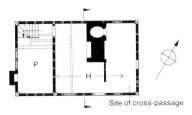

Fig 123 *Hangingwood Cottage, Standon: plan and section*

wing to N (correctly NE), of the mid 17th century, and a range to S, which is not demonstrably earlier. The cross-wing, of two storeys with cellar and attics, has an internal chimney-stack with fireplaces in both ground-floor rooms; the two first-floor fireplaces may also be original; to N of the stack a staircase (now removed) rose from cellar to attic and to S a lobby gave access from the S range to both ground-floor rooms. The S range may replace an earlier building, there being now no room describable as a hall; in the S range and adjoining the wing is a staircase of mid 17th-century appearance, parts of which appear to be old; to S of the staircase are three service rooms; the W side of the range is taken up by a corridor leading from the wing to a kitchen to S. The kitchen, of one storey and attic only, may have had a wooden chimney originally; it also has a ceiling which extends into the slightly wider two-storey range to N, a structural curiosity for which no satisfactory explanation can be offered. To E a gabled staircase turret is probably not later than *c*1700. In the 19th century a wing gabled to W was added in the re-entrant angle formed by the S range and wing; it incorporates a narrow entrance-hall adjoining the wing and leading to the staircase, and a reception room to S.

(77849)
Rigery's Farm (TL 364208)

incorporates to N part of a late medieval house, probably the open hall, which extended to S. In the 17th century a chimney-stack was inserted and presumably the two bays to S were added or rebuilt then, although this is a surprisingly late period for an end-jetty. The ground-floor room is unusually long in relation to its width and looks as if it should have a partition at the binding-beam, which was encased at the time of visit; however, such a proportion is not unknown in houses of the period (cf The Abbot's House, Abbots Langley (Fig 2), room to NW). The conjoined diagonal shafts of the chimney-stack rise from a square base which is level with the ridge of the hall roof; consequently the shafts are partly masked by the higher roof to

S. This may indicate either that the end-jettied block is later than the stack or that the masking is the consequence of defective design. The staircase is to W of the stack; a wing gabled to W was added in the re-entrant angle in the 18th century.

For illustrations, see *English Houses 1200–1800*, Figs 59 (plate), 60.

(77850)
Standon Lordship (TL 392214)

was held by the families of Clare (from 1086) and Mortimer (from 1368), then by the Dukes of York, and in the early 16th century by Catherine of Aragon and Jane Seymour successively. The medieval house was evidently of some importance since it appears to have been the residence from time to time of the great lords who owned it; this may be implied in the early 15th century by the exemption of the manor from the exactions of the harbingers of the royal household and their exclusions from

Fig 124 *Plashes, Standon: development diagrams*

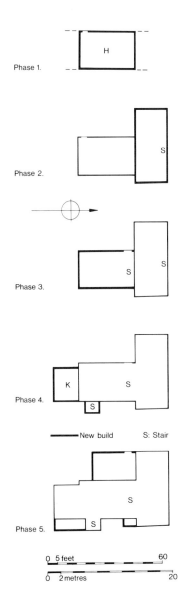

lodging there.[1] It was a sufficiently good house for Sir Ralph Sadler, after being appointed in 1539 to various offices connected with the Lordship, to receive Thomas Cromwell; in 1540 he obtained a grant of the manor[2] and subsequently built a house. Its size, said to be due to the steward having built it larger than his absent master intended,[3] may rather be related to Sadler's reputation as the richest commoner in England and to his tenure of office in 1540–3 as one of the principal secretaries of the state;[4] it is known from an engraving of c1700[5] and a plan made in the early 19th century before demolition. The S (hall) range had on the porch a tablet bearing the initials R S and a shield of arms (a lion rampant sinister parted per fess in a field ermine) and flanked by two smaller tablets bearing the date 1546;[6] the wooden frame of the hall door also bore Sadler's initials in the spandrels. Perhaps the courtyard plan was complete by 1561 when Queen Elizabeth first stayed there; if not then, certainly by 1578 on her second visit.[7] The W or gatehouse range, part of which is all that survives of the house, is probably Sadler's work, the wide arched opening, moulded, being of that date. The hall was in the middle of the S range; there were apparently service rooms to E and a parlour to W of it. Two windows lighting the cellars[8] are blocked; each has hollow-chamfered jambs and head and a wooden lintel. In the W range the most remarkable feature was the provision of four newel staircases flanking the entrance. The lower courses of the NW and SW flanking turrets remain; the brickwork in the chimney-stack adjoining the SW turret is largely original; and much of the brickwork immediately adjoining the stack, into which two modern windows have been inserted, is probably original. Otherwise the walls are of 1872 and many of the details must be after 1927. Drawings of 1834[9] and 1837[10] show that little else of the 16th-century work can have survived. A point about the W range is that all drawings of the entrance front show the windows to N of the gateway lower than those to S, so perhaps this range was of two builds. Presumably the range to N provided lodgings. The E range appears to have been earlier than that to N, judging by their awkward junction, although the former had perhaps been rebuilt by the time the plan was drawn. A suggestion that John Thorpe (1565–c1655) was responsible for additions to Sadler's house[11] appears to be a confusion with an architect of the same name who incorporated the ruin into a hunting lodge in 1872.

The subsequent development of the house cannot be followed in detail. Part of it was in use as a farmhouse c1800, with a small shelter shed for cattle built in front.[12] The house was in repair until sold by the heirs of William Plumer who died

in 1822; by 1894 it had been largely demolished with only the gateway and the block immediately to S remaining.[13] In 1872 that part was rebuilt and enlarged as a hunting lodge for the second Duke of Wellington.[14]

For illustrations, see *English Houses 1200–1800*, Figs 88 (plate), 89.

Notes
1. VCH III, 353.
2. VCH III, 353–4.
3. Fuller *Worthies*, Vol II, 41.
4. *DNB*.
5. Chauncy I, 340.
6. Oldfield Vol VI, 91.
7. Nichols 1821–3, I, 100; II, 106.
8. Drapentier, Chauncy 1700.
9. Buckler Vol II, 83.
10. James Wilcox.
11. Heal 1943, 111.
12. Oldfield Vol VI, 86; Nichols 1821–3, II, 108.
13. Buckler Vol II, 83.
14. VCH III, 354–5.

(77851)
Sutes (TL 366189)

derives its name from the family of Robert Swote whose name appears in the Subsidy Roll of 1330;[1] possibly it was built by Robert himself but may be somewhat later. To N and W the walls rise directly from the surviving arms of a moat.

The house comprises a main range to S and a cross-wing to N; the former incorporates two bays and the short screens-passage bay of a comparatively small aisled hall, of which the W aisle and service bay to S have been demolished. On the first floor can be seen the posts, plates and curved braces of the aisled construction, and, incorporated in a later partition, the tie-beam, arch-braces and the foot of the crown-post which formed the spere-truss. The wing has closely spaced, plain joists of large scantling; it was extended to N in the early 16th century (cf Clintons, Little Hadham). Subsequent alterations and additions took place principally in the 17th century, although the lack of original detail makes their dating problematic. When the W aisle was demolished a first floor was inserted over the nave and E aisle and a chimney-stack with lobby-entrance built in the nave; the room to N of the stack was then the hall and that to S the parlour. About the same time a kitchen was created in the wing by the addition of an internal chimney-stack, and a staircase in a

Fig 125 *The Grange, No. 3 High Street, Puckeridge, Standon: first-floor plan*

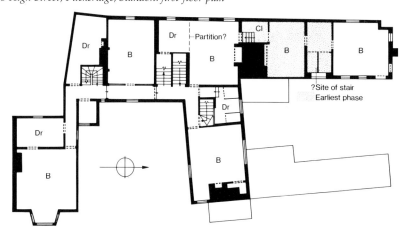

turret in the re-entrant angle to E was built. At what period the presumed service end of the aisled hall was demolished is uncertain; perhaps in the early 19th century when much of the exterior was weatherboarded and the remainder plastered.[2]

Notes
1. Gover, Mawer and Stenton 1938, 199.
2. RCHME 1910, 208.

(77852)
Town Farm, Mill End (TL 396225),

of c1500, comprised an open hall, probably a bay in series with it to W, and a two-storey cross-wing to E. The wing has a cambered tie-beam with chamfered arch-braces; some framing is exposed to N. The length of the hall is uncertain because the setting-out is irregular; it is nearly 20 ft (6 m) wide by only about 18 ft (5·5 m) long so far as can now be traced; the bearer carrying the upper floor of the bay to W is supported by inserted posts and may encroach on the hall. In the late 16th century a chimney-stack was inserted in the hall, backing on to the wing; it has moulded wooden jambs and a cambered lintel and was presumably of timber and plaster originally. Then or perhaps in the 18th century, when the stack was rebuilt in brick, the hall and adjoining bay were heightened to two storeys. In the late 18th century the house was refronted in brick with pilasters, string course and parapet, and fireplaces were provided in the room to SW and the parlour to E.

(77853)
The Grange, No. 3 High Street, Puckeridge,

so called in a deed of 1727, was 'heretofore the Crown'.[1] Its plan shows that the building was an inn by the late 17th century. An inn called The Crown continued to exist in 1753, presumably by mere transferral of the sign, and later amalgamated with The Falcon (see page 176).

The oldest part is to N (Fig 125); although little original work is visible its low proportions and a tie-beam cut through for access on the first floor suggest it was a late-medieval open hall; the bay to N may be contemporary but has been heightened. The range to S, of two storeys, is dated to c1800 by a moulded lintel in the ground-floor room to N, which appears to have formed part of a timber chimney-stack; the stack may have served a second fireplace inserted in the former hall to N, where a plain timber lintel remains. Since the plan as enlarged is unlike that of a normal dwelling house the building may already have been an inn of modest size, with one or more staircases (cf 27 Leyton Road, Harpenden). Not until the late 17th century did it definitely become The Crown inn, when two wings and galleries were added to the S part and probably two staircases, one to S and the other in the wing to NE. The wing to NE, with a large fireplace, was a kitchen. The wing to SE has, on the ground floor, a single lofty room (cf The Grange, High Street, Stevenage). The first floor of the inn comprised three bedrooms with fireplaces, each with an unheated room, perhaps a dressing room or closet, adjoining; and there were attic bedrooms. The chimney-stack in the middle of the street range was rebuilt in brick with two square shafts flanking an octagonal one. At this period the old house to N was linked to the rest only by a ground-floor passage, suggesting it may have provided an inferior kind of accommodation; the upper floor had been inserted by then.

The present rendering and fenestration date from the early 19th century; the staircases are all of that period, the middle one being an addition; and the SE wing was refurbished with barge-boards and the bay window renewed.

Notes
1. Johnson 1963, Pt 2, 11.

(77854)
Thorpe House, No. 19 High Street, Puckeridge (TL 386213)

was built c1500; the form of its plan (Fig 126) and structure suggest it was built as an inn on a restricted site. The street (W) range as built comprised an open hall between two cross-wings. The wider wing to S incorporates a high waggon entrance leading to the yard and a cross-passage providing access to the inn; the passage appears to have been separated from the hall by a screen, in the lower part of which must have stood the doorway now reset between the chimney-breast and staircase, since its head beam is moulded and embattled on both sides. In the upper part of the screen, a post tenoned into the N wall-plate of the wing has a shaped head and was apparently a spere-post. In the hall the E wall has indications of a large window; the framing to N lacks the peg-holes for a bench that are commonly found in a house, but the E wall-plate has a dovetail joint in the right place for a canopy beam. The present division of the N bay may perpetuate something like the original arrangement with a staircase to E. A second staircase, necessary to reach the upper floor over the entrance, may have risen from the yard to the floored space over the passage, with a second flight to reach the room over the waggonway. Possibly the service rooms lay to S of the waggonway; the building there now appears to be of later date than the inn but could not be examined.

The later history of the building was not recovered satisfactorily. A floor and chimney-stack were inserted in the hall in the late 16th century; the lintel of the fireplace suggests the stack originally may have been of timber. A wing was added to E at about this time; a carved and moulded bearer shows that it incorporated an important room. The hall was heightened c1700 and the chimney-stack rebuilt in brick with a fireplace in the chamber over the hall.

(77855)
Nos 30/32 High Street, Puckeridge (TL 386235)

were built in the late 16th century as a three-cell house with a continuous jetty to E. It had an internal chimney-stack and probably a lobby-entrance but in recent years has been

Fig 126 *Thorpe House, No. 19 High Street, Puckeridge, Standon: plan*

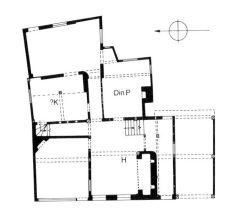

completely gutted of all but the structural partitions. The roof has clasped-purlins and windbraces.

(77856)
No. 52 High Street, Puckeridge

is a late medieval Wealden house; the roof, of crown-post type with braces to the collar-purlin, is hipped with a small smoke gablet to S and is gabled to N. The upper room to N extended over the cross-passage. In the late 16th century a floor was inserted in the hall and jettied to give a flush front; a chimney-stack was also inserted backing on to the cross-passage; it had moulded timber jambs and lintel, and since there is no sign of coeval brickwork or chimney-shafts the stack may have been of timber originally. A

wing to SW with hip roof is probably a 17th-century kitchen; to W a range of two storeys was added parallel to the house in the early 19th century, perhaps to provide a dining room.

(77857)
The Crown and Falcon Inn, No. 33 High Street, Puckeridge
(TL 386233)

was presumably built as an inn because it incorporated a wide vehicle entrance; otherwise it appears to have been an orthodox three-cell house with a continuous jetty.[1]

Note

1. Plans of 1883 and 1946, RCHME archive; Buckler Vol II, 61.

Fig 127 *Bonningtons, Stanstead Abbots: reconstruction of original plans*

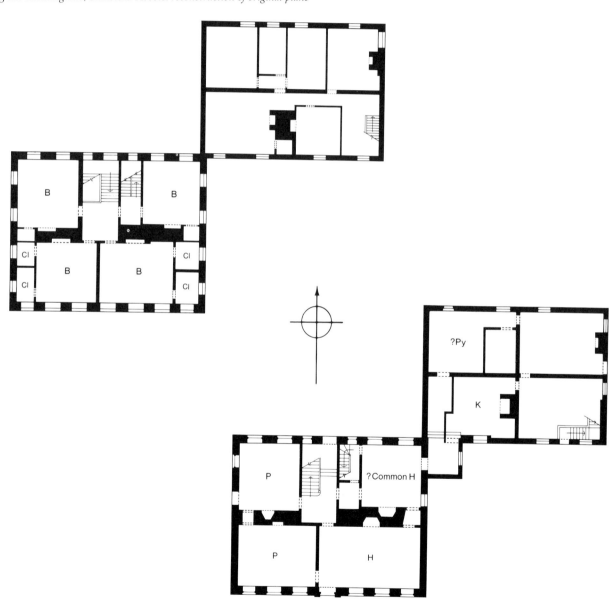

STANSTEAD ABBOTS

(77858)
Bonningtons (TL 408131)

is first mentioned in an abstract of title[1] stating that `Ralph Skynner alias Byde built the seat of Bonnington Hall and converted several parts of the lands contiguous thereto into gardens, orchards, walks and fishponds'. It appears to have replaced the `Messuage wherein George Ansell then dwelt standing on Bonnington's Hill' which changed hands in 1686. John Byde, son of Ralph, `hath of late years [c1725] laid out a great deal of money in lasting improvements on the premises'. The house is of brick and of two storeys with attics, and was built c1690. A reconstruction of the original plan (Fig 127) shows the pairs of closets which survive at the ends of the principal first-floor rooms and it is possible that similar closets existed on the ground floor too. Little evidence of John Byde's work remains but it can be guessed that he replaced mullion-and-transom windows with sashes. The service quarters are built corner-to-corner with the house and have always been joined, originally only on the ground floor, by a lobby-like structure. By 1833 a verandah had been added along the front and also a conservatory at the SW corner. In 1858 Bonningtons had dining, drawing and morning rooms, library, ten bedrooms, three dressing rooms and four servants' rooms (Fig 128).[2] In 1863 the house was the seat of Salisbury Baxendale, Sheriff in that year.

Fig 128 *Bonningtons, Stanstead Abbots: 1858 plans*

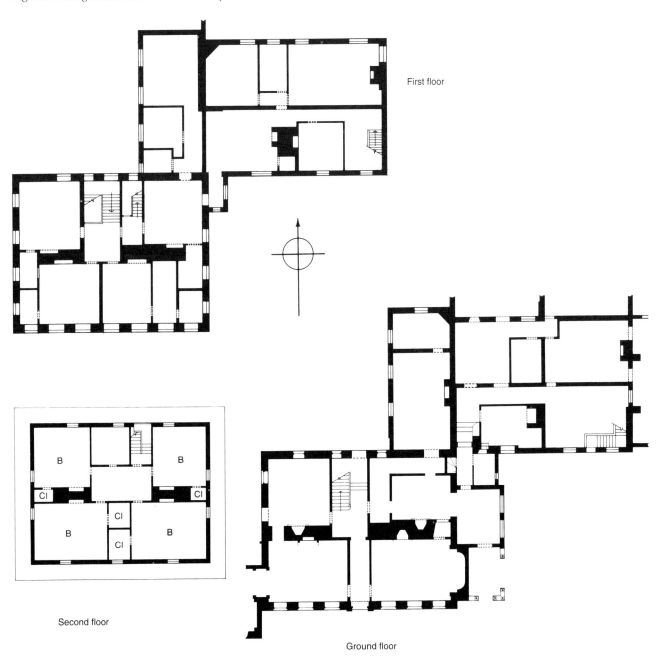

First floor

Second floor

Ground floor

177

Notes
1. HRO, D/EB 1630 T6.
2. Advertisement in *The Hertfordshire Mercury and County Press*, 5 June 1858.

(81063)
No. 77 High Street,

of two storeys, was built in the early 16th century; the plan then comprised hall to E and parlour or service room to W and an internal chimney-stack, probably with lobby-entrance to N. A slight difference in height between the E and W rooms suggests that the first floors are of different date; to E of the stack are two brackets, one with a simple moulding, which may be part of a timber chimney-stack; possibly the hall originally was open to the roof, the bay to W being of two storeys. In the SW corner of the W room two mortises for joists running parallel to the wall may have formed a landing at the head of a staircase. A bay was added to W *c*1800 and the entrance transferred to an outshot to S. The first-floor windows were fitted with triangular-headed lights and the dormer windows with cusped barge-boards; the chimney-stack is probably of the same date.

(77859)
The Red Lion Inn, No. 1 High Street (TL 386119),

was built in the late 15th century and comprised an open hall between two cross-wings jettied to S (Fig 129); some framing exposed in the W wing on the first floor includes, in the E wall, to S, a blocked four-light window with diamond-mullions which looked out over the hall roof. In the mid–late 17th century the open hall was replaced by a somewhat wider one of two storeys, jettied, with attics, thus creating an imposing elevation in which two wide gabled wings flank three narrower gables in the main range. The 17th-century framing is plain, with tension-braces and arch-braces of shallow curvature. At this period the building became an inn (if it were not so earlier). The early 19th-century staircase rises to a large landing off which open a room to S and probably two rooms in the E wing, and, in the bay to W, a corridor; the staircase and corridor were in the normal relation to the inn yard before the building was extended in the 19th century. The internal partition forming the corridor is timber framed and has, to W, two adjacent doorways (blocked) into a large room (*c*.21 ft x 14 ft (6·4 m x 4·3 m)) which was perhaps the dining room; the latter has a bolection-moulded fireplace and doorways into the two front bedrooms adjoining to E and W. All the rooms of the middle range have plaster ceilings and ceilings were also inserted into the wing rooms, although there is no evidence that the roof space was utilised in any way. In the 19th century the inn was enlarged to N.

Fig 129 The Red Lion Inn, Stanstead Abbots: plan

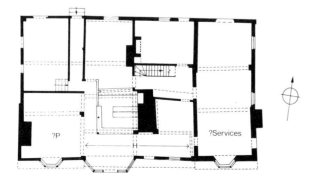

(77860)
Rye House (TL 386099)

was built by Sir Andrew Ogard, a naturalised Dane, to whom a licence to crenellate was issued in 1443.[1] William Worcester notes that `the building of the Inner Court with brick and the rooms with the cloister cost, including repairs, a total of 2 [2,000?] marks and more'.[2] What was meant by `repairs' is uncertain because the house and its new moat appear to have been built on an unencumbered site. In 1683 it was the scene of the Rye House Plot to murder Charles II and the Duke of York, and after the failure of this attempt a plan and elevation of the house were published;[3] they are now the only evidence of the house itself, which was rebuilt, except for the gatehouse, about the end of the 17th century. Despite some uncertainties of interpretation stemming from alterations between the 1440s and 1680s, the plan is of great interest as the house of a soldier-of-fortune who became rich through the French wars.[4]

The only 15th-century work remaining is the gatehouse,[5] which was joined to the bay or cross-wing at the lower end of the hall. In the gatehouse the moulded entrance-arch had, carved in the spandrels, Ogard's coat of arms and its supporters;[6] the first-floor chamber, lit by two oriel windows, was reached by a newel staircase and intercommunicated with rooms over pantry and buttery; these service rooms presumably occupied the site of the kitchen shown there in 1685. The hall was 34 ft long by 24 ft (10·4 m x 7·3 m)[7] and is likely to have been of two bays with a narrower screens bay to E; it had an oriel window. Adjoining the house, probably to S, was the cloister; and there was a chapel served by the `priests, clerks and choristers, of whom there were 16 every day, with four priests, to a cost of £100 per year'.[8] Excavations in 1857 under `a square tower' revealed `a subterranean apartment with an iron door, having a latticed window'.[9] All these buildings lay within the curtain wall which had corner turrets with cross-shaped loops. To E the outer courtyard was flanked by two symmetrically disposed ranges; the range to S had two external fireplaces and was perhaps lodgings; that to N probably comprised stables and barns.

In 1559 the house was sold to William Frankland, a London mercer,[10] whose son William sold it to Sir Edward Baesh in 1620.[11] Reference to `the capital messuage of the manor wherein William Frankland now dwells, and the farmhouse, lying near or adjoining thereunto, wherein John Stayre now dwells' suggests that the S range of the outer court may have been the farmer's house. After the Restoration the N range became a malting-house; drawings[12] show the oasthouse. By 1683 the cloister and all its buildings had been removed, the hall divided into two rooms and an upper floor and gabled attics inserted, a staircase added to N of the parlour wing and the putative service rooms converted into a kitchen. In 1662 Sir Ralph Baesh paid tax on 11 hearths;[13] in 1664 and 1665 Mr Richard Walcote, the only person paying for 11 hearths in Stanstead Abbots, presumably lived in Rye House. By the time of the 1683 Plot Richard Rumbold, maltster, was tenant.[14]

Not many years later most of the house was pulled down and replaced by an L-shaped block of two storeys and attic, with mullion-and-transom windows. Subsequently it was used as Stanstead parish workhouse; by 1838 the maltings had disappeared;[15] thereafter a tavern was built in the forecourt.[16] The range to N of the gatehouse was rebuilt, shoddily, and castellated,[17] probably in 1857 when the excavation referred to above took place. In recent years the gatehouse was unroofed and restored.

For illustrations, see *English Houses 1200–1800*, Figs 31 (plate), 32, 308 (plate).

Notes
1. *Cal Chart*, 1427–1516, 38.
2. Worcester *Itineraries*, 49.
3. *A True Account and Declaration of the Horrid Conspiracy Against the Late King, His Present Majesty and the Government...* (1685).
4. McFarlane 1973, 27, 95, 183–4.
5. Smith, T P 1975, 111–50.
6. Oldfield Vol VI, 125.
7. Worcester *Itineraries*, 47.
8. Ibid.
9. *Gent Mag* (1857) (i), 710–11; Proc Soc Ants **4** (1856–9), 67–8.
10. VCH III, 370–1.
11. PRO CP 43/146, M 35–6.
12. Charnock; Luppino.
13. PRO E179/375/30.
14. Andrews 1902–4, 43.
15. Drawing, James Wilcox.
16. Cussans 1870–3, Vol I (i), 34.
17. Illustration, Andrews 1902–4; Smith, T P 1975, 112.

(77861)
Stanstead Bury (TL 399111),

a manor house, was owned by the Augustinian Abbey of Waltham in the 15th century; in 1522 it was leased to John Rodes of London for 61 years[1] and in 1531 ownership passed to the Crown by exchange. The late medieval W wing was built by the abbey or one of its tenants. By 1542 Rodes' lease had been terminated and the manor was in the possession of Philip Paris Esq., at a nominal rent of 7s 7d per annum.[2] In 1556 it was stated: 'The manor place is in decay and will ask much reparation in timber and tiling £40'.[3] In 1559 it was granted to Edward Baesh Esq., who was 'General Surveyor of Victuals for the Navy Royal',[4] Sheriff in 1571 and 1584 and died in 1587. To his time belongs some painted glass with an unidentified coat of arms and the date 1563,[5] which refers to additions to N and E. In 1587 the 'circuit' of the house comprised 15 acres and there were 100 deer in the park.[6] Baesh's widow Jane, who died in 1614, was still living at Stanstead Bury in February 1593.[7] By the mid 17th century a second house had been built some 30–40 ft (9–12 m) to SW of the first;[8] it appears on an estate map of 1781.[9] Although the date of this second house is uncertain, the irregular fenestration[10] may imply that a comparatively early building was heightened or altered in the mid 17th century. A two-storey gatehouse[11] entered through a four-centred arch was probably built by Edward Baesh. His house was large enough to entertain Queen Elizabeth on progress twice, 17–22 September 1571 and 14–20 August 1576,[12] and a gatehouse would be in keeping with such state.

From Edward Baesh the manor descended in 1587 to his son Ralph (d.1598) and his grandson Edward, who died without issue in 1653. Probably the house was by then substantially as Drapentier depicted it *c*1700[13] because the manor descended to Edward Baesh's cousin Ralph, who had impoverished himself in the service of Charles I and was permitted by private Act of Parliament to sell part of the estate to raise the sum of £300 per annum.[14] In 1662 Sir Ralph Baesh paid for 35 hearths[15] and in 1664 Lady Baesh paid for 39.[16] Their son Edward sold the remainder of the estate *c*1676 to Sir Thomas Field, who was Sheriff in 1683. His son Edmund, who succeeded him in 1689 'within Age',[17] altered the E elevation after the making of the engraving *c*1700 and probably before he was Sheriff in 1703. In 1794 the house was separated from the manor and sold to George Porter and in 1802 passed by marriage to Captain Robert Jocelyn RN;[18] and it was probably Jocelyn who refaced the S

elevation and demolished the second house to SW. In 1852 Captain Edward Spencer Trower became tenant of Stanstead Bury and in 1907 his descendant Mr Spencer Trower bought it. In 1930–1 Sir William Gosselin Trower carried out extensive alterations including building a new north house as a servants' wing and moving the entrance from S to W.[19]

The W wing (Fig 130) is part of a late medieval open-hall house; it had a crown-post roof, the tie-beams and crown-posts of which have been removed, leaving the peg-holes in the collar-beams as the only evidence of a collar-purlin.

Probably the first addition was the brick range to E; behind panelling in the staircase-hall are a moulded plinth, the NE corner of the chimney-stack with simulated quoins in plaster, and, high up in the wall, a blocked window with wooden lintel, all of the 16th century and not closely datable. The principal storey stood above an undercroft.[20] The function of this range is uncertain. The width (about 22 ft (6·7 m)) and the lateral fireplace are appropriate for a hall range but if so its position in relation to the presumed medieval hall implies a complete recasting of the house.

The next addition (Fig 131) is the large square block to N, presumably comprising parlour with great chamber above and cellar below. The latter was entered to W from a timber-framed stair turret, by a doorway with chamfered frame and carved stops facing the stairs; and to N by a similar doorway, facing outwards, which implies the existence of some coeval structure there. The cellar, now partly filled and with all openings blocked, had *c*1907 'a blocked window in the east wall, probably originally an outside wall; in the south wall...are two small triangular-headed niches'.[21] The niches can no longer be seen; the blocked window coincides with a ground-floor opening in brickwork about 4 ft 6 ins (1·5 m) thick with no sign of a straight joint in it, and may be a chimney-stack with the fireplace enlarged to make a doorway at a different level. The date 1563 in the reset glass does not conflict with the door stops but is uncomfortably (though not impossibly) early for the patterned framing, assuming that has been correctly restored. This block is likely to have formed part of the house in which Edward Baesh entertained Elizabeth I in 1571 and 1576. Possibly by this time the second house had been built. A drawing of *c*1800[22] shows large mullion-and-transom windows (possibly of the early 17th century) on the first floor, below which are windows of four lights, perhaps of the 16th century; evidently the principal rooms were on the first floor.

When the E range was built is difficult to say, except that it was after 1563 and before 1653 (see above); the room functions are uncertain; probably staircases preceded both the present main stair and one to NW.

After Edmund Field's remodelling the E range comprised entrance-hall with staircase-hall to S and parlour or drawing room to N; the former parlour perhaps became the dining room. Probably then the S range was reduced in importance; the floor levels were altered to make them level with those in the rest of the house; the upper part was a half-storey or semi-attic.

In the early 19th century the entrance was moved to S where a new entrance-hall was created, flanked by two chimney-stacks; the range was heightened by a few courses of brick and reroofed, and the elevations to SE were rendered. The plans of the house[23] show it prior to the alterations of 1930.

For an illustration, see *English Houses 1200–1800*, Fig 217.

Notes
1. VCH III, 369.
2. Cussans 1870–3, Vol I (i), 30.
3. PRO E315/391, fo 118.

4.   Chauncy I, 383.
5.   VCH III, 370, n69.
6.   Inquisition *post mortem*, PRO C142/215/269.
7.   PRO E115/19/54.
8.   Engraving, Chauncy II, 382; Oldfield Vol VI, 118.
9.   HRO 71024/2.
10. Oldfield Vol VI, 118.
11. Chauncy 1700.
12. Colthorpe and Bateman 1977, 19, 28.
13. Chauncy 1700.
14. Chauncy I, 382; Kingston 1894, 188.
15. PRO E179/375/30.
16. PRO E179/248/27.
17. Chauncy II, 383.
18. Title deeds in possession of Mr A G Trower; VCH III, 369.
19. Inf. Mr A G Trower.
20. Chauncy 1700.
21. VCH III, 370.
22. Oldfield Vol VI, 118.
23. Copyright Mr A G Trower.

Fig 130 *Stanstead Bury, Stanstead Abbots: plan*

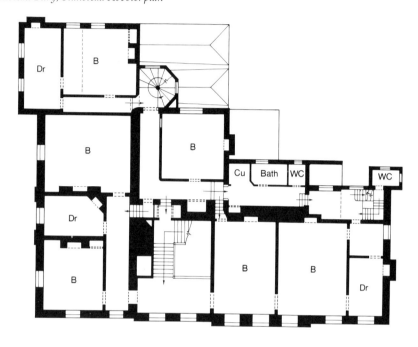

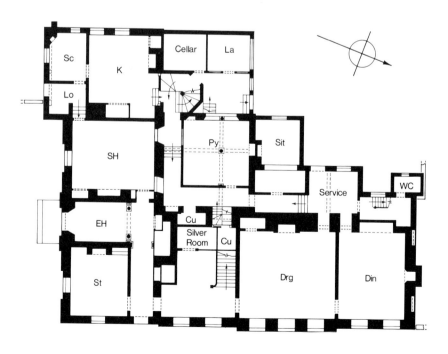

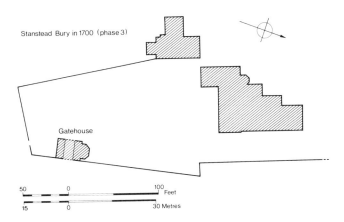

Fig 131 *Stanstead Bury, Stanstead Abbots: 1700 block plan*

STANSTEAD ST MARGARETS

(77862)
The Manor House (TL 380117)

and demesne lands were separated from the manor (originally called Thele) in 1359. In the late 17th century the capital messuage appears to have been divided between co-heirs, for in 1685 Thomas Wale, citizen and goldsmith of London, sold one-quarter and one-third of a quarter of it to Robert Peter the elder, citizen and girdler of London.[1] This division may be responsible for the peculiarities of plan in the existing house.

The house is of several periods, now hard to disentangle after alterations in the 19th and early 20th centuries. The principal elements of the existing building are two gabled wings of unequal length standing to E and W of a late 17th-century chimney-stack which had square shafts with diagonal fillets. The taller wing to E projects slightly beyond the other as if originally jettied to N and subsequently underbuilt; the wing may be earlier than the stack, perhaps of *c*1600. The lower and longer wing may replace a hall range truncated to W. A late 17th-century wing to S has a lateral stack to E for a kitchen fireplace; to S is a service room and above are unheated bedrooms. Possibly the W and S wings are close in date and represent a rebuilding almost as thorough as that at Hammond's Farm, Pirton, though quite different in its results. There is now no evidence of the division of the capital messuage implied in 1685.

Note
1. VCH III, 474.

STEVENAGE

(77863)
Bragbury (TL 269212)

was described in 1610 as a messuage held of the manor of Friars in Standon by Thomas Mitchell, Gent., on whom it had been settled by his father Thomas Mitchell senior in 1602.[1] The oldest part of the house, comprising a hall range and flanking cross-wings, is likely to have been built by *c*1600 although nothing datable to that period survives and the existence of such a house has to be inferred from later work; but if Bragbury is correctly identifiable with Bragbury Hall Farm shown in a small sketch of 1584,[2] the inference is confirmed. About the third quarter of the 17th century it was refaced, a rear block and stair turret were

added, and it had a cupola. During the 18th century it was owned by Francis Pym, MP for Bedfordshire, and by 1819 was in the hands of William Manfield, Esq., who removed the cupola.[3] Later in the 19th century bay windows were added to N and W and then and subsequently the interior was greatly altered, leaving virtually no old detail.

The house (Fig 132) incorporates two cross-wings of different length and a hall range with somewhat higher roof, an appearance which suggests that the original hall range has been rebuilt, probably when refronting took place in the late 17th century. To S (rear) the space between the wings was filled by a large room and a short staircase wing to E; a small block of one-room plan was added to W. Fireplaces in the hall and room behind it discharged into a chimney-stack with three square flues. The hall was both room and entrance; possibly the room to S was a rear hall, like that at Tyttenhanger, Ridge; the room to E had a wide fireplace as for a kitchen, although other service rooms lay to SW. Upstairs is a lobby by which the three principal rooms were approached (cf Tyttenhanger); possibly the dining room was over the hall, the withdrawing room to E, and a bedchamber and closets to W. In the 19th century the characteristic plan of a longitudinal passage with rooms on both sides was adopted, and the house was rendered and refronted with iron trelliswork on two storeys.

Notes
1. PRO C142/32/107; VCH III, 80.
2. HRO, D/EAS.
3. Neale 1819–29, Vol II.

(77864)
The Grange, No. 5 High Street

(formerly The Swan Inn), a large inn of generally 18th-century appearance with large 19th-century additions in the courtyard, may incorporate a timber-framed building of *c*1600 or earlier, evidence of which is hardly definite enough to permit its plan to be reconstructed. The range to W has binding-beams and bearers, mostly encased in boards or plaster, in both ground and first-floor rooms; an internal chimney-stack with wide fireplace

Fig 132 *Bragbury, Stevenage: location diagram showing original hall and cross-wing*

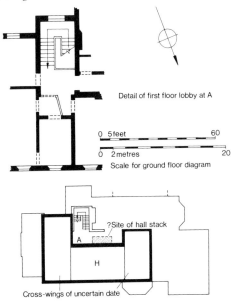

Detail of first floor lobby at A

Scale for ground floor diagram

?Site of hall stack

Cross-wings of uncertain date

to S probably served the hall; the lack of a fireplace to N is consistent with the insertion of the stack into an open hall, backing on to a cross-passage. The position, in the room to S of the hall, of a beam near the W wall, suggests that it is one of two binding-beams in what was formerly a cross-wing jettied to W. The N range and the kitchen to E are of uncertain date, probably late 16th or early 17th century. In the S wing, reset in the N wall to E, is a doorway with moulded jambs and head and bar stops bearing some ornament now defaced; it is of the third quarter of the 17th century. This part of the building can hardly be very different in date from the alterations to the W range, which included a timber gallery and staircase of c1670–80 with moulded handrail and twisted balusters. Probably the W end of the S wing was rebuilt then; it now comprises a large room on the ground floor and offices above, none of which contains datable old details, so that it might be regarded as a much later alteration; only a straight joint in the wall to S shows that the brickwork is earlier than that to E. This unusually wide block may be compared to one in a similar position at The Grange, Standon; it perhaps served much the same function as an assembly room of the late 18th century. To the same period belongs the rebuilding of the S part of the W range and the insertion of a staircase adjoining the covered gateway to N; a corner fireplace in the range to N may be coeval. In 1715 the `messuage or inn called The Swan', leased by Bridgett Noodes of London in 1711 to James Green of Stevenage, innholder, was sublet by him to John Greatorex.[1]

In the early 18th century the E part of the S wing was refaced and extended N to the kitchen; a staircase was built to serve all the E part of the inn including the chambers over the kitchen; there was no way past the `assembly room' to the street range. In the mid 18th century a staircase was built adjoining the covered gateway, and later, perhaps c1770–80, the inn was refronted; the windows have segmental heads; in the middle is a two-storey bay window; entrance from the street was through a small passage room to the main staircase. In 1779, and no doubt much earlier, Quarter Sessions were meeting at The Swan.[2] There is little evidence of alteration in the 19th century. In the present century, when the building became a school, a block of rooms was added to E.

For an illustration, see *English Houses 1200–1800*, Fig 288.

Notes
1. HRO, Lytton 46705.
2. HRO, *Sessions Books* 1752–99, Vol VIII, 517.

(77865)
No. 3 High Street,

has a main range facing W and, to SE, a late medieval wing comprising an open hall about 17 ft (5·2 m) square and an E bay with nothing to show whether it was of one storey or two; whatever lay to W has been removed, but because the shorter of the two hall bays is at this end the cross-passage and service rooms were presumably here. The street range and a short wing in the re-entrant angle are of the late 17th century; the former, drawn c1800,[1] had nine bays and was remarkable principally for the two narrow end bays, which, like the middle bay, were emphasised by breaking forward the eaves cornice above them. Why they should have been so treated is difficult to understand; the windows to S lit a small staircase and perhaps those to N lit another, or a narrow closet. The principal staircase is of the late 17th century; there were then three ground-floor rooms, each with a fireplace, in the front range, the middle room being a large hall; the kitchen was perhaps to N, since the rear wing, where it might be expected, has no fireplace of the requisite size.

This point is reinforced by the early Victorian alterations to the house which moved the entrance one bay to S and added bay windows to what had perhaps always been the two principal reception rooms.

For illustrations, see *English Houses 1200–1800*, Figs 269 (plate), 270 (plate), 271.

Note
1. Oldfield Vol VI, 193; `Gone' added in a later hand.

(77866)
No. 37 High Street,

of the early 16th century, incorporates an open hall flanked by two narrow cross-wings. In the hall can be seen the wall-plates, the cambered tie-beam and curved braces of the open truss and, embedded in a partition, one original rafter of steep pitch, probably part of a crown-post roof. The S wing originally comprised one large first-floor room; to W (front) the tie-beam, cambered on top and with a flat soffit, has a shutter groove running its full length; the middle truss is arch-braced, with crown-post and two-way braces. The N wing may also have had a crown-post roof. In the 17th century a chimney-stack and upper floor were built in the hall, the former backing on to a cross-passage, and the walls were raised to accommodate two storeys. The proportions of the hall (c17 ft long x 19 ft wide (5·2 m x 5·8 m)) suggest that the cross-passage was in the wing to S. All evidence of subsequent change was removed in a recent restoration. A conveyance of 1929[1] describes the building as formerly a public house called `The Old Castle'.

Note
1. National Westminster Bank Archives.

(77867)
No. 68 High Street,

of brick and of two storeys and attics and a small cellar, was built in the second quarter of the 18th century. Old plans[1] enable the original room dispositions to be reconstructed with a fair degree of certainty. Behind the imposing E elevation of eight bays the house was only one room in depth. The entrance led directly into the staircase-hall; the two principal rooms lay at the ends of the house, the larger being to S; the middle part of the house was occupied by a small heated room, a passage to the rear doorway and an unheated service room; the off-centre position of the chimney-breast to N suggests there was a narrow room to W. Upstairs the rooms follow the same plan. A difficulty in interpreting the plan is the absence of a kitchen; this may have been in a rear wing although the first-floor windows do not allow much space for its roof to abut the main range. In the present century the building has been much altered to adapt it as a bank.

For illustrations, see *English Houses 1200–1800*, Figs 278 (plate), 279.

Note
1. Made available by Barclays Bank Ltd.

(77868)
The White Lion PH, 60 High Street,

incorporates to S the cross-wing, jettied to E, of a late medieval house with open hall; the wing adjoins what was formerly a comparatively low carriage entrance, wider than a normal cross-passage, which, if it is an original feature, suggests the building was always an inn (cf Thorpe House, No. 19 High Street, Puckeridge, Standon). This is not certain; only in the late 17th century, when the remainder of the building was rebuilt, did it definitely become an inn. To N of the carriage entrance are two rooms with an internal chimney-stack between them. A staircase to W, reached easily from the yard, rises to a gallery from which two principal bedrooms are approached through a lobby adjoining the stack; to S the gallery gives access to bedrooms over the gateway and wing and to the attic rooms over the principal bedrooms; one attic room has a small fireplace with four-centred head. Alterations carried out in 1976 exposed some framing, including a small two-light ovolo-moulded window; the bearer in the ground-floor room to N of the entrance also has an ovolo-moulding.

(77869)
No. 2 Letchmore Road (TL 235248)

comprises a hall and two cross-wings jettied to N; probably the parlour wing was to E and the service wing to W. The hall and each storey of the wings are close-studded with a middle rail; the open truss has a double hollow chamfer running through posts and tie-beam; the roof has clasped-purlins. In the 17th century a chimney-stack and lobby-entrance were built, blocking the cross-passage; the stack was probably of timber; the coeval first floor in the hall has comparatively slight joists. In the mid 17th century a fireplace was added to the parlour. In the 18th century the hall stack was rebuilt in brick and a fireplace added to W; then, if not earlier, the former hall became the kitchen and service rooms were created to E within the former hall. Both wings retained staircases until the present century, when that to E was removed.

The house served as Stevenage Workhouse from 1759 to 1835, and as a school where straw plaiting was taught from then until 1855; it then became the office and residence of the manager of the local gas company until 1936, when it reverted to being a private residence.[1]

Note
1. Inf. Mr E R Moore.

(77870)
The Old Bury (TL 239262)

stands to W of the parish church and is probably Stevenage manor house. The manor belonged to Westminster Abbey from c1062 until the Dissolution and was subsequently given to the bishopric of London.[1] The house was built in the late 15th century and comprised an open hall and coeval cross-wing to W; the wall-plates of the hall are jointed into the wing-framing; the wing, jettied to S, was probably at the upper end of the hall. Probably a further bay stood to E. A few smoke-blackened rafters with lap joints for collar-beams imply a crown-post roof; the wing has a crown-post roof with two-way braces. In 1647 the manor house, described as `newly erected' by the then tenant George Banister, comprised hall, parlour, kitchen, two butteries, milk house, brewhouse, with several chambers over them.[2] Banister's work included the building of a brick chimney-stack and a first floor in the hall, and the wing to E; the wing has an axial bearer and was therefore not jettied. The stack blocks the cross-passage and has to E and W fireplaces with four-centred heads, splayed at the back; the latter feature shows that the hall was not used for cooking but had become a parlour – perhaps a dining parlour – with a second parlour to E. The unheated room to N of the latter was perhaps one of the butteries. The staircase is in a turret to N of the hall. Banister probably also added the chimney-stack in the W wing to convert it into a kitchen. In the early 18th century the W wing was extended to N by the addition of a two-storey block with

braces to the bearers, perhaps for a granary (cf Old Ramerick, Ickleford). In the early 19th century the staircase was rebuilt; corridors were built on both ground and first floors and the former hall, by then a dining room, was widened to S.

Notes
1. VCH III, 141.
2. Parliamentary Survey, Guildhall MS 12036.

(77871)
Shephall Bury (approx TL 256229),

a manor, belonged to St Albans Abbey from before the Conquest to the Dissolution; its subsequent descent is uninformative about the house. A drawing of c1800[1] shows that the medieval hall, still open to the roof or a ceiling at eaves level, remained; it had late 18th-century sash windows and a round-headed doorway with fanlight. At each end of the hall were two gabled wings. This house was demolished c1865.[2]

Notes
1. Oldfield Vol V, 525.
2. VCH II, 444.

(77872)
Stebbing Farm (TL 222261)

was built in 1442–3.[1] In November 1440 Robert Hunnesden paid 4d for a burnt toft, formerly Robert Hynton's, for which the rent had previously been 18d. In the same rental John Stebbing paid 24s 8d for lands called Lorkyns, now Larkins, a field immediately N of Stebbing Farm. At a court held on 26 April 1442 William Wulgate received a toft called Hyntons for a rent of 12d on condition that he should build a house by the feast of St Peter ad Vincula (1 August) 1443, the lord finding him sufficient timber. Robert Hunnesden and John Stebbing were admitted as pledges for his building the house.[2] The pledges were not distrained at the court held in October 1443; in the next

Fig 133 *Stebbing Farm, Stevenage: plan and section*

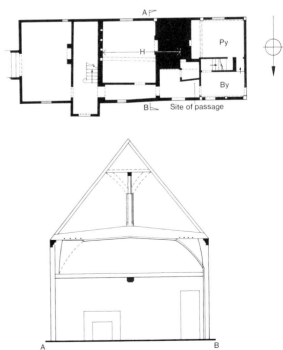

rental (1477) William Stebbing 'de Hathengrene' pays a rent (Redditing de Stebbing) of 26s for land called Lorkyns, etc., ie, he pays John Stebbing's old rent plus 18d for the toft formerly Hyntons; and the house perpetuates the name of John Stebbing, who died in 1466. The evidence shows that William Wulgate, who was for a time a tenant of the manor, either built the house himself in 1442–3 or ensured that John Stebbing who entered on the farm immediately afterwards did so.

The house originally comprised three bays (Fig 133), the two to E being the hall; the tie-beam of the open truss is hollow-chamfered continuously with the wall-posts; the crown-post is rebated and formerly had four-way struts; the wall-plates are moulded and stopped. To W, where no old detail remains, were probably accommodated pantry and buttery with chamber above. In the early 17th century a chimney-stack was built next to the open truss and backing on to the screens-passage, and a first floor was inserted in the hall; it is considerably higher than the floor over the service end. The placing of the stack to S suggests there was a staircase to N. In the late 17th century a single-storey kitchen and service wing was added to W. In the 18th century a second fireplace, backing on to the existing stack and blocking the entrance-passage, was added; thereafter the entrance was perhaps to N. In the mid 19th century a two-storey brick block was added to E comprising a large entrance and staircase-hall and a sitting room.

For illustrations, see *English Houses 1200–1800*, Figs 41 (plate), 294.

Notes
1. Inf. Mr H O N Farris, from Wymondley court rolls and rentals (PRO).
2. Farris 1975–6, 34.

STOCKING PELHAM

(77873)
Cottage at Crab's Green (TL 455287)

of the 18th century, is a single-storey building of poor-quality timber-framing, clad partly in plaster and partly in weatherboarding. The plan (Fig 134) comprised four ground-floor rooms; room use is conjectural. In recent years it has been enlarged and renovated.

Fig 134 *Cottage at Crab's Green, Stocking Pelham: plan*

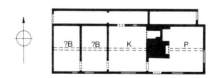

TEWIN

(77874)
Marden Hill (TL 279140)

was a manor of St Albans Abbey from c1050 to the Dissolution. In the late 16th century it came into the possession of Edward North,[1] whose grandson Hugh, succeeding to the property in 1653, 'erected a fair House'.[2] His estate was divided between two daughters; neither his name nor the daughters' married names appear in the Hearth Tax returns of 1663. By 1785 the property was in the hands of Robert Mackay, for whom Francis

Carter designed the present house,[3] and of whom Carrington remarked that he 'did wrong, pulled a Good house down'.[4] The plan[5] is square, the principal storey being raised above a basement in which the kitchen was in the SE corner. It appears originally to have comprised the entrance-hall to S flanked by morning and dining rooms and opening into a staircase-hall of equal width; to W of the latter is a bow-ended drawing room and to E a passage to the service block. Opening off the drawing room and occupying the NW corner of the house was the library; to NE, opening off what was perhaps called the gentlemen's room, was an apsidal-ended water closet. To E, connected by a two-storey corridor, is a service range aligned N–S. In 1818 the house was bought by Claude-George Thornton who immediately commissioned Sir John Soane to alter it.[6] Soane's alterations, which were comparatively minor, included building a porch and moving the existing double flight of stone steps to the garden side (N); he enlarged the dining room to N to provide an arched recess for the sideboard and altered the position of doorways and fireplaces in the morning and drawing rooms; and probably built a new staircase which had winders rather than the short middle flight with two landings of the original. Thornton, who was Sheriff in 1838, died in 1866. On the death of his son and heir in the following year[7] the house was advertised as recently decorated and repaired, with 15 bedrooms, 3 dressing rooms, boudoir, drawing and dining rooms, morning room, library and gentlemen's room, 2 WCs, principal and secondary staircases, butler's pantry, footmen's room, housekeeper's room, kitchen and other service rooms.[8] 'Recently repaired' may include the extension over the porch of the room over the entrance-hall and the doorway with pedimented head on console brackets; and probably the staircase was altered then, re-using Soane's balusters, to provide a single flight dividing into two flights to the first-floor landing. Subsequent alterations have affected mainly the service rooms. In recent years the house has been converted into flats.

Notes
1. VCH III, 482.
2. Chauncy I, 541.
3. Colvin 1978, 198; Oldfield Vol VI, 222.
4. Carrington *Diary*, 182.
5. Hussey 1941, 328–33.
6. Stroud 1961, 112; Hussey 1941, 328–33.
7. VCH III, 482.
8. The *Hertfordshire Mercury and County Press*, 17 August 1867.

(77875)
Queen Hoo Hall (TL 278161),

a reputed manor,[1] was bought by John Smyth in 1584 and leased in February 1589 by his son James to Affabell Partridge, goldsmith of London,[2] in terms implying that the building was only recently finished: 'For the better encouragement of Affabel Partridge to build upon the premises James Smythe grants to him all such bricks as James hath now lying in Brantfield and all his timber trees ready felled within the manor', and also grants licence to dig chalk and sand for lime and bricks. Under the covenant Partridge undertook, firstly, to use these materials for 'such necessary buildings, offices and fences about the mansion house' as he should think convenient, and, secondly, not to alter 'the brick mansion house newly built' except to improve it.[3]

The S (properly SE) elevation is framed by two very shallow wings with three-light mullion-and-transom windows on ground and first floors and three-light dormer windows in the attics. A wash drawing of 1818[4] shows these attics with, not windows, but three panels all pierced by a cruciform loop, and there were two similar panels in the W gable. The symmetry created by the wings is not maintained by the openings between the bays, because the three-room ground plan (Fig 135) entailed placing the doorway off-centre. It is remarkable that all six principal rooms on two floors have fireplaces, and that there are no

Fig 135 *Queen Hoo Hall, Tewin: plan*

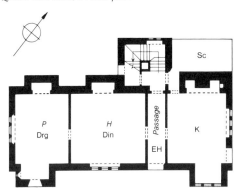

service rooms on the ground floor, only a cellar under the kitchen. Upstairs were three chambers of which the middle one, over hall and passage, is so large that it may have been subdivided. The chamber over the parlour has wall-paintings of two periods. The earlier scheme consists of a frieze representing a moulded cornice with inset panels having scroll ornament; above was a representation of wooden panelling, also with scrolls. Over the fireplace is what is said to be a later and apparently unfinished Old Testament scene, perhaps King Solomon worshipping false gods,[5] consisting of horses, figures and monsters in red outline. The staircase turret has a timber-framed newel about 2 ft 6 ins square (0·8 m) used as cupboards; on the top landing in the wall to E the stubs of what looks like the chamfered and stopped jamb of a doorway, plastered, may conceivably be a bricklayer's error. It is not certain that all three attic rooms, corresponding to those on the floor below, are original. Those to E and W are lit by two-light windows in the gables as well as from the front but are spanned by roof trusses with tenoned purlins which incorporated collar-beams and braces now removed.

By the early 17th century the house had passed into the possession of Sir Henry Boteler, who died in 1609,[6] and in 1634 was occupied by his second son Ralph.[7] Subsequently it became a farmhouse. A pedimented wooden porch, fireplace in the attic to W and a scullery are all of *c*1800,[8] when the house was occupied by farmers named Whittenbury;[9] it is the setting of Joseph Strutt's *Queenhoo-Hall, a Romance...*, written in 1808. In 1851 it was occupied by Jane Bilton, farmer, and her three daughters, with one agricultural labourer living in; later it became two cottages; in 1903 it was put in order as one residence[10] and was restored and a new doorway made in the W bay; and in the late 1950s it was again restored and the wall-paintings uncovered.[11]

Notes
1. VCH III, 482.
2. For whom see Reddaway 1960–8, 184 and index.
3. HRO, 40980.
4. Luppino.
5. Cornforth 1962, 596, 'painted perhaps for James Smythe'; Croft-Murray 1962–70, Vol II, 314*a*.

6. VCH III, 483.
7. *Visitations*, 30.
8. Oldfield Vol VI, 212; Luppino (1828); Buckler Vol IV, 183–4, of 1832–3.
9. Carrington *Diary*, 28, 39; survey, 1804, HRO D/P22 29/2.
10. *EHAST* 1927, 395.
11. *EHAST* 1945–9, 167; Cornforth 1962, 598.

(77876)
Tewin House (approximately TL 267142)
was purchased by Thomas Mountford who died in 1632,[1] and whose son Dr John Mountford, canon residentiary of St Paul's and rector of Therfield (see The Old Rectory, Therfield), built a 'fair House near the Church'.[2] In the early 1650s it was bought by the Boteler family,[3] Sir Francis Boteler paying for 15 hearths in 1663. After his death in 1690 his daughter sold the house to William Gore who made 'a fair Addition' to it.[4] In 1715 it was purchased by General Joseph Sabine[5] who, between 1716 and 1718, built what may have been a completely new house.[6] The house was drawn *c*1800[7] and appears in the background of a painting of Colonel J and Mrs Sabine.[8] A Colonel Sabine lived at Tewin Water briefly in the 1730s.[9] The house was said to have cost close on £40,000 sterling to build and furnish; two rooms in particular were 'really works of art'.[10] One was

composed of the finest and rarest marbles brought expressly from Italy and Greece, and the ceiling is painted in fresco by a clever Roman painter. The second is still more beautiful, being a hall or grand staircase composed of rare and precious woods, but the work manship is far superior to the material, the artist having encrusted these woods in a wonderfully clever manner with tints and colours, and has succeeded in shaping them into lovely forms, figures and landscapes, in perfect imitation of nature.

The walls of a third room were painted with battle scenes of the Duke of Marlborough's campaigns.[11] Tewin House was described in 1788[12] as a 'spacious, uniform house 100 ft front, attached and detached offices'; the mansion house comprised eight chambers and two dressing rooms on the attic storey, four chambers and three dressing rooms on the principal storey, a spacious marble hall and staircase, two drawing rooms, eating room and tea room on the ground floor, and vaults and cellaring under the body of the house. Servants' offices adjoined the house to N and around the courtyard were the brewhouse, wash-house, bakehouse and laundry.

The house was bought in 1788 by Charles Schreiber, 'a Dutch man', on whose death his son William 'made Great Alterations in the offices of the House, for the Worse, and Distroyd the fine Engin which used to Serve the House and Offices with water and then Sunk a Well, a great Simpleton'.[13] In 1804 it came into the hands of the 5th Earl Cowper, who in 1807 pulled it down to enlarge the grounds of Panshanger.[14] At the time the house was demolished, in 1807, it was said to have '27 windows East front 27 in West front and 9 in Each end, fine large Sashes, all Brick with large Corner Stones, flat Roof'.[15] The accounts for taking down the house mention the cleaning of 909,100 bricks in all, and the total cost of the work was £394 8*s* 7*d*.[16]

For an illustration, see *English Houses 1200–1800*, Fig 190 (plate).

Notes
1. VCH III, 484.
2. Chauncy I, 540.
3. VCH III, 484.
4. Chauncy I, 541.

5.   *DNB*.
6.   Carrington *Diary*, 145.
7.   Oldfield Vol VI, 216; Clutterbuck.
8.   Sold by Christie, June 1974.
9.   Carrington *Diary*, 23.
10. de Saussure 1902, 307.
11. Croft-Murray 1962–70, Vol I, 262.
12. HRO, Particulars, D/EPT 2129.
13. Carrington *Diary*, 47.
14. VCH III, 484.
15. Carrington *Diary*, 145.
16. HRO, Panshanger Estate ledger, D/EP 18.

(77877)
Tewin Water (TL 256145)

is the manor house of Tewin. From the late 13th century to the Dissolution the manor belonged to the priory of St Bartholomew, Smithfield, and except between 1544 and *c*1622, when it was in the hands of the Wrothe family, its owners are unlikely to have lived at Tewin until the manor came into the hands of James Fleet.[1] `Esqre Fleet, a gentleman of Great fortune', came to live here *c*1714[2] and was Sheriff in 1718; he repaired and beautified the capital messuage[3] and died in 1733. His widow survived kidnapping and twenty years of confinement in Ireland, returned to Tewin Water and died, aged 98, in 1789.[4] After her death the estate came to the 3rd Earl Cowper, who had purchased the reversion ten years earlier.[5] He is said to have pulled the old house down and built another which was occupied by Lord Townsend; Oldfield's drawing of it[6] shows a three-storey front of seven bays with a further bay projecting at each end. In 1797 the Earl gave this house to Henry Cowper, clerk assistant of the House of Lords,[7] who promptly called in the architect John Thomas Groves to rebuild it again;[8] a note accompanying the drawing states that Henry Cowper `has lately altered and embellished it'. Humphry Repton, who was called in at the same time to replan the park, remarked of Groves' work: `tho it may almost be deemed an entire new building, yet he was confined by the old house to the present level of his floors'.[9] A watercolour in the *Red Book* apparently shows Groves' first design from SE; on the opposite page are pencil notes in Henry Cowper's hand: `No roof seen/Chimneys stand the other way/No bow to the Atticks/No recess between the bows/Side windows in the bows narrower than the middle.'[10] The first, third and fourth points were altered in the house as built; Groves may already have incorporated the fifth in his design; only the second was not ignored. The Repton view shows that

Fig 136 *Tewin Water: plan*

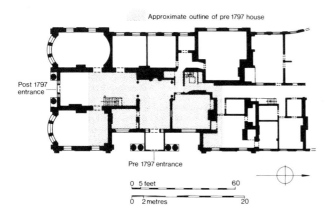

the entrance was then, as it had been earlier, to E; the narrow wings of the earlier house[11] appear to be incorporated in the larger blocks terminating the portico; the space between the blocks is of approximately seven bays, as appears in the attic storey. Although the plan today (Fig 136) incorporates some elements earlier than the elevation depicted by Oldfield, it is difficult to reconstruct the 18th-century or earlier plan. A large chimney-stack directly opposite (to N of) the S entrance and which survives only on the ground floor is likely to be of the 17th century; the grandiose late 19th-century staircase to S and the smaller early 19th-century staircase in a square well to N, stand in much the same relation to the stack as in some late 17th-century houses, eg Brent Pelham Hall and Wyddial Hall; and the relation between the lesser staircase and the room to S which looks like a large parlour is also found in such houses. Little is known about the house thereafter prior to the extensive repairs in 1892, including alteration of the sanitary arrangements, on the entry of the Earl of Limerick.[12] Subsequently it became the country residence of Alfred Beit, diamond millionaire and partner of Cecil Rhodes, who died there in 1906.[13] Limerick and Beit enlarged the house and renovated the interior so thoroughly, transferring the entrance to W, that hardly a single earlier fitting remains. Private occupation ceased in 1946.[14]

Notes
1.   VCH III, 481.
2.   Carrington *Diary*, 23.
3.   VCH III, 481.
4.   Carrington *Diary*, 23–4.
5.   Neale 1818–29, Vol II.
6.   Oldfield Vol VI, 226.
7.   *DNB*.
8.   Carrington *Diary*, 35; Colvin 1978, 367.
9.   *Red Book*, HRO, C2404.
10. Inf. Miss E Lynch, HRO.
11. Oldfield Vol VI, 227.
12. HRO, Panshanger Papers, Box 32.
13. *DNB* Second Supplement 1.
14. *Newsletter* **8**, 1957.

THERFIELD

(81094)
The Old Rectory (TL 335369)

belonged to Ramsey Abbey from the late 12th century until the Dissolution, when it passed to the dean and chapter of St Paul's. The grant in 1336 of a toft in Therfield for the enlargement of the rectory presages its importance in the 15th century when the E wing, a comparatively complex structure of its kind, was built by a wealthy rector. At the Dissolution courts were held in the rectory.[1] In so far as its relatively simple mouldings can be compared with the elaborate and closely dated sequences found in Cambridge,[2] a date towards the end of the 15th century is probable, when Edward Shouldham (d.1503), who was Master of Trinity Hall and rebuilt the church roof, was rector.[3] From 1513 to 1516 John Yonge, DCL, Master of the Rolls and diplomatist,[4] held the living.

An open hall adjoined the wing; its existence in 1625 is implied by a parsonage terrier,[5] which does not mention chambers over the hall. John Mountford (or Montfort), DD, admitted rector in 1640, `rebuilt the greatest part of the parsonage with brick at his own charge',[6] and although hardly any of his work can now be seen it probably included the hall range. Evidently the rebuilding was finished by April 1643, when Mountford petitioned the Sequestration Committee concerning the loss, among other things, of his library, `value of £1,000 at least'; later it was said that `they first permitted him to build the parsonage house, new almost from the ground, and then turned him out without suffering him to sleep one night in it (or but one at most) though it cost him a thousand pounds'.[7]

In 1661 complaint was made that Marmaduke Tenant, `rector and minister of Therfield', did not conduct the service according to the Book of Common Prayer;[8] in the following year he paid for 11 hearths[9] but was turned out soon afterwards.[10] In 1665 `the dean of Polles', Francis Turner, subsequently bishop of Ely and a non-juror,[11] paid for 11 hearths.[12] Alterations to the rectory were undertaken by Henry Etough, a converted Jew, who was rector from 1734 to 1757 and was satirised as Tophet by Thomas Gray;[13] `at his coming to his living...he borrowed £800 and laid it out putting his house and appurtenances into good repair and a decorous state; and afterwards was very attentive to keep them so'.[14] Nevertheless Charles Weston, who became rector in 1762, `pulled down the greatest part of the parsonage house in a ruinous condition and rebuilt it',[15] and it is to him that the present appearance of the house is largely due. A library was added in 1800 by Dr Charles Moss, bishop of Oxford and a noted pluralist,[16] who was described in 1805 as `resident when not waiting on His Majesty as res. of St Paul's'.[17] More work was undertaken in 1875 by the Revd J G Hall, who borrowed £500 from the Governors of Queen Anne's Bounty to restore the fabric of the chancel and the rectory.[18] Only during the Commonwealth and the last hundred years of ecclesiastical ownership did the house cease to be occupied by eminent clerics whose energies were largely expended outside the parish. It was sold by the Church Commissioners in 1970.

The house now comprises two distinct parts (Fig 137), the more important being the E wing, which is one of the most interesting remains of medieval domestic architecture in the county, both for its intrinsic quality and the light it throws on the planning of a wealthy medieval rectory. It has rendered walls of flint rubble with chalk dressings, and comprised a gabled range running N and S with two shorter blocks projecting to E. Only the N elevation has kept much of its medieval appearance; it has a circular stair turret and a window with a principal mullion flanked by two pairs of cinquefoiled lights; to E is a square-headed two-light window now made into a door, above which are two taller first-floor windows, that to E of one light and that to W of two lights.

The ground floor formed a single room nearly three times as long as it is wide, with identical four-light windows to N and S.

A doorway to N opened into a small room, perhaps a study, lit only to N by the mutilated two-light window; another doorway to S opened into a larger room, which apparently had, at the SW corner, another round stair turret. A door, to NE, now blocked, suggests that the room had a service function and perhaps some internal partitioning.

On the first floor the short wing to NE was a chapel in which, to E, is the outline of a tall window with two-centred head; to N a single-light window lit the tiny presbytery and a two-light window to W of it lit the larger, but still very small, nave. A large first-floor chamber is reached by a second door a few steps higher up the staircase; the resulting difference in the ceiling height of the ground-floor rooms corresponds to their relative importance. No original details of this chamber remain except, perhaps, the roof, which appears to have a waggon ceiling plastered at the S end. (The two-light window in the N wall to W is of 1875, replacing an 18th-century sash window.)[19]

To S is a narrow range now of one storey but of two storeys in 1910.[20] It incorporates a 15th-century window of one cinquefoiled light and two small circular windows with quatrefoil cusping, but rendering of the walls makes it uncertain whether the windows are in their original positions or reset; their placing does not correspond with any obvious room divisions and none appear in drawings done in 1875 prior to restoration. Nevertheless a long narrow wing serving a comparatively minor function can be paralleled in other late medieval houses; and the siting of the doorway, so awkwardly cut through the former newel stair, must have been necessitated by the existence of the wing. A likely use for the outer end of the first floor of such a wing is as a latrine.

The hall was probably timber framed; since the stone E wing survived it is reasonable to suppose that some part of the hall would have survived had it been built of the same material. An original stone doorway on the first floor of the wing must have led into an upper room or gallery at the E end of the hall range.

The 1625 terrier shows that the rectory was large by comparison with contemporary rectories and even lay manor houses. The hall, `on the west side of the entry', had, beyond it, two parlours, a study, `one other little new built parlour' and a pantry, and upstairs, four chambers, study and `turrett'; `On the E side of the hall...a little lower chamber, a cellar, a kitchen, a larder and a scullery'; and `Without on the south side, a little walking cloister, one other kitchen, brewhouse, bolting house, dairy house and coal house'.

Little trace remains of the partial rebuilding by John Mountford. It included refacing the angle buttress and the W

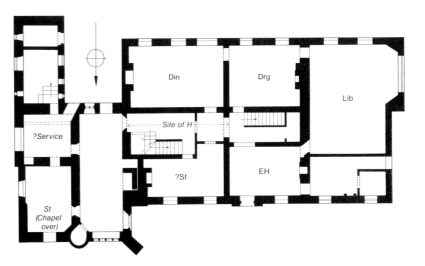

Fig 137 *The Old Rectory, Therfield: plan*

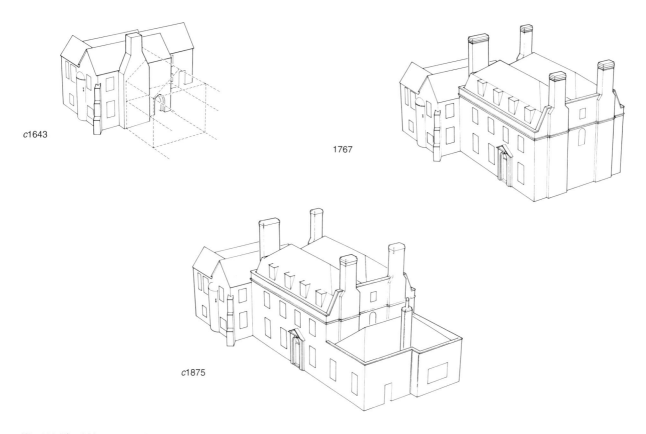

*c*1643

1767

*c*1875

Fig 138 *The Old Rectory, Therfield: development plans*

return of the N wing in brick; in the latter are the chamfered jambs of a wide window. The chimney-stack to W of the wing may be his work (Fig 138); the fireplace has a flat lintel, chamfered continuously with the jambs, which is appropriate for the period and unlike the moulded original openings. Although this characteristic is the only positive evidence for the date of the fireplace, the projection of the stack into the hall also points to its being a later insertion; perhaps there were two fireplaces back-to-back. It may have been at this period that the two E projections of the medieval wing were joined and reroofed. The inventory of John Standish, rector, dated 27 January 1687[21] lists fewer rooms than might be expected: little parlour, hall, great parlour, kitchen, buttery, cellar; coalhouse, woodhouse, wellhouse (presumably in or near the cloister); parlour chamber, green chamber, best chamber, chamber over the kitchen; the library of books; garretts and chapel. The reappearance of a chapel is an interesting indication of changes in religious sentiment that had come about since 1625.

Charles Weston's rebuilding undertaken in 1767 made the house what it is today (Fig 138). On the site of the hall and W wing he built a double-depth brick house which, on the garden (S) side, is of five bays and completely symmetrical, whereas the front (N) has four bays and an asymmetrical entrance. Possibly the presence of the big 17th-century chimney-stack produced this asymmetry and a somewhat unconventional plan, which embodies a comparatively large entrance-hall with fireplace. The room to SW was a parlour or drawing room, that to SE probably the dining room, and that to NE perhaps a study, for which there is otherwise no provision. The library, of one storey only, was added in 1800 and modified by the addition of a bay window in 1875 (Fig 138). The main staircase is in early 19th-century style

and the entrance-hall, staircase-hall and landing are in a classical idiom, but how much of all this is modern reproduction work is difficult to determine. One feature that has disappeared in this century is the timber `covered-way' reminiscent of a cloister walk, which was added parallel to the SE wing by the Revd J G Hall in 1875, to give access to a wash-house.

For illustrations see *English Houses 1200–1800*, Figs 28 (plate), 29.

Notes
1. VCH III, 282.
2. RCHME 1959, 393.
3. Hale 1884, 23.
4. *DNB.*
5. Lincolnshire RO, Terr 14/56.
6. Parish register, HRO, D/P107/3/1.
7. Matthews 1948, 201.
8. HRO, *Quarter Sessions Minute Books* 4, 48.
9. PRO E179/375/30.
10. Matthews 1934, 480.
11. *DNB.*
12. PRO E179/248/1.
13. Gray *Poetical Works*, 95, 271–3.
14. *Gent Mag* 1786 (i), 281.
15. Parish register, HRO, D/P107/3/1.
16. *DNB.*
17. Lincolnshire RO, Diocese Survey 1805, SPE/8.
18. HRO, D/P107/3/10.
19. Drawing, HRO, D/P107/3/27.
20. RCHME 1910, 218–19.
21. HRO, Prob 4/5165.

THORLEY

(77878)
Moor Hall (TL 467188)

was a small estate belonging to the Augustinian Priory of Merton. In 1544 it was acquired by Clement Newce[1] and in 1611 was described as a capital messuage owned by William Newce Esq. and in the tenure of Richard Godfrey.[2] It is a late medieval house comprising an open hall with two-storey bays to N and S; the latter have chamfered bearers with pegged-and-tenoned floor joists; above the hall a few rafters and the closed truss to E are blackened by smoke; to S of the inserted chimney-stack is the sawn-off W end of a tie-beam; probably the roof was of crown-post type. In the early 17th century an upper floor was inserted in the hall and a staircase wing was added to E; a chimney-stack must have been added in the hall but since no trace of it now remains it was presumably of timber. A short addition to N, perhaps of c1700, may be contemporary with a range roofed parallel to it and terminating at the staircase wing; the brick chimney-stack in the hall is probably of the late 18th century; in the mid 19th century the house was refaced in brick to E, with slight additions.

Notes
1.   VCH III, 375.
2.   PRO C142/327/99.

(77879)
Thorley Hall (TL 476188),

formerly moated, was built by a member of the Gerbergh family, who held the manor from the mid 13th century until 1390. It incorporates some of the roof structure of a timber-framed aisled hall of c1300. Thomas Gerbergh, who in 1278 laid claim to certain liberties of the manor, and was assessed for a third part of a knight's fee in 1303,[1] is a likely builder, but if not, then his son John Gerbergh. In the early–mid 15th century the hall was reduced in width to heighten the walls; the roof was rebuilt as a single span and a wing was added to S. These changes were probably made by John Leventhorpe who held the manor from 1419 until 1435 or later,[2] although they have been ascribed to the early 14th century.[3] In the late 16th and early 17th centuries the house declined in status when it was leased out to, among others, John Dale, `who was, while he lived, Fermer of Thorley Hall', and who died in 1606.[4] In 1691 it was bought by John

Fig 139 *Thorley Hall, Thorley: plan*

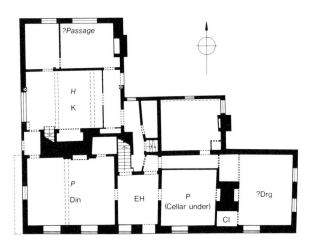

Billers, a haberdasher of London,[5] no doubt as his country retreat, for although Sheriff in 1697 he was described in 1699 as `Mr Billers, of London'.[6] After his death in 1712 it was sold to Moses Raper and in 1724 the outhouses were described as being part in his own occupation, part of Robert Flack, farmer;[7] evidently the house had by then become a residence. Matthew Raper FRS was the only subsequent owner of note, from 1748 to 1778.[8] The aisled hall (Fig 139) was of two bays, probably with a screens-passage to S; it had octagonal posts with moulded capitals and passing-braces. In the early 15th century the posts of the open truss were cut just below the capitals and the upper parts supported on a tie-beam; a crown-post roof was substituted for the passing-braces; the aisles were rebuilt slightly narrower than before; and a wing of three bays with crown-post roof was added to S. In the 17th century a chimney-stack with four conjoined diagonal shafts was inserted at the S end of the hall, perhaps on the site of the screens-passage, and an upper floor was built; the tie-beam over the hall was cut away to make a chamber over the hall; hall, parlour and chamber over the hall all had fireplaces. Between 1691 and c1700 John Billers enlarged the wing to E[9] and removed the entrance to E. The enlarged wing comprised an entrance-hall with two arched openings, one leading to the staircase which is partly housed in a turret to N, and the other to a back door (cf 99 Fore Street, Hertford). Probably the room to W of the entrance-hall, the former parlour, then became a dining room, with the kitchen to N; and the two rooms to the E were perhaps the parlour with a cellar underneath and drawing room (Fig 139). The N end of the hall declined in importance and was probably pantry and dairy. By 1834[10] a one-storey block had been added to E of the staircase. The room to E on both floors, hitherto lit only from S, were each provided with a window to E. Then or later the block to E of the staircase was heightened to two storeys and provided with a chimney-stack, and the N end of the hall was lowered and given a lean-to roof.

Two old wells and associated brick culverts draining into the Invat were discovered in 1903.[11]

For illustrations, see *English Houses 1200–1800*, Figs 21 (plate), 291.

Notes
1.   VCH III, 374.
2.   Ibid, 375.
3.   Hewett 1980, 266.
4.   *Gent Mag* 1811 (ii), 112.
5.   VCH III, 375.
6.   VCH *Herts Families*, 273.
7.   Guildhall MS 11936, 19, 98.
8.   VCH *Herts Families*, 273.
9.   Drawing, Buckler Vol II, 88.
10. Ibid.
11. Gerish and Andrews 1902–4, 297–303.

(77880)
Twyford House (TL 496192)

was sold in 1650 by Francis Barrington of Thorley, Gent., to William Hayle, who was rector of Great Hallingbury 1643–89;[1] it was then described as a messuage, not a manor, although its superior status is attested by a dove-house.[2] The present house was built towards the close of the 17th century, perhaps by Dr Hale of Dunmow, Essex who stands second, after `Mr Billers, of London' (and of Thorley Hall), in the list of freeholders in Thorley in 1699.[3] Extensive alterations in the 19th century and division into flats make investigation difficult (Fig 140), so that the following interpretation is extremely tentative. The house is akin to those small manor houses or seats which comprise two blocks or wings at either end of an entrance-hall (see *English Houses 1200–1800*, pp 33–4); a reconstruction of the ground and first-floor plans has been attempted (Fig 141); details of doorways and lobbies are uncertain. An unusual feature in a house of this class is that the hall chimney-stack is placed axially, to E, rather than laterally (but cf the somewhat later Lockleys, Welwyn). Adjoining the ground-floor room to NE and the chamber over the hall are partitions which correspond to pairs of closets (cf Bonningtons, Stanstead Abbots). The width of the wings to W and the positions of chimney-stacks suggest that each had a staircase (cf Julians, Rushden). In a deed of 1727 the house is called `a messuage or mansion-house'; in the early 19th century it passed by marriage to George Frere and was considerably altered. The space between the wings was enclosed to provide a new staircase and the S wing was extended to W, the new room having a hipped roof of steep pitch. These changes took place before 1834.[4] Soon afterwards Lewis Vulliamy suggested to George Frere that a third storey should be added to the extension[5] but this proposal was not adopted and a staircase turret was built instead. In 1845 Vulliamy added stables.[6] In 1893 the house descended to Laurie Frere on his father's death and in 1894 alterations were carried out by the architect F S Brereton, including the addition of a studio window.[7]

Notes
1. Venn and Venn 1922–7, Vol II, 282.
2. Deed, HRO, D/EWO T26.
3. VCH *Herts Families*, 273.
4. Buckler Vol II, 89.
5. HRO, D/EWO E30, letter with sketch and plan, 1 August 1835.
6. Colvin 1978, 858.
7. Inf. Miss E Lynch, HRO, who supplied other details.

Fig 140 *Twyford House, Thorley: ground and first-floor plans*

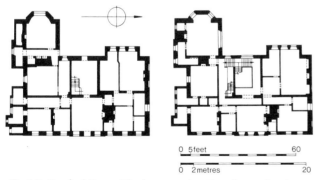

Fig 141 *Twyford House, Thorley: reconstruction of ground and first-floor plans*

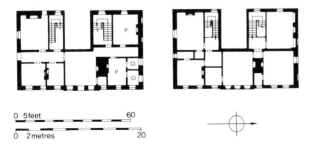

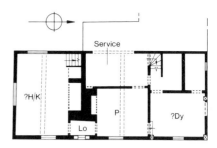

Fig 142 *Little Barwick, Thundridge: plan*

THUNDRIDGE

(77881)
Little Barwick Farm (TL 386188),
ostensibly of the mid or late 17th century, is a two-cell internal-chimney house of two storeys and attics facing E, with a lower and later bay to N. Hints of an earlier origin are its unusual width (20 ft (6 m)) for its plan form (Fig 142) and apparent date, and evidence of heightening to N; above an internal offset at about the height of the first floor the wall leans slightly (cf Chells Manor, Aston). In the late 17th century the room to S, which has the larger of the two back-to-back fireplaces and from which the staircase rises, was the hall; to N was the parlour with service room to W. Late 17th-century features include the staircase, with moulded balusters, and an original fireplace in the first-floor room to S. The bay to N, of two storeys but lower than the main part of the house, and re-using much old timber, was added *c*1700; it appears to have been a dairy and service rooms with bedchamber above. In the 19th century fireplaces were provided in the attics and a wing added to NW.

(82741)
Sawtrees Farm (TL 387179),
a manor house, is first recorded in the early 15th century and seems always to have been at lease.[1] It is a large house with a long range to N (correctly NE) forming the bar of a T-plan, and a shorter one to S forming the stem. The N range is of the early–mid 16th century; the greater part of it, about 60 ft (18 m) in length and excluding the two bays to W, has a continuous jetty to S; the plan comprises three rooms, two large ones to E and W with lateral stacks and a small one between them about 15 ft square (4·5 m) occupied by a pantry with a later passage to S. The small room has a bearer moulded with seven rolls; the entrance is to S and perhaps always was. The hall, with chamfered bearer, is probably the room to W; the somewhat larger parlour (*c*25 ft x 16 ft (7·5 m x 5 m)), its binding-beams and bearer moulded with an ogee and a hollow chamfer, is to E; above the latter is a great chamber which has a fireplace with four-centred head and crown-post with four-way struts; to W the roof has only lengthwise struts. No indications of staircases remain; possibly one (or two) were in turrets to N (cf Redcoats, Wymondley). To W is a two-bay building, possibly of the 16th century; it appears to have been open to the roof and may have been a kitchen and another service room. The S wing was added in the early–mid 17th century, partly masking both the hall and the unheated room; it comprises a parlour (*c*21 ft x 15 ft (6·5 m x 4·5 m)) with lateral fireplace to W and a small unheated room to N in which is a newel staircase; the latter gives access by corridors to the whole house. The new ground-floor room was perhaps a dining room, served from the adjoining hall which may then have acquired the additional function of a kitchen. In the late 17th century a fireplace was added to the chamber over

the hall by building a chimney-stack on beams in the hall; the stack does not continue to the ground. In the 18th and 19th centuries the exterior was rendered, the lateral stacks to N were rebuilt and the inserted stack cut off below the roof.

Note
1. VCH III, 379.

(77882)
Thundridge Bury (TL 367174)

was the moated house of a manor that belonged from 1330 onwards to the Lincolnshire family of Disney; in 1555 it was purchased by John Gardiner of London[1] and remained with his descendants until its demolition in 1811. Arms and a crest were granted to John Gardiner in 1546.[2] The house is said, on architectural grounds, to have been built `about the reign of Henry VII'[3] and to be first mentioned in 1534–5.[4] It was described in 1811 as having a hall 40 ft square (12 m), `decorated in a manner which might be called etching on plaster' and not in colours, with the labours of Hercules. In rooms to N, where parts of the original work were exposed, were painted a fishing scene and the hunting of a wild bull; these may have been in the two parlours, each 36 ft by 18 ft (11 m x 5·5 m). All this wall decoration was probably of the 16th century. Edward Gardiner Esq. was Sheriff in 1628; his son, also Edward, was Sheriff in 1656 and was assessed for 16 hearths in 1663.[5] Illustrations[6] suggest that the house was refronted in the mid–late 17th century; the principal (W) elevation was probably symmetrical, of at least nine bays, comparatively low but extended by one bay and heightened to W. A chimney-stack which survived the final demolition was built in brickwork of English bond; it serves three fireplaces to S, on three floors, this being the only indication that the house had attics.[7] During the 18th century Thundridge Bury was leased to tenants, including John Cheshyre Esq., who was Sheriff in 1750. Late in that century the house appears to have been enlarged to W.

Notes
1. VCH III, 378.
2. *Visitations*, 57.
3. *Gent Mag* 1811 (i), 609.
4. *Gent Mag* 1811 (ii), 305.
5. PRO E179/248/24/11.
6. Oldfield Vol VI, 266; engraving of *c*1811, *Gent Mag* 1811 (i), 609.
7. RCHME 1910, 221; Gerish 1902–4, 138–9.

(77883)
White Hind House (formerly PH) (TL 359173),

of the mid 16th century, is a continuous-jetty house facing W, of three-room plan; a former partition to N of the hall has mortises for the paired doorways to service rooms; to E a staircase rises from the site of the cross-passage; the hall itself has been gutted and its original chimney-stack removed; in the parlour to S the stair trap adjoining the gable-end wall is visible. On the first floor is a wall-painting of large multi-petalled flowers drawn freehand in black outline on the plaster, probably of the early 17th century. Extensive alterations, probably including the creation of a low wide vehicle entrance, are dated by an external plaster roundel inscribed `Restored 1848'; a corresponding roundel to N inscribed `Built 1563' refers to the admittance of John Brett to a tenement called le White Hind, taken from a court roll[1] and not necessarily to the building of the house.

Note
1. Extract in house.

TRING

(77884)
Grove Farm Cottages (SP 933123)

is a late medieval cruck-built house aligned N–S and comprising an open hall, a bay to N also open to the roof, and a continuation to S of unknown length. Probably the bay to N was at the upper end of the hall; the partition between them has been removed and a beam just above head height shows no possible position for a doorway except to E where the soffit is concealed. Such a position, instead of the twin doorways customary for service rooms, suggests this was the parlour end. In the 16th or 17th centuries the chimney-stack was inserted at the lower end of the hall, a lobby-entrance presumably replaced a cross-passage, and upper floors were inserted throughout. An E wing was added, possibly in the late 17th century, and a lean-to along the remainder of the E side may be partly of that date. In the 19th century that part to S of the hall and also the chimney-stacks were rebuilt and the house was refaced in brick to W.

The interest of the house lies in its development, which resembles that of many longhouses.

For an illustration, see *English Houses 1200–1800*, Fig 298 (plate).

(77885)
Pendley Manor (SP 942118)

was the residence of several sheriffs of whom the first to be Sheriff of Herts was John Aignel in 1312, and the second Sir Robert Whittingham in 1433. Whittingham built at least part of the important house which is the subject of John Oliver's engraving of *c*1700;[1] the date of the house is uncertain. In 1506 it was stated that about eighty years before `there was no great mansion-house' at Pendley; subsequently Whittingham enclosed the village, razed it, and `built the said place at the West end there as the town sometimes stood'.[2] Building-works after *c*1426 would accord with his being Sheriff a few years later, but a licence in 1440 to empark 200 acres[3] has been taken as a *terminus post quem* for the house,[4] which was definitely in existence by 1449 when `the hall of Penley' is mentioned.[5] A date *c*1430 is perhaps the most likely. The engraving is taken from an outer courtyard looking through to an inner one which had a cloister with a four-centred arch with sunk spandrels, and beyond it some indeterminate tracery. At some time after 1472[6] the house passed to the Verney family who, between 1480 and 1589, provided two sheriffs for Hertfordshire (1499, 1589) and six for Buckinghamshire (1480, 1511, 1524, 1540, 1557, 1558);[7] the jettied ranges of the outer courtyard are likely to be of the 16th century and no doubt the house underwent many changes. One chimney-stack is built against a jetty (cf Redcoats, Wymondley); the others are represented with octagonal or diagonal shafts, some of which are likely to be the work of Sir Richard Anderson, who was Sheriff of Hertfordshire in 1610 and created baronet in 1643; his son of the same name was probably responsible for the sash windows. Much of this house must have been demolished by the middle of the 18th century, when the principal elevation (to N) of 11 bays had a Palladian appearance,[8] although some older work may have been incorporated behind the façade and in the two wings to S.[9] This house was tenanted[10] by Dr Richard Warren, the most eminent physician of his day,[11] who died in 1797. By 1803 it was owned by R B Harcourt Esq.;[12] subsequently it is said to have been abandoned and finally burnt in 1835.[13] The present house was built sometime after 1871.[14]

For an illustration, see *English Houses 1200–1800*, Fig 35 (plate).

Notes

1. Chauncy II, 560; a painting dated 1804 by Augustus Charles de Pugin (Christie's Sale Catalogue, 24 March 1982, No. 89) is merely a derivative of this.
2. VCH II, 285, citing court roll.
3. VCH II, 285.
4. Munby 1977, 133–4.
5. PRO SC 2/176/120, Albury court roll.
6. VCH II, 284.
7. Viney 1965.
8. Oldfield Vol I, 59.
9. Block plan of 1799, HRO, D/EX 234, II.
10. Oldfield Vol I, 59, caption.
11. *DNB*.
12. HRO, 56476.
13. Williams 1980, 74–5 (not necessarily reliable).
14. Cussans 1879–81, Vol III (ii), 18.

(32409)
Tring Park (SP 926111),

a manor house of Tring, belonged to the Crown from before the Conquest. A Parliamentary Survey[1] does not mention a manor house. The manor was acquired by Henry Guy, then secretary to the Treasury,[2] in 1680:[3] he had no doubt bought an estate and begun building some years earlier. He built a house to the design of Sir Christopher Wren, and Wren himself refers in a letter dated 14 May 1682 to a proposed visit to Tring.[4] These facts point to a start date in the late 1670s rather than 1669–71[5] or *c*1670,[6] and a mention is made in March 1682 of `ye place where Harry Guy lives'.[7] Chauncy, who illustrated the house,[8] makes no mention of its building. The most notable event in its history was William III's dining with Guy in June 1690.

The house appears to have been built as nearly perfectly symmetrically as could be, the front and rear (N and S) elevations being almost identical.[9] It was built over a basement. Roger North described the house in his manuscript *Of Building*:

Mr Guy's house is of three ranges; and one thing post-nate *in the contrivance, at the entrance, is remarkable. The staires ascending to the first or hall floor are not without, but within a room, that serves as a portch. This was not so in the first design, but altered. And in so large an house, where a room can be spared for the use of a porch, it is very convenient.*[10]

Elsewhere he remarks:

And at first the ascent was all without, with a broad paved landing before the cheif door. But by I know not what criticisme, that was not thought convenient...at length those staires were disbanded, and the poor vestibule, which I thought the cheif ornament to the avenew, was condemned to a stair raised all within the door... This vestibule is no other than a porch.[11]

In the RIBA Drawings Collection is one sheet of drawings labelled on the reverse side `The severall Plans and Uprights of Mr Gore's house of Tring in Hartford Shire' and another sheet on smaller paper with a different watermark, showing a plan and elevation of the house, which appears to be more or less contemporary with the first. The drawings are dated *c*1730. They accord with North's description of the approach and principal rooms save in two particulars, that there is a `broad paved landing' before the front door, and there are no stairs in the `porch', which is more appropriately described as a vestibule. The plan and other drawings appear to show Wren's original conception, whereas Oliver's engraving[12] shows the entrance as

altered. The room designations given by North are shown on the plan. The long section showing the S side of the hall is slightly confusing. Doorways in this drawing and the one of the opposite side have the openings shown in a dark colour; what looks like a doorway but is in a lighter colour was presumably a cupboard put there to produce symmetry with a real doorway opposite; yet what is shown similarly on plan as another cupboard, at the foot of the great staircase, is given a dark opening as if it was a doorway. These discrepancies cannot now be reconciled. The first-floor plan, in so far as it can be deduced from the present arrangement and the 18th-century ground plan, may have comprised two identically planned ranges of rooms to N and S of the central axis; the transverse gallery at the stair head gave access on each side to an ante-room flanked by two large dressing rooms, which were in turn flanked by a smaller bedroom with staircase adjoining.

The RIBA drawing of the N front is not particularly accurate: it shows the niches as being the same height as the windows, which they are not, quoins where there are pilasters, four attic windows, not six, and no *œil-de-bœuf* in the pediment. A simpler doorway and the suppression of the pedimented window could represent alterations, but not the other matters.

In 1705 Guy conveyed the manor to `Sir William Gore, a Merchant of London',[13] from whom it descended in 1707 to his son, also William, who commissioned Bridgeman in the early 1720s to make extensive alterations to the garden.[14] A plan said to be of Tring Park attributed to Bridgeman[15] shows symmetrically disposed outbuildings which do not appear in an early 18th-century engraving[16] and may never have existed; so different is the outline of the house as drawn from the very distinctive shape of the actual building that the plan may refer to some other house. Smaller and less regularly arranged buildings, some perhaps of *c*1700, were depicted in 1839.[17] James Gibbs designed ornamental garden buildings.[18]

In 1786 house and manor were sold to Sir Drummond Smith, who made considerable alterations before being Sheriff in 1789. He moved the entrance to E and built a coach-porch there; enlarged the S of two projections to W;[19] replaced the eaves cornices by parapets; and refurbished a ground-floor room to S with a plaster ceiling. He was probably responsible for altering the ceiling at the head of the staircase; Wren designed it so that `from the seiling a shell is lifted up, cuppolo-wise over the gallery, which looks well underneath, but above is a monster',[20] but in 1808 the `handsome Gallery or Ball Room' had a circular dome in the centre.[21] Perhaps by then the house was occupied by a tenant, `— Grant, Esqr.'.[22] A drawing of 1832[23] shows that the first-floor three-light window to S had been given an Italianate form with a lowered sill. When Baron Lionel Nathan de Rothschild bought the estate in 1872 he improved the attic storey by building French-style pavilion roofs, generally enriched the exterior and added a large polygonal block to SW; at the same time the interior was extensively refitted in the Wren manner, including a new staircase and a deeper cove over the hall; and a new gallery, canted out as a bay window, was added to W of the hall.

For illustrations, see *English Houses 1200–1800*, Figs 140 (plate), 141, 209 (plate).

Notes

1. PRO E/317/29 (Herts).
2. *DNB*.
3. VCH II, 283.
4. Wren Soc 1935, 23.
5. Hill and Cornforth 1966, 242.
6. Colvin 1978, 925.

7. Thompson 1875, 130.
8. Chauncy II, 558.
9. Buckler Vol I, 182, dated 1839.
10. Colvin and Newman 1981, 73–4.
11. Ibid, 129.
12. Chauncy 1700.
13. Defoe *Tour* 1927, 395.
14. Willis 1977, 59–60.
15. Ibid, Plate 45*a*.
16. *Vitruvius Britannicus*, Vol IV, 104–5.
17. Buckler Vol I, 182.
18. Colvin 1978, 343.
19. HRO, D/EX 234 ph; enclosure map 1799.
20. Colvin and Newman 1981, 74.
21. Britton and Brayley 1808, Vol VII, 146.
22. Clutterbuck
23. Buckler Vol I, 181.

TRING RURAL

(77886)
Betlow Farm (SP 899172)

was built in the 15th century. The manor of Betlow, first recorded in the late 13th century, was held after 1625 with Tiscot, and the house (at approximately SP 896170) is said to have disappeared about the end of the 19th century;[1] the foundations were removed during the Second World War.[2] This house may have replaced Betlow Farm as the manor house; alternatively Betlow Farm is a tenement carved out of the manor. It was built as an open hall with a storeyed bay at each end; the hall is of two equal bays, divided by an open truss of some elaboration in which blocking pieces fill the spandrels of the arch-braces; this may point to a date in the mid 15th century. In the late 16th century an upper floor and central chimney-stack with two ground-floor fireplaces were inserted in the hall; first-floor fireplaces were added *c*1700; and in the early 19th century the house was refaced in brick to E and a kitchen wing of one storey was added, also to E.

A first-floor room had a wall-painting (now destroyed) with a frieze of indecipherable black-letter texts above a geometrical floral design typical of the late 16th or early 17th century.

For an illustration, see *English Houses 1200–1800*, Fig 69.

Notes
1. VCH II, 288.
2. Inf. Mr C Chandler.

Fig 143 *No. 13 Tring Road, Wilstone, Tring Rural: ground and first-floor plans*

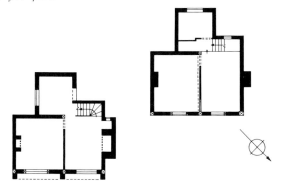

(81105)
No. 13 Tring Road, Wilstone (SP 904140),

of the late 15th century (Fig 143), is of two storeys and of two unequal bays, neither of which was heated originally, and has a bold jetty to NE. The joists are of large scantling; at the NW corner there was formerly a stair trap, the stairs rising to NE (front); the doorway between the two upstairs rooms, now blocked, stands partly over the jetty. In the late 17th century a staircase-projection was added to SW and a chimney-stack to NW; the upper part of the stack was later modified, probably to prevent down-draught. Subsequent alterations are of little historical importance.

WALKERN

(77887)
Manor Farm,

of brick, of two storeys and attics and of L-shaped plan, was built towards the end of the 17th century, perhaps incorporating an earlier timber-framed building to NW. The front range, facing SE, comprises hall and parlour; the staircase is opposite the entrance, in the re-entrant angle of the SW wing, in which is the kitchen; the pantry is in a lean-to to NE of the staircase. To NW, parallel with the front range, is what may be an earlier structure, gabled to SW and NE, of uncertain purpose; it had been converted to bakehouse and brewhouse. Three large bedrooms correspond to the L-plan below. In recent years the house has been considerably altered.

(77888)
Rooks Nest Farm (TL 287258)

is a large farmhouse of L-shaped plan which was built in two distinct parts; the front range is of brick and of the mid 17th century, the slightly lower rear wing is timber framed with brick nogging and is a generation or more later, possibly 1701. Since neither part is self-contained the process of alternate development has to be invoked to explain the house, ie the front range was added to or replaced its predecessor, retaining for a time the whole or part of the earlier house, which was subsequently rebuilt. The front range, of two storeys and attics, is of cruciform plan with a two-storey porch to E balancing the stair turret to W of the internal chimney-stack; the hall, to S, is slightly larger than the parlour to N; the chamber over the hall has an original fireplace with four-centred head. On the S face of the stair turret a mortar flashing sloping down from E to W indicates the existence of a pent roof antedating the present one to E of the wing; although its length is uncertain it suggests that the wing to W is secondary. Some weathering of the door-frame from the hall (now dining room) to N shows that the door was originally on the outside of the house.

In the 19th century a brewhouse wing was added, the pantry converted into a parlour, and the lean-to rebuilt as a larder.

For illustrations, see *English Houses 1200–1800*, Figs 168 (plate), 169.

WARE

(77889)
Amwell House (TL 358139),

now Ware College of Further Education, is said to have been built by John Scott, the Quaker poet (1730–83),[1] on what evidence is not clear. His father, a linendraper, moved to Amwell in 1740; after 1760 Scott, by then a poet, paid occasional

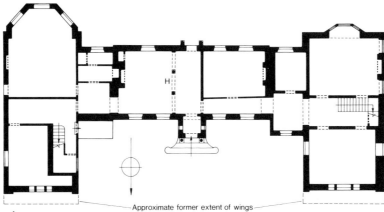

Fig 144 *Amwell House, Ware: plan*

visits to London, presumably while living at Ware; and in November 1770 `took a house at Amwell'.[2] It is not known if Scott's father did any building or when he died, or when Scott himself built the grotto admired by Samuel Johnson.[3] Scott is said to have defrayed the cost of improving the road from Ware to Hertford, which passes Amwell House, in 1768.[4] An engraving of 1811[5] shows the garden elevation much as now. (An engraving of *c*1823[6] linking Scott with a house having a main range and two cross-wings and of early 17th-century appearance may simply be a mistake.) Matters are further confused by the fact that the present house, although of 18th-century brick, has a plan (Fig 144) unlike anything that might be expected then, and by reproduction Georgian detail.

The five middle bays, originally of two storeys and distinguished by the later rubbing down and colouring of the brickwork, are probably of the early 18th century. Two rooms flanked an entrance-hall; there is no sign of a staircase. Subsequently this range was heightened to three storeys, and wings of two storeys were added, each with a staircase. The resulting plan runs contrary to the general 18th-century tendency towards centralisation around a staircase (cf Bayley Hall, Hertford), and the placing of the chimney-stacks within the main range rather than laterally is a vernacular practice. So different is the house from what might be expected of a successful linen draper or an aspiring poet and gentleman that it may represent the piecemeal rebuilding of an older house comparable to New Hall, Ware, which has similarly proportioned hall and wings. Some early 18th-century detail includes staircases with twisted fluting to the balusters, moulded cornices, and panelling.

In 1906 the house was bought to accommodate the Girls' Grammar School;[7] in 1964 it became a College of Further Education; and in 1973 the wings were truncated to widen the road.

Notes
1. *DNB*.
2. Ibid.
3. Jones 1974, 169–71, following Andrews 1899–1901*a*, 15–31.
4. Hunt, E M 1949, 38.
5. Britton and Brayley 1808, Vol VII, opposite p 246.
6. NMR, source untraced.
7. VCH III, 383.

(77890)
Nos 14/16 Baldock Street
incorporates a late 16th-century building of which the moulded binding-beams and bearers are exposed. In the last quarter of the 17th century it was rebuilt as an inn; the street (W) elevation was refronted in brick and extended to N to make five bays; mullion-and-transom windows survive on the first floor. The street range was widened to E to provide corridors on both floors and a wing was added to SE. A principal staircase, with turned balusters and moulded handrail, faces a doorway from the courtyard and gave access to all first-floor rooms. Two rooms in this wing, which lies along the plot boundary, now have only indirect lighting; this may arise from extension of the building to S. In the 19th century the inn was divided in order to form two shops with living accommodation.

(77891)
No. 20 Baldock Street
is a small, late medieval house of two bays, one of which was an open hall; it had a clasped-purlin roof with windbraces. An upper floor was inserted, a chimney-stack built, and the walls heightened in the late 17th century; the present rendered front and sash windows are of the early 19th century, as is the extension to E.

(77892)
No. 23 Baldock Street,
built *c*1600, is of two storeys and has to S a covered carriageway as if for an inn; the entrance has a depressed four-centred head and foliage in the spandrels. The staircase is unusual in not being accessible from the yard. The original disposition of the rooms facing the street is hard to reconstruct, even the size of the hall; kitchen and service rooms were to W. On the first floor short landings from the staircase give access to five rooms. The only attic, in the W wing, is jettied to S.

(77893)
The Old Bull's Head PH, No. 26 Baldock Street,
of two storeys and two bays and jettied to W, is of the early 16th century; it has a crown-post roof with two-way braces. There is no trace of an original fireplace, not even in the larger of the two ground-floor rooms where one might be expected. A drawing of 1836[1] shows the present first-floor bay windows, which have ovolo-moulded mullions and transoms; they appear to be additions of *c*1600. In the late 17th century a wide gabled wing including a new staircase was added to E; attic rooms with dormer windows[2] were probably also of the late 17th century, as a chamfered and stopped beam in the first-floor room to N confirms. Thin console brackets in pairs below the eaves are unrelated to structural timbers and must have been added not long before 1836;[3] ground-floor bay windows may also be of the early 19th century. Subsequently a carriageway was driven

through the adjoining building to S to give access to the yard; and in the late 19th century a clubroom was built at the end of the NE wing.

Notes
1. Buckler Vol IV, 76.
2. Ibid; now removed.
3. Ibid.

(77894)
No. 45 Baldock Street,

of *c*1500, is of two storeys, the upper storey jettied to E, with crown-post roof; it was apparently of two-room plan and has no sign of an original chimney-stack. All old details are concealed by alterations of the 19th century.

(77895)
Place House, No. 21 Bluecoat Yard (TL 359143),

formerly the manor house of Ware,[1] is an aisled hall and can be dated by mouldings to the time of Thomas, Lord Wake (1297–1349).[2] An earlier date, `the close of the thirteenth century', suggested initially on the basis of a splayed and tabled scarf joint in an arcade-plate,[3] was subsequently said to be supported by the mouldings.[4] The manor descended by marriage to Richard III, after whose death Henry VII granted it in 1487 to his mother Margaret Beaufort, Countess of Richmond.[5] She held it until 1509[6] and during her tenure the house was enlarged and the remarkable movable screen, still in its original position, was provided; the person whose initials, R W, are carved on the screen has not been identified. Between 1575 and 1587 the manor was acquired by Thomas Fanshawe who built Ware Park and leased out the old manor house.

By 1635, as appears from a Chancery suit,[7] the house may have been in dual occupation. In November 1635 Humfrey Packer of Hertford, Gent., as part of a marriage contract between his son Edward Packer of Ware, Gent., and Margaret, daughter of Edward Sams, grocer of London, had settled upon Margaret Place House and The Cross Keys in Ware. In 1640, when Edward sued his father to carry out the agreement, the latter said that he

had dwelt in one of the houses...for divers years, had bestowed great costs and charges in the wainscoting, repairing and adding buildings to same, and implanting fruit trees in the garden and orchard, as the defendant had no other dwelling place of his own and hoped that the complainant would be a dutiful son, and allow him to abide.[8]

The reference to garden and orchard can only be to Place House; an inn in the market-place[9] is an unlikely residence for a gentleman; and there is clear evidence that Place House was divided in the 17th century. Part of Humfrey Packer's work may have been the building or alteration of the E wing, replacing the original service bay. Other work, probably of a minor nature, took place in 1657, a date painted, with the initials W [?] (second initial indistinct), on the screen. A `Map' made 7 October 1685, prior to the purchase in the following November by the governors of Christ's Hospital of `the Capital Messuage and ground called The Place at Ware', shows the house in outline, without internal detail, and an accompanying schedule lists 31 rooms and outbuildings. To adapt the house as a school the W wing and minor buildings were demolished and to accommodate children a range of 12 `Nurses Houses' was built over the old orchard to the W.[10] Thereafter changes were few and of a minor nature, little being done even after the school moved away in 1760,[11] until the medieval house was restored in 1977.

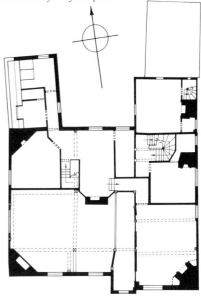

Fig 145 *Place House, No. 21 Bluecoat Yard, Ware: ground and first-floor plans*

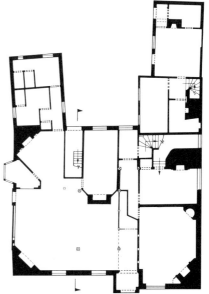

Fig 146 *Place House, No. 21 Bluecoat Yard, Ware: section*

Extension for school 1687-9

Screen c.1500

The nave of the aisled hall (Fig 145) is of two unequal bays, and excluding the screens-passage, which was separated from it by a spere-truss, was square; the columns are octagonal, with moulded capitals and, below the moulded base, an integral square pad at the foot, resting directly on the natural gravel; the mouldings of the tie-beams are carried round the hall as cornices; the roof has crown-posts. To W two dovetailed housings for tie-beams in the wall-plate of the demolished wing establish that the wing was of three bays, its ground-floor walls being flush with those of the aisles. To E of the passage the arcade-posts have mortises for braces rising to the truncated wall-plates of a further bay in series with the hall (Fig 146). The

Fig 147 Place House, No. 21 Bluecoat Yard, Ware: development perspectives

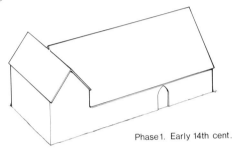

Phase 1. Early 14th cent.

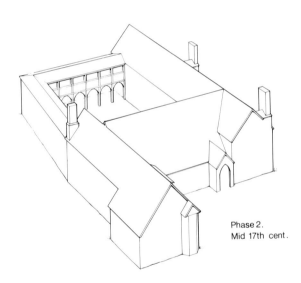

Phase 2.
Mid 17th cent.

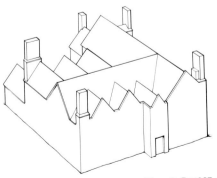

Phase 3. By 1687-9

movable screen of *c*1500 has two octagonal posts with moulded bases and caps, and a moulded head-beam; the lower part of the screen is plain, the upper part has two registers of four carved panels, in one of which are the initials R W; the Tudor rose and pomegranate are carved on panels and shafts. Other work probably done at this time includes the lengthening of the W wing to S. The description of the hall in the 1685 survey[12] as being `wainscoted round' with `one large table, three seats fixed to the wainscot, and one large form, together with a press or cupboard' may well represent the appearance of the hall when the screen was put in. A `cloister' of uncertain date, probably late medieval, extended to N of the W wing for about 50 ft (15 m) and then turned E to join the E wing (Fig 147).

The first major alteration now identifiable was the building of the E wing, which cannot be dated very precisely; it is of two storeys with attics and a cellar; the attics, like the panelling and staircase, are of the early 17th century and can perhaps be ascribed to Humfrey Packer. In 1657, the date painted on the screen with the initials W [?], the principal ground-floor room was painted with a representation of panelling accurate enough to depict the wooden pegs at the joints, and a frieze of bold addorsed scrolls. In the 1685 survey the rooms `On the East end of the hall' are as follows: `Parlour with a fireback in it and one wainscot bench', which may refer to the S room with a corner fireplace; and a series of service rooms – buttery, cellar, pantry, kitchen and `closet with a window board, shelved round' – the last room presumably being unglazed. Upstairs were four chambers, that over the kitchen `with a closet'; they probably correspond to the room to N and a little cupboard-like space to S of the chimney-stack; and there was also `half the long gallery'. The other half of this gallery appears in the list of rooms `On the west end of the Hall', so the cloister enclosing a garden was of two storeys.[13] But preceding this half of the gallery comes a list of a dozen rooms, beginning with a `Buttery joining to the Cloisters' and followed by a `Kitchen (so called) wainscoted round with 2 seats fixed and a sideboard fixed'; the impression thus given of a parlour wing converted to other purposes is reinforced by a `wainscoted larder looking into the courtyard with a bench fixed'; and there were a buttery, `the entry' and two cellars. The first room listed is `A chamber over the parlour wainscoted round', ie parlour was the proper designation of the `kitchen (so called)'; thereafter come `one earth-floored chamber over the back house' and a closet adjoining, and chambers over kitchen and buttery. These are followed by the `backhouse' which, its position in the list suggests, was separate from the other ground-floor rooms, and `one woodhouse in the courtyard' with a chamber over, which formed a wing to W of the main S wing. From this description it appears that Place House in the 1670s had an open hall, at each end of which was a self-contained suite of rooms.

In November 1685 Christ's Hospital purchased Place House, and between June 1687 and November 1689 various craftsmen were paid over £730,[14] much of which must have gone in building the timber-framed and plastered range of 12 `Nurses' Houses' (Fig 148). The W wing of Place House and the cloisters were demolished; the E wing was refurbished as the Schoolmaster's house with an additional corner fireplace; the whole was probably given new windows. But the principal alteration was to the hall; the S aisle was heightened to make it equivalent to two full storeys with a flat plaster ceiling; the N aisle was demolished and replaced by a wider structure, spanned by an arch of roughly finished timber encased in boards, which springs from the N post of the open truss and rises to a flat plastered ceiling; and the old nave was ceiled over at collar-beam level. So altered the ground floor provided a large

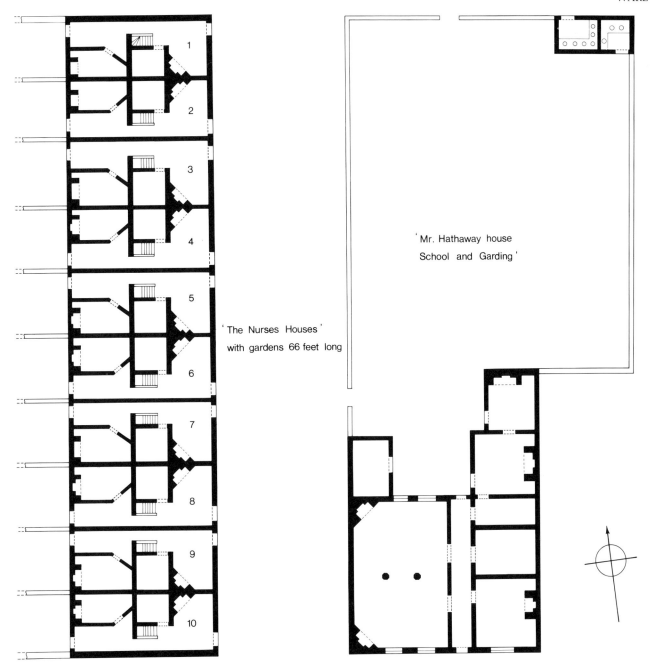

Fig 148 *Place House, No. 21 Bluecoat Yard, Ware: plan of house and nurses' range*

'The Nurses Houses'
with gardens 66 feet long

'Mr. Hathaway house
School and Garding'

school room, with fireplaces in the NW and SW corners and new doors filling the spaces between the late medieval screen and the earlier speres. It appears on two late 17th-century plans,[15] neither altogether accurate. One marks 'The new Wall yt. was built between Mr Roberts garden and the Nurses garden', which is probably the brick wall for which William Birchel was paid £50 in July 1693; this plan shows the hall posts wrongly. The other is later and was perhaps made not long before the school was moved in 1760; it shows the school benches while omitting the corner fireplaces.

In the late 18th century an upper floor was inserted in the school room, a chimney-stack built in the nave of the aisled hall, adjoining the spere-truss, and a staircase built in the NW corner of the former school room. In the 19th century a short N wing

was added to NW. The use to which Place House was put has not been traced continuously, but since it was a day and boarding school run by the Misses Medcalf in 1839[16] and by Martha Medcalf in 1851 it may have served the purpose since 1760; it ceased between 1878 and 1882.[17] In 1977, as part of a general renovation, the later intrusions were removed from the open hall.

For illustrations, see *English Houses 1200–1800*, Figs 23 (plate), 42, 67 (plate), 292 (plate).

Notes
1. Hunt, E M 1949, 9–10.
2. *DNB*.
3. Gibson 1971, 2.

4. Hewett 1980, 122–3 and Fig 356.
5. *Cal Pat* 1485–94, 155.
6. VCH III, 387.
7. PRO C2, Charles I P46 (24).
8. Ibid.
9. Hunt, E M 1949, 101.
10. Guildhall, Christ's Hospital Archives, Building Accounts, 1680–97.
11. Page 1953, 27.
12. Guildhall, Christ's Hospital Archives.
13. `Map' 1685, Guildhall, Christ's Hospital Archives.
14. Guildhall, Christ's Hospital Archives, Building Accounts, 28 November 1680 to 19 June 1697.
15. Guildhall, Christ's Hospital Archives.
16. Advertisement, *Herts and Beds Reformer*, 14 December 1839.
17. *Kelly* 1851, 1878, 1882.

(77896)
No. 17 Bridgefoot Street (TL 359142),

comprising two formerly separate buildings, was demolished in 1957[1] and is mentioned here for the structural peculiarity observed in both buildings, of two crown-posts placed close together. Although it cannot be explained with certainty, this is probably the result of adding a new roof to an existing one and jointing the new collar-purlin to the old one in order to achieve greater stability.

Note
1. Mercer 1975, 170, 171.

(77897)
No. 9 Church Street (TL 355144),

called The Manor House, was formerly the rectory and acquired its name from its association with the rectory manor. Although the present house is claimed to incorporate a building of the alien Benedictine priory of Ware, no part of the present structure can be dated with any confidence before the 17th century. The plan is anomalous and difficult to interpret, principally because the L-shaped main range aligned N–S is long and narrow (88 ft x 15–16 ft (26·8 m x *c*.3·7 m)). The room to N, now the drawing room, has a fireplace discharging into a large 17th-century chimney-stack to E with two diagonally set shafts flanking a square one. To S is a staircase-hall, the former front entrance to W now being masked by a conservatory. The most difficult part of the house to explain is the dining room, to E of which is a mass of plastered or otherwise concealed brickwork, part of which can be accounted for by a large fireplace, but there must be something more than that. To S again was perhaps a service room originally. This plan has a general resemblance to that of The George Hotel, Bishops Stortford, and other jettied buildings with two large chimney-stacks to rear. In the early 18th century a short wing was added to SW; it has an internal chimney-stack serving two fireplaces, that to W for a kitchen; the chimney-stack has a corbelled-out cap. Possibly this wing extended to W to provide service rooms. A first-floor room to S (study) has an early 17th-century overmantel and panelling, perhaps all reset. A valuation of 1778 states that `the rectory house and all other buildings upon this estate are very large and spacious'.[1]

Towards the middle of the 19th century a service stair was built to S; ground and first-floor corridors were to E; the present staircase, not necessarily in the position of the old one, was built; and the whole house was refenestrated and new fireplaces, doors, windows and ceiling cornices provided. A curious feature of the ground-floor corridor is a short beam of large scantling, aligned with the binding-beam in the dining room. The two beams can hardly be continuous, and it is just possible that there was once a wing to E here, with a fireplace in the shallow projection which encroaches on the corridor.

Note
1. Trinity College, Cambridge, Box 44, IVD.

(77898)
The French Horn Inn, No. 56 High Street,
with Nos 52/54 High Street,

formerly comprised the sizeable inn of that name; division into several properties and partial demolition make the plan difficult to interpret. The principal range to S fronting the High Street had three wings to N; to W of the middle wing a mid 17th-century staircase with heavy carved balusters may originally have been approached through the wing from the courtyard to E. A 19th-century staircase in the E courtyard rises to a gallery adjoining the front range. An assembly room was built *c*1770 on the site of a malting.[1] The SW corner of the inn was set back by several feet *c*1840 in order to widen the street.[2]

For an illustration, see *English Houses 1200–1800*, Fig 287 (plate).

Notes
1. Johnson 1962, Pt 1, 98.
2. Hunt, E M 1945–9, 138.

(77899)
No. 63 High Street

formerly had, in a first-floor room, a compass ceiling; on the end walls the segmental spaces above the panelling were filled with elaborate strapwork executed in plaster and bearing the initials I H S and the date 1624; there was also an overmantel of the same date.[1]

Note
1. Andrews 1905–7, 269–71 with drawings.

(77900)
No. 75 High Street,

of two storeys, jettied to E, and of two bays, revealed richly moulded timber details when drastically altered in 1972;[1] it is probably of the late 15th century.

Note
1. *Newsletter* **33**, 1973.

(77901)
No. 84 High Street,

forming part of the encroachment on the W market-place called Middle Row, is partly late 15th century and partly mid 17th century. Two interpretations are possible: first, that there was originally an open hall with a cross-wing to E, the hall having been rebuilt subsequently;[1] or secondly that what looks like a wing is an unheated building comparable to No. 94 High Street, the later structure to W being a rebuilding of whatever stood on the adjoining site, if anything. There is no conclusive evidence; a reason for preferring the second interpretation is that the plan of the W part bears none of the traces of origin that such rebuilt halls usually do (cf No. 32 Bridge Street, Hitchin).

A carpenter's numeral 1111 on the truss to N suggests[2] that there was formerly a third bay projecting some 15 ft (4·5 m) to W into High Street. The W range had an internal chimney-stack with fireplaces facing N and S, not E and W as might be expected if the stack had been built within an open hall roofed E and W. In this part are moulded plaster ceilings, one on each floor. The building was refenestrated in the 18th century and the ground floor to S altered in the 19th century.

Notes
1. *Newsletter* **34**, 1974 and 41, 1976.
2. *Newsletter* **38**, 1975.

(77902)
No. 87 High Street,

now the Public Library, was built in the late 18th century, perhaps *c*1770–80. It faces N, is of brick, and of three storeys with cellars, with an older timber-framed wing of two storeys and attics to S. In the late 19th century the lowest storey was rusticated and a portico and an entablature from which pairs of columns standing on independent bases break forward were added. The plan comprised only two large rooms divided by a narrow entrance-hall, the staircase being in a shallow projection to S; the kitchen, from which the cellar is reached, is in the rear wing, with other service rooms to S. On the first floor were two bedrooms, each with a dressing room, with two bedrooms and a minor room to S.

(77903)
House `on the north side of...Gilpin House',

possibly on the site of No. 92 High Street, formed part of Middle Row which encroaches on the W market-place at Ware. It was of the early 15th century and had windows with cinquefoiled ogee-headed lights and trefoiled spandrels facing to N and S along the street, so that it was built freestanding. It was perhaps jettied but a confusion of compass points[1] makes it uncertain on which sides. It was demolished in 1898.

Note
1. Andrews 1899–1901b, 265–9.

(77904)
No. 94 High Street,

probably of the 15th century, forms part of the infilling of the W market-place. Although narrow, being slightly less than 12 ft (3·7 m) wide, it is of two storeys with cellar and of two bays with a bold jetty to S (Fig 149). Mortises suggest there was a small shop at the front with a doorway and one unglazed window; the first floor was undivided. To W on the ground floor was a light partition screening off some attached structure now removed. The two bays have neither stair trap nor fireplace. A third bay added to N in the early 16th century has a crown-post roof and an original stair trap; the latter was blocked when a chimney-stack was added *c*1700.

Fig 149 *No. 94 High Street, Ware: plan*

Later stair

For an illustration, see *English Houses 1200–1800*, Fig 237 (plate).

(77905)
No. 2 West Street

incorporates two bays of what must have been a three-bay building at right-angles to the street. It was originally open from

the ground, the roof being blackened by smoke; the surviving open truss combines passing-braces and arch-braces; no trace of a louvre exists except a gablet above the hipped end of the roof to N. A valley rafter to E indicates that this building, which is of uncertain purpose, was originally part of a larger one. A date of *c*1260 is claimed on the basis of carpentry joints but all that can safely be said is that such a date is not impossible.[1]

Note
1. Gibson et al 1980–2, 126–43.

(81120)
No. 8 West Street,

of brick and originally of two storeys and attics, was built in the early 18th century. It faces S and was refronted and heightened to three storeys in the early 19th century. The double-pile plan comprises four rooms flanking a narrow hall which traverses the house; a servants' staircase to NW appears to be a 19th-century addition. There is much bolection-moulded panelling, most of it probably late 19th-century reproduction work.

WARE RURAL

(77907)
Blakesware (approximately TL 406163),

a manor, was purchased in 1664 by Sir Thomas Leventhorp of Sawbridgeworth, who `rebuilt this House and made it a very fair Seat'.[1] On his death in February 1683 the house was sold to John Plummer who `much improved it by Building',[2] perhaps before becoming Sheriff in 1689. It is the subject of Charles Lamb's `Blakesmoore in H-shire' in *Essays of Elia*. It was of two storeys and attics. The principal elevation was surmounted by five curvilinear gables[3] and was probably of eleven bays. In the middle was a two-storey pedimented porch separated by one bay from two flanking projections of similar appearance; these corresponded to the three middle gables. The principal rooms, to judge by the grouping of the chimney-stacks, lay to the left of the entrance. To right of the entrance and joined to the house by a short connecting block was a building projecting forward at right-angles, surmounted by a large ventilator; this was perhaps a kitchen. The interior fittings and furnishings were sold on 17 April 1822 and the structure itself, in lots for demolition, on 22 May.[4] The catalogues are perhaps sufficiently detailed to permit a reconstruction of the house. Two drawings show the house in course of demolition.[5] A new house was begun by Mrs Gosselin in about 1875.[6]

For an illustration, see *English Houses 1200–1800*, Fig 147 (plate).

Notes
1. Chauncy I, 414.
2. Salmon 1728, 246.
3. Oldfield Vol VI, 380 and Clutterbuck; Cussans 1879–81, Vol III (ii), 314, is inaccurate.
4. CRO, 296/B 671, Cockett and Nash sale books.
5. BL Add MS 32352, fos 90, 91.
6. Cussans 1879–81, Vol III (ii), Addenda, 314.

(77908)
Fanhams Hall

is not easily distinguished from Fanhams Hall Farm in documents. In 1699, when John Evans, citizen and clothmaker of London bought it, it is described as the `messuage, tenement or farmhouse...called Fanhams Hall'.[1] `A Survey of Fanham Hall

Farme belonging to Mr. Jn⁰ Evans' dated 1716[2] shows an internal-chimney house of five bays which is more likely to be a farmhouse than the Hall. John Evans, who died in 1729, probably built the earliest part of the present house, and in 1771, when William Plumer of Gilston Park bought it, it was still described as the `messuage, tenement and farm house and farm called Fanhams Hall'.[3] Possibly farmhouse and Hall were not more clearly distinguished because they were close together, a situation found elsewhere in the county (see *English Houses 1200–1800*, p 106). Plumer leased out the house; a mortgage of 1784[4] mentions Fanhams Hall and `the farmhouse called Fanhams Hall Farm'. By c1800, when Oldfield captioned a drawing `A small Seat in Ware uninhabited lately',[5] the gentry house must have been clearly differentiated. In 1822 Plumer's widow Jane sold the `messuage with the farm house and farm called `Fanhams Hall'[6] to Samuel Adams, `banker and gent., of Ware'. A conveyance of 1851 to Philip Longmore[7] refers to the `capital messuage, farmhouse and farm called Fanhams Hall at Ware' and in that year the Hall was occupied by a coltbreaker.[8] In 1859 it was sold to Henry Page of Ware, a maltster who acquired a large fortune and undertook building-works, the precise extent of which has not been discovered, including glass by William Morris's firm.[9] Captain Richard Page Croft enlarged the house in 1901;[10] and from him it descended to Sir Henry Page Croft, 1st Lord Croft.[11] Since 1950 it has been used as a training centre and offices.

The early 18th-century house was of two storeys and attics and c58 ft by 48 ft (18 m x 14·5 m) overall, with a front of seven bays to S. It appears to have resembled Langleybury, Abbots Langley, in outline, the middle part of the N elevation being recessed to give light to the principal staircase. Only the E elevation, which now faces an internal courtyard, retains any 18th-century detail; six windows, three on each floor, have flat-arched heads and aprons; two wider segmental-headed windows are later copies and also have aprons and moulded brick bands mark the first and second floors. The Oldfield drawing[12] shows that c1800 the house was of three storeys; this corresponds to the courtyard elevation in which the top storey is rendered above the band and the windows have no aprons. All the brickwork has been rubbed down and tuck-pointed. The drawing shows the elevation to E, of five bays, with two boldly projecting first-floor bay windows carried on columns; although the windows dwarfed the doorway this was perhaps the entrance, because the roofs and chimney-stacks correspond with those of the entrance front in a Victorian photograph;[13] this shows that the house had by then been enlarged to S. In 1901 the house was greatly enlarged and altered and given a generally Elizabethan appearance; the interior is a mixture of that and Queen Anne style, the W staircase being of the latter kind, with the freestanding plan characteristic of the period.

Notes
1. National Westminster Bank Archives, 758/1, Parcel C.
2. Ibid.
3. Ibid.
4. Ibid.
5. `Fathoms Hall', Oldfield Vol VI, 384–5.
6. National Westminster Bank Archives, 758/1 Parcel B.
7. Ibid.
8. Census.
9. Sewter 1975, 71, under `Farnham Hall (?)'.
10. *Architectural Review* XVIII (July–Dec 1905), 270.
11. *DNB*.
12. Oldfield Vol VI, 384–5.
13. NMR.

(77909)
Hall House, Baker's End (TL 395171)
is late medieval and comprises a small open hall, a jettied cross-wing to E and a two-storeyed service bay to W. The two doors to the service rooms have hollow-chamfered four-centred heads and part of a similar door-head remains to N; close-studding is exposed in the hall; the open truss has a rebated crown-post roof with two-way braces. In the mid 17th century a brick chimney-stack was built backing on to the cross-passage; it is set to S to allow for a staircase. A fireplace was added in the parlour in the late 17th or early 18th century. In the 19th century the house was divided into three cottages; in recent years it has been restored to single occupancy.

(77910)
Morley House, Wareside (TL 387152)
was enlarged and refurbished as a neo-Georgian house by Raymond Erith in 1956. Prior to that it is said to have been two 17th-century cottages, one of T-plan, the other of L-plan, which had been joined together in the 18th century. Some such explanation may be necessary to explain the present rambling plan but too little old work is now visible to confirm it.

(77911)
New Hall (TL 390162)
is first mentioned in 1326 when the vill called Le Newehalle, comprising two messuages and land, was granted to Waltham Abbey, in whose possession it remained until the Dissolution.[1] In 1546 the tenement or manor of Newhall[2] was held by John Dodington senior and in 1563 by Thomas Thoroogood.[3] The house is of the late 15th century and comprised an open hall, a jettied cross-wing to W and a service bay to E (Fig 150). In the 17th century an unusual transformation converted it into a house intended for dual occupation. An upper floor was inserted in the hall, which was heightened, and a chimney-stack was built partly in the cross-passage; the present fireplaces and chimney-shafts are of the late 17th century and may replace a timber stack serving only the hall. This provided one of the two household units, entered through a lobby beside the stack. The service bay was heightened and its upper floor raised and a jettied cross-wing was added to E; the wing comprised two ground-floor rooms, the front one unheated and the rear one with a wide kitchen fireplace. This, with the service room, comprised the second unit, entered by the cross-passage. Two staircases were necessary. The site of the original one serving the W wing was not observed; it was replaced by a mid–late 17th-century staircase in a rear wing of slight projection. In the E unit a 19th-century staircase in the former service bay is probably in the same position as the original one.

Fig 150 *New Hall, Ware Rural: plan*

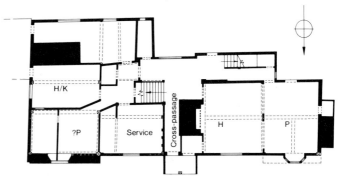

The significance of New Hall lies in the dual but nevertheless interdependent occupancy, comparable to that at Walnut Tree Farm, Pirton. The W unit appears to have comprised, by the end of the 17th century, hall and parlour, both with fireplaces, and a small storeroom adjoining the staircase; the E unit comprised a combined hall and kitchen, an unheated parlour, and the service room of the original house. Possibly meals were taken in the W hall, so that the house was still used in much the old way, yet the two front doors and two staircases establish that it comprised two households. Subsequent alterations, though numerous, are comparatively unimportant; they include the rebuilding of the porch and alteration of the E staircase.

For illustrations, see *English Houses 1200–1800*, Figs 179 (plate), 180 (plate).

Notes
1. VCH III, 391.
2. PRO C/142/74/102.
3. Inquisition *post mortem*, PRO C/142/135/77.

(77912)
Newhouse Farm (TL 392152)

is of brick and is dated to the last quarter of the 17th century by a three-course brick band; the kneelers and coping of the gables; the square finials of the rear (W) gables; and the size of the chimney-stack to S. The staircase balusters are of two different designs, both consistent with this date, but one of them may be the result of an antiquarian restoration of which there is other evidence. Originally the plan (Fig 151) comprised two principal rooms at the front and kitchen and service rooms in the two wings to W. Access from hall and kitchen to parlour and service wing was probably by a pent-roofed way between the wings corresponding to the present inner partition (cf the earlier roof of this kind at Rooks Nest Farm, Walkern).

Fig 151 *Newhouse Farm, Ware Rural: plan*

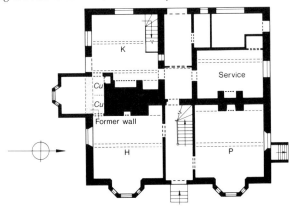

In the mid 19th century bay windows were added to E; in the early 20th century a small wing was added to S; the space between the original wings was enclosed to form an entrance-hall; and antiquarian restoration including the alteration of the staircase and panelling of the first-floor rooms in 17th-century style was undertaken.

(77913)
Tudor Cottage, Baker's End (TL 395169),

of *c*1500, comprises hall to S, which may have been truncated, and jettied cross-wing to N. The wing was formerly divided into two rooms; a doorway with four-centred head and sunk spandrels is reset. An upper floor and a chimney-stack were built in

the hall *c*1700; the smallness of the base of the stack points to its partial or complete rebuilding in the 19th century, when the house was shortened.

(77914)
Ware Park (approximately TL 333144)

had its origins in a park which was in existence by 1349[1] and formed part of the manor of Ware. Between 1570 and 1575 Thomas Fanshawe, Remembrancer of the Exchequer and several times MP,[2] purchased first the manor and then the park[3] and built a new manor house in the park which superseded Place House, Ware. By October 1573 the work was well advanced; payment was made at London for 8,000 tiles, and in December there was a further payment for 132 iron bars for the new building. An undated note intended for Fanshawe lists the work yet to be done; it includes six bay windows to be made in the gallery; 'the upper floor of the same gallery to be made with a compass roofe'; and work on various lodgings, including 'your own lodgings'. Among the rooms mentioned are the hall, and the chamber and hall chamber over it; the great parlour; the lower parlour and the grand chamber over it; and the great kitchen and the great chamber over it. There was a chapel.[4]

Fanshawe's son Sir Henry devoted himself to creating a garden.[5] Henry's son Thomas, by then Viscount Fanshawe, paid for 33 hearths in 1666[6] but having been ruined by the Civil War was forced to sell Ware Park to Sir Thomas Byde in 1668 for £26,000.[7] The following year Byde was Sheriff.

In 1774 Thomas Hope Byde, who was born in 1752, inherited the estate[8] and is said to have rebuilt the house on a new site.[9] The house faced the park to SW, the imposing front elevation, of three bays with semi-octagonal projections at each end, had a high basement with small windows and a simple classical porch at the entrance; above, the principal storey had tall windows surmounted by sunk panels; there was an attic storey.[10] To rear was an L-shaped block;[11] the block to NE probably contained family rooms, that to NW service rooms. A sketch of one of the principal rooms shows an 18th-century fireplace in a room with a domed ceiling.[12] William Palmer, who acquired the house between 1853 and 1858,[13] was of Ware Park when Sheriff in 1848; he presumably had a lease on the house, and appears to have rebuilt it. A late 19th-century photograph[14] showing an Italianate house with a tower suggests that little if any 18th-century work remained. In 1886 J H E Parker, RN, was Sheriff; two years later the house was advertised to be let furnished.[15] The house was burnt in 1911 and subsequently rebuilt.

Notes
1. VCH III, 386.
2. *DNB*.
3. PRO Close Roll, C54/971/10.
4. 'The Manner of Consecrating Sir Thomas Fanshawe's Chapel at Ware Park by the Bishop of Durham', BL Add MS 29586, fos 26–8.
5. Fea 1905, 284–8.
6. PRO E170/248/28.
7. Fea 1905, 230.
8. VCH III, 388.
9. Cussans 1870–3, Vol I (i), 140.
10. Oldfield Vol VI, 376; Charnock; Brayley 1808, Vol VII, 253.
11. Dury and Andrews 1766.
12. Luppino.
13. VCH III, 388.
14. NMR.
15. *The Hertfordshire Mercury and County Press*, 22 December 1888.

(77915)
Westmill House (TL 338163),

of the mid 17th century and of two storeys and attics, comprises a main range to W and a wing to N forming an L-shaped plan. The W range comprised two principal rooms with lateral fireplaces to E and a small service room between them. Probably the hall was to S with entrance directly into it, a partition perhaps corresponding to the position of a screen; the parlour to N was perhaps primarily a dining parlour, its fireplace back-to-back with that of the kitchen to E; their common chimney-stack has a lobby-entrance to N. The staircase was in the re-entrant angle; only the top flights from first floor to attic remain. In the chamber over the kitchen is a fragment of a 17th-century wall-painting, a Corinthian capital and part of the shaft. A refronting of the house with sash windows and pedimented doorcase is dated by a rain-water head with I T/1781 in relief; a staircase-hall was formed in the entrance, and a study or office from the service room to N; a wing now demolished to E of the hall was probably of this date.

WATFORD

(39642)
Cassiobury Park (approximately TQ 096973)

was a manor belonging to St Albans Abbey at the time of the Domesday Survey,[1] and in the course of the 13th century became sufficiently important to give its name to the Hundred which comprised all the abbey lands in Hertfordshire. Nevertheless, despite mention of brick cellars 'in front of the present house' and a drawing of a pointed door-head (see below), there is insufficient evidence to support the contention[2] that the large post-Reformation house incorporated monastic buildings; on the contrary, a reference in 1541 to the farm on the site of Cashiobury[3] and Richard Morrison's petition in July 1545 for a lease of the site of the manor[4] suggest there were no buildings of any consequence there. The manor passed to the Crown at the Dissolution and in 1545 was granted to Sir Richard Morrison; 'he began a fair and large House in this Place...and had prepared Matrices for the finishing thereof, but before the same could be half built, he was forced to fly beyond the Seas'. Dying at Strasbourg in 1556, he was succeeded by his son Charles, who completed the house and was Sheriff in 1579. His grandson, also Sir Charles, came into the estate in 1600[5] and was created baronet in 1611; a rain-water head dated 1603[6] is the only evidence of his building activity. Subsequently the house passed by marriage to Arthur Capell, whose estates, forfeited under the Commonwealth, were recovered at the Restoration by his son Arthur, who was created Earl of Essex in 1661;[7] he changed his place of residence from Hadham Hall to Cassiobury in 1668–9,[8] and Hugh May remodelled the house for him c1677–80.[9] A drastic reconstruction 'in the castellated style' was carried out c1800–5 by James Wyatt for the 5th Earl.[10] Although the house was completely demolished in 1927 it is presented here for its intrinsic interest and for the light it sheds on the problems of house planning in the 17th century.

A considerable part of the pre-Restoration H-plan house survived until c1800, and some fragments until 1927. An 18th-century engraving of the house from SE[11] shows a W wing which was evidently a lodgings range, that part to S of the main range comprising four units, each with a shallow bay window of two storeys, and three doorways. The grouping of the diagonal chimney-shafts (4:2:2:4) suggests that there were four sets of lodgings, each with a large chamber and a correspondingly large fireplace served by two shafts, and a smaller chamber

with a smaller fireplace needing only one chimney-shaft; a fifth set lay to N; each had a wing, probably for a staircase to W.[12] The W wing appears hardly to have extended to N of the main range. To W was a small detached brick building of two storeys with small ground-floor windows, as if for an undercroft, and a tall mullion-and-transom window rising above the eaves into a stepped gable. If anything can be ascribed to Sir Richard Morrison it is this. Adjoining it to E was a medieval-looking doorway with a pointed, moulded head. Presumably kitchen and service rooms were here. Little is known about the remainder of the 16th and early 17th-century house. A wooden doorway with an unusual moulding in its square head and jambs was found 'embedded in the wall near the tower in 1927';[13] the tower was near the SW corner of Wyatt's house and so the doorway establishes the length of the main range in the 16th century. Brickwork painted with a diaper-based pattern was exposed 'on the back wall of Lord Essex's Dressing Room (formerly outside E wall)'[14] and it is unfortunate that this room can no longer be located precisely. The same is true of the rain-water head, dated 1603. Drawings of the house in the 18th century show, in the main range, three chimney-stacks with diagonal shafts, all of which must be of 1603 or earlier, and although there is nothing to prove that the E wing existed by then, it is likely (cf The Grove, Sarratt).

Hugh May's work seems to have comprised the refacing and refurbishing of the main range and the complete rebuilding of the E wing. John Evelyn noted that 'The House is new, a plaine fabric...The *Tympanum* or Gabel at the front is a Bass-relievo of Diana hunting cut in Portland stone'.[15] He disapproved of 'The middle Dores being round...but when the Hall is finish'd as his Lordship designs it, being an Oval *Cupol'd* together with the other wing, it will be a very noble Palace.' Illustrations show that the E wing had panelled chimney-stacks throughout, which, taken in conjunction with the width of this range and its planning, must mean that this part of the house had been wholly rebuilt by May. This may be the basis of Evelyn's comment: 'I believe he [Essex] onely meant to repair at first', for repair, however extensive, was what he must have done to the main range. As well as rebuilding the entrance-hall with its cupola, May created a series of state rooms and must have added a loggia ('Cloisters') to N of the main range; the loggia was flanked by two staircases, presumably to permit access to the principal first-floor rooms without either going through other rooms, or using corridors. In the E wing, circulation on the ground floor, and no doubt on the first floor too, was assured by corridors; one staircase served the private rooms above Lord Essex's suite and the other, the grandest staircase in the house, was placed at the N end of the wing to give access to the important rooms above the State Bedroom. Whether, in May's conception, the Great Library was upstairs, as it was c1800, is not certain. It is extraordinary that part of the old house was allowed to remain, and many must have echoed the surprise implied in an 18th-century comment: 'the Middle and the East Wing is modern, and in good repair; but the West wing is very old, and by no means corresponding with the other Parts of the House'.[16]

Alterations during the 18th century are not documented; they include the insertion of two Venetian windows to give more light in the two small rooms flanking the Drawing Room; and a bow-ended extension to S of the E wing, with another Venetian window on the first floor. An aerial perspective[17] showing the W wing in late 17th or early 18th-century style, matching the rest, is false. Wyatt pulled down the S end of the E wing and incorporated most of the remainder into a Gothic courtyard house. May's principal rooms were preserved; the principal staircase was also retained, although it appears to have been moved from the N end of the E wing to a position near the re-entrant angle of the E and S wings. A visitor in 1825 noted that `The old rooms...have not been much deffaced. A fine ceiling above stairs is thrown away in a bed Ro...'.[18] The loggia was transformed into the Great Cloister; the W Cloister formed the entrance-hall; and a corridor – surprisingly, not Gothicised – ran along the E side of the courtyard. To N the service rooms are principally remarkable for their complexity and the octagonal kitchen. Work which cannot now be specified was carried out by Sir Jeoffrey Wyatville after the death of James Wyatt in 1813.[19]

For illustrations, see *English Houses 1200–1800*, Figs 97 (plate), 138 (plate), 139.

Notes

1. VCH II, 453.
2. Ibid, 454.
3. PRO Ministers' Accounts, SC 6/1619.
4. PRO E318/782.
5. VCH II, 453,
6. Anderson, WCL 2959.
7. *DNB*.
8. Minet 1914, 72.
9. Colvin 1978, 545.
10. Britton 1837, 27.
11. Hertford Museum.
12. Drawing of W front, Britton 1837, Plate 3.
13. Anderson, HM.
14. Anderson, WCL 2958.
15. Evelyn *Diary*: 17 April 1680.
16. Defoe *Tour* Vol II, 166.
17. Kip 1709, 28.
18. Harris 1971, 11–12.
19. Colvin 1978, 561.

(77916)
Frogmore House, Lower High Street,

of brick and of three storeys, presents problems of interpretation. A rain-water head near the S corner is dated 1716. The SE elevation of five bays, has, in the two principal storeys, tall, narrow windows each with a shallow sunk panel above; the parapet was probably treated similarly. Originally the house was entered on this side. The present front doorway to SW is of *c*1900 and leads past the foot of the staircase (cf Golden Parsonage, Great Gaddesden), all of which is reproduction work, as the sinuous ramping of the handrail and wall panels confirms. Consequently the doorway from the present staircase-hall to the SE room must be part of the *c*1900 arrangement, and fits panelling in that room which must also be reproduction work. Similar arguments show that virtually all the interior is of the same period.

The house is now divided into three flats, of which only the one on the ground floor could be examined.

(77917)
Garston House (TL 117000),

a manor first recorded in the 13th century, was purchased in 1453 by Abbot John of Wheathampstead for St Albans Abbey.[1] He was probably responsible for building a cross-wing (cf The Old Rectory Therfield); nothing is known about the open hall which lay to W. The wing had a lofty upper storey with a three-light traceried window.[2] The hall range was apparently rebuilt in the late 17th century, perhaps by John Marsh who owned the house in 1672 when it was licensed for Nonconformist worship,

and who died in 1681.[3] In the mid 18th century it was leased by Isaac Hawkins Browne the elder, minor poet and MP for Wenlock;[4] and towards the end of the century by Josiah Dornford (1764–97), miscellaneous writer and Inspector-General of the army accounts in the Leeward Islands;[5] all the windows of the N (entrance) front were renewed in Gothick style and battlements added in his time. During the 19th century a verandah and single-storey wing for a billiard room were added to E but otherwise the appearance of the house was little altered when it was sold in 1918[6] and demolished. Excavation of the site in 1956 revealed flint footings and 13th-century pottery.[7]

Notes

1. *Chronica Monastici S. Albani, Reg Abbat*, Vol 1, 188.
2. Meynell, two drawings 1799.
3. VCH II, 460.
4. *DNB*; *Court and City Register* 1751, 38.
5. *DNB*; Oldfield Vol VII, 76; Brett Smith 1923.
6. HRO, SC 484.
7. Inf. Mr B F Rawlins.

(81141)
The George Inn

had, in the yard, a freestanding building of two storeys with open jettied gallery of six bays off which three equidistantly spaced doors opened into three rooms. It was demolished in 1897.[1]

For an illustration, see *English Houses 1200–1800*, Fig 250 (plate).

Note

1. Photograph 1894, Anderson, WCL.

(77918)
Nos 137/139, High Street,

at the S corner of Carey Place, is timber framed, of two storeys and was perhaps built in 1614. The plan, aligned E–W, comprises two rooms with internal chimney-stack; on the first floor the fireplace in the front room (to W) had the painted Stuart royal arms with crest and mantling and the date 1614;[1] the whole of the adjoining wall has a painted representation of panelling, now concealed. In the early 18th century the building was refenestrated, rendered and reroofed.[2]

Notes

1. Now in Watford Museum.
2. Castle 1977*a*, 20.

(77919)
Nos 177/179, High Street

comprised a street range facing W (correctly SW) and a long wing to E. Four bays (formerly five) at the end of the wing are of *c*1500 and were probably a warehouse; they appear always to have been of two storeys and had a crown-post roof braced to the collar-purlin. The street range, of three bays and jettied to W, was built in the 16th century; it has no trace of any original fireplace. A late 16th-century building links these two structures; the chimney-stack, of brick, is built within the warehouse; the ground-floor fireplace, for the hall, has moulded timber jambs and lintel; the first-floor fireplace in the chamber above has only a moulded lintel. These two rooms are the first indication that the building served a domestic as well as a commercial function. It has since been demolished.[1]

Note

1. Castle 1977*b*, 176–85.

(77920)
No. 194 High Street,

of three storeys, now Watford Museum, was the headquarters of Benskins Brewery from 1818 until 1972. A rain-water head bears the date 1775 and initials E A D (for Edmund and Ann Dawson).[1] The plan comprised four rooms of varying sizes grouped around a narrow entrance-hall and staircase-hall. A plan dated 1807,[2] showing dual occupancy, was probably drawn when the house was divided; the circumstances of division are unknown (Fig 152). There is no key to the tinting of the plan but since the dividing wall, the smaller of the two staircases, two large bow windows at the rear and a reduction in the size of one fireplace differ from the rest, they no doubt represent the necessary alterations, which also entailed making a second front doorway beside the original one; and each house was provided with its own laundry with what was no doubt servant accommodation above, in a flanking wing. The two ground-floor rooms of each house are labelled `Eatg Room' and `Breakfast Parlour'.

Fig 152 *No. 194 High Street, Watford: plan dated 1807, when the house was divided (top); existing plan (bottom)*

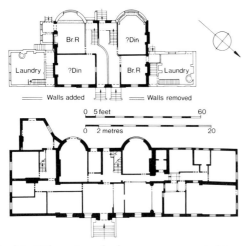

In the late 19th century the house was converted in part into offices and then and subsequently was greatly altered. It was acquired by Watford Borough Council on 5 November 1976 for conversion into a museum.

Notes
1. Inf. Mrs H Poole.
2. In the possession of Allied Breweries.

(77921)
Little Cassiobury

was built in the late 17th century and is said to have been a dower house of the Earls of Essex.[1] Its front (W) elevation is remarkable for the end bay windows which, inside, provide hardly more than window seats. The plan comprises an entrance-hall which is flanked by two slightly smaller rooms, each leading to a minor room to E; the staircase is E of the hall behind the chimney-stack; the first-floor rooms correspond. The first major addition appears to have been a large room to SE and smaller rooms adjoining it to N; to NE the kitchen may be a reconstruction of the original. In 1930 the house was `rehabilitated' by Clough Williams-Ellis;[2] the present arrangement of the staircase dates from then, and probably much else. In 1939 it was converted into offices for Hertford County Council, when several rooms lost their fittings.

Notes
1. VCH III, 447.
2. Hastings 1938, 162.

(77922)
Watford Place (TL 110962),

a large house built at the end of the 18th century,[1] is the successor of two earlier buildings, both of which appear to have been grouped together under that name, although one of them, for part of its history, was called The Lecturer's House. The latter, the residence of the holder of the lectureship founded and endowed by Lady Elizabeth Russell in 1610, was added to the endowment by Dame Dorothy Morrison soon after Lady Elizabeth (her daughter) died in 1611. Michael Heydon, by a lease dated 18 October 1613, granted `all that capital messuage or dwelling house called Watford Place situate in Newe Street' to Dame Dorothy for 100 years,[2] and in 1740 the Russell Trustees purchased it as the house `commonly called Watford Place'.[3] This house is known in outline from a plan of 1824,[4] when it was exchanged for other property, and from two early 19th-century views,[5] and the porch survived until 1965. It was built in the mid–late 16th century, facing E with a cross-wing to W. The wing was probably of mixed construction with brick and timber framing; it had a stepped gable and two octagonal shafts, the latter standing on trefoiled corbels and having crenellated caps; to E a two-storey bay window lit the hall and great chamber, and to E again was a two-storey porch. By the 18th century a boldly jettied upper storey over a carriageway had been added to the wing. The plan of 1824 suggests that a wing to SE was a later addition.

Some distance to S a second brick house faced E to St Mary's churchyard; it was of the late 16th century and incorporated part of a house of *c*1500; the latter survived until *c*1750; to E was a later wing. This must have been the house occupied by Thomas Hobson of the Inner Temple, Clerk of the Petty Bag, who died 30 August 1679 `at his House call'd Watford Place'.[6] It was demolished in the first quarter of the 19th century.[7] Although it is impossible to reconstruct the history of the two houses in any detail they seem to have had a generally similar development.

The present Watford Place was built by Archibald Paxton, Esq.; two prints of it in the house bear the date 1797 and the caption to Oldfield's drawing[8] refers to it as `a newly erected mansion'. In April 1822 Paxton's son-in-law Stewart Marjoribanks, `having bought Watford Place, commenced making considerable alterations';[9] these included removal of the top storey and the addition of the steps and porticoed front concealing the ground floor, so producing the present Italianate appearance. In 1825 Marjoribanks sold the house to Mr Jonathan King, who took possession of it on 6 December.[10] In 1851[11] the grounds had just been divided up as building plots. The fittings of the house are now entirely of the mid 19th century.

Notes
1. This account incorporates information from Mr B F Rawlins.
2. Chauncy II, 363.
3. Rudd 1930–2, 99.
4. HRO.
5. Clutterbuck Vol I; watercolour in private collection, photographed for RCHME files.
6. Chauncy II, 463.
7. Rawlins 1974, 12–15; 1975, 10.
8. Oldfield Vol VII, 72.
9. Diary of Charles Hayward, Watford Central Library.
10. Ibid.
11. HRO, SC, D ELS B 487.

WATFORD RURAL

(77923)
Oxhey Hall (TQ 103943),

the house of one part of the manor of Oxhey, was formerly enclosed within a moat of which the N, S and W arms remain; it now has the appearance of a Victorian farmhouse of brick with roofs of Welsh slate. The complicated descent of the manor[1] throws little light on the house prior to the 16th century. By *c*1500 the site of the manor of Oxhey, called Oxhey Hall, was in the possession of Randolph Billington, who sold it to John Brown. Subsequently the estate was owned successively by George Newdigate and his son John; the latter disposed of it by two conveyances dated 1566 and 1571 to Francis Haydon, who sold it to John Franklyn (d.1596). These frequent sales and a lack of information about the owners make it difficult to connect anyone with the existing building, which appears to be no more than the lodgings range of a much larger house, but since only the Newdigates were in possession for any length of time they are most likely to have built it (but cf Queen Hoo, Tewin, where James Smyth left the house after only five years). By 1604 the manor was leased to John Anderson or Polter. In 1621 the probate inventory of John Anderson the younger of Oxhey Hall, yeoman,[2] lists hall, parlour, boulting room and cellar; followed by wash-house, milk house and kitchen, which were perhaps detached, or a detached range; chambers over hall, cellar and parlour, and the servants' chamber, the last-named possibly

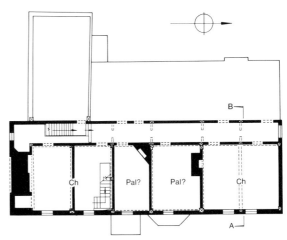

Fig 154 *Oxhey Hall, Watford Rural: first-floor plan*

Fig 153 *Oxhey Hall, Watford Rural: cross-section*

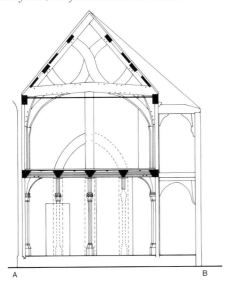

being over the boulting house; and finally the stable and mill house. These rooms are too few for the quite different kind of household implied by the surviving building. Either Oxhey Hall was in divided occupation, the part described being largely service rooms, or it comprised two separate houses.

Behind the mid 19th-century brick front is a timber-framed building of two storeys, the timber throughout being of unusually large scantling. The room to N has a remarkably elaborate ceiling of 16 square panels formed by the binding-beams and bearers, all of which are of deep section and moulded. Each panel frames chamfered boards cut to a quatrefoil shape with square flower terminals on each cusp, and is subdivided into four small panels by two slight chamfered timbers with a floral boss at the intersection. The principal beams have bosses, some

modern, at the intersections, and at each end is a bracket springing from the moulded capital of a semi-octagonal shaft carved in the solid of each wall-post. Where the framing is exposed it is in large panels with bracing in a herring-bone pattern. The whole decorative scheme, which is of the early 16th century, is of a richness unparalleled in the county. The room to S has exposed joists and a wide and probably original fireplace. The middle part of the house on the ground floor is wholly Victorian in appearance, but upstairs the principal posts, with arch-braces springing from moulded capitals and rising to cambered tie-beams, are mostly exposed. On both ground and first floor, passages to E run the full length of the building; they are spanned by two-centred arches springing from moulded capitals and corresponding to the bays of the main structure. The roof has tenoned purlins; four bays have a rather plain finish with one purlin on each side and raking struts; the two bays to N have two purlins and are divided by an open truss with reverse-curved braces (Fig 153). Mortises in the W wall-plate establish the positions of the four doorways, and chamfers on the E plate show the positions of the principal windows.

These details permit interpretation of the building as a lodgings range placed within a moated enclosure and associated with a house the site of which is unknown. It comprises two large first-floor rooms to N and S and two smaller ones in the middle (Fig 154); all were open to the roof and were reached by doors from the corridor. The room to N was better finished and the adjoining room larger than their counterparts to S, and this near-symmetry suggests that each pair of rooms formed a suite, not necessarily interconnected. Probably there was a comparable arrangement on the ground floor, the more important rooms being to N; and the existence of two relatively small and unimportant rooms in the middle may explain why it was so easy to transform them into their present Victorian guise without leaving a trace of antiquity. Probably the original staircase was on the site of the present one because only there, in the W wall of the corridor, do the wall-posts not correspond to the bays of the main structure, which may imply a stair giving access to a W range as well as to the existing corridor.

The present wing to W and the chimney-stack to S of the main range were probably built in the early 17th century; the wing roof has clasped-purlins and windbraces. In the early 18th century a chimney-stack was inserted to heat the two N rooms on each floor of the main range. In 1754 the probate inventory of Daniel Lovett, late of Oxhey Hall,[3] lists kitchen, passage, the best parlour, scullery, pantry, brewhouse, cellars, four chambers, the room over the passage, the lumber room and men's room.

About the 1860s or 1870s the house was refronted and extended at the back.

For illustrations, see *English Houses 1200–1800*, Figs 96 (plate), 297 (plate), 302 (plate).

Notes
1. VCH II, 455–9.
2. HRO, A25/2716.
3. HRO, Prob 3/53/2.

(77924)
Oxhey Place (TQ 112932)

was an estate formed out of the manor of Oxhey Hall;[1] in 1605 it was purchased by Sir James Altham,[2] Baron of the Exchequer, who built a house at the cost of £3,100.[3] John Heydon bought it in 1639 and in 1662 paid for 21 chimneys.[4] He sold it in 1668 to Sir William Bucknall, who `built a fair House'[5] described in the Particular as `a very spacious and large house'. In 1688 Sir John Bucknall demolished a large part of the old mansion and built a large square mansion of brick,[6] and although neither Chauncy nor Salmon mention this the date is likely enough because Bucknall became Sheriff in 1692. The only drawing of the house[7] shows an elevation which appears originally to have been seven bays wide and perhaps only of two storeys; this may have been the extent of the 1670 work. The third storey and two flanking bays at each end may be additions of 1688. After surveys by Mr Gwilt and Mr Wyatt another Sir William Bucknall pulled the house down in 1799 and sold the materials `by catalogue' for £1,693. An intended new house at that time, for which James Lewis submitted designs, was not actually built.[8]

Notes
1. VCH II, 456.
2. *DNB*.
3. HRO, Particular of *c*1682.
4. PRO E179/375/30.
5. Chauncy II, 357.
6. Cussans 1879–81, Vol III (ii), 174–5.
7. Oldfield Vol VII, 84.
8. HRO, Gorhambury MS IX, E10, 11.

WATTON-AT-STONE

(77925)
No. 93 High Street (TL 302192)

incorporates the cross-wing of a small, late medieval house, the hall of which has been rebuilt. The wing, probably of the 16th century, is narrow and of two bays with a crown-post roof which has slight two-way braces. The hall range is of two-room lobby-entrance plan; the part adjoining the wing is of two storeys and has some re-used smoke-blackened rafters; the remaining part, in separate occupation, is of one storey and attics and may incorporate the structure of the medieval hall.

(77926)
Watton Woodhall (TL 318189),

`a large Pile of Brick, with a fair Quadrangle in the Middle of it',[1] was burnt in 1771.[2] Its representation on a map of 1766[3] is too schematic to be trustworthy but shows an elongated courtyard and also the three projections of the entrance front facing SE; a drawing of the ruins was made in August 1775.[4] The house was clearly of several builds, the earliest identifiable part being perhaps the gatehouse, which was flanked by two semi-octagonal turrets; the gateway had a four-centred arch with a large window above and two chimney-shafts of moulded brick. To left (SW) of the gatehouse the hall, above an undercroft, is identifiable by its tall windows, and adjoining it is the gabled parlour wing. To the right (NE) of the gatehouse a range of two storeys had a chimney-stack with two fluted shafts; an adjoining corner block was somewhat higher and perhaps later. A considerable part of the house was presumably the work of Sir Philip Boteler, who succeeded to the manor in 1514[5] and was Sheriff in 1533 and 1540; Sir John Boteler, who succeeded in 1545 and was Sheriff in 1556; and Philip Boteler, who was Sheriff in 1578.

For an illustration, see *English Houses 1200–1800*, Fig 94 (plate).

Notes
1. Chauncy II, 56.
2. Carrington *Diary*, 22.
3. Dury and Andrews 1766.
4. Bodl, Gough Maps 11, fo 42*r*.
5. VCH III, 162.

WELWYN

(77927)
Danesbury (TL 233171),

formerly St John Lodge, was described in 1775 as a new house, built by Mary (née Schuyler) the wife of Captain the Hon Henry St John; some years after her death in 1784 the house was sold to a family connection, General Cornelius Cuyler, serving in the British army.[1] A drawing of *c*1800[2] shows a Palladian house of three storeys and of seven bays facing SW with semi-octagonal bay windows of full height to NW and SE; its overall plan was square (Fig 155). The house was leased *c*1816 to William Blake, a banker, who purchased it in 1824; sale particulars of that year describe it as having a paved entrance-hall, `a capital Drawing Room with Bow, and a noble Eating Room, with Bow', each 36 ft by 24 ft (11 m x 7 m); over the latter was a drawing or morning

Fig 155 *Danesbury, Welwyn: development plans*

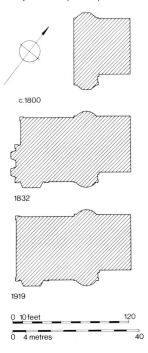

c.1800

1832

1919

0 10 feet   120
0 4 metres   40

room, and over the former the principal bedroom, with dressing room.[3] Rooms this size fill the SW front and imply that the entrance had been moved, perhaps to NW (Fig 156). Presumably Blake rebuilt the bay windows as bows; by 1832 he had refronted the house by adding a large block of two storeys to SW, creating a fairly plain pilastered front with several boldly projecting bay windows on the ground floor;[4] it is not clear how the problem of lighting so large a double-pile house was solved but no doubt a staircase-hall was needed in the addition, and this was top-lit. The Blake family occupied the house until 1919 when it was sold to Mr A E Barton;[5] soon after it was gutted by fire.[6] The addition of 1824–32 was demolished and the remainder immediately rebuilt with two bow windows to SW as well as those to NW and SE: the interior is in the Queen Anne style; the house was renamed from a mistaken antiquarian supposition.[7] Since c1945 it has been a hospital.

Notes
1. Johnson 1960, 41.
2. Oldfield Vol VII, 194.
3. HRO, D/EX69 E4.
4. Buckler Vol IV, 199.
5. HRO, SC D/ERy B485.
6. *The Hertfordshire Mercury and County Press*, 11 September 1920.
7. Johnson 1960, 41.

Fig 156 *Danesbury, Welwyn: plan*

0 5feet   60
0   2metres   20

(77928)
Lockleys (TL 237159),

a manor, is first recorded in 1303; later in the 14th century the capital messuage was stated to be ruined.[1] Nothing definite is known about the `fair seat' which existed in 1700;[2] the most likely builder is George Horsey of Digswell,[3] who acquired Lockleys in 1566, was Sheriff in 1572 and died in 1587. Edward Wingate, to whom it was sold in 1624, was a Parliamentarian[4] who became a Commissioner of Excise under Charles II and died in 1685; he devoted his energies to the grounds[5] and paid for 12 hearths in 1673.[6] In 1715 Ralph Wingate paid tax on 30 windows[7] and in that year sold the estate to Edward Searle Esq. of London, merchant, who built the present house in 1717. It was described a few years later as `elegantly built and situated, especially if we

look at it in its Summer Perfection',[8] but its quite advanced detailing is belied by the archaic plan of a hall flanked by cross-wings (Fig 157). Although, so far as can now be seen, it was rebuilt in a single campaign, no breaks being visible in the brick-work, it incorporated in the early 19th century a wing to NE with a roof of steep pitch;[9] and in the N wing a chamfered

Fig 157 *Lockleys, Welwyn: plan c1720*

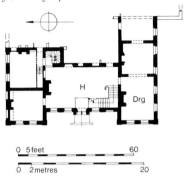

0 5feet   60
0   2metres   20

bridging-joist is apparently unrelated to the room it is now in. Moreover the hall is larger than was usual in the early 18th century, and has features which suggest the refashioning of an older house: there is a staircase in the re-entrant angle between hall and N wing, cutting across one of the windows of the hall range; a blocked doorway opposite the front entrance; and a lofty recess, rising the full height of the hall and the room above, placed where a lateral fireplace or a window might be expected. Little can be said about room uses except that the kitchen was probably in the block to NE; and although the secondary stair-case is much inferior to the main one it is more than a servants' stair, because, in providing the only access to the second floor, it probably led to some chambers used by the family. To N of the house were stables, wash-house, laundry, dairy and brewhouse forming one side of the yard;[10] Sir George Shee, who had been successively Undersecretary for Home, War and Colonies[11] bought Lockleys c1815 and perhaps added to SE a wing which had, on the first floor, a lofty ballroom conspicuous by its tall windows; an unsigned and undated architect's sketch[12] of the floor construction of this room, which has brick arches, may well be of Shee's time. The wing appears in a drawing of 1832[13] but may antedate Shee's death in 1825. In 1911 the house underwent an extensive restoration by Sir Reginald Blomfield for Mrs Neale, to whom the estate had descended by marriage.[14] Most of the interior fittings are of that date. From 1924 onwards the house has been used as a school.

Notes
1. VCH III, 167.
2. Chauncy II, 30.
3. *Visitations*, 114-15.
4. Kingston 1894, 5, 11.
5. Chauncy II, 30.
6. PRO E179/375/31.
7. HRO, LT Misc 10.
8. Salmon 1728, 204.
9. Clutterbuck.
10. SC 10 November 1812 (typescript in house, original in possession of Captain R Neale).
11. Tipping 1920, 51.
12. In possession of Captain R Neale.
13. Buckler Vol IV, 198.
14. Tipping 1920, 54.

(77929)
The Old Rectory (TL 231161),[1]

formerly a moated site, lost its original function in 1730 when Edward Young[2] became rector and moved to his house called Guessens, also in Welwyn, and although the house was occupied by his successor from 1765 until c1775 it has been in lay occupation ever since.[3] In May 1518 the rector was non-resident and the rectory was said to be ruinous[4] so the present buildings are likely to be of later date. In 1663 Gabriel Towerson, Minister, paid for seven hearths.[5] In 1709 the rectory was described as a house of brick and timber, tiled, having three rooms paved and others floored; there were also two barns each of three bays and a porch, two stables, a carthouse and a granary.[6] In 1715 and again in 1724 and 1730 the Revd Mr Otley paid the maximum window tax on 30 or more windows.[7] In 1733 Mrs Mary Wingate and Mrs Beaver paid for the parsonage, the Revd Dr Young appearing later in the list. A map of c1810[8] shows the present range extending farther E and two outbuildings; some of these extra buildings may be those referred to in 1709. Adam Burditt, coachman, was in occupation in 1851.[9] An abstract of title dated 1906 names seven tenants. The house comprises two two-storeyed and jettied timber-framed buildings facing S and a later addition to W; the middle part, which was of one room on each floor originally, is wider than that to E but both have clasped-purlin roofs of two bays, with curved windbraces; to W evidence has been found of a wide chimney-stack; another large stack remains to E. Possibly these two adjoining structures can be explained by piecemeal rebuilding; to a hall 'ruinous' in 1518 was added the large solar or chamber block, and subsequently the hall was replaced by a much smaller structure, now the E part (cf 40, Stocks Road, Aldbury). A lower two-storey range to W is late 17th century. A narrow and slightly lower weatherboarded range was added parallel to the earlier buildings and possibly in stages, in the 18th century; even with this the 30 or more windows of 1715 are difficult to find.

Notes
1. This account incorporates information from Mr Tony Rook.
2. *DNB*.
3. Rook 1979, 34–6.
4. Lincoln *Visitations*, Vol II, 111.
5. PRO E/179/248/23.
6. Lincolnshire RO, Terr/22.
7. HRO, LT Misc 10.
8. Redrawn, Rook 1979, 37.
9. Census.

WELWYN GARDEN CITY

(60014)
Digswell House (TL 230143),

recorded as a manor before the Conquest, was acquired by John Perient in 1414;[1] Thomas Peryent Esq. was Sheriff in 1498 and died in 1539. His will mentions the hall, parlour, parlour chamber, great chamber above the parlour and the chamber within the great chamber.[2] Thomas Perient senior was Sheriff in 1576. Thereafter the house declined in importance. A drawing of c1800[3] shows what was probably a late-medieval hall range with an oriel window of full height but ground and first-floor windows for the remainder. Entry was through a two-storey porch; at each end were two gabled wings, those at the service end being lower than those at the upper end; the latter had some 18th-century detail, including a Venetian window. In 1786 the

estate was bought by Henry Cowper,[4] who by 1804 had demolished the old house and was building a new one[5] to designs by Samuel Wyatt.[6] The house has now been subdivided to serve a community of artists and craftsmen.

For an illustration, see *English Houses 1200–1800*, Fig 47 (plate).

Notes
1. VCH III, 83.
2. Ward 1953, 66–7.
3. Oldfield Vol II, 552.
4. VCH III, 83.
5. Carrington *Diary*, 108.
6. Colvin 1978, 958.

(77930)
Ludwick Hall (TL 255116),

a manor house, was held by the Ludwick family from the early 13th century until 1414 when it passed to John Perient.[1] It was built in the first half of the 15th century and comprised a hall of two bays with cross-wing to E and service bay to W. The hall is of two unequal bays (10 ft and 12 ft 6 ins (3·1 m and 3·8 m)); to W was the cross-passage and to E a bench, the peg-holes for which are visible; the posts of the open truss have been cut back and the arch-braces and tie-beam removed. The wing to E was jettied to N; in the W bay the first-floor joists, close-spaced and of large scantling, are laid E–W. In the 16th century the hall was divided by a partition immediately to W of the open truss; part of it remains in the roof, heavily blackened to W, clean to E. In the late 16th century a wing was added to W; about 8 ft (2·4 m) from the S wall a binding-beam has mortises for a partition; the bay to S has smoke-blackened rafters suggesting that this was a kitchen, perhaps with a service room to N. In the 17th century an upper floor and brick chimney-stack were inserted in the hall and a lobby-entrance was created. In the late 18th century ground and first-floor fireplaces were added to the E wing. A single-storey brick wing built c1800 to N of the W wing was probably a kitchen because about the same time a cellar was built to S of the wing and the old kitchen and the adjoining bay were provided with a fireplace, to make either a parlour or a farm office.

For an illustration, see *English Houses 1200–1800*, Fig 48.

Note
1. VCH III, 105.

WESTMILL

(77932)
Westmill Bury (TL 371270),

the manor house of Westmill, descended with Hamels, Braughing, from the late 16th century and was occupied as a farmhouse from the beginning of the 18th century.[1] It is of two storeys and attics and of brick, facing N (correctly NW), and was built in the first quarter of the 18th century. The plan, which has altered considerably in the present century and is thus somewhat uncertain as to its original form, is c58 ft 6 ins x 37 ft (18 m x 11 m) overall and is divided by a transverse brick wall flanking the passage-like hall to W into two not quite equal parts, that to E being the larger. The front hall has to E a staircase to the cellars and, approached from the rear (S), one to the first floor, which has certainly been reset although all the details are ostensibly original. Four ground-floor rooms each have a gable-wall fireplace; the room to NW has been subdivided and a secondary staircase has been built in that to SW, flanking a passage from entrance-hall to an early 19th-century service wing to W. All the rooms except that to NE are oblong, with the fireplace on one of the short sides. The first floor now has five bedrooms, that to N of the staircase being without a fireplace; originally the plan may have provided dressing rooms or closets for the four principal rooms.

Note
1. VCH III, 399.

(77931)
Wakeley (TL 341268)

at the time of the Conquest was divided into three holdings, only one of which was a manor;[1] its descent does not explain the present house, which comprises two separate houses built in line some 4 ft (1·2 m) apart and aligned NE–SW (N–S for description); both are ostensibly of c1600 but have indications of earlier origin. That to S is of three-cell internal-chimney plan, the rooms from N to S being kitchen, hall and small service room. No 17th-century detail remains but the placing of the Victorian staircase within the hall to E suggests that it may replace two earlier ones sited at the ends of the house in late medieval fashion. The house to N is of T-plan with cross-wing to S. The hall range has roof trusses devoid of smoke-blackening and a lateral stack to W; the hall fireplace is of c1700. The oldest datable feature is a two-light ovolo-moulded window of the 17th century and the chimney-stack is of the late 17th century but the form of the plan is earlier and points to the piecemeal rebuilding of an earlier house. The two houses may have been linked together on the ground floor. In the 19th century the houses were joined together and a porch and staircase were added.

For an illustration, see *English Houses 1200–1800*, Fig 185 (plate).

Note
1. VCH IV, 20–2.

WESTON

(77933)
Howell's Farm (TL 280278),

named from John de Hauile who was living in 1294,[1] incorporates a late medieval cross-wing; the open hall associated with it, which must have been of considerable size, has been demolished. By 1580 it was in the possession of the Kimptons, who established themselves as a gentry family, but whether Howells

Fig 158 Bride Hall, Wheathampstead: plan

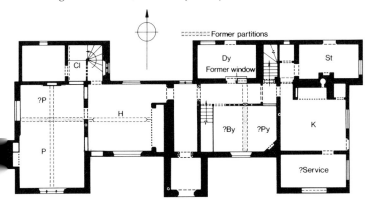

or Darnells in this parish was their seat is not clear.[2] From the late 17th century until the 1970s Howells was a farmhouse and then became purely a residence.

The wing is of three bays, jettied to E, and originally had neither fireplace nor internal partitions; and since there is no obvious break in the ground-floor joists for a staircase the latter was perhaps external, as at Clintons, Little Hadham. (For a comparable later wing see The Abbot's House, Abbots Langley.) The ends of the wall-plate are shaped and the roof has crown-posts down-braced to the tie-beam. The former hall stood to N. In the 16th century a chimney-stack with one octagonal flue and glazed bricks which may have formed a simple pattern was added to S; the ground-floor fireplace is large for a parlour but perhaps the latter had taken over some of the functions of the hall. In the late 17th century a short wing was added to S to provide a parlour and a chamber with a fireplace with a depressed four-centred head; the chamfered plinth to S of the old stack, and its cutting away in the passage, prove that the parlour chimney is an addition. At the same time a first-floor fireplace was added to the old stack and three diagonal shafts capped the whole. A staircase was added to S of the stack, and the old wing was extended c.4 ft (1·2 m) to E to accommodate it and provide a flush E wall; this alteration probably accompanied the demolition of the open hall. A short wing to SW, of two storeys, probably a dairy, was also added.

In the early 18th century the wing to SW was extended, probably as a brewhouse, and a new staircase, of which some re-used balusters remain, was built between the SW and SE wings, facing the entrance; and if the room to W of the entrance were formed then, with a passage to S, the plan approximated to that of a new-built house of the period. Then or later in the century a kitchen was added to NW. The house underwent careful restoration c1970.

For an illustration, see *English Houses 1200–1800*, Fig 9.

Notes
1. Gover, Mawer and Stenton 1938, 146.
2. Inquisition *post mortem*, PRO C/142/308/118; *Visitations*, 69.

WHEATHAMPSTEAD

(77934)
Bride Hall (TL 190159),

a manor house, descended in 1543 by marriage to Sir John Boteler, whose son Sir Philip sold it to George Perient in 1597. The Botelers were the only people to own it for any length of time before 1608, when it was put into the hands of trustees for Sir John Garrard, Bart.[1] The house, which is of brick, was probably built in the time of Sir Philip Boteler; it is dated to the late 16th century by the original stepped outline of the porch gable;[2] the W wing may have been similar because, like the porch, it now has tumbled brickwork in the S gable. The plan (Fig 158), unusual for a manor house in having the hall chimney-stack backing on to the cross-passage, may be explicable as the result of changes during a piecemeal rebuilding of an older house, the phases of which cannot be closely dated. In the first of them the form of the hall fireplace, as well as its vernacular position, suggests that it may have been intended for cooking; a timber-framed partition separated the hall from the wing to W; the wing originally comprised to S a larger room and a smaller one to N with fireplaces; that to S was no doubt an unheated parlour in the sense of bedchamber; from the room to N a doorway opened into a staircase turret, probably to a closet under the stair which was reached directly from the hall. To E of the entrance-passage is an axial passage lit, originally, by a window *c*5 ft 3 ins (1·6 m) wide; three doors to S led to the cellar and two service rooms (cf Aston Bury); to N a staircase turret matched that to W. The E wing comprised kitchen and a service room to S; the latter has to W a stair trap, possibly original, for a servants' staircase; a beam between the rooms, now largely masked by a brick wall, is chamfered to N and plain to S. The first-floor rooms are open to ceilings under the collar-beams; the W wing roof has collar-rafters. In the late 17th century a chimney-stack was added to the W wing with ground and first-floor fireplaces, the former being painted with vertical bands of black and white triangles. In the 18th century several ground-floor windows were rebuilt and partitions were renewed in brick; a fireplace was added to N of the W wing; a dairy and office were added to NE; the eaves throughout were rebuilt with a serrated course of brick.[3] Subsequently fireplaces were added in the bedrooms to E of the internal stack and probably also in that to NE. In the mid 1920s the house underwent a thorough-going restoration, using late 16th-century detail to renew 18th-century windows.

Notes
1. VCH II, 435, 299.
2. Buckler Vol III, 183.
3. Ibid.

(77935)
The Old Farmhouse, Bury Farm,

of the early 16th century, belongs to the same architectural type as guildhalls, church houses or similar special-purpose buildings and resembles the Guildhall, Ashwell (Nos 57–61 High Street). It is jettied on both long walls to N and S and comprises three rooms on each floor, the middle room being of two bays. Doorways and windows have moulded jambs and four-centred heads. Chimney-stacks were built in the hall and to N of the W bay in the 18th century.

For an illustration, see *English Houses 1200–1800*, Fig 243 (plate).

(77936)
Castle Farm (TL 157146),

formerly Creswell Farm,[1] is of the late 17th century and of mixed construction, brick on the ground floor and timber framed above. It is square in plan (Fig 159) with central chimney-stack and lobby-entrance to E; room uses are conjectural; the staircase is approximately in its original position; to NW is a cellar. These divisions are matched on the first floor, where a small fireplace with chamfered four-centred head and high stops to the jambs still has its original plaster finish. The service wing to S is of later construction but may, by analogy with larger houses, replace an original one.

Fig 159 *Castle Farm, Wheathampstead: plan*

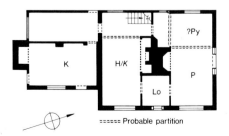

====== Probable partition

Note
1. VCH II, 296.

(77937)
Cottage at Gustard Wood Common

(demolished; precise location unknown) had a roof of raised-aisled (or queen-post) construction supporting a crown-post with four-way struts; it was unusual in having a purely decorative crown-strut. It was probably of the early 15th century. The width and quality of the building (*c*21 ft (6·5 m)) suggests it was of quite high status.[1]

For an illustration, see *English Houses 1200–1800*, Fig 293.

Note
1. Davys 1888, 13–14.

(77938)
Delaport Farm (TL 175153)

is of two principal parts, neither complete in itself; that to NE, of two bays and of the late 16th century, comprises hall and chamber above; the chimney-stack by analogy backed on to a wide cross-passage. In the 17th century a third bay to SW replaced whatever stood there; the gable chimney-stack and fireplace are set to NW as if to allow for an unheated service room (removed) to SE; this bay may have been built by James Delaport who purchased land in the parish in 1663.[1] Extensive alterations in the present century have obscured the development of this house.

Note
1. VCH II, 296.

(77939)
Lamers or Lamer Park (TL 181160)

was a manor, taking its name from the important family of de la Mare. In 1608 it was conveyed to trustees of Sir John Garrard, Bart., who, in 1617, obtained a charter of free warren on his estate.[1] A particular of the manor, undated but of the early 17th century,[2] opens with `a faire brick house' which was valued, with its gardens, orchards and outhouses, at £1,500; there was also a park. Sir John Garrard, who was one of the leading Parliamentarians in Hertfordshire and was Sheriff in 1643, 1644 and the first half of 1645, had presumably engaged in building-works of some kind which were commemorated by heraldic glass dated 1632; there was also glass dated 1610.[3] A drawing of Lamer House `from an old sketch taken before it was rebuilt'[4] shows a building of very unusual appearance with large mullion-and-transom windows, dormer windows and a three-storey porch, all of which might be of *c*1632, but the strangest features are three tall round crenellated towers quite without parallel in Hertfordshire. In the absence of the original, which has not been located, not much reliance can be placed on the redrawing. In 1673 Sir John Garrard paid for 20 hearths;[5] he died in 1686.[6] In 1690 another Sir John Garrard, son of the first, was Sheriff. The last representative of the line was Sir Benet Garrard, who is said to have demolished the old house about 1761 and built a new one; he died in 1767.[7] An inventory of the household furniture taken in July 1767 after Sir Benet's death[8] opens with a list of 10 rooms in the old building which includes Sir Benet's bed-chamber and ends with a breakfast parlour; it then proceeds to the breakfast parlour in the new building, so that part at least of the old house was incorporated in the new. For some years the house was leased out; in 1781 it was occupied by John Stuart, Lord Cardiff.[9] A plan made in 1794 (Fig 160)[10] for Sir Benet's successor Charles Drake, who took the name Garrard, does not

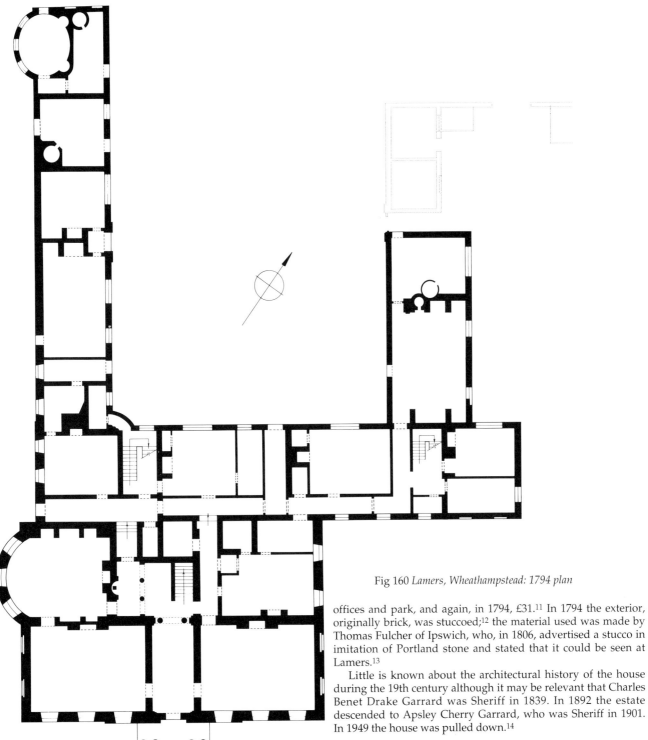

Fig 160 *Lamers, Wheathampstead: 1794 plan*

offices and park, and again, in 1794, £31.[11] In 1794 the exterior, originally brick, was stuccoed;[12] the material used was made by Thomas Fulcher of Ipswich, who, in 1806, advertised a stucco in imitation of Portland stone and stated that it could be seen at Lamers.[13]

Little is known about the architectural history of the house during the 19th century although it may be relevant that Charles Benet Drake Garrard was Sheriff in 1839. In 1892 the estate descended to Apsley Cherry Garrard, who was Sheriff in 1901. In 1949 the house was pulled down.[14]

Notes
1. VCH II, 299.
2. HRO, 27362.
3. RCHME 1910, 239.
4. HRO, MS caption added to page proof of VCH II, 299, but omitted from final publication.
5. PRO E179/375/31.
6. Monumental Inscription, Oldfield Vol VII, 253.

suggest that any part of the old building then survived, although it is noticeable that the back (N) wall of the rectangular block forming the principal part of the house built in the 1760s is in fact staggered as if to join older work. In 1792 the sum of £59 was paid to Daniel Tidd for carpenter's work at Lamer House,

7. Ibid.
8. HRO, 27284.
9. *Royal Kalendar* 1781, 13.
10. HRO, 80232B.
11. HRO, 80232A.
12. BL Add MS 9063, fo 768.
13. Colvin 1978, 324.
14. *About Wheathampstead*, 47.

(77940)
Mackerye End (TL 156155),

a manor, belonged to the Brockett family from 1558 to 1628 and then had three owners before coming into the possession of Thomas Hunsden, who paid tax on 12 hearths at Michaelmas 1662 and 13 in 1673;[1] he rebuilt the house in 1665.[2] All datable features are of the mid–late 17th century. Following its incorporation in the Lamer estate in 1681, Mackerye End lost its former importance and consequently suffered comparatively little alteration for a house of its size. The design of the symmetrical front elevation emphasises the wings, which have pedimented gables and had wider windows than the main range; they also have tall chimney-shafts with carved ornament whereas the stack serving the hall had, in 1907, three square shafts rising to a single deep cap, the whole embellished only by mouldings.[3] To N and E the windows have brick architraves with lugs top and bottom.

The plan (Fig 161) can be explained using an inventory dated

Fig 161 *Mackerye End, Wheathampstead: ground and first-floor plans*

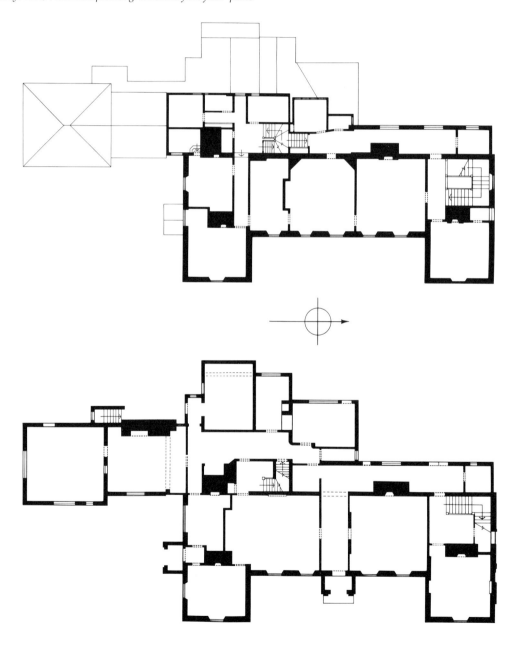

27 April 1734,[4] which represents room usage much as it had been nearly seventy years earlier; excerpts from the entries of architectural relevance are given in the Appendix. Room names are indicated on the reconstructed plan of 1665 (see *English Houses 1200–1800*, Fig 112); certain points require comment. The partition separating hall from entrance appears to incorporate short screens (cf Tyttenhanger, Ridge). Possibly a doorway to NE of the hall gave access to the parlour. Originally the staircase was lit to N by two windows uniform with those to E and perhaps also by windows to W; they are difficult to reconcile with the existing staircase. Possibly at least one flight cut across a window, as happened later at Lockleys, Welwyn, but if this practice is anachronistic the staircase must have been altered in the late 19th century; and the present arrangement does not allow adequately for a room `under the best stairs'. If alteration has taken place it occurred when the rear corridors were added in the late 19th century. The principal first-floor rooms were separated from the rest of the house by an unbroken studded partition[5] forming the S wall of the `Chamber in the Gallery'. To SW and parallel to the brick house is a timber-framed range of two storeys which appears, from the position of its principal posts, to have extended to S. (A similar range, also containing the secondary staircase, formerly existed at Brent Pelham Hall.) The roof truss to W of the S wing appears to stand on the wall-plate of this building although the actual points of junction are concealed, and if this is so the timber range is either coeval with the brick house or antedates it. The framing is not closely datable and some of its peculiarities must be due to alteration, but it is likely to be coeval with the chimney-stack, which is late 17th century, probably 1665. A wide fireplace existed to W of this stack in 1910,[6] and since the space is so small (under 7 ft (2·1 m)) the gabled single-storey timber-framed building to W may be of the same date. The butler's room lacks fire-irons in the inventory and was presumably unheated; underneath is a cellar. On the second floor the long garrett with clock in the cupola occupied the main range; the principals of the roof trusses there are chamfered with comparatively elaborate stops below the collar-beam. Not precisely located on this floor were `the uper store room'; the cheese loft; the garrett next to it, which alone on this floor had andirons; and `the maids' room garrett'. This accounts for 12 of the fireplaces paid for in 1673; the thirteenth may have been in a small building parallel to the kitchen, where what may have been another late 17th-century chimney-stack, now rebuilt, stood;[7] this was probably the brew-house. In the mid 18th century the secondary staircase was rebuilt; a rococo plaster ceiling was put in the hall; and the front windows were lengthened and fitted with hung sashes. All this work was probably done during the occupation of Thomas Garrard, who was Recorder of St Albans from 1713 to 1758.[8] In 1881 the corridors to W were added;[9] probably then a round-headed staircase window was put in and the staircase was altered; mullion-and-transom windows were restored and two small bedrooms, each with an art nouveau fireplace, were formed in the middle of the house. In the 1920s the dining room was given its present form with a wide recess to S and the middle bedroom was created.

For illustrations, see *English Houses 1200–1800*, Figs 111 (plate), 112, 113, 309 (plate).

Notes
1. PRO E179/375/30, 31 respectively.
2. Not late 16th century (RCHME 1910, 239).
3. Anderson, WCL 2129.
4. In the possession of Mr D Cory-Wright.
5. Inf. Mr D Cory-Wright.
6. RCHME 1910, 239.
7. Anderson, WCL 2129.
8. Howard and Fowler 1889, 30; Monumental Inscription, Wheathampstead Church.
9. Inf. Mr D Cory-Wright.

(77941)
Mackerye End Farm,
now called the Manor House (TL 157157), of two storeys and attics, is an unusually large and elongated example of a lobby-entrance plan; it appears to be no earlier than the late 17th century although certain anomalous features are difficult to explain. It is aligned N–S; the S half has a large internal chimney-stack with lobby-entrance to E and the site of a former staircase, leaving space for a passage between parlour to N and hall to S. The parlour has a binding-beam with a few peg-holes but not enough for a partition; to W the post supporting the beam is cut off for a window; the N wall incorporates framing for a bay window now removed. The hall has a wide fireplace; to E two studs or posts rise to the plaster ceiling; the binding-beam has a very narrow chamfer. To N are two small service rooms to E and W of a passage and staircase; to N again is the kitchen, with wide fireplace to N. The kitchen is said to be a later addition[1] but no clear evidence of this was noted. On the first floor the room over the hall has a bolection-moulded fireplace and shelf moulded like a cornice. The attic storey is a later insertion. In the 19th century a range was parallel to hall and parlour, to E; it comprised an entrance-hall flanked by two rooms; the old house was then rendered and refenestrated.

For an illustration, see *English Houses 1200–1800*, Fig 176 (plate).

Note
1. *About Wheathampstead*, 31.

(77942)
Old Raisins (TL 155167)
represents the piecemeal rebuilding by the process of alternate development of a long-house older than any part of the surviving building. The bay to S, comprising the hall with chamber above, is of the mid–late 17th century and has framing superior to that elsewhere in the house; the chimney-stack is coeval with it. The hall was entered from a cross-passage in the inferior part of the house to rear (N) of the stack. It is remarkable that this bay should have a lateral fireplace rather than one backing on to the hall stack, since the two must be fairly close in date; the stepped offsets and diagonal shaft of the former are of the mid 17th century and, typologically, precede the shaft of the hall stack. The wide kitchen fireplace no doubt represents a change of use here. The bay to N has thin framing, probably of the early 18th century, and incorporates a dairy to N, service rooms adjoining the kitchen, and a staircase. The dairy remained in use until this century, when further alterations took place.

A drawing of 1829[1] suggests that `Raisins Farm' was then little more than the two S bays and a lean-to to N but its accuracy in detail is doubtful. In 1858 thatching, perhaps of the lower part of the house, was undertaken at Raisins Farm; in 1893 alterations and repairs to the value of £65 4s 6d were undertaken at Raisin Cottages.[2]

For illustrations, see *English Houses 1200–1800*, Figs 160 (plate), 161.

Notes
1. HRO, 42051.
2. HRO, 80235(4).

(77943)
The Swan PH, No. 56 High Street (TL 176138),

of *c*1500, is of four bays; the middle two formed an open hall, those at the ends were perhaps of two storeys. The roof has clasped-purlins; the open truss has a cambered tie-beam and arch-braces. In the third quarter of the 17th century a two-storey bay with ovolo-moulded bearer was added to S; the chimney-stack has a corbelled cap. Then or somewhat earlier a chimney-stack and upper floor were inserted in the hall. In the early 19th century the ground floor was refronted in brick and three bay windows added. In 1824 the `house formerly the Swan Inn', with three parlours and seven chambers, is mentioned; also the Swan PH, with good-sized parlour, smaller kitchen, small bar, wash-house, pantry, two cellars and three chambers.[1] The present Swan incorporates part or the whole of these buildings.

Note

1. HRO, Box 13, Particulars of Lord Melbourne's Estates.

(77944)
Turners Hall Farm (TL 158162)

is late medieval and comprises an open hall with a two-storeyed bay to W and a two-storeyed cross-wing to E which is probably an addition. Although its size and particularly width (21 ft (6·5 m)) suggest a manor house it has not been identified with any known manor,[1] and seems to have been part of the manor of Kinsbourne Hall or Annables. The `tenement and lands called Turnours' are first mentioned in 1521,[2] when they are leased by Edward Hawte of London, Gent., to John Hunt. In 1549 it is the messuage and in 1587 and 1620 the `tenement messuage or farme' called Turners.[3]

The hall was of two unequal bays; the open truss has a cambered tie-beam with double hollow-chamfer and arch-braces and the roof has clasped-purlins. The partition to E has paired doorways for pantry and buttery (blocked); that to W has doorways to N and S and peg-holes intended to support a bench; to S a mortise about 6 ft 6 ins (2 m) from the floor for a bench-end. The two-storeyed bay to W was divided into two rooms by a partition flush with the S face of the bearer; presumably the better-finished room to S was an unheated parlour and that to N a service room containing a staircase.

Alterations in the mid 17th century probably include the wing to E, comprising kitchen to S and service room, although it lacks datable detail; a brick chimney-stack was built adjoining the open truss and backing on to the cross-passage; and an upper floor was inserted in the hall, carried on moulded binding-beams and bearer; a break in the mouldings of the binding-beam to E suggests that a staircase stood to S of the stack. In the late 19th century the house was refronted in flint with brick dressings and a staircase was built to E of the chimney-stack, making the former cross-passage into an entrance and staircase-hall.

Notes

1. VCH II, 308.
2. HRO, 41512.
3. HRO, 41522, 41551, 41579.

(60027)
Waterend House (TL 203138)

was a manor held by the Brockett family in the 15th and 16th centuries. Nothing in the house is of that period although the date 1549, no longer visible, is said to be cut on one of the rafters.[1] After the death of Sir John Brockett in 1598 the descent

of the manor becomes obscure until 1621, when it was in the possession of Sir John Garrard of Lamers. The house is said to have been built *c*1610 by Sir John Jennings, whose family lived here for many years;[2] the letter I is worked in blue headers at the E end of the N wall. It was refaced in the late 17th century. When J C Buckler drew the house in 1834 it had its present appearance, but there are reasons for thinking it had already undergone restoration. A drawing of 1845,[3] when the tenant was a farmer, shows at the front a second doorway absent in 1834. In the present century there has been considerable restoration.

The evidence of a 16th-century building is principally in the hall. About 6 ft (1·8 m) from the front (N) wall and parallel to it is a beam with no trace of mortises; terminating on it and spanning the remaining width of the hall (*c*17 ft (5·2 m)) is a bearer which has mortises for a studded partition with a doorway in the middle (cf High Trees, Great Munden), as if forming a screens-passage; and in the E wing unevenness in the plaster ceiling suggests that a partition aligned with the former beam has been removed. These features are explicable by postulating a timber-framed house of half-H plan.

In the mid–late 17th century the house was enlarged by making the hall flush with the wings and extending both wings to E to form a half-H plan; all this was done and the remainder of the house refaced in brickwork of English bond. The ground plan then comprised a large hall about 24 ft (7·3 m) square with lateral fireplace to S; a wing to W with an internal chimney-stack and wide fireplace to N for a kitchen, and smaller unheated room to N and S with cellars beneath; a wing to E with an internal stack and two smaller fireplaces for parlours, the room to N being unusually long (*c*20 ft x 15 ft 6 ins (6·1 m x 4·6 m)); the principal newel staircase is in the re-entrant angle of the W wing; a smaller one is to W of the chimney-stack of the E wing; a third at the NE corner of the W wing may replace an original staircase. It is surprising that the principal staircase does not adjoin the parlour wing. On the first floor above the first-mentioned beam in the hall is a partition forming a corridor, against which chamfered tie-beams are stopped. This work is difficult to date. The brickwork in English bond and the comparatively small size of the E chimney-stack suggest the mid–late 17th century, yet the date 1692 inscribed on the plaster above a first-floor fireplace in the wing is too late for the octagonal chimney-shafts with moulded caps and bases.

Some of the difficulty may be due to antiquarian restoration, probably by Charles Benet Drake Garrard who came into possession in 1825.[4] Drawings dated 1832[5] show the house with every detail in what would then have been considered Elizabethan style, including the chimney-stacks; but the entrance doorway has a four-centred arch with sunk spandrels which seem never have to been built, and the ground-floor windows in the wing to W differ from those in the drawing. Relieving arches are depicted above the shallow bay windows to N and although the brickwork there has been repaired it is unlikely that arches have been removed. Moreover the stack of six shafts on the W chimney-stack includes one or two serving an early 19th-century fireplace added to make a new kitchen at the S end of the W wing. Evidently J C Buckler was either showing a client what the house should look like or sketching what the latter intended. In 1845 it was said that `the inside is not so remarkable as the exterior... There is no good staircase in it, nor any large room. Nothing at all ornamented on the inside; while the exterior is so handsome...it seems to be in perfect order at present, tho' little has apparently been done to it'.[6] The absence of any large room suggests that the hall was then subdivided, which may be connected with a second entrance into it. Restoration of fireplaces, windows and other features took place in the present century.

Notes
1. RCHME 1910, 200; VCH II, 434.
2. Cussans 1879–81, Vol III (ii), 232; VCH II, 434.
3. Field nd.
4. VCH II, 434.
5. Buckler Vol III, 181–2.
6. Field nd.

WIDFORD

(77945)
Abbotts Farm (TL 420153)

has slight indications of being a late medieval three-cell house with a chimney-stack built backing on to a cross-passage c1600. The house was enlarged and drastically altered in 1913.[1]

Note
1. Inf. Mrs D Pawle.

(77946)
Goddards (TL 421159),

of two storeys and of brick, was built in the second quarter of the 18th century. The ground plan comprises four rooms flanking a narrow entrance-hall to E and a wider staircase-hall to W, the kitchen being in a single-storey block to N; the latter is timber framed and too long to have been solely a kitchen; a scullery and brewhouse are possible uses for part of it. In the early 19th century the house became an academy for young gentlewomen run by the Misses Elizabeth and Jane Norris and was visited by Charles Lamb when holidaying in the district.[1] In 1899 Charles Nelson Tween, son of one of the Misses Norris who had married a farmer, heightened the kitchen, enlarged the house to N, extended the main staircase to the attic and put in plate-glass windows.[2] It was enlarged to S in the 1960s.

Notes
1. Hine 1949, 263.
2. Ibid.

(77947)
Nether Hall (TL 423160),

of the 19th century and of brick, rendered, incorporates to W a wing of c1500, of two storeys, originally jettied; the open hall was replaced by a mid-Victorian gabled block of two storeys and attics roofed parallel to the wing.

(77948)
The Old Cottage, High Street (TL 420159),

of the 17th century, is timber framed and was probably intended to be plastered; the roof is of thatch. Originally most of the house was open to the roof, only the bay to S being lofted over. A chimney-stack was built in the 18th century, perhaps replacing a timber stack; the hall and room to N were floored over; and a dormer window was provided to light the room over the hall.

WIGGINTON

(77949)
The Old Cottage,

of two storeys and of two-room plan, was built in the early 17th century. To E is the hall, with gable-end chimney flanked by the entrance to E, and to W a narrow inner room, perhaps originally subdivided. This is one of the classic longhouse-derivative forms.

To N two contiguous ranges gabled to N have been added to create a squarish overall plan; the range to W is a kitchen, with fireplace to N, and is probably of c1700; that to E is later.

WYDDIAL

(77950)
Beauchamps (TL 382313),

a manor recorded under the name Alfladewick in Layston parish before the Conquest, belonged to the Beauchamp family between c1278 and c1420 and by the late 16th century to the Baesh family; in 1587 it was described as the `manor or farm of Affledwick alias Beauchamps'.[1] In 1653 it descended to Ralph Baesh,[2] who built a `fair House' with materials from Ardeley Place which were given him by his relative by marriage, Justinian Sherburne.[3] Beauchamps is timber framed, so presumably the materials were timber, although no conspicuous existence of re-used timber was observed. The house is an unusually large version of the internal-chimney, lobby-entrance plan with a ground plan of four rooms in line and wings to NE and NW each containing a staircase and service rooms. The room to E of the internal stack was the kitchen, with a wide fireplace; to E again was a parlour with a passage to the yard between it and the pantry and staircase to N. To W of the stack was the hall and beyond it a parlour with cellar beneath. On the first floor intercommunication between the E and W sides of the house may have been possible but was evidently not part of the normal pattern of circulation (cf Aston Bury). Two bedrooms with fireplaces flanked the internal stack; to E and W was an important bedroom with dressing room to N.

Ralph Baesh conveyed Beauchamps `by force of an Act of Parliament'[4] to John Taylor, subsequently rector of Westmill, who was holding it in 1669.[5] The name Baesh does not appear in the Hearth Tax returns for 1662–3 so the house was at lease before then, perhaps to Henry Taylor, Gent., and John Sibley, who paid for 11 hearths in 1662 and 1663.[6] In 1673 Ralph Taylor paid for 10 hearths.[7] There is little evidence of alteration to the house, which became, after 1731, part of the Wyddial Hall estate. At the Census of 1851 it was occupied only by an agricultural labourer. Not many years later, perhaps in the 1860s, it was refronted in polychrome brick; the internal stack was pierced to form an entrance-hall and a corridor was added to N.

Notes
1. PRO C142/215/269.
2. VCH IV, 82.
3. Chauncy I, 126.
4. Ibid, 264.
5. VCH IV, 82.
6. PRO E179/375/30; E179/248/23.
7. PRO E179/375/31.

(77951)
Former Parsonage House, W of church
(approximately TL 373317)

appears in two drawings of 1831.[1] It was of L-shaped plan with a short two-storeyed jettied range of two bays facing S and a longer range at right-angles to N. The jettied block is likely to have been late medieval and the whole has a general resemblance to a house with an open hall and a cross-wing facing the street, like the Old Post Office, Offley.

Note
1. Buckler Vol II, 181–2.

(77952)
Wyddial Bury (TL 373316)

is a continuous-jetty house of the early–mid 16th century facing to N; it may have had a timber chimney-stack for a fireplace in the hall to E; to E of the hall is a smaller service room; to W of the stack was probably the cross-passage, there being no evidence of an original fireplace on this side; all evidence of the room to W has been obliterated. A range to S, forming the stem of a T-shaped plan, was added c1600; it appears to have been a kitchen with an unheated room to S; two bearers dying into the rear (S) of the stack suggest that the latter was originally of timber. In the late 17th century the S range was extended to S, probably for a brewhouse, and both chimney-stacks were rebuilt in brick. In the mid 19th century the W end of the N range was refaced and a wing was added to W, both using polychrome brick. Then or later the octagonal shafts of the two principal stacks were rebuilt.

(77953)
Wyddial Hall (TL 373317),

a manor house, incorporates an early 16th-century house of brick known from an engraving of c1700 by Drapentier.[1] In 1494 Humphrey and Margery Wellisbourne inherited the manor and on Humphrey's death in 1516 Margery settled it on their son Arthur. The house appears to have been built in the early 16th century; a timber doorway with four-centred head, discovered in 1733, bore characters in relief which were variously interpreted as 1000, 1016 and 1390[2] but are more likely to represent 1516; the door-head is probably the right-hand one of a pair, with 15 in the left-hand and 16 in the right-hand spandrel, heraldic badges in the two middle spandrels, and all with foliage carving and shield à bouche according with the date.[3] Another indication of building-works, probably in the Tudor period, is provided by the window painted with the arms of France and England quarterly which was found in the offices.[4] In 1568 the manor came to John Gill, who was Sheriff in 1575, and in 1643 to Richard Goulston who created a park.[5] At Michaelmas 1662 Goulston paid for 19 hearths and in May 1663 for 22.[6] His son James Goulston of Wyddial was Sheriff in 1684 but did not succeed his father until 1686; presumably the house was divided. Francis Goulston, who was Sheriff in 1730, gave the house its present appearance; in the course of building-works in August 1733 he observed the doorway mentioned above. John Thomas Ellis MP, who succeeded to the estate in 1780, discovered the painted glass in the course of altering the offices. In 1834 the architect C N Cumberlege exhibited at the Royal Academy designs for further alterations; the present large service wing and staircase may have been built by Charles Heaton-Ellis who owned the Hall from 1836 to 1865. Subsequent changes have been mainly decorative.

The plan of the early 16th-century house has been reconstructed (*English Houses 1200–1800*, Figs 7 and 8) from the Drapentier engraving and the existing structure, of which the hall chimney-stack and porch remain, greatly altered; the screens between hall and cross-passage are perpetuated by two Doric columns; and the putative pair of doorways of 1516 may have been at the S end of the hall, to E and W. The reasons for supposing that the entrance-passage was floored over are the existence of a two-storey porch and a change of floor level in the attics corresponding to the Doric columns. To N of the hall were service rooms with cellars beneath in which, in 1909, could be seen 16th-century brickwork and the three-light mullioned windows depicted in 1700.[7] Francis Goulston's description of the Hall as `a Timber-built House'[8] no doubt refers to a house of brick with timber partitions. The earliest known alterations are

of the 17th century when the roof was rebuilt with tenoned purlins and the attics were lit by gabled dormer windows above a parapet. At this time a cupola was built; the porch was perhaps heightened; and the rooms to N of the entrance-passage were refenestrated with four-light mullion-and-transom windows. The plan suggests that the service rooms were transformed into a large parlour with fireplace and chimney-stack to W; the stack can be identified in Drapentier's and Oldfield's drawings as standing to right of the porch, with two diagonal flues, and being nearer the front of the house than the hall stack. The increased importance of this end of the house accounts for the unusual position of the principal staircase, unrelated to the entrance-hall, and may be related to joint occupation such as that by Richard Goulston and his son James the Sheriff. To N a short wing to W may have existed by c1700. On present knowledge it is impossible to fit in the 22 hearths paid for in 1663. Speculative though some of these points are, they serve to explain why the remodelling of the 1730s resulted in a plan quite uncharacteristic of the period. An upper floor was inserted in the hall; the main range was made two rooms deep throughout, with a kitchen to W of the hall; and the wing to SW was enlarged, probably for service rooms. The early 19th-century work ascribed to Heaton-Ellis included rebuilding the staircase and adding to N a servants' staircase; that to S was also rebuilt as a newel staircase approached through a lobby with a curved wall broken by niches; both principal staircases convey striking spatial effects. A service wing was added to NW and some rooms in the wing to SW were provided with fireplaces; this is probably why one of the chimney-stacks projects into the corridor. In the present century internal detail has been renewed in period style.

For illustrations, see *English Houses 1200–1800*, Figs 1 (plate), 2 (plate), 3 (plate), 4, 5 (plate), 6 (plate), 7, 8.

Notes
1. Chauncy I, 221.
2. *Phil Trans* **39** (1735–6), 119–31.
3. Inf. the late Mr S E Rigold.
4. `A Descriptive sketch of Wyddial...' by H G Oldfield (1789), BL, King's Topog. Coll XV, 90*e* .
5. Chauncy I, 223.
6. PRO E179/375/30.
7. RCHME 1910, 244.
8. *Phil Trans* **39** (1735–6), 122.

WYMONDLEY

(77954)
Delamere, Great Wymondley (TL 213282),

is named from the family of de la Mare who held it from 1275 to c1375. When sold in 1438 to John Pulter it was for the first time called a manor rather than a tenement or messuage; a terrier of the mid 15th century shows that the holding was of 185 acres (75 has). Pulter was succeeded in 1452 by his son, also John, who was Sheriff of Bedfordshire in 1453 and died in 1482.[1] John Pulter the younger is the likely builder of a timber-framed cross-wing about 17ft (5·2 m) wide, parts of which are incorporated in the house; the hall connected with it stood to W. Edward Pulter, who died in 1572, was the last of the family to live at Delamere; he bought the manor of Cottered where his son, also Edward, was established, and thereafter the house was let to tenants. In the mid 17th century the house was rebuilt in brick as a double-pile incorporating to W about half the width of the former cross-wing. Oldfield depicted the house c1800 as it is today but with a white building to W, presumably timber framed and looking like a barn;[2] and an enclosure map of 1811[3] shows this building returning at some 20 ft (6·1 m) as a wing to N about 75 ft (23 m) long. According to Oldfield's caption, `what now remains is only part of the original house. From the foundations remaining it appears to have been nearly three times the magnitude of what remains, for besides another piece of building like this there appears to have been a centre part which must have made it a considerable Mansion.' The rebuilt house has an unusual symmetrical S elevation, marred only by the entrance which is placed slightly off-centre. The plan[4] comprised, to S, hall (to W) and parlour, each with a closet flanking the gable-wall fireplace, and lit by a two-light transomed window; to N the staircase is flanked by a service room, perhaps a pantry, to W, and an entrance-lobby and small room with fireplace to E. The dispositions on the first floor are not clear in detail but certainly comprised two principal and one or two lesser rooms, one of the former (to W) being perhaps the dining room; closets flanked the chimney-stacks. In the attic the room to E, with a late 17th-century fireplace, was evidently another bedchamber of some importance. In 1803, when Delamere was described as `The Farm...rented by Mr Joseph Prime', it had `a good Kitchen, Parlour, Dairy, two Pantries, with a back kitchen, and two cellars, four bed Rooms, and one Servants bed Room, one dark Garret, and Cheese loft'.[5]

Notes
1. Inf. Mr H O N Farris, from Great Wymondley court rolls, HRO.
2. Oldfield Vol VII, 413.
3. HRO, QS/E 81.
4. VCH III, 182.
5. HRO, 60952A.

(77955)
Manor House, formerly Manor Farm (TL 213286),

Great Wymondley, was so named in the 19th century; the holding arose from the strips of demesne land acquired by William Wilshere after buying the manorial rights in 1806; the strips were consolidated at the time of enclosure (1811). The house can be identified with a free tenement held by John Smyth `lying by the highway leading to Hitchin on the south and the lord's tenement called Lymberys, in the tenure of the said John, abutting on the highway leading to Baldock to the east'.[1] The house is of the 15th century; the open hall has been rebuilt; to E and W are wings with exposed Kentish framing, that to W, the service wing, being the larger; weathering on the E wall of the wing to W shows that the hall eaves were quite low. The wing to W appears to have been converted into a parlour in the mid 16th century; the axial partition was removed then and a frieze of black-letter texts above geometric and floral patterns was added. The hall, of two bays, and jettied porch to S are of the early 17th century; to W a large fireplace backs on to another for the kitchen, converted from the former parlour; the porch leads to a lobby-entrance and, originally, a staircase adjoining the stack; and a chimney-stack with two diagonal shafts was added to the E wing, for ground and first-floor fireplaces. At this period the house was extensively decorated with wall-paintings in the parlour and all first-floor rooms except that over the porch; they include scrolls, panels and other common motifs. Possibly additions to N are also of the early 17th century; they comprise a service room adjoining the hall and staircases to the chamber over the parlour and the cellar beneath it, which are not closely datable. The house underwent careful restoration in 1977.

Note
1. Inf. Mr H O N Farris, from Great Wymondley court rolls, HRO.

(77956)
Redcoats (TL 207265)

was not a manor, only a tenement of the manor of Great Wymondley. It is remarkable for being jettied on the long walls to E and W and to N, for the number of rooms with fireplaces, and for the unusually high quality of its detail. The evidence of ownership is inconclusive as to the builder.[1] It may have been John Sturgeon, who owned the estate from c1481 until c1492, was Sheriff in 1479 and 1485, and referred in his will to `my place called Radcotes'; a first-floor fireplace has enriched mouldings, parallels for which are ascribed to c1470–80, eg a bay window at Neville Holt, Leicestershire.[2]

The house is divided on each floor into two large rooms and a small one. Lateral chimney-stacks are built against the jetties to E and W and a staircase to E. The middle ground-floor room, about 31 ft x 18 ft (9·5 m x 5·5 m), was the hall; to S one doorway of the cross-passage remains, with hollow-chamfered four-centred head and hollowed spandrels; until recently a similar doorway, reset, stood where a screen between passage and hall might be expected; and a window of two four-centred lights with moulded mullions, possibly reset, stands above the doorway which originally led to the staircase turret. To E a window of c1800 occupies the approximate site of the original one. To N the parlour has a fireplace of which only the moulded stone jambs and brick relieving arch remain; it does not face the middle of the room as the hall fireplace does (excluding the width of the passage) but is set about 3 ft (1 m) to S, as if to allow for some piece of furniture to N. The wall to S has been rebuilt. To S of the hall was an unheated service room, apparently undivided because the axial bearer is not mortised for a partition; a staircase stood against the S wall, the site of the trap being indicated by comparatively recent joists, with a two-light window to E to light the foot of the stair as well as that part of the room.

The first-floor partitions do not correspond exactly with those below, and the room to N, which is as long as the hall and wider by the width of the two jetties, extends to S over it. The hollow-chamfered jambs of the stone fireplace are enriched with paterae; to N a range of two-light windows about 6 ft (2 m) above the floor is divided by three studs into four pairs, with hollow-chamfered jambs and square heads; to N is an open truss of two chamfered orders, the chamfers being returned at the ends on to small solid brackets and short wall-posts (now removed). At the original stair head, panelling formed a small lobby from which a doorway (blocked) led to the rooms over hall and parlour. Over the hall a room, smaller than that to N, has a stone fireplace with four-centred head and spandrels with dragons; to S a three-light window (blocked) has moulded mullions; its sill is at normal height, approximately 3 ft 6 ins (1 m) above the floor. Whether this room intercommunicated with that to S is not clear. The latter had windows of three lights to W and of two lights to E, both being somewhat to N, as if the S part of the room were functionally, if not structurally, separate, eg for a staircase. All first-floor rooms were open to the roof.

In the late 17th century the building of a staircase and axial partitions made six or seven first-floor rooms out of three; the parlour was reduced in size to accommodate the new stair, which may have resembled the existing one of the late 19th century. The transverse beam in the hall was replaced by one with late 17th-century mouldings. The chimney-stack to E was enlarged to provide a fireplace for one of the new rooms and a single-storey timber-framed building, probably a kitchen, was added to E.

For illustrations, see *English Houses 1200–1800*, Figs 44, 45, 312 (plate).

Notes
1. Inf. Mr H O N Farris.
2. Garner and Stratton 1929, Plate 144.

(77957)
Titmore Green Farm (TL 214263)

is late medieval and comprised an open hall, originally with low eaves, with jettied cross-wing to N and bay to S in series with the hall. Apart from some exposed brickwork at the front the exterior is everywhere roughcasted and all the chimney-stacks were rebuilt in the 19th century. Few original features are exposed inside. A jettied wing replaced the bay to S *c*1600. In the later 17th century the house was greatly altered. The hall was heightened to two storeys and a lateral chimney-stack added to W; it is surprising that the open hearth was not replaced earlier than this; perhaps the evidence has been removed. The first floor is supported by a bearer about 17 ft 6 ins (5·3 m) long although binding-beams would have been shorter; possibly a studded screens partition reduced its unsupported length originally. A chimney-stack inserted to S converted the service wing into a kitchen, the pantry being removed to a narrower wing added to W. A staircase wing to N of the hall chimney-stack is large enough to have accommodated some other function as well, perhaps a dairy. Somewhat later a fireplace was added to the parlour. In the 19th century the front was partly rebuilt in brick and a passage built to W connecting the two wings.

(32405)
Wymondley Bury (TL 217271)

For a description of this house see Mercer 1975, 171–2.

For an illustration, see *English Houses 1200–1800*, Fig 40 (plate).

(77958)
Wymondley Hall, formerly Wymondley Hall Farm (TL 215274),

is of the late 16th century and comprises a main range with jettied cross-wing to S of the hall and service bay to N; the wing has, on the first floor, a pedimented bay window. The hall was entered by opposite doors to N, with lateral fireplace to E; the bay to N was formerly two rooms, the mortises for the partition being exposed; the wing to S comprised a large room with lateral fireplace and a smaller one, probably including a staircase, to E; both chimney-stacks have diagonal shafts. In the mid 17th century bay windows were added to W and perhaps then the exterior was rendered, as it was in 1841;[1] a staircase turret adjoining the hall chimney-stack to N may be of this date; and the service rooms were converted into a kitchen by the addition of a fireplace to N, the added stack having three square flues with a triangular fillet on each face. In the late 19th century a gabled wing of brick was added to N, minor additions were made to E, and the elevation was refaced in brick. Then or later the timbers of the W elevation were exposed.

Note
1. Buckler Vol III, 107.

(77959)
Wymondley Priory (TL 218279),

a small house of Augustinian canons founded before 1218, was dissolved in 1537[1] and granted to James Needham, Clerk of the King's Works.[2] What Needham did to adapt the priory buildings is uncertain; a fragmentary wall-painting (destroyed) is perhaps of his time; part of the cloisters may have remained *c*1700[3] and fragmentary stone walls still stood near the house *c*1800,[4] but the existing house, incorporating 13th-century windows which appear to be the W end of a claustral building about 21 ft (6·5 m) wide, is a mid 17th-century building. It is essentially the work of George Needham who inherited and `much improved it' in 1688,[5] was assessed for 16 hearths in 1662[6] and died in 1669. The plan[7] comprised a range of three rooms which were, from N to S, pantry, entrance-passage, hall and parlour; hall and parlour have lateral fireplaces to E, the former placed back-to-back with the kitchen in a wing to E. All the elevations were gabled; there was a two-storey porch capped by a small cupola.[8] In the late 18th century Thomas Browne, Garter King of Arms and `eminent land surveyor', resided here.[9] Additions were made to N in the 19th century. In recent years the house was completely gutted, leaving only the principal structural features internally, in the course of restoration.

Notes
1. Knowles and Hadcock 1953, 160.
2. *DNB*; *King's Works* Vol III (i), 14; Monumental Inscription, Oldfield Vol VII, 440–1.
3. Chauncy II, 110.
4. Oldfield Vol VII, 418.
5. Chauncy II, 110.
6. PRO E179/375/30
7. VCH III, 182.
8. Oldfield Vol VII, 418.
9. *DNB*; Eden 1979, 48.

Appendix

No. 27 LEYTON ROAD, HARPENDEN

'An Inventory of the Goods and Chattells of William Edwards Late of Harpenden in the County of Hartford Innhoulder deceased taken and Appraised this 28th day of September Anno Dom' 1719.

A Barne a Stable and hogglaye – Sett up upon the premisses by ye said Wm Edwards with other Outhouses

A Cart house sett up upon the West

ye Hale Chamber 2 Feather beads and bedsteads... [and] a Table a Court Cubbord an old Cheere

ye 2 Rooms over ye Kittchin an Old Feather bead [and] beadstedd... a pr. of handirons 2 Flock Bedds [and] beadsteads 3 Chesters an old Trunk 2 Stools and a Cheere

ye 2 Rooms over ye Parler 6 Flockbeads [and] beadsteads with a Smale Table

another Roome over ye Hale 2 Featherbeads... & beadsteads a pr. of Smale Handirons 5 Chayres & a Table

a Small Roome over ye Closett a Flock bead...

a Clock Standing upon the Stare Case

ye Hall a Table 8 Cheares a Screene a pott shelfe a pr. of Handirons... & 2 Formes

ye Back Roome 3 Tables 8 Cheares a pr. of handirons Fire Shovells & Tongs...

ye Brewhouse...

ye Kittchin 2pr. of handirons Fire Shovell & Tongs Bellows ...dresser & Shelves a Table Cheares...

ye Seller.'

[Total Value £151. 11. 00]

HATFIELD HOUSE

Hatfield 30 September 1611

(The numbering of rooms in the inventories corresponds to that in Fig 102 in *English Houses 1200–1800*. Where the position of a room cannot be identified with certainty, it is followed by `?'.)

39	Hall
42	Greate Parlor
44	Ante chamber
45	Your ho. boke-chamber
48	Your ho. bedchamber
47	Pallett Chamber to your ho. bedchamber
51	Corner Chamber to the south easte
50	Second Chamber Southwarde
49	the thyrde Chamber to the court for a Pallet Chamber
46	Pallitt chamber in the entrie on the West side of your Ho. bokechamber
18	Great Chamber
20	Withdrawing Chamber
23	Kings bed chamber
22	Pallitt chamber to the Kings bedchamber
26	Corner chamber Southward next to the Kings bedchamber
25	Seconde Chamber
24	thyrde Chamber to the Court for a Pallitt Chamber
21	Ante Chamber at the west end of the Kings Withdrawing Chamber
19	Lobbie betwene the great chamber and the gallerrye
16	Gallerie
13	within drawing chamber
14	Bedchamber adjoyneinge to it
15?	Pallett Chamber next to it
11	Greate Chamber
9	The within drawinge chamber
7?	(Passage to the upper Closett (Closet above Chapel))
4	Quens bedchamber
5a	Pallett chamber adjoneing
1	Corner chamber south-weste
2	Middle Chamber towards the Southe
3	Corner Chamber towards the Southe West for a Pallet Chamber
6	Ante chamber adjoning to the Upper Chappell
10	Lobbie betwene the gallerie and the Chappell
33	Chappell
32	Chaplins chamber
29	Ante Chamber South-eastwarde
28	Middle Chamber southwards being for a bedchamber
27	Corner Chamber southwestwards for a pallett chamber
63	Corner chamber northwest for My Lorde Cranborne
61	Next chamber adjoyneinge for a bedchamber for my Lo Cranborne
59	Pallett chamber to my Lo Cranborns chamber
68	Ante chamber
70	Bed chamber
72	Pallett chamber

3 Garrett chambers southwarde for servants
    Next 3 garratt chambers southwarde for servants
    Next 2 garratt chambers southwarde for servants
65 Wardrobe
66 the Armorye
    In the Kitchen Larders and Butteries in Mr Shawes
      keepinge

1621

39 Hall
41a Passage to Parlore
42 Parlore
44 Dying Roome
45 Drawing Chamber
48 Your lo. bedchamber
57 the weomens Chamber
50 Your lo. booke chamber
47 the lobbies
49 My la. Eliz nurserie
46 wast Roome
39a passage
38 Abners chamber
37 Stewards dyning Rome
33 Chappell below
32 Mr Buckes Chamber
29 His mans Chamber
28 Sweetemeate howse
27 Sir Arthur Capells chamber
30 My yonge lords Nurserie
31 Pallet Roome to it
17 Upon the great steares
18 Greate Chamber
20 Kings lyinge Chamber
23 Kings bed chamber
26 Pallet roome next the Kings bedchamber
25 Chamber over yr lo. booke chamber
24 My ladie Annes nurserie
21 With drawing Chamber on the Kinges side
20 Lobbie
16 [Gallery] (contents listed)
14 Bedchamber next the gallerie
13 Chamber next to it Northward
11 Greate Chamber on the queens side
9 With drawing Chamber on the queens side.
7 Passage to the chapell
4 Bedchamber on the queens side
1 Palett Roome next to it
2 Midle chamber on the queens side
3 Pallet chamber to the chappell chamber
6 Chappell chamber
8 Chappell above
10 Lobbie
67 Chamber next the Armorie
    Clymes chamber
    Jeromes chamber
    Mr Franclines chamber
    Mr Sowthworthes chamber (1)
    Mr Turwhitts chamber   (2)
    his mans chamber

    Clerke of the Kitchens chamber
    Miles and Matt Johnsons chamber
    Mr Francies Gardenars chamber
    Matt Johnsone studdie
    In my lordes Closett
    Mr Francies Garnars studdie
    Mrs Swallowes Clossett
    Mr Turwhitts studdie
    Myles his studdie
    Paules studdie

1629

18 Greate Chamber on Kinges side
20 Withdrawinge chamber on the Kinges side
23 Kinges bed Chamber
22 Lobbie to the Kinges Chamber
26 Pallet Roome to the Kinges bedchamber
25 Middle Chamber on the Kinges side
24 Pallet Roome to the middle chamber on the
    Kinges side
21 Little drawing Chamber to the Kinges bedd
    Chamber
19 Lobbie betwixt the gallerie and the great
    Chamber on the Kinges side
16 Gallarie
10 Lobbie Roome att the end of the gallarie by the
    Chapple
13 Gallarie Chamber
14 Chamber over the Pantrie
11 Greate Chamber on the Queenes side
12 Withdrawing chamber on the Queenes side
4 Queenes beddchamber
1 Pallett Chamber to the Queenes Chamber
2 Middle chamber on the Queenes side
3 Pallet Chamber to the Chapple chamber
6 Chapple Chamber
5 Lobbie Roome to the Queenes bedchamber
7/8 Upper Chapple
33 Lower Chapple
32 Chapple Chamber below
31 Pallett Roome to the Chapple Chamber below
28 Sweetmeat House
27 Wett Nurserie Chamber
30 My La. Elizabeth Chamber
29 Mr younge Lo.s Chamber
41 In the great Staires on the Kinges side
39 Hall
39a the entrie betwixt the hall and the Kitchin
42 Great Parlour
44 dyninge Roome next to the great Parlour
45 withdrawinge Chamber to the dyninge Room
46 My Lo: dressinge Chamber
47a Mr Lo:s stoole house
47b In the lobbie going to my La: Chamber
49 Chamber next to the Lobbie
50 Middle Chamber of the low Roomes
51 Gentlewomens Chamber
51a My La: Closset betwixt my la: bedchamber and
    gentlewomens

48 My la: bedchamber
43 Lobbie Roome betwixt my Lo:s dressing Chamber and the great staires
65 Wardroppe
    Mr Brownes Chamber
    Chamber next to Mr Brownes
    Mr Kerkhams Chamber   (3)
    Clerkes Chamber
54? pallat Roome next to the staire head
53? Mris Francklins Chamber
52? the little Roome to Mris Francklins
    Mr Garratts Chamber
    Mr Southworthes Chamber (1)
70 Middle Chamber over the great Chamber on the Kinges side
    Matthew Plowmans Chamber
    Monsieur Durands Chamber
    Abner Stansbies Chamber
    Miles Matthewes Chamber

1638

18 Greate Chamber one the Kings side
20 Withdraweing Chamber one the Kings side
23 Kings bedd Chamber
22 Lobby to the Kings Chamber
26 Pallett Chamber, now my La. Eliz Cecills chamber
25 Middle Chamber on the Kings side
27 Pallatt Roomes to the mydle Chamber on the Kings side
19 Lobby betwixt the gallery and the great chamber on the Kings side
21 little draweing Chamber to the Kings beddchamber
16 Gallary
10 Lobby att the end of Gallary
13 Gallary Chamber
14 Chamber over pantry
11 Great Chamber on the Queenes side
9 Withdraweing Chamber, the Queens side
4 Queens bedd chamber
1 Pallatt Chamber to the Queenes side
2 Middle chamber on the Queenes side
3 Pallatt Chamber to Chappell chamber
6 Chapell chamber
5 Lobby
7/8 Upper Chappell
33 Lower Chappell
32 Chapell Chamber now Sir Arthur Capells
31 Pallatt Roome
28 Preserving Roome
30 Wett Nursery
27 My La. Katherns Chamber
29 Yonge Lo:s Chamber next the Court
41 Great stayres of the kings side
39 Hall
38? Stewards Roome
42 Greate Parlour
43 dyneing Roome next to the Parlour

44 Withdraweing Chamber
46 My Lo:s dressing Chamber
47a My Lo:s stoole house
49 My Lo: Howards Chamber on the ground next the Court
47b Lobby betwixt My Lo: Howards
50 Middle Chamber of the Lower rooms
51 Gentlewomens Chamber
51a My La: Elizabeths Clossett
48 My La:s beddchamber
48c My La:s stoolehowse
57 My Lo: Cranbournes Chamber over the Chappell
63 Mr Roberts Cicills Chamber
    Mr Fryer the Tutors Chamber
    Nicholas Lamprer Mr Cicills mans Chamber
56 Midle Chamber which was the Clarke of the kitchins
55 Mrs Brownes Chamber
56 the outward Roome
53 Mr Garratts Chamber
52 Pallatt Roome
    Dr Wincopps Chamber
    his study
    Mr Plowemans chamber
    Abner Stansbeys chamber
    Will: Kings Chamber
    Mr Ashtons Chamber

1646

18 Greate Chamber on the Kings side
20 Withdrawing Chamber on the Kings side
23 Kings Bedchamber
26 Pallet chamber to the Kinges Bedchamber
22 Loby to the Kings Bedchamber
25 Midle Chamber on the Kings side now a Nursury
27 Pallett room to the midle chamber on the Kings side
21 Little withdrawing chamber to the Kings bechamber
19 Lobby betwene the gallary and the Greate chamber on the Kings side
16 Gallary
10 Lobby Roome att the end of the Gallary by the Chappell
13 Gallery chamber
14 chamber over the Pantry
11 Greate chamber on the Queenes side
9 Withdrawing chamber on the Queenes side
4 Queenes bedchamber
1 Pallet chamber to the Queenes bedchamber
2 Midle chamber on the Queenes side
3 Pallet chamber to the chappell chamber
6 Chappell chamber
5 lobby roome to the Queenes bedchamber
7/8 Upper chappell
33 Lower chappell (and in the church)
32 Chappell Chamber below

221

31	Pallet roome to it	13	WC
28	Preservinge howse	14	Hornbeam Bedroom
27	My Lord Cranbornes dressing chamber	15	Housemaids' Bedroom
30	My Lord Cranbornes bedchamber	16	Housekeeper's Bedroom
29	Lady Cranbornes gentlewomens chamber	17	Stillroom maid
41	Greate staires on the Kings side	18	Rose Bedroom
42	Dyning Roome below Stairs	19	Stillroom Maid
43	Withdrawinge roome next to it	20	Groom of Chambers
44	Second drawing chamber to the Dyneinge Roome	21	Oak Dressing Room
46	My lords dressing Chamber	22	Chaplain's Bedroom
49	the Lady Lisles bedchamber	23	Ash Dressing Room
50	the Lord Lisles dressing chamber	24	Lime Dressing Bedroom
51	Gentlewomens chamber	25	Walnut Dressing Bedroom
51a	My Ladies closett betweene my Lords dressing chamber and the gentlewomens Chamber	26	Work Room
		27	Chestnut Bedroom
48	My Ladies bedchamber	28	King James's Bedroom
47c	My Ladies stoole howse	29	Kitchen Maid
38?	Stewards roome	30	Prince Albert's Bedroom
63	Chamber over the dineing Roome on the Queenes side	31	Holly Bedroom
		32	Queen Anne's Bedroom
61	Lady Mary Cecills chamber	33	Beech Bedroom
59	Lady Maries nurses chamber	34	Cromwell's Bedroom
57	next chamber in the row	35	Footman's Bedroom
58	The outward roome to it	36	Wellington's Bedroom
55	Next Chamber now Mr Robert Cecylls chamber	37	Fir Room
56	Outward roome to Mr Cecills chamber	38	Store Room
52	Pallett roome next to the staire head	39	Kitchen Maids' Bedroom
53	Mr Garrards Chamber	40	Queen's Bedroom
54	Outward roome to it	41	Nursery Kitchen
68	Chaplaines Chamber	42	Magnolia Room
70	Study	43	Valet's Bedroom
72	Mr Markhams Chamber	44	Housemaid's Bedroom
74	the Butlers chamber	45	Night Nursery
76	Middle chamber over the Kings bedchamber	46	Nursemaid's Bedroom
77	Chamber at the staire head	47	Steward's Bedroom
78	Outward roome to it	48	Pine Room
79	Chamber on the east side of it	49	Larch Room
		50	Mahogany Room
		51	Day Nursery
		52	Poplar Room

Household officers:

John Southworth, Receiver-General, 1624–31
Edmund Tirwhitt, Gentleman of the Horse, 1623–30
Roger Kirkham, Receiver-General 1633–46,
    Steward of the Household 1643–44
(This information was communicated by
Mr Harcourt-Williams.)

Hatfield attic 19th-century room names

1	Beech Room
2	Chestnut Room
3	Hazel Room
4	Elm Stairs
5	Elm Room
6	Hornbeam Room
7	Holly Room
8	Maple Room
9	Lime and Ash Bedroom
10	Sycamore Room
11	Walnut Bedroom
12	Oak?

MACKERYE END, WHEATHAMPSTEAD

`An inventory of the goods belonging to Mackrey End taken this 27th day of April 1734.'

Best parlour: wainscoted all over; three pairs window curtains, ten walnut chairs, two mahogany card tables, one mahogany other table, marble chimney-piece and slab, new fire hearth, grate for burning wood with two dogs, `a wood lock and key with a barr and bolt going into the garden, and a latch to the little door'.

In the passage: a large wainscot table.

Under the best stairs: a light closet with five shelves and a table.

Hall: wainscoted half way, a long table, six joint stools, a bench, six Turkey-work chairs, two pairs of large andirons, one pair of dogs.

In the passage: a wooden lock and key and two bolts to the stair foot door.

Common parlour: wainscoted all over, three pairs of window curtains, ten walnut chairs, a wainscot table, a little mahogany table for a side board, a grate for burning wood with two dogs, a marble chimney-piece and slab, a new fire hearth, a latch to the strong door into the passage.

Butlers room

Larder

The two kitchens: a long table, a form, two joint stools, four chairs. A form in the back kitchen to wash upon.

Brewhouse

Over the great staircase: a large picture of Juno.

Chamber over the best parlour: wainscoted all over, a bedstead, two pairs window curtains, a brass grate for burning wood with two dogs, `one shelf and four rows of pins in the closet and part thereof paper'd half way'.

Large chamber over the hall: wainscoted all over, a bedstead, three rods, curtains, a new grate, three bolts to the doors, three pairs of window curtains, four rods, two dogs, two brass andirons.

Chamber in the gallery: papered all over, a bedstead, a rod, `blew camblet furniture curtains', a pair of brass andirons, two dogs.

Chamber over the little parlour: wainscoted all over, chest of drawers, four cane chairs, a table, three pairs of window curtains and two rods, two chimney hooks, a brass lock and key to the little door, a lock and key to the great door, a shelf in the little passage, two dogs with brass fireshovel and tongs and a broom.

In the closet: a bench, some pegs, shelves and hangings.

The room over the kitchen: papered all over, a bedstead, a rod, curtains, four cane chairs, a pair of window curtains and rod, three locks, three keys, two bolts and a latch, a wooden chimney-piece, two brass dogs, and two andirons.

In the two closets: shelves, pegs, two stools, a desk to write on, four pictures.

Chamber over the back kitchen: featherbed, `an armed chair and stool work't', two other chairs, pair of andirons.

The upper store room: a sweetmeat cupboard, a chest, a still, a table.

Cheese loft

In the garret next to it: two bedsteads, two dogs, two brass andirons, two bolts to the door.

Maids' room garret: a bedstead.

Long garret: `a clock compleat with diall and weights', three doors with two locks, keys and a latch.

Abbreviations

BHH	*The Building of Hatfield House*
BL	British Library
BM	British Museum
Bodl	Bodleian Library, Oxford
CL	*Country Life*
CRO	Cambridgeshire County Record Office
DNB	*The Dictionary of National Biography*
EHAST	*Transactions of the East Hertfordshire Archaeological Society*
Gent Mag	*Gentleman's Magazine*
HH & G	*Hatfield House and Gardens*
HGA	*The Herts Genealogist and Antiquary*
Herts Arch	*Hertfordshire Architecture*
Herts P and P	*Hertfordshire Past and Present*
HRO	Hertfordshire County Record Office
JBAA	*Journal of the British Architectural Association*

NMR	National Monuments Record
Phil Trans	*Philosophical Transactions of the Royal Society*
PRO	Public Record Office
Proc Soc Ants	*Proceedings of the Society of Antiquaries of London*
RCAHM (Wales)	Royal Commission on Ancient and Historical Monuments in Wales
RCHME	Royal Commission on the Historical Monuments of England
RIBA	Royal Institute of British Architects
StAAST	*Transactions of the St Albans and Hertfordshire Architectural and Archaeological Society*
TSPES	*Transactions of St Paul's Ecclesiological Society*
V & A	Victoria and Albert Museum
VCH	The Victoria History of the Counties of England
WAM	Westminster Abbey Muniments

Primary Sources

A Whitford Anderson, drawings in Hertford Museum (not numbered).

A Whitford Anderson, photographs in Watford Central Library. References to these are followed by date or number where known.

H C and R T Andrews, a collection of engravings, photographs, etc, in Hertford Museum. Cited only where ultimate source of illustration is not known.

Beechwood Park, Flamstead: a collection of plans and drawings dating from the late 17th to early 20th centuries and listed by H M Colvin and J Harris (unpublished MS). Most of the collection was still in the possession of Beechwood Park preparatory school when the house was visited in 1976.

John Hickman Binyon, MS book on Northaw (where he lived 1829–79); HRO D/P73 29/3.

Bosanquettina, Bosanquet family, members of, small album of drawings c.1812, Ashmolean Museum, Oxford.

Charlotte Bosanquet, drawings, 1842–3, Ashmolean Museum, Oxford.

John and John Chessell Buckler, drawings by, in HRO unless otherwise stated; references followed by volume and number.

Census, 1851 Census Returns, PRO.

John Charnock (1759–1807), drawings in National Maritime Museum.

W B Gerish Collection in HRO: mostly newspaper cuttings of the late 19th and early 20th centuries.

Richard Gough (1735–1809), antiquary. Unpublished folio collection of engravings of British topography in forty-six volumes, Bodleian Library, Oxford. Hertfordshire is covered in volume XI.

Guildhall Library: Christ's Hospital Archives.

The Building of Hatfield House: a MS volume of excerpts from the Hatfield MSS compiled in the early 20th century by R T Gunton, librarian to the 3rd Marquess of Salisbury.

Hatfield House and Gardens: a MS volume of excerpts from the Hatfield MSS compiled in the early 20th century by R T Gunton, librarian to the 3rd Marquess of Salisbury.

Charles Hayward's Diary, MS, 4 vols (1822, 1825, 1826, 1827) in Watford Central Library.

J W Jones, collection of drawings, etc, to illustrate grangerised Clutterbuck; BL, 5 vols, Add MSS, 32348–52.

Luppino drawings, St Albans Public Library; see *English Houses 1200–1800*, Chapter 1, note 10.

Drawings in the collection of Godfrey Meynell.

G E Moodey, drawings deposited in HRO.

Munden Year by Year, bound volume of papers relating to Munden in the possession of Viscount Knutsford.

H G Oldfield, drawings in HRO.

Royal Kalendar, The Royal Kalendar...or Annual Register...for the Year 1781... A New Edition Corrected to the 8th of February, of the Royal Kalendar; or Complete and Correct Annual Register for England, Scotland, Ireland and America for the Year 1781,... London, printed for J Almon and J Debrett.

Soane Note Books in Sir John Soane's Museum, 13 Lincoln's Inn Fields, London.

James Wilcox, drawings in Hertford Museum; see *English Houses 1200–1800*, Chapter 1, note 11.

Bibliography

About Wheathampstead (by Harpenden and St Albans WEA, 1974).

Alcock, N W 1981. *Cruck Construction: an Introduction and Catalogue* (CBA Research Report 42).

Alcock, N W and Barley, M W 1972. `Medieval roofs with base-crucks and short principals'. *Antiq J* **52**, 132–68.

Alcock, N W and Laithwaite, M 1973. `Medieval houses in Devon and their modernisation'. *Medieval Archaeol* **17**, 100-25.

Ambler, L 1913. *The Old Halls and Manor Houses of Yorkshire, with some other houses built before the year 1700.*

Andrews, C B (ed) 1936. *The Torrington Diaries.*

Andrews, H C 1905–7. `Notes on No. 63 High Street, Ware'. *EHAST* **3**, 269–71
   1908–9. `Hammond's Farm, Pirton'. *EHAST* **4**, 27–31.

Andrews, R T 1899–1901*a*. `Scott's Grotto, Amwell' *EHAST* **1**, 15–31.
   1899–1901*b*. `Ancient Buildings at Ware'. *EHAST* **1**, 265-9.
   1902–4. `The Rye House Castle and the manor of Rye'. *EHAST* **2**, 32–45.

Archer, M 1976. `Beast, bird or flower: stained glass at Gorhambury House'. *CL* **159** (January–June), 1451–4, 1562–4.

Archer-Thompson, W 1939–40. *The Draper's Company History of the Company's Properties and Trusts,* 2 vols.

Aubrey *Brief Lives. Brief Lives* (ed A Powell, 1945).

Aylott, G nd. *The Story of Letchworth Hall* (reprinted Letchworth).
   1912–14. `The Tylers' Guildhall, Hitchin. *EHAST* **5**, 78–81.

Bacon, Francis 1625. *Essays* (Everyman edition, 1973).

Bailey, G and Hutton, B 1966. *Crown-Post Roofs in Hertfordshire.* Hitchin.

Baker, J L 1980. `"Smoke deflectors" in hall houses'. *Surrey Archaeol Collect* **72**, 268–9.

Bedal, K 1978. *Historische Hausforschung.* Münster.

Beresford, G 1974. `The medieval manor of Penhallam, Jacobstow, Cornwall'. *Medieval Archaeol* **18**, 90–145.
   1975. *The Medieval Clay Land Village: Excavations at Goltho and Barton Blount* (Society for Medieval Archaeology monograph **6**).
   1978. `Excavations at the deserted medieval village of Caldecote...an interim report'. *Hertfordshire's Past* **4** (Spring), 3–14.

Beresford, M W 1957. *New Towns of the Middle Ages.*

Beresford, M W and Finberg, H P R 1973. *English Medieval Boroughs: A Handlist.* Newton Abbot.

Beresford, M W and St Joseph, J K 1979. *Medieval England: An Aerial Survey,* 2nd edn. Cambridge.

Biddle, M 1976. `Towns' in D M Wilson (ed) *The Archaeology of Anglo-Saxon England,* 99–150.

Biddle, M, Barfield, L and Millard, A. 1959. `The excavation of The More, Rickmansworth'. *Archaeol J* **116**, 136–99.

Blair, J 1987. `The 12th-century Bishop's Palace at Hereford'. *Medieval Archaeol* **31**, 59–79.

Blake, W 1911. *An Irish Beauty of the Regency.*

Boalch, D H 1978. *The Manor of Rothamsted,* 2nd edn.

Borenius, T and Charlton, J 1936. `Clarendon Palace: an interim report'. *Antiq J* **16**, 55–84.

Boswell, J 1785. *Journal of a Tour to the Hebrides with Samuel Johnson* (Everyman edition, 1941).

Braudel, F 1981. *Civilisation and Capitalism: Vol I. The Structures of Everyday Life* (revised edn, S Reynolds).

Bray, J M 1928–33. `The Ashwell Museum'. *EHAST* **8**, 210–11.

Brett Smith, H F B 1923. Introduction in I H Browne the Elder, *A Pipe of Tobacco.* Oxford.

Brigg, W 1895. `Hertfordshire deeds'. *HGA* **1**, 87–96.
   1897 `Church terriers'. *HGA* **2**, 66–71.
   (ed) 1902. *The Parish Registers of Aldenham 1559-1659.* St Albans.

Britton, J 1837. *The History and Description of Cassiobury Park.*

Britton, J and Brayley, E W 1808. *The Beauties of England and Wales: Vol VII, Hertfordshire.*

Brown, J E 1909. *Chantry Certificates for Hertfordshire.* Hertford.

Builder, The (London, 1843–).

Building News. (London, 1855–1926)

Burke's *Landed Gentry,* 19th edn.

Busby, J H 1933. *Harpenden Hall* (privately printed). Harpenden.

Butler, A S G 1950. *The Architecture of Sir Edwin Lutyens,* 3 vols. London.

Butterfield, W 1908. *Alterations in and about Hatfield House since 1868* (privately printed).

C[arlile], J W nd. `Archaeological studies on the two manors of Ponsbourne and Newgate Street. Hertford'. (Bound up with Part 3 of *EHAST* **3** (1905-7), separately paginated).

Carrington *Diary. Memorandoms for...* (ed W Branch Johnson, 1973). Chichester.

Carson, C *et al* 1981. `Impermanent architecture in the southern American colonies'. *Winterthur Portfolio* **16**, 135–96.

Carswell, J 1960. *The South Sea Bubble.*

Castle, S A 1977*a. Timber-Framed Buildings in Watford.* Chichester.

1977*b*. `A late-medieval timber-framed building in Watford'. *Herts Archaeol* **5**, 176–85.

Charles, F W B 1967. *Medieval Cruck-Building and its Derivatives* (Society for Medieval Archaeology monograph **2**).

Chauncy, Sir H 1826. *The Historical Antiquities of Hertfordshire*. (First published 1700, London. References are to the 2nd edn of 1826 (2 vols, London and Bishop's Stortford), reprinted 1975, Dorking, with Introduction by Carola Oman).

Cherry, M 1989. `Nurstead Court, Kent: a reappraisal'. *Archaeol J* **146**, 451–64.

Chronica Monastici S Albani
  Annales Monastici. *Monasterii S. Albani* (ed H T Riley, 2 vols, 1870–1, Rolls Series).
  Gesta Abbatum Monasterii S. Albani (ed H T Riley, 3 vols, 1867-9, Rolls Series).
  Registrum Abbatiae Johannis Whethamstede (ed H T Riley, 2 vols, 1870–3, Rolls Series).

Clapham, A W and Godfrey, W H nd [1913]. *Some Famous Buildings and Their Story*.

Clarendon, Lord 1702–4. *History of the Rebellion and Civil Wars in England* (ed Macray, 6 vols, 1881). Oxford.

Clark, P and Slack, P 1976. *English Towns in Transition*. Oxford.

Clarkson, S F 1887. `The Saunders Almshouses at Flamstead...'. *StAAAST* **1**, Part IV, 88–90.

Clutterbuck, R. *The Topography of Hertfordshire*: the author's grangerised copy (in HRO), in 6 vols, of his *The History and Antiquities of the County of Hertford* (3 vols, 1815–27).

Cobb, J W 1883. *History of Berkhamsted*.

Colman, G and Colman, S 1964–6. `A thirteenth-century aisled house: Purton Green Farm, Stansfield'. *Proc Suffolk Inst Archaeol Hist* **30** (published 1967), 150–65.

Colthorpe, M and Bateman, L H 1977. *Queen Elizabeth and Harlow*. Harlow.

Colville, D nd [*c*.1972]. *North Mymms – Parish and People*. Letchworth.

Colvin, H M 1971. `Edward VI at Hunsdon House'. *Burlington Magazine* **113**, 210.
  1978. *A Biographical Dictionary of British Architects 1600–1840*, 2nd edn.

Colvin, H M and Harris, J nd. Typescript catalogue of plans and drawings for Beechwood Park, Flamstead.

Colvin, H M and Newman, J (eds) 1981. *Of Building. Roger North's Writings on Architecture*.

Conzen, M R G 1960. `Alnwick, Northumberland: a study of town-plan analysis'. *Trans Inst Brit Geogr* **27**, 1–127.

Cornforth, J 1962. `Queen Hoo Hall, Hertfordshire'. *CL* **131**, January–June, 594–8.
  1963. `A Stuart maltsters house'. *CL* **134**, July–December, 676–9

Courtney, P 1989. `Excavation in the outer court of Tintern Abbey'. *Medieval Archaeol* **33**, 99–143.

Crabbe, G (ed) 1851. *The Poetical Works of the Rev. George Crabbe*, new edn.

Croft-Murray, E 1962–70. *Decorative Painting in England*, 2 vols.

Cussans, J P 1870–81. *History of Hertfordshire*.
  Volume *I* (1870–3):
    (i) Braughing Hundred
    (ii) Edwinstree Hundred
    (iii) Odsey Hundred.
  Volume *II* (1874–8):
    (i) Hitchin Hundred
    (ii) Hertford Hundred
    (iii) Broadwater Hundred.
  Volume *III* (1879–81):
    (i) Dacorum Hundred
    (ii) Cashio Hundred.
  (Reprinted 1972, Wakefield, with Introduction by W Branch Johnson)

Daniell, H C N 1923–7. `Popes Manor, Essendon'. *EHAST* **7**, 148–60.

Davies, R (ed) 1863. `The Life of Marmaduke Rawdon of York'. *Camden Soc* **85**, reprinted London, New York.

Davys, The Revd Canon [Owen W] 1888. `Wayside chapel: notes on an ancient cottage at Gustard Wood Common...'. *StAAAST*, 13–14.

Defoe *Tour. A Tour Through the Whole Island of Great Britain*, 3rd edn, 4 vols, 1742.

Defoe *Tour* 1927. Edited with an introduction by G D H Cole.

de Saussure, C 1902. *A Foreign View of England...*

de Sorbière, S 1667. *Voyage to England* (first published Cologne; English translation, *Voyage to England: done into English; with observations by T Sprat*, 1709).

Dineley, T 1888. *Progress of the 1st Duke of Beaufort Through Wales 1684*.

Dollman, F T and Jobbins, J R 1861–3. *Analysis of Ancient Domestic Architecture in Great Britain*, 2 vols.

Downes, K 1969. *Hawksmoor*.

Drinkwater, N 1964. `The Old Deanery, Salisbury'. *Antiq J* **44**, 41–59.

Dulley, A J F 1978. `Housing and society in Aldenham'. *Herts Archaeol* **6**, 78–95.

Dunnage, W 1815. MS *History of Hitchin*.

Dury, A and Andrews, J 1766. *A Topographical Map of Hartford-shire: from an actual survey* (9 sheets; facsimile published at a reduced scale by Hertfordshire Publications, 1980).

Eden, R 1979. *Dictionary of Land Surveyors*. Folkestone.

Edwards, J 1974. *Cheshunt in Hertfordshire*. Cheshunt.

EHAST 1912–14. `Excursions 1913'. *E Herts Archaeol Soc Trans* **5**, 212-20.
  1927. `Excursions 1927'. *E Herts Archaeol Soc Trans* **7**, 393–408.
  1940–2. `Henry George Oldfield and the Dimsdale Collection of Hertfordshire Drawings'. *E Herts*

Archaeol Soc Trans **11**, 212–24.

1945–9. `120th Excursion'. *E Herts Archaeol Soc Trans* **12**, 156–67.

Eland, G (ed) 1947. *The Shardeloes Papers*.

Emery, A 1970. *Dartington Hall*. Oxford.

Evelyn *Diary. The Diary of John Evelyn* (ed E S de Beer, 6 vols, 1955).

Faull, M C and Moorhouse, S A (eds) 1981. *West Yorkshire: An Archaeological Survey to AD 1500*, 4 vols. Wakefield.

Farris, H O N 1975-6. `Stebbing Farm' (letter). *Herts Countryside Magazine* **30**, 34.

Fea, A (ed) 1905. *Memoirs of Lady Fanshawe*.

Field, F J nd. `A summer at Welwyn', unpublished MS, Welwyn Garden City Library.

Fiennes *Journeys. The Journeys of Celia Fiennes* (ed C Morris, 1947).

Fischer Fine Art Ltd, February–March 1981. *Catalogue Architectural Drawings*.

Fitzherbert. *Book of Husbandrie* (ed Revd Walter W Skeat, *The Book of Husbandry by Master Fitzherbert*, English Dialect Society, Series D, Miscellaneous, 1882).

Fletcher, J M 1965-6. `Three medieval farmhouses in Harwell'. *Berkshire Archaeol J* **62**, 46–69.

1979. `The Bishop of Winchester's medieval manor-house at Harwell, Berkshire, and its relevance in the evolution of timber-framed halls'. *Archaeol J* **136**, 173–92.

Fletcher, J M and Spokes, P S 1964. `The origin and development of crown-post roofs'. *Medieval Archaeol* **8**, 152–83.

Fletcher, M 1972. `Pope's Farm'. *Herts Arch Review* **5**, 83–6.

Fox, Sir Cyril and Lord Raglan 1951–4. *Monmouthshire Houses*, 3 parts (Part *I* 1951; Part *II* 1953; Part *III* 1954). Cardiff.

Fraser, S E Joan nd. *The History of Offley Place* (pamphlet, Hertfordshire County Council).

Fuller *Worthies. The Worthies of England* (ed J Nicholls, 2 vols, 1811).

1905–7. `Brent Pelham Hall and its owners'. *EHAST* **3**, 51–60.

1907. *Sir Henry Chauncy, Kt.* Bishop's Stortford.

Gerish, W B and Andrews, R T 1902–4. `Notes on the manor of Thorley Hall and the subterranean passages discovered there...'. *EHAST* 2, 297–303.

Gibbs, A E 1890. *The Corporation Records of St Albans*. St Albans.

Gibbs, H C 1908. *History of Briggens*, MS in possession of Lord Aldenham.

1915. *The Parish Registers of Hunsdon 1546-1837*, St Albans.

Gibbs, J 1728. *A Book of Architecture*.

Gibson, A V B 1971. `Some timber-framed buildings in East Herts and their dating'. *Hertfordshire Past and Present* **11**, 2–15.

1973. `A "half-Wealden" in Bishop's Stortford'. *Herts Archaeol* **3**, 127–30.

1974–6. `A base-cruck hall at Offley'. *Herts Archaeol* **4**. 153–7.

Gibson, A V B *et al* 1980–2. `Investigation of a 13th-century building at No. 2 West Street, Ware'. *Herts Archaeol* **8**, 126–43.

Girouard, M 1959*a*. `Salisbury Hall, Hertfordshire – I'. *CL* **126**, 22 October 1959, 596–9.

1959*b*. `Salisbury Hall, Hertfordshire – II'. *CL* **126**, 29 October 1959, 708–11.

1962. `Trevalyn Hall, Denbighshire'. *CL* **132**, 78–81.

1973. *The Victorian Country House*.

1978. *Life in the English Country House: A Social and Architectural History*. New Haven and London.

Godfrey, W H 1911. *The English Staircase*.

Gover, J E B, Mawer, A and Stenton, F N 1938. *The Place-Names of Hertfordshire* (English Place-Name Society). Cambridge.

Granville *Autobiography. The Autobiography and Correspondence of Mary Granville* (Mrs Delany).

Gravett, K 1981. `The Clergy House, Alfriston: a reappraisal'. *National Trust Studies*, 103–8.

Gray, Thomas *Poetical Works. Poetical Works* (ed J Bradshaw, 1907).

Gunther, R T 1928. *The Architecture of Sir Roger Pratt...from his Note-Books*. Oxford.

Garner, T and Stratton, A 1929. *The Domestic Architecture of England During the Tudor Period*, 2 vols, 2nd edn.

The Gentleman's Magazine Library. Being a classified collected of the chief contents of *The Gentleman's Magazine* from 1731–1868. (Edited G L Gomme, 1883).

Gentleman's Magazine, *Library of English Topography* 5, published *c*.1900.

George, D 1931. *England in Transition*.

Gerish, W B 1901. `The Great and Little Hormeads'. *Home Counties Magazine* **3**, 110–13.

1902–4. `Thundridge Bury'. *EHAST* **2**, 135–9.

Habakkuk, H J 1955. `Daniel Finch, 2nd Earl of Nottingham: his house and estate' in J H Plumb (ed) *Studies in Social History*, 139–78.

Hale, G 1884. `Therfield'. *StAAAST*, 19–28.

Hale, W H (ed) 1858. `The Domesday of St Paul's...'. *Camden Soc* **69**.

Hall, R de Z 1972. *A Bibliography on Vernacular Architecture*. Newton Abbot.

Harbord, R G 1952. *The Parish of Ardeley*. Ardeley.

Harding, J 1974. `Surrey, Dunsfold'. *Medieval Archaeol*. **18**, 215.

le Hardy, W (ed) 1961. *Guide to the Hertfordshire Record Office, Part I*. Hertford.

Harris, J 1961. `Raynham Hall, Norfolk'. *Archaeol J* **118**, 180–7.

1970. *Sir William Chambers*.

1971. `C R Cockerell's *Ichnographica Domestica*'. *Architectural History* **14**, 5–29.

1981. *The Palladians*.

Hastings, R 1938. `Swan song of a house: Little Cassiobury, Watford'. *CL* **84**, 13 August 1938, 162–3.

Hatfield and its People, Books 1–12 (by members of Hatfield WEA, 1959–64, Hatfield).

Heal, Sir Ambrose 1943. `A great country house in 1623'. *Burlington Magazine* **82**, 108–16.

Heath, J 1676. *Chronicle of the Late Intestine War*, 2nd edn

Hemp, W J and Gresham, C A 1942–3. `Park, Llanfrothen, and the unit system'. *Archaeol Cambrensis* **97**, 98–112.

Hertford Civic Society, *Newsletter* 1978, 2.

The Herts and Beds Reformer. See *The Reformer and Herts, Beds, Essex, Cambridge and Middx Advertiser*.

Hertfordshire Countryside Magazine (Hitchin, 1946–).

The Herts Genealogist and Antiquary (3 vols, 1895–8, ed W Brigg).

The Herts Guardian, Agricultural Journal and General Advertiser for Hertfordshire, Buckinghamshire, Cambridgeshire and Middlesex. (Hertford, 1852–1902).

The Hertfordshire Illustrated Review (St Albans 1893, 10 issues only).

The Hertfordshire Mercury and County Press (Hertford, 1772–).

Hertfordshire Past and Present (Hertford, 1960–75/6).

Hertfordshire's Past (Hertford, 1976–).

Hewett, C 1980. *English Historic Carpentry*. Chichester.

Hill, O and Cornforth, J 1966. *English Country Houses: Caroline 1625–1685*.

Hine, R L nd (Stagenhoe). `History of Stagenhoe'. Unpublished typescript, HRO 71038.

nd (Sun Hotel). *The Story of the Sun Hotel*. Hitchin.

1923–7. `Hitchin'. *EHAST* **7**, 302–3.

1927–9. *The History of Hitchin*, 2 vols.

1949. *Charles Lamb and His Hertfordshire*.

1951. *Relics of an Un-common Attorney*.

Hodgson, V T 1902. `Mural paintings at Rothamsted'. *StAAAST* NS 1 (1895–1902), 378–84.

Holmes, G 1979, `The professions and social change in England, 1680–1730' (The Raleigh Lecture on History). *Proc Brit Acad* **65**, 313–54

Home Counties Magazine (London, 1901–).

Horn, W and Born, E 1965. *The Barns of...Great Coxwell and Beaulieu St Leonards*. Berkeley and Los Angeles.

Hoskins, W G 1955. *The Making of the English Landscape*.

Howard, R L and Fowler, H 1889. `Mackerye End House and its inhabitants'. *StAAAST*, 27–31.

Hubbard, E 1986. *Clwyd (Denbighshire and Flintshire)*. (The *Buildings of Wales* series).

Hughson, David (pseud) 1805–9. *London, Being an Accurate History...Perambulation*, 6 vols.

Hunt, E M 1945–9. `Ware: the French Horn'. *EHAST* **12**, 138–9.

1949. *History of Ware*. Hertford.

Hunt, J A 1902–4. `Rawdon House, Hoddesdon'. *EHAST* **2**, 11–17.

Hussey, C 1924. `Aldenham House, Hertfordshire'. *CL* **55**, 23 February 1924, 282–90.

1941. `Marden Hill, Hertfordshire'. *CL* **90**, 22 August 1941, 328-33.

1943. `The King's Lodge, Abbots Langley, Hertfordshire'. *CL* **93**, 9 April 1943, 660–3.

1947. `Julians, Hertfordshire'. *CL* **101** (January–June, 1160–3.

1956. `St Paul's Walden Bury'. *CL* **119** (January–June) 472–5; 532–5.

1958. *English Country Houses: Late Georgian 1800–1840*.

1963. *English Country Houses: Mid Georgian 1760–1800*, revised edn.

1965. *English Country Houses: Early Georgian 1715–60*, revised edn.

Jackson, C (ed) 1875. *The Autobiography of Mrs Alice Thornton....* Surtees Society, Vol LXII.

James, T B and Robinson, A M 1988. *Clarendon Palace: The History and Archaeology of a Medieval Palace and Hunting Lodge near Salisbury, Wiltshire*. (Society of Antiquaries of London Research Report XLV).

Johnson, E A and Weaver, O J 1962–3. Interim report (typescript) for St Albans and Hertfordshire Architectural and Archaeological Society.

Johnson, W Branch 1960. *Welwyn Briefly*. Welwyn 1962 and 1963. *Hertfordshire Inns*, 2 parts, Letchworth.

Jones, B 1974. *Follies and Grottoes*, 2nd edn.

Jones, S R 1968. `Domestic buildings (in Tewkesbury Borough)' in VCH *A History of Gloucestershire*, Vol VIII, 110–69.

1971. `Moorland and non-moorland long-houses'. *Trans Devonshire Assoc* **103**, 35–75.

1975–6. `West Bromwich (Staffs) Manor-house'. *Trans South Staffs Archaeol Soc* **17**, 1–63.

Jones, S R and Smith, J T 1958. `Manor House, Wasperton'. *Trans Birmingham and Warwickshire Archaeol Soc* **76**, 19–28.

1960. `The Great Hall of the Bishop's Palace, Hereford'. *Medieval Archaeol* **4**, 69–80.

1963–72. `The houses of Breconshire', Parts I–VII. *Brycheiniog* **9–16**.

1963. Part I The Builth District. **9**, 1–77.

1964. Part II The Hay and Talgarth District. **10**, 69–183.

1965. Part III, The Brecon District. **11**, 1–149.

1966/7. Part IV The Crickhowell District. **12**, 1–91.

1968/9. Part V The Defynnog District. **13**, 1–85.

1972. Part VI The Faenor (Vaynor) and Penderyn District. **16**, 1–37.

1972. Part VII The Ystradgynlais District. **16**, 39–78.

Jones, T 1809. *History of the County of Brecknock* (ed Baron Glanusk, 4 vols, 1911–30. Brecon).

Keller, F-E 1986. `Christian Ellesten's drawings of Roger Pratt's Clarendon House and Robert Hookes'

Montague House'. *Burlington Magazine* **128** (October issue), 732–7.

Kelly's Directory of Hertfordshire. 1882, 1890, 1899, 1911, 1912 and 1928.

Kingsford, P N 1971. `A London merchant: Sir William Baker'. *History Today.* **21**, 338–48.

Kingston, A 1894. *Hertfordshire During the Great Civil War and Long Parliament.* London and Hertford.

King's Works. The History of the King's Works (gen ed H M Colvin), Vols II (1963), III (1975), IV (1982), V (1976).

Kinneir Tarte, F W 1895–1902. `Mural colour decoration at Mr H J Thurnall's house'. *StAAAST* NS **1**, 385–6.

Kip, W 1709. *Britannia Illustrata.*

Kirby, D 1974. `Beadle House, Hertford, formerly Dimsdale House – an essay in conservation problems'. *ERA,* Journal of the Eastern Region of the Royal Institute of British Architects **37** (March–April 1974), 29–31.

Kitton, F G 1892. *Hertfordshire Country Houses.*

1895–1902. `The Old inns of St Albans'. *StAAAST* NS **1**, 233–61.

Knebworth House, 1974. A guidebook to Knebworth House.

Knowles, D and Hadcock, R N 1953. *Medieval Religious Houses: England and Wales.*

L— 1909. `Mantles and overmantels at Childwickbury'. *CL* **25** (January–June), 918–19.

Laslett, P 1965. *The World We Have Lost.*

Law, C M 1972. `Some notes on the urban population of England and Wales in the 18th century'. *Local Hist* **10**, 13–16.

Lees-Milne, J 1970. *English Country Houses: Baroque 1685–1715.*

Leland *Itinerary. The Itinerary of John Leland* (ed L Toulmin Smith, 5 vols, 1907).

Lincoln *Visitations.* Visitations in the Diocese of Lincoln 1517–1531 (ed A Hamilton Thompson 1940–7, 3 vols, Lincoln Record Society).

Lincoln, Rutland & Stamford Mercury (Stamford, 1695–).

Linstrum, D 1972. *Sir Jeffrey Wyattville.*

Lloyd, N 1925. *A History of English Brickwork from Medieval Times to the End of the Georgian Period.* London and New York.

1931. *A History of the English House from Primitive Times to the Victorian Period.* London and New York.

Lobel, M D (gen ed) 1969. *Historic Towns Vol I.* London and Oxford.

Longman, G 1967. *Bushey Then and Now.* Bushey.

Lucas *Diary. A Quaker Journal...the Diary...of William Lucas of Hitchin (1804–61)* (ed G E Bryant and G P Baker, 2 vols, 1934).

Lucas, G 1908–11*a*. `The Old Hall, Pirton'. *EHAST* **4**, 31–3.

1908–11*b*. `Julians, Rushden'. *EHAST* **4**, 76–81.

1908–11*c*. `Hinxworth Place'. *EHAST* **4**, 159–78.

Lugar, R 1828. *Villa Architecture, a Collection of Views, With Plans, of Buildings Executed in England, Scotland....*

Luttrell, N 1857. *A Brief Historical Relation of State Affairs,*

6 vols. Oxford.

Lutyens, E J T and Andrews, H C 1945–9. `No. 16 Bull Plain, Hertford, Herts'. *EHAST* **12**, 40–1.

M[anchester], A 1945–9. `Hertford: 130 Fore Street' *EHAST* **12**, 135-6.

Machin, R A 1976. *Probate Inventories and Manorial Excepts of...Yetminster.* Bristol.

1978. *The Houses of Yetminster.* Bristol.

Manor House, guidebook. A guidebook to the Manor House, Little Gaddesden, written *c.*1970.

Matthews, The Revd A G 1934. *Calamy Revised, Being a Revision of E Calamy's Account of the Ministers and Others Ejected and Silenced, 1660–2.* Oxford.

1948. *Walker Revised, Being a Revision of J Walker's Suffering of the Clergy During the Grand Rebellion 1642–60.* Oxford.

Mayes, P 1967. `Lincolnshire: South Witham'. *Medieval Archaeol* **11**, 274–5.

McFarlane, K B 1973. *The Nobility of Later Medieval England.* Oxford.

Mercer, E 1962. *English Art 1553–1625* (Oxford History of English Art, Vol V). Oxford.

1975, *English Vernacular Houses: A Study of Traditional Farmhouses and Cottages.*

Michelmore, D J H 1979. *A Current Bibliography of Vernacular Architecture* (Vernacular Architecture Group).

Middlesex and Herts Notes and Queries, I–IV, 1895–8, edited by W J Hardy. (Incorporated with the *Home Counties Magazine* after 1898).

Millington, G 1981. *Little Berkhamsted.* Little Berkhamsted.

Minet, W MS. Manuscript account by W Minet of his restoration of Hadham Hall. In HRO, 70899 (unpaginated).

1914. *The Manor of Hadham Hall* (privately published).

Mitchell, R 1801. *Plans, etc,...of Buildings Erected in England and Scotland; With an Essay to Elucidate the Grecian, Roman and Gothic Architecture.*

Moody, A S 1961. `The renovation of the "Christopher Inn", French Row, St Albans, 1950–4'. With notes on the structure history by P K Baillie-Reynolds. *StAAAST,* 50–64.

Morris, E F 1902–4. `Hyde Hall, Sawbridgeworth'. *EHAST* **2**, 203–9.

Munby, L M 1974. *Hertfordshire Population Statistics.* Hitchin.

1977. *The Hertfordshire Landscape.*

(ed) 1963. *History of Kings Langley.*

Nares, G 1956*a*. `Moor Place, Hertfordshire – I'. *CL* 119, January–June, 156–9.

1956*b*. `Moor Place, Hertfordshire – II'. *CL* 119, January–June, 204–7.

Neale, J P 1819–29. *Views of the Seats of Noblemen and*

Gentlemen in England, Wales, Scotland and Ireland, from drawings by J P Neale, 6 vols (unpaginated).

Newman, J 1976. *West Kent and the Weald (The Buildings of England* series), 2nd edn.

Newsletter 1955, 1957, 1958, 1963, 1965, 1971, 1973, 1974, 1975, 1976. Written, illustrated and published for the East Herts Archaeological Society by G E Moodey.

Newton brochure. Brochure (nd, *c*.1912) issued by the long-established firm of Frank Newton, builders and decorators of Hitchin; copy in NMR.

Nichols, J 1982–3. *Progresses of Queen Elizabeth*, 3 vols, 2nd edn (first published 1788–1805).

Norman, F H 1902–4. `Moor Place, Much Hadham'. *EHAST* **2**, 143–50.

Northampton Mercury (Northampton, 1721–1931; continued as *Mercury and Herald*, 1931–).

Notes on Hatfield House, dictated by James, 2nd Marquess of Salisbury, to Mary, Marchioness of Salisbury, in 1866–7 and edited by her; privately printed in 1886.

Oldfield. see *EHAST* 1940–2.

Ollard, R 1979. *The Image of the King*.

Oman, C 1975. `Introduction' in Sir H Chauncy's *The Historical Antiquities of Hertfordshire* (2nd edn, 1826).

Oswald, A 1938*a*. `Beechwood Park, Hertfordshire – I'. *CL* **84**, 12 November 1938, 474–8.

 1938*b*. `Beechwood Park, Hertfordshire – II'. *CL* **84**, 19 November 1938, 498–502.

Paddick, E W 1971. *Hoddesdon*. Hoddesdon, Hertfordshire.

Page, F 1953. *Christ's Hospital, Hertford*.

Page, W 1920. `The origins and forms of Hertfordshire towns and villages'. *Archaeologia* **69**, 47–60.

Paine, J 1783. *Plans...of Noblemen* [sic] *and Gentlemen's Houses...York*, 2 vols, 2nd edn.

Pantin, W A 1969. `Medieval inns' in E M Jope (ed) *Studies in Building History*, 166–91.

Parker, V 1971. *The Making of King's Lynn*. Chichester.

Particulars 1721. *The Particulars and Inventories of the...Directors of the South Sea Company; and of Robert Surnam...said Company. Together with Abstracts of the Same*, 2 vols.

Paul, R W 1894. *Vanishing London*.

Pelham, E C 1971. *The Oaklands Story 1921–1971* (published privately).

Pepys *Diary. The Diary of Samuel Pepys* (ed R Latham and W Matthews, 11 vols, 1970–83).

Petchey, M 1974–6. `Aston Bury, Aston'. *Herts Arch* **4**, 179–80.

Pevsner, Sir N and Cherry B 1977. *Hertfordshire (The Buildings of England* series), 2nd edn.

Philosophical Transactions of the Royal Society, 1665– .

Phil Trans 1735–6. `An extract of a letter from Mr John Cope to Dr Alexander Stuart...concerning an antient date found at Widgel Hall in Hertfordshire'. *Philosophical Transactions of the Royal Society*, **39**, 19.

`Remarks on an antient date...' by Mr John Ward. *Philosophical Transactions of the Royal Society* **39**, 120–1.

`Part of a letter from Francis Gulston [sic] Esq to Mr John Ward'. *Philosophical Transactions of the Royal Society*, **39**, 122–3.

Platt, C 1978. *Medieval England*.

Poole, H and Fleck, A 1976. *Old Hitchin*. Hitchin.

Rahtz, P A 1979. *The Saxon and Medieval Palaces at Cheddar* (British Archaeological Reports: British Series **65**). Oxford.

Raine, J 1882. *History...of North Durham*.

Rawlins, B F 1974. `Excavations on the former Stonemason's Yard site, George Street, Watford'. *Bull Watford and SW Herts Arch Soc* **19**, Spring 1974, 12–15.

 1975. `Excavations on the former Stonemason's Yard site, George Street, Watford'. *Bull Watford and SW Herts Arch Soc* **21**, Spring 1975, 10.

RCAHM (Wales) 1988. *An Inventory of the Ancient Monuments in Glamorgan. Vol IV Domestic Architecture from the Reformation to the Industrial Revolution part II: Farmhouses and Cottages*.

RCHME. *An Inventory of the Historical Monuments in*:
Hertfordshire (1910)
Essex. Volume I. North-West Essex (1916).
    Volume III. North-East Essex (1922).
    Volume IV. South-East Essex (1923).
Huntingdonshire (1926).
Middlesex (1937).
Dorset. Volume I. West Dorset (1952; reprinted with amendments in 1974).
    Volume II. South-East: Parts I and II; Central: Part 1 (1970, 3 vols, continuous pagination).
    Volume V. East Dorset (1975).
Cambridge. City of Cambridge. Parts I and II (1959).
    Volume I. West Cambridgeshire (1968).
    Volume II. North-East Cambridgeshire (1972).
City of Salisbury. Volume I (1980).
 1962. *Monuments Threatened or Destroyed. A Select List: 1956–62*.
 1981. *Hotels and Restaurants: 1830 to the Present Day* (by P Boniface).
 1986. *Rural Houses of West Yorkshire 1400–1830*.
 1987. *Houses of the North York Moors*.

Reddaway, T F 1960–8. `Elizabethan London – Goldsmith's Row in Cheapside, 1558–1645'. *Guildhall Miscellany* **2**, 181–206.

The Reformer and Herts, Beds, Essex, Cambridge and Middlesex Advertiser (Hertford,1835–41; continued as *The Hertfordshire Mercury and Reformer*, 1844–68; continued as *The Hertfordshire Mercury and County Press*, 1868–71; continued as *Hertfordshire Mercury and County Press*, 1872–).

Renn, D 1971. *Medieval Castles in Hertfordshire*. Chichester.

Reynolds, S 1977. *An Introduction to the History of English Medieval Towns*. Oxford.

Rickman, L 1928–33. `Brief Studies...of Much Hadham'. *EHAST* **8**, 288–312.

Rickmansworth Historian, 1961– . Rickmansworth.

Rigold, S E 1973. `The Town House, Barley'. *Hertfordshire Archaeol* **3**, 94–9.

Rigold, S E and Rouse, E Clive 1973. `Piccotts End: a probable medieval guest house and its wall paintings'. *Hertfordshire Archaeol* **3**, 78–89.

Roberts, E 1974. `Totternhoe stone and flint in Hertfordshire churches'. *Medieval Archaeol* **18**, 66–89.

Roberts, G 1844. *Life, Progresses and Rebellion of James, Duke of Monmouth*, 2 vols.

Roberts, J H 1979. `Five medieval barns in Hertfordshire'. *Hertfordshire Archaeol* **7**, 159–80.

Rogers, J S 1933–5. `The manor and houses at Gorhambury'. *StAAAST*, NS **4**, 35–112.

Rook, T 1979. `History begins at home'. *Hertfordshire's Past* **7**, Autumn 1979, 34–7.

Roskell, J S 1957. `Sir William Oldhall, Speaker in the Parliament of 1450–1'. *Nottingham Medieval Studies* **5**, 87–112.

Rouse, E Clive 1989. `Domestic wall and panel paintings in Hertfordshire'. *Archaeol J* **146**, 423–50.

Report: MS report in RCHME archives.

Rudd, H 1930–2. `The old almshouses of Watford'. *StAAAST*, 99–108.

Rufinière du Prey, P de la 1979. `John Soane, Philip Yorke and their quest for Primitive Architecture'. *National Trust Studies* 1979, 28–38.

Salmon, N 1728. *The History of Hertfordshire*.

Salzman, L F 1952. *Building in England Down to 1540*. Oxford.

Sandall, K 1975. `Aisled halls in England and Wales'. *Vernacular Architect* **6**, 19–27.

1986. `Aisled halls in England and Wales'. *Vernacular Architect* **17**, 21–35.

Sangster, P 1972. *Balls Park* (place of pubn not known).

Scattergood, B P 1933–5. `The Old Bull and Bennetts Butts, Harpenden'. *StAAAST*, NS **4**, 276–92.

Sewter, A C 1975. *The Stained Glass of William Morris and His Circle*.

Silcox-Crowe, N 1985. `Sir Roger Pratt' in R Brown (ed) *The Architectural Outsiders*, 1–20.

Slater, T R 1980. *The Analysis of Burgages in Medieval Towns* (Department of Geography, University of Birmingham).

Smith, J T 1953. `Shrewsbury: topography and architecture to the middle of the 17th–century' (unpublished MA thesis, University of Birmingham).

1955. `Medieval aisled halls and their derivatives'. *Archaeol J* **112**, 76–94.

1960. `Medieval roofs: a classification'. *Archaeol J* **115**, 111–49.

1971. `Lancashire and Cheshire houses: some problems of architectural and social history'. *Archaeol J* **127**, 156–81.

1974. `The early development of timber buildings: the passing-brace and reversed assembly'. *Archaeol J* **131**, 238–63.

1978. `A clay fireback at Hitchin, Herts'. *Post-Medieval Archaeol* **12**, 127–8.

1981. `Mittelalterliche Dachkonstruktion in Nordwesteuropa' in Claus Ahrens (ed) *Frühe Holzkirchen im nordlichen Europa*, 379–90. Hamburg.

Smith, P 1975. *Houses of the Welsh Countryside: A Study in Historical Geography*.

Smith, T P 1975. `Rye House and aspects of early brickwork in England'. *Arch J* **132**, 111–50.

Steensberg, A 1952. *Bondehuse og Vandmoller i Danmark gennem 2000 ar* (Farms and Watermills in Denmark during 2000 years). Copenhagen.

Stone, L 1955. `The building of Hatfield House'. *Arch J* **112**, 100–28.

1965. *Social Change and Revolution in England 1540–1640*.

Stone, L and Stone J 1972. `Country houses and their owners in Hertfordshire 1540–1879' in William O Aydelotte, Allan G Bogue and Robert William Fogel (eds) *The Dimensions of Quantitative Research in History*, 56–123.

Strong, R, Binney, M and Harris, J 1974. *The Destruction of the Country House 1875–1975*.

Stroud, D 1961. *The Architecture of Sir John Soane*.

1962. *Humphrey Repton*.

1975. *Capability Brown*.

Styles, P 1957. `Introduction' in M Walker (ed) *Warwick County Records XCVIII, Hearth Tax Returns 1*. Warwick.

Summer, W H 1904. *Memories of Jordans and the Chalfonts* (made available by Mr C F Stell).

Summerson, Sir J 1953. *Architecture in Britain 1530–1830*.

1958–9. `The idea of the villa'. *J Roy Soc Arts* **107**, 570–87.

1959a. `The building of Theobalds, 1504–1585'. *Archaeologia* **97**, 107–26.

1959b. `The classical country house in 18th-century England'. *J Roy Soc Arts*, July 1959 (reprinted in *The Unromantic Castle* (1990), 79–120).

(ed) 1966. The Book of Architecture of John Thorpe in the Soane Museum. Walpole Society, Vol XL.

T— 1910. `Astonbury, Hertfordshire'. *CL* **27**, 26 March 1910, 450–8.

Tate, W E 1945–9. `A hand list of Hertfordshire Enclosure Acts and awards'. *EHAST* **12**, 18–31.

Tawney, R H 1958. *Business and Politics Under James I*. Cambridge.

Thieme, U and Becker, F 1907–50. *Allegmeines Lexikon der bildendun Künstler*, 37 vols. Leipzig.

Thompson, E M (ed) 1875. `Letters of H Prideaux'. Camden Soc, NS 15.

Thraliana (edited K C Balderston, 1942). Oxford.

Tilden, P 1954. *True Remembrances*.

The Times (1788–).

Tipping, H A 1920. `Lockleys, Hertfordshire'. *CL* 48 (July–Dec), 48–55.

1920–37. *English Houses. Period III*, 9 vols. London and New York.

1925a. `Bayfordbury – I, Hertfordshire'. *CL* **67**, 17 January 1925, 92–9.

1925b. `Bayfordbury – II, Hertfordshire'. *CL* **67**, 24 January 1925, 124–33.

Tregelles, J A 1908. *A History of Hoddesdon*. Hertford.

Trevor Davis, F 1890–1. `Notes on Aston Bury'. *StAAAST*, 63–7.

TSPES 1881–5. `XL: Saturday June 11 1881, visit to Berkhamsted'. *Transactions of the St Paul's Ecclesiological Society* **1**, *xxv–xxviii*.

Turner, T H and Parker, J H 1851–9. *Domestic Architecture in England*, 3 vols. Oxford.

Vallans, William 1590. *A Tale of Two Swannes* (Short Title Catalogue 2490, reprinted Oxford 1769).

van Koughnet, Lady Jane 1815. *History of Tyttenhanger*. London.

Venn, J and Venn J A 1922–27. *Alumni Cantabrigiensis*, 4 vols.

The Victoria History of the Counties of England.

1902–14 *Hertfordshire*, 4 vols.

1902–37 *Northants*, 4 vols.

1904–13, *Bedfordshire,* 3 vols.

1906–24 *Berkshire*, 4 vols.

1907–76 *Glos*, 11 vols.

1907 *Hertfordshire Families* (ed D Warrand).

1911–89 *Middlesex*, 9 vols.

1926–36 *Huntingdonshire*, 3 vols.

Viney, E 1965. *Sheriffs of Bucks*. Aylesbury (privately printed).

Visitations. The Visitation of Hertfordshire (ed W E Metcalf, 1886). Harleian Society.

Vitruvius Britannicus, 3 vols 1967.

Vol I: *Vitruvius Britannicus* vols I, II and III by Colin Campbell, London 1715–1725.

Vol II: *Vitruvius Britannicus* `Volume The Fourth', announced London 1739; and *Vitruvius Britannicus* vols IV and V, by John Woolfe and James Gandon, London 1802–8.

Vol III: *The New Vitruvius Britannicus* by George Richardson, London 1802-1808; and Index.

W — , L 1911. `Temple Dinsley, near Hitchin, Hertfordshire'. *CL* **29** (January–June), 562–72.

1912. `Balls Park, Hertford'. *CL* **31** (January-June), 578–87.

Walker, M (ed) 1957. *Warwick County Records XCVIII, Hearth Tax Returns 1*. Warwick.

Ward, D 1953. *Digswell From Domesday to Welwyn Garden City*. Welwyn.

Weaver C J and Poole, D 1961. `The Crown and Anchor Inn,

St Albans: an interim report'. *StAAAST*, 43–9.

Weaver, L 1925. *Houses and Gardens by Sir Edwin Lutyens*.

Weinbaum, M 1937. *The Incorporation of Boroughs*. Manchester.

West, S E 1970. `Brome, Suffolk. The excavation of a moated site, 1967'. *J Brit Archaeol Ass* 3 ser **33**, 80–121.

Western, H G 1975. *A History of Ickleford* (published privately).

Wheathampstead and Harpenden 3 parts (by Harpenden and St Albans WEA, 1973-5).

Williams, D 1980. *Master of One*.

Willis, B 1801. *Willis' Survey of St Asaph* (enlarged edn, in 2 vols by Edward Edwards).

Willis, P 1977. *Charles Bridgeman*.

Winterton, W R 1969. `The Mettkerkes of Rushden'. *Herts P and P* **9**, 33–40.

Wood, M 1936–8. `A later fifteenth-century house in George Street, St Albans'. *StAAAST* NS **5**, 99–104.

Wood, M E 1948. `Thirteenth-century domestic architecture in England'. *Archaeol J* **105** (Supplement), 1–150.

1951. `Little Wenham Hall'. *Archaeol J* **108**, 190–1.

1965. *The English Medieval House*.

Worcester *Itineraries. William Worcestre Itineraries* (ed and transl J H Harvey, 1969). Oxford.

Wren Soc 1935. `Miscellaneous Designs and Drawings by Sir Chr. Wren and others...', edited by A T Bolton and H D Hendry (Oxford).

Yaxley, S (ed) 1973. *History of Hemel Hempstead*. Hemel Hempstead.

Young, A 1770. *A Six Months' Tour Through the North of England*, 4 vols.

1804. *A General View of the Agriculture of Hertfordshire*.

Index of Names and Places

Subject Index